Geometry Second Edition

Scott, Foresman

About the cover. The picture below shows a sculpture titled *Cube,* 1969, by Isamu Noguchi. The sculpture is 8.4 meters tall, made of steel and aluminum, and painted red.

Geometry Second Edition

Scott, Foresman

Christian R. Hirsch
Mary Ann Norton
Dwight O. Coblentz
Andrew J. Samide
Harold L. Schoen

Scott, Foresman and Company
Editorial Offices: Glenview, Illinois

Regional Offices: Sunnyvale, California ·
Tucker, Georgia · Glenview, Illinois ·
Oakland, New Jersey · Dallas, Texas

Authors

Readers and Consultants

Christian R. Hirsch
Professor of Mathematics
Western Michigan University
Kalamazoo, Michigan

Mary Ann Norton
Director of Mathematics K-12
Spring Independent School District
Houston, Texas

Dwight O. Coblentz
Director and Mathematics Coordinator
Department of Education
San Diego County
San Diego, California

Andrew J. Samide
Mathematics Teacher
Wheaton North High School
Wheaton, Illinois

Harold L. Schoen
Professor of Mathematics and Education
The University of Iowa
Iowa City, Iowa

Loretta M. Braxton
Professor of Mathematics
Virginia State University
Petersburg, Virginia

Cecilia Cooper
Mathematics Faculty
William Rainey Harper College
Palatine, Illinois

Sidney Sharron
Supervisor, Instructional Media
and Resources Branch
Los Angeles City Unified School District
Los Angeles, California

ISBN: 0-673-23432-0

Contents

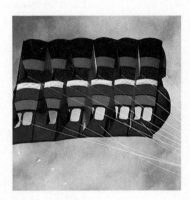

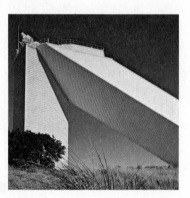

Chapter 9   Area of Polygons and Circles 398

Chapter 10   Solids 442

Symbols and Abbreviations

$\angle APB$ angle with vertex P, page 31

a apothem, page 423

$\doteq$ is approximately equal to, page 281

A area, page 401

B area of base of a solid, page 354

b base of a polygon, page 401

$\odot R$ circle with center R, page 354

C circumference of a circle, page 427

$\cong$ is congruent to, page 26

$\ncong$ is not congruent to, page 125

$\leftrightarrow$ corresponds to, page 166

$\cos A$ cosine of angle A with measure of $\angle A$ given in degrees, page 336

cm^3 cubic centimeter, page 454

PQ distance between points P and Q; length of $\overline{PQ}$, page 24

h height; length of altitude, page 401; length of a lateral edge, page 448

L.A.   lateral area, page 448

d length of diameter, page 354

r length of radius, page 394

s length of a side of a regular polygon, page 150; length of a side of a square, page 401; length of an arc of a circle, page 427; slant height of a solid, page 465

$\overleftrightarrow{AB}$ line containing points A and B, page 8

$\overset{\frown}{AQB}$ major arc of circle with endpoints A and B; point Q is on arc, page 374

$m\angle C$ measure of angle C in degrees, page 33

$m\overset{\frown}{AB}$ measure of arc AB in degrees, page 375

$\overset{\frown}{AB}$ minor arc with endpoints A and B, page 374

(x, y) ordered pair of numbers, page 327

$\parallel$ is parallel to, page 108

$\nparallel$ is not parallel to, page 123

$\square$ parallelogram, page 218

p perimeter of a polygon, page 423

$\perp$ is perpendicular to, page 42

$\not\perp$ is not perpendicular to, page 125

π pi, page 428

$\mathscr{R}$ plane named by letter r, page 8

T point named by letter t, page 8

$P_1P_2 \ldots P_n$ polygon with n vertices, P_1, P_2, $\ldots$, P_n, page 422

$\overrightarrow{RT}$ ray with endpoint R that contains point T, page 18

$\overline{RT}$ segment with endpoints R and T, page 18

$\sim$ is similar to, page 266

$\sin A$ sine of angle A with measure of $\angle A$ given in degrees, page 336

m slope of nonvertical line, page 530

cm^2 square centimeter, page 402

$\tan A$ tangent of angle A with measure of $\angle A$ given in degrees, page 336

T.A.   total area, page 448

$\triangle ABC$ triangle with vertices A, B, and C, page 138

V volume, page 453

Chapter 1

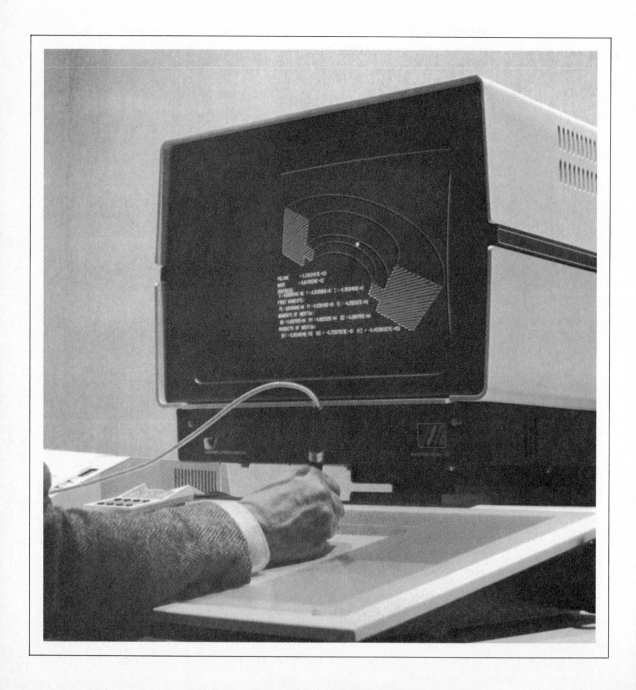

Introduction to Geometry

Geometric ideas and the logical, step-by-step reasoning used in studying geometry are important in computer graphics and computer-aided design.

1. The photograph on the opposite page shows an industrial designer using computer graphics. Describe the geometric figures that appear in the photograph.

The list of instructions below produced the design at the right. The instructions are in the computer language LOGO. "RIGHT 90" means "Rotate the pointer 90 degrees (a quarter turn) to the right." A complete rotation is 360 degrees.

RIGHT 90
FORWARD 50
RIGHT 90
FORWARD 50
RIGHT 90
FORWARD 50
RIGHT 90
FORWARD 50

2. Modify the instructions so that the computer would produce a design of the same shape but different size.

3. Modify the instructions so that the computer would produce a differently shaped four-sided design.

4. Sketch the design that would be produced by the list of computer instructions below.

RIGHT 30
FORWARD 50
RIGHT 120
FORWARD 50
RIGHT 120
FORWARD 50

5. Combine the two lists of computer instructions in an order that would produce the outline of a house.

Geometry in the Real World

Over 6000 years ago, geometry was used to measure land and construct buildings. In fact, the term *geometry* means "earth measure." Geometry consisted of a collection of facts about the size, shape, and position of plots of land, of buildings, as well as of the pyramids. These facts were the results of experimentation and observation.

Some early geometric methods were very accurate. The sides of the Great Pyramid at Gizeh, shown here, are accurate to within 1 centimeter in 180 meters.

We, too, will be interested in studying the size, shape, and position of objects in the real world. To do this it is often helpful to reduce them to simpler forms. A geometer concentrates only on the outline of the figure; that is, on the lines, angles, planes, and intersections.

The Pyramid at Gizeh might be represented as shown at right. The pyramid could be described as consisting of a square base and four triangular faces of the same size and shape.

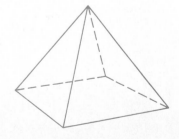

It is important to be able to make drawings to represent objects and to describe objects geometrically.

Example

Represent the object in each photograph with a drawing. Give a geometric description of the object.

Solution

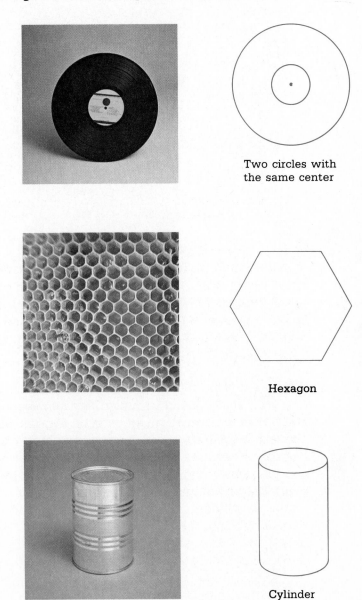

Two circles with the same center

Hexagon

Cylinder

The geometry of ancient Egypt provided practical methods for solving important everyday problems. However, relying on measurement and on the appearance of figures sometimes led to inaccuracies and erroneous conclusions. The diagrams below suggest how appearances can be misleading.

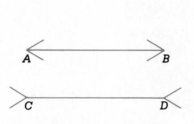

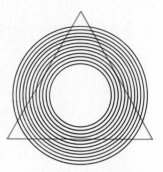

Is it further from
A to B or from C to D?

Are the sides of the blue figure straight?

To avoid such errors, the Greeks did not accept measurements or observations to justify geometric relationships. Their approach to geometry was based upon abstraction and logical reasoning. Geometric properties were accepted only if they could be logically derived from a few basic assumptions.

We, too, will be interested in developing geometry as a mathematical system in which logical reasoning is used to reach conclusions about geometric figures. However, we will also emphasize the usefulness of geometry in everyday life. In this course, you will see how the formal study of geometry can provide a language for describing the physical world and methods for analyzing and drawing conclusions about real-world phenomena.

Class Exercises

Match each photograph with one of the drawings. Use the drawing to give a possible geometric description of the object.

1.

3.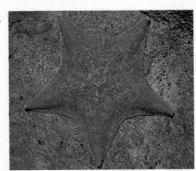

2.

4.

a.

c.

b.

d.

Written Exercises

Set A

To obtain a driver's license in some states, drivers must be able to identify certain traffic signs by their shape and color alone. Choose the appropriate sign and write a geometric description of the shape.

1. Stop   **4.** School crossing

2. Yield   **5.** Railroad crossing

3. Warning   **6.** Road construction

a.   **c.**   **e.**

b.   **d.**   **f.**

Knowledge of geometry is important in many careers. Exercises 7-10 illustrate some questions that a civil engineer might consider in designing a parking lot for a shopping mall.

7. What is one advantage of angle parking as on the left of the entrance?

8. What is one advantage of perpendicular parking as on the right of the entrance?

9. How can you make sure that the parking lines are parallel?

10. Estimate how long each parking line should be.

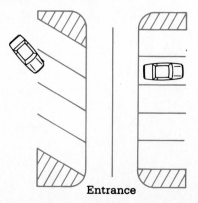

Entrance

11. Are the three cylinders in this picture the same size?

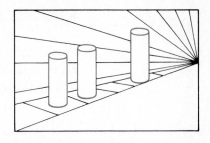

Set B

The illusion in exercise 11 is created because the artist violated a geometric principle of perspective art. Study the method used below to locate the third pole in a proper perspective drawing of equally tall, equally spaced poles.

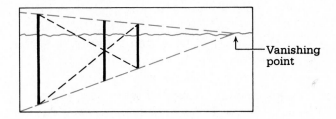

Vanishing point

12. Trace the drawing above. Then draw three more poles in proper perspective.

Drafters often make six "plane perspective" drawings to show how an object looks from front, back, top, bottom, and each side. Dotted lines are used for edges that cannot be seen from a particular view.

13. One side view of the given object is shown. Draw and label the other five views.

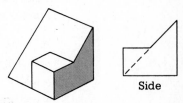

Side

14. Gestalt psychologists use geometry in their study of human perception. What is represented by these figures and their background?

1.2   Points, Lines, and Planes

Point, line, and *plane* are the basic concepts of geometry. Each is an abstraction based on our experience in the physical world.

A star in the night sky suggests the idea of a **point.** Points have no size. They are represented with dots and are named with capital letters.

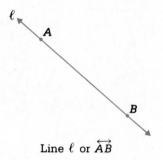

Points *C, D, P,* and *Q*

A straight, thin wire suggests the idea of a **line.** A line extends infinitely far in both directions and has no width. A line is represented by a stroke of a pencil, with an arrowhead at each end. Lines can be named with lower-case letters. If *A* and *B* are two points on a line, the line can also be named $\overleftrightarrow{AB}$ (read "line *AB*").

Line ℓ or $\overleftrightarrow{AB}$

A flat surface such as a hockey rink suggests the idea of a **plane.** A plane extends infinitely far in all directions and has no thickness. Planes can be represented with four-sided figures and named with capital script letters.

Plane *E*

In mathematics, a good definition of a word tells what that word means using terms that are already known. But you have to start with some basic words. It is customary in geometry to begin with the basic terms *point, line,* and *plane.* These are **undefined terms** in this course.

The following definitions use our three undefined terms.

| Definition | **Space** is the set of all points. |

"Cubic Space Division," a lithograph by the Dutch artist
M. C. Escher, illustrates portions of some of the many planes
in space. The edges of the girders illustrate possible
relationships among lines.

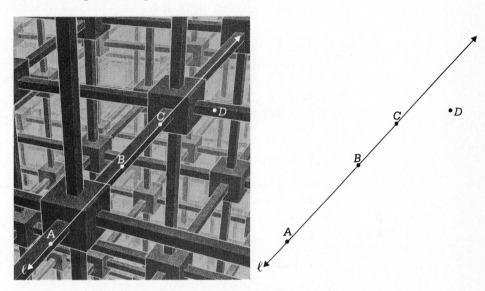

Observe that points *A*, *B*, and *C* are contained in line ℓ. Such
points are called collinear. Are points *A*, *B*, and *D* collinear?

Definition   **Collinear points** are points that are contained in one line.

Points that are not contained in one line are said to be
noncollinear. Unless otherwise specified, points may be
assumed to be collinear whenever they appear that way in a
diagram.

Definition   **Coplanar points (or lines)** are points (or lines) that are contained
in one plane.

Points *Q*, *R*, *S*, and *T* are coplanar,
since each is contained in plane *E*.
Lines *m* and *k* are coplanar because
they are both contained in plane *E*.

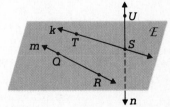

Points or lines that are not contained in the same plane are **noncoplanar.** Points Q, R, S, and U are noncoplanar. Lines m and n are also noncoplanar.

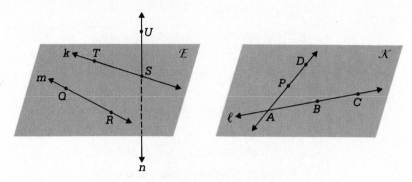

We use "in" and "on" to mean "contained in." Line ℓ and $\overleftrightarrow{AD}$ are *in* plane $\mathcal{K}$. Points A, B, and C are *on* line ℓ.

Point B is **between** points A and C. The word "between" is only used to describe collinear points. Thus P is not between A and C, since A, P, and C are noncollinear. However, P is between A and D.

The intersection of two sets is the set of elements that the two sets have in common. Lines and planes are sets of points, so their intersections are sets of points.

In the diagram at the right, the intersection of lines m and n is point X. Line k intersects plane $\mathcal{E}$ at point Y. Planes $\mathcal{E}$ and $\mathcal{H}$ intersect in line n.

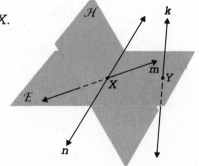

In this text, "two lines" means "two distinct or different lines"; "four points" means "four distinct or different points"; and so on.

Class Exercises

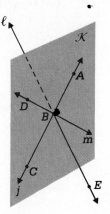

1. Points *A*, *C*, and __?__ are collinear.
2. Points *A*, *B*, *D*, and __?__ are coplanar.
3. Give another name for $\overleftrightarrow{BE}$.
4. Points *C*, *D*, *B*, and __?__ are noncoplanar.
5. Points *A*, *B*, and __?__ are noncollinear.
6. Give another name for line *j*.
7. List three points which are coplanar and collinear.
8. List two lines which are coplanar.
9. Name a point between *A* and *C*.

Written Exercises

Set A

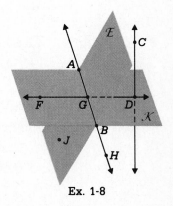

1. List three collinear points.
2. List three noncollinear points.
3. Name the intersection of $\overleftrightarrow{AB}$ and $\overleftrightarrow{FD}$.
4. Name the intersection of plane *E* and plane *K*.
5. List four coplanar points.
6. List four noncoplanar points.
7. Name a point between *G* and *H*.
8. Name a point between *F* and *D*.

Ex. 1-8

[9-13] Tell whether a point, a line, or a plane is suggested by each object.

9. A table top

10. The sharp end of a pin

11. A grain of sand

12. A parking lot

13. A telephone wire

14. **a.** Mark two points, *P* and *Q*, on a sheet of paper.
    b. Use a straightedge or ruler to draw a line which contains them.
    c. Can you draw another line containing *P* and *Q*?
    d. What can you conclude about the number of lines that contain two given points?

15. Use a sheet of cardboard to represent a plane and the tips of three sharpened pencils to represent points.
    a. If the points are collinear, how many planes can contain all three points?
    b. If the points are noncollinear, how many planes can contain all three points?
    c. What can you conclude about the number of planes that contain three given points?

[16-23] Use a straightedge or ruler to draw a diagram to illustrate each description. Label your diagram.

16. Point *P* is contained in two lines.

17. Points *A*, *Q*, and *S* are coplanar.

18. Point *M* is not contained in line *ℓ*.

19. Line *t* contains points *Q* and *R*, but does not contain points *P* and *S*.

20. Plane *𝒦* contains points *A*, *B*, and *C*, but does not contain point *D*.

21. Points *Q* and *R* are contained in the intersection of planes *ℋ* and *𝒦*.

22. Point *X* is between *A* and *B* and *A* is between *X* and *Y*.

23. Line *m* intersects $\overleftrightarrow{DE}$ at a point *F* such that *E* is between *D* and *F*.

Set B

Two special subsets of a line are shown below.

24. Using our undefined terms and the idea of "between," write a definition for segment *AB*.

A ———————————————— B
Segment *AB*

25. Write a definition for ray *AB* using the words "segment" and "between."

A •——————————————•——→ B
Ray *AB*

26. Three coplanar lines may have 0, 1, 2, or 3 points of intersection. Using a straightedge or ruler, draw a diagram to illustrate each case.

27. What are the possible numbers of points of intersection for four coplanar lines? Draw a diagram for each case.

28. Draw four coplanar lines that have the maximum number of points of intersection.
    a. Suppose a fifth line is drawn that intersects each of the four lines at distinct points. How many new points of intersection are there?
    b. What is the maximum number of points of intersection for five coplanar lines?

29. Using the reasoning suggested in exercise 28, determine the maximum number of points of intersection for
    a. 6 coplanar lines   c. 8 coplanar lines
    b. 7 coplanar lines   d. 12 coplanar lines

30. Think about a cardboard box and the planes and points suggested by the sides and corners. Using a straightedge, draw a single diagram that illustrates all of these descriptions.
    a. Point A is in the intersection of planes E, F, and K.
    b. Points C and B are both in the intersection of planes E and F.
    c. Points P and Q are both in the intersection of planes F and K.
    d. Points S and T are both in the intersection of planes E and K.

Set C

31. A **row** is defined to be four collinear points. How can ten lights be fixed to the wall of a videogames center so that each light is in exactly two rows?

32. Draw any two lines ℓ and m. Mark points A, C, and E on ℓ. Mark points B, D, and F on m. Label the intersection of $\overleftrightarrow{CF}$ and $\overleftrightarrow{DE}$ point P; the intersection of $\overleftrightarrow{AF}$ and $\overleftrightarrow{BE}$ point Q; and the intersection of $\overleftrightarrow{AD}$ and $\overleftrightarrow{BC}$ point R. What appears to be true about points P, Q, and R?

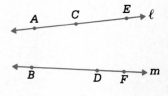

33. Repeat exercise 32 using a different pair of lines. Is your conclusion the same?

1.3 Basic Postulates

In lesson 1.2, we introduced three undefined terms—point, line, and plane. We give meaning to these terms by assuming certain facts about them. The statements that we assume are called **postulates.** These postulates lead to other facts about points, lines, and planes. Our first postulate simply ensures the existence of points.

Postulate 1
Points Postulate

Space contains at least four noncoplanar, noncollinear points. A plane contains at least three noncollinear points. A line contains at least two points.

Your intuition about lines should tell you that you can draw a line through any two points. If lines were not straight, you could draw more than one line. But since lines are straight, you can draw only one. The next postulate guarantees that there is one such line and no others.

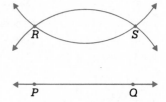

Postulate 2
Line Postulate

Two points are contained in one and only one line.

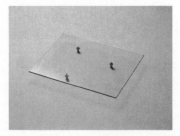

The model above suggests that three noncollinear points are contained in a plane. Do you think a second plane could also contain these three points? The next postulate ensures that there is only one such plane.

Postulate 3
Plane Postulate

Three noncollinear points are contained in one and only one plane.

The phrases "exactly one" and "unique" have the same meaning as "one and only one." The word "determine" means "are contained in one and only one." Postulates 2 and 3 can be restated as follows.

Postulate 2: Two points determine a line.
Postulate 3: Three noncollinear points determine a plane.

Postulate 4

Flat Plane
Postulate

If two points are contained in a plane, then the line through them is contained in the same plane.

These packaging dividers suggest that two planes need not intersect. However, if they do intersect, their intersection is always a line.

Postulate 5

Plane
Intersection
Postulate

If two planes intersect, they intersect in a line.

Physical examples of this postulate are in every classroom. Can you find one?

Class Exercises

[1-5] State the postulate that justifies your answer for each exercise.

1. How many lines contain points *A* and *B*?

2. List three points that determine plane $\mathcal{K}$.

3. Is $\overleftrightarrow{AC}$ contained in plane $\mathcal{K}$?

4. Is there a point in plane $\mathcal{E}$ not on $\overleftrightarrow{AB}$?

5. Name the intersection of planes $\mathcal{E}$ and $\mathcal{K}$.

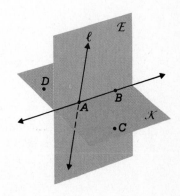

Written Exercises

Set A

[1-6] Complete each statement.

1. Two points are contained in one and only one __?__ .
2. If two planes intersect, their intersection is a __?__ .
3. Three noncollinear points are contained in exactly one __?__ .
4. At least four __?__ , noncollinear points are contained in space.
5. If P and Q are in a plane, then __?__ is in the same plane.
6. A __?__ contains at least two points.

[7-11] State the postulate that applies to the situation.

7. A camera tripod has three legs instead of four.
8. The location of two endposts determines the position of a fence.
9. To tear paper in a straight line, it helps to crease it first.
10. Cove moldings are sometimes placed along the intersection of a ceiling and a wall. These moldings are straight strips.

11. To check the flatness of a board, a carpenter places a ruler across it in several directions and looks for any space between the ruler and the board.

[12-15] Complete each statement with *always*, *sometimes*, or *never*.

12. Two points are __?__ collinear.
13. Three points __?__ determine a plane.
14. Four points are __?__ coplanar.
15. A line and a point not on the line are __?__ coplanar.

[16-21] The information in the first column is given. State the postulate(s) that support the corresponding conclusion.

Given information	Conclusion
16. *P* and *Q* are points in space.	There is exactly one line containing points *P* and *Q*.
17. *A* and *B* are points in plane *E*.	$\overleftrightarrow{AB}$ is contained in plane *E*.
18. *D*, *E*, and *F* are noncollinear points.	There is exactly one plane containing points *D*, *E*, and *F*.
19. Points *S* and *T* are each in planes *H* and *K*.	The intersection of planes *H* and *K* is $\overleftrightarrow{ST}$.
20. *ℓ* is a line in space.	*ℓ* contains at least two points.
21. Plane *K* contains $\overleftrightarrow{XY}$.	Plane *K* contains a point *Z* not on $\overleftrightarrow{XY}$.

[22-23] These facts are given:

a. *A* and *B* are two points.
b. Line *ℓ* contains *A* and *B*.
c. Line *m* contains *A* and *B*.

22. What must be true about lines *ℓ* and *m*?

23. State the postulate that supports your conclusion in exercise 22.

[24-25] These facts are given:

a. Line *ℓ* contains points *A* and *B*.
b. *A* and *B* are each contained in two planes *K* and *H*.

24. What must be true about planes *K* and *H* and line *ℓ*?
25. State the postulate(s) that support your conclusion in exercise 24.

26. What is the maximum number of planes determined by four points, no three of which are collinear?

27. What is the maximum number of planes determined by five points, no three of which are collinear?

Segments and Rays

The distance to the moon has been measured to within six centimeters by using a laser beam. To do this, a beam of light from an observatory at A is aimed at a reflecting surface at B on the moon. The time required for the light to travel to the moon and back is measured. Points A and B together with the points on the path of the beam between A and B provide a physical model of a line segment.

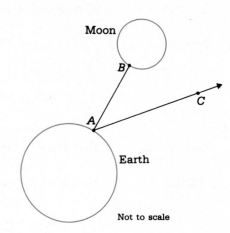

Not to scale

Definition A **segment**, $\overline{RT}$, is the set of points R and T and all the points between R and T.

The **endpoints** of $\overline{RT}$ (read "segment RT") are points R and T.

Notice that if a laser beam is aimed away from the moon, it can be used to measure distances to objects further out in space. The set of points on the path of the beam starting at A and extending without end through C is an example of a ray.

Definition A **ray**, $\overrightarrow{RT}$, is the set of points $\overline{RT}$ and all points S such that T lies between R and S.

The endpoint of $\overrightarrow{RT}$ (read "ray RT") is point R.

Each point on a line determines two rays with the same endpoint. For example, point A determines rays $\overrightarrow{AB}$ and $\overrightarrow{AC}$. $\overrightarrow{AB}$ and $\overrightarrow{AC}$ are called opposite rays.

Definition

Rays $\overrightarrow{AB}$ and $\overrightarrow{AC}$ are **opposite rays** if points A, B, and C are collinear and A is between B and C.

Example 1

Name the intersection of $\overrightarrow{PQ}$ and $\overrightarrow{SR}$.

Solution

$\overrightarrow{PQ}$ includes $\overline{PQ}$ and all the points on ℓ to the right of Q. $\overrightarrow{SR}$ includes $\overline{SR}$ and all the points on ℓ to the left of R. Therefore, the intersection of $\overrightarrow{PQ}$ and $\overrightarrow{SR}$ is $\overline{PS}$.

Example 2

Describe geometrically the graph of $x \geq 4$.

Solution

Graph $x \geq 4$ on a number line.

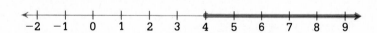

The graph of $x \geq 4$ is a ray.

Every line in a plane separates the plane into two **half-planes** or **sides** of the line. At right, ℓ separates plane $\mathcal{E}$ into half-planes $\mathcal{H}_1$ and $\mathcal{H}_2$.

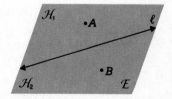

The half-plane $\mathcal{H}_1$ contains all the points X such that $\overline{AX}$ does not intersect ℓ. Two points A and B are said to be in **opposite half-planes** if A and B are not on ℓ and $\overline{AB}$ intersects ℓ. Line ℓ is the **edge** of each half-plane, but is not contained in either half-plane.

Class Exercises

1. How many endpoints does a segment have?
2. How many endpoints does a ray have?
3. How many endpoints does a line have?
4. Name the endpoint(s) of $\overline{DE}$.
5. Do $\overline{AB}$ and $\overline{BA}$ name the same segment? Explain.
6. Name the intersection of $\overline{AB}$ and $\overrightarrow{AB}$.
7. Name the endpoint(s) of $\overrightarrow{PQ}$.
8. Do $\overrightarrow{ST}$ and $\overrightarrow{TS}$ name the same ray? Explain.
9. Must $\overrightarrow{QP}$ and $\overrightarrow{QR}$ be opposite rays? Explain.
10. Must $\overrightarrow{QP}$ and $\overrightarrow{QR}$ be opposite rays if points Q, P, and R are collinear? Explain.

11. Into how many half-planes does a line separate a plane?
12. Does a half-plane contain the edge of the half-plane?

Written Exercises

Set A

1. Name two segments.
2. Name two rays that are not opposite rays.
3. List two other ways of naming $\overrightarrow{BE}$.
4. Name the intersection of $\overline{DB}$ and $\overline{CA}$.
5. Name the intersection of $\overrightarrow{BD}$ and $\overrightarrow{CE}$.
6. Name the intersection of $\overrightarrow{DC}$ and $\overrightarrow{BC}$.
7. Name two different rays that have D as their endpoint.
8. Name a pair of rays that have C as their endpoint.
9. Give another name for $\overrightarrow{CB}$.
10. Name the intersection of $\overrightarrow{DA}$ and $\overline{BC}$.
11. Name two half-planes.
12. Name two points that are in the same half-plane.

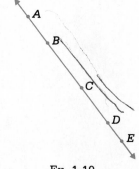

Ex. 1-10

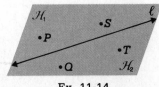

Ex. 11-14

13. Name the edge of one of the half-planes.

14. Name two points that are in opposite half-planes.

[15-22] Draw a diagram to illustrate the information given.

15. Point Q is on $\vec{DE}$, but Q is not on $\overline{DE}$.
16. $\vec{AB}$ and $\vec{AX}$ are opposite rays.
17. $\vec{RS}$ and $\vec{RT}$ are the same ray.
18. $\overline{AB}$ and $\overline{BC}$ are noncollinear.
19. $\vec{PQ}$ and $\vec{PT}$ are noncollinear.
20. Points X, Y, Q, and Z are collinear, and $\vec{XY}$ and $\vec{QZ}$ do not intersect.
21. The intersection of two rays $\vec{BC}$ and $\vec{AC}$ is $\overline{AB}$.
22. $\overline{XY}$ is in plane E, and X and Y are in opposite half-planes with edge m.

Set B

[23-26] Describe geometrically the number-line graph of each inequality.

23. $x \le 2$ 25. $x > 8 \ or \ x \le 8$
24. $-3 \le x \le 9$ 26. $x \le 1 \ or \ x \ge -1$

27. In plane E, P and Q are on opposite sides of line m, and Q and T are on opposite sides of line m. Are P and T on the same or opposite sides of line m?

28. In plane K, A and B are on opposite sides of line ℓ, and B and C are on the same side of line ℓ. Are A and C on the same or opposite sides of line ℓ?

[29-34] Suppose points are arranged in a plane so that no three of them are collinear.

29. Find the number of rays, each containing two of the given points, that can be drawn using the specified number of points as endpoints. Record your results in a table like the one given below.

Number of points	2	3	4	5	6
Number of rays	2	?	12	?	?

30. Look for a pattern in the table for exercise 29. Predict the number of rays that can be drawn using 10 points.

31. Which expression gives the number of rays that can be drawn using n points?
a. n **b.** $2n$ **c.** $n^2 - 4$ **d.** $n(n - 1)$

32. Find the number of segments that can be drawn using the given number of points as endpoints. Record your answers in a table like the one given below.

Number of points	2	3	4	5	6
Number of segments	?	?	?	?	?

33. How many segments can be drawn using 8 points?

34. Write an expression that gives the number of segments that can be drawn using n points.

Set C

35. There are 28 football teams in the National Football League. In conducting the annual player draft, the home office of each team must have direct telephone lines to the offices of each of the other teams. How many direct telephone lines are required?

Algebra Review   Solving Linear Equations

Example

Solve $\frac{2}{3}(x + 4) = 7 - (x + 1)$.

Solution

$$2(x + 4) = 21 - 3(x + 1) \quad \text{Multiply both sides by 3.}$$
$$2x + 8 = 21 - 3x - 3 \quad \text{Remove parentheses.}$$
$$2x + 8 = 18 - 3x \quad \text{Simplify.}$$
$$5x = 10 \quad \text{Combine like terms.}$$
$$x = 2 \quad \text{Multiply both sides by } \tfrac{1}{5}.$$

Solve.

1. $3x + 5 = 23$ **4.** $15 = 3x - 9$

2. $3.2 = 5x + 0.7$ **5.** $135 - 83a = 882$

3. $9 + \frac{1}{2}w = 14$ **6.** $6n - 19 + \frac{1}{2}(n - 8) = 52$

Progress Check

Lesson 1.1
Page 2

1. How did the approaches to geometry of the ancient Egyptians and the early Greeks differ?

2. Make a drawing and give a possible geometric description of the object in the photograph below.

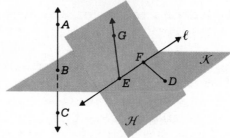

Items 3-14

Lesson 1.2
Page 8

3. Points *A*, *B*, and *C* are __?__ points.

4. Points *E*, *F*, *D*, and *G* are __?__ points.

5. Point *B* is __?__ points *A* and *C*.

6. The intersection of $\overleftrightarrow{AC}$ and plane $\mathcal{K}$ is __?__ .

Lesson 1.3
Page 14

7. Name points that determine line ℓ.

8. Name points that determine plane $\mathcal{H}$.

9. The intersection of planes $\mathcal{H}$ and $\mathcal{K}$ is __?__ .

10. State the postulate that guarantees that $\overleftrightarrow{BD}$ is in plane $\mathcal{K}$.

Lesson 1.4
Page 18

11. Name two segments with endpoint *F*.

12. Name two rays with endpoint *E*.

13. Name a pair of opposite rays.

14. Line ℓ separates plane $\mathcal{K}$ into two __?__ .

Linear Measure

A ruler can be used to measure the distance between two points. For example, the distance in centimeters between points *A* and *B* is 6.

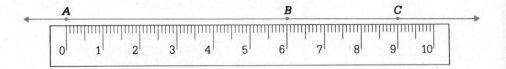

The distance in centimeters between *B* and *C* is 3. The distance would be the same even if the ruler were moved along the line so that *B* was above the 2 on the scale. This fact is formalized in the following postulate.

Postulate 6

Ruler
Postulate

For every pair of points there is a unique positive real number called the distance between them.

The distance between points *A* and *B* is denoted *AB*. Above, *AB* = 6 and *BC* = 3.

When a unit is not specified in this book, you can assume it to be centimeters, meters, feet, or any convenient unit. Unless otherwise specified, you should assume that the same unit is used for all the measurements in a diagram.

The **length** or **linear measure** of a segment is the distance between its endpoints. Note that $\overline{AB}$ represents a set of points, whereas *AB* represents the length of the segment, which is a real number.

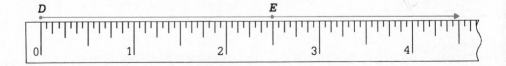

How many points *F* can you find on $\overrightarrow{DE}$ such that *DF* = 4 units? Postulate 7 generalizes this property.

Postulate 7

Segment
Construction
Postulate

On any ray, there is exactly one point at a given distance from the endpoint of the ray.

Postulate 7 is called the Segment Construction Postulate because it describes, for example, the method used by a roofing contractor to measure and cut a section of gutter to a specified length.

From the endpoint R of the gutter, there is only *one* point Q such that the length of $\overline{RQ}$ is 14 feet.

How might the contractor measure a 20-foot section of gutter using a 16-foot tape measure? One possible method is shown below.

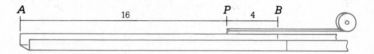

Since P is between A and B, $AP + PB = AB$. Thus, $AB = 20$. Postulate 8 formalizes this idea.

Postulate 8

Segment
Addition
Postulate

If point P is between points A and B, then $AP + PB = AB$.

Note that in the equation $AP + PB = AB$, we are adding real numbers (lengths), not segments.

Definition	A **midpoint** of a segment $\overline{RT}$ is a point S between R and T such that $RS = ST$.

R   S   T

This definition means that if S is a midpoint of $\overline{RT}$, then $RS = ST$ and S is between R and T. It also means that if S is between R and T and $RS = ST$, then S is the midpoint of $\overline{RT}$.

| **Postulate 9**
Midpoint
Postulate	A segment has exactly one midpoint.

Plane $\mathcal{K}$ intersects $\overline{AB}$ at point C, the midpoint of $\overline{AB}$. We say that plane $\mathcal{K}$ *bisects* $\overline{AB}$. Sets of points such as a plane, a line, a ray, a segment, or even a single point can bisect a segment.

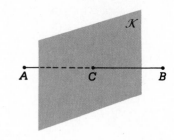

Definition	A **bisector of a segment** is a set of points whose intersection with the segment is the midpoint of the segment.

A **counterexample** is a statement or diagram that shows that a given statement is not always true.

Example

Give a counterexample for the following statement: If line ℓ intersects $\overline{FG}$, then ℓ bisects $\overline{FG}$.

Solution

$\overline{FG}$ has a midpoint, call it M. The diagram at the right is a counterexample for the given statement since it shows line ℓ intersecting $\overline{FG}$ and ℓ is not a bisector of $\overline{FG}$.

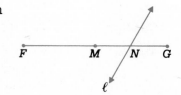

Definition	**Congruent segments** are segments that have the same length.

The symbol $\cong$ means "is congruent to." Thus $\overline{AB} \cong \overline{CD}$ means that $\overline{AB}$ and $\overline{CD}$ are congruent segments. By the definition of congruent segments, $\overline{AB} \cong \overline{CD}$ whenever $AB = CD$, and vice versa.

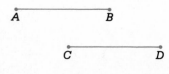

You are familiar with circles. The definition of circle is in terms of point, plane, and distance.

Definition   A **circle** is the set of points in a plane at a fixed distance (the **radius**) from a fixed point (the **center**).

The figure at right displays some of the terms associated with circles. It also pictures a compass, an instrument for drawing circles.

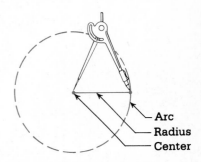

Arc
Radius
Center

The ancient Greeks used only two instruments when making geometric constructions. The straightedge, an unmarked ruler, was used for drawing lines. The compass was used for drawing circles. We also only use those instruments. The following construction applies the Segment Construction Postulate.

Construction 1   Construct a segment congruent to a given segment.

Given $\overline{AB}$

Construct   A segment congruent to $\overline{AB}$.

Method   Step 1: Draw a line ℓ with a straightedge. Choose any point on ℓ; call it X.

Step 2: Put the compass point on A and the compass pencil on B. The **compass radius** is now AB.

Step 3: Using X as the center and AB as the compass radius, draw an arc that intersects line ℓ. Label the point of intersection Y.

Then $\overline{XY} \cong \overline{AB}$.

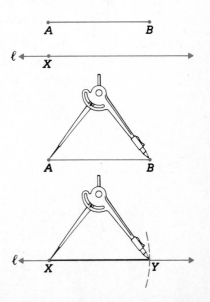

Class Exercises

[1-6] State the postulate or definition that supports the statement.

1. For two points P and Q, $PQ \neq -7$.
2. If $AB = CD$, then $\overline{AB} \cong \overline{CD}$.
3. If point R is between points S and T so that $SR = 6$ and $RT = 8$, then $ST = 14$.
4. If X is on $\overrightarrow{AB}$ and $AX = 7$, then there is not another point Y on $\overrightarrow{AB}$ such that $AY = 7$.
5. If B is between A and C, and $AB = BC$, then B is the midpoint of $\overline{AC}$.
6. If $\overleftrightarrow{CD}$ bisects $\overline{AB}$ at M, then M is the midpoint of $\overline{AB}$.
7. Name the instruments that we will use to make geometric constructions.

Written Exercises

Set A

1. If $BD = 6$, then $DB =$ __?__ .
2. If $AD = 10$ and $\overline{AD} \cong \overline{BE}$, then $BE =$ __?__ .
3. If $AC = 7$ and $CE = 5$, then $AE =$ __?__ .
4. If $BD = 8$ and C is the midpoint of $\overline{BD}$, then $BC =$ __?__ .
5. If $BE = 12$ and $DE = 3$, then $BD =$ __?__ .
6. If $\overline{AC} \cong \overline{CE}$ then C is the __?__ of $\overline{AE}$.

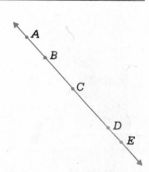

7. Explain how a clerk in a fabric store applies the Segment Construction Postulate when cutting ribbon from a spool for a customer.

8. The distance of an air flight between Chicago and New York can be determined by using a map. Which postulate explains why it makes no difference whether you measure from Chicago to New York or vice versa?

9. A third-down football play involved a 20-yard pass from scrimmage followed by a 15-yard run.
   a. How many yards were gained on the play?
   b. On which postulate is your conclusion based?

10. To cut a 36-cm rod in half, you can measure 18 cm from one end of the rod. Which postulate guarantees that it makes no difference from which end you measure?

[11-16] The information in the first column is given. State the postulate or definition that supports the corresponding conclusion.

Given information	Conclusion
11. $\overline{PQ} \cong \overline{ST}$	$PQ = ST$
12. Points A and B	AB is a positive real number.
13. Plane $\mathcal{F}$ bisects $\overline{CD}$ at point P.	P is the midpoint of $\overline{CD}$.
14. $\overline{XY}$	$\overline{XY}$ has only one midpoint.
15. $AB = DE$	$\overline{AB} \cong \overline{DE}$
16. Point Q is the midpoint of $\overline{MN}$.	$\overline{MQ} \cong \overline{QN}$

Set B

[17-20] Sketch a counterexample for each statement.

17. If points P, Q, and R are collinear, then $PQ + QR = PR$.

18. If $\overline{AM} \cong \overline{MB}$, then M is the midpoint of $\overline{AB}$.

19. If point P is on line m, there is only one point on m at a given distance from P.

20. If $\overline{RS} \cong \overline{AB}$, and $\overline{RS}$ bisects $\overline{AB}$ at point M, then M is the midpoint of $\overline{RS}$.

21. Point B is between points A and C and $AC = 24$. If BC is three times AB, find AB.

22. Point Q is between points P and R and $PR = 41$. If PQ is 8 more than twice QR, find PQ.

23. Which postulate in this lesson ensures that any line contains infinitely many points?

24. An assembly line manufacturing process involves tasks which are performed by one robot at station X_1 and by another robot at station X_2. Where along the line should a supply depot be located so that the sum of the distances traveled by the two robots to the depot is as small as possible?

$$X_1 \rule{4cm}{0.4pt} X_2$$

25. Repeat exercise 24 for the case of a robot at each of 3 collinear stations.

$$X_1 \quad X_2 \rule{3cm}{0.4pt} X_3$$

26. Repeat exercise 24 for the case of a robot at each of 4 collinear stations.

$$X_1 \quad X_2 \quad X_3 \quad X_4$$

27. Repeat exercise 24 for the case of a robot at each of n collinear stations.

$$X_1 \ X_2 \quad X_3 \ X_4 \ \cdots \quad X_n$$

Construction Exercises

[1-4] Construct a segment congruent to the given segment.

1. $P \rule{4cm}{0.4pt} Q$

3. $E \rule{4cm}{0.4pt} F$

2. $G \rule{4cm}{0.4pt} H$

4. $R \rule{3cm}{0.4pt} S$

[5-11] Given: $\overline{AB}$ and $\overline{CD}$. Construct a segment of the required length.

$$A \rule{5cm}{0.4pt} B \qquad C \rule{6cm}{0.4pt} D$$

5. $AB + CD$

8. $AB + 2(CD)$

6. $2(AB)$

9. $4(AB) - CD$

7. $CD - AB$

10. $2(DC - AB)$

11. If $AB = 6$ and $CD = 10$, construct $\overline{XY}$ so $XY = 2$.

1.6   Angles and Angle Measure

The distance a soccer ball travels depends on two factors: the force with which it is kicked, and the angle formed by the initial path of the ball and a horizontal ray.

Definition

An **angle** is the union of two noncollinear rays which have the same endpoint.

The rays are called the **sides** of the angle and their common endpoint is the **vertex.**

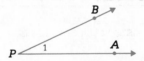

The sides of the angle above are $\overrightarrow{PA}$ and $\overrightarrow{PB}$; the vertex is P. The angle can be denoted by $\angle APB$, $\angle BPA$, $\angle P$, or $\angle 1$. Notice that when three letters are used, the letter of the vertex is the middle letter.

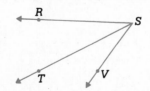

When two or more angles have the same vertex, using a single-letter name causes confusion. In the figure above, no angle should be named $\angle S$. Instead use three letters: $\angle RST$, $\angle TSV$, or $\angle VSR$.

An angle determines three sets of points in a plane: the points on the angle, those in its interior, and those in its exterior. The half-planes shown in the diagram below help illustrate the formal definitions that follow.

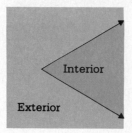
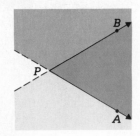

Definition The **interior** of ∠APB is the intersection of two half-planes: the side of $\overleftrightarrow{PA}$ containing B and the side of $\overleftrightarrow{PB}$ containing A.

Definition The **exterior** of an angle is the set of points in the plane which do not belong to the interior of the angle or to the angle itself.

Unless otherwise specified, points may be assumed to be in the interior (or exterior) of an angle when a diagram shows them in that position.

To measure an angle, place a protractor on it as shown in one of the drawings below.

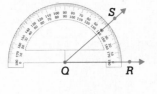
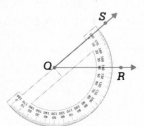
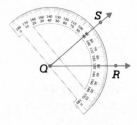

| Zero of outer scale on a ray | Zero of inner scale on a ray | Subtract the numbers on one scale |

No matter which method is used, the measure of ∠SQR is the same. Postulate 10 states that this is true for all angles.

Postulate 10	For every angle there is a unique real number r, called its **degree**
Protractor Postulate	**measure,** such that $0 < r < 180$.

If the degree measure of $\angle SQR$ is 40, we write $m\angle SQR = 40$. Or we say that $\angle SQR$ is an angle of 40° (read "40 degrees").

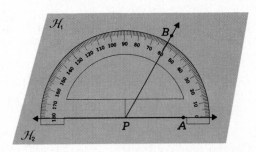

Protractors can also be used to draw an angle with a given measure. In the diagram above, $\overrightarrow{PB}$ was drawn so that $m\angle APB = 60$. Can you draw another 60° angle in $\mathcal{H}_1$ using $\overrightarrow{PA}$ as a side?

Postulate 11	Let $\mathcal{H}_1$ be a half-plane with edge $\overleftrightarrow{PA}$. There is exactly one ray $\overrightarrow{PB}$
Angle Construction Postulate	with B in $\mathcal{H}_1$ such that $\angle APB$ has a given measure.

Using the diagram at the right, find $m\angle APB$, $m\angle BPC$, and $m\angle APC$. How are the measures of $\angle APB$, $\angle BPC$, and $\angle APC$ related? Postulate 12 generalizes this observation.

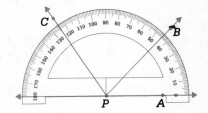

Postulate 12	If B is in the interior of $\angle APC$, then
Angle Addition Postulate	$m\angle APB + m\angle BPC = m\angle APC$.

In the Angle Addition Postulate, measures of angles are added. These measures are real numbers. So algebra may be used to rewrite $m\angle APB + m\angle BPC = m\angle APC$ as $m\angle BPC = m\angle APC - m\angle APB$.

Just as segments have midpoints, angles have bisectors.

<table>
<tr><td>Definition</td><td>A bisector of an angle APC is a ray $\overrightarrow{PB}$ such that B is in the interior of ∠APC and m∠APB = m∠BPC.</td></tr>
</table>

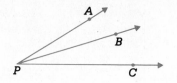

<table>
<tr><td>Postulate 13
Angle Bisector
Postulate</td><td>An angle has exactly one bisector.</td></tr>
</table>

If you compare Postulates 10–13 with Postulates 6–9, you will notice many striking similarities. This is reasonable, since the process for measuring segments is similar to the process for measuring angles. The following definition completes the list of similar properties for linear measure and angle measure.

<table>
<tr><td>Definition</td><td>Congruent angles are angles that have the same measure.</td></tr>
</table>

When ∠A and ∠B are congruent, we write ∠A ≅ ∠B.

Class Exercises

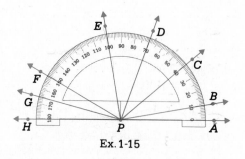

Ex. 1-15

1. Name a point in the interior of ∠EPG.

2. Name a point in the exterior of ∠BPD.

3. Name the vertex of ∠HPF.

4. Name seven angles that have $\overrightarrow{PG}$ as a side.

[5-12] Give the measure of each angle.

5. ∠APC	**7.** ∠APE	**9.** ∠APG	**11.** ∠FPB
6. ∠BPD	**8.** ∠EPD	**10.** ∠CPD	**12.** ∠GPD

[13-14] Give the bisector of each angle.

13. ∠*DPB*   **14.** ∠*HPF*

15. Name an angle congruent to ∠*EPC*.

Written Exercises

Set A

1. Name ∠1 in two other ways.

2. Name all the angles shown which have $\overrightarrow{EF}$ as a side.

3. Name all the angles shown.

4. Name a point in the interior of ∠*GEF*.

5. Name a point in the exterior of ∠2.

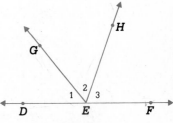

Ex. 1-10

6. Is the union of $\overrightarrow{ED}$ and $\overrightarrow{EG}$ an angle? Explain.

7. Is the union of $\overrightarrow{ED}$ and $\overrightarrow{EF}$ an angle? Explain.

8. If $\overrightarrow{EH}$ is the bisector of ∠*GEF*, what can you conclude about ∠2 and ∠3?

9. What information is needed to conclude that $\overrightarrow{EG}$ is the bisector of ∠*DEH*?

10. Using $\overrightarrow{EF}$ as a side, can you draw another angle whose measure is the same as that of ∠*GEF*? Explain.

11. $m\angle APB + m\angle BPC = m\angle\ \underline{?}$

12. $m\angle DPB + m\angle BPA = m\angle\ \underline{?}$

13. $m\angle BPD - m\angle CPD = m\angle\ \underline{?}$

14. $m\angle BPD - m\angle BPC = m\angle\ \underline{?}$

15. If $\overrightarrow{PC}$ is the bisector of ∠*DPB* and $m\angle CPD = 28$, then $m\angle BPC = \underline{?}$

16. If $\overrightarrow{PC}$ is the bisector of ∠*DPB* and $m\angle DPB = 62$, then $m\angle DPC = \underline{?}$

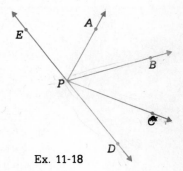

Ex. 11-18

17. If $m\angle APC = 87$ and $m\angle CPD = 28$, find $m\angle APD$.

18. If $m\angle BPD = 72$ and $m\angle CPD = 26$, find $m\angle BPC$.

1.6 Angles and Angle Measure

35

19. A drafting student drew the angle at the right. What is $m\angle PQR$? Which postulate is used to get this measure?

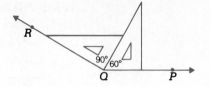

Set B

[20-25] Draw a sketch, if possible, to illustrate each situation. Otherwise, write *not possible*.

20. Two angles whose intersection is a point

21. Two angles whose intersection is a segment

22. Two angles whose intersection is a ray

23. Two angles whose intersection is a line

24. The vertex of $\angle 1$ is in the interior of $\angle 2$ and vice versa.

25. $\angle 3$ and $\angle 4$ have the same vertex, and the interior of $\angle 3$ is contained in the interior of $\angle 4$.

26. A point X is in the interior of $\angle PQR$. If $m\angle PQX = 40$ and $m\angle PQR = 110$, find $m\angle XQR$.

[27-28] Point P is between points A and B. Points C, E, and D are in the same half-plane with edge $\overleftrightarrow{AB}$. Point C is in the interior of $\angle APE$. $\overrightarrow{PE}$ bisects $\angle DPC$.

27. Make a diagram to illustrate the situation.

28. If $m\angle APC = 72$ and $m\angle CPD = 70$, find $m\angle APE$.

The U.S. Army Artillery Corps uses a semicircular protractor divided into 3200 units. This unit of angle measure is called a *mil*.

29. Modify the postulates of this lesson so that they would be useful to the Artillery Corps.

30. Would the changes in angle measure from degrees to mils require changes in any definitions in this lesson?

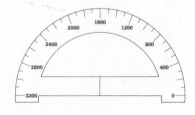

31. Give the mil measure of a 90° angle. Of a 135° angle.

Set C

[32-33] A creative geometry student suggested that the measure of an angle ABC be determined as follows:

a. Choose X on $\overrightarrow{BA}$ such that $BX = 1$ unit.
b. Choose Y on $\overrightarrow{BC}$ such that $BY = 1$ unit.
c. The measure of $\angle ABC$ is the length of $\overline{XY}$.

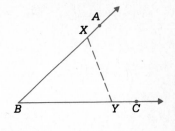

32. Draw angles with degree measures of 30, 60, and 90 and find their measures as defined above.

33. Are Postulates 10, 11, and 12 still satisfied when angles are measured in this new way? Explain.

34. Determine the number of angles formed by 20 coplanar, noncollinear rays that have a common endpoint. **Hint** Solve some simpler, related problems and look for a pattern in the results.

Construction Exercises

___

Construction 2 Construct an angle congruent to a given angle.

Given | $\angle FGH$

Construct | $\angle PQR \cong \angle FGH$

Method | Step 1: Draw ray $\overrightarrow{QR}$.

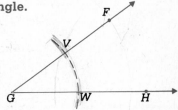

Step 2: With G as center, construct an arc which intersects $\overrightarrow{GF}$ and $\overrightarrow{GH}$. Label the points of intersection V and W, respectively.

Step 3: With center Q and radius GV, construct an arc which intersects $\overrightarrow{QR}$ at S.

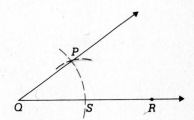

Step 4: With center S and radius VW, construct an arc which intersects the arc in step 3 at P.

Step 5: Draw $\overrightarrow{QP}$.

Then $\angle PQR \cong \angle FGH$.

<u>**Construction 3**</u>   **Construct the bisector of a given angle.**

Given $\angle ABC$

Construct $\overrightarrow{BD}$, the bisector of $\angle ABC$

Method   Step 1: With B as center, construct an
arc that intersects $\overrightarrow{BA}$ and $\overrightarrow{BC}$ at X
and Y respectively.

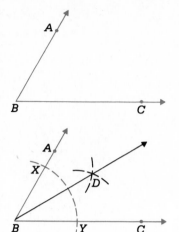

Step 2: With X and Y as centers, and
a radius greater than $\frac{1}{2} XY$, construct
two intersecting arcs. Label the
intersection D.

Step 3: Draw $\overrightarrow{BD}$.

Then $\overrightarrow{BD}$ bisects $\angle ABC$.

[1-4] Trace each angle and construct a congruent angle.

1.

3.

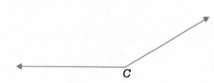

2.

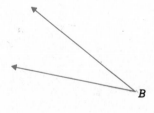

4.

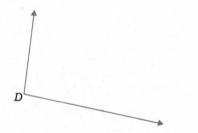

5. Construct an angle $\angle F$ so that $m\angle F = m\angle A + m\angle B$.

6-9. Trace the angles in exercises 1-4 above and bisect each
angle.

10. Construct an angle $\angle G$ so that $m\angle G = \frac{1}{2}(m\angle B + m\angle D)$.

Career   Navigator

Andrea Wiley is a navigator. She uses degree measure to specify the direction in which an airplane or ship is moving.

The angle between due north and the craft's line of motion gives the direction of the motion. This angle is always measured clockwise from the north and is called the **course** of the craft.

There are 360 degrees in a complete revolution. Courses are given by three-digit numbers between 000° and 359° inclusive.

The courses shown at the right are 040° and 225° respectively.

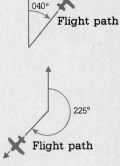

Exercises

1. Give the course of a ship which sails
   a. North
   b. East
   c. South
   d. West
   e. Northeast
   f. Southeast
   g. Southwest
   h. Northwest

2. A ship sails on a course of 210°. Through what angle must it turn to follow a course of 325°? Sketch a diagram showing the two courses.

3. A plane flies on a course of 160°. Which of the eight compass directions is nearest the plane's course?

1.7   Special Angles and Pairs of Angles

Knowledge of special angles and pairs of angles is very important to artisans who create intricate stained-glass designs and to many other people.

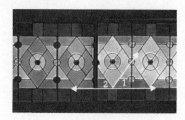

Angles can be classified according to their measures.

Definition   A **right angle** is an angle whose measure is 90.
An **acute angle** is an angle whose measure is less than 90.
An **obtuse angle** is an angle whose measure is greater than 90.

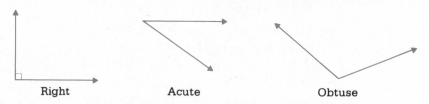

The mark, ⌐, is used to indicate a right angle.

Special terms are also used to classify pairs of angles related by their measures.

Definition   **Complementary angles** are two angles whose measures have a sum of 90. Each angle is called the **complement** of the other.

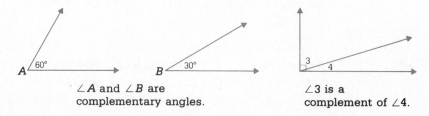

∠A and ∠B are
complementary angles.

∠3 is a
complement of ∠4.

Supplementary angles are two angles whose measures have a sum of 180. Each angle is called a **supplement** of the other.

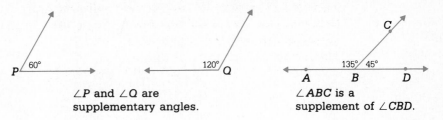

∠P and ∠Q are
supplementary angles.

∠ABC is a
supplement of ∠CBD.

Angles can also be related by position.

Definition **Adjacent angles** are two coplanar angles with a common side and no common interior points.

At the right, ∠APB and ∠BPC are adjacent angles with $\overrightarrow{PB}$ as their common side.

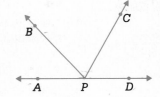

∠BPD and ∠BPC also have $\overrightarrow{PB}$ as a common side. However, they have interior points in common so they are not adjacent.

Adjacent angles such as ∠APB and ∠BPD, whose noncommon sides form a line, are given a special name.

Definition A **linear pair** of angles is a pair of adjacent angles whose noncommon sides are opposite rays.

Angles in a linear pair are related by measure as well as by position.

Postulate 14 The angles in a linear pair are supplementary.
Supplement
Postulate

Since ∠5 and ∠6 are a linear pair, they are supplementary, and $m\angle 5 + m\angle 6 = 180$.

In the photograph on page 40, $m\angle 2 = 130$. What is $m\angle 1$?

When two lines intersect, they form four linear pairs of angles. The pairs are $\angle 1$ and $\angle 2$, $\angle 2$ and $\angle 3$, $\angle 3$ and $\angle 4$, and $\angle 4$ and $\angle 1$. The two lines also form two pairs of "opposite angles," such as $\angle 1$ and $\angle 3$. These are called vertical angles.

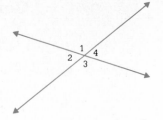

Definition   **Vertical angles** are two angles whose sides form two pairs of opposite rays.

In the physical world, two lines are often constructed so they intersect to form a 90° angle. This relationship occurs so frequently that such lines are given a special name.

Definition   **Perpendicular lines** are lines that intersect to form a right angle.

If $\overleftrightarrow{AC}$ and $\overleftrightarrow{DF}$ are perpendicular, we write $\overleftrightarrow{AC} \perp \overleftrightarrow{DF}$ (read "$\overleftrightarrow{AC}$ is perpendicular to $\overleftrightarrow{DF}$").

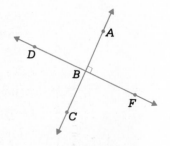

Rays and segments are said to be perpendicular if the lines containing them are perpendicular. Thus $\overrightarrow{AC} \perp \overrightarrow{DF}$, $\overrightarrow{FD} \perp \overline{BC}$, and so on.

Name some physical examples of perpendicularity that are in your classroom.

Definition   A **perpendicular bisector** of a segment is a line which is perpendicular to the segment and contains its midpoint.

In the figure above, $\overleftrightarrow{AC} \perp \overleftrightarrow{DF}$. If in addition $DB = BF$, then $\overleftrightarrow{AC}$ is a perpendicular bisector of $\overline{DF}$.

Class Exercises

1. Name a right angle.
2. Explain why ∠*BPC* is a right angle.
3. Name four acute angles.
4. Name four obtuse angles.
5. Name eight pairs of adjacent angles.
6. Name a pair of complementary angles.
7. Name two supplements of ∠*BPE*.
8. Name six linear pairs of angles.
9. Name six pairs of vertical angles.
10. Name a pair of perpendicular rays.
11. If *BP* = *PD*, then __?__ is the perpendicular bisector of __?__ .

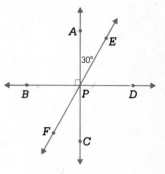

Ex. 1-11

12. ∠*R* and ∠*S* are complementary and *m*∠*R* = 50. Find *m*∠*S*.
13. ∠*P* and ∠*Q* are supplementary and *m*∠*P* = 10. Find *m*∠*Q*.
14. ∠*X* and ∠*Y* are a linear pair and *m*∠*Y* = 75. Find *m*∠*X*.

Written Exercises

Set A

1. Name two right angles.
2. Name three obtuse angles.
3. Name ten acute angles.
4. Name eight pairs of adjacent angles.
5. Name four linear pairs of angles.
6. Name two pairs of complementary angles.
7. Name five pairs of supplementary angles.
8. Name two pairs of perpendicular lines.

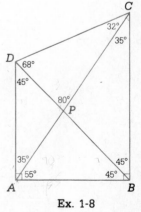

Ex. 1-8

[9-14] Find the measure of the complement of ∠*A*.

9. *m*∠*A* = 5
10. *m*∠*A* = 72
11. *m*∠*A* = 45
12. *m*∠*A* = 56
13. *m*∠*A* = 38
14. *m*∠*A* = *r*

[15-20] Find the measure of the supplement of ∠P.

15. $m\angle P = 31$ **17.** $m\angle P = 43$ **19.** $m\angle P = 75$

16. $m\angle P = 152$ **18.** $m\angle P = 137$ **20.** $m\angle P = r$

[21-24] State whether the numbered angles are adjacent. If they are not adjacent, explain why not.

21. 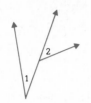   **22.** 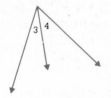   **23.** 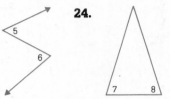   **24.**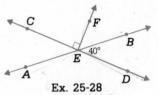

25. $m\angle AED = $ __?__   **27.** $m\angle BEF = $ __?__

26. $m\angle FED = $ __?__   **28.** $m\angle AEF = $ __?__

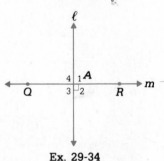

Ex. 25-28

29. What kind of angle is ∠2?

30. Is $\ell \perp m$? Explain.

31. What kind of angle is ∠1? Explain.

32. What kind of angle is ∠3? Explain.

33. If two lines are perpendicular, how many right angles are formed?

34. Line ℓ is a perpendicular bisector of $\overline{QR}$. Name a pair of congruent segments.

Ex. 29-34

Set B

The figure at the right shows a part of a square-cornered picture frame of uniform width.

35. What kind of angles are ∠1 and ∠2?

36. At what angles should the pieces be cut to form a right-angled corner?

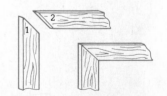

37. ∠A and ∠B are complementary angles. $m\angle A$ is 4 times $m\angle B$. Find $m\angle A$ and $m\angle B$.

38. ∠C and ∠D are supplementary angles. $m\angle C$ is 30 more than 5 times $m\angle D$. Find $m\angle C$ and $m\angle D$.

A goniometer is used by geologists to measure the angle between the faces of mineral crystals.

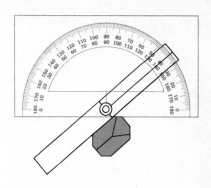

39. What is the measure of the angle between the two faces of the crystal shown?

40. How is this method of measurement related to Postulate 14 and the definitions in this lesson?

41. Suppose that $\angle 1$ and $\angle 2$ are a linear pair, and that $\angle 2$ is a right angle. What can you conclude about $\angle 1$? Why?

42. Suppose that $\angle 1$ and $\angle 2$ are a linear pair, and that $\angle 1 \cong \angle 2$. What can you conclude about $\angle 1$ and $\angle 2$? Why?

Set C

43. The measure of a supplement of an angle is 40 more than 3 times the measure of its complement. Find the measure of the angle.

44. If $\angle A$ is acute, $\angle B$ is a supplement of $\angle A$, and $\angle C$ is a complement of $\angle A$, find $m\angle B - m\angle C$.

Construction Exercises

| Construction 4 | Through a point on a given line, construct a line perpendicular to the given line. |

Given   Point P on line m

Construct $\overleftrightarrow{PQ} \perp m$

Method   Step 1: With P as center and a convenient radius, construct arcs intersecting m at two points, A and B.

Step 2: With A and B as centers and a radius greater than AP, construct two intersecting arcs. Label the point of intersection Q.

Step 3: Draw $\overleftrightarrow{PQ}$.

Then $\overleftrightarrow{PQ} \perp m$ at P.

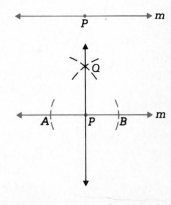

Construction 5   Construct the perpendicular bisector of a given segment.

Given $\overline{AB}$

Construct   The perpendicular bisector of $\overline{AB}$

Method   Step 1: With A and B as centers and
                radius greater than $\frac{1}{2}AB$, construct
                two pairs of intersecting arcs. Label
                the points of intersection of the
                arcs P and Q.

                Step 2: Draw $\overleftrightarrow{PQ}$.
                $\overleftrightarrow{PQ}$ is the perpendicular bisector of $\overline{AB}$.

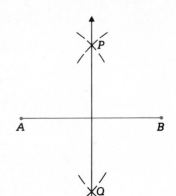

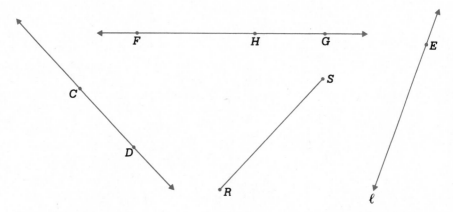

1. Trace $\overleftrightarrow{CD}$. Construct a line perpendicular to $\overleftrightarrow{CD}$ through C.
2. Trace line ℓ. Construct a line perpendicular to ℓ through E.
3. On one drawing, construct $\overline{XZ} \perp \overline{ZT}$, then $\overline{XY} \perp \overline{ZX}$, then
   $\overline{TV} \perp \overline{TZ}$, with $\overleftrightarrow{TV}$ intersecting $\overleftrightarrow{XY}$ at W.
4. Construct the perpendicular bisector of $\overline{CD}$.
5. Trace $\overline{FG}$ and find its midpoint by construction.
6. Construct a segment whose length is $\frac{1}{2}(FH)$.
7. Trace $\overline{RS}$. Construct t, the perpendicular bisector of $\overline{RS}$,
   intersecting $\overline{RS}$ at V. On t, mark points X and Y so that
   $VX = VY = RV$. Draw $\overline{RX}$, $\overline{XS}$, $\overline{SY}$, and $\overline{RY}$. Use a protractor
   to find the number of right angles and angle bisectors in
   the figure.

Using BASIC

Complements and Supplements

The computer program below is written in the language called BASIC. The program can be used to compute and print the measures of the complements and supplements of six acute angles.

```
100 PRINT "ANGLE", "COMP.", "SUPP."
110 PRINT "MEAS.","MEAS.","MEAS."
120 PRINT
130 FOR I = 1 TO 6
140 READ A       A is measure of given angle.
150 LET C = 90 - A    C is measure of the complement.
160 LET S = 180 - A    S is measure of the supplement.
170 PRINT A, C, S
180 NEXT I
190 DATA 20, 45, 50, 75, 80, 89
200 END
```

1. RUN the program and use its output to discover a relationship between the complement and supplement of an acute angle.

2. Test your conjecture for exercise 1 by using a different set of measures of acute angles in line 190.

3. Explain why the program cannot be used with measures of obtuse or right angles.

4. Revise the program so that it can be used with measures of any angle by adding the following lines:

```
145 IF A > = 90 THEN 175
172 GOTO 180
175 PRINT A, "NONE", 180-A
```

RUN the modified program with these measures as data:

$$30, 110, 70, 90, 1, 150$$

★ 5. How might the original program be modified so that it would handle ten angle measures as input data?

★ 6. Write a program to identify integer angle measures from 1 to 90 where the measure A of the angle is equal to the difference between the measure S of its supplement and twice the measure C of its complement.

Inductive Reasoning

Postulates 1-14 describe some of the obvious relationships among geometric figures. In this lesson we will consider a method for discovering new geometric relationships which are not necessarily obvious.

Galileo, an Italian astronomer and physicist, made a number of discoveries concerning pendulums. By experimenting he collected the following data.

Time of swing (in seconds)	1	2	3	4	5
Pendulum length (in units)	1	4	9	16	?

Examine the table for a pattern. How long would a pendulum be if it required 5 seconds to complete one swing? The correct answer, 25 units, can be verified experimentally. In general, the data suggest that if it takes n seconds to complete one swing, the length of the pendulum is n^2.

The process of forming a conclusion based upon examination of several specific cases is called **inductive reasoning.**

Heron, a Greek mathematician, used inductive reasoning to discover that the angle at which a ball strikes a flat surface is congruent to the angle at which it rebounds.

$\angle 1 \cong \angle 2$

In the following diagrams of game tables, a ball is shot from corner A at a 45° angle. On each table, Heron's discovery is used to draw the path of the ball. The numbers indicate where and in what order the ball strikes the various sides. In what corner does the ball always end up?

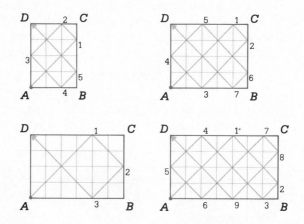

Using inductive reasoning, you might conclude that if the width of the game table is 4 units, the ball will always end up in corner D.

However, the diagram at the right of a 4-by-8 table shows that this conclusion is not correct. Here the ball ends up in corner B.

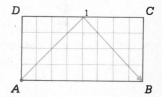

This illustrates an important aspect of inductive reasoning—conclusions that seem reasonable for some cases may not apply to all cases. Therefore, you must be cautious when using inductive reasoning.

Yet inductive reasoning is extremely important in everyday life as well as in mathematics and the sciences because it is the way we usually get ideas to try out and verify.

Class Exercises

1. A gardener experimented with a new fertilizer, using it on alternate rows of a garden. The rows with the new fertilizer gave the better yield. Should the gardener recommend this fertilizer to the Garden Club? Explain.

2. A football scout for the Broncos observed that in the first three games of the season, the Chiefs always threw a pass on second down. The Chiefs' fourth game is against the Broncos. What kind of defense should the Broncos use against the Chiefs on second down?

The first three diagrams show the number of pieces of pizza determined by 1, 2, and 3 cuts, respectively.

3. Predict the number of pieces determined by 4 cuts. Check your conclusion by counting the pieces in the fourth diagram.

4. What type of reasoning did you use in exercise 3?

5. Predict the number of pieces determined by 5 cuts. By *n* cuts.

Written Exercises

Set A

Give an example of how inductive reasoning might be used by:

1. An automobile driver

2. A medical researcher

3. Draw a pair of intersecting lines. Use a protractor to measure each angle in a pair of vertical angles. Repeat the procedure three times. How do the measures of vertical angles appear to be related?

4. Draw a linear pair of angles. Then draw the bisector of each angle. Measure the angle formed by the bisectors. Repeat the procedure with a different linear pair. What conclusion is suggested by your findings?

5. **a.** Draw a semicircle like the one above.
   b. Choose a point P on the semicircle and draw $\angle APB$.
   c. What is $m\angle APB$?
   d. Choose another point Q and find $m\angle AQB$.
   e. What appears to be true about the angle formed in each case?
   f. Check your conjecture with several more points.

Set B

On the circle at the right, three points are marked and connected. Four nonoverlapping regions are formed.

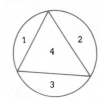

6. Copy and complete the table below. Draw a new circle for each case. Mark points on the circle. Connect all pairs of points with segments. Count the regions.

Number of points	1	2	3	4	5
Number of regions	?	?	4	?	?

7. Predict how many regions would be formed if six points were chosen. Check your prediction.

[8-10] By placing segments end to end, you can separate a plane into nonoverlapping regions as shown. Figure **a** separates the plane into two regions: points inside the figure and points outside.

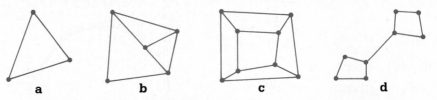

a   b   c   d

8. Copy and complete the table below. For each figure, count the number of segments or edges *E*, the number of points or vertices *V*, and the number of regions *R*.

Figure	a	b	c	d
Edges	?	?	?	?
Vertices	?	?	?	?
Regions	2	?	?	?

9. Write a formula relating *V*, *R*, and *E*.

10. How many regions would be formed by a figure with 6 vertices and 8 edges? Check your conjecture with a drawing.

11. In the game tables on page 49, look at the ratios of the table widths to lengths. Use the reduced form of the ratios to predict in which corner of a 4-by-*n* table the ball will end up. (Let *n* be any positive integer.)

12. Predict the number of times the ball will hit the sides of a 4-by-*n* table before ending up in a corner.

Geometry Maintenance

1. Name three undefined terms in geometry.

2. If *M* is the midpoint of $\overline{PQ}$, then __?__ = __?__ .

3. If *S* is between *V* and *W*, then __?__ + __?__ = __?__ .

4. ∠*A* is a supplement of ∠*B*. *m*∠*A* = 36. Find *m*∠*B*.

Excursion   Dihedral Kaleidoscope

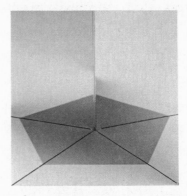

A **dihedral angle** is the union of two noncoplanar half-planes with a common edge, together with the common edge. A two-mirror kaleidoscope is a physical example of a dihedral angle. Designers use kaleidoscopes to discover patterns for wallpaper, floor coverings, and fabrics.

Make a kaleidoscope using two mirrors hinged with tape. Draw a line 10 cm long on a sheet of paper. Position the mirrors as shown above. Adjust the mirrors so that you can see a figure with 5 congruent sides.

a. Carefully trace the angle formed by the mirrors.
b. Remove the mirrors and use a protractor to measure the angle you drew. This is the measure of the dihedral angle formed by the mirrors.

1. Complete the table below by adjusting the mirrors until you see a figure with the indicated number of sides.

Number of sides	3	4	5	6	7	8
Measure of dihedral angle	_?_	_?_	72	_?_	_?_	_?_

2. What measure would the angle have if the figure had 10 sides?

3. Write a formula relating the measure m of the dihedral angle and n, the number of sides in the figure.

Chapter Summary

1. Point, line, and plane are the undefined terms of geometry. (page 8)

2. Postulates are statements which are accepted without proof. Postulates give meaning to the undefined terms. (page 14)

3. Two points are contained in exactly one line. Three noncollinear points are contained in exactly one plane. (page 14)

4. If B is between A and C, then $AB + BC = AC$. (page 25)

5. In the diagram at the right, if $AB = BC$, then B is the midpoint of $\overline{AC}$, and vice versa. (page 26)

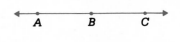

6. Congruent segments have the same length. (page 26)

7. If P is in the interior of $\angle ABC$, then $m\angle ABP + m\angle PBC = m\angle ABC$. (page 33)

8. In the diagram at the right, if $m\angle 1 = m\angle 2$, then $\overrightarrow{BP}$ is the bisector of $\angle ABC$, and vice versa. (page 34)

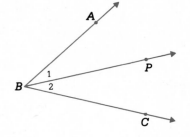

9. Congruent angles have the same measure. (page 34)

10. Angles are classified as acute, right, or obtuse. (page 40)

11. Pairs of angles can be classified as:
    complementary   adjacent   a linear pair
    supplementary   vertical
    (pages 40-42)

12. Perpendicular lines form a right angle. (page 42)

13. If $\ell \perp \overline{AB}$ at its midpoint, then ℓ is a perpendicular bisector of $\overline{AB}$. (page 42)

14. Inductive reasoning is the process of reaching a general conclusion after observing several specific cases. The conclusion may be true or false. (page 48)

Chapter Review

Lesson 1.1
Page 2

1. Geometry involves the study of the _?_ , _?_ , and _?_ of objects in the real world.

2. Make a drawing of the object in the photograph.

Lesson 1.2
Page 8

[3-5] Use the diagram at the right.

3. Name three collinear points.

4. Name four coplanar points.

5. Name three noncollinear points.

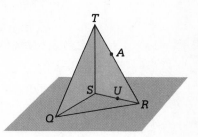

Lesson 1.3
Page 14

[6-8] True or false

6. Three points are contained in exactly one plane.

7. If points P and Q are in plane $\mathcal{E}$, then $\overleftrightarrow{PQ}$ is in plane $\mathcal{E}$.

8. The intersection of two planes, $\mathcal{H}$ and $\mathcal{K}$, is a point A.

Lesson 1.4
Page 18

9. Name the endpoints of $\overline{DE}$.

10. Point P is between points S and T. Name a pair of opposite rays.

11. Into how many half-planes does a line separate a plane?

Lesson 1.5
Page 24

12. Point D is between points A and G such that $AG = 18$ and $DG = 7$. Find AD.

13. Two segments are congruent if _?_ .

14. Point R is the midpoint of $\overline{QS}$ and $QR = 11$. Find QS.

Lesson 1.6
Page 31

[15-19] $m\angle RYT = 90$

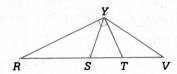

15. Name all the angles with vertex Y.

16. Name a point in the interior of $\angle SYV$.

17. Name a point in the exterior of $\angle RYT$.

18. If $m\angle SYV = 75$ and $m\angle RYS = 42$, find $m\angle RYV$.

19. If $\overrightarrow{YS}$ is the bisector of $\angle RYT$, find $m\angle SYT$.

Lesson 1.7
Page 40

[20-26] $m\angle DEB = 90$.

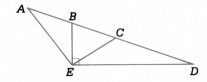

20. Name a right angle.

21. Name an obtuse angle.

22. Name an acute angle.

23. Name a pair of complementary angles.

24. Name a pair of supplementary angles.

25. Name two pairs of adjacent angles with vertex E.

26. Name two linear pairs of angles.

27. If $\angle A \cong \angle B$ and $\angle A$ is a complement of $\angle B$, find $m\angle B$.

28. If $\angle X \cong \angle Y$ and $\angle Y$ is a supplement of $\angle X$, find $m\angle Y$.

29. Two perpendicular lines form __?__ pairs of vertical angles.

Lesson 1.8
Page 48

30. Predict the next two numbers in this sequence of triangular numbers.

1   3   6   10

31. What type of reasoning did you use in item 30?

Chapter Test

1. Give two other names for line ℓ.

2. Give another name for $\overrightarrow{DC}$.

3. Name a pair of opposite rays.

4. $AG + GB = \underline{\quad ? \quad}$

[5-9] Answer the question, and then state a postulate or definition to support your answer.

5. How many lines contain points A and F?

6. How many planes contain points A, C, and F?

7. Is $\overleftrightarrow{BE}$ contained in plane $\mathcal{K}$?

8. If $\underline{\quad ? \quad}$, then $\overline{AE} \cong \overline{BF}$.

9. If $\underline{\quad ? \quad}$ and $\underline{\quad ? \quad}$, then m is a perpendicular bisector of $\overline{AB}$.

10. Points E and F are in the same $\underline{\quad ? \quad}$ with edge $\overleftrightarrow{AB}$.

11. $m\angle PTQ = \underline{\quad ? \quad}$

12. $m\angle QPT + m\angle TPR = m\angle \underline{\quad ? \quad}$

13. $m\angle PRS - m\angle SRT = m\angle \underline{\quad ? \quad}$

14. Name an obtuse angle.

15. Name a right angle.

16. $\angle QPT$ and $\angle \underline{\quad ? \quad}$ are adjacent angles.

17. Name a pair of complementary angles.

18. Name two pairs of vertical angles.

19. Name two points in the interior of $\angle QPR$.

20. Name two supplements of $\angle PTR$.

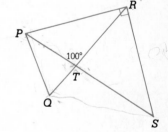

21. The measure of $\angle V$ is five times the measure of its supplement, $\angle W$. Find $m\angle V$ and $m\angle W$.

22. Use inductive reasoning to predict the next three pentagonal numbers.

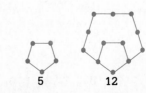

1   5   12

Chapter 2

Proof in Geometry

A reporter at a balloon race needed to report which balloon and balloonist placed first, second, third, and fourth. He had the following information:

a. The winners were Anne, Betty, Carl, and Dean, not necessarily in that order.

b. The winning balloons were colored all white; yellow and red; green, blue, and white; and white with multicolors.

c. Dean finished before the all-white balloon and after the green, blue, and white balloon.

d. The winning balloon did not have white on it.

e. Carl finished before Dean and after Anne.

Can you piece the information together for the reporter?

1. Use clue c. In which two positions could the all-white balloon be? Why?

2. Use clue c again. In which two positions could the green, blue, and white balloon be?

3. Look at clue d. Which balloon was first?

4. Combine the results from exercises 2 and 3. In which position must the green, blue, and white balloon be?

5. Use clue c to find in which position the all-white balloon finished.

6. Which balloon filled the remaining position?

7. Use clues c and e to determine who owned each balloon.

If clues a-e are true, is any other solution to the puzzle possible? Using agreed-upon statements to logically argue that other statements are true is called deductive reasoning. In this chapter you will learn to form deductive arguments to show that geometric statements are true.

2.1 Deductive Reasoning

The guidelines in the curriculum handbook for Roseville High School state that students need 20 credits in grades 9 through 12 to graduate. Also advanced courses are offered to students who score at the 92nd percentile or above on the standardized test in a subject area.

How many credits should a student complete each year?

A student has percentile scores of 94, 92, and 86 in English, mathematics, and science, respectively. In which advanced courses may the student enroll?

Your answers to these questions are a result of **deductive reasoning.** Deductive reasoning is the use of logical principles to draw necessary conclusions.

In algebra you used deductive reasoning and properties of real numbers to solve equations.

Example 1   Solve $3x + 5 = 17$.

Solution

$$3x + 5 = 17$$
$$ -5 = -5 \quad \text{Reflexive property of equality}$$
$$3x = 12 \quad \text{Addition property of equality}$$
$$\tfrac{1}{3} = \tfrac{1}{3} \quad \text{Reflexive property of equality}$$
$$x = 4 \quad \text{Multiplication property of equality}$$

In example 1 each statement is justified by a property of real numbers. Since the properties of real numbers will also be used in geometry, the ones that will be needed are listed below.

Properties of Real Numbers

For all real numbers a, b, c, and d:

$a = a$	Reflexive property of equality
If $a = b$, then $b = a$.	Symmetric property of equality
If $a = b$ and $b = c$, then $a = c$.	Transitive property of equality
If $a = b$ and $c = d$,	
then $a + c = b + d$	Addition property of equality
and $a - c = b - d$	Subtraction property of equality
and $ac = bd$	Multiplication property of equality

$a(b + c) = ab + ac$ Distributive property

Exactly one of these is true:
     $a = b$, $a > b$, or $b > a$ Trichotomy property

If $a > b$ and $b > c$, then $a > c$.	Transitive property of inequality
If $a > b$, then $a + c > b + c$	Addition property of inequality
and $a - c > b - c$	Subtraction property of inequality
If $a > b$ and $c > 0$, then $ac > bc$	Multiplication properties of inequality
If $a > b$ and $c < 0$, then $ac < bc$	
If $a = b$, then a may replace b in any equation or inequality.	Substitution principle

In geometry each statement in a deductive argument is justified by a property of real numbers, definition or postulate.

Example 2   Use a deductive argument to show that $QR = QS - RS$.

$\underset{\bullet}{Q} \quad \underset{\bullet}{R} \rule{3cm}{0.4pt} \underset{\bullet}{S}$

Solution

Because R is between Q and S, $QR + RS = QS$.	Segment Addition Postulate
$RS = RS$	Reflexive property of equality
Since $QR + RS = QS$ and $RS = RS$, $QR = QS - RS$.	Subtraction property of equality

Class Exercises

[1-3] Fill in the conclusion to the deductive argument.

1. "Does Jim have a physical education class?"
   "Jim is a sophomore, and all sophomores have physical education, so __?__."

2. "Is 596,732,204,978,640 evenly divisible by 8?"
   "Any number is evenly divisible by 8 if the number formed by its last 3 digits is evenly divisible by 8, so __?__."

3. "If you practice every day, you will learn to play better."
   "I do practice every day, so __?__."

[4-11] State the definition, postulate, or real-number property that justifies the statement.

4. If $AB = CD$, then $CD = AB$.

5. If $AB = RS$ and $RS = CD$, then $AB = CD$.

6. If Q is between A and T, then $AQ + QT = AT$.

7. If $m\angle K > m\angle J$, then $2m\angle K > 2m\angle J$.

8. If $AB = CD + DT$ and $CD + DT = OT$, then $AB = OT$.

9. If $m\angle R = 40$ and $m\angle W = 50$, then $m\angle R + m\angle W = 90$.

10. If $AC = AB + BC$ and $BD > AC$, then $BD > AB + BC$.

11. $m\angle A = m\angle A$

Written Exercises

Set A

[1-2] Write the conclusion of the argument.

1. "A pint is a pound the world around."
   This carton of milk contains 2 pints.
   Therefore this carton weighs __?__.

2. Only persons who are 16 years old before September 1 will be allowed to take driver's education this year.
   Kathy will be 16 on November 18.
   Therefore Kathy __?__.

[3-4] Use the warranty below.

> This clock is warranted for one year from the date of purchase against defects in materials and workmanship. During this period such defects will be repaired or the product will be replaced at the company's option without charge. This warranty does not cover damage caused by misuse or negligence.

3. The hour hand of the clock was missing when the clock was purchased.
   Therefore, the company __?__ .

4. The clock was left outside in the rain one month after its purchase.
   Therefore, the company __?__ .

[5-14] State the property of real numbers that justifies the statement.

5. If $x = 5$ and $y = 3$, then $x + y = 5 + 3$.

6. If $6 > 3$ and $c > 0$, then $6c > 3c$.

7. If $s = t$ and $t = r$, then $s = r$.

8. $2(4x + 5) = 8x + 10$

9. If $3x = 12$, then $x = 4$.

10. If $AB + BC = AC$, then $AB = AC - BC$.

11. $3p - 6q = 3(p - 2q)$

12. If $AC = AB + BC$ and $AB + BC = QR$, then $AC = QR$.

13. If $LN = LM + MN$ and $MN = QS$, then $LN = LM + QS$.

14. If $2(AX) = 2(BY)$, then $AX = BY$.

[15-22] State the postulate or definition that justifies the statement.

15. If P is between A and B, then $AP + PB = AB$.

16. If $\overrightarrow{FG}$ is in the interior of $\angle PFQ$, then
    $m\angle PFG + m\angle GFQ = m\angle PFQ$.

17. If M is the midpoint of $\overline{AC}$, then $AM = MC$.

18. If $RS = PQ$, then $\overline{RS} \cong \overline{PQ}$.

19. If $m\angle 1 + m\angle 2 = 180$, then $\angle 1$ and $\angle 2$ are supplementary.

20. If $\angle P$ is obtuse, then $m\angle P > 90$.

21. If $\overrightarrow{RT}$ is the bisector of $\angle ORB$, then $m\angle ORT = m\angle TRB$.

22. If $\angle T \cong \angle V$, then $m\angle T = m\angle V$.

[23-26] Complete the deductive argument.

23. Show that if $\overleftrightarrow{AM}$ bisects $\overline{CD}$ at point M, then $CM = MD$.

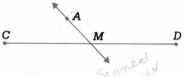

Since $\overleftrightarrow{AM}$ bisects $\overline{CD}$ at M,   Definition of __?__
M is the midpoint of $\overline{CD}$.
Since M is the midpoint   Definition of __?__
of $\overline{CD}$, then $CM = MD$.

24. Show that if $AQ = QB$ and $QB = BR$, then $\overline{AQ} \cong \overline{BR}$.

Since $AQ = QB$ and   __?__ property of equality
$QB = BR$, then $AQ = BR$.
Because $AQ = BR$,   Definition of __?__
then $\overline{AQ} \cong \overline{BR}$.

25. Show that if $\angle 1$ and $\angle 2$ are a linear pair, then $m\angle 1 + m\angle 2 = 180$.

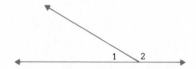

If $\angle 1$ and $\angle 2$ are a linear pair,   __?__ Postulate
then they are supplementary.
If $\angle 1$ and $\angle 2$ are supplementary,   __?__
then $m\angle 1 + m\angle 2 = 180$.

26. Show that if $\angle Q$ and $\angle R$ are right angles, then $m\angle Q + m\angle R = 180$.

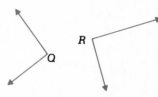

Since $\angle Q$ and $\angle R$ are right   __?__
angles, $m\angle Q = 90$ and $m\angle R = 90$.
Then $m\angle Q + m\angle R = 90 + 90 = 180$.   __?__

[27-32] Write a deductive argument. Justify each statement with a definition, postulate, or property of real numbers.

27. Show that if *B* is the midpoint of $\overline{AC}$, then $\overline{AB} \cong \overline{BC}$.

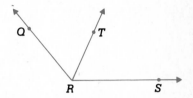

28. Show that if $\overrightarrow{RT}$ bisects $\angle QRS$, then $\angle QRT \cong \angle TRS$.

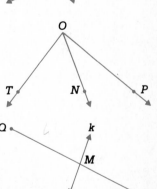

29. Show that if *B* is in the interior of $\angle XYZ$, then $m\angle XYZ - m\angle BYZ = m\angle XYB$.

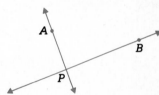

30. Show that if $m\angle APB = 90$, then $\overrightarrow{AP} \perp \overleftrightarrow{PB}$.

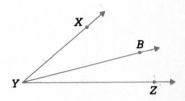

31. Show that if $\angle TON$ and $\angle NOP$ are complements, then $m\angle TOP = 90$.

32. Show that if *k* bisects $\overline{QR}$ at *M*, then $\overline{QM} \cong \overline{RM}$.

[33-34] Write a deductive argument to justify the given statement.

33. If *N* is the midpoint of $\overline{JS}$, then $JN = \frac{1}{2}(JS)$.

34. If $\overrightarrow{QR}$ bisects $\angle SQT$, then $2(m\angle SQR) = m\angle SQT$.

Two-Column Proofs

A computer programmer must organize the steps of a program and clearly explain the processing that these steps do. In geometry we also need to organize and clearly report the steps taken to reach a conclusion.

The two-column table below presents an answer to the following question:

In the diagram at the right, if $\angle FED$ and $\angle DEW$ are complementary, why must $\angle FEW$ be a right angle?

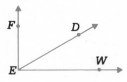

Statements	Reasons
1. $\angle FED$ and $\angle DEW$ are complementary.	1. This was *given* as true.
2. $m\angle FED + m\angle DEW = 90$	2. The *definition of complementary angles* states their sum is 90.
3. $m\angle FEW = m\angle FED + m\angle DEW$	3. Since D is in the interior of $\angle FEW$, statement 3 is true by the *Angle Addition Postulate*.
4. $m\angle FEW = 90$	4. Since the angle measures in statements 2 and 3 are real numbers, statement 4 is true by the *transitive property of equality*.
5. $\angle FEW$ is a right angle.	5. This follows from statement 4 and the *definition of right angle*.

A deductive argument such as the one on page 66 is called a **proof.** Compare the proof below with the one on page 66. Notice that only a few words are needed to justify a statement in a proof. The numeral in brackets after reason 2 shows which previous statement was used to obtain statement 2.

Given   ∠FED and ∠DEW are complementary.

Prove   ∠FEW is a right angle.

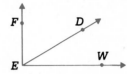

Proof

Statements	Reasons
1. ∠FED and ∠DEW are complementary.	1. Given
2. m∠FED + m∠DEW = 90	2. Def. of complementary angles [1]
3. m∠FEW = m∠FED + m∠DEW	3. Angle Addition Post.
4. m∠FEW = 90	4. Transitive property of equality [2, 3]
5. ∠FEW is a right angle.	5. Def. of right angle [4]

The table above is called a **two-column form** for reporting a proof. We will use this form for most of the proofs in this book.

A statement that is proved is called a **theorem.** After a theorem is proved, it may be used as a reason in future proofs.

Parts of a Two-Column Proof

1. Given: statement of all known facts about the problem
2. Prove: statement of the conclusion
3. Diagram: illustration of the problem
4. Statements: numbered statements that follow logically from the given information and previous statements
5. Reasons: the postulates, theorems, definitions, or properties of real numbers that justify the statements

---

A photographer uses a paper cutter to trim excess paper from prints. Theorem 2.1 guarantees that the angles formed are congruent. The proof of Theorem 2.1 is in the class exercises.

Theorem 2.1   All right angles are congruent.

The proofs of Theorems 2.2 and 2.3 rely on the real-number properties of segment lengths and angle measures. The proofs of the parts of Theorem 2.2 are exercises 6-8. The proof of Theorem 2.3 is in the exercises of lesson 2.6.

Theorem 2.2   Congruence of segments is reflexive, symmetric, and transitive.

Theorem 2.3   Congruence of angles is reflexive, symmetric, and transitive.

Class Exercises

Fill in the reasons in the proof of Theorem 2.1.

Given: $\angle A$ and $\angle B$ are right angles.
Prove: $\angle A \cong \angle B$

Statements	Reasons
1. $\angle A$ and $\angle B$ are right angles.	1. __?__
2. $m\angle A = 90$	2. __?__
3. $m\angle B = 90$	3. __?__
4. $m\angle A = m\angle B$	4. __?__
5. $\angle A \cong \angle B$	5. __?__

Written Exercises

Set A

[1-5] Supply the missing reasons in each proof.

1. Given: O is between N and W.

Prove: $NO = NW - OW$

Statements	Reasons
1. O is between N and W.	1. ?
2. $NO + OW = NW$	2. ?
3. $OW = OW$	3. ?
4. $NO = NW - OW$	4. ?

2. Given: $RY = RO$

Prove: $PR + RY = PO$

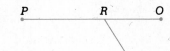

Statements	Reasons
1. $PR + RO = PO$	1. ?
2. $RY = RO$	2. ?
3. $PR + RY = PO$	3. ?

3. Given: $m\angle AOD = 90$

Prove: $\overleftrightarrow{AO} \perp \overleftrightarrow{OD}$

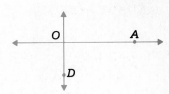

Statements	Reasons
1. $m\angle AOD = 90$	1. ?
2. $\angle AOD$ is a right angle.	2. ?
3. $\overleftrightarrow{AO} \perp \overleftrightarrow{OD}$	3. ?

4. Given: $\angle ENA \cong \angle AND$

Prove: $\overrightarrow{NA}$ bisects $\angle END$.

Statements	Reasons
1. $\angle ENA \cong \angle AND$	1. ?
2. $m\angle ENA = m\angle AND$	2. ?
3. $\overrightarrow{NA}$ bisects $\angle END$.	3. ?

5. Given: $\overleftrightarrow{AB}$ bisects $\overline{CD}$ at M.

Prove: $CM = DM$

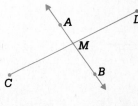

Statements	Reasons
1. $\overleftrightarrow{AB}$ bisects $\overline{CD}$ at M.	1. ?
2. M is the midpoint of $\overline{CD}$.	2. ?
3. $CM = DM$	3. ?

[6-8] Complete the proof of Theorem 2.2.

6. Congruence of segments is reflexive.
Given: Any segment $\overline{AB}$
Prove: $\overline{AB} \cong \overline{AB}$

Statements	Reasons
1. $\overline{AB}$ is any segment.	1. ?
2. $AB = AB$	2. ?
3. ?	3. Def. of ? [2]

7. Congruence of segments is symmetric.
Given: $\overline{AB} \cong \overline{XY}$
Prove: $\overline{XY} \cong \overline{AB}$

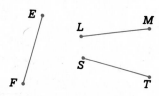

Statements	Reasons
1. ?	1. Given
2. $AB = XY$	2. ?
3. $XY = AB$	3. ?
4. $\overline{XY} \cong \overline{AB}$	4. ?

8. Congruence of segments is transitive.
Given: $\overline{EF} \cong \overline{LM}$, $\overline{LM} \cong \overline{ST}$
Prove: $\overline{EF} \cong \overline{ST}$

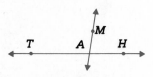

Statements	Reasons
1. $\overline{EF} \cong \overline{LM}$	1. ?
2. $EF = LM$	2. ?
3. ?	3. Given
4. ?	4. Def. of congruent segments [3]
5. $EF = ST$	5. ?
6. ?	6. Def. of congruent segments [5]

9. Given: $\overleftrightarrow{MA}$ and $\overleftrightarrow{TH}$ intersect at A.
Prove: $\angle MAT$ and $\angle MAH$ are supplementary.

Statements	Reasons
1. ?	1. Given
2. $\angle MAT$ and $\angle MAH$ are ?	2. Def. of linear pair
3. ?	3. Supplement Post. [2]

Drawing and Using Diagrams

Drafters must be certain that their drawings convey correct information. Project engineers must interpret correctly the drawings supplied them. Drawing and using diagrams are important parts of geometry also.

Use the diagram at the right. What statements can you make about ∠EOD and ∠COD? About ∠AOB and ∠BOC?

Did you assume that the points were coplanar? Would your statements be the same if the points were not coplanar?

If points A, B, C, D, and E were not coplanar, they might appear as in the diagram at the right. To avoid confusion, all diagrams in this book are plane figures, unless otherwise stated or the planes are shown.

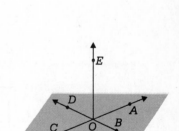

You may assume from a diagram that:
Points and lines are coplanar.
Points and rays are collinear.
Angles are adjacent, vertical, or linear pairs.
A point is between two others or in the interior of an angle.

You may not assume that lines are perpendicular, or that segments or angles have the same measure.

A diagram is an aid in visualizing geometric relationships. It should contain all the information in the Given, but no additional assumptions.

Pairs of angles or segments that are given as congruent may be marked as shown below.

$\angle A \cong \angle T$
$\angle B \cong \angle S$
$\angle C \cong \angle R$
$\overline{AB} \cong \overline{ST}$
$\overline{BC} \cong \overline{RS}$
$\overline{AC} \cong \overline{RT}$

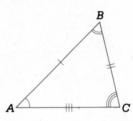
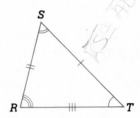

Example

Select the best diagram for the following proof.

Given: $\overline{AN} \cong \overline{NB}$; $\overline{BO} \cong \overline{OC}$; $\overline{CP} \cong \overline{PD}$; $\overline{DM} \cong \overline{MA}$

Prove: $MN = OP$

a.
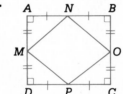

b.
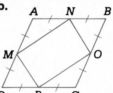

c.
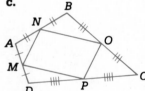

Solution

Diagram **c** is best, since diagrams **a** and **b** both have information marked that was not part of the Given.

In the proof of a theorem, the diagram is often drawn first, so that the letters in the diagram can be used in writing the Given and Prove. In Theorem 2.4 the diagram contains names for the two lines and the point of intersection.

Theorem 2.4

If two lines intersect, they intersect in one and only one point.

Given

ℓ and m intersect.

Prove

ℓ and m intersect at P and only at P.

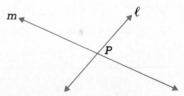

The proof of Theorem 2.4 is in lesson 3.4. The diagram, Given, and Prove for Theorems 2.5 and 2.6 are exercises 25 and 26. Their proofs are in lessons 2.6 and 3.4.

Theorem 2.5 A line and a point not on the line are contained in one and only one plane.

Theorem 2.6 Two intersecting lines lie in one and only one plane.

Class Exercises

1. Select the best diagram for the given information.
   Given: Vertical angles $\angle DOE$ and $\angle LOW$; $\angle ODE \cong \angle OWL$

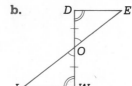

a. **b.** **c.**

[2-8] Can the information be obtained from the diagram?

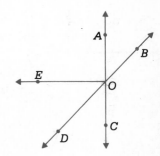

2. $\overrightarrow{OE}$, $\overrightarrow{OA}$, and $\overrightarrow{OB}$ are coplanar.
3. $\overrightarrow{OB}$ and $\overrightarrow{OD}$ are collinear.
4. $\overrightarrow{OD}$ bisects $\angle EOC$.
5. $\overrightarrow{OA} \perp \overrightarrow{OE}$
6. $m\angle DOE + m\angle EOA = m\angle DOA$
7. $\angle AOB$ and $\angle BOC$ form a linear pair.
8. $\overline{AO} \cong \overline{BO}$

[9-12] True or false

9. Two lines can intersect in more than two points.
10. Two intersecting lines lie in a plane.
11. A line and a point lie in one and only one plane.
12. If two lines look perpendicular, that information should be added to the Given.

Written Exercises

Set A

[1-5] State the postulate, theorem, definition, or property of real numbers that supports the statement.

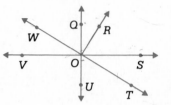

1. ∠*ROS* and ∠*SOT* are adjacent angles.
2. *UO* + *OQ* = *UQ*
3. ∠*VOW* and ∠*WOS* are supplementary.
4. ∠*SOT* and ∠*WOS* are supplementary.
5. *m*∠*QOR* + *m*∠*ROS* = *m*∠*QOS*

6. Select the best diagram, given $\overline{JX} \perp \overline{JN}$, $\overline{NY} \perp \overline{JN}$, and $\overline{JX} \cong \overline{NY}$.

a. 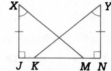 b.  c.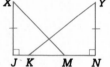

7. Select the best diagram, given $\overline{AY} \cong \overline{BX}$ and ∠*X* ≅ ∠*Y*.

a. 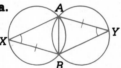 b. 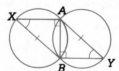 c.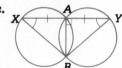

[8-17] Use a straightedge to draw a diagram; then label it. If the diagram cannot be drawn, explain why.

8. $\overleftrightarrow{QR}$ bisects $\overline{ST}$ at point *X*.
9. ∠*ABG* and ∠*CBG* are supplementary.
10. ∠*WAD* and ∠*DAY* are complementary and adjacent.
11. ∠1 and ∠2 are adjacent angles whose noncommon sides are perpendicular.
12. $\overline{AB}$ and $\overline{AQ}$ bisect each other.
13. $\overrightarrow{AB}$ bisects ∠*CDA*.
14. ∠*X* and ∠*Y* are complements of ∠*W*.
15. ∠5 and ∠6 are supplements of ∠7.
16. ∠*P* and ∠*Q* are supplementary; ∠*C* and ∠*D* are supplementary; *m*∠*Q* = *m*∠*D*.
17. $\overrightarrow{OA} \perp \overrightarrow{OB}$; $\overrightarrow{OB} \perp \overrightarrow{OG}$; *A*, *B*, *G*, and *O* are coplanar.

18. Which theorem explains why identifying a row and a column locates just one desk in a classroom?

19. Which theorem explains why a skier's pole point and uphill ski determine a plane for stability?

20. Which theorem explains why the skeleton of a kite can be covered by a flat surface?

Set B

[21-24] Draw and label a diagram for the statement.

21. In a plane, $\overrightarrow{OA}$, $\overrightarrow{OB}$, and $\overrightarrow{OC}$ are such that $m\angle AOC - m\angle BOC = m\angle AOB$.

22. In a plane, $\overrightarrow{BE} \perp \overleftrightarrow{AC}$ at B; $\overrightarrow{BD}$ bisects $\angle ABE$.

23. $\angle 1$ and $\angle 2$ are a linear pair; $\overrightarrow{OC}$ bisects $\angle 1$; $\overrightarrow{OA}$ bisects $\angle 2$.

24. In a plane, $\overleftrightarrow{AD}$ bisects $\overline{QR}$ at point M.

25. Draw and label a diagram for Theorem 2.5. Then state the Given and Prove.

26. Draw and label a diagram for Theorem 2.6. Then state the Given and Prove.

[27-37] Tell whether the statement is true or false, given $\angle AOC$ is a right angle and $\overrightarrow{OD}$ bisects $\angle EOC$.

27. $\angle 1$ and $\angle 2$ are complementary.

28. $\angle 5$ and $\angle BOE$ are supplementary.

29. $\angle 3 \cong \angle 4$

30. $\angle 3 \cong \angle 2$

31. $\angle 6$ is acute.

32. $\angle GOB$ is obtuse.

33. $\angle 2$ and $\angle 3$ are complementary.

Set C

34. $\angle 1$ and $\angle 6$ are complementary.

35. $m\angle 5 + m\angle 6 = 2(m\angle 3)$

36. $m\angle 2 + 2(m\angle 4) + m\angle 5 = 180$

37. $m\angle 1 + m\angle 4 = m\angle 3 + m\angle 2$.

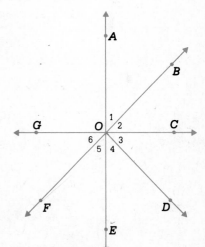

Career   Furniture Designer

Dorothy Jackson designs furniture.
She uses basic geometric ideas to
design and build new products.

Exercises

Name a postulate, theorem, or definition that justifies each
step she used to build a prototype of a teakwood table.

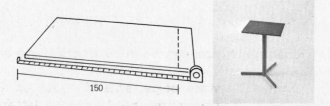

1. To cut the table top, she first marked a point on the edge
   of a sheet of lumber 150 cm from one end.
2. She marked another point 150 cm from the same end and
   connected them to determine a cutting line.
3. She designed a pedestal base with three legs to ensure
   that the table would not wobble.

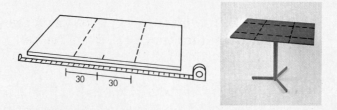

4. To locate a position for mounting the base, she found two
   numbers on the tape measure, each 30 cm from the center
   of one edge.
5. To drill the holes for mounting the base, she drew a line
   20 cm from each side and drilled where the lines met.

2.4 "If . . . Then" Statements

Deductive reasoning is used every day.

Father: If you get an A on your math test tomorrow, we'll go to the ball game on Saturday.

Jim, next day: I got an A on my math test.

What conclusion can be drawn from these statements?

Logic is the study of patterns of reasoning. Reasoning patterns may be represented by using letters for important statements.

p: Jim gets an A on the math test.
q: Jim and his father go to the ball game.

　　Father: If p, then q.
　　　　Jim: p
Deduction: q

If the statements made by Jim and his father are true, then the conclusion—that they will go to the ball game on Saturday—must be true.

A statement of the form "If p, then q" is a **conditional** statement. It is often written "$p \Rightarrow q$" (read "p implies q").

The "if" clause of a conditional statement is the **hypothesis,** and the "then" clause is the **conclusion.**

What are the hypothesis and conclusion of this statement? If $\angle A$ is a right angle, then $m\angle A = 90$.

Example 1	What can be deduced from this pair of statements?

If our team wins, I will be happy.
I am happy.

Solution	No deduction can be made, because there are many reasons why you might be happy. This pattern is not the same as the first pattern.

$p{\Rightarrow}q$ is true.
   q is true.

No deduction about p is possible.

When a conditional statement is true, and the conclusion is known to be true, it is still possible for the hypothesis to be false.

Often a conditional statement must be rewritten to put it into "if . . . then" form.

Example 2	Write these statements in "if . . . then" form.

1. All moons revolve around a planet.
2. A four-sided figure is a square only if all sides are congruent.

Solution	1. If a heavenly body is a moon, then it revolves around a planet.

2. If a four-sided figure is a square, then all its sides are congruent.

When a theorem is in "if . . . then" form, the hypothesis is the Given, and the conclusion is the Prove. Thus, it is often helpful to restate theorems in "if . . . then" form.

Theorem 2.7	Supplements of congruent angles are congruent.

Restatement   If two angles are congruent, then their supplements are congruent.

Given $\angle 1$ and $\angle 3$ are supplementary;
$\angle 2$ and $\angle 4$ are supplementary;
$\angle 1 \cong \angle 2$

Prove $\angle 3 \cong \angle 4$

Proof

Statements	Reasons
1. $\angle 1$ and $\angle 3$ are supplementary. $\angle 2$ and $\angle 4$ are supplementary.	1. Given
2. $m\angle 1 + m\angle 3 = 180$ $m\angle 2 + m\angle 4 = 180$	2. Def. of supp. $\angle$s [1]
3. $m\angle 1 + m\angle 3 = m\angle 2 + m\angle 4$	3. Substitution [2]
4. $\angle 1 \cong \angle 2$	4. Given
5. $m\angle 1 = m\angle 2$	5. Def. of $\cong$ $\angle$s [4]
6. $m\angle 3 = m\angle 4$	6. Subtraction prop. of equality [3, 5]
7. $\angle 3 \cong \angle 4$	7. Def. of $\cong$ $\angle$s [6]

A **corollary** is a theorem that follows directly from another theorem. The proof of the following corollary of Theorem 2.7 uses only the reflexive property of angle congruence and Theorem 2.7. Its proof is exercise 28.

Theorem 2.8	Supplements of the same angle are congruent.

A similar theorem and corollary are true for complementary angles. Their proofs are exercises 29 and 30.

Theorem 2.9	Complements of congruent angles are congruent.

Theorem 2.10	Complements of the same angle are congruent.

Class Exercises

[1-3] Identify the hypothesis and conclusion.

1. If there is a good wind today, then I'll go sailing.
2. If you are a good driver, you remain constantly alert while you drive.
3. If two angles are congruent, then they have the same measure.

[4-10] Restate each sentence in "if . . . then" form and identify the hypothesis and conclusion.

4. Students that fail the exam will not graduate.
5. All persons have the right to life, liberty, and the pursuit of happiness.
6. I'll go to the movies only if it rains.
7. A good crop implies that the weather has been good.
8. Two angles are congruent if their complements are congruent.
9. Two intersecting line segments lie in a plane.
10. Supplements of the same angle are congruent.

Written Exercises

Set A

[1-4] Identify the hypothesis and conclusion.

1. If $AB = CD$, then $\overline{AB}$ and $\overline{CD}$ are collinear.
2. If two rays have the same endpoint, then the rays are collinear.
3. If ab is even and b is odd, then a is even.
4. If two angles are vertical angles, then they are congruent.

[5-12] Write the statement in "if . . . then" form.

5. $\overleftrightarrow{CD}$ bisects $\overline{AB}$ at E implies that E is the midpoint of $\overline{AB}$.
6. All triangles have three sides.
7. When two planes intersect, their intersection is a line.
8. The equation $x = 4$ is true if $3x = 12$ is true.

9. Two angles form a linear pair only if they are supplementary.

10. Two angles have a common side if they are adjacent.

11. Complements of congruent angles are congruent.

12. Every pair of points is collinear.

[13-18] In the diagram $m\angle DPB = 30$.

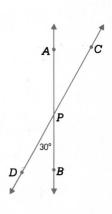

13. How are $\angle APD$ and $\angle DPB$ related by position?

14. What is $m\angle APD$? Why?

15. What is $m\angle APC$? Why?

16. Is $\angle APC \cong \angle DPB$? Why?

17. Would the answer to exercise 16 change if $m\angle DPB = 50$?

18. Would the answer to exercise 16 be the same regardless of $m\angle DPB$?

Set B

[19-20] Write an "if . . . then" statement for the proof.

19.

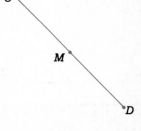

Statements	Reasons
1. C, D, and M are collinear; $\overline{CM} \cong \overline{DM}$	1. Given
2. $CM = DM$	2. Def of $\cong$ seg. [1]
3. M is the midpoint of $\overline{CD}$.	3. Def. of midpt. [2]

20.

Statements	Reasons
1. $AB + BC = AC$	1. Given
2. $BC = BC$	2. Reflexive prop. of equality
3. $AB = AC - BC$	3. Subtraction prop. of equality [1, 2]
4. $BC = XB$	4. Given
5. $AB = AC - XB$	5. Substitution [3, 4]

[21-23] Write the postulate in "if . . . then" form.

21. Postulate 3   22. Postulate 6   23. Postulate 14

[24-27] Analyze the pair of sentences by representing the clauses with *p* and *q*. Write the conclusion or explain why none is possible.

24. If you have a dollar, then you can skate at the park.
Leslie has a dollar.

25. Complements of congruent angles are congruent.
$\angle 2$ and $\angle 4$ are congruent.

26. All right angles are congruent.
$\angle Q$ and $\angle T$ are congruent.

27. Two intersecting lines lie in a plane.
$\overleftrightarrow{AB}$ and $\overleftrightarrow{OR}$ intersect at point *M*.

28. Complete the proof of Theorem 2.8.

Given: __?__

Prove: $\angle 2 \cong \angle 3$

Statements	Reasons
1. __?__	1. Given
2. $\angle 1 \cong \angle 1$	2. __?__
3. $\angle 2 \cong \angle 3$	3. __?__

Set C

29. Prove Theorem 2.9.
30. Prove Theorem 2.10.

Geometry Maintenance

1. State three ways in which a plane may be determined.
2. If $m\angle P = 19$, find the measures of its supplement and complement.

[3-6] $\overrightarrow{BM}$ bisects $\angle ABN$, $\overrightarrow{BN}$ bisects $\angle MBC$, and $m\angle ABC = 108$.

3. $\angle 1 \cong \angle$ __?__
4. $\angle 3 \cong \angle$ __?__
5. Find $m\angle 1$.
6. If $m\angle 5 = m\angle ABC$, find $m\angle 4$.

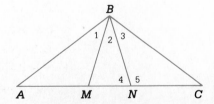

Progress Check

Lesson 2.1
Page 60

[1-4] Write the property of real numbers that supports the statement.

1. If $AB + BC = AC$, then $BC = AC - AB$.

2. If $2x = 14$, then $x = 7$.

3. $2(XY + YZ) = 2(XY) + 2(YZ)$

4. If $CD + DE = CE$ and $DE = QR$, then $CD + QR = CE$.

Lesson 2.2
Page 66

5. Complete the proof.

Given: $\overleftrightarrow{XY}$ bisects $\overline{AB}$ at Q.

Prove: $\overline{AQ} \cong \overline{BQ}$

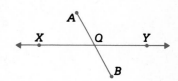

Statements	Reasons
1. $\overleftrightarrow{XY}$ bisects $\overline{AB}$ at Q	1. ?
2. Q is the midpoint of $\overline{AB}$.	2. ?
3. $AQ = BQ$	3. ?
4. $\overline{AQ} \cong \overline{BQ}$	4. ?

Lesson 2.3
Page 71

6. Given: A, B, and C are collinear; $\angle BAP$ and $\angle CAP$ are a linear pair; and $\overrightarrow{AP}$ bisects $\angle SAT$. Draw a diagram.

[7-11] Can the statement be assumed from the diagram?

7. K is in the interior of $\angle ABC$.

8. $\angle ABK \cong \angle CBK$

9. $\overrightarrow{BK} \perp \overline{AC}$

10. A, C, and K are collinear.

11. $\angle CKB$ and $\angle AKB$ are a linear pair.

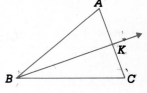

Lesson 2.4
Page 77

12. Write Postulate 2 in "if . . . then" form.

[13-16] Give the hypothesis and conclusion.

13. If $5y - 3 = 12$, then $y = 3$.

14. Supplements of the same angle are congruent.

15. All right angles are congruent.

16. If two points lie in a plane, then the line containing them lies in the plane.

In Chapter 1, our geometry began with three undefined terms—point, line, and plane. These undefined terms were used to define other geometric terms. Postulates stated certain relationships among these geometric terms.

Using the postulates, definitions, and properties of real numbers, we proved a few theorems. The definitions, postulates, properties of real numbers, and theorems make up our inventory of geometric facts. Any statement from the inventory can be used as a reason in a proof.

But how do you get the statements in a proof? As we prove Theorem 2.11 we will show you how the inventory can help you think of the appropriate statements in a proof.

Theorem 2.11	Vertical angles are congruent.

Restatement	If two angles are vertical angles, then they are congruent.
Given	$\angle 1$ and $\angle 2$ are vertical angles.
Prove	$\angle 1 \cong \angle 2$

Keeping in mind what is to be proved, study the diagram and the Given. Do they suggest any relationships?

Vertical angles are given. The definition of vertical angles tells you that they are formed by two pairs of opposite rays. Not much help.

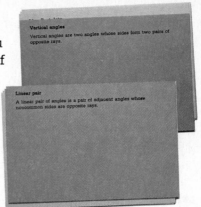

What other definition(s) mention opposite rays? Look through your inventory. The definition of a linear pair of angles also mentions opposite rays.

Look at the diagram again. Do you see a linear pair of angles? ∠1 and ∠3 form a linear pair, and ∠2 and ∠3 also form a linear pair.

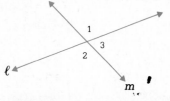

What else in the inventory mentions a linear pair of angles? The Supplement Postulate tells you that a linear pair of angles are supplementary. So ∠1 and ∠3 are supplementary, and ∠2 and ∠3 are also supplementary.

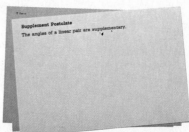

Now you have two angles, ∠1 and ∠2, each supplementary to ∠3. What do you know about two angles that are supplementary to the same angle? Look through your inventory to find statements that mention supplementary angles in the if-clause. Theorem 2.8 tells you that ∠1 ≅ ∠2.

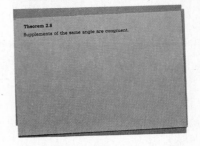

This thinking can be summarized in a Plan for Proof.

Find two linear pairs of angles in the diagram. Use the Supplement Postulate and Theorem 2.8 to get ∠1 ≅ ∠2.

Now the proof can be completed, using the Plan for Proof as a guide. The proof is shown below.

Theorem 2.11   Vertical angles are congruent.

Restatement   If two angles are vertical angles, then they are congruent.

Given   ∠1 and ∠2 are vertical angles.

Prove   ∠1 ≅ ∠2

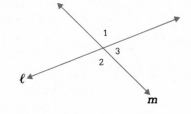

Plan for Proof   Find two linear pairs of angles in the diagram.
Use the Supplement Postulate and Theorem 2.8 to get ∠1 ≅ ∠2.

Statements	Reasons
1. ∠1 and ∠2 are vertical angles.	1. Given
2. ∠1 and ∠3 are a linear pair. ∠2 and ∠3 are a linear pair.	2. Def. of linear pr.
3. ∠1 and ∠3 are supplementary. ∠2 and ∠3 are supplementary.	3. Supplement Post. [2]
4. ∠1 ≅ ∠2	4. Supplements of the same ∠ are ≅. [3]

The Plan for Proof of Theorem 2.12 is exercise 20.

Theorem 2.12   If one angle of a linear pair is a right angle, then the other angle is also a right angle.

Class Exercises

1. List four types of statements that belong to the inventory of geometric statements.
2. Search the inventory to find four ways to prove that two segments are congruent.
3. Search the inventory to find as many ways as possible to prove that two angles are congruent.

[4-7] Use the current inventory to find at least four statements that can be proved from the given information.

4. Given: $\angle FOD$ is a right $\angle$; $\overrightarrow{OP}$ bisects $\angle DOF$.

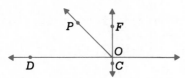

6. Given: $\angle QPR$ is a right $\angle$; $\overrightarrow{PX}$ bisects $\overline{QR}$.

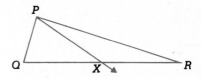

5. Given: $\overline{WY}$ and $\overline{XZ}$ bisect each other.

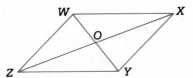

7. Given: $\angle 1 \cong \angle 2$; $GM = MN$; $MN = NI$

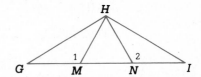

Written Exercises

Set A

[1-5] Use the figure at the right.

1. If $m\angle 3 = 110$, find:

    a. $m\angle 1$ **b.** $m\angle 2$ **c.** $m\angle 4$

2. If $m\angle 1 = \frac{1}{2}m\angle 3$, find:

    a. $m\angle 1$ **b.** $m\angle 2$ **c.** $m\angle 3$

3. Suppose $\angle 1$ and $\angle 2$ are supplements. What can you conclude about k and ℓ?

4. Suppose $\angle 1$ and $\angle 2$ are complements. What is $m\angle 2$?

5. Suppose $m\angle 1$ were increased by 10. What effect would this have on

    a. $m\angle 2$?   **b.** $m\angle 3$?   **c.** $m\angle 4$?

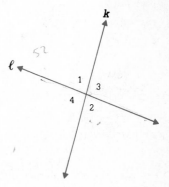

[6-7] Solve for x.

6.

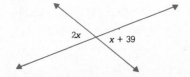

7.

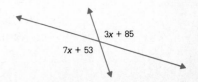

[8-11] Arrange the steps for a Plan for Proof in order.

8. Given: Y is between X and Z;
   Z is between X and W.
   Prove: $XY + YZ + ZW = XW$

   a. Since Y is between X and Z, use the Segment Addition Postulate to get (1) $XY + YZ = XZ$.
   b. Then substitute (1) into (2) to get $XY + YZ + ZW = XW$.
   c. Since Z is between X and W, use the Segment Addition Postulate to get (2) $XZ + ZW = XW$.

9. Given: B is in the interior of $\angle APC$.

   Prove: $m\angle APC - m\angle APB = m\angle BPC$

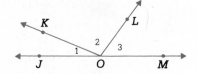

   a. Since B is in the interior of $\angle APC$, use the Angle Add. Post. to get $m\angle APC = m\angle APB + m\angle BPC$.
   b. Then use the Subtraction property of equality to get $m\angle APC - m\angle APB = m\angle BPC$.

10. Given: $\overrightarrow{OL}$ and $\overrightarrow{OK}$ lie in the same half-plane with edge $\overleftrightarrow{JM}$
    Prove: $m\angle 1 + m\angle 2 + m\angle 3 = 180$

   a. Substitute to get $m\angle 1 + m\angle 2 + m\angle 3 = 180$.
   b. Since $\angle JOL$ and $\angle 3$ are a linear pair, they are supplements by the Supplement Postulate.
   c. Use Angle Add. Post. to get $m\angle 1 + m\angle 2 = m\angle JOL$.
   d. By def. of supplements, $m\angle JOL + m\angle 3 = 180$.

11. Given: $AM = MN$; $MN = NC$
    Prove: $AC = 3MN$

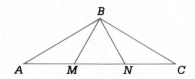

   a. Substitute for AN to get $AC = AM + MN + NC$.
   b. Substitute again using the given information.
   c. Use Segment Addition Postulate to get $AC = AN + NC$ and $AN = AM + MN$.
   d. Add to get $AC = 3MN$.

[12-19] Write a Plan for Proof.

12. Given: ∠*ABC* is a right angle.

Prove: ∠1 and ∠2 are complementary.

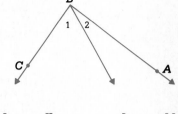

13. Given: *JK = LM*

Prove: *JL = KM*

14. Given: *PQ > RS*

Prove: *PR > QS*

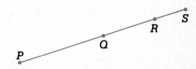

15. Given: ∠*EPH* is a right angle.

Prove: ∠3 ≅ ∠4

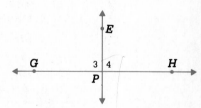

16. Given: *m∠DEF = m∠TXU*;
$\overrightarrow{XU}$ bisects ∠*TXW*.

Prove: *m∠DEF = m∠UXW*

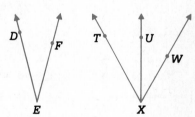

17. Given: ∠1 ≅ ∠4

Prove: ∠2 ≅ ∠3

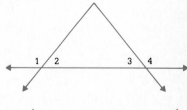

18. Given: ∠*ABD* and ∠*CDB* are right angles; ∠2 ≅ ∠4

Prove: *m∠1 = m∠3*

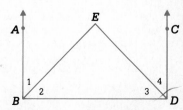

19. Given: $\angle EBC$ is a right angle;
$\overrightarrow{BE}$ bisects $\angle DBF$.

Prove: $m\angle ABD = m\angle CBF$

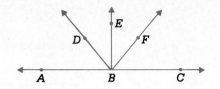

20. Write a Plan for Proof for Theorem 2.12.

Set C

21. Prove Theorem 2.12.

22. Prove: The bisectors of a linear pair of angles are perpendicular.

[23-24] Solve for x and y.

23. 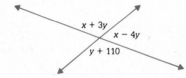   **24.**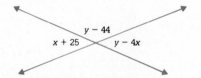

Algebra Review

Example

Solution

Solve for x and y: $x + 3y = 18$ (1)
$\qquad\qquad\qquad\qquad 3x - 5y = 12$ (2)

Addition Method

Multiply equation (1) by -3.
Add the equations.

$$-3x - 9y = -54$$
$$\underline{3x - 5y = 12}$$
$$-14y = -42$$

Substitution Method

Solve equation (1) for x.
Substitute into equation (2).

$$x + 3y = 18 \Rightarrow x = 18 - 3y$$
$$3(18 - 3y) - 5y = 12$$
$$54 - 9y - 5y = 12$$
$$-14y = -42$$

Solve for y. $y = 3$
Then solve for x. $x + 3(3) = 18 \Rightarrow x = 9$

Check the solution $(9, 3)$ in both equations.

Solve and check.

1. $m + n = 4$ **2.** $5x + 7y = 2$ **3.** $5x + 5y = 35$
$ 5m - 3n = 4$ $ x = y + 4$ $ 3x + 2y = 18$

Using BASIC

Optimal Locations

A chain of seven restaurants is to be supplied from a new warehouse located along a freeway. The chain can be represented by a number line with coordinates as shown.

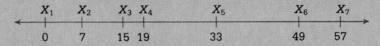

```
100 REM TOTAL DISTANCE TO N COLLINEAR POINTS
110 INPUT "ENTER NUMBER OF POINTS";N
120 FOR I = 1 TO N        I is the index for restaurant locations.
130 PRINT "ENTER COORDINATE OF POINT ";I;
140 INPUT X(I)
150 NEXT I
160 PRINT "ENTER MINIMUM POINT TO TEST,"
170 PRINT "MAXIMUM POINT, AND INCREMENT."
180 INPUT MIN,MAX,INC
190 PRINT
200 PRINT "TEST POINT","SUM"
210 FOR T = MIN TO MAX STEP INC
220 LET S = 0        S holds sum of distances for current test point.
230 FOR I = 1 TO N
240 LET D = ABS(X(I) - T)    D is distance from Ith
250 LET S = S + D            restaurant to test point.
260 NEXT I
270 PRINT T,S
280 NEXT T
290 INPUT "TEST ANOTHER INTERVAL (YES OR NO)? ";A$
300 IF A$ = "YES" THEN 160
310 END
```

1. Where should the warehouse be located so that the sum of the distances from the restaurants to the warehouse is as small as possible?

2. Where should the warehouse be located if an eighth restaurant is added to the chain at coordinate 38?

3. If the restaurant at 49 gets twice the business of each of the other restaurants, where should the warehouse be located?

Writing A Proof

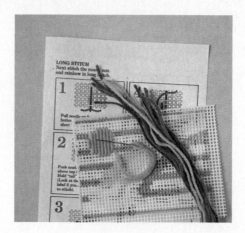

Most tasks can be simplified by breaking them down into steps. In geometry a theorem can be proved using the following steps.

Step 1: If necessary, restate the theorem in "if . . . then" form.

Step 2: Draw and label an appropriate diagram.

Step 3: State the Given and Prove in terms of the diagram.

Step 4: Develop a Plan for Proof.

Step 5: Write the proof in two-column form.

Here is a proof of Theorem 2.13 with each step shown.

Theorem 2.13   Two perpendicular lines form four right angles.

Step 1   Restatement: If two lines are perpendicular, then they form four right angles.

Step 2

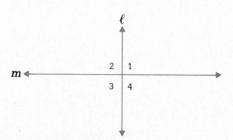

Step 3   Given: $\ell \perp m$

Prove: $\angle 1$, $\angle 2$, $\angle 3$, and $\angle 4$ are right angles.

Step 4   Plan for Proof

Use the definition of $\perp$ lines to get
one right $\angle$, say $\angle 1$.
Use the linear pair $\angle 1$ and $\angle 2$ and
Theorem 2.12 to show $\angle 2$ is a right angle.
Use the appropriate linear pairs and
Theorem 2.12 to show $\angle 3$ and $\angle 4$ are right $\angle$s.

Step 5

Statements	Reasons
1. $\ell \perp m$	1. Given
2. The intersection of ℓ and m contains one rt. $\angle$, say $\angle 1$.	2. Def. of $\perp$ lines [1]
3. $\angle 1$ and $\angle 2$ are a lin. pr.	3. Def. of lin. pr.
4. $\angle 2$ is a rt. $\angle$.	4. If one $\angle$ of a lin. pr. is a rt. $\angle$, then the other is also. [2, 3]
5. $\angle 2$ and $\angle 3$ are a lin. pr.	5. Def. of lin. pr.
6. $\angle 3$ is a rt. $\angle$.	6. If one $\angle$ of a lin. pr. is a rt. $\angle$, then the other is also. [4, 5]
7. $\angle 3$ and $\angle 4$ are a lin. pr.	7. Def. of lin. pr.
8. $\angle 4$ is a rt. $\angle$.	8. If one $\angle$ of a lin. pr. is a rt. $\angle$, then the other is also. [6, 7]
9. $\angle 1$, $\angle 2$, $\angle 3$, and $\angle 4$ are rt. $\angle$s.	9. Steps 2, 4, 6, and 8

Theorem 2.14   If the angles in a linear pair are congruent, then the lines containing their sides are perpendicular.

The proof of Theorem 2.14 is exercise 12.

Class Exercises

[1-2] If $\angle 1 \cong \angle 2$, prove that $\angle 3 \cong \angle 4$.

1. Give a Plan for Proof.

2. Write a two-column proof.

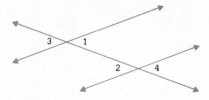

[3-4] If $\overline{AB} \perp \overline{BC}$, prove that $\angle 5$ and $\angle 6$ are complementary.

3. Give a Plan for Proof.

4. Write a two-column proof.

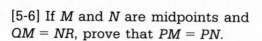

[5-6] If M and N are midpoints and $QM = NR$, prove that $PM = PN$.

5. Give a Plan for Proof.

6. Write a two-column proof.

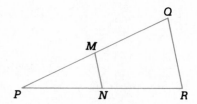

Written Exercises

Set A

[1-3] Prove Theorem 2.3. You may use the proof of Theorem 2.2 on page 70 to help you.

1. Congruence of angles is reflexive.
   Given: Any angle $\angle A$
   Prove: $\angle A \cong \angle A$

2. Congruence of angles is symmetric.
   Given: $\angle B \cong \angle C$
   Prove: $\angle C \cong \angle B$

3. Congruence of angles is transitive.
   Given: $\angle D \cong \angle E$; $\angle E \cong \angle F$
   Prove: $\angle D \cong \angle F$

4. Given: $\angle 1$ is a right angle;
   $\angle 1 \cong \angle 2$
   Prove: $\angle 2$ is a right angle.

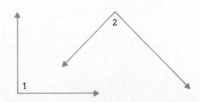

5. Given: ∠1 and ∠2 are supplementary.

Prove: ∠1 ≅ ∠3

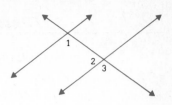

6. Given: A is the midpoint of $\overline{PR}$;
$AQ = AP$

Prove: $AQ = AR$

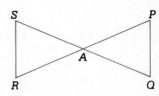

7. Given: ∠1 ≅ ∠4

Prove: ∠2 ≅ ∠3

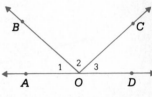

8. Given: B and C lie in the same half-plane with edge $\overrightarrow{AD}$.

Prove: $m\angle 1 + m\angle 2 + m\angle 3 = 180$

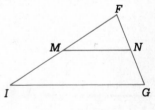

9. Given: $\overline{MN}$ bisects $\overline{FI}$ and $\overline{FG}$;
$FM > FN$

Prove: $MI > NG$

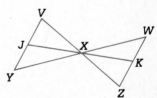

10. Given: $\overrightarrow{XJ}$ bisects ∠VXY;
$\overrightarrow{XK}$ bisects ∠WXZ.

Prove: ∠VXJ ≅ ∠WXK

11. Prove: If two angles are congruent and supplementary, then they are both right angles.

12. Prove Theorem 2.14.

13. Prove: A line and a point not on the line lie in a plane.
Hint Use Postulates 1, 2, and 3.

14. Prove: Two intersecting lines lie in a plane.

2.7   Converses

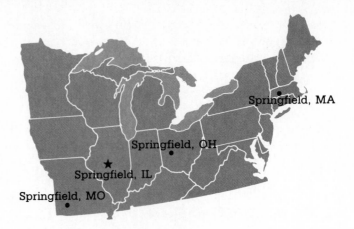

Use the map to decide if each statement is true or false.

Statement 1: If a city is the capital of Illinois, then the city is named Springfield.

Statement 2: If a city is named Springfield, then it is the capital of Illinois.

Notice that the hypothesis and conclusion of statement 1 are interchanged to form statement 2. Statement 2 is called the converse of statement 1.

Definition

A **converse** of a conditional statement is formed by interchanging the hypothesis and conclusion.

If a statement is represented symbolically as $p \Rightarrow q$, then its converse is $q \Rightarrow p$. What is the converse of $q \Rightarrow p$?

Example 1

Write the converse of these statements. Tell whether each converse is true or false.

1. If two lines are perpendicular, then they form four right angles.

2. Four collinear points are coplanar.

Solution

1. The converse: If two lines form four right angles, then they are perpendicular. The definition of perpendicular lines ensures that this statement is true.

2. The statement in "if . . . then" form is: If four points are collinear, then they are coplanar. Its converse is: If four points are coplanar, then they are collinear. This statement is false, as the diagram at the right illustrates.

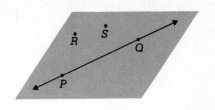

Notice that a statement and its converse must be examined separately to determine whether each is true or false.

If a statement and its converse are both true, then they can be rewritten as one "if and only if" statement.

Example 2   Rewrite these two statements as one "if and only if" statement.

   1. If $\overrightarrow{AC}$ bisects $\overline{BD}$, then $\overrightarrow{AC}$ contains the midpoint of $\overline{BD}$.

   2. If $\overrightarrow{AC}$ contains the midpoint of $\overline{BD}$, then $\overrightarrow{AC}$ bisects $\overline{BD}$.

Solution $\overrightarrow{AC}$ bisects $\overline{BD}$ if and only if $\overrightarrow{AC}$ contains the midpoint of $\overline{BD}$.

This solution is the definition of a bisector of a segment. Every definition is an "if and only if" statement, although the statement may not always appear in this form.

Example 3   Prove: The angles of a linear pair are congruent if and only if the lines containing their sides are perpendicular.

Solution   The "if and only if" statement must first be separated into two statements that are converses of each other. Then each statement must be proved.

Part I If the angles of a linear pair are congruent, then the lines containing their sides are perpendicular.
Part II If the sides of a linear pair of angles are perpendicular, then the angles are congruent.

Part I is Theorem 2.14, which was proved in lesson 2.6. The proof of Part II is exercise 25.

2.7 Converses

Class Exercises

[1-4] Give the converse of each statement. Tell whether you think the converse is true or false.

1. If $x = 3$, then $2x + 5 = 11$.
2. Vertical angles are congruent.
3. I get sick if I eat too much candy.
4. A minor planet revolves around the sun only if the planet is an asteroid.

[5-8] The converse of a conditional statement is given. What is the original statement?

5. If q, then r.
6. $p \Rightarrow n$
7. h, if k.
8. p only if q.

[9-11] Use this statement: Two congruent segments have the same length.

9. Write the statement in "if . . . then" form.
10. What is the converse? Is it true?
11. Write the sentence and its converse as one "if and only if" statement.

Written Exercises

Set A

[1-6] True or false

1. The converse of a true statement is always true.
2. Theorems are always "if and only if" statements.
3. Definitions are always "if and only if" statements.
4. The converse of "p, if q" is "if q, then p."
5. "r if and only if s" means both "if r, then s" and "if s, then r."
6. A pair of angles are vertical angles if and only if they are congruent.

[7-16] Write the converse of the statement and tell whether you think the converse is true or false.

7. If three sides of a triangle are congruent, then the three angles are congruent.

8. A linear pair of angles is supplementary.

9. Every square is a rectangle.

10. Every rectangle is a square.

11. All right angles are congruent.

12. If two angles are a linear pair, then the sum of their measures is 180.

13. If two angles are complementary, then the sum of their measures is 90.

14. If $\angle A \cong \angle B$, then $\angle B \cong \angle A$.

15. If two angles are adjacent, then they have a common ray.

16. If two angles are not congruent, then the angles are not vertical angles.

Set B

[17-20] Write two conditional statements from the "if and only if" statement.

17. $\overrightarrow{OA}$ bisects $\angle XOY$ if and only if $m\angle XOA = m\angle AOY$.

18. Two angles are supplementary if and only if the sum of their measures is 180.

19. $\angle E \cong \angle F$ if and only if $m\angle E = m\angle F$.

20. Two angles form a linear pair if and only if they are adjacent and supplementary.

[21-24] Write a definition of the term using "if and only if."

21. Perpendicular lines   **23.** Right angle
22. Congruent angles   **24.** Complementary angles

25. Prove Part II of example 3 on page 97.

Set C

26. Prove: An angle is acute if and only if its supplement is obtuse.

27. Prove: An angle is a right angle if and only if it is congruent to a right angle.

Excursion   Logic

A **statement** is a sentence that is
either true or false but not both.

Every statement has a **negation**, a
second statement that is true
whenever the first statement is
false, and false whenever the first
statement is true. The symbol $\sim p$
(read "not p") represents the
negation of statement p.

Example 1

Form the negation of each statement.

1. The Lings own a sailboat.
2. $\angle X$ is obtuse.

Solution

1. The Lings do not own a sailboat.
2. $\angle X$ is not obtuse, *or* $\angle X$ is acute or right.

You are familiar with the converse of an "if . . . then"
statement. By using negations, two other statements can be
formed from an "if . . . then" statement.

The **inverse** is formed by negating both the hypothesis and
conclusion. The **contrapositive** is formed from the original
statement by negating the hypothesis and conclusion and
then interchanging them.

Example 2

Write the converse, inverse, and contrapositive of this
statement: If $\angle 1$ and $\angle 2$ are vertical angles, then $\angle 1$ and $\angle 2$
are congruent.

Solution

Converse: If $\angle 1$ and $\angle 2$ are congruent, then $\angle 1$ and $\angle 2$ are
vertical angles.

Inverse: If $\angle 1$ and $\angle 2$ are not vertical angles, then they are
not congruent.

Contrapositive: If $\angle 1$ and $\angle 2$ are not congruent, then they
are not vertical angles.

The original statement is true by Theorem 2.11. Which other statement is true? Which statements are false? These statements exemplify an important logical principle: If a statement is true, then its contrapositive is true; if a statement is false, then its contrapositive is false.

Two statements that must either both be true or both be false are called **equivalent** statements. Hence a statement and its contrapositive are equivalent statements.

Now look at the converse in example 2. Can you form the contrapositive of this statement? Upon examination, this contrapositive is seen to be the same as the inverse of the original statement. Therefore the converse and inverse of a statement are also equivalent statements.

We can summarize these relationships symbolically, using $\Leftrightarrow$ for "is equivalent to."

"If . . . then" statement	$(p{\Rightarrow}q){\Leftrightarrow}(\sim q{\Rightarrow}\sim p)$	Contrapositive
Converse	$(q{\Rightarrow}p){\Leftrightarrow}(\sim p{\Rightarrow}\sim q)$	Inverse

Exercises

[1-4] Write the negation of each statement.

1. $\angle A$ and $\angle B$ are complements.

2. It is not raining.

3. $x > 3$

4. $y = 4$

[5-7] Write the converse, inverse, and contrapositive of each statement. Classify each as true or false.

5. If the Lings sail along the western coast of Florida, then they sail on the Gulf of Mexico.

6. If $\angle 1$ is an acute angle, then $m\angle 1 < 90$.

7. If $\angle A$ and $\angle B$ are right angles, then $\angle A \cong \angle B$.

8. Let $\sim t{\Rightarrow}\sim s$ be the converse of a statement. Write its inverse and contrapositive.

9. Let $\sim r{\Rightarrow}p$ be the contrapositive of a statement. Write its converse and inverse.

Chapter Summary

1. Deductive reasoning is the use of logical principles to draw conclusions. (page 60)

2. A proof written in two-column form contains:
   a. the restatement, if necessary
   b. a diagram
   c. the Given and Prove
   d. the statements
   e. the reasons (page 67)

3. A theorem is a statement that is proved. (page 67)

4. The reasons in a proof can be properties of real numbers, definitions, postulates, previously proved theorems, and the given information. (page 67)

5. A diagram for a proof should be labeled and the given information should be marked. (page 72)

6. An "if . . . then" statement is a conditional statement. The "if" part is the hypothesis, and the "then" part is the conclusion. (page 77)

7. If $p \Rightarrow q$ is true and p is true, then q is true. (page 77)

8. The hypothesis of a theorem identifies the given information; the conclusion identifies what is to be proved. (page 78)

9. The converse of a conditional statement is formed by interchanging the hypothesis and conclusion. (page 96)

10. If both a statement and its converse are true, they can be combined into one "if and only if" statement. (page 97)

11. Some important theorems are:
    a. All right angles are congruent. (page 68)
    b. Supplements of congruent angles (or the same angle) are congruent. (page 79)
    c. Complements of congruent angles (or the same angle) are congruent. (page 79)
    d. Vertical angles are congruent. (page 84)
    e. Two perpendicular lines form four right angles. (page 92)

Chapter Review

Lesson 2.1
Page 60

1. Write the conclusion to this deductive argument:

If two angles are a linear pair, then the sum of their measures is 180.

$\angle 1$ and $\angle 2$ are a linear pair.

Therefore __?__ .

State the real-number property that justifies the statement.

2. If $3x + 5 > 17$, then $3x > 12$.

3. If $r = s$ and $s = t$, then $r = t$.

4. $AB = AB$

5. If $QR = AB$ and $AB + CD < UV$, then $QR + CD < UV$.

Lesson 2.2
Page 66

6. Supply the missing reasons.

Given: A is between X and Y

Prove: $XY - XA = AY$

X ———————————— A — Y

Statement	Reasons
1. A is between X and Y	1. __?__
2. $XY = XA + AY$	2. __?__
3. $XA = XA$	3. __?__
4. $XY - XA = AY$	4. __?__

Lesson 2.3
Page 71

[7-9] Use a straightedge to draw a diagram for each exercise. Label each diagram.

7. $\angle 1$ and $\angle 2$ are complements of $\angle 3$.

8. $\overleftrightarrow{XY}$ is the perpendicular bisector of $\overline{PR}$.

9. $\angle 4$ and $\angle 5$ are adjacent and congruent.

[10-13] Give the definition(s), postulate(s), or theorem(s), that justify the statement.

10. $\angle BXC$ and $\angle CXD$ are supplementary.

11. $\angle AXB \cong \angle CXD$

12. $\angle 1$ and $\angle 2$ are adjacent angles.

13. $AX + XC = AC$

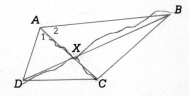

Lesson 2.4
Page 77

[14-17] Write the hypothesis and conclusion of each statement.

14. If $6y + 12 = 24$, then $y = 2$.

15. The angles of a linear pair are supplementary.

16. Two angles are congruent if they are vertical angles.

17. Two angles are adjacent only if they have a common side.

[18-19] Write the Given and Prove.

18. If $\overrightarrow{XY}$ bisects $\angle AXB$, then $\angle AXY \cong \angle BXY$.

19. Supplements of the same angle are congruent.

Lesson 2.5
Page 84

[20-23] Use this statement: The sides of vertical angles that are supplementary are perpendicular.

20. Write the sentence in "if . . . then" form.

21. Draw a diagram and label it.

22. Write the Given and Prove.

23. Write a Plan for Proof.

Lesson 2.6
Page 92

24. Given: $\overleftrightarrow{JK} \perp \overleftrightarrow{MN}$
Prove: $\angle JON \cong \angle KON$

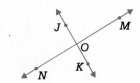

25. Given: $m\angle 1 = m\angle 3$
Prove: $m\angle 2 + m\angle 3 = 180$

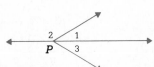

Lesson 2.7
Page 96

[26-29] Write the converse of the statement.

26. If $\angle 1$ and $\angle 2$ are vertical angles, then $\angle 1 \cong \angle 2$.

27. All right angles are congruent.

28. If $JK = KH$, then $\overrightarrow{KB}$ bisects $\overline{JH}$.

29. Two angles are acute if they are complementary.

30. Write this statement as two conditional statements: A rectangle is a square if and only if it has four congruent sides.

Chapter Test

[1-6] True or false

1. A line and a point not on a line are coplanar.

2. If $\angle P \cong \angle Q$, then $\angle P$ and $\angle Q$ are vertical angles.

3. The "if" part of a theorem identifies what is to be proven.

4. Congruence of angles is transitive.

5. The converse of a true conditional statement can be false.

6. If $\angle 1$ and $\angle 2$ are complementary to the same angle, then $\angle 1 \cong \angle 2$.

[7-8] Use this statement: The supplement of an acute angle is obtuse.

7. Write the statement in "if . . . then" form.

8. Write the converse of the statement.

9. Write this statement as two conditional statements: Two adjacent angles are complementary if and only if their noncommon sides are perpendicular.

10. Find $m\angle QOS$, given $\angle TOR \cong \angle ROV$ and $m\angle SOT = 10$.

11. Solve for x.

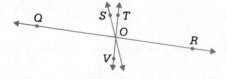

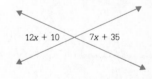

12. Supply the missing reasons.

Given: $m\angle 4 = m\angle 3$
Prove: $\angle 3$ and $\angle 5$ are supplementary.

Statements	Reasons
1. $m\angle 4 = m\angle 3$	1. ___?___
2. $\angle 4$ and $\angle 5$ are a linear pair.	2. ___?___
3. $\angle 4$ and $\angle 5$ are supplementary.	3. ___?___
4. $m\angle 4 + m\angle 5 = 180$	4. ___?___
5. $m\angle 3 + m\angle 5 = 180$	5. ___?___
6. $\angle 3$ and $\angle 5$ are supplementary.	6. ___?___

Parallel Lines and Planes

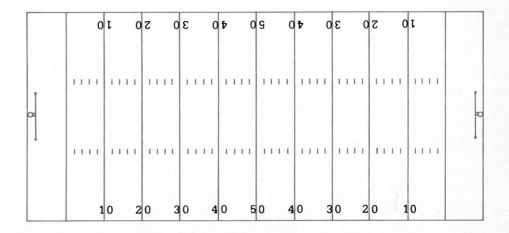

Coplanar lines that do not intersect are called parallel lines. Think about extending the markings on the football field to suggest lines.

1. In a plane, if two lines are perpendicular to the same line, do you think they must be parallel? Give an example from the picture.

2. In a plane, if a line is perpendicular to one of two parallel lines, must it be perpendicular to the other? Give an example.

3. In a plane, if two lines are parallel to a third line, must they be parallel to each other? Give an example.

3.1   Parallel Lines and Transversals

Think of the points suggested by the corners of this game.

$\overleftrightarrow{AB}$ and $\overleftrightarrow{CD}$ do not intersect. Yet both lines are in the plane determined by A, B, and C. $\overleftrightarrow{AB}$ and $\overleftrightarrow{CD}$ are called parallel lines, and we write $\overleftrightarrow{AB} \parallel \overleftrightarrow{CD}$.

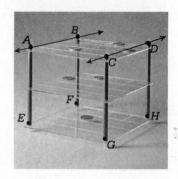

Definition	

Parallel lines are lines which are coplanar and do not intersect.

Segments and rays are parallel if the lines containing them are parallel. For example, $\overline{AC} \parallel \overline{EG}$ and $\overrightarrow{CD} \parallel \overrightarrow{EF}$.

$\overleftrightarrow{AC}$ and $\overleftrightarrow{EF}$ do not intersect, but they are not coplanar, so they are not parallel. They are skew lines.

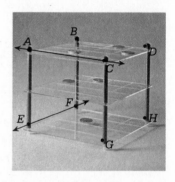

Definition	

Skew lines are two lines that are not coplanar.

$\overleftrightarrow{AB}$ and $\overleftrightarrow{DH}$ are skew lines as well.

Definition	

Two planes, or **a line and a plane,** are **parallel** if and only if they do not intersect.

The plane containing A, D, and B is parallel to the plane containing E, H, and F and is also parallel to $\overleftrightarrow{GH}$.

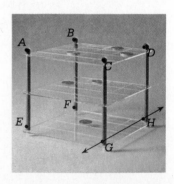

Definition	A **transversal** is a line which intersects two coplanar lines in two distinct points.

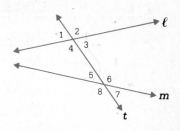

The two lines ℓ and m are said to be "cut" by the transversal t.

The eight angles formed have special names.

Interior angles	$\angle 3$, $\angle 4$, $\angle 5$, $\angle 6$
Exterior angles	$\angle 1$, $\angle 2$, $\angle 7$, $\angle 8$
Alternate interior angles	$\angle 3$ and $\angle 5$, $\angle 4$ and $\angle 6$
Corresponding angles	$\angle 1$ and $\angle 5$, $\angle 2$ and $\angle 6$, $\angle 3$ and $\angle 7$, $\angle 4$ and $\angle 8$

These terms can be given formal definitions, as in exercises 9 and 10.

Alternate interior angles, such as $\angle 2$ and $\angle 3$, have different vertices, are on opposite sides of the transversal, and lie "between" the two lines.

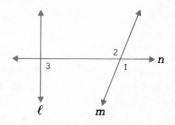

Corresponding angles, such as $\angle 1$ and $\angle 3$, are on the same side of the transversal and are in "corresponding" positions relative to the two given lines.

Special markings are sometimes used to show that lines in a figure are parallel. In the figure at the right, $m \parallel n$ and $j \parallel k$.

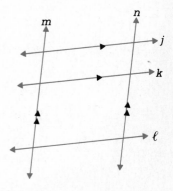

Class Exercises

[1-6] In the figure below, you may assume that lines and planes that appear to be parallel are parallel.

1. Name three pairs of parallel lines.
2. Name three pairs of skew lines.
3. Name three pairs of parallel planes.
4. Name a line parallel to the plane containing points *T*, *U*, and *V*.
5. Name a line parallel to the plane containing points *T*, *X*, and *Y*.
6. Name three lines parallel to the plane containing points *X*, *Y*, and *W*.

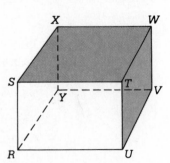

[7-12] Refer to the figure at the right.

7. Identify the transversal.
8. Name two pairs of alternate interior angles.
9. Name four pairs of vertical angles.
10. Name four pairs of corresponding angles.
11. If $m\angle 1 = 100$ and $m\angle 5 = 70$, what are the measures of the other six angles?
12. If $m\angle 3 = 95$ and $m\angle 8 = 85$, what are the measures of the other six angles?

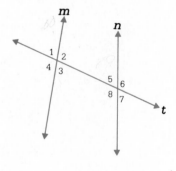

Written Exercises

Set A

[1-2] Name each transversal and list the lines that it cuts.

1.

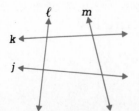

2.

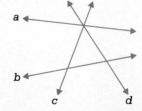

Chapter 3   Parallel Lines and Planes

[3-8] Classify each pair of angles.

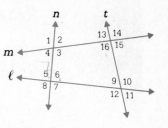

3. ∠4 and ∠6   **6.** ∠3 and ∠7

4. ∠2 and ∠16   **7.** ∠3 and ∠5

5. ∠2 and ∠14   **8.** ∠1 and ∠13

[9-10] Draw a diagram to help complete each definition.

9. Let *t* be a transversal intersecting lines ℓ and *m* at points *P* and *Q*, respectively. Let *A* be a point on ℓ and *B* a point on *m* such that *A* and *B* are on opposite sides of *t*. Then __?__ and __?__ are alternate interior angles.

10. If ∠1 and ∠2 are alternate interior angles and ∠2 and ∠3 are vertical angles, then __?__ and __?__ are corresponding angles.

[11-14] Which letters shown contain each item?

A E F H M N T V W X Y Z

11. Transversals   **13.** Parallel segments

12. Corresponding angles   **14.** Alternate interior angles

Set B

[15-20] Tell whether each statement is true or false. If false, sketch a counterexample. Do not assume that points or lines are coplanar, unless so given.

15. Two lines parallel to the same line must be parallel.

16. A line parallel to a plane is parallel to every line in the plane.

17. Two lines perpendicular to the same line must be parallel.

18. In a plane, two lines perpendicular to the same line must be parallel.

19. Two lines which lie in parallel planes must be skew.

20. In a plane, if a line intersects one of two parallel lines, then it must intersect the other.

Set C

21. Explain why at least two skew lines exist.

In the map at the right, the diagonal street forms congruent corresponding angles with two other streets whenever the other streets are parallel, and *only* if they are parallel. This suggests Postulate 15.

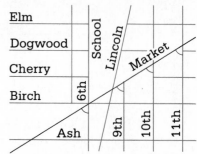

Postulate 15

Parallel Lines Postulate

Two coplanar lines cut by a transversal are parallel if and only if corresponding angles are congruent.

Postulate 15 consists of two "if . . . then" statements:

If two parallel lines are cut by a transversal, then corresponding angles are congruent. (2 lines $\parallel \Rightarrow$ corr. $\angle$s $\cong$)

If two lines are cut by a transversal so that corresponding angles are congruent, then the lines are parallel. (Corr. $\angle$s $\cong \Rightarrow$ 2 lines $\parallel$)

When two coplanar lines are cut by a transversal, four pairs of corresponding angles are formed. We can prove that if there is one pair of congruent corresponding angles, then there are four pairs.

Given $\angle 1 \cong \angle 5$

Prove $\angle 2 \cong \angle 6$; $\angle 3 \cong \angle 7$; $\angle 4 \cong \angle 8$

Plan for Proof   Since $\angle 1$ and $\angle 2$ are supplementary and $\angle 5$ and $\angle 6$ are supplementary, use Theorem 2.7 to show that $\angle 2 \cong \angle 6$. Use vertical angles to show $\angle 3 \cong \angle 7$ and $\angle 4 \cong \angle 8$.

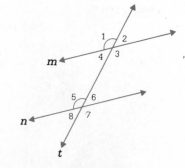

So given any single pair of congruent corresponding angles, you may use Postulate 15 to show that lines are parallel.

Theorem 3.1   If a transversal is perpendicular to one of two parallel lines, then it is perpendicular to the other.

Given   Lines ℓ and m cut by transversal t; $\ell \| m$; $t \perp \ell$

Prove $t \perp m$

Plan for Proof   Label corresponding angles, $\angle 1$ and $\angle 2$.
Use Postulate 15 to show $\angle 1 \cong \angle 2$.
Show $\angle 2$ is a right angle.

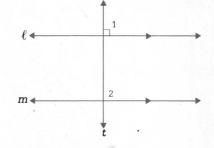

Proof

Statements	Reasons
1. Lines ℓ and m cut by transversal t; $t \perp \ell$	1. Given
2. $\angle 1$ is a right angle.	2. Two $\perp$ lines form 4 rt. $\angle$s [1]
3. $m\angle 1 = 90$	3. Def. of a rt. $\angle$ [2]
4. $\ell \| m$	4. Given
5. $\angle 1 \cong \angle 2$	5. 2 lines $\| \Rightarrow$ corr. $\angle$s $\cong$ [1, 4]
6. $m\angle 1 = m\angle 2$	6. Def. of $\cong$ $\angle$s [5]
7. $m\angle 2 = 90$	7. Substitution [3, 6]
8. $\angle 2$ is a right angle.	8. Def. of a rt. $\angle$ [7]
9. $t \perp m$	9. Def. of $\perp$ lines [8]

Theorem 3.2 is a direct result of Postulate 15; its proof is exercise 17.

Theorem 3.2   In a plane, if two lines are perpendicular to the same line, then they are parallel.

Given   Coplanar lines n, m, and t; $n \perp t$; $m \perp t$

Prove $n \| m$

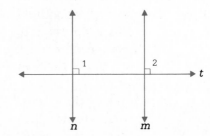

Class Exercises

[1-4] Which postulate or theorem supports each conclusion?

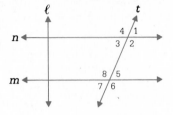

1. Given: $n \parallel m$; Conclusion: $\angle 1 \cong \angle 5$

2. Given: $\ell \perp n$, $n \parallel m$; Conclusion: $\ell \perp m$

3. Given: $\angle 1 \cong \angle 5$; Conclusion: $n \parallel m$

4. Given: $\ell \perp n$, $m \perp \ell$; Conclusion: $n \parallel m$

Written Exercises

Set A

[1-14] Use the figure at the right.

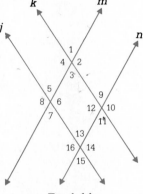

1. Assume that $j \parallel k$. Name five pairs of congruent corresponding angles.

2. Assume that $m \parallel n$. Name five pairs of congruent corresponding angles.

[3-8] Assume that $m\angle 3 = 102$, $j \parallel k$, and $m \parallel n$. Find the measure of each angle.

  3. $\angle 11$ **5.** $\angle 10$ **7.** $\angle 9$

  4. $\angle 7$ **6.** $\angle 6$ **8.** $\angle 5$

Ex. 1-14

[9-14] For each pair of congruent angles given, tell which pair of lines must be parallel.

  9. $\angle 1 \cong \angle 5$ **11.** $\angle 8 \cong \angle 16$ **13.** $\angle 10 \cong \angle 14$

  10. $\angle 4 \cong \angle 12$ **12.** $\angle 3 \cong \angle 7$ **14.** $\angle 3 \cong \angle 11$

15. The crossarms of a telephone pole are perpendicular to the pole. State the theorem that explains why the crossarms are parallel.

16. The opposite sides of two intersecting streets are parallel. What are the measures of the angles formed at the other three corners?

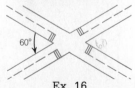

17. Write a proof for Theorem 3.2.

Ex. 16

18. Given: $\angle 1 \cong \angle 3$
    Prove: $\angle 2 \cong \angle 4$
19. Given: $\overleftrightarrow{BC} \| \overleftrightarrow{DE}$; $\angle 1 \cong \angle 2$
    Prove: $\angle 2 \cong \angle 3$
20. Given: $\angle 1 \cong \angle 3$; $\angle 1 \cong \angle 2$
    Prove: $\angle 3 \cong \angle 4$

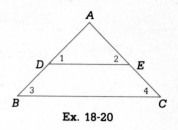

Ex. 18-20

Set B

[21-24] Given: $\overleftrightarrow{AC} \| \overleftrightarrow{DB}$. Find x and the measure of each angle.

21. $m\angle 1 = 3x - 10$; $m\angle 2 = x + 70$
22. $m\angle 1 = x + 27$; $m\angle 2 = 2x - 36$
23. $m\angle 1 = 910 - 3x$; $m\angle 2 = x - 90$
24. $m\angle 1 = 2(x + 40)$; $m\angle 2 = 11x + 44$

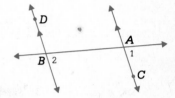

25. If Theorem 3.2 did not specify that the lines were "in a plane," would it be a true statement? Explain.

26. Given $\ell \| m$ and $m\angle 1 = 75$, find $m\angle 2$ and $m\angle 4$.

27. See exercise 26. Try other measures for $\angle 1$ and write a general "if . . . then" statement about pairs of angles such as $\angle 2$ and $\angle 4$.

28. Write a plan for proving your statement in exercise 27.

29. If $m\angle 3 = 115$ and $m\angle 4 = 65$, what can you conclude about lines ℓ and m? Write a plan for a proof justifying your answer.

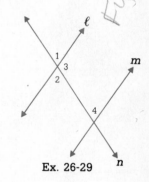

Ex. 26-29

30. To cut timbers to fit snugly, a carpenter can make $\overleftrightarrow{BE} \| \overleftrightarrow{CF}$. To do this, carpenter's squares are aligned along $\overleftrightarrow{BC}$ as shown. Why does this guarantee that $\overleftrightarrow{BE} \| \overleftrightarrow{CF}$?

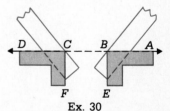

Ex. 30

Set C

31. Prove: If two parallel lines are cut by a transversal, then the bisectors of corresponding angles are parallel.

32. Prove the converse of the statement in exercise 31.

3.3   Parallel Lines and Interior Angles

When two parallel lines are cut by a transversal, corresponding angles are congruent. It is easy to prove that alternate interior angles are also congruent.

Theorem 3.3   **If two parallel lines are cut by a transversal, then alternate interior angles are congruent. (2 lines ‖ ⇒ alt. int. ∠s ≅)**

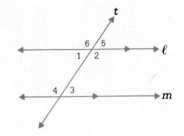

Given   Lines ℓ and m cut by transversal t; ℓ‖m

Prove   ∠1 ≅ ∠3; ∠2 ≅ ∠4

Plan for Proof   Show vert. angles, ∠1 and ∠5, are ≅.
Show corr. angles, ∠5 and ∠3, are ≅.
By transitivity, ∠1 ≅ ∠3.
Use a similar argument for ∠2 and ∠4.

Proof

Statements	Reasons
1. Lines ℓ and m cut by transversal t; ℓ‖m	1. Given
2. ∠1 ≅ ∠5	2. Vert. ∠s are ≅.
3. ∠5 ≅ ∠3	3. 2 lines ‖ ⇒ corr. ∠s ≅. [1]
4. ∠1 ≅ ∠3	4. Congruence of ∠s is transitive. [2, 3]
5. ∠2 ≅ ∠6	5. Vert. ∠s are ≅.
6. ∠6 ≅ ∠4	6. 2 lines ‖ ⇒ __?__ [1]
7. ∠2 ≅ ∠4	7. __?__ [5, 6]

Theorem 3.4   **If two lines are cut by a transversal so that alternate interior angles are congruent, then the lines are parallel.
(Alt. int. ∠s ≅ ⇒ 2 lines ‖)**

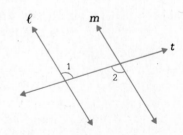

Given   Lines ℓ and m cut by transversal t;
∠1 ≅ ∠2

Prove   ℓ‖m

The proof of Theorem 3.4 is exercise 28.

In the diagram at the right, ∠1 and ∠2 are called **interior angles on the same side of the transversal.** So are ∠3 and ∠4.

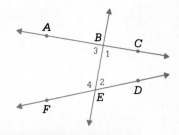

To investigate the measures of these angles when the lines are parallel, look at the parallel rulers below.

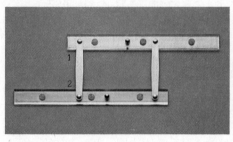

In the first picture, it appears that $m\angle 1 = m\angle 2$. However, in the second picture, $m\angle 1$ has increased while $m\angle 2$ has decreased. The angles are no longer congruent, but the *sum* of their measures remains the same. That sum is 180.

Theorem 3.5

If two parallel lines are cut by a transversal, then interior angles on the same side of the transversal are supplementary.
(2 lines ∥ ⇒ int. ∠s on same side supp.)

Given   Lines ℓ and m cut by transversal t; $\ell \parallel m$

Prove   ∠1 and ∠2 are supplementary; ∠3 and ∠4 are supplementary.

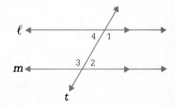

Theorem 3.6

If two lines are cut by a transversal so that interior angles on the same side of the transversal are supplementary, then the lines are parallel. (Int. ∠s on same side supp. ⇒ 2 lines ∥)

The proofs of Theorems 3.5 and 3.6 are exercises 29 and 30.

Many of the theorems in this chapter provide ways of proving angles congruent. Other theorems provide ways of proving lines parallel.

Ways to Prove Lines Parallel

Show that:

Two corresponding angles are congruent.
Two alternate interior angles are congruent.
Two interior angles on the same side of a transversal
    are supplementary.
A transversal is perpendicular to two given lines.
The lines are coplanar and do not intersect.

Properties of Parallel Lines

If two lines are parallel:

They are coplanar and do not intersect.
All pairs of corresponding angles are congruent.
Both pairs of alternate interior angles are congruent.
Both pairs of interior angles on the same side of a transversal
    are supplementary.
A transversal perpendicular to one line is perpendicular to
    the other.

Class Exercises

[1-6] If $\ell \parallel m$, what is the measure
of $\angle 5$ in each case?

1. $m\angle 2 = 80$ **4.** $m\angle 1 = 104$

2. $m\angle 3 = 98$ **5.** $m\angle 4 = 73$

3. $m\angle 8 = 76$ **6.** $m\angle 5 = 2(m\angle 2)$

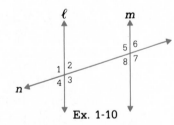

Ex. 1-10

[7-10] If $m\angle 2 = 75$, what must be the measure of each of the
following angles for ℓ and m to be parallel?

7. $\angle 8$ **8.** $\angle 5$ **9.** $\angle 6$ **10.** $\angle 7$

Written Exercises

Set A

What is the measure of ∠12 in each case?

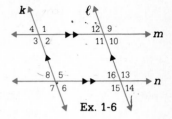

1. $m\angle 2 = 75$ 4. $m\angle 8 = 80$

2. $m\angle 1 = 110$ 5. $m\angle 14 = 72$

3. $m\angle 16 = 68$ 6. $m\angle 5 = 104$

Ex. 1-6

[7-12] Is the given fact enough to deduce that $\ell \parallel m$? If so, state the theorem or postulate that applies.

7. $\angle 1 \cong \angle 5$ 10. $m\angle 6 + m\angle 3 = 180$

8. $\angle 6 \cong \angle 4$ 11. $m\angle 2 + m\angle 3 = 180$

9. $\ell \perp t, m \perp t$ 12. $\angle 2 \cong \angle 4$

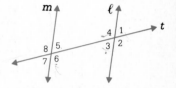

[13-18] For each given fact, tell which lines must be parallel. If none are necessarily parallel, write *none*.

13. $\angle 3 \cong \angle 10$ 16. $\angle 7 \cong \angle 19$

14. $\angle 5 \cong \angle 15$ 17. $\angle 3 \cong \angle 12$

15. $\angle 12 \cong \angle 5$ 18. $\angle 10 \cong \angle 18$

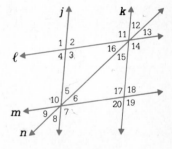

[19-21] The drawing shows a carpenter's bevel, a tool used to draw parallel line segments.

19. How are $m\angle 1$ and $m\angle 3$ related?

20. How does Postulate 15 assure that $\overleftrightarrow{AB} \parallel \overleftrightarrow{CD}$?

21. What is $m\angle 2 + m\angle 3$?

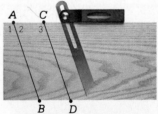

22. In the ladder at the right, the rungs are perpendicular to the sides. State three theorems that explain why the rungs are parallel.

23. Are the sides of the ladder necessarily parallel? Explain.

24. Given: $\ell \parallel m$, $\angle 1 \cong \angle 4$. Prove: $n \parallel t$

25. Given: $\ell \parallel m$, $\angle 2 \cong \angle 5$. Prove: $n \parallel t$

26. Given: $\ell \parallel m$, $n \parallel t$. Prove: $\angle 2 \cong \angle 4$

27. Given: $\ell \parallel m$, $n \parallel t$. Prove: $\angle 1 \cong \angle 5$

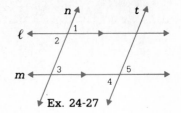

Ex. 24-27

Set B

28. Prove Theorem 3.4.

29. Prove Theorem 3.5.

30. Prove Theorem 3.6.

31. Given: $\overleftrightarrow{BC} \parallel \overleftrightarrow{EF}$, $m\angle 1 + m\angle 4 = 180$
Prove: $\overleftrightarrow{BA} \parallel \overleftrightarrow{ED}$

32. Given: $\overleftrightarrow{BC} \parallel \overleftrightarrow{EF}$; $\overleftrightarrow{BA} \parallel \overleftrightarrow{ED}$
Prove: $\angle 1$ and $\angle 4$ are
supplementary.

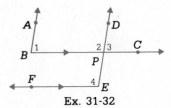

Ex. 31-32

33. Given: $\overleftrightarrow{HJ} \parallel \overleftrightarrow{ML}$; $\overleftrightarrow{HG} \parallel \overleftrightarrow{KL}$
Prove: $\angle 5 \cong \angle 8$

34. Refer to exercises 32 and 33 to
complete the following theorem:
"If the sides of two coplanar angles
lie in parallel lines, then the angles
are either __?__ or __?__."

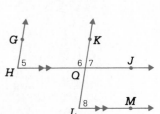

Ex. 33-34

[35-40] Given: $\ell \parallel m$. Find x.

35. $m\angle 3 = 2x + 16$; $m\angle 5 = 7x - 4$

36. $m\angle 4 = 3x + 19$; $m\angle 6 = 2(x + 10)$

37. $m\angle 4 = 8x - 80$; $m\angle 5 = -2x + 116$

38. $m\angle 3 = 3x + 36$; $m\angle 6 = 10x - 12$

39. $m\angle 3 = x^2 - 2x$; $m\angle 6 = 3x + 108$

40. $m\angle 3 = x^2 + 2x$; $m\angle 7 = -x + 70$

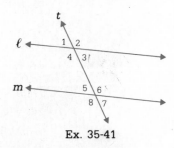

Ex. 35-41

41. $\angle 1$ and $\angle 7$ are **alternate exterior angles**, as are $\angle 2$ and $\angle 8$.
State and prove two theorems about alternate exterior
angles similar to Theorems 3.3 and 3.4.

Set C

42. Prove: If two parallel lines are cut by a transversal, then
the bisectors of alternate interior angles are parallel.

43. Prove the converse of the statement in exercise 42.

3.4   Indirect Proof

Look at the stairway in this lithograph by Maurits Escher. Could such a stairway exist in the real world? Consider the following example of **indirect reasoning**.

Either (1) the stairway could not exist in the real world *or* (2) the stairway could exist in the real world.

Suppose the stairway could exist.

Then each stair would be at a higher level than the previous stair. So after completing a circuit, a monk would be at a level higher than where he began.

But this contradicts the fact that after completing a circuit, each monk is on the level at which he began.

Therefore, the assumption that the stairway could exist *is false.*

We conclude that the stairway could not exist in the real world.

Example	Use indirect reasoning to justify the conclusion in this article from a company's newsletter.

Jennifer Gibson is our new sales representative. During her first 6 months on the job, she opened 20 new accounts. Note that this means she must have added 4 or more new accounts during one of those months.

Solution	**Alternatives**	*Either* (1) she added 4 or more new accounts during one of the months *or* (2) she added fewer than 4 new accounts each month.
	Assumption	*Suppose* she added fewer than 4 new accounts each month.
	Argument	*Then* she added 3 or fewer new accounts each month. So her total could be 6 times this number—18 or fewer new accounts.
	Contradiction	*But this contradicts* the fact that she added 20 new accounts.
	Conclude (2) is false.	*Therefore, the assumption* that she added fewer than 4 new accounts each month *is false.*
	Conclude (1) is true.	*We conclude* that she added at least 4 new accounts during at least one of the months.

Indirect reasoning can be used in geometry proofs.

Steps in an Indirect Proof

1. Assume that the opposite of the statement to be proved is true.
2. Argue to a contradiction of a known fact—a postulate, theorem, definition, algebraic property, or given fact.
3. Conclude that the assumption is false.
4. Conclude that the statement to be proved is true.

The proof of Theorem 2.4 was postponed because its second part involves an indirect proof. We now prove it.

Theorem 2.4	**If two lines intersect, then they intersect in one and only one point.**

Given
Two lines, ℓ and m, intersect.

Prove
Part I: Lines ℓ and m intersect in at least one point.

Part II: Lines ℓ and m intersect in only one point.

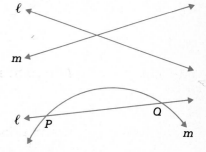

Part I
We know that the intersection of ℓ and m contains at least one point because it is given that the lines intersect.

Part II
Either (1) ℓ and m intersect in only one point *or* (2) ℓ and m intersect in two or more points.

Suppose ℓ and m intersect in two or more points. Call two of these points P and Q.

Then the two points, P and Q, would be contained in two lines, ℓ and m.

But this contradicts the fact that, by the Line Postulate, two points are contained in one and only one line.

Therefore, the assumption that ℓ and m intersect in two or more points *is false.*

We conclude that ℓ and m intersect in only one point.

Class Exercises

[1-6] State what you would assume to prove each statement indirectly.

1. $\angle A \cong \angle B$ **3.** $\ell \perp m$ **5.** $\ell \not\parallel m$

2. $\ell \parallel m$ **4.** $m\angle A \neq 60$ **6.** A, B, and C are collinear.

Written Exercises

1. In 1983, Emily was shopping for a used car. One car had an "Unleaded Fuel Only" decal. Such decals first appeared on cars in 1975. Emily concluded that the car was eight years old or less. Write an indirect argument to show that Emily is correct.

2. The announcement below was not printed clearly. On what day and date were the tryouts scheduled?

> Sophomore Class Play Tryouts
> he Little Theater
> rsday at 7:00
> ary 30

[3-8] Write the theorem, postulate, or definition that each statement contradicts.

3. Lines m and n intersect in points A and B.

4. Right $\angle PXQ$ and acute $\angle QXR$ form a linear pair.

5. Planes $\mathcal{E}$ and $\mathcal{K}$ contain intersecting lines m and t.

6. On $\overrightarrow{AB}$, points C and D are both 6 units from A.

7. Points R, S, and T are midpoints of $\overline{AB}$.

8. $\angle A$ is an obtuse angle with measure 48.

[9-14] Complete this proof of the second part of Theorem 2.5: A line and a point not on the line lie in only one plane.

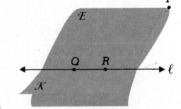

Given: Point P not on line ℓ
Prove: P and ℓ lie in only one plane.

9. *Either* (1) __?__ *or* (2) P and ℓ lie in two or more planes.

10. *Suppose* __?__ . Call two of these planes $\mathcal{E}$ and $\mathcal{K}$.

11. *Then* line ℓ lies in both __?__ . By the __?__ Postulate, ℓ contains at least two points, Q and R. It is given that P does not lie on $\overleftrightarrow{RQ}$ (that is, line ℓ), so three noncollinear points, __?__ , __?__ , and __?__ , all lie in $\mathcal{E}$ and also all lie in $\mathcal{K}$.

12. *But this contradicts* the fact that, by the Plane Postulate, three noncollinear points ___?___ .

13. *Therefore, the assumption* that ___?___ is ___?___ .

14. *We conclude* that ___?___ .

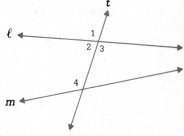

15. Given: $\ell \not\parallel m$
    Prove: $\angle 1 \not\cong \angle 4$

16. Given: $\angle 3 \not\cong \angle 4$
    Prove: $\ell \not\parallel m$

17. Given: $m\angle 4 + m\angle 2 \neq 180$
    Prove: $\ell \not\parallel m$

18. Given: $\ell \not\parallel m$ and $t \perp \ell$
    Prove: $t \not\perp m$

Ex. 15-18

Set B

[19-22] Are the two given statements contradictory?

19. $\ell \parallel m$; point P lies on ℓ and m.

20. $\angle D$ is acute; $m\angle D = 63$

21. Point B is between points A and C; $BC > AC$

22. $\angle R$ and $\angle T$ are complementary; $\angle R \cong \angle T$

23. Pat did 90 sit-ups in 2 minutes. Write an indirect argument to show that she must have done 20 or more sit-ups during at least one 30-second interval.

24. In the mystery below, whom does the inspector suspect?

> At 8:45 P.M., Mrs. Wilson's maid knocked on the library door and got no answer. The door was locked from the inside. The maid called Inspector Sharpe and a professor friend. When the door was forced open, Mrs. Wilson was found dead. Nearby was a half-empty teacup, a tiny unstoppered vial, and a typewritten note that said, "Blessed are the poor for they shall be happy." The window was open. When the two men went outside to inspect the grounds, Charles, the wealthy widow's sole heir, arrived. He was told his aunt was poisoned and said, "How terrible! Poisoned? Who did it? Why was the door locked? Had my aunt been threatened?" He explained he had been working late at the office and was stopping by on his way home.

Set C

25. Given: $\ell \parallel m$; plane $\mathcal{E}$ contains m; plane $\mathcal{E}$ does not contain ℓ.
    Prove: Plane $\mathcal{E} \parallel \ell$

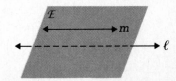

3.5 Parallels and Perpendiculars to a Line

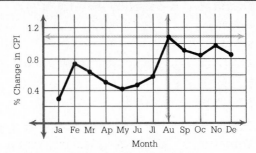

Month

To interpret a point on a graph such as the one above, we draw lines parallel and perpendicular to the horizontal axis. The intersections of these lines with the axes give the month and the value for that month.

Theorem 3.7 assures us that there is exactly one such parallel and exactly one such value for any given point.

The proof uses a line not given in the theorem. $\overleftrightarrow{PA}$ is an **auxiliary line**. To use an auxiliary line, you must justify it with a theorem or postulate. (See reason 2 below.)

Theorem 3.7   Through a point not on a given line, there is exactly one line parallel to the given line.

Given   Line ℓ; point P not on ℓ

Prove   Part I: There is one line through P parallel to ℓ.
Part II: There is only one line through P parallel to ℓ.

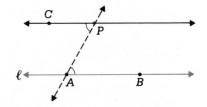

Part I

Statements	Reasons
1. Choose 2 points, A and B, on ℓ.	1. Points Postulate: A line contains at least 2 points.
2. Draw $\overleftrightarrow{PA}$.	2. Line Postulate: _?_.
3. In the half-plane with edge $\overleftrightarrow{PA}$ not containing B, draw a ray, $\overrightarrow{PC}$, such that $m\angle CPA = m\angle PAB$.	3. Angle Construction Postulate
4. $\angle CPA \cong \angle PAB$	4. Def. of $\cong$ $\angle$s [3]
5. $\overleftrightarrow{CP} \parallel \ell$	5. Alt. int. $\angle$s $\cong$ $\Rightarrow$ 2 lines $\parallel$ [4]

Part II

Either (1) there is only one line through P parallel to ℓ *or* (2) there are two or more lines through P parallel to ℓ.

Suppose there are two or more lines through P parallel to ℓ. Call two of these lines $\overleftrightarrow{PC}$ and $\overleftrightarrow{PD}$ as shown.

Then $\angle DPA \cong \angle PAB$ because when parallel lines are cut by a transversal, alternate interior angles are congruent. For the same reason, $\angle PAB \cong \angle CPA$. So $\angle DPA \cong \angle CPA$ because congruence of angles is transitive.

But this contradicts the fact that, by the Angle Construction Postulate, there is exactly one such angle with a given measure.

Therefore, the assumption that there are two or more lines through P parallel to ℓ *is false.*

We conclude that there is only one line through P parallel to ℓ.

Theorem 3.8 is a corollary to Theorem 3.7. The indirect proof of Theorem 3.8, exercise 26, uses only definitions and Theorem 3.7.

__Theorem 3.8__

In a plane, if two lines are parallel to the same line, then they are parallel to each other.

Given

$\ell \parallel m;\ m \parallel n$

Prove

$\ell \parallel n$

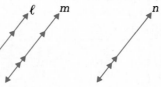

__Theorem 3.9__

In a plane, through a point on a given line, there is one and only one line perpendicular to the given line.

The proofs of the two parts of Theorem 3.9 are exercises 1-4 and 13-18.

Theorem 3.10 is a corollary to Theorem 3.9; its proof is exercise 20.

Theorem 3.10   In a plane, a segment has exactly one perpendicular bisector.

When a football player is tackled, a referee places the ball to establish the *line of scrimmage,* a line perpendicular to the sideline through the ball.

This is an application of Theorem 3.11. Its proof is exercise 25.

Theorem 3.11   Through a point not on a given line, there is one and only one line perpendicular to the given line.

Given	Line ℓ and point P not on ℓ
Prove	Part I: There is one line through P perpendicular to ℓ. Part II: There is only one line through P perpendicular to ℓ.
Plan for Proof	Part I: Use Theorem 3.9 to draw $m \perp \ell$ at some point A on ℓ. Use Theorem 3.7 to draw n through P parallel to m. Use Theorem 3.1 to show $n \perp \ell$.
	Part II: Suppose there are two lines j and k through P perpendicular to ℓ. Use Theorem 3.2 to argue to a contradiction.

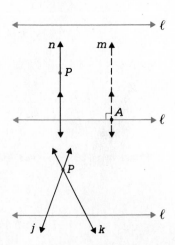

Class Exercises

Tell whether each statement is true or false.

1. There is exactly one line parallel to $\overleftrightarrow{RT}$ through S.

2. $\overleftrightarrow{QT}$ and $\overleftrightarrow{QU}$ can both be parallel to $\overleftrightarrow{SR}$.

3. There is exactly one line perpendicular to $\overleftrightarrow{RT}$ through point T.

4. There is exactly one line perpendicular to $\overleftrightarrow{RS}$ through Q.

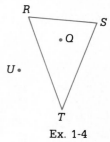

Ex. 1-4

Written Exercises

Set A

[1-4] Prove Theorem 3.9, Part I.

Given: Line ℓ in plane $\mathcal{K}$; point P on ℓ
Prove: There is one line in $\mathcal{K}$ through P perpendicular to ℓ.

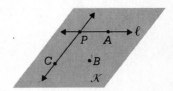

Statements	Reasons
1. Let A be another point on ℓ and let B be another point in $\mathcal{K}$, not on ℓ.	1. _?_ .
2. In the half-plane with edge ℓ containing B, there is exactly one ray, $\overrightarrow{PC}$, such that $m\angle APC = 90$.	2. _?_ .
3. $\angle APC$ is a right angle.	3. _?_ .
4. $\overleftrightarrow{PC} \perp \ell$	4. _?_ .

[5-10] State the postulate or theorem that justifies each statement.

5. Draw $\overleftrightarrow{DB}$.

6. Choose P on $\overrightarrow{BA}$ such that $BP = CD$.

7. Let M be the midpoint of $\overline{BC}$.

8. Draw line m through A parallel to $\overleftrightarrow{BC}$.

9. Draw line m through D so $m \perp \overleftrightarrow{BC}$.

10. In the plane containing A, B, and C, draw ℓ perpendicular to $\overleftrightarrow{AC}$ at D.

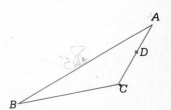

[11-12] Refer to the figure at the right.

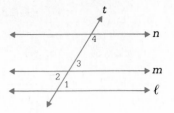

11. Given: $\ell \parallel n$; $\angle 1 \cong \angle 2$
    Prove: $m \parallel n$

12. Given: $\angle 1 \cong \angle 3$; $m \parallel n$
    Prove: $\angle 1$ and $\angle 4$ are supplementary.

[13-18] Complete this proof of Theorem 3.9, Part II.

Given: Line ℓ in plane $\mathcal{K}$ and point P on ℓ
Prove: There is only one line in $\mathcal{K}$
through P perpendicular to ℓ.

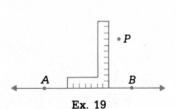

13. *Either* (1) there is only one line in $\mathcal{K}$
    through P perpendicular to ℓ *or*
    (2) there are two or more ? .

14. *Suppose* ? . Call two of the lines $\overleftrightarrow{PC}$
    and $\overleftrightarrow{PD}$.

15. *Then* $m\angle DPA =$? and
    $m\angle CPA =$? .

16. *But this contradicts* the Angle
    Construction Postulate, ? .

17. *Therefore, the assumption* ? *is* ? .

18. *We conclude that* ? .

19. Explain how a carpenter's square can
    be used to draw a line through a
    point P parallel to $\overleftrightarrow{AB}$.

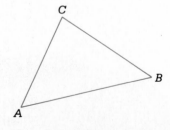

Ex. 19

Set B

20. Prove Theorem 3.10.

[21-24] Can an auxiliary line be drawn to meet
each set of conditions? Justify your answer.

21. Draw the perpendicular bisector of
    $\overline{AB}$ through C.

22. Draw the angle bisector of $\angle C$.

23. Draw a line perpendicular to $\overleftrightarrow{AB}$
    through C.

24. Draw the angle bisector of $\angle C$
    perpendicular to $\overleftrightarrow{AB}$.

25. Prove Theorem 3.11, Parts I and II.

26. Write an indirect proof of Theorem 3.8.

27. Prove indirectly: In a plane, if a line intersects one of two parallel lines, then it also intersects the other.

[28-30] Given: $\overleftrightarrow{AB} \parallel \overleftrightarrow{DE}$.

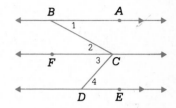

28. $m\angle 1 = m\angle 2$; $m\angle 4 = 42$; $m\angle 3 = $ __?__
What theorems justify your answer?

29. $m\angle 1 = 40$; $m\angle 2 = 40$; $m\angle 4 = 50$;
$m\angle BCD = $ __?__

30. $\overleftrightarrow{CF} \parallel \overleftrightarrow{DE}$; $m\angle 1 = 30$; $m\angle 4 = 45$;
$m\angle BCD = $ __?__

31. Given: $\overleftrightarrow{PQ} \parallel \overleftrightarrow{ST}$
Prove: $m\angle QRS = m\angle 1 + m\angle 4$

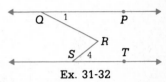

Ex. 31-32

Set C

32. Is the converse of the theorem in exercise 31 also true? If so, prove it; if not, give a counterexample.

33. If the words "in a plane" were not in Theorems 3.8, 3.9, and 3.10, would they still be true?

Construction Exercises

Construction 6   Through a point not on a given line, construct a line parallel to the given line.

Given   Point P not on line ℓ

Construct   A line through P parallel to ℓ

Method   Step 1: Pick any point A on ℓ. Draw $\overleftrightarrow{AP}$ to determine $\angle 1$.

Step 2: Using $\overrightarrow{PA}$ as one ray, construct $\angle 2$ on the side of $\overrightarrow{PA}$ opposite $\angle 1$ so that $\angle 1 \cong \angle 2$. Label the point where the arcs meet Q.

Step 3: Draw $\overleftrightarrow{PQ}$.
Then $\overleftrightarrow{PQ} \parallel \ell$.

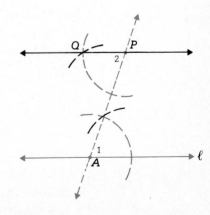

<u>**Construction 7**</u> **Through a point not on a given line, construct a line that is perpendicular to the given line.**

Given   Point *C* not on line *m*

Construct   A line through *C* perpendicular to *m*

Method   Step 1: With *C* as center, draw an arc that intersects *m* at two points *E* and *F*.

Step 2: Using the same radius with *E* and *F* as centers, construct two arcs that intersect at a point *D* which is different from *C*.

Step 3: Draw $\overleftrightarrow{CD}$.

Then $\overleftrightarrow{CD} \perp m$.

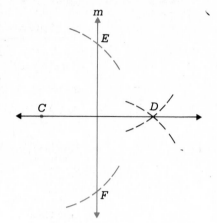

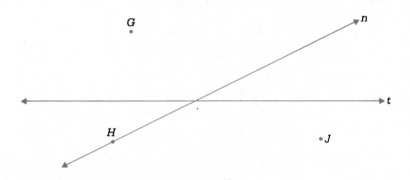

[1-6] Trace the drawing above as needed.

1. Construct a line parallel to *n* through *G*.
2. Construct a line parallel to *t* through *G*.
3. On what theorem is the construction of a parallel based?
4. Construct a line perpendicular to *n* through *H*.
5. Construct a line perpendicular to *t* through *G*.
6. Construct a line perpendicular to *n* through *J*.

7. Draw a large triangle. Through each vertex, construct a line that is parallel to the opposite side.
8. Draw a large triangle. Through each vertex, construct a line that is perpendicular to the opposite side.

Progress Check

Lesson 3.1
Page 108

[1-4] Is each statement always, sometimes, or never true?

1. Coplanar lines ℓ and m intersect.

2. A transversal intersects two coplanar lines in two distinct points.

3. Skew lines j and k intersect in exactly one point.

4. Parallel lines h and k are not coplanar.

[5-6] Refer to the figure at the right.

5. $\angle 3$ and ? are corresponding angles.

6. $\angle 3$ and ? are alternate interior angles.

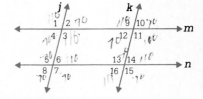

Lesson 3.2
Page 112

[7-10] Given: $j \parallel k$; $m \parallel n$; $m\angle 3 = 110$. Find each measure.

7. $m\angle 7$ 9. $m\angle 11$

8. $m\angle 2$ 10. $m\angle 15$

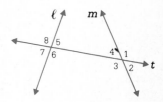

Lesson 3.3
Page 116

[11-14] For each pair of congruent angles, tell which pair of lines you can conclude are parallel.

11. $\angle 2 \cong \angle 8$ 13. $\angle 6 \cong \angle 1$

12. $\angle 6 \cong \angle 11$ 14. $\angle 3 \cong \angle 7$

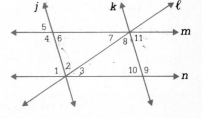

Lesson 3.4
Page 121

15. State what you would suppose to start an indirect proof that $j \parallel k$.

16. Given: In plane $\mathcal{E}$, transversal $t \perp k$, $t \not\perp j$
    Prove: $j \not\parallel k$

Lesson 3.5
Page 126

17. What postulate or theorem would justify the statement, "Draw $\overleftrightarrow{PR}$"?

18. Given: $m \parallel n$
    Prove: There is at least one line t through A perpendicular to both m and n.

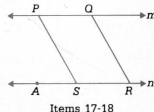

Items 17-18

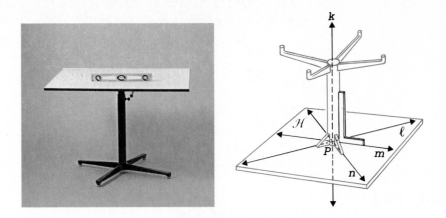

In assembling a pedestal table, it is important to make the top of the table level. This can be done by attaching the top so it is perpendicular to the vertical leg. The idea of a plane perpendicular to a line is formalized below.

Definition

A line and a plane that intersect **are perpendicular** if and only if every line in the given plane which passes through the point of intersection is perpendicular to the given line.

In the drawing at the right above, to say that $k \perp \mathcal{H}$ at P means that $k \perp \ell$, $k \perp m$, and $k \perp n$.

Theorem 3.12

If two planes are perpendicular to the same line, then the planes are parallel.

Given $\mathcal{H} \perp \ell$ at P; $\mathcal{E} \perp \ell$ at R

Prove $\mathcal{H} \parallel \mathcal{E}$

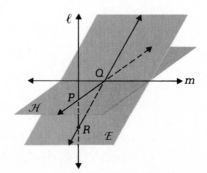

Proof	*Either* (1) $\mathcal{H} \parallel \mathcal{E}$ or (2) $\mathcal{H}$ and $\mathcal{E}$ intersect.

Suppose $\mathcal{H}$ and $\mathcal{E}$ intersect. *Then* their intersection is a line m. Choose a point Q on m and draw $\overrightarrow{PQ}$ and $\overrightarrow{RQ}$. By the Flat Plane Postulate, $\overleftrightarrow{PQ}$ lies in $\mathcal{H}$ and $\overleftrightarrow{RQ}$ lies in $\mathcal{E}$. By the definition of a line perpendicular to a plane, $\ell \perp \overleftrightarrow{PQ}$, and $\ell \perp \overleftrightarrow{RQ}$. Then there are two lines through Q perpendicular to ℓ.

But this contradicts Theorem 3.11.

Therefore, the assumption that $\mathcal{H}$ and $\mathcal{E}$ intersect *is false*.

We conclude that $\mathcal{H} \parallel \mathcal{E}$.

Theorem 3.13	**If two parallel planes are cut by a third plane, then the lines of intersection are parallel.**
Given	Plane $\mathcal{R} \parallel$ plane $\mathcal{S}$; plane $\mathcal{T}$ cuts $\mathcal{R}$ and $\mathcal{S}$ in lines m and n, respectively.
Prove	$m \parallel n$

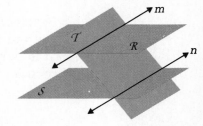

Proof	

Statements	Reasons
1. m lies in planes $\mathcal{R}$ and $\mathcal{T}$; n lies in planes $\mathcal{S}$ and $\mathcal{T}$.	1. Given
2. m and n are coplanar.	2. Def. of coplanar [1]
3. Plane $\mathcal{R} \parallel$ plane $\mathcal{S}$	3. ___?___ .
4. m and n do not intersect.	4. Def. of $\parallel$ planes [1, 3]
5. $m \parallel n$	5. ___?___ [2, 4]

Class Exercises

1. Can each of three lines be perpendicular to the other two? Explain or sketch an example.

2. Given: plane $\mathcal{K} \perp$ line ℓ. Draw $\mathcal{K}$ and ℓ, then draw $m \parallel \ell$ and $n \parallel \ell$. How do m, n, and $\mathcal{K}$ seem to be related?

3. Given: $\mathcal{H} \perp m$; $\mathcal{K} \parallel \mathcal{H}$; $\mathcal{E} \parallel \mathcal{H}$. Draw planes $\mathcal{H}$, $\mathcal{E}$, and $\mathcal{K}$ and line m. How do m, $\mathcal{K}$, and $\mathcal{E}$ seem to be related?

Written Exercises

Set A

[1-6] Given: Lines j, k, and n in plane $\mathcal{H}$; j and m in plane $\mathcal{E}$; k and ℓ in plane $\mathcal{F}$

1. If $\mathcal{E} \parallel \mathcal{F}$, how are j and k related?
2. If $\mathcal{E} \parallel \mathcal{F}$, is ℓ necessarily parallel to m?
3. If $j \perp n$ and $k \perp n$, what conclusion, if any, can you draw about j and k?
4. If $j \perp n$ and $k \perp n$, what conclusion, if any, can you draw about $\mathcal{E}$ and $\mathcal{F}$?
5. If $\mathcal{E} \parallel \mathcal{F}$ and $\mathcal{E} \perp n$, what are four conclusions that you can draw about the lines shown?
6. If $n \perp \mathcal{E}$ and $n \perp \mathcal{F}$, what are six conclusions that you can draw about the lines and planes shown?

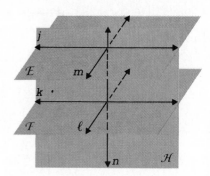

Set B

[7-14] Is each statement always, sometimes, or never true?

7. Two lines perpendicular to the same line are perpendicular.
8. Two lines perpendicular to the same line are parallel.
9. Two lines perpendicular to the same plane intersect.
10. Two lines perpendicular to the same plane are parallel.
11. Two lines parallel to the same plane are parallel.
12. Two lines parallel to the same plane are skew.
13. Two planes parallel to the same plane are parallel.
14. Two planes parallel to the same line are parallel.

Set C

15. Given: $n \perp \mathcal{H}$ at P; $\mathcal{H} \parallel \mathcal{K}$
Prove: n intersects $\mathcal{K}$

16. Given: $n \perp \mathcal{H}$ at P; n intersects $\mathcal{K}$ at Q; $\mathcal{H} \parallel \mathcal{K}$; R is a point on $\mathcal{K}$.
Prove: $\overleftrightarrow{RQ} \perp n$

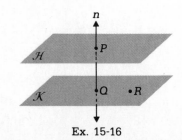

Ex. 15-16

Career   Contractor

Jim Washington is a contractor. He was hired to convert an old warehouse into a dinner theater.

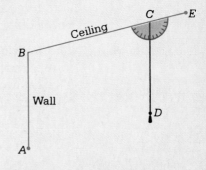

1. Jim built a short, open staircase up to the stage. What angle should each step make with the crossbar so that the steps will be parallel to the floor?

2. What theorem or postulate justifies your answer in exercise 1?

3. What should the measure of ∠A be for the handrail to be parallel to the crossbar?

4. What theorem or postulate does this illustrate?

5. The height of the stage is 108 cm. What is the "drop" from one step to the next?

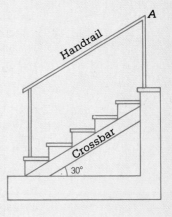

To find the angle between the slanted ceiling and the wall, ∠ABC at the right, Jim used a protractor and a plumb line (a string with a weight).

6. If the protractor indicates that $m\angle BCD = 78$, what is $m\angle DCE$?

7. What is $m\angle ABC$? Explain.

3.7   Triangles

Engineers and architects use triangular components to enhance the beauty and stability of their designs.

A **triangle** is the union of the three segments determined by three noncollinear points.

If A, B, and C are noncollinear, the union of $\overline{AB}$, $\overline{BC}$, and $\overline{AC}$ is triangle ABC, denoted by $\triangle ABC$.

A, B, and C are the **vertices** of the triangle; $\overline{AB}$, $\overline{BC}$, and $\overline{AC}$ are its **sides.** $\angle A$, $\angle B$, and $\angle C$ are the **angles** of $\triangle ABC$.

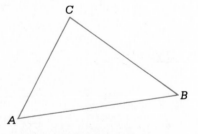

A side of a triangle is **opposite** an angle if the side does not contain the vertex of the angle. (The angle is opposite the side as well.) In $\triangle ABC$, $\overline{AB}$ is opposite $\angle C$. Which side is opposite $\angle A$? Which angle is opposite $\overline{AC}$?

The **interior** of a triangle is the intersection of the interiors of its angles. The **exterior** of a triangle is the set of points in the plane which do not belong to the triangle or to its interior.

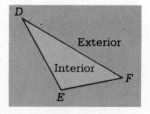

Triangles may be classified in terms of their angles.

Definition

An **acute triangle** is a triangle with three acute angles.
A **right triangle** is a triangle with a right angle.
An **obtuse triangle** is a triangle with an obtuse angle.

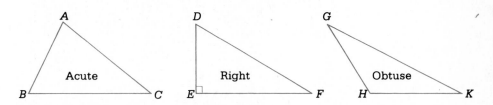

In a right triangle, the side opposite the right angle is called the **hypotenuse**. The other two sides are the **legs**. The hypotenuse of $\triangle DEF$ is $\overline{DF}$; the legs are $\overline{ED}$ and $\overline{EF}$.

Definition

An **equiangular triangle** is a triangle with three congruent angles.

$\triangle LMN$ at the right is equiangular.

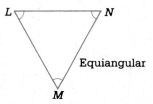

· Triangles can also be classified in terms of their sides.

Definition

A **scalene triangle** is a triangle with no two sides congruent.
An **isosceles triangle** is one with at least two sides congruent.
An **equilateral triangle** is one with three congruent sides.

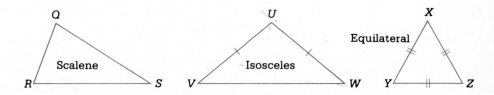

In an isosceles triangle, the congruent sides are called the **legs**; the third side is the **base**. The angle opposite the base is the **vertex angle**. The angles opposite the congruent sides are the **base angles**.

In $\triangle UVW$, the legs are $\overline{UV}$ and $\overline{UW}$; the base is $\overline{VW}$. $\angle U$ is the vertex angle and the base angles are $\angle V$ and $\angle W$.

Class Exercises

1. Name all of the triangles shown in the diagram.

2. Name the vertices, sides, and angles of △ABC.

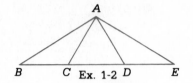

Ex. 1-2

[3-10] Use the diagrams at the right.

3. △ _?_ is acute.

4. △ _?_ is obtuse.

5. △ _?_ is equiangular.

6. △ _?_ is a right triangle.

7. The hypotenuse of the right triangle is _?_ .

8. _?_ and _?_ are the legs of the right triangle.

9. △ _?_ is scalene.

10. △ _?_ is equilateral.

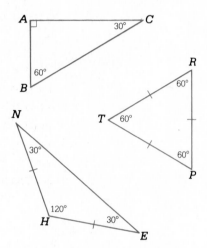

Written Exercises

Set A

[1-6] Draw a triangle that satisfies the given conditions.

1. Scalene and acute
2. Scalene and right
3. Scalene and obtuse

4. Isosceles and obtuse
5. Isosceles and right
6. Equilateral and acute

[7-8] Given: ∠S is a right angle.

7. What kind of triangle is △RST?

8. Name its legs and its hypotenuse.

[9-11] Given: $\overline{GF} \cong \overline{GH}$

9. What kind of triangle is △FGH?

10. Name its vertex angle and base angles.

11. Name its base and its legs.

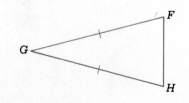

12. a. Use a protractor to draw a large
triangle with angles of 90°, 60°,
and 30°.

b. Draw the trisectors of the angles.
(Trisectors divide an angle into
three congruent angles.)

c. Label the points where adjacent
trisectors of different angles
intersect. (See the figure.)

d. Draw the triangle determined by
these points of intersection.

e. Guess what kind of triangle $\triangle ABC$
is. Check your guess with a ruler.

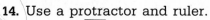

Ex. 12-13

13. Repeat exercise 12 with a triangle
with angles of 75°, 60°, and 45°.

14. Use a protractor and ruler.

a. Draw $\overline{AB}$ with $AB = 3$ cm.

b. Draw $\angle ABC$ with measure 60 and $BC = 2(AB)$.

c. What is $m\angle ACB$? What is $m\angle CAB$?

15. Repeat exercise 14 with $AB = 2$ cm.

16. Write an indirect proof: A triangle cannot have two right
angles.

17. How many triangles are determined by 4 coplanar points,
no 3 of which are collinear? By 5 such points?

Construction Exercises

1. Given: $\overline{AB}$ and $\overline{CD}$
Construct: Right $\triangle PQR$ with legs $\overline{PQ}$ and $\overline{PR}$; $\overline{PQ} \cong \overline{AB}$
and $\overline{PR} \cong \overline{CD}$.

2. Given: $\overline{AB}$; $AB = 6$ cm
Construct: Equilateral $\triangle XYZ$ with $\overline{XY} \cong \overline{AB}$.

3. Repeat exercise 2 using $AB = 8$ cm. What seems to be true
about the angles of an equilateral triangle?

3.8　The Angles of a Triangle

A concrete model frequently suggests relationships that can be established by proof. This model of a triangle is first folded so that B lies on $\overline{AC}$ and the fold is parallel to $\overline{AC}$. Then it is folded so that A and C are at B.

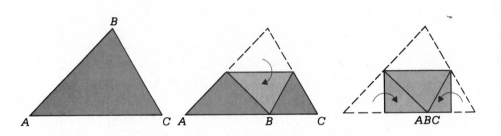

It appears that $m\angle A + m\angle B + m\angle C = 180$. Results like this with several triangles suggest the following theorem.

Theorem 3.14　**The sum of the measures of the angles of a triangle is 180.**

Given	$\triangle ABC$
Prove	$m\angle A + m\angle ABC + m\angle C = 180$
Plan for Proof	Use Thm. 3.7 to draw $\overleftrightarrow{DE} \parallel \overleftrightarrow{AC}$ through B. Show $m\angle 1 + m\angle 2 + m\angle 3 = 180$. Use alt. int. $\angle$s and substitution.

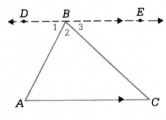

Proof

Statements	Reasons
1. Through B draw $\overleftrightarrow{DE} \parallel \overleftrightarrow{AC}$.	1. Through a point not on a given line ___?___ .
2. $\angle 1$ and $\angle ABE$ are supp.	2. Supplement Postulate
3. $m\angle 1 + m\angle ABE = 180$	3. ___?___ [2]
4. $m\angle 2 + m\angle 3 = m\angle ABE$	4. Angle Addition Post.
5. $m\angle 1 + m\angle 2 + m\angle 3 = 180$	5. Substitution [3, 4]
6. $\angle 1 \cong \angle A$; $\angle 3 \cong \angle C$	6. 2 lines $\parallel \Rightarrow$ ___?___ [1]
7. $m\angle 1 = m\angle A$; $m\angle 3 = m\angle C$	7. Def. of $\cong$ $\angle$s [6]
8. $m\angle A + m\angle ABC + m\angle C = 180$	8. Substitution [5, 7]

The following theorems are corollaries of Theorem 3.14. Their proofs are exercises 9-11.

Theorem 3.15	If two angles of one triangle are congruent to two angles of another triangle, then the remaining angles are congruent.

Theorem 3.16	The acute angles of a right triangle are complementary.

Theorem 3.17	Each angle of an equiangular triangle has measure 60.

In the triangle at the right, side $\overline{AC}$ has been extended. $\angle 1$ is called an **exterior angle** of $\triangle ABC$ since it forms a linear pair with $\angle BCA$, one of the angles of the triangle. $\angle A$ and $\angle B$ are called the **remote interior angles** with respect to $\angle 1$.

Note that when all sides of a triangle are extended, there are two exterior angles at each vertex. In the diagram, each numbered angle is an exterior angle.

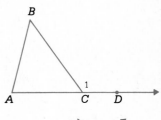

In $\triangle XYZ$,

$$m\angle XYZ + m\angle X + m\angle Z = \underline{\ ?\ }, \text{ and}$$
$$m\angle XYZ + m\angle 7 = \underline{\ ?\ }.$$

How are $m\angle 7$, $m\angle X$, and $m\angle Z$ related? Your answer should suggest Theorem 3.18.

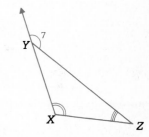

Theorem 3.18	The measure of an exterior angle of a triangle is equal to the sum of the measures of its two remote interior angles.

Theorem 3.19	The measure of an exterior angle of a triangle is greater than the measure of either of its remote interior angles.

The proofs of Theorems 3.18 and 3.19 are exercises 17 and 18.

Class Exercises

[1-5] Given △XYZ, find m∠X.

1. m∠Y = 30 and m∠Z = 100. 50

2. △XYZ is equiangular. 60

3. An exterior angle at X has measure 50. 30

4. ∠X and an exterior angle at X have the same measure. 90

5. An exterior angle at Z has measure 125; m∠Y = 80. 45

[6-8] Find m∠1 in each diagram.

6.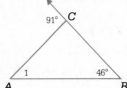

7.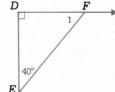

8.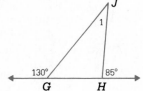

Written Exercises

Set A

[1-6] Find the measure of each angle in △PQR.

1. m∠P = 87; m∠Q = 63

2. ∠P is a right angle; m∠Q = 53

3. m∠P = 5x; m∠Q = 7x; m∠R = 8x − 20

4. m∠P = 40; m∠Q = 2x + 15; m∠R = 3x

5. m∠Q = 4x + 7; m∠R = 3(x − 2); the measure of an exterior angle at P is 85.

6. m∠P = 8x; m∠Q = 7x; the measure of an exterior angle at R is 2(x + 65).

[7-8] Given: ∠B ≅ ∠DEF; ∠C ≅ ∠F.
Explain why each statement is true.

7. ∠A ≅ ∠D

8. m∠D < m∠EGF.

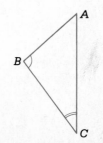
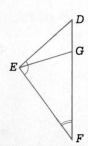

9. Prove Theorem 3.15.

10. Prove Theorem 3.16.

11. Prove Theorem 3.17.

12. Given: △HGJ and △MKJ are
right triangles.
Prove: ∠H ≅ ∠M

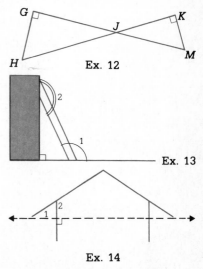

Ex. 12

13. One end of a support brace was
cut at an angle (∠1) of 115°. At
what angle should the other end
of the brace be cut?

Ex. 13

14. The *pitch* (m∠1) of the roof at
the right is 35°. What is the
measure of the angle (∠2) that
the attic ceiling makes with the
outside wall of the house?

Ex. 14

Set B

[15-16] To measure ∠1, a machinist would place *angle
gauge blocks* as shown. The blocks used in the diagram
indicate that m∠4 = 41 and m∠2 = 27.

15. Prove that m∠1 = 68.

16. Draw and label a diagram to help
explain how to use these two
blocks to check whether an
angle has a measure of 14.

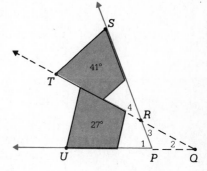

17. Prove Theorem 3.18.

18. Prove Theorem 3.19. (Recall that "a > b" means that
a = b + c for some positive number c.)

19. Given: $\overline{CD} \perp \overline{AB}$; ∠A ≅ ∠B
Prove: $\overrightarrow{CD}$ bisects ∠ACB

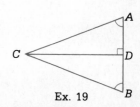

Ex. 19

20. Prove: The measure of any exterior angle of an equiangular triangle is 120.

21. Prove: The sum of the measures of the exterior angles of a triangle, one at each vertex, is 360.

22. Prove: A triangle cannot have two obtuse angles.

23. Given: $\triangle MAY$ with $\angle M \cong \angle Y$
    Prove: $m\angle NAM = 2(m\angle M)$

24. Given: $\overline{JU} \parallel \overline{NE}$; $\overline{EJ} \parallel \overline{NU}$
    Prove: $\angle 1 \cong \angle 2$

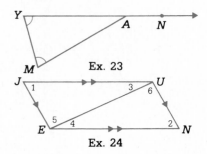

Ex. 23

Ex. 24

Set C

25. When a light ray strikes a smooth surface such as a facet of a jewel, the angle at which the ray strikes the surface is congruent to the angle at which the ray leaves the surface. The sparkle of a diamond results from light being reflected from facet to facet and back through its top directly to the eye of the observer. In the cross sections of the two diamonds shown below, the diamond at the left has been cut too deeply—$\angle Y$ is too small. Use the figure at the right below to prove that if $\angle B$ at the base of the diamond is cut at 90°, then the entering and exiting rays will be parallel.

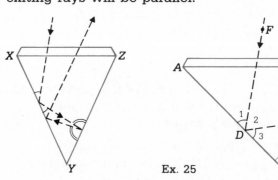

Ex. 25

26. Prove: If two parallel lines are cut by a transversal, then the bisectors of the interior angles on the same side of the transversal are perpendicular.

27. Prove the converse of the statement in exercise 26.

3.9   Polygons

The faces of a crystal are geometric figures whose edges are line segments. Such figures are called polygons.

A **polygon** is the union of three or more coplanar segments such that each segment intersects exactly two other segments, one at each endpoint, and no two intersecting segments are collinear. The first two figures below are polygons; the last one is not.

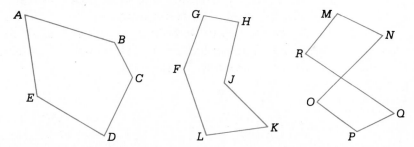

$\overline{AB}$, $\overline{BC}$, and $\overline{LK}$ are **sides** of the polygons above. $\angle BCD$ and $\angle DEA$ are **angles** of the polygons, and A, F, and H are **vertices** of the polygons.

In the polygon at the right, $\overline{ST}$ and $\overline{TU}$ are **consecutive sides** since they intersect. $\angle STU$ and $\angle TUV$ are **consecutive angles.** A polygon is named by listing its vertices in **consecutive order,** so this polygon might be named $STUVW$ or $VUTSW$.

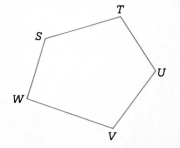

Polygons separate a plane into three sets of points: the polygon, its interior, and its exterior. If each line that contains a side of the polygon contains no points in the interior of the polygon, the polygon is **convex**. *ABCDE* is convex. *FGHJKL* is **nonconvex**. We are interested primarily in convex polygons.

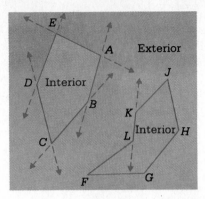

A segment joining two nonconsecutive vertices is a **diagonal** of the polygon. $\overline{XV}$ is one diagonal of *VWXYZ*. How many diagonals does *VWXYZ* have altogether?

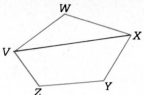

Polygons are classified by the number of sides they have.

Number of sides	Name of polygon	Number of sides	Name of polygon
3	Triangle	8	Octagon
4	Quadrilateral	9	Nonagon
5	Pentagon	10	Decagon
6	Hexagon	15	15-gon
7	Heptagon	n	n-gon

In an **equiangular polygon,** all the angles are congruent. In an **equilateral polygon,** all the sides are congruent. A **regular polygon** is a convex polygon which is both equiangular and equilateral.

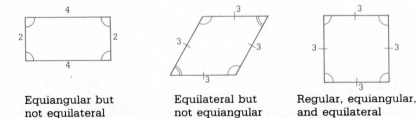

Equiangular but not equilateral   Equilateral but not equiangular   Regular, equiangular, and equilateral

The **perimeter** of a polygon is the sum of the lengths of its sides. Each figure above has a perimeter of 12.

Class Exercises

[1-4] If the figure is not a polygon, explain why it is not. If the figure is a polygon, tell whether it is convex or nonconvex, then classify it by its number of sides.

1.

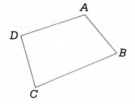

3.

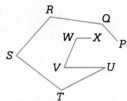

2.

4.

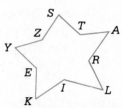

[5-10] Use the figure at the right.

5. Name the sides of the polygon.
6. Find its perimeter.
7. Name a pair of consecutive angles.
8. Name a pair of consecutive sides.
9. Name a pair of nonconsecutive sides.
10. Name all the diagonals through *C*.

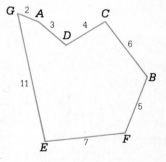

Written Exercises

[1-6] Name the parts of polygon *ABCDEF*.

1. The vertices
2. The sides
3. The angles
4. Two consecutive sides
5. Two consecutive angles
6. Two nonconsecutive sides

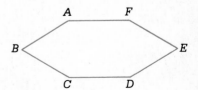

[7-9] Use a protractor and ruler to decide whether each polygon is convex, nonconvex, equiangular, equilateral, or regular.

7. convex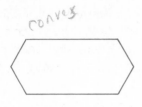

8. noncovex

9.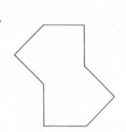

10. What is the perimeter of a regular nonagon if each side measures 15?

11. How long is each side of an equilateral hexagon with perimeter 96?

12. A quadrilateral has sides of lengths $2x$, $2x + 1$, $2x - 1$, and $3x$. Find the perimeter in terms of x.

13. If the perimeter of the quadrilateral in exercise 12 is 18, find x and the length of each side.

14. How many diagonals can you draw from each vertex of a polygon with 6 sides? 10 sides?

Set B

15. A regular decagon and a regular 13-gon have the same perimeter. The length of one side of the 13-gon is 5.4. How long is each side of the decagon?

16. Write an expression for the perimeter of a regular n-gon if each side has length s.

17. Copy and complete the table. You may want to draw the polygons.

No. of sides	3	4	5	6	7	8
No. of diagonals from each vertex	?	?	2	?	?	?
Total no. of diagonals	?	?	5	?	?	?

18. How many diagonals does a decagon have? Check your answer with a drawing.

19. Use exercises 17 and 18 to write expressions for (a) the number of diagonals from each vertex of an *n*-gon and (b) the total number of diagonals.

20. If every student in your geometry class shakes hands once with each other student, how many handshakes would be involved? **Hint** Represent each student with a vertex of a polygon and use segments connecting vertices to represent handshakes.

21. A volleyball league has seven teams, and each team is to play each other team twice. How many matches are played? How many weeks will it take if three matches are played in the league each week?

22. Given: *ABCD* with diagonal $\overline{AC}$
    Prove: $m\angle BAD + m\angle B + m\angle BCD + m\angle D = 360$

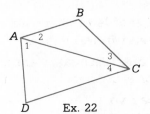

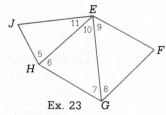

Ex. 22   Ex. 23

23. Given: *EFGHJ* with diagonals $\overline{EG}$ and $\overline{EH}$
    Prove: $m\angle JEF + m\angle F + m\angle FGH + m\angle GHJ + m\angle HJE = 540$

Set C

24. Use a protractor to draw a large regular hexagon. (The measure of each angle is 120.) Draw the angle trisectors. Connect the points of intersection of adjacent trisectors consecutively. What kind of figure is formed? Is it regular?

Geometry Maintenance

1. $\angle A$ and $\angle B$ are complementary; $\angle A$ and $\angle C$ are supplementary. Find $m\angle B$ and $m\angle C$ if $m\angle A$ is
   a. 14   **b.** 39   **c.** *x*   **d.** $180 - y$

2. __?__ points determine a plane. __?__ points determine a line.

3. Are the angles of a linear pair supplementary, complementary, or neither?

3.10 The Angles of a Polygon

Snowflakes are fascinating examples of geometry in nature. No two snowflakes are alike. Yet every snowflake is shaped like a regular hexagon or could be framed by one.

Since the sum of the measures of the angles of a triangle is the same for all triangles, perhaps the sum is the same for other convex polygons of a given number of sides.

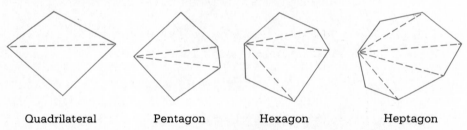

| Quadrilateral | Pentagon | Hexagon | Heptagon |

In each polygon above, all possible diagonals from one vertex have been drawn. In each case, the sum of the measures of the angles of the polygon is the sum of the measures of the angles of the triangles.

Polygon	Number of sides	Number of triangles	Sum of the measures of the angles
Quadrilateral	4	2	$(2)180 = 360$
Pentagon	5	3	$(3)180 = 540$
Hexagon	6	4	$(4)180 = 720$
Heptagon	7	5	$(5)180 = 900$
n-gon	n	$n - 2$	$(n - 2)180$

Theorem 3.20	The sum of the measures of the angles of a convex polygon of n sides is $(n - 2)180$.

Example 1   Find the sum of the measures of the angles of a convex polygon with 12 sides.

Solution   Sum of the measures of the angles $= (n - 2)180$
$= (12 - 2)180$
$= 1800$

Example 2   Find the measure of one angle of a regular polygon with 20 sides.

Solution   Sum of the measures of the angles $= (n - 2)180$
$= (20 - 2)180$, or 3240

Measure of one angle $= 3240 \div 20$, or 162

In this pentagon, the sides have been extended in succession to form an exterior angle at each vertex.

The table below describes this pentagon and any convex n-gon.

	5	n
Number of vertices	5	n
Sum of interior and exterior angles at one vertex	180	180
Sum of interior and exterior angles at *all* vertices	$180(5) = 900$	$180n$
Sum of interior angles	$(5 - 2)180 = 540$	$(n - 2)180$
Sum of exterior angles (sum of interior and exterior $\angle$s minus sum of interior $\angle$s)	$900 - 540 = 360$	$180n - (n - 2)180 =$ $180n - 180n - 360 = 360$

| **Theorem 3.21** | The sum of the measures of the exterior angles of a convex polygon, one angle at each vertex, is 360. |

The proofs of Theorems 3.20 and 3.21 are omitted.

Example 3

The measure of an angle of a regular polygon is 135. Find the measure m of each exterior angle and n, the number of sides.

Solution

$m = 180 -$ (measure of an angle of the polygon)
$= 180 - 135$, or 45

$n =$ number of sides
$=$ number of vertices
$=$ (sum of measures of exterior angles) $\div 45$
$= 360 \div 45$, or 8

Class Exercises

Tell whether each statement about a convex pentagon is true or false. If false, explain why.

1. The sum of the measures of its angles is 640.

2. The measure of each angle is always 108.

3. The sum of the measures of the exterior angles is 360.

4. If it is regular, each exterior angle has measure 72.

5. The sum of the measures of the exterior angles is $(5 - 2)180$.

Written Exercises

Set A

[1-8] Find the sum of the measures of the angles of a convex polygon with the given number of sides.

1. 4   **3.** 6   **5.** 8   **7.** 40

2. 5   **4.** 7   **6.** 9   **8.** 60

[9-12] The number of sides of a regular polygon is given. Find the measure of each angle.

9. 4   **10.** 7   **11.** 10   **12.** n

[13-16] The measure of an exterior angle of a regular polygon is given. Find the number of sides.

13. 45   **14.** 60   **15.** r **16.** 72

[17-20] The sum of the measures of the angles of a convex polygon are given. Find the number of sides.

17. 900   **18.** 720   **19.** 1260   **20.** 2340

Set B

[21-23] The figures at the right show how to draw a regular hexagon with a T-square and 30-60-90 triangles.

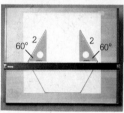

21. In the first figure, how is the 60° angle of each triangle related to the hexagon? Why is 60° correct?

22. In the second figure, how is each 60° angle related to the interior angle of the hexagon?

23. What kind of right triangle would you use with a T-square to draw a regular octagon?

[24-27] The measure of one angle of a regular polygon is given. Find the number of sides.

24. 140   **25.** 144   **26.** 150   **27.** 165

28. The sides of a regular pentagon can be extended to form a five-pointed star. What is the measure of the angle at each of the five points?

Set C

29. Prove indirectly: A convex hexagon must have at least one angle whose measure is 120 or greater.

Excursion   Tessellations with Polygons

A tessellation, or tiling, is an arrangement of polygon shapes that completely covers a plane surface without overlapping and without leaving gaps.

Tessellation patterns are commonly found on wallpaper, tiled floors and walls, and fabrics. The floor and ceiling of your classroom might be tessellated with squares.

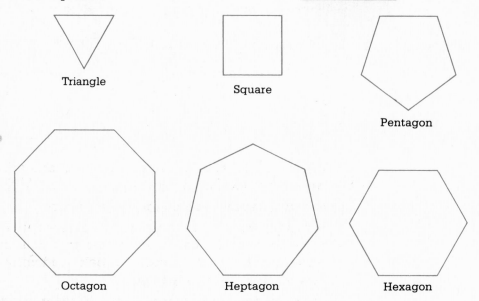

Triangle

Square

Pentagon

Octagon

Heptagon

Hexagon

1. For each regular polygon above:
   a. mark a point P on a sheet of plain paper;
   b. trace the polygon so that P is one of the vertices; and
   c. see if repeated tracings of the polygon will cover the region around the point with no overlaps or gaps.

2. Use exercise 1 to complete the table below.

Number of sides in the polygon	3	4	5	6	7	8
Does the polygon tessellate?	?	Yes	?	?	?	?
Measure m of one angle	?	90	?	?	?	?
Is m a factor of 360?	?	Yes	?	?	?	?

3. If a regular polygon shape forms a tessellation, what is true of the measure of each angle?

4. Can other regular polygon shapes be used as tiles besides those shown on page 156? Explain.

5. Some tessellations use several regular polygons. In each figure below, explain why the polygon shapes fit together.

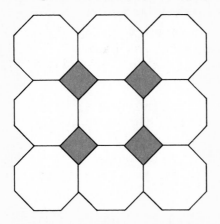 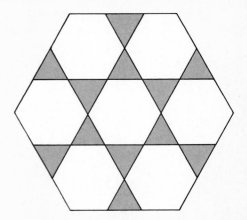

6. Draw a tessellation using only squares and equilateral triangles traced from page 156.

7. Create a tessellation of your own design.

8. Maurits Escher created about 150 different tessellations. Some of them are based on regular polygons that tessellate. For each tessellation below, identify the regular polygon that it is based on.

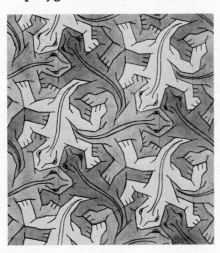 

Chapter Summary

1. Two lines either intersect, are parallel, or are skew. Two planes either intersect or are parallel. (page 108)

2. If two parallel lines are cut by a transversal,
   a. then corresponding angles are congruent.
   b. then alternate interior angles are congruent.
   c. and the transversal is perpendicular to one of the lines, then it is perpendicular to the other.
   d. then interior angles on the same side of the transversal are supplementary. (page 118)

3. Two lines cut by a transversal are parallel if
   a. corresponding angles are congruent.
   b. alternate interior angles are congruent.
   c. both lines are perpendicular to the transversal.
   d. interior angles on the same side of the transversal are supplementary. (page 118)

4. In a plane, through a point on a line, there is exactly one line perpendicular to the given line. (page 127)

5. Through a point not on a given line, there is exactly one line parallel to the given line and exactly one line perpendicular to the given line. (pages 126–128)

6. A line perpendicular to a plane is perpendicular to each line in the plane that passes through the point of intersection. (page 134)

7. The sum of the measures of the angles of a triangle is 180. (page 142)

8. The measure of an exterior angle of a triangle is equal to the sum of the measures of its remote interior angles. (page 143)

9. Regular polygons are convex polygons that are both equiangular and equilateral. (page 148)

10. The sum of the measures of the interior angles of a convex n-gon is $(n - 2)180$. The sum of the measures of the exterior angles of a convex polygon, one angle at each vertex, is 360. (pages 153–154)

Chapter Review

Lesson 3.1
Page 108

[1-3] Name each of the following.

1. A transversal
2. A pair of alternate interior angles
3. A pair of corresponding angles

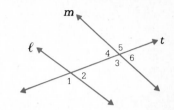

Lesson 3.2
Page 112

[4-6] Given: $\ell \parallel m$ and $n \perp \ell$

4. If $m\angle 4 = 80$, then $m\angle 8 = $ _?_ .
5. $m\angle 2 = $ _?_ .
6. If $m\angle 9 = 90$, then n and t _?_ .

Lesson 3.3
Page 116

[7-8] Given: $\ell \parallel m$

7. If $m\angle 7 = 120$, then $m\angle 5 = $ _?_ .
8. $m\angle 5 + m\angle 8 = $ _?_ .

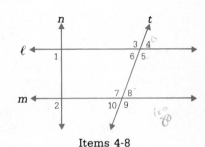

Items 4-8

9. A board is cut in half to be used as two rafters in constructing a roof. What theorem explains why $\angle 1$ and $\angle 2$ are congruent?

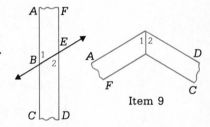

Item 9

Lesson 3.4
Page 121

10. State the definition, postulate, or theorem that this statement contradicts: "Point A lies in both of the parallel lines m and n."

11. Wayne scored five goals in two hockey games. Write an indirect argument to show that Wayne must have scored a "hat trick" (at least three goals in one game) in one of these two games.

Lesson 3.5
Page 126

[12-14] Given: Plane $\mathcal{K}$ with noncollinear points P, Q, and R.

12. What theorem or postulate is used to draw the auxiliary line $\overleftrightarrow{QR}$?

13. How many lines in plane $\mathcal{K}$ are perpendicular to $\overleftrightarrow{QR}$ through Q?

14. How many lines are parallel to $\overleftrightarrow{QR}$ through P?

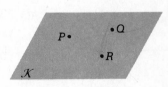

**Lesson 3.6
Page 134**

[15-20] Given: Lines j, k, and n in plane $\mathcal{T}$; ℓ and j in $\mathcal{R}$; m and k in $\mathcal{S}$; lines intersect in points P and Q. Classify each statement as always, sometimes, or never true.

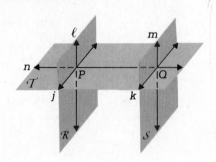

15. If $\mathcal{R} \parallel \mathcal{S}$, then $j \parallel k$.

16. If $j \parallel k$, then $j \parallel m$.

17. If $j \parallel k$, then $\mathcal{R} \parallel \mathcal{S}$.

18. If $n \perp \mathcal{R}$, then $\ell \perp j$.

19. If $n \perp \mathcal{R}$ and $n \perp \mathcal{S}$, then $\mathcal{R} \parallel \mathcal{S}$.

20. If $m \perp \mathcal{T}$, then $m \perp k$ and $m \perp n$.

**Lesson 3.7
Page 138**

21. Draw an acute isosceles triangle and name its legs, vertex angle, base angles, and base.

22. Draw a scalene right triangle and name its legs and its hypotenuse.

23. Draw an isosceles right triangle. Name its legs.

**Lesson 3.8
Page 142**

[24-26] Given: $\angle D \cong \angle H$ and $\angle F \cong \angle K$

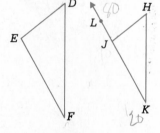

24. If $m\angle D = 55$ and $m\angle F = 20$, then $m\angle E = \underline{\ ?\ }$.

25. If the measure of an exterior angle at J is 70, then $m\angle HJK = \underline{\ ?\ }$.

26. If $m\angle K = 20$ and $m\angle HJL = 80$, then $m\angle H = \underline{\ ?\ }$.

**Lesson 3.9
Page 147**

[27-29] Draw a convex polygon $ABCD$.

27. Name all the diagonals of $ABCD$.

28. What additional information is necessary in order to conclude that $ABCD$ is a regular polygon?

29. Write an expression for the perimeter of $ABCD$.

**Lesson 3.10
Page 152**

30. The sum of the measures of the angles of a convex polygon of n sides is $\underline{\ ?\ }$.

31. The measure of an exterior angle of a regular hexagon is $\underline{\ ?\ }$.

32. The measure of each angle of a regular pentagon is $\underline{\ ?\ }$.

Chapter Test

[1-8] Is each statement always, sometimes, or never true?

1. Two planes that have no points in common are parallel.

2. If two parallel lines are cut by a transversal, then interior angles on the same side of the transversal are supplementary.

3. Two lines perpendicular to the same line are parallel.

4. Through a point not on a given line, there are two lines perpendicular to the given line.

5. In right $\triangle ABC$, $m\angle A + m\angle B = 112$.

6. Equilateral $\triangle DEF$ is isosceles.

7. Right $\triangle PQR$ is isosceles.

8. Right $\triangle XUZ$ is scalene.

[9-12] Given: $j \parallel k$; $\ell \parallel t$

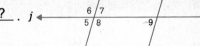

9. $m\angle 2 = m\angle\ \underline{\ ?\ } = m\angle\ \underline{\ ?\ } = m\angle\ \underline{\ ?\ }$.

10. If $m\angle 5 = 40$, then $m\angle 3 = \underline{\ ?\ }$.

11. If $m\angle 2 = 95$, then $m\angle 5 = \underline{\ ?\ }$.

12. $m\angle 3 + m\angle 8 + m\angle 9 + m\angle 4 = \underline{\ ?\ }$.

[13-15] Given: Regular pentagon $ABCDE$.

13. The sum of the measures of the angles of $ABCDE$ is $\underline{\ ?\ }$.

14. The sum of the measures of the exterior angles of $ABCDE$ is $\underline{\ ?\ }$.

15. The measure of one exterior angle of $ABCDE$ is $\underline{\ ?\ }$.

16. If $m\angle 4 = 80$ and $m\angle 1 = 20$, then $m\angle 2 = \underline{\ ?\ }$.

17. Can this statement be used in a proof with the figure at the right? "Draw $\overleftrightarrow{CE}$ so that $\overrightarrow{CE}$ bisects $\angle KCP$ and $\overleftrightarrow{CE} \parallel \overleftrightarrow{AP}$."

Items 16-17

18. Given: Parallel planes $\mathcal{E}$ and $\mathcal{K}$ cut by plane $\mathcal{T}$. Prove indirectly that $\overleftrightarrow{AB} \parallel \overleftrightarrow{CD}$.

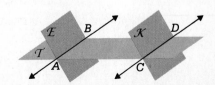

Cumulative Test   Chapters 1-3

Select the best answer for each item.

1. A straight thin wire suggests the idea of a(n) __?__.

   a. Point   c. Plane

   b. Line   d. Angle

2. Points A, B, and C are collinear. Which of these statements must be true?

   a. A, B, and C are coplanar.

   b. A, B, and C are noncoplanar.

   c. B is between A and C.

   d. $\overleftrightarrow{AB}$ and $\overleftrightarrow{BC}$ are noncoplanar.

3. On a number line, the graph of $x \geq 2$ is a(n) __?__.

   a. Line   c. Ray

   b. Segment   d. Point

4. On $\overleftrightarrow{AB}$ there is(are) __?__ point(s) 6 units from A.

   a. 0   c. 2

   b. 1   d. More than 2

5. Given $\overrightarrow{AB}$, there is an angle, $\angle BAC$, such that $m\angle BAC = 27$. This result is guaranteed by the __?__ Postulate.

   a. Protractor

   b. Angle Construction

   c. Angle Addition

   d. Supplement

6. According to the Multiplication property of inequality, if $MN > PQ$, then __?__.

   a. $-3MN < -3PQ$ c. $MN \neq PQ$

   b. $3MN = 3PQ$ d. $4MN < 4PQ$

7. The process of forming a conclusion based upon the examination of several specific cases is called __?__.

   a. Inductive reasoning

   b. Deductive reasoning

   c. Indirect reasoning

   d. Argument by counterexample

8. B is between A and C and $\angle ABD$ is a right angle. $m\angle CBD = $ __?__.

   a. 45   b. 135   c. 60   d. 90

9. Given: $\angle 1$ and $\angle 2$ are vertical $\angle$s; $m\angle 1 = 90$

   Prove: $m\angle 2 = 90$

   Statements

   1. $\angle 1$ and $\angle 2$ are vertical $\angle$s; $m\angle 1 = 90$
   2. $\angle 2 \cong \angle 1$
   3. $m\angle 2 = m\angle 1$
   4. $m\angle 2 = 90$

   The reason for step 4 is __?__.

   a. Definition of congruent angles

   b. Transitive prop. of equality

   c. Vertical $\angle$s are $\cong$.

   d. Given

10. In a proof using this figure, you may assume that __?__.

   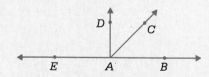

   a. A is the midpoint of $\overline{BE}$.

   b. $\overrightarrow{AB}$ and $\overrightarrow{AE}$ are opposite rays.

   c. $\overleftrightarrow{AD} \perp \overleftrightarrow{BE}$ d. $\overrightarrow{AC}$ bisects $\angle BAD$.

11. Using the diagram below, $x = \underline{\quad?\quad}$.

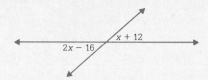

    a. 40   **b.** 28   **c.** 14   **d.** 4

12. In a plane, $\overleftrightarrow{RS} \perp k$ and $\overleftrightarrow{RT} \perp k$. Therefore, $\underline{\quad?\quad}$.

    a. $\overleftrightarrow{RS} \parallel \overleftrightarrow{RT}$ **c.** R is on k.

    b. $\overleftrightarrow{RS} \perp \overleftrightarrow{RT}$ **d.** T is on $\overleftrightarrow{RS}$.

13. $\overleftrightarrow{AB} \parallel \overleftrightarrow{CD}$ if we can show that $\angle \underline{\ ?\ } \cong \angle \underline{\ ?\ }$.

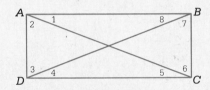

    a. 3, 7   **c.** 1, 5

    b. 2, 6   **d.** 1, 2

14. You wish to prove this statement indirectly: The sum, $a + b$, of two negative numbers a and b is negative. What do you assume at the start?

    a. a and b are negative numbers.

    b. $a + b$ is not negative.

    c. a and b are not negative.

    d. $a + b$ is negative.

15. Given point P on line k; R, Q, and k are coplanar; $\overleftrightarrow{PQ} \perp k$; and $\overleftrightarrow{PR} \perp k$. Then $\underline{\quad?\quad}$.

    a. $\angle PQR$ is a right angle.

    b. P, Q, and R are not coplanar.

    c. P, Q, and R are collinear.

    d. $\overleftrightarrow{PQ} \perp \overleftrightarrow{PR}$

16. If planes $\mathcal{S}$ and $\mathcal{R}$ are parallel, which statement is true?

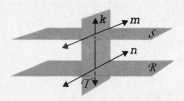

    a. $k \perp m$ **c.** Plane $\mathcal{T} \perp$ plane $\mathcal{S}$

    b. $m \parallel n$ **d.** None of these

17. A triangle with an acute angle is called $\underline{\quad?\quad}$.

    a. Acute   **d.** Not enough

    b. Scalene   information

    c. Equiangular

18. In the triangle, $x = \underline{\quad?\quad}$.

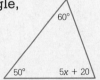

    a. 10   **b.** 110   **c.** 70   **d.** 18

19. A 7-sided polygon is a(n) $\underline{\quad?\quad}$.

    a. Hexagon   **c.** Pentagon

    b. Heptagon   **d.** Octagon

20. Two perpendicular lines form four right angles. The restatement of this theorem in "if ... then" form is:

    a. If two lines are perpendicular, then they form four right angles.

    b. If two lines form four right angles, then they are perpendicular.

    c. Two lines are perpendicular if and only if they form four right angles.

    d. None of the above is correct.

Congruent Triangles

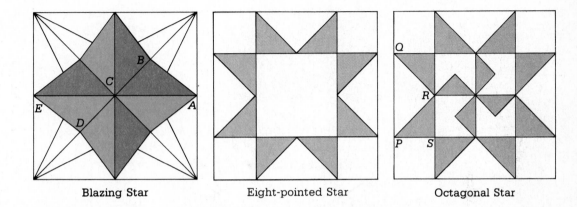

Blazing Star   Eight-pointed Star   Octagonal Star

In quilt designs, repeated uses of the same figure help produce an orderly and balanced result. They also simplify the making of the quilt.

1. Which of the designs above was used repeatedly in the quilt on page 164?

2. A cardboard pattern was used to cut the red triangular pieces in the "Blazing Star" design so that each piece would be the same size and shape. Could the same pattern be used for the orange triangles in that design?

3. Do you think that the pattern used for △ABC could be used to make △PQR in the "Octagonal Star" design? To make △RSP?

4. When △ABC is cut out, the longest edge of the pattern is used to draw $\overline{AC}$. Which part of △CDE is drawn with the same edge of the pattern?

5. Which angle of △CDE is drawn with the same corner of the pattern as ∠B in △ABC?

4.1   Congruence of Triangles

 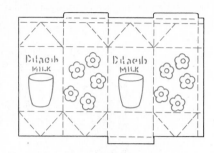

Objects that are cut from a pattern, like the milk cartons pictured here, are identical in size and shape. This real-world idea has a mathematical counterpart in the idea of congruence.

To check if two triangles are congruent, pair each vertex of one triangle with a vertex of the other. Several pairings are possible; one special pairing is shown below.

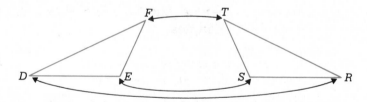

Each side and each angle of one triangle corresponds to a side or angle of the other. The symbol $\leftrightarrow$ means "corresponds to."

Angles: $\angle D \leftrightarrow \angle R,\ \angle E \leftrightarrow \angle S,\ \angle F \leftrightarrow \angle T$

Sides: $\overline{DE} \leftrightarrow \overline{RS},\ \overline{EF} \leftrightarrow \overline{ST},\ \overline{DF} \leftrightarrow \overline{RT}$

This correspondence is special because each part of one triangle is congruent to its corresponding part. If such a correspondence can be set up, the triangles are congruent. That is, $\triangle DEF \cong \triangle RST$.

Definition   Two **triangles** are **congruent** if and only if there is a correspondence between the vertices such that each side and each angle is congruent to its corresponding side or angle.

In the diagram at the right, six pairs of congruent parts are shown.

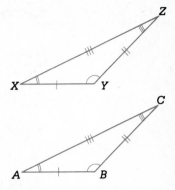

$$\angle A \cong \angle X \quad \angle B \cong \angle Y \quad \angle C \cong \angle Z$$
$$\overline{AB} \cong \overline{XY} \quad \overline{BC} \cong \overline{YZ} \quad \overline{AC} \cong \overline{XZ}$$

You can conclude that $\triangle ABC \cong \triangle XYZ$. The order of the letters tells how the vertices are paired. For example, $\triangle ABC \not\cong \triangle XZY$ since $\angle B \not\cong Z$.

If $\triangle OLD \cong \triangle NEW$, then the definition of congruent triangles states that any or all of the six pairs of corresponding parts are congruent. For example, you may conclude that $\overline{DO} \cong \overline{WN}$. Name two other pairs of segments that are congruent.

When we use the definition of congruent triangles to conclude that pairs of sides or angles are congruent, we give as the reason, "Corresponding parts of congruent triangles are congruent." This is abbreviated as "Corr. parts of $\cong$ $\triangle$s are $\cong$." Remember that this is simply part of the definition of congruent triangles.

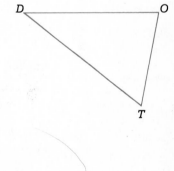

An **included angle** for two sides of a triangle is an angle whose rays contain the two sides of the triangle. An **included side** for two angles of a triangle is a side whose endpoints are the vertices of the angles. Thus, $\angle O$ is included between $\overline{DO}$ and $\overline{TO}$. The side included between $\angle D$ and $\angle T$ is $\overline{DT}$.

Since congruence of segments and congruence of angles are reflexive, symmetric, and transitive, these properties hold for congruence of triangles as well.

Theorem 4.1 Congruence of triangles is reflexive, symmetric, and transitive.

Class Exercises

[1-4] Given: $\triangle XYZ \cong \triangle RTS$. Tell how you would mark the indicated part of $\triangle RTS$.

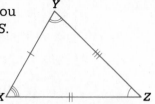

1. $\overline{RS}$ 3. $\angle R$
2. $\overline{TS}$ 4. $\angle S$

5. In $\triangle XYZ$, which side is included between $\angle Y$ and $\angle Z$?

6. In $\triangle XYZ$, which angle is included between $\overline{XY}$ and $\overline{ZX}$?

7. If $\triangle XYZ \cong \triangle RTS$, then $\triangle XZY \cong \triangle \underline{\ ?\ }$, $\triangle YXZ \cong \triangle \underline{\ ?\ }$. $\triangle YZX \cong \triangle \underline{\ ?\ }$, $\triangle ZXY \cong \triangle \underline{\ ?\ }$, and $\triangle ZYX \cong \triangle \underline{\ ?\ }$.

[8-13] Tell whether each statement appears to be true or false.

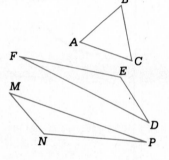

8. $\triangle ABC \cong \triangle DEF$ 11. $\triangle FED \cong \triangle PMN$
9. $\triangle DEF \cong \triangle MNP$ 12. $\angle F \cong \angle P$
10. $\triangle DEF \cong \triangle NMP$ 13. $\triangle ABC \cong \triangle BAC$

Written Exercises

Set A

[1-2] Given: $\triangle PAS \cong \triangle TEL$

1. List three pairs of congruent sides.
2. List three pairs of congruent angles.

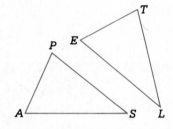

Given: $\triangle XYZ \cong \triangle JKL$.
Is each statement true or false?

3. $\triangle YZX \cong \triangle KLJ$ 5. $\triangle XZY \cong \triangle JLK$
4. $\triangle YXZ \cong \triangle KJL$ 6. $\triangle YZX \cong \triangle KJL$

Tell whether each statement appears to be true or false.

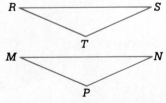

7. $\triangle MNP \cong \triangle RST$ 9. $\triangle MNP \cong \triangle STR$
8. $\triangle MNP \cong \triangle SRT$ 10. $\triangle MNP \cong \triangle RTS$

[11-14] List the six pairs of congruent corresponding parts of the given triangles.

11. $\triangle ABE \cong \triangle CBD$ **13.** $\triangle EBD \cong \triangle DBE$

12. $\triangle ABD \cong \triangle CBE$ **14.** $\triangle ABC \cong \triangle CBA$

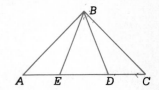

Set B

15. Ed measured the lengths of the shadows of a tree and a pole and found that they were the same length. He assumed that $\angle A$ and $\angle C$ were congruent since both were formed by the sun's rays and the ground.

  a. Is $\overline{AB} \cong \overline{CD}$? Why?
  b. The pole and the tree are both vertical. Why does this mean that $\angle B \cong \angle D$?
  c. Do $\triangle ABT$ and $\triangle CDP$ appear to be congruent?
  d. How do you think the heights of the tree and the pole compare?

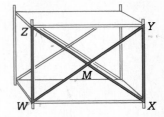

16. For the scaffold at the right, M is the midpoint of $\overline{WY}$ and $\overline{XZ}$.

  a. Name an angle congruent to $\angle WMZ$.
  b. Which segment is congruent to $\overline{WM}$? To $\overline{ZM}$?
  c. Do $\triangle ZMW$ and $\triangle XMY$ appear to be congruent?

17. Prove that congruence of triangles is reflexive.

18. Prove that congruence of triangles is symmetric.

19. Prove that congruence of triangles is transitive.

Set C

20. Given: $\triangle ABC \cong \triangle CBA$
  Prove: $\triangle ABC$ is isosceles.

21. Given: $\triangle ABC \cong \triangle CBA$; $\triangle ABC \cong \triangle ACB$
  Prove: $\triangle ABC$ is equilateral.

22. Prove that if two triangles are congruent and one of them is scalene, then the other is scalene.

23. State a possible definition for congruence of two convex n-gons.

Excursion   Equivalence Relations

Tom has a set of 780 baseball cards. Tom sorts his cards in a variety of ways. The table below gives some of the sorting rules or *relations* that he uses and the groups of cards that result.

Relation Card A __?__ Card B	No. of groups	Type of groups
"Shows a player in the same league as"	2	American League National League
"Shows a player on the same team as"	26	One for each major league team
"Shows the same player as"	Many	One for each player

As with baseball cards, relations between triangles can be used to sort triangles into groups.

Relation	No. of groups	Type of groups
"Is congruent to"	Many	One for each collection of triangles of the same size and shape

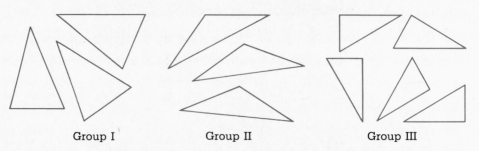

Group I   Group II   Group III

Only three groups are pictured here. There are infinitely many groups, each containing infinitely many triangles.

The congruence relation for triangles and the relations for baseball cards have something in common. Each relation classifies the objects into groups so that *every* object is in *one and only one* group. Such a relation is called an equivalence relation.

<table>
<tr><td>Definition</td><td>An equivalence relation for a set is a relation defined for that set which is reflexive, symmetric, and transitive.</td></tr>
</table>

Theorem 4.1 states that congruence of triangles is an equivalence relation for the set of triangles. There are many relations in mathematics that are *not* equivalence relations.

Example | Is the relation "is longer than" an equivalence relation for line segments?

Solution | First check for the transitive property: If $AB > CD$ and $CD > EF$, then $AB > EF$. This statement is true.

Now check for the symmetric property: If $AB > CD$, then $CD > AB$. This statement is *not* true.

Since "is longer than" for segments is not symmetric, it is not an equivalence relation.

Exercises

Tell whether the relation is an equivalence relation for baseball cards. Explain.

1. "Shows a player who plays the same position as"
2. "Shows a player who bats with the same hand as"

Is each relation an equivalence relation for the given set?

3. "Is perpendicular to" for the set of lines
4. "Is the same shape as" for the set of triangles
5. "Is congruent to" for the set of line segments

The SSS, SAS, and ASA Postulates

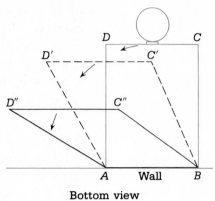

Bottom view

Some basketball goals are designed to swing sideways to the wall when the gym is used for other sports. The corners are hinged so the frame is not rigid. The angle at corner B changes as the goal is swung towards the wall.

To use the goal for basketball, a rigid frame is needed. So a brace is added to form $\triangle ABE$. When the brace is bolted at points A and E, the distances AB, BE, and EA are constant. Postulate 16 below explains why the angle at corner B then has a constant measure and the frame is kept rigid.

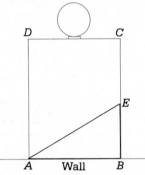

Postulate 16

SSS Postulate

If three sides of one triangle are congruent to the corresponding parts of another triangle, then the triangles are congruent.

Given: $\overline{AB} \cong \overline{XY}$; $\overline{BC} \cong \overline{YZ}$; $\overline{CA} \cong \overline{ZX}$

Conclusion: $\triangle ABC \cong \triangle XYZ$

The SSS Postulate allows you to show that two triangles are congruent using only three pairs of corresponding parts.

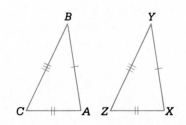

To measure the width of a pond, Ron and Leah place a marker at point P and stand at the two ends of the pond. Leah paces off the distance from L to P, then continues walking straight ahead for the same number of paces, stopping at L' (read "L prime"). Ron locates R' in the same way. Ron then walks 17 paces from R' to L'. How wide is the pond?

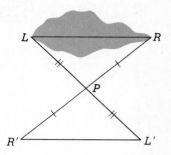

If $\triangle LRP \cong \triangle L'R'P$, then $\overline{LR}$ and $\overline{L'R'}$ are the same length. Why? To show that the triangles *are* congruent, Ron and Leah can use the vertical angles, $\angle RPL$ and $\angle R'PL'$, and the SAS Postulate.

Postulate 17	If two sides and the included angle of one triangle are congruent
SAS Postulate	to the corresponding parts of another triangle, then the triangles are congruent.

Given: $\overline{AC} \cong \overline{XZ}$
$\angle C \cong \angle Z$
$\overline{CB} \cong \overline{ZY}$

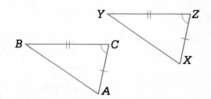

Conclusion: $\triangle ABC \cong \triangle XYZ$

In the name "SAS Postulate," the A is in the middle because the angle must be the *included* angle. If $\angle A \cong \angle X$ were given instead of $\angle C \cong \angle Z$, the SAS Postulate would not apply.

The idea of an included angle or side is important in Postulate 18 as well.

Postulate 18	If two angles and the included side of one triangle are congruent
ASA Postulate	to the corresponding parts of another triangle, then the triangles are congruent.

Given: $\angle A \cong \angle X$
$\overline{AB} \cong \overline{XY}$
$\angle B \cong \angle Y$

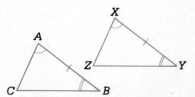

Conclusion: $\triangle ABC \cong \triangle XYZ$

Example   Use the markings shown to decide
             whether the triangles must be
             congruent. If they are congruent, write
             the correspondence and tell which
             postulate applies.

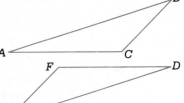

Solution   If $M \leftrightarrow B$, $A \leftrightarrow L$, and $R \leftrightarrow E$, then
             $\triangle MAR \cong \triangle BLE$ by the SAS Postulate.

Class Exercises

[1-4] Which postulate justifies
$\triangle ABC \cong \triangle DEF$?

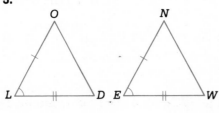

1. Given: $\overline{AC} \cong \overline{DF}$; $\overline{AB} \cong \overline{DE}$; $\overline{BC} \cong \overline{EF}$
2. Given: $\overline{EF} \cong \overline{BC}$; $\overline{AB} \cong \overline{DE}$; $\angle B \cong \angle E$
3. Given: $\angle C \cong \angle F$; $\angle E \cong \angle B$; $\overline{BC} \cong \overline{EF}$
4. Given: $\overline{DF} \cong \overline{AC}$; $\overline{DE} \cong \overline{AB}$; $\angle D \cong \angle A$

[5-8] Use the markings to decide whether the triangles must
be congruent. If they are congruent, write the
correspondence and tell which postulate applies.

5.

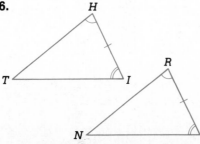

7.

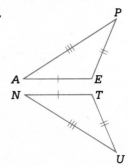

6.

8.

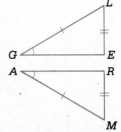

Written Exercises

Set A

[1-3] The goal is to prove △NOW ≅ △ART.

1. To use the SSS Postulate, show that
   $\overline{NO}$ ≅ _?_ , $\overline{OW}$ ≅ _?_ , and $\overline{NW}$ ≅ _?_ .

2. Given ∠W ≅ ∠T. To use the SAS Post.,
   show that $\overline{AT}$ ≅ _?_ and $\overline{RT}$ ≅ _?_ .

3. Given $\overline{OW}$ ≅ $\overline{RT}$. To use the ASA Post.,
   show that _?_ and _?_ .

[4-6] The goal is to prove △TAR ≅ △WON.

4. To use the SSS Postulate, show that
   $\overline{NW}$ ≅ _?_ , $\overline{OW}$ ≅ _?_ , and $\overline{NO}$ ≅ _?_ .

5. Given ∠W ≅ ∠T. To use the SAS Post.,
   show that $\overline{AT}$ ≅ _?_ and $\overline{RT}$ ≅ _?_ .

6. Given $\overline{OW}$ ≅ $\overline{AT}$. To use the ASA Post.,
   show that _?_ and _?_ .

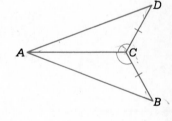

Ex. 1-6

[7-8] Supply the missing reasons.

7. Given: $\overline{CD}$ ≅ $\overline{CB}$; ∠ACD ≅ ∠ACB
   Prove: △ACD ≅ △ACB

Statements	Reasons
1. $\overline{CD}$ ≅ $\overline{CB}$	1. _?_
2. ∠ACD ≅ ∠ACB	2. _?_
3. $\overline{AC}$ ≅ $\overline{AC}$	3. _?_
4. △ACD ≅ △ACB	4. _?_

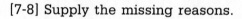

8. Given: ∠XZY ≅ ∠WZV; Z is the midpoint of $\overline{YV}$; ∠Y and
   ∠V are right angles.
   Prove: △XYZ ≅ △WVZ

Statements	Reasons
1. ∠XZY ≅ ∠WZV	1. _?_
2. Z is the midpt. of $\overline{YV}$.	2. _?_
3. YZ = ZV	3. _?_
4. $\overline{YZ}$ ≅ $\overline{ZV}$	4. _?_
5. ∠Y and ∠V are rt. ∠s.	5. _?_
6. ∠Y ≅ ∠V	6. _?_
7. △XYZ ≅ △WVZ	7. _?_

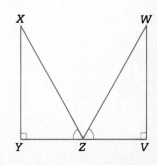

[9-12] Prove: △ABC ≅ △CDA

9. Given: $\overline{AD} \cong \overline{CB}$; $\overline{AB} \cong \overline{CD}$
10. Given: $\overline{BC} \| \overline{AD}$; $\overline{AD} \cong \overline{CB}$
11. Given: $\overline{AB} \| \overline{CD}$; $\overline{AB} \cong \overline{CD}$
12. Given: $\overline{AB} \| \overline{CD}$; $\overline{AD} \| \overline{BC}$

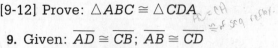

13. List the congruent parts in △MNP and △FGH.

14. Does △MNP appear to be congruent to △FGH? Do you think there is an "AAA Congruence Postulate"? Why?

15. List the congruent parts in △XYZ and △DEF.

16. Does △XYZ appear to be congruent to △DEF? Do you think there is an "SSA Congruence Postulate"? Why?

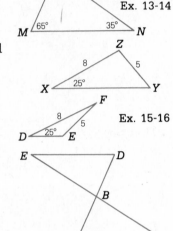

Ex. 13-14

Ex. 15-16

Set B

[17-20] Prove: △ABC ≅ △DBE

17. Given: B is midpt. of $\overline{AD}$; ∠A ≅ ∠D
18. Given: B is midpt. of $\overline{AD}$ and $\overline{CE}$.
19. Given: $\overline{AC} \| \overline{DE}$; $\overline{AC} \cong \overline{DE}$
20. Given: $\overline{AC} \| \overline{DE}$, B is midpt. of $\overline{CE}$

21. To measure the distance OP across a lake, lay off $\overline{PR}$ and $\overline{OR}$. Then use a surveyor's transit to lay out $\overline{RF}$ so that ∠FRO ≅ ∠PRO. Choose S on $\overrightarrow{RF}$ so that $\overline{RS} \cong \overline{RP}$. Draw $\overline{OS}$. Prove △PRO ≅ △SRO. Why does OP = OS?

[22-23] Prove: △MRP ≅ △NRP

22. Given: $\overline{PM} \cong \overline{PN}$; ∠MPR ≅ ∠NPR
23. Given: $\overline{PR} \perp \overline{MN}$; R is midpt. of $\overline{MN}$.

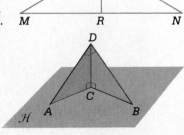

Set C

24. Given: $\overline{DC} \perp \mathcal{H}$; ∠ADC ≅ ∠BDC
    Prove: △ACD ≅ △BCD

The AAS, LL, HA, and LA Theorems

When Mary replaced the braces on a drop-front desk, she knew that $\angle ABC$ and $\angle DEF$ were congruent and that $\overline{AC}$ and $\overline{EF}$ were the same length. She now needs only to sight along $\overleftrightarrow{AD}$ to see whether $\angle BAC$ and $\angle EDF$ have the same measure. If they do, then the AAS Theorem below assures that the triangles formed are congruent and that the braces will appear evenly attached.

Theorem 4.2 AAS Theorem	If two angles and the side opposite one of the angles in one triangle are congruent to the corresponding parts of another triangle, then the triangles are congruent.

Given

$\angle P \cong \angle S$; $\angle Q \cong \angle T$, $\overline{QR} \cong \overline{TU}$

Prove

$\triangle PQR \cong \triangle STU$

Plan for Proof

Show $\angle R \cong \angle U$ by Theorem 3.15. Use the ASA Postulate.

Do you think there is an SSA congruence theorem? Below are two noncongruent triangles that can be formed with sides of length 19 cm and 14 cm and a nonincluded angle of 40°. So SSA cannot be used to prove that triangles are congruent.

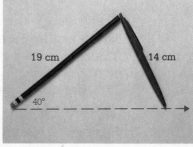

The following theorems can be helpful in right triangles.

Theorem 4.3
LL Theorem

If two legs of one right triangle are congruent to the corresponding parts of another right triangle, then the triangles are congruent.

Theorem 4.4
HA Theorem

If the hypotenuse and an acute angle of one right triangle are congruent to the corresponding parts of another right triangle, then the triangles are congruent.

Theorem 4.5
LA Theorem

If a leg and an acute angle of one right triangle are congruent to the corresponding parts of another right triangle, then the triangles are congruent.

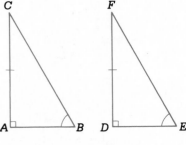

Case I

Given
Rt. △s ABC and DEF with rt. ∠s at A and D; $\overline{AC} \cong \overline{DF}$; $\angle B \cong \angle E$

Prove
$\triangle ABC \cong \triangle DEF$

Plan for Proof
Show $\angle A \cong \angle D$ by Theorem 2.1.
Use AAS.

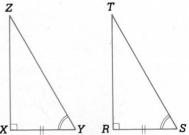

Case II

Given
Rt. △s XYZ and RST with rt. ∠s at X and R; $\overline{XY} \cong \overline{RS}$; $\angle Y \cong \angle S$

Prove
$\triangle XYZ \cong \triangle RST$

Plan for Proof
Show $\angle X \cong \angle R$ by Theorem 2.1.
Use ASA.

The proof of the LA Theorem requires two cases since the given leg can either be opposite the given acute angle (Case I) or be part of one of its rays (Case II).

The proofs of the AAS, LL, HA, and LA Theorems are exercises 15, 16, 17, and 18, respectively.

Class Exercises

[1-4] Which postulate or theorem justifies △*MIN* ≅ △*SEC*?

1. Given: $\overline{SE} \cong \overline{MI}$; $\angle M \cong \angle S$; $\angle I \cong \angle E$
2. Given: $\overline{NI} \cong \overline{CE}$; $\angle M \cong \angle S$; $\angle I \cong \angle E$
3. Given: Rt. $\angle$s at C and N;
   $\overline{MN} \cong \overline{SC}$; $\angle M \cong \angle S$
4. Given: Rt. $\angle$s at C and N;
   $\overline{MN} \cong \overline{SC}$; $\overline{IN} \cong \overline{EC}$

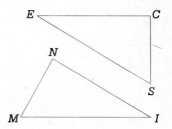

[5-8] Tell whether each pair of triangles must be congruent. If so, write the correspondence and tell why.

5.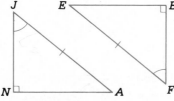

7.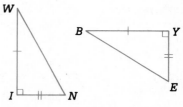

6.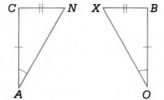

8.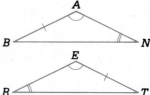

Written Exercises

Set A

[1-4] The goal is to prove △*TAN* ≅ △*RED*.

1. Given: $\overline{TA} \cong \overline{RE}$ and $\angle T \cong \angle R$. To use
   the AAS Thm., show $\angle \underline{?} \cong \angle \underline{?}$.
2. Given: Rt. $\angle$s at A and E. To use the
   LL Thm., show $\overline{TA} \cong \underline{?}$ and
   $\underline{?} \cong \underline{?}$.
3. Given: Rt. $\angle$s at A and E, and
   $\angle T \cong \angle R$. To use the HA Thm.,
   show $\underline{?} \cong \underline{?}$.
4. Given: Rt. $\angle$s at A and E, and
   $\angle T \cong \angle R$. To use the LA Thm., either
   show $\underline{?} \cong \underline{?}$ or show $\underline{?} \cong \underline{?}$.

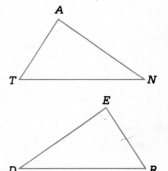

5. Given: $\overline{BC} \perp \overline{AD}$; $\angle A \cong \angle D$
Prove: $\triangle ABC \cong \triangle DBC$

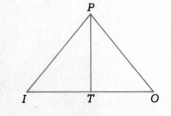

Statements	Reasons
1. $\overline{BC} \perp \overline{AD}$	1. ?
2. $\angle ACB$ and $\angle DCB$ are rt. $\angle$s.	2. ?
3. $\triangle ABC$ and $\triangle DBC$ are rt. $\triangle$s.	3. ?
4. $\overline{BC} \cong \overline{BC}$	4. ?
5. $\angle A \cong \angle D$	5. ?
6. $\triangle ABC \cong \triangle DBC$	6. ?

6. Given: $m\angle RST = m\angle USV = 90$;
S is the midpt. of $\overline{RU}$ and $\overline{TV}$.
Prove: $\triangle RST \cong \triangle USV$

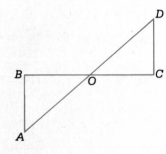

Statements	Reasons
1. $m\angle RST = m\angle USV = 90$	1. ?
2. $\angle RST$ and $\angle UVS$ are rt. $\angle$s.	2. ?
3. $\triangle RST$ and $\triangle USV$ are rt. $\triangle$s.	3. ?
4. S is the midpoint of $\overline{RU}$ and $\overline{TV}$.	4. ?
5. $RS = SU$; $TS = SV$	5. ?
6. $\overline{RS} \cong \overline{SU}$; $\overline{TS} \cong \overline{SV}$	6. ?
7. $\triangle RST \cong \triangle USV$	7. ?

[7-10] Prove: $\triangle AOB \cong \triangle DOC$

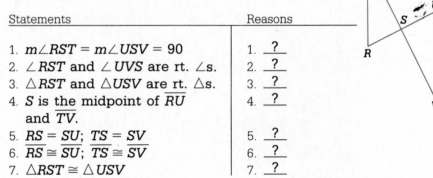

7. Given: $\angle A \cong \angle D$; $\overline{AB} \cong \overline{DC}$

8. Given: O is the midpoint of $\overline{AD}$;
$\angle B \cong \angle C$

9. Given: $\overline{AB} \perp \overline{BC}$; $\overline{DC} \perp \overline{BC}$;
O is the midpoint of $\overline{AD}$.

10. Given: $\overline{AB} \perp \overline{BC}$; $\overline{DC} \perp \overline{BC}$; $\overline{AB} \cong \overline{CD}$

[11-14] Prove: $\triangle TIP \cong \triangle TOP$

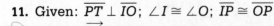
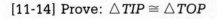
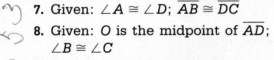

11. Given: $\overline{PT} \perp \overline{IO}$; $\angle I \cong \angle O$; $\overline{IP} \cong \overline{OP}$

12. Given: $\overrightarrow{PT}$ bisects $\angle IPO$; $\angle I \cong \angle O$

13. Given: $\overline{IP} \cong \overline{OP}$; T is midpt. of $\overline{IO}$.

14. Given: $\overline{PT} \perp \overline{IO}$; $\angle I \cong \angle O$

[15-18] Prove each theorem.

15. The AAS Theorem   **17.** The HA Theorem

16. The LL Theorem   **18.** The LA Theorem, Cases I and II

Set B

19. Given: $\overleftrightarrow{RT}$ bisects $\angle SRW$ and $\angle STW$
Prove: $\triangle RST \cong \triangle RWT$

20. Given: V is midpt. of $\overline{SW}$ and $\overline{RT}$
Prove: $\triangle RVW \cong \triangle TVS$

21. Given: $\overline{RS} \perp \overline{ST}$; $\overline{RW} \perp \overline{WT}$;
$\overrightarrow{TR}$ bisects $\angle STW$.
Prove: $\triangle RST \cong \triangle RWT$

22. Given: $\overline{RS} \perp \overline{ST}$; $\overline{RW} \perp \overline{WT}$; $\overline{ST} \parallel \overline{RW}$
Prove: $\triangle RST \cong \triangle TWR$

23. Given: $\overline{WT} \parallel \overline{RS}$; $\overline{RW} \parallel \overline{ST}$
Prove: $\triangle RSW \cong \triangle TWS$

24. Given: $\overline{RS} \cong \overline{TW}$; $\overline{RW} \cong \overline{ST}$
Prove: $\triangle RST \cong \triangle TWR$

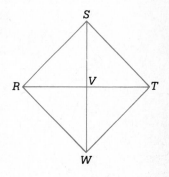

Ex. 19-24

[25-28] Given: P, Q, R, and S are noncoplanar; $\angle RSP$, $\angle RSQ$, and $\angle QSP$ are right angles.

25. Given: $\overline{PS} \cong \overline{SQ}$
Prove: $\triangle PSR \cong \triangle QSR$

26. Given: $\overline{PS} \cong \overline{RS}$
Prove: $\triangle PSQ \cong \triangle RSQ$

27. Given: $\angle PQS \cong \angle PRS$
Prove: $\triangle PQS \cong \triangle PRS$

28. Given: $\angle PRS \cong \angle QRS$
Prove: $\triangle PSR \cong \triangle QSR$

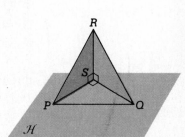

Cele wants to cut the brass piece shown for end $ABCDE$ of the magazine stand. She knows B is the midpoint of $\overline{RS}$.

29. Explain how Cele could use the LL Theorem to cut the brass piece.

30. Explain how Cele could then use the LA Theorem to cut the brass piece for the other end.

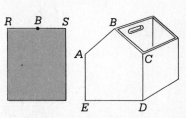

31. To measure the height AC of a pole, a surveyor stood at B and measured $\angle ABC$. She then marked off $\overrightarrow{BE}$ so $m\angle ABE = m\angle ABC$. She next marked off $\overrightarrow{AF}$ so $m\angle BAF = 90$. Let D be the intersection of $\overrightarrow{AF}$ and $\overrightarrow{BE}$. Explain why $\triangle ABC \cong \triangle ABD$. What ground measurement could the surveyor make to find the height of the pole?

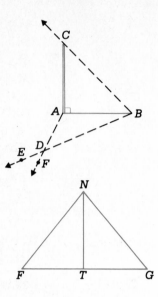

32. Newport (N) is due north of Tiffin (T). Fairfield (F) is 52 km due west of Tiffin, and Grove City (G) is 52 km due east. Show that $\triangle FTN \cong \triangle GTN$. Explain why Fairfield and Grove City are an equal distance from Newport.

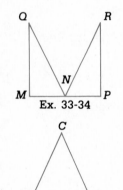

Set C

33. Given: $\angle M \cong \angle P$; $\angle MNR \cong \angle PNQ$; $\overline{QM} \cong \overline{MP}$; $\overline{RP} \cong \overline{MP}$
    Prove: $\triangle MNQ \cong \triangle PNR$

34. Given: $\angle M \cong \angle P$; $\angle MNR \cong \angle PNQ$; $\overline{QN} \cong \overline{NR}$
    Prove: $\triangle MNQ \cong \triangle PNR$

Ex. 33-34

35. Given: $\overline{EB} \perp \overline{AC}$; $\overline{AD} \perp \overline{EC}$; $\overline{AC} \cong \overline{EC}$; $\angle CAD \cong \angle CEB$
    Prove: $\triangle CAD \cong \triangle CEB$

36. Given: $\overline{EB} \perp \overline{AC}$; $\overline{AD} \perp \overline{EC}$; $\overline{CA} \cong \overline{CE}$; $\overline{BC} \cong \overline{DC}$
    Prove: $\triangle APB \cong \triangle EPD$

37. Repeat exercise 35 without using the given information that $\angle CAD \cong \angle CEB$.

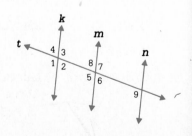

Ex. 35-37

Geometry Maintenance

[1-5] Given: $k \parallel m$; $m\angle 5 = 114$

1. $m\angle 3 = \underline{\ ?\ }$ 3. $m\angle 2 = \underline{\ ?\ }$

2. $m\angle 1 = \underline{\ ?\ }$ 4. $m\angle 4 = \underline{\ ?\ }$

5. If $m\angle 9 = 114$, then $n \parallel \underline{\ ?\ }$ and $n \parallel \underline{\ ?\ }$.

4.4   Proving Corresponding Parts Congruent

One way of proving that segments or angles are congruent is to show first that they are corresponding parts of congruent triangles. Then use "Corr. parts of $\cong$ $\triangle$s are $\cong$."

Example 1

Show that if the legs of a director's chair are attached at their midpoints, then the edge of the chair seat will be parallel to the floor.

Solution

Draw $\overline{AC}$ and $\overline{BD}$ as in the diagram at the right to represent the legs.

Given

E is the midpoint of $\overline{AC}$ and $\overline{BD}$.

Prove

$\overline{AB} \parallel \overline{CD}$

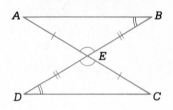

Plan for Proof

Show $\triangle ABE \cong \triangle CDE$ by SAS.
Use corr. parts to show $\angle B \cong \angle D$.
Use alt. int. $\angle$s to show $\overline{AB} \parallel \overline{CD}$.

Proof

Statements	Reasons
1. E is the midpoint of $\overline{AC}$ and $\overline{BD}$.	1. Given
2. $AE = EC$; $DE = EB$	2. Def. of midpoint [1]
3. $\overline{AE} \cong \overline{EC}$; $\overline{DE} \cong \overline{EB}$	3. Def. of $\cong$ segments [2]
4. $\angle AEB \cong \angle CED$	4. Vertical $\angle$s are $\cong$.
5. $\triangle ABE \cong \triangle CDE$	5. SAS Postulate [3, 4]
6. $\angle ABD \cong \angle CDB$	6. Corr. parts of $\cong$ $\triangle$s are $\cong$. [5]
7. $\overline{AB} \parallel \overline{CE}$	7. Alt. int. $\angle$s $\cong$ $\Rightarrow$ 2 lines $\parallel$ [6]

Example 2

Prove that the bisector of the vertex angle of an isosceles triangle is perpendicular to the base.

Given

$\overrightarrow{CM}$ bisects $\angle ACB$; $\overline{AC} \cong \overline{BC}$

Prove

$\overline{CM} \perp \overline{AB}$

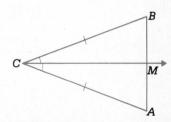

Plan for Proof

Show $\triangle ACM \cong \triangle BCM$ by SAS.
Use corr. parts to show $\angle AMC \cong \angle BMC$.
Use Thm. 2.14 to show $\overline{CM} \perp \overline{AB}$.

Ways to Prove Triangles Congruent

Show that the triangles are congruent to the same triangle.

Show that the following parts are congruent:

All six pairs of corresponding parts (Definition)
Three pairs of corresponding sides (SSS)
Two pairs of corresponding sides and their included
    angles (SAS)
Two pairs of corresponding angles and their included
    sides (ASA)
Two pairs of corresponding angles and a pair of
    corresponding, nonincluded sides (AAS)

Show that right triangles have the following congruent parts:

Both pairs of corresponding legs (LL)
Hypotenuses and a pair of acute angles (HA)
A pair of corresponding legs and a pair of corresponding
    acute angles (LA)

Example 3   Draw a diagram showing the postulates and theorems on
which the AAS Theorem depends.

Solution   Examine the Plan for Proof of the AAS Theorem (page 177). It
shows that the ASA Postulate is used with Theorem 3.15,
which is a corollary of Theorem 3.14. The proof of Theorem
3.14 (page 142) leads to other postulates and theorems.
Continue until no new theorems are cited.

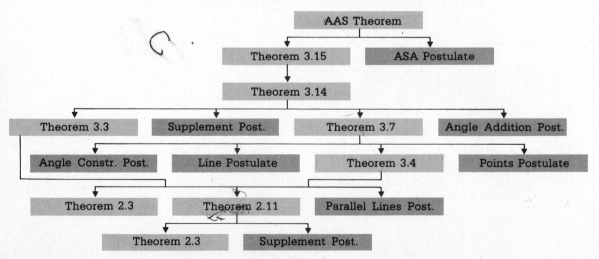

Class Exercises

Given: $\overline{AD} \cong \overline{BC}$; $\overline{AB} \cong \overline{CD}$. The goal is to prove $\overline{AB} \parallel \overline{CD}$.

1. $\overline{AC}$ is a transversal cutting $\overline{AB}$ and $\overline{CD}$. Name a pair of alternate interior angles.

2. You can show that $\overline{AB} \parallel \overline{CD}$ if you first show that $\angle 1$ and $\angle 2$ are __?__.

3. $\angle 1 \cong \angle 2$ if $\triangle ABC \cong$ __?__.

4. You can show the triangles are congruent by the __?__ Postulate.

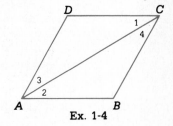

Ex. 1-4

Name triangles that you might prove congruent to prove each statement.

5. $\overline{RS} \cong \overline{TS}$ 8. $\angle RSV \cong \angle TSV$

6. $\overline{RU} \cong \overline{TU}$ 9. $\angle SVR \cong \angle SVT$

7. $\angle 1 \cong \angle 2$ 10. $\overline{SV} \perp \overline{RT}$

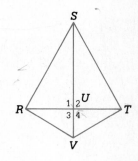

Written Exercises

Set A

1. Given: $\overline{WZ} \cong \overline{YZ}$; $\angle 1 \cong \angle 2$
   Prove: $\angle 3 \cong \angle 4$

2. Given: $\overline{WX} \cong \overline{YX}$; $\overline{WZ} \cong \overline{YZ}$
   Prove: $\angle 1 \cong \angle 2$

3. Given: $\angle 1 \cong \angle 2$; $\angle 3 \cong \angle 4$
   Prove: $\overline{WZ} \cong \overline{YZ}$

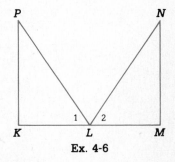

Ex. 1-3

4. Given: $\overline{PK} \cong \overline{NM}$; $\overline{KL} \cong \overline{ML}$; rt. $\angle$s at K and M
   Prove: $\overline{PL} \cong \overline{NL}$

5. Given: $\angle P \cong \angle N$; $\angle 1 \cong \angle 2$; $\overline{PK} \cong \overline{NM}$
   Prove: $\angle K \cong \angle M$

6. Given: $\overline{PL} \cong \overline{NL}$; $\overline{PK} \cong \overline{NM}$; L is the midpoint of $\overline{KM}$.
   Prove: $\angle K \cong \angle M$

Ex. 4-6

7. Complete the proof in example 2, page 183.

8. Given: $\angle 2 \cong \angle 3$; $\angle B \cong \angle D$
Prove: $\overline{AB} \cong \overline{CD}$

9. Given: $\overline{AB} \cong \overline{CD}$; $\angle 2 \cong \angle 3$
Prove: $\overline{AD} \parallel \overline{CB}$

10. Given: $\overline{AD} \perp \overline{CD}$; $\overline{AB} \perp \overline{BC}$; $\angle 1 \cong \angle 4$
Prove: $\overline{AB} \cong \overline{CD}$

11. Given: $\overline{AB} \perp \overline{BC}$; $\overline{AD} \cong \overline{BC}$; $\angle 1 \cong \angle 4$
Prove: $\overline{AD} \perp \overline{DC}$

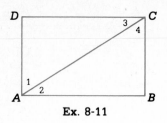

Ex. 8-11

Set B

12. If a carpenter's square is placed in the interior of $\angle XYZ$ such that $XY = ZY$ and $XW = ZW$, then W lies on the angle bisector. Explain.

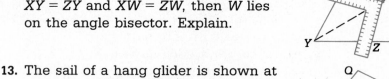

13. The sail of a hang glider is shown at the right. If $PQ = PS$ and $RQ = RS$, then $\angle Q$ and $\angle S$ will have the same measure. Explain.

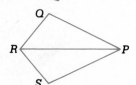

14. To find the distance from B to A across an expressway, you could use the brim of a hat. Sight point A along the brim of the hat. Then, without raising or lowering your head, turn to sight point C. Explain why $BA = BC$.

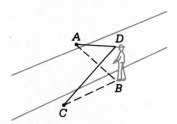

[15-17] Draw a diagram as in example 3 showing the postulates and theorems on which each theorem depends.

15. HA Theorem　　**16.** LL Theorem　　**17.** LA Theorem

18. When a billiard ball bounces off a side of a billiard table, the angles at which the ball hits and rebounds are congruent. Show that a ball shot from P to the midpoint B of the end of the table will rebound to a point P' such that $CP = AP'$.

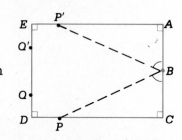

Set C

19. Show that a ball shot from Q to B will rebound to a point Q' such that $DQ = EQ'$.

4.5 Overlapping Triangles

The five-pointed star, called a pentagram, is often found in nature. In the diagram at the right, a pentagram (black) is drawn inside a regular pentagon. How many triangles are there in the figure? Be careful. Many of the triangles overlap one another.

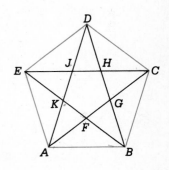

The identification and use of overlapping triangles is important in the study of geometry.

Example	Use the diagram above.
Given	Regular pentagon *ABCDE*
Prove	$\overline{AC} \cong \overline{BE}$

Solution

It may help you to draw the triangles separately so the corresponding parts of the triangles are more obvious.

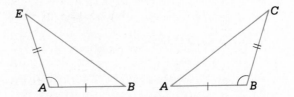

Plan for Proof

Show that $\overline{AB} \cong \overline{AB}$.
Use the definition of a regular polygon.
Use ASA and corresponding parts.

To get one pair of triangles congruent, it is sometimes necessary first to prove that another pair is congruent.

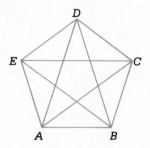

Given   Regular pentagon *ABCDE*

Prove   △*ACE* ≅ △*BEC*

Plan for Proof   Draw △*ACE* and △*BEC* separately.
$\overline{AE} \cong \overline{BC}$ by the definition of a regular pentagon.
Show that $\overline{EC} \cong \overline{EC}$.
To get $\overline{AC} \cong \overline{BE}$, first get
△*ABE* ≅ △*BAC* by SAS. (See page 187.)
Then use SSS.

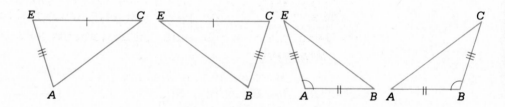

Proof

Statements	Reasons
1. *ABCDE* is a regular pentagon.	1. Given
2. $\overline{AE} \cong \overline{BC}$	2. Def. of regular pentagon [1]
3. ∠*EAB* ≅ ∠*CBA*	3. Def. of regular pentagon [1]
4. $\overline{AB} \cong \overline{AB}$	4. Congruence of segments is __?__ .
5. △*ABE* ≅ △*BAC*	5. SAS Postulate [2, 3, 4]
6. $\overline{BE} \cong \overline{AC}$	6. Corr. parts of ≅ △s are ≅. [5]
7. $\overline{EC} \cong \overline{EC}$	7. __?__ .
8. △*ACE* ≅ △*BEC*	8. SSS Postulate [2, 6, 7]

Class Exercises

List the six pairs of corresponding parts for the congruent triangles given.

1. △*ABD* ≅ △*BAC*   **3.** △*CAB* ≅ △*BDC*

2. △*DEC* ≅ △*BEA*   **4.** △*DEC* ≅ △*AEB*

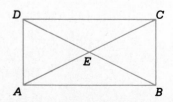

[5-10] Given: $\angle UXY \cong \angle UZY$; $\overrightarrow{YU}$ bisects $\angle XYZ$. The goal is to prove $\overline{XZ} \perp \overline{UY}$.

5. To show $\overline{XZ} \perp \overline{UY}$, first show $\angle\ \underline{?}\ \cong \angle\ \underline{?}\ $ or $\angle\ \underline{?}\ \cong \angle\ \underline{?}\ $.

6. To show $\angle 1 \cong \angle 2$, first show $\triangle\underline{?}\ \cong \triangle\underline{?}\ $.

7. To show $\triangle XVY \cong \triangle ZVY$, use the common side and angle bisector to get two pairs of congruent corresponding parts: $\underline{?}\ \cong \underline{?}\ $ and $\angle\underline{?}\ \cong \angle\underline{?}\ $.

8. To get $\triangle XVY \cong \triangle ZVY$, show $\angle\underline{?}\ \cong \angle\underline{?}\ $ and use the AAS Theorem, or show $\underline{?}\ \cong \underline{?}\ $ and use the SAS Postulate.

9. To get $\overline{XY} \cong \overline{ZY}$, first show $\triangle UYX \cong \triangle UYZ$ by the $\underline{?}\ $ Theorem, using the given facts and common side.

10. Using exercises 5-9, write the statements for a two-column proof.

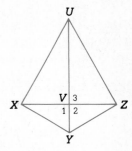

Written Exercises

Set A

[1-6] Does this information show that $\triangle KGH \cong \triangle JHG$? Why?

1. $\angle GHK \cong \angle HGJ$; $\angle KGH \cong \angle JHG$
2. $\overline{KH} \cong \overline{GJ}$; $\overline{KG} \cong \overline{HJ}$
3. $\angle GKH \cong \angle HJG$; $\overline{KG} \cong \overline{JH}$
4. $\angle KGH \cong \angle JHG$; $\overline{GJ} \cong \overline{KH}$
5. $\angle GHJ$ and $\angle HGK$ are rt. $\angle$s; $\overline{KG} \cong \overline{JH}$
6. $\overline{KG} \perp \overline{GH}$; $\overline{JH} \perp \overline{GH}$; $\angle GKH \cong \angle HJG$

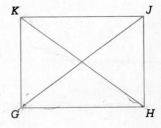

[7-12] Does this information show that $\triangle XYV \cong \triangle ZYU$? Why?

7. $\overline{XY} \cong \overline{ZY}$; $\overline{YU} \cong \overline{YV}$
8. $\angle X \cong \angle Z$; $\overline{XV} \cong \overline{ZU}$
9. $\angle X \cong \angle Z$; $\overline{XY} \cong \overline{ZY}$
10. $\overline{XY} \cong \overline{ZY}$; $\overline{XV} \cong \overline{ZU}$
11. $\angle X \cong \angle Z$; $\angle XVY \cong \angle ZUY$
12. $\angle XVY$ and $\angle ZUY$ are rt. $\angle$s; $\overline{XY} \cong \overline{ZY}$

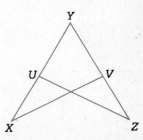

[13-16] Prove: $\triangle ADB \cong \triangle BCA$

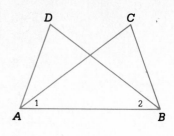

13. Given: $\overline{AD} \cong \overline{BC}$; $\angle DAB \cong \angle CBA$
14. Given: $\angle DAB \cong \angle CBA$; $\angle 1 \cong \angle 2$
15. Given: $\angle D \cong \angle C$; $\angle 1 \cong \angle 2$
16. Given: $\overline{AD} \cong \overline{BC}$; $\overline{DB} \cong \overline{CA}$

[17-20] Prove: $\triangle RTV \cong \triangle STU$

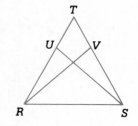

17. Given: $\overline{UT} \cong \overline{VT}$; $\angle TVR \cong \angle TUS$
18. Given: $\angle TRV \cong \angle TSU$; $\overline{RT} \cong \overline{ST}$
19. Given: $\overline{RV} \cong \overline{SU}$; $\angle TRV \cong \angle TSU$
20. Given: $\angle TVR \cong \angle TUS$; $\overline{RV} \cong \overline{SU}$

Set B

[21-24] Prove: $\triangle ABD \cong \triangle FEC$

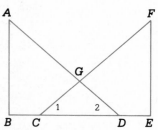

21. Given: $\angle B$ and $\angle E$ are rt. $\angle$s;
$\overline{BC} \cong \overline{DE}$; $\angle 1 \cong \angle 2$
22. Given: $\angle B$ and $\angle E$ are rt. $\angle$s;
$\angle A \cong \angle F$; $\overline{BC} \cong \overline{DE}$
23. Given: $\overline{AB} \perp \overline{BE}$; $\overline{FE} \perp \overline{BE}$; $\overline{AB} \cong \overline{EF}$;
$\overline{BC} \cong \overline{DE}$
24. Given: $\overline{AB} \perp \overline{BE}$; $\overline{FE} \perp \overline{BE}$; $\overline{AD} \cong \overline{FC}$;
$\angle 1 \cong \angle 2$

[25-27] Refer to the bridge sketched at the right.

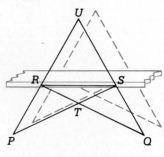

25. Name three pairs of triangles in the
support structure of the bridge which
appear to be congruent.

26. Explain why $\triangle PRS \cong \triangle QSR$ if
$\overline{PR} \cong \overline{QS}$ and $\overline{PS} \cong \overline{QR}$.

27. If $\overline{UP} \cong \overline{UQ}$ and $\overline{UR} \cong \overline{US}$, how do you
know that $\triangle UPS \cong \triangle UQR$?

28. Given: $\angle KMN \cong \angle PNM$;
$\angle KNM \cong \angle PMN$
Prove: $\overline{KO} \cong \overline{PO}$

29. Given: $\overline{NK} \cong \overline{MP}$; $\overline{PN} \cong \overline{KM}$
Prove: $\overline{MO} \cong \overline{NO}$

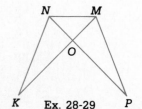

Ex. 28-29

[30-32] In the tower at the right, piece $\overline{AC}$ must be replaced.
$\overline{AD} \cong \overline{BC}$ and $\angle ADC \cong \angle BCD$.

30. Name the overlapping triangles that can be proved congruent with the given information.

31. Prove that those triangles are congruent.

32. The replacement piece, $\overline{AC}$, will be congruent to which segment? Why?

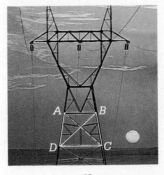

33. Given: V is the midpoint of $\overline{XZ}$; $\overline{UY} \perp \overline{XZ}$
    Prove: $\angle UXY \cong \angle UZY$

34. Given: $\overline{UY} \perp \overline{XZ}$; $\overrightarrow{UY}$ bisects $\angle XUZ$.
    Prove: $\overline{XY} \cong \overline{ZY}$

35. Given: $\overline{XU} \cong \overline{ZU}$; $\overline{XY} \cong \overline{ZY}$
    Prove: $\overline{UY} \perp \overline{XZ}$

36. Given: $\overleftrightarrow{UY}$ bisects $\angle XUZ$ and $\angle XYZ$.
    Prove: $\overline{UY} \perp \overline{XZ}$

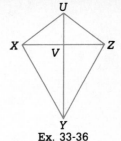

Ex. 33-36

[37-40] Given: Regular pentagon $ABCDE$. List all triangles congruent to the given triangle.

37. $\triangle ABC$ 39. $\triangle ABG$

38. $\triangle ABD$ 40. $\triangle ABF$

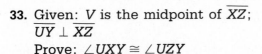

Set C

41. Given: $\overline{AF} \cong \overline{CD}$; $\overline{DE} \cong \overline{FE}$
    Prove: $\angle EFD \cong \angle EDF$

42. Given: $\overline{AF} \cong \overline{CD}$; $\angle EFD \cong \angle EDF$
    Prove: $\overline{DE} \cong \overline{FE}$

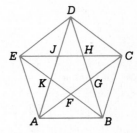

Ex. 41-42

43. Given: $\angle 1 \cong \angle 2$; $\overline{RW} \cong \overline{RS}$
    Prove: $\overline{VU} \cong \overline{TU}$

44. Given: $\overline{RS} \cong \overline{RW}$; $\overline{VW} \cong \overline{TS}$
    Prove: $\angle 1 \cong \angle 2$

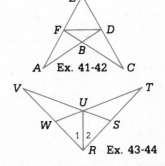

Ex. 43-44

45. In $\triangle ABC$ and $\triangle DEF$, $\overline{AC} \cong \overline{DF}$, $\angle A \cong \angle D$, and $\angle C \cong \angle F$.
    Prove $\triangle ABC \cong \triangle DEF$ without using the AAS Theorem, the SSS Postulate, or the ASA Postulate.

Progress Check

Lesson 4.1
Page 166

[1-2] Given: $\triangle ABC \cong \triangle DEF$

1. List the pairs of corresponding sides.

2. List the pairs of corresponding angles.

Lesson 4.2
Page 172

Which postulate justifies $\triangle XYZ \cong \triangle SRT$?

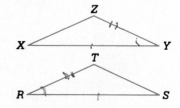

3. Given: $\overline{XY} \cong \overline{RS}$; $\angle Y \cong \angle R$; $\overline{YZ} \cong \overline{RT}$

4. Given: $\overline{XY} \cong \overline{RS}$; $\overline{XZ} \cong \overline{ST}$; $\overline{YZ} \cong \overline{RT}$

5. Given: $\angle Z \cong \angle T$; $\angle X \cong \angle S$; $\overline{XZ} \cong \overline{ST}$

Lesson 4.3
Page 177

Which theorem justifies $\triangle MPR \cong \triangle NPR$?

6. Given: $\overline{RP} \perp \overline{MN}$; $\angle M \cong \angle N$

7. Given: $\overline{RP} \perp \overline{MN}$; $\overline{MP} \cong \overline{PN}$

8. Given: $\angle M \cong \angle N$; $\angle MRP \cong \angle NRP$

9. Given: $\overrightarrow{AC}$ bisects $\angle BAD$; $\overline{AB} \perp \overline{BC}$; $\overline{AD} \perp \overline{DC}$
Prove: $\triangle ABC \cong \triangle ADC$

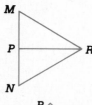

Lesson 4.4
Page 183

[10-13] Name triangles that you might prove congruent to prove each statement.

10. $\overline{MP} \cong \overline{OP}$

12. $\overrightarrow{NP}$ bisects $\overline{MO}$.

11. $\angle MNP \cong \angle ONP$

13. $\overline{NP} \perp \overline{MO}$

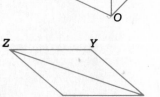

14. Given: $\overline{YZ} \parallel \overline{XW}$; $\overline{YZ} \cong \overline{XW}$
Prove: $\overline{XY} \cong \overline{WZ}$

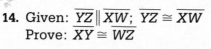

Lesson 4.5
Page 187

[15-18] Name a pair of congruent triangles.

15. Given: $\overline{AB} \cong \overline{CD}$; $\angle ABC \cong \angle BCD$

16. Given: $\overline{AD} \cong \overline{BC}$; $\angle ADB \cong \angle DBC$

17. Given: $\overline{AB} \cong \overline{CD}$; E bisects $\overline{AC}$ and $\overline{BD}$.

18. Given: $\angle ABD \cong \angle DCA$; $\angle CAD \cong \angle ADB$

19. Given: $\overline{AB} \cong \overline{DC}$; $\angle ABD \cong \angle CDB$
Prove: $\triangle ADE \cong \triangle CBE$

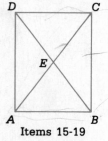

Items 15-19

4.6 Using Congruence to Justify Constructions

Constructions have appeared in previous chapters. Using the congruent triangle postulates and theorems, you can now justify these constructions.

Construction 3 Construct the bisector of a given angle.

Given	$\angle ABC$
Construct	$\overrightarrow{BD}$, the bisector of $\angle ABC$

Method
Step 1: With B as center, construct an arc that intersects $\overrightarrow{BA}$ and $\overrightarrow{BC}$ at X and Y, respectively.

Step 2: With X and Y as centers and a radius greater than $\frac{1}{2}(XY)$, construct two intersecting arcs. Label the intersection D.

Step 3: Draw $\overrightarrow{BD}$.

Then $\overrightarrow{BD}$ bisects $\angle ABC$.

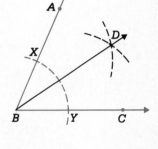

Plan for Justification
Draw $\overline{XD}$ and $\overline{YD}$; $\overline{BX} \cong \overline{BY}$ and $\overline{XD} \cong \overline{YD}$ by construction.
Show $\triangle BXD \cong \triangle BYD$ by SSS.
Then $\angle XBD \cong \angle YBD$ by corr. parts.

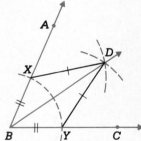

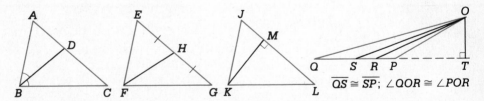

$\overline{QS} \cong \overline{SP}; \angle QOR \cong \angle POR$

Segments relating to a triangle can be constructed. An **angle bisector of a triangle** is the segment from any vertex to the opposite side on the ray bisecting the angle. $\overline{BD}$ and $\overline{OR}$ are angle bisectors. A **median of a triangle** is the segment from any vertex to the midpoint of the opposite side. $\overline{FH}$ and $\overline{OS}$ are medians. An **altitude of a triangle** is the perpendicular segment from any vertex to the line containing the opposite side. $\overline{KM}$ and $\overline{OT}$ are altitudes.

<u>**Construction 8**</u>   **Construct the altitude from a given vertex of a triangle.**

Given $\triangle ABC$

Construct $\overline{CG}$ with G on $\overleftrightarrow{AB}$ and $\overline{CG} \perp \overleftrightarrow{AB}$

Method   Step 1: With C as center, draw an
                arc that intersects $\overleftrightarrow{AB}$ at two points
                E and F; extend $\overleftrightarrow{AB}$ if necessary.

                Step 2: With E and F as centers and
                radius greater than $\frac{1}{2}(EF)$, construct
                a pair of arcs intersecting at D.

                Step 3: Draw $\overrightarrow{CD}$. Label the
                intersection of $\overrightarrow{CD}$ and $\overleftrightarrow{AB}$ as G.

                $\overline{CG}$ is the desired altitude.

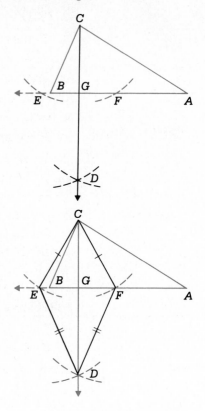

Plan for   Draw $\overline{CE}$, $\overline{CF}$, $\overline{DE}$, and $\overline{DF}$.
Justification $\overline{CE} \cong \overline{CF}$ and $\overline{DE} \cong \overline{DF}$ by
                construction.
                Show $\triangle CDE \cong \triangle CDF$ by SSS.

                Get $\angle GCE \cong \angle GCF$ and $\overline{CG} \cong \overline{CG}$.
                $\triangle GCE \cong \triangle GCF$ by SAS.
                $\angle EGC$ and $\angle FGC$ form a linear pair
                and are congruent, so use Thm. 2.14.

Class Exercises

1. If $\overline{RV} \perp \overline{TS}$, then $\overline{RV}$ is a(n) __?__
   of $\triangle RST$.

2. If V is the midpoint of $\overline{ST}$, then $\overline{RV}$ is
   a(n) __?__ of $\triangle RST$.

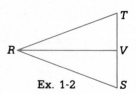

Ex. 1-2

[3-5] True or false

3. A straightedge can be used to
   measure the length of a segment.

4. If A is the center of an arc through
   B and C, then $\overline{AB} \cong \overline{AC}$.

5. If an arc is drawn with the compass
   radius used in exercise 4 and with D
   as center, then $\overline{DE} \cong \overline{AB}$.

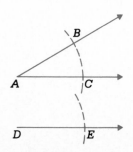

[6-11] Refer to the construction at the right of an angle congruent to a given angle. (Construction 2)

6. The center for the arc through D and E is ___?___ .

7. How are BD and BE related?

8. The center for the arc through P and R is ___?___ .

9. How are QP and QR related?

10. How are BE and QP related?

11. P is the intersection of two arcs. One is the arc through P and R with center Q. The center of the other arc is ___?___ ; its radius copies the distance between points ___?___ and ___?___ .

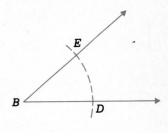

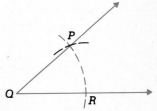

Written Exercises

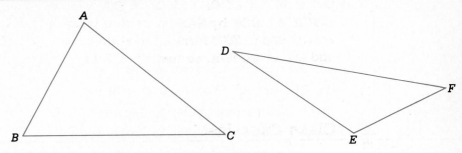

Set A

[1-10] Trace the figures above as needed.

1. Construct the bisector of $\angle ABC$.

2. Construct an angle congruent to $\angle DEF$.

3. Construct the midpoint of $\overline{AC}$.

4. Construct a segment twice as long as $\overline{EF}$.

5. Construct a right angle.

6. Divide $\overline{DE}$ into four congruent parts using only compass and straightedge.

7. Construct the median of $\triangle ABC$ from A to $\overline{BC}$.

8. Construct the median of $\triangle ABC$ from C to $\overline{AB}$.

9. Construct the altitude of $\triangle DEF$ from E to $\overline{DF}$.

10. Construct the altitude of $\triangle DEF$ from F to $\overleftrightarrow{DE}$.

4.6 Using Congruence to Justify Constructions

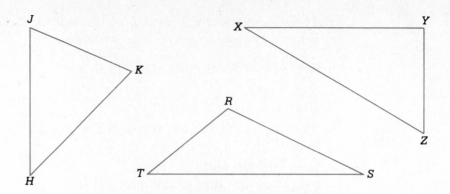

[11-13] Trace the figures above as needed.

11. Construct a triangle congruent to $\triangle XYZ$ by using the SAS Postulate.

12. Construct a triangle congruent to $\triangle RST$ by using the ASA Postulate.

13. Construct a triangle congruent to $\triangle HJK$ by using the SSS Postulate.

[14-21] Construct each figure and write a plan to justify your construction. Trace the figures above as needed.

14. An angle congruent to $\angle R$

15. The perpendicular bisector of $\overline{XZ}$

16. A line perpendicular to $\overleftrightarrow{HJ}$ through J

17. A line perpendicular to $\overleftrightarrow{RS}$ through T

18. A 45° angle

19. A 60° angle

20. A 120° angle

21. A 135° angle

[22-24] Draw a triangle with sides of 10 cm, 12 cm, and 13 cm.

22. Construct the three angle bisectors.

23. Construct the three medians.

24. Construct the three altitudes.

Set C

25. Construct a triangle with angles of 120° and 15° and write a plan to justify your construction.

4.7　Isosceles Triangles and the HL Theorem

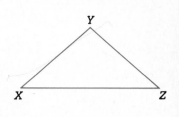

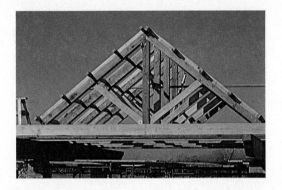

The rafters which support most roofs are the legs of isosceles triangles. In the diagram at the right above, $\overline{YX} \cong \overline{YZ}$. Note that the base angles of $\triangle XYZ$ appear to be congruent. This suggests the Isosceles Triangle Theorem.

Theorem 4.6
Isosceles
Triangle
Theorem

If two sides of a triangle are congruent, then the angles opposite those sides are congruent.

Given　　　　$\triangle ABC$ with $\overline{AC} \cong \overline{BC}$

Prove　　　　$\angle A \cong \angle B$

Plan for Proof　Draw $\overline{CD}$ where D is the midpoint of $\overline{AB}$.
Show $\triangle ADC \cong \triangle BDC$ by SSS.
Then use corresponding parts.

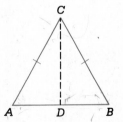

Proof

Statements	Reasons
1. $\overline{AC} \cong \overline{BC}$	1. Given
2. Let D be the midpoint of $\overline{AB}$.	2. Midpoint Postulate
3. Draw $\overline{CD}$.	3. Line Postulate
4. $AD = DB$	4. Def. of midpoint [2]
5. $\overline{AD} \cong \overline{DB}$	5. Def. of $\cong$ segments [4]
6. $\overline{CD} \cong \overline{CD}$	6. Congruence of segments is reflexive.
7. $\triangle ADC \cong \triangle BDC$	7. SSS Postulate [1, 5, 6]
8. $\angle A \cong \angle B$	8. Corr. parts of $\cong \triangle$s are $\cong$. [7]

The converse of the Isosceles Triangle Theorem is also true.

Theorem 4.7   If two angles of a triangle are congruent, then the sides opposite those angles are congruent.

Given $\triangle ABC$ with $\angle A \cong \angle B$

Prove $\overline{AC} \cong \overline{BC}$

Plan for Proof   Draw $\overrightarrow{CE}$, the bisector of $\angle ACB$.
Let D be the intersection of $\overleftrightarrow{AB}$ and $\overleftrightarrow{CE}$.
Show $\triangle ACD \cong \triangle BCD$ by AAS.
Then $\overline{AC}$ and $\overline{BC}$ are corresponding parts.

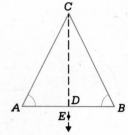

The following theorems are corollaries of Theorems 4.6 and 4.7, respectively. Their proofs are exercises 14 and 15.

Theorem 4.8   An equilateral triangle is also equiangular.

Theorem 4.9   An equiangular triangle is also equilateral.

The next theorem is useful in proving that two right triangles are congruent. Its proof is exercise 34.

Theorem 4.10   If the hypotenuse and a leg of one right triangle are congruent to
HL Theorem   the corresponding parts of another right triangle, then the triangles are congruent.

Given $\triangle ABC$ and $\triangle DEF$ are right $\triangle$s with rt. $\angle$s at E and B; $\overline{AC} \cong \overline{DF}$; $\overline{BC} \cong \overline{EF}$

Prove $\triangle ABC \cong \triangle DEF$

Plan for Proof   Draw $\overleftrightarrow{DE}$.
Choose G on the ray opposite $\overrightarrow{ED}$ so $\overline{EG} \cong \overline{AB}$ and draw $\overline{FG}$.
Show $\triangle ABC \cong \triangle GEF$ by SAS or LL.
Get $\overline{AC} \cong \overline{GF}$ by corr. parts.
Use $\overline{AC} \cong \overline{DF}$ to get $\overline{DF} \cong \overline{GF}$.
Apply the Isosceles $\triangle$ Thm.
Show $\triangle GEF \cong \triangle DEF$ by AAS, HA, or LA.
Use transitivity to get $\triangle ABC \cong \triangle DEF$.

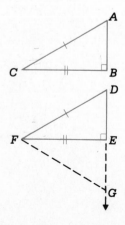

Class Exercises

1. $\triangle ABC$ is equilateral. How are $\angle A$, $\angle B$, and $\angle C$ related? What are their measures?

2. $\triangle ABC$ is equiangular. How are $\overline{AB}$, $\overline{BC}$, and $\overline{AC}$ related?

3. Given: Equiangular $\triangle ABC$; $AB = 2x - 3$; $BC = 21 - x$. Find AC.

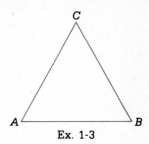

Ex. 1-3

4. Combine Theorems 4.6 and 4.7 into a single "if and only if" statement.

5. Write Theorems 4.8 and 4.9 in "if . . . then" form.

6. Combine Theorems 4.8 and 4.9 into a single "if and only if" statement.

Written Exercises

Set A

1. The measure of the vertex angle of an isosceles triangle is 50. Find the measure of each base angle.

2. The measure of a base angle of an isosceles triangle is 50. Find the measure of the other two angles.

[3-6] Given: $\angle 4 \cong \angle 5$

3. $AC = 12$ and $BC = 2x + 4$. Find x.
4. $AC = 2x - 9$ and $BC = 11$. Find x.
5. $AC = 3x$ and $BC = x + 4$. Find BC.
6. $AC = x - 3$ and $BC = 2x - 8$. Find AC.

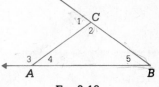

Ex. 3-12

[7-12] Given: $\overline{AC} \cong \overline{BC}$

7. $m\angle 1 = 100$; $m\angle 2 = \underline{?}$ 10. $m\angle 1 = 100$; $m\angle 4 = \underline{?}$
8. $m\angle 1 = 100$; $m\angle 4 + m\angle 5 = \underline{?}$ 11. $m\angle 1 = 100$; $m\angle 3 = \underline{?}$
9. $m\angle 3 = 120$; $m\angle 2 + m\angle 5 = \underline{?}$ 12. $m\angle 3 = 120$; $m\angle 2 = \underline{?}$

[13-15] Prove each theorem.

13. Theorem 4.7   14. Theorem 4.8   15. Theorem 4.9

16. A plot of ground is sketched on the right. Explain why the three sides of the plot must be of equal length.

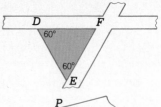

17. The frame of a gabled roof is sketched at the right. Find the measure of the angle formed at the peak *P* of the roof and the length *QR* of the crossbeam.

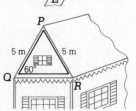

18. Given: $\overline{XY} \perp \overline{TZ}$; $\overline{YZ} \perp \overline{XV}$; $\overline{TW} \cong \overline{VW}$
Prove: $\angle WXZ \cong \angle WZX$

19. Given: $\overline{XY} \perp \overline{TZ}$; $\overline{YZ} \perp \overline{XV}$; $\angle YXZ \cong \angle YZX$
Prove: $\triangle TYZ \cong \triangle VYX$

20. Given: $\overline{XY} \cong \overline{ZY}$; $\overline{XW} \cong \overline{ZW}$
Prove: $\triangle XTW \cong \triangle ZVW$

21. Given: $\overline{XY} \perp \overline{TZ}$; $\overline{YZ} \perp \overline{XV}$; $\overline{XY} \cong \overline{ZY}$
Prove: $\overline{XW} \cong \overline{ZW}$

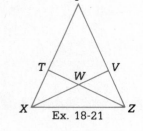

Ex. 18-21

[22-25] Draw a figure and write a Given and Prove for each statement.

22. If a triangle is isosceles, then the median from the vertex angle bisects the vertex angle.

23. If an altitude of a triangle is also a median, then the triangle is isosceles.

24. The median from the vertex angle of an isosceles triangle is the perpendicular bisector of the base.

25. The altitudes to the congruent sides of an isosceles triangle are congruent.

Set B

26. Prove the statement in exercise 22.

27. Prove the statement in exercise 23.

28. Prove the statement in exercise 24.

29. Prove the statement in exercise 25.

30. Write the converse of the statement in exercise 22. Is the converse true?

31. Prove the converse of the statement in exercise 23.

Chapter 4   Congruent Triangles

32. Prove: The altitude from the vertex angle of an isosceles triangle bisects the vertex angle.

33. Prove the converse of the statement in exercise 32.

34. Write a two-column proof of the HL Theorem.

35. Draw a diagram showing the postulates on which the HL Theorem depends. (See page 184.)

36. Rafters $\overline{AB}$ and $\overline{AC}$ are the same length. Braces $\overline{DE}$ and $\overline{FG}$ are placed so that $\overline{BE} \cong \overline{GC}$, $\overline{DE} \perp \overline{BC}$, and $\overline{FG} \perp \overline{BC}$. Explain why the braces must be the same length.

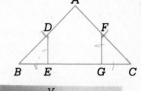

37. Two braces of equal length support a shelf. Explain why you would attach the braces to the wall the same distance below the shelf.

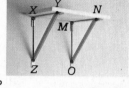

38. Ann needs to cut 10 triangular pieces from a board 12 inches wide. $\triangle PQR$ is a sketch of a single piece. How long does the board need to be?

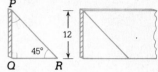

39. Given: $\overline{AC} \cong \overline{BC}$; $\angle 1 \cong \angle 2$
Prove: $\angle CAD \cong \angle CBD$

40. Given: $\overline{AC} \cong \overline{BC}$; $\overline{AD} \cong \overline{BD}$
Prove: $\overline{CD} \perp \overline{AB}$

41. Given: $\overline{AB} \perp \overline{CD}$; $\angle CAB \cong \angle CBA$
Prove: $\angle DAB \cong \angle DBA$

42. Given: $\overline{AB} \perp \overline{CD}$; $\overline{AD} \cong \overline{DB}$
Prove: $\angle CAB \cong \angle CBA$

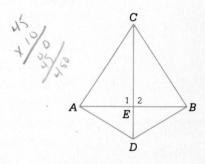

43. Prove: The medians to the congruent sides of an isosceles triangle are congruent.

44. Use exercise 43 to prove that the three medians of an equiangular triangle are congruent.

Set C

45. Prove: The base angles of an isosceles triangle are acute.

46. Write an indirect proof of the HL Theorem.

47. Prove Theorem 4.6 without auxiliary lines. (See exercises 13 and 14, page 169.)

4.8 Inequalities in One Triangle

Recall that $a > b$ means there is a positive real number c such that $a = b + c$. For real numbers a, b, c, and d, we say that a and b are **unequal in the same order** as c and d if (1) $a > b$ and $c > d$, or (2) $a < b$ and $c < d$.

Theorem 4.11 If the lengths of two sides of a triangle are unequal, then the measures of the angles opposite those sides are unequal in the same order.

Given $\triangle ABC$, $CB > CA$

Prove $m\angle CAB > m\angle B$

Plan for Proof Choose D on $\overline{CB}$ so $CD = CA$; draw $\overline{AD}$.
Show $\angle 1 \cong \angle 3$ by the Isosceles $\triangle$ Thm.
Show $m\angle 3 > m\angle B$ by Thm. 3.19.
Substitute to show $m\angle 1 > m\angle B$.
$m\angle CAB = m\angle 1 + m\angle 2$ by the Angle Add. Post.
Use def. of $>$ and transitivity.

The converse of Theorem 4.11 is also true.

Theorem 4.12 If the measures of two angles of a triangle are unequal, then the lengths of the sides opposite those angles are unequal in the same order.

Given $\triangle ABC$; $m\angle A > m\angle B$

Prove $CB > CA$

Proof   Either (1) $CB > CA$ or (2) $CB \not> CA$. Suppose $CB \not> CA$.
Then either $CB = CA$ or $CB < CA$.

If $CB = CA$, then $m\angle A = m\angle B$ by the Isosceles Triangle Theorem. But this contradicts the Given. Thus, $CB \neq CA$.

If $CB < CA$, then $m\angle A < m\angle B$ by Theorem 4.11. But this contradicts the Given. Thus, $CB \not< CA$.

Therefore, the assumption that $CB \not> CA$ is false. We conclude that $CB > CA$.

Chapter 4   Congruent Triangles

The following important inequality relates the lengths of the sides of a triangle. Its proof is exercise 27.

Theorem 4.13

Triangle
Inequality
Theorem

The sum of the lengths of any two sides of a triangle is greater than the length of the third side.

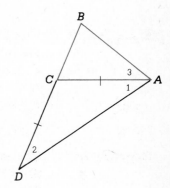

Given $\triangle ABC$

Prove $AC + CB > AB$

Plan for Proof   Choose D on the ray opposite to $\overrightarrow{CB}$ so
$DC = AC$.
Draw $\overline{AD}$ and show $m\angle 1 = m\angle 2$.
Show $m\angle BAD > m\angle 2$.
Use Thm. 4.12 to show $DB > AB$.
Show $DB = DC + CB$, then substitute.

Example 1   The lengths of two sides of a triangle are 6 and 8. Find the range of possible lengths x for the third side.

Solution   By the Triangle Inequality Theorem, $6 + 8 > x$, $x + 6 > 8$, and $x + 8 > 6$. For all three inequalities to hold, x must lie in the range $2 < x < 14$.

Example 2   Light moving through a single substance (at a constant speed) travels by the shortest path. Light from a lamp at L is reflected by a mirror on $\overline{MN}$ to an observer at O. To find the path light takes from L to O via the mirror, draw $\overline{OP} \perp \overline{MN}$. Choose O' on $\overrightarrow{OP}$ so $OP = O'P$. Draw $\overline{LO'}$. Let R be the intersection of $\overline{LO'}$ and $\overline{MN}$. Show that the path from L to R to O is the shortest path; that is, for any other point Q on $\overline{MN}$, show that $LQ + QO > LR + RO$.

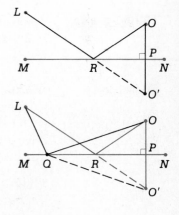

Solution

$LQ + QO' > LO'$	$\triangle$ Inequality Thm.
$LO' = LR + RO'$	Segment Add. Post.
$\triangle QPO \cong \triangle QPO'$; $\triangle RPO \cong \triangle RPO'$	LL Theorem
$QO' = QO$; $RO' = RO$	Corresponding parts
$LQ + QO > LR + RO$	Substitution

The following theorem is a corollary of the Triangle Inequality Theorem. Its indirect proof is exercise 30.

Theorem 4.14   Points *A*, *B*, and *C* are collinear and *B* is between *A* and *C* if *AB* + *BC* = *AC*.

"The shortest path between two points is a straight line." This familiar restatement of the Triangle Inequality Theorem explains why the distance between two points is defined as the length of the line segment between them. The distance from a point to a line or to a plane is also defined to be the length of the "shortest path."

Theorem 4.15   The perpendicular segment from a point to a line is the shortest segment from the point to the line.

Given $\overleftrightarrow{XY}$ with point *P* not on $\overleftrightarrow{XY}$; $\overline{PQ} \perp \overleftrightarrow{XY}$; *M* is any point on $\overleftrightarrow{XY}$ other than *Q*.

Prove   *PM* > *PQ*

Plan for Proof   In $\triangle PMQ$, $m\angle MQP = 90$.
Show $m\angle MQP > m\angle PMQ$.
Then *PM* > *PQ*.

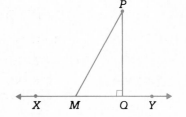

Theorem 4.16   The perpendicular segment from a point to a plane is the shortest segment from the point to the plane.

Definition   The **distance from a point to a line (or plane)** not containing the point is the length of the perpendicular segment from the point to the line (or plane).

Class Exercises

[1-6] Can a triangle have sides of the given lengths?

1. 11, 9, 16   **3.** 15, 8, 6   **5.** *x*, 2*x* + 1, 2*x* + 2

2. 5, 7, 9   **4.** 6, 2, 8   **6.** 2*y*, 2*y* − 7, 2*y* + 9

7. Name the shortest and longest sides of $\triangle ABC$.

8. Name the angles of $\triangle DEF$ of smallest and largest measure.

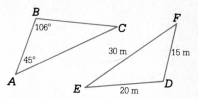

9. Write Theorems 4.11 and 4.12 as a single "if and only if" statement.

10. In the figure, the distance from P to line m appears to be __?__ .

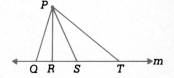

Written Exercises

Set A

[1-6] The lengths of two sides of a triangle are given. Find the range of possible lengths x for the third side.

1. 5, 7   **3.** 3.6, 2.1   **5.** 2.5, 7.5

2. 18, 16   **4.** 7, $3\frac{1}{2}$ **6.** 8, 8

[7-9] Name the shortest and longest sides of each triangle.

7. 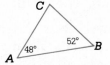   **8.**   **9.**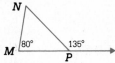

[10-12] Name the angles of smallest and largest measure.

10. 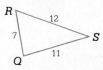   **11.** 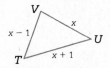   **12.**

13. Given: C is in the interior of $\angle DAB$.
Prove: $m\angle BAC < m\angle BAD$

14. Given: C is in the interior of $\angle BAD$.
Prove: $m\angle BAD > m\angle CAD$

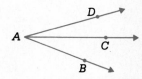

15. Given: $\angle YXZ$ is a right angle.
Prove: $YZ > XZ;\ YZ > XY$

16. Given: $YZ > XZ;\ \overline{XY} \cong \overline{XZ}$
Prove: $m\angle X > m\angle Z;\ m\angle X > m\angle Y$

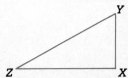

17. Prove Theorem 4.15.   **18.** Prove Theorem 4.16.

Set B

19. Given: $m\angle B > m\angle A$; $m\angle E > m\angle D$
Prove: $AD > BE$

20. Given: $AC > BC$; $CE > CD$
Prove: $\overline{AB} \not\parallel \overline{DE}$

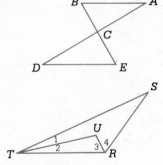

21. Given: $ST > RS$; $\angle 1 \cong \angle 2$; $\angle 3 \cong \angle 4$
Prove: $TU > UR$

22. Given: $TU > UR$; $\angle 1 \cong \angle 2$; $\angle 3 \cong \angle 4$
Prove: $ST > RS$

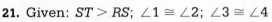

[23-24] Given: $\triangle XYZ$. Find the distance from Y to $\overleftrightarrow{XZ}$.

23. Rt. $\angle Z$; $XY = 5$; $XZ = 3$; $YZ = 4$

24. Altitude $\overline{YN}$; median $\overline{YM}$; $YN = 11$; $YM = 15$

25. Given: $\overline{BC} \perp \overline{AD}$; $\overline{AC} \perp \overline{AB}$
Prove: $BC > AD$

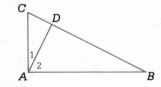

26. Given: $\overline{AC} \perp \overline{AB}$; $\overline{AD} \perp \overline{BC}$; $AB > AC$
Prove: $m\angle 1 < m\angle 2$

27. Prove the Triangle Inequality Theorem.

28. The air distances from New York to Chicago, Montreal, and Washington, D.C. are 714 mi., 331 mi., and 205 mi., respectively. Use the Triangle Inequality Theorem to find maximum and minimum air distances between Chicago and Montreal, Montreal and Washington, and Chicago and Washington.

29. Four stores are located at the vertices of convex quadrilateral $ABCD$. They are supplied from a warehouse at P, the intersection of the diagonals. Show that the sum of the distances from each store to P is less than the sum of the distances to any other point (such as Q).

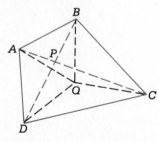

Set C

30. Write an indirect proof for Theorem 4.14.

31. Prove that the perimeter of a convex quadrilateral is greater than the sum of the lengths of its diagonals.

Chapter 4   Congruent Triangles

Career   Carpenter

Carlos Perez is a carpenter. Some objects that Carlos has built are shown below. When Carlos makes a duplicate of an object, he uses the same measurements.

State the postulate or theorem which guarantees that the triangle for a duplicate object will be congruent to the triangle for the original object.

1. Top of a corner desk;
   AF, FE

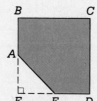

3. Rafters for a garage roof;
   XY, YZ, XZ

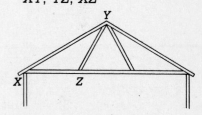

2. Side of a secretary desk;
   RQ, m∠RQL

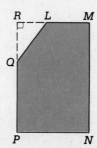

4. Section of a wall planter;
   m∠Y, m∠Z, YZ

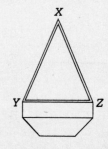

Inequalities in Two Triangles

Top views of a door are shown below. The door and the opening in the frame are each 70 cm wide. As the door is opened, the angle at H becomes larger and the distance between the edge of the door and the frame becomes greater. This suggests the Hinge Theorem given below.

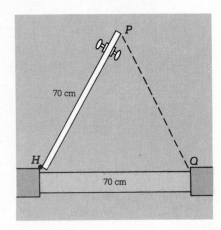

Theorem 4.17

Hinge Theorem

If two sides of one triangle are congruent to two sides of another triangle and the measures of the included angles are unequal, then the lengths of the third sides are unequal in the same order.

Given	$\overline{AC} \cong \overline{DF}$; $\overline{AB} \cong \overline{DE}$; $m\angle A > m\angle D$	
Prove	$BC > EF$	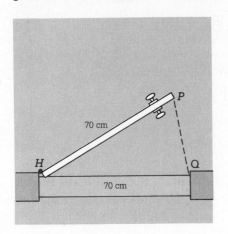
Plan for Proof	Draw $\overrightarrow{AG}$ so $\angle BAG \cong \angle EDF$. Show that $\overrightarrow{AG}$ is in the interior of $\angle BAC$. Choose H on $\overrightarrow{AG}$ so that $\overline{AH} \cong \overline{DF}$; draw $\overline{BH}$. Since $\overline{AB} \cong \overline{DE}$, $\triangle ABH \cong \triangle DEF$ by SAS. Show $\overline{BH} \cong \overline{EF}$.	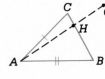

Case I If H lies on $\overline{BC}$:

$BH + HC = BC$ by the Segment
Addition Postulate.
Show $BC > BH$.
Substitute to show $BC > EF$.

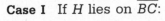

Case II If H does not lie on $\overline{BC}$:

Draw $\overrightarrow{AJ}$, the bisector of $\angle CAH$.
Let K be the intersection of $\overrightarrow{AJ}$ and $\overline{CB}$.
Draw $\overline{KH}$.
Use transitivity to show $\overline{AC} \cong \overline{AH}$.
Show $\triangle ACK \cong \triangle AHK$ by SAS.

Show $\overline{KC} \cong \overline{KH}$.
Use the Triangle Inequality Thm. to show
$BK + KH > BH$.
Substitute to show $BK + KC > BH$.
Use the Segment Addition Post. and
substitution to show $BC > EF$.

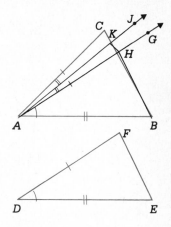

The converse of the Hinge Theorem is also true.

<table>
<tr><td>**Theorem 4.18**</td><td>If two sides of one triangle are congruent to two sides of another triangle and the lengths of the third sides are unequal, then the measures of the angles included between the congruent sides are unequal in the same order.</td></tr>
</table>

Given $\overline{XY} \cong \overline{RS}$; $\overline{XZ} \cong \overline{RT}$; $ZY > TS$

Prove $m\angle X > m\angle R$

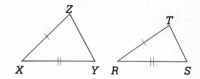

Proof   Either (1) $m\angle X > m\angle R$ or (2) $m\angle X \not> m\angle R$. Suppose
$m\angle X \not> m\angle R$. Then either $m\angle X < m\angle R$ or $m\angle X = m\angle R$.

If $m\angle X < m\angle R$, then $ZY < TS$ by the Hinge Theorem. But
this contradicts the Given. Thus, $m\angle X < m\angle R$ is false.

If $m\angle X = m\angle R$, then $\triangle XYZ \cong \triangle RST$ by SAS and $\overline{ZY} \cong \overline{TS}$.
But this contradicts the Given. Thus, $m\angle X = m\angle R$ is false.

Therefore, the assumption that $m\angle X \not> m\angle R$ is false. We
conclude that $m\angle X > m\angle R$.

Class Exercises

[1-3] Fill in the blank with > or <.

1.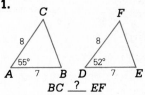

BC _?_ EF

2.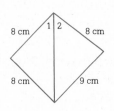

XY _?_ RS

3.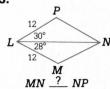

MN _?_ NP

[4-6] Tell whether ∠1 or ∠2 has the greater measure.

4.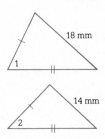

5.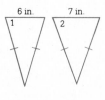

6.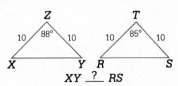

Written Exercises

Set A

[1-4] Fill in the blank with > or <.

1. If $\overline{AE} \cong \overline{CB}$, $m\angle ABC = 100$, $m\angle BAE = 78$, then AC _?_ BE.

2. If $\angle EAD \cong \angle CBD$, $AD = 5$, $BD = 7$, then $m\angle E$ _?_ $m\angle C$.

3. If $\angle R \cong \angle V$, $RT = 13$, $TV = 10$, then $m\angle RWT$ _?_ $m\angle VWT$.

4. If $ST = TU$, $m\angle WTS = 92$, $m\angle WTU = 88$, then SW _?_ UW.

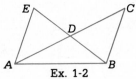

Ex. 1-2

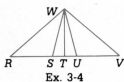

Ex. 3-4

5. Given: $\overline{GH} \cong \overline{GJ}$; $m\angle HGK > m\angle JGK$
Prove: $HK > JK$

6. Given: $\overline{GH} \cong \overline{GJ}$; $HK > JK$
Prove: $m\angle HGK > m\angle JGK$

Ex. 5-6

Chapter 4 Congruent Triangles

7. Given: $\overline{VW} \cong \overline{XY}$; $m\angle WXY > m\angle VWX$
Prove: $WY > VX$

8. Given: $\overline{VW} \cong \overline{XY}$; $WY > VX$
Prove: $m\angle WXY > m\angle VWX$

9. Given: $\overline{VW} \cong \overline{XY}$; $\overline{WZ} \cong \overline{XZ}$; $WY > VX$
Prove: $m\angle YXZ > m\angle VWZ$

10. Given: $\overline{VW} \cong \overline{XY}$; $\angle ZWX \cong \angle ZXW$;
$m\angle WXY > m\angle VWX$
Prove: $YZ > VZ$

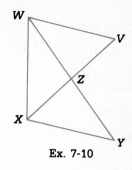

Ex. 7-10

11. Given: $\overline{AD} \cong \overline{BC}$; $m\angle BAD < m\angle ABC$
Prove: $BD < AC$

12. Given: $\overline{AD} \cong \overline{BC}$; $BD < AC$
Prove: $m\angle BAD < m\angle ABC$

13. Given: $\overline{AD} \cong \overline{BC}$; $\overline{AD} \parallel \overline{BC}$;
$\angle BAD$ is acute.
Prove: $BD < AC$

14. Given: $\overline{AD} \cong \overline{BC}$; $\overline{AD} \parallel \overline{BC}$; $BD < AC$
Prove: $\angle ABC$ is obtuse.

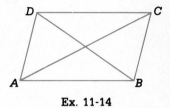

Ex. 11-14

Set B

15. Given: $\overline{MQ} \cong \overline{NQ}$; $\overline{PN} \cong \overline{RM}$; $PQ > QR$
Prove: $SM > SN$

16. Given: $\overline{MQ} \cong \overline{NQ}$; $\overline{PN} \cong \overline{RM}$; $SN < SM$
Prove: $QR < PQ$

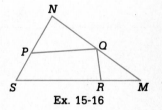

Ex. 15-16

17. Given: $\overline{AD} \cong \overline{BD}$; $m\angle ADE < m\angle BDE$
Prove: $AE < BE$

18. Given: $\overline{AD} \cong \overline{BD}$; $BC < AC$
Prove: $m\angle BDC < m\angle ADC$

Set C

19. Given: $\angle BAD \cong \angle ABD$;
$m\angle ADE < m\angle BDE$
Prove: $BC < AC$

20. Given: $\angle BAD \cong \angle ABD$; $BC < AC$
Prove: $m\angle ADE < m\angle BDE$

21. Given: $\overline{AD} \cong \overline{BD}$; $AE < BE$
Prove: $m\angle BDC < m\angle CDA$

22. Given: $\angle ABD \cong \angle BAD$; $m\angle BDC < m\angle CDA$
Prove: $AE < BE$

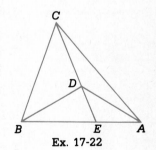

Ex. 17-22

4.9 Inequalities in Two Triangles

Chapter Summary

1. Corresponding parts of congruent triangles are congruent. (page 167)

2. Two triangles can be proved congruent by the
   a. SSS Postulate (page 172)
   b. SAS Postulate (page 173)
   c. ASA Postulate (page 173)
   d. AAS Theorem (page 177)

3. Two right triangles can be proved congruent by the
   a. LL Theorem (page 178)
   b. HA Theorem (page 178)
   c. LA Theorem (page 178)
   d. HL Theorem (page 198)

4. Two sides of a triangle are congruent if and only if the angles opposite those sides are congruent. (pages 197-198)

5. The lengths of two sides of a triangle are unequal if and only if the measures of the angles opposite those sides are unequal in the same order. (page 202)

6. **Triangle Inequality Theorem** The sum of the lengths of any two sides of a triangle is greater than the length of the third side. (page 203)

7. The perpendicular segment from a point to a line (or plane) is the shortest segment from the point to the line (or plane). Its length is the distance from the point to the line (or plane). (page 204)

8. **Hinge Theorem** If two sides of one triangle are congruent to two sides of another triangle and the measures of the included angles are unequal, then the lengths of the third sides are unequal in the same order. (page 208)

9. If two sides of one triangle are congruent to two sides of another triangle and the lengths of the third sides are unequal, then the measures of the angles included between the congruent sides are unequal in the same order. (page 209)

Chapter Review

Lesson 4.1
Page 166

[1-3] Given: $\triangle KLM \cong \triangle RST$

1. List the pairs of congruent sides.
2. List the pairs of congruent angles.
3. Name the side included between $\angle RST$ and $\angle STR$.

Lesson 4.2
Page 172

4. If $\angle B \cong \angle E$, then $\triangle ABC \cong \triangle DEF$ by the __?__ Postulate.
5. If $\overline{AC} \cong \overline{DF}$, then $\triangle ABC \cong \triangle DEF$ by the __?__ Postulate.
6. Given: $\overline{JK} \cong \overline{NO}$; $\angle HJK \cong \angle MNO$; $\angle JKH \cong \angle NOM$. What conclusion can you draw and why?

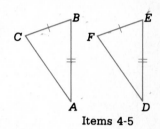

Items 4-5

Lesson 4.3
Page 177

[7-9] Which postulate or theorem justifies $\triangle RST \cong \triangle WXY$?

7. $\overline{RT} \cong \overline{WY}$; $\angle S \cong \angle X$; $\overline{TR} \perp \overline{RS}$; $\overline{YW} \perp \overline{XW}$
8. Rt. $\angle$s at R and W; $\overline{RS} \cong \overline{WX}$; $\overline{RT} \cong \overline{WY}$
9. $\overline{ST} \cong \overline{XY}$; $\angle T \cong \angle Y$; $\overline{TR} \perp \overline{RS}$; $\overline{YW} \perp \overline{WX}$

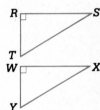

10. Given: C is the midpoint of $\overline{BD}$; $\angle A \cong \angle E$; $\angle B \cong \angle D$
    Prove: $\triangle ABC \cong \triangle EDC$
11. Given: C is the midpoint of $\overline{BD}$; $\overline{AC} \parallel \overline{ED}$; $\overline{AC} \cong \overline{DE}$
    Prove: $\triangle ABC \cong \triangle ECD$

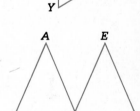

Items 10-11

Lesson 4.4
Page 183

12. Given: $\angle K \cong \angle F$; $\overline{HK} \cong \overline{HF}$
    Prove: $\overline{FG} \cong \overline{JK}$
13. Given: $\overline{FG} \perp \overline{KF}$; $\overline{JK} \perp \overline{KF}$; $\overline{GH} \cong \overline{JH}$
    Prove: $\overline{FH} \cong \overline{KH}$
14. Given: H is midpt. of $\overline{KF}$ and $\overline{GJ}$.
    Prove: $\overline{FG} \parallel \overline{JK}$

Items 12-14

Lesson 4.5
Page 187

15. Given: $\overline{XY} \perp \overline{VZ}$; $\overline{VW} \perp \overline{XZ}$; $\overline{VW} \cong \overline{XY}$
    Prove: $\triangle XYZ \cong \triangle VWZ$
16. Given: $\overline{YT} \cong \overline{WT}$; $\overline{VT} \cong \overline{TX}$
    Prove: $\overline{YZ} \cong \overline{ZW}$

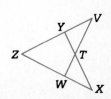

Lesson 4.6
Page 193

17. Draw $\overline{AB}$. Construct an isosceles right triangle with $\overline{AB}$ as a leg.

18. Draw $\overline{PQ}$. Choose a point R not on $\overleftrightarrow{PQ}$. Construct a line through R perpendicular to $\overleftrightarrow{PQ}$. Write a plan for justification.

[19-21] Is each statement sometimes, always, or never true?

19. The median of $\triangle ABC$ through A is parallel to $\overleftrightarrow{BC}$.

20. The altitude of $\triangle ABC$ from A intersects $\overline{BC}$ at a right angle.

21. A triangle has three angle bisectors.

Lesson 4.7
Page 197

22. $m\angle B = \underline{\ ?\ }$

23. $AB = \underline{\ ?\ }$ cm

24. $BC = \underline{\ ?\ }$ cm

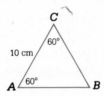

25. Given: $\overline{XZ} \cong \overline{YZ}$. Prove: $\angle 1 \cong \angle 2$

26. Given: $\angle 1 \cong \angle 2$. Prove: $\overline{XZ} \cong \overline{YZ}$

27. Given: $\overline{XZ} \cong \overline{YZ}$; $\overline{ZW} \perp \overline{XY}$.
Prove: $\overline{ZW}$ bisects $\overline{XY}$.

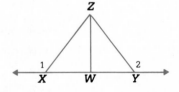

Lesson 4.8
Page 202

28. The smallest angle of $\triangle DEF$ is $\underline{\ ?\ }$. Its largest angle is $\underline{\ ?\ }$.

29. In $\triangle FED$, $\overline{FG}$ is the median, $\overline{FH}$ is the altitude, and $\overline{FJ}$ is the angle bisector from F. Which of the three segments is shortest?

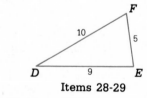

Items 28-29

30. Find the possible values for x.

31. If $m\angle J > m\angle K$, what are possible values for x?

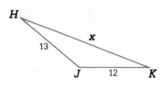

Lesson 4.9
Page 208

32. Given: $\overline{AD} \cong \overline{BC}$; $m\angle CAD < m\angle ACB$
Prove: $CD < AB$

33. Given: $\overline{AD} \cong \overline{BC}$; $AB > CD$
Prove: $m\angle ACB > m\angle CAD$

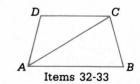

Items 32-33

Chapter Test

[1-7] Tell whether each statement is always, sometimes, or never true. Explain.

1. If $\triangle ABC \cong \triangle DEF$, then $\overline{BC} \cong \overline{EF}$.

2. If $\triangle ABC \cong \triangle DEF$, then $\overline{CB} \cong \overline{ED}$.

3. The base angles of an isosceles right triangle are 30° angles.

4. The perpendicular segment from a vertex of a triangle to the opposite side is a median.

5. A median of a triangle bisects a side of the triangle.

6. The sum of the lengths of two sides of a triangle is greater than the length of the third side.

7. If the measures of two angles of a triangle are unequal, then the sides opposite those angles are congruent.

[8-11] Which postulate or theorem justifies $\triangle ABC \cong \triangle DEF$?

8. $\angle C \cong \angle F$; $\overline{AC} \cong \overline{DF}$; $\overline{BC} \cong \overline{EF}$

9. $\angle C \cong \angle F$; $\angle D \cong \angle A$; $\overline{AB} \cong \overline{DE}$

10. $\overline{AC} \cong \overline{DF}$; $\overline{AB} \cong \overline{DE}$; $\overline{BC} \cong \overline{EF}$

11. $\angle C$ and $\angle F$ are rt. $\angle$s; $\overline{AB} \cong \overline{DE}$; $\overline{BC} \cong \overline{EF}$

[12-14] Solve for x.

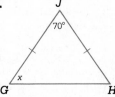

12.

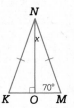

13.

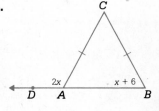

14.

15. Given: $\overline{PQ} \cong \overline{QR}$; $m\angle PQS < m\angle RQS$
    Prove: $PS < RS$

16. Given: $\overline{PQ} \cong \overline{QR}$; $PS < RS$
    Prove: $m\angle PQS < m\angle RQS$

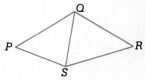

17. Given: $\overline{AF} \cong \overline{DE}$; $\angle A \cong \angle D$; $\angle F \cong \angle E$
    Prove: $\overline{AB} \cong \overline{CD}$

18. Given: $\overline{AF} \cong \overline{BE}$; $\overline{AF} \parallel \overline{BE}$; $\overline{AC} \cong \overline{BD}$
    Prove: $\overline{FC} \parallel \overline{DE}$

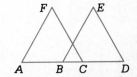

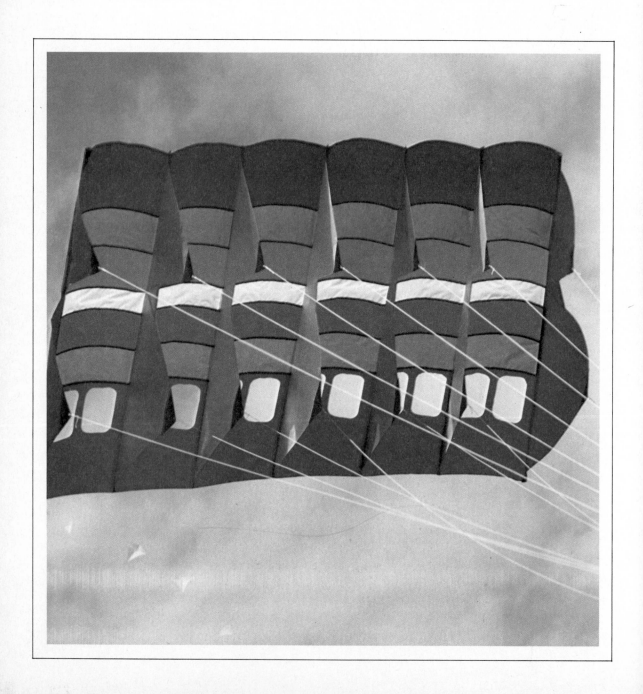

Using Congruent Triangles

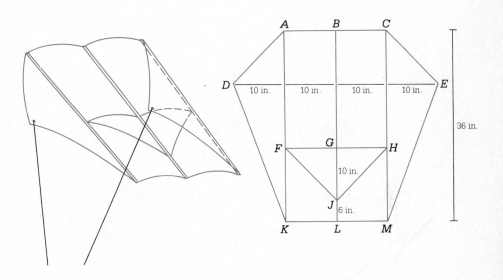

The multicelled kite on page 216 is composed of several adjoining kites. Each cell is a kite called a Scott Sled. Use the pattern for a Scott Sled above to answer these questions. You may assume that lines that look perpendicular are perpendicular.

1. Find *AF*.
2. Name a square using the labeled points.
3. Use the labeled points to name eight rectangles.
4. A trapezoid such as *AFJB*, has exactly one pair of parallel sides. Name five other trapezoids.

In this chapter, several types of quadrilaterals will be defined. By drawing one or both diagonals, you will use the properties of triangles to prove the properties of quadrilaterals.

5.1   Quadrilaterals

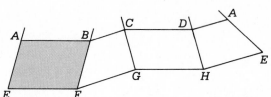

Tony Merlo is a sheet metal worker. He makes transition
pieces for heating, ventilating, and air-conditioning ducts. He
uses patterns containing quadrilaterals similar to the one
above to form the pieces.

In the shaded quadrilateral, $\overline{AB}$ and $\overline{EF}$ do not have a
common vertex. These two sides are called **opposite sides.**

Which quadrilaterals in the pattern
appear to have exactly one pair of
opposite sides parallel? These
figures are called trapezoids.

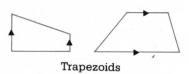

Trapezoids

Definition A **trapezoid** is a quadrilateral with exactly one pair of opposite
sides parallel.

Which quadrilaterals in the pattern
appear to have two pairs of opposite
sides parallel? These figures are
called parallelograms.

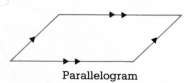

Parallelogram

Definition A **parallelogram** is a quadrilateral in which both pairs of
opposite sides are parallel.

We write parallelogram $PQRS$ as $\square\,PQRS$.

Certain parallelograms have special names.

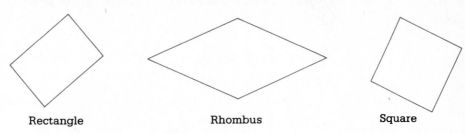

Rectangle   Rhombus   Square

Definition   A **rectangle** is a parallelogram with four right angles.

Definition   A **rhombus** is a parallelogram with four congruent sides.

Definition   A **square** is a rectangle with four congruent sides.

Class Exercises

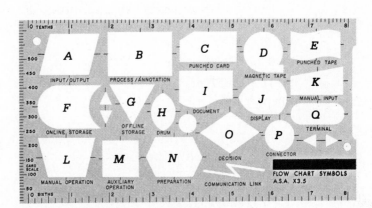

The template above is used to draw flow charts. List all the figures that appear to be:

1. Quadrilaterals
2. Trapezoids
3. Parallelograms
4. Rectangles
5. Squares
6. Rhombuses
7. Regular polygons
8. Rectangles that are not rhombuses
9. Rhombuses that are not rectangles
10. Shapes that are not polygons

Written Exercises

Set A

[1-10] True or false. If false, explain.

1. Every parallelogram is a quadrilateral.
2. Some parallelograms are not squares.
3. Every square is a trapezoid.
4. Every trapezoid is a convex polygon.
5. Some quadrilaterals are neither trapezoids nor parallelograms.
6. Some rectangles have no congruent angles.
7. Some parallelograms are not plane figures.
8. No trapezoids are rectangles.
9. A figure could be both a square and a parallelogram but not a rectangle.
10. Some rectangles are rhombuses.

[11-16] Refer to the diagram at the right.

11. $m \angle U = $ __?__
12. $m \angle S = $ __?__
13. $m \angle MNT = $ __?__
14. $m \angle RMN = $ __?__
15. $m \angle UMN = $ __?__
16. $m \angle MNS = $ __?__

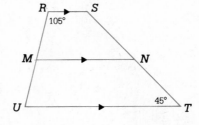

[17-22] Each quadrilateral in the pattern for the transition piece below is a trapezoid.

17. Name the parallel sides of trapezoid *ABYX*.
18. Name the parallel sides of trapezoid *BCZY*.
19. $m \angle 1 = $ __?__
20. $m \angle 2 = $ __?__
21. $m \angle 3 = $ __?__
22. $m \angle 4 = $ __?__

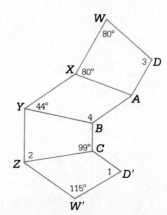

23. If the perimeter of rhombus *QRST* is 72*b*, what is the length of one side in terms of *b*?

24. If the length of one side of square *ABCD* is 3*y* − 4 what is the perimeter of the square in terms of *y*?

[25-26] Given rhombus *ABCD* and square *JKLM*. Find the length of each side.

25.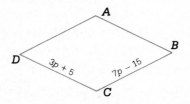

26.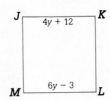

[27-28] Given □*EFGH* and trapezoid *QRST*. Find the measure of the designated angles.

27.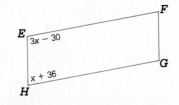

28.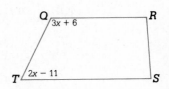

29. Given: □*RUBY*
Prove: ∠*R* and ∠*U* are supplementary;
∠*U* and ∠*B* are supplementary.

30. Given: Trapezoid *OPAL*;
∠*O* ≅ ∠*P*; $\overline{OP} \parallel \overline{AL}$
Prove: ∠*L* and ∠*P* are
supplementary.

Set B

[31-34] Decide if each statement is true or false. If it is true, explain. If it is false, give a counterexample.

31. If a quadrilateral has three right angles, then it is a rectangle.

32. If a parallelogram has one right angle, then it is a rectangle.

33. If two pairs of consecutive angles of a quadrilateral are supplementary, then the quadrilateral is a parallelogram.

34. If a quadrilateral has two right angles, then it is a parallelogram.

5.1 Quadrilaterals

221

35. Given: $\square ABCD$
Prove: $\angle A \cong \angle C$; $\angle B \cong \angle D$

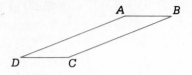

[36-38] Follow these steps to get an unexpected result.

a. Draw a large triangle, $\triangle ABC$. Let X be any point between B and C.

b. Draw a segment through X which is parallel to $\overline{AB}$. (You can put lined paper under your drawing to help you.) Label the intersection with $\overline{AC}$ point Y.

c. Draw a segment through Y parallel to $\overline{BC}$. Label the intersection with $\overline{AB}$ point Z.

d. Draw a segment through Z parallel to $\overline{AC}$. Label the intersection with $\overline{BC}$ point X'.

e. Repeat steps **b-d,** starting with X' instead of X. Label the new points Y', Z', and X''.

36. What appears to be true about X and X''?

37. At what point on $\overline{BC}$ would X and X' coincide?

38. Assuming that your answer to exercise 36 is true, name six parallelograms and three trapezoids in your drawing whose vertices are the labeled points.

Set C

39. Given: Quadrilateral $PLUM$; $\angle P \cong \angle U$; $\angle L \cong \angle M$
Prove: $PLUM$ is a parallelogram.

40. Prove that quadrilateral $PEAR$ is a trapezoid if the angle bisectors of $\angle P$ and $\angle R$ are perpendicular but the angle bisectors of $\angle P$ and $\angle E$ are not perpendicular.

Geometry Maintenance

1. Write the converse of the SSS Postulate.

2. Is the converse true or false?

3. Write the SSS Postulate and its converse as one *if and only if* statement.

4. Is the *if and only if* statement true or false?

5.2 Properties of Parallelograms

One property of a parallelogram is given in its definition: it is a quadrilateral with two pairs of opposite sides parallel.

A diagonal of a parallelogram divides it into two triangles. Comparing these triangles in the figure at the right suggests another property of parallelograms stated in Theorem 5.1.

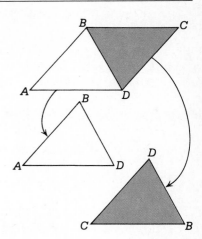

Theorem 5.1	A diagonal and the sides of a parallelogram form two congruent triangles.

Given $\square ABCD$ with diagonal $\overline{DB}$

Prove $\triangle ABD \cong \triangle CDB$

Plan for Proof   Use alt. int. $\angle$s to show $\angle 1 \cong \angle 2$ and $\angle 3 \cong \angle 4$. Use ASA to show that $\triangle ABD \cong \triangle CDB$.

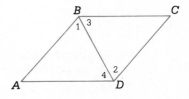

Proof

Statements	Reasons
1. $\square ABCD$ with diagonal $\overline{BD}$.	1. Given
2. $\overline{BD} \cong \overline{DB}$	2. Congruence of segments is reflexive.
3. $\overline{AB} \parallel \overline{CD}$	3. Def. of $\square$ [1]
4. $\angle 1 \cong \angle 2$	4. _?_
5. $\overline{AD} \parallel \overline{BC}$	5. _?_
6. $\angle 3 \cong \angle 4$	6. _?_
7. $\triangle ABD \cong \triangle CDB$	7. ASA Post. [2, 4, 6]

Two corollaries of Theorem 5.1 give additional properties of parallelograms. Their proofs are exercises 18 and 19.

Theorem 5.2	Opposite sides of a parallelogram are congruent.

Theorem 5.3   Opposite angles of a parallelogram are congruent.

Still another property results from drawing both diagonals.

Theorem 5.4   The diagonals of a parallelogram bisect each other.

Given $\square ABCD$ with diagonals $\overline{AC}$ and $\overline{BD}$

Prove $\overline{AC}$ and $\overline{BD}$ bisect each other.

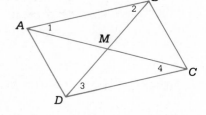

Plan for Proof   Use Theorem 5.2 and ASA to show
that $\triangle ABM \cong \triangle CDM$.
Then show that M is the midpoint of
$\overline{AC}$ and $\overline{BD}$.

Proof

Statements	Reasons
1. $\square ABCD$	1. Given
2. $\overline{AB} \cong \overline{CD}$	2. Opp. sides of a $\square$ are $\cong$. [1]
3. $\overline{AB} \parallel \overline{CD}$	3. Def. of $\square$ [1]
4. $\angle 1 \cong \angle 4$; $\angle 2 \cong \angle 3$	4. 2 lines $\parallel \Rightarrow$ _?_
5. $\triangle ABM \cong \triangle CDM$	5. ASA Post. [2, 4]
6. $\overline{AM} \cong \overline{CM}$; $\overline{BM} \cong \overline{DM}$	6. _?_
7. $AM = CM$; $BM = DM$	7. Def. of $\cong$ seg. [6]
8. M is the midpt. of $\overline{AC}$ and $\overline{BD}$	8. Def. of midpt. [7]
9. $\overline{AC}$ and $\overline{BD}$ bisect each other.	9. Def. of bisect [8]

The properties of parallelograms are summarized below.

Properties of Parallelograms

1. Opposite sides are parallel.
2. A diagonal and the sides form two congruent triangles.
3. Opposite sides are congruent.
4. Opposite angles are congruent.
5. Diagonals bisect each other.

The distance between two parallel lines is the length of a segment drawn from any point on one line perpendicular to the other line. Thus, the distance between parallel lines *m* and *n* at the right is *AB*, *CD*, or *EF*. These distances seem to be equal. You can use the properties of parallelograms to prove this as a theorem.

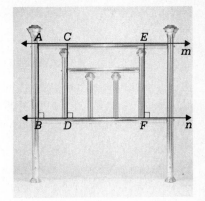

Theorem 5.5 The distance between two given parallel lines is constant.

Given $\ell \parallel k$; P and Q are any two points on ℓ; $\overline{PR} \perp k$; $\overline{QS} \perp k$

Prove $PR = QS$

Plan for Proof Show that $PQSR$ is a parallelogram. Use Theorem 5.2 to show $PR = QS$.

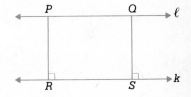

Proof

Statements	Reasons
1. P and Q are on ℓ; $\overline{PR} \perp k$; $\overline{QS} \perp k$; $\ell \parallel k$	1. Given
2. $\overline{PR} \parallel \overline{QS}$	2. In a plane __?__
3. $PQSR$ is a $\square$	3. Def. of $\square$ [1, 2]
4. $\overline{PR} \cong \overline{QS}$	4. Opp. sides of a $\square$ are $\cong$. [3]
5. $PR = QS$	5. Def. of $\cong$ seg. [4]

Class Exercises

[1-5] Given: $\square LEFT$

1. Name a pair of parallel lines.
2. Name a pair of congruent angles.
3. Name a pair of congruent sides.
4. Name a pair of supplementary angles.
5. Why is $\triangle LFT \cong \triangle FLE$?

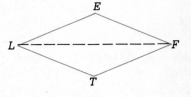

[6-12] Given: ▱ *WING*

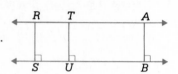

6. If $m \angle GWI = 115$, then $m \angle GNI = \underline{\ ?\ }$.

7. If $WI = 12$, then $GN = \underline{\ ?\ }$.

8. If $m \angle WGN = 85$, then $m \angle WIN = \underline{\ ?\ }$.

9. If $WX = 11.5$, then $NX = \underline{\ ?\ }$.

10. If $GI = 38$, then $XI = \underline{\ ?\ }$.

11. If $GI = 15$, $WI = 6$, and $IN = 12$, then
$GN + GW = \underline{\ ?\ }$.

12. If $m \angle WGI = 20$ and $m \angle WIG = 40$, then $m \angle WIN = \underline{\ ?\ }$.

[13-14] Given: $\overleftrightarrow{AR} \parallel \overleftrightarrow{SB}$; $\overline{RS} \perp \overleftrightarrow{SB}$; and $\overline{TU} \perp \overleftrightarrow{SB}$

13. How do you know that $\overline{RS} \parallel \overline{TU}$?

14. If $RS = 8$ and $\overline{AB} \perp \overleftrightarrow{SB}$, then $AB = \underline{\ ?\ }$.

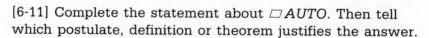

Written Exercises

Set A

[1-5] Given: ▱ *HIJK*

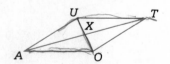

1. If $HI = 18$, find KJ.

2. If $m \angle HIJ = 135$, find $m \angle HKJ$.

3. If $HO = 10$, find HJ.

4. If the distance from K to $\overleftrightarrow{HI}$ is 15,
what is the distance from I to $\overleftrightarrow{KJ}$?

5. If $m \angle HJK = 30$ and $m \angle JHK = 40$, find $m \angle KHI$.

[6-11] Complete the statement about ▱ *AUTO*. Then tell
which postulate, definition or theorem justifies the answer.

6. $AX = \underline{\ ?\ }$

7. $\overline{AU} \parallel \underline{\ ?\ }$

8. $\triangle AUT \cong \underline{\ ?\ }$

9. $\angle AOU \cong \underline{\ ?\ }$

10. $AO = \underline{\ ?\ }$

11. $\angle UAO \cong \underline{\ ?\ }$

[12-14] Write the theorem in "if . . . then" form.

12. Theorem 5.2   **13.** Theorem 5.3   **14.** Theorem 5.4

Chapter 5 Using Congruent Triangles

[15-17] Write the converse of the theorem. Decide whether the converse seems true or false.

15. Theorem 5.2   **16.** Theorem 5.3   **17.** Theorem 5.4

18. Prove Theorem 5.2.
  Given: $\square ABCD$
  Prove: $\overline{AB} \cong \overline{CD}$; $\overline{AD} \cong \overline{BC}$

19. Complete this proof of Theorem 5.3.
  Given: $\square EFGH$
  Prove: $\angle EHG \cong \angle EFG$; $\angle HEF \cong \angle HGF$

Statements	Reasons
1. _?_	1. Given
2. Draw $\overline{EG}$ and $\overline{FH}$.	2. _?_
3. $\triangle EFG \cong \triangle GHE$	3. _?_
4. $\angle EHG \cong \angle$ _?_	4. _?_
5. $\triangle HEF \cong \triangle FGH$	5. _?_
6. _?_	6. _?_

[20-27] Given: $\square TAXI$. Solve for y or z or both.

20. $AX = 3y$; $TI = 2y + 10$

21. $m \angle TAX = 2y - 5$; $m \angle TIX = 3y - 20$

22. $AM = 6y + 4$; $IM = 4y + 26$

23. $m \angle XTI = 4y - 5$; $m \angle TXA = 3y + 10$

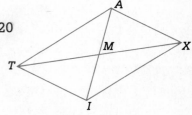

Set B

24. $TM = 3z$; $TX = 3z + 18$

25. $MI = 6y - 5$; $AI = 2y + 15$

26. $AT = 7y + z$; $XI = y + 28$; $TI = y + z$; $AX = 5$

27. $m \angle TIX = 2z + y$; $m \angle TAX = z + 20$; $m \angle ATI = z - y$

28. The DeCarlo family needs to replace four vertical slats in a railing. Which theorem guarantees that the four slats have the same length?

29. David wants to hang a rectangular mirror in the center of a hallway wall. The wall is 96 cm by 222 cm. The mirror is 46 cm by 92 cm. Explain how Theorem 5.4 suggests a way to determine the position of the mirror.

30. Given: $\square CTGD$; $\overline{CO} \perp \overline{DG}$; $\overline{AG} \perp \overline{CT}$
Prove: $\triangle COD \cong \triangle GAT$

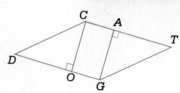

31. Given: $\square GRIN$; $\square GLAD$
Prove: $\angle A \cong \angle I$

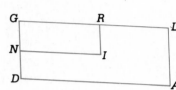

32. Given: $\overline{AB} \parallel \overline{GH}$; $\overline{CD} \parallel \overline{AB}$; $\overline{GH} \parallel \overline{EF}$; $\overline{FD} \perp \overline{CD}$; $\overline{CE} \perp \overline{EF}$
Prove: $\overline{CE} \cong \overline{DF}$

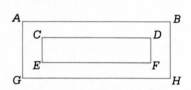

33. Given: $\square EFGH$; $\overline{EG} \cong \overline{FH}$
Prove: $\angle HEF$ is a right angle.

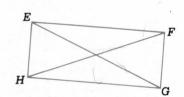

Set C

34. Given: $\triangle MNQ$ is equilateral; $\angle 1 \cong \angle 2 \cong \angle 3$
Prove: $PQRS$ is a parallelogram.

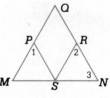

35. Given: $\square TUVW$; $\overline{TX} \cong \overline{VY}$
Prove: $\overline{XY}$ bisects $\overline{UW}$.

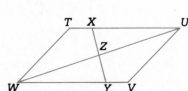

36. Is every side of a regular octagon parallel to another side? Explain.

Quadrilaterals That Are Parallelograms

To make a quilt like the one above, Ellen Jacob needed a pattern for a parallelogram. On a rectangular sheet of cardboard, she marked P on $\overrightarrow{AB}$ so that $AP = 15$ cm. She drew $\overrightarrow{PQ}$ at the proper angle. Then on $\overrightarrow{QD}$, she marked R so that $QR = AP$.

Theorem 5.6 guarantees that $APQR$ is a parallelogram.

Theorem 5.6   If two sides of a quadrilateral are parallel and congruent, then the quadrilateral is a parallelogram.

Given   Quadrilateral $ABCD$; $\overline{AD} \parallel \overline{BC}$; $\overline{AD} \cong \overline{BC}$

Prove $ABCD$ is a parallelogram.

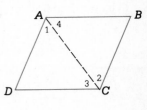

Plan for Proof   Draw $\overline{AC}$.
Show $\angle 1 \cong \angle 2$ and $\triangle ACB \cong \triangle CAD$ by SAS.
Then show $\angle 3 \cong \angle 4$ and $\overline{AB} \parallel \overline{CD}$.

Proof

Statements	Reasons
1. Quadrilateral $ABCD$	1. Given
2. Draw $\overline{AC}$.	2. _?_ Postulate
3. $\overline{AC} \cong \overline{CA}$	3. _?_
4. $\overline{AD} \parallel \overline{BC}$; $\overline{AD} \cong \overline{BC}$	4. Given
5. $\angle 1 \cong \angle 2$	5. 2 lines $\parallel \Rightarrow$ _?_ . [4]
6. $\triangle ACB \cong \triangle CAD$	6. SAS Postulate [3, 4, 5]
7. $\angle 3 \cong \angle 4$	7. _?_
8. $\overline{AB} \parallel \overline{CD}$	8. Alt. int. $\angle$s $\cong \Rightarrow$ _?_ . [7]
9. $ABCD$ is a parallelogram.	9. Def. of $\square$ [4, 8]

The converses of Theorems 5.2 and 5.4 provide two additional methods for proving that a quadrilateral is a parallelogram. The proofs of these theorems are exercises 18 and 19.

Theorem 5.7   If both pairs of opposite sides of a quadrilateral are congruent, then the quadrilateral is a parallelogram.

Given   Quadrilateral $ABCD$; $\overline{AB} \cong \overline{CD}$; $\overline{BC} \cong \overline{AD}$

Prove $ABCD$ is a parallelogram.

Plan for Proof   Draw $\overline{BD}$.
Show $\triangle ABD \cong \triangle CDB$ by SSS.
Then $\angle 1 \cong \angle 2$, so $\overline{AB} \parallel \overline{CD}$.
Use Thm. 5.6.

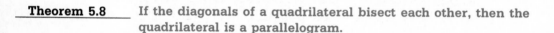

Theorem 5.8   If the diagonals of a quadrilateral bisect each other, then the quadrilateral is a parallelogram.

Given   Quadrilateral $ABCD$; diagonals $\overline{AC}$ and $\overline{BD}$ bisect each other.

Prove $ABCD$ is a parallelogram.

Plan for Proof   Show $\triangle AOB \cong \triangle COD$ by SAS.
Show $\overline{AB} \cong \overline{CD}$ and $\overline{AB} \parallel \overline{CD}$.
Then use Thm. 5.6.

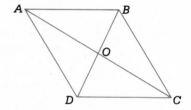

Ways to Prove a Quadrilateral is a Parallelogram

Show that:

def of parallelogram

1. Both pairs of opposite sides are parallel.
2. Both pairs of opposite sides are congruent.
3. One pair of opposite sides is parallel and congruent.
4. The diagonals bisect each other.

Class Exercises

[1-8] State the definitions or theorems which justify that *ABCD* is a parallelogram.

1. Given: $AX = 8$; $DX = 7$;
   $AC = 16$; $BD = 14$

2. Given: $m \angle ADC = 125$; $m \angle CBA = 125$;
   $m \angle DAB = 55$; $m \angle DCB = 55$

3. Given: $\overline{DC} \parallel \overline{AB}$; $\overline{AD} \parallel \overline{BC}$

4. Given: $\overline{CD} \cong \overline{AB}$; $\overline{AD} \cong \overline{BC}$

5. Given: $\overline{CD} \parallel \overline{AB}$; $\overline{AX} \cong \overline{CX}$

6. Given: $\angle 1 \cong \angle 2$; $\angle 3 \cong \angle 4$

7. Given: $\angle 1 \cong \angle 2$; $\overline{CD} \cong \overline{AB}$

8. Given: X is the midpoint of $\overline{BD}$ and $\overline{AC}$.

[9-11] Show that the statement will *not* guarantee that a quadrilateral is a parallelogram by finding a counterexample.

9. One pair of sides is congruent and another pair of sides is parallel.

10. The diagonals are perpendicular.

11. One diagonal is the perpendicular bisector of the other.

Written Exercises

Set A

1. The diagram shows parallel rulers constructed so that $PQ = RS$ and $PR = QS$. Why is $\overline{PR} \parallel \overline{QS}$ for all positions of the rulers?

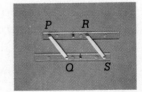

2. Jason built a frame for a bookcase. How can he use Theorem 5.6 to position the shelves parallel to the base of the frame?

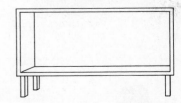

3. Assume that the wall standards shown are parallel. Where would the fourth shelf support be placed so that the shelves are parallel? State the theorem that supports your conclusion.

4. In the photo $WX = YZ$. If each cable was lowered 60 feet from the rooftop, why is $WXYZ$ a parallelogram?

[5-10] Find x so that $ABCD$ is a parallelogram. Tell which theorem or definition justifies your answer.

5. $AM = 10$; $CM = 10$; $DM = 9$; $BM = x$

6. $AD = 7$; $AB = 12$; $CD = 12$; $BC = x$

7. $m\angle 1 = x$; $m\angle 3 = 40$; $m\angle 5 = 50$; $m\angle 7 = 40$

8. $DM = 6$; $BM = 6$; $AC = 17$; $CM = x$

9. $m\angle 4 = m\angle 8 = 38$; $m\angle 7 = x$; $m\angle ADC = 153$

10. $m\angle 1 = 43$; $m\angle ADC = 105$; $m\angle 2 = m\angle 6 = x$

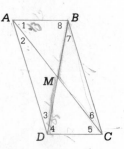

[11-16] Prove that $QRST$ is a parallelogram.

11. Given: $\overline{ST} \parallel \overline{QR}$; $\overline{TX} \cong \overline{RX}$

12. Given: $\angle TQR$ and $\angle QRS$ are supplementary; $\angle QRS$ and $\angle RST$ are supplementary.

13. Given: $\angle 1 \cong \angle 2$; $\angle QTS \cong \angle SRQ$

14. Given: $\overline{TX} \cong \overline{RX}$; $\overline{QX} \cong \overline{XS}$

15. Given: $\angle 1 \cong \angle 2$; $\angle 3 \cong \angle 4$

16. Given: $\angle TQR$ and $\angle QTS$ are supplementary; $\angle TSR$ and $\angle SRQ$ are supplementary; $\angle SRQ \cong \angle QTS$.

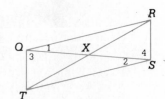

17. Draw a quadrilateral which is not a parallelogram. Locate the midpoint of each side. Connect the midpoints in order. What appears to be true about the quadrilateral formed?

18. Prove Theorem 5.7.

19. Prove Theorem 5.8.

20. Prove the converse of Theorem 5.3: If both pairs of opposite angles of a quadrilateral are congruent, then the quadrilateral is a parallelogram.

[21-24] Find x and y so that $KMNO$ is a parallelogram.

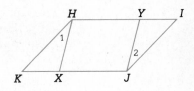

21. $KM = x + y$; $MN = 2y + 6$;
ON $= 2x - 7$; $KO = 3y$

22. $KM = x + y$; $ON = 3x - 4y$;
$m\angle MKN = x + 5$; $m\angle KNO = 2x - 10$

23. $m\angle KOM = 6y + 1$; $m\angle KMO = 3x + 2$;
$m\angle MON = 2x + 8$; $m\angle OMN = 4y + 7$

24. $KP = 2x + 4$; $MP = 6 + 3y$; $NP = 15 - y$; $OP = x + 4$

25. Given: $\square HIJK$; $\angle 1 \cong \angle 2$
Prove: $HXJY$ is a parallelogram.

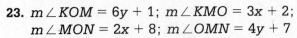

26. Given: $\overline{AX} \cong \overline{CX}$; $\overline{CY} \cong \overline{BY}$;
$\overline{XY} \cong \overline{ZY}$
Prove: $ABZX$ is a parallelogram.

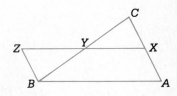

27. Prove: If the sum of the lengths of any two consecutive sides of a quadrilateral is a constant, then the quadrilateral is a parallelogram.

28. Given: $ABCD$ is a square;
$\overline{AY} \cong \overline{CW}$; $\overline{XW} \perp \overline{AC}$; $\overline{YZ} \perp \overline{AC}$
Prove: $WXYZ$ is a parallelogram.

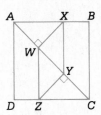

29. Given: Quadrilateral $FINE$; $\overline{IF} \cong \overline{FE} \cong \overline{EN}$; $\angle E \cong \angle I$
Prove: $FINE$ is a parallelogram.

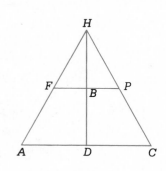

The design specifications for the truss, or bridge support, have points P and F as the midpoints of $\overline{CH}$ and $\overline{AH}$, respectively. What appears to be true about $\overline{FP}$ and $\overline{AC}$?

Point B is the midpoint of $\overline{HD}$. What seems to be true about $\overline{BF}$ and $\overline{AD}$?

Your observations should be consistent with Theorem 5.9. Its proof is exercise 18.

Theorem 5.9   **If a segment joins the midpoints of two sides of a triangle, then it is parallel to the third side, and its length is one-half the length of the third side.**

Given $\triangle ABC$; X is the midpoint of $\overline{AC}$; Y is the midpoint of $\overline{BC}$.

Prove $\overline{XY} \parallel \overline{AB}$ and $XY = \frac{1}{2}(AB)$

Plan for Proof   Locate Z on $\overrightarrow{XY}$ so that $XZ = 2(XY)$.
Draw $\overline{BZ}$.
Show $\triangle BZY \cong \triangle CXY$ by SAS.
Then $\angle 1 \cong \angle 2$ so $\overline{AX} \parallel \overline{BZ}$.
Show $\overline{BZ} \cong \overline{AX} \cong \overline{CX}$.
By Thm. 5.6, $ABZX$ is a $\square$, so $\overline{XY} \parallel \overline{AB}$.
Show $XY = \frac{1}{2}(XZ) = \frac{1}{2}(AB)$.

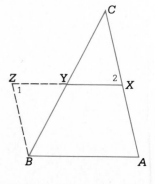

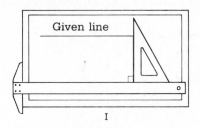
Given line

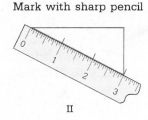
Mark with sharp pencil

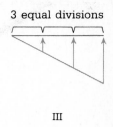
3 equal divisions

I

II

III

Cheryl Hollatz is a student in a drafting class. In mechanical drawing, she must divide a line segment into three equal parts. Her technique is shown above.

Theorem 5.10 guarantees that the segments in step III are congruent. Its proof is exercise 19.

Theorem 5.10   **If three or more parallel lines cut off congruent segments on one transversal, then they cut off congruent segments on every transversal.**

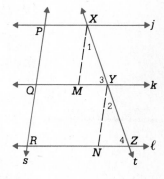

Given
$j \parallel k \parallel \ell$; j, k, and ℓ are cut by transversals s and t; $\overline{PQ} \cong \overline{QR}$

Prove
$\overline{XY} \cong \overline{YZ}$

Plan for Proof
Draw a line through X and a line through Y parallel to s.
Label the points of intersection with k and ℓ, M and N, respectively.
Then $PQMX$ and $QRNY$ are $\square$s.

Show $\overline{MX} \cong \overline{QP}$ and $\overline{RQ} \cong \overline{NY}$ to get $\overline{MX} \cong \overline{NY}$.
Show $\angle 3 \cong \angle 4$.
Show $\overline{MX} \parallel \overline{NY}$, so $\angle 1 \cong \angle 2$.
Then $\triangle XMY \cong \triangle YNZ$ by AAS.
Hence $\overline{XY} \cong \overline{YZ}$.

Note that the proof of Theorem 5.10 is planned for only three parallel lines. This plan could be generalized to prove the theorem for any number of parallel lines.

Class Exercises

[1-5] Given: A and B are midpoints of $\overline{XZ}$ and $\overline{YZ}$.

1. If $AB = 7$, then $XY = \underline{\ ?\ }$.
2. If $XY = 13$, then $AB = \underline{\ ?\ }$.
3. If $AB = 2s + 1$, then $XY = \underline{\ ?\ }$.
4. If $AB = 15$, and $XY = 3c + 15$, then $c = \underline{\ ?\ }$.
5. If $XY = p$, then $AB = \underline{\ ?\ }$.

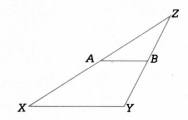

[6-9] $\overleftrightarrow{AD} \parallel \overleftrightarrow{BE} \parallel \overleftrightarrow{CF}$ and $\overline{AB} \cong \overline{BC}$.

6. Explain why $\overline{DE} \cong \overline{EF}$.
7. If $\overline{AM}$ intersects $\overleftrightarrow{BE}$ at X, why is X the midpoint of $\overline{AM}$?
8. If $DE = 5$, then $DF = \underline{\ ?\ }$.
9. If $DF = 13$, then $EF = \underline{\ ?\ }$.

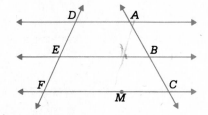

Written Exercises

Set A

[1-4] Given: X and Y are midpoints of $\overline{AB}$ and $\overline{BC}$.

1. If $AC = 13$, then $XY = \underline{\ ?\ }$.
2. If $XY = 3.3$, then $AC = \underline{\ ?\ }$.
3. If $XY = r$ and $AC = 3r - 30$, then $r = \underline{\ ?\ }$.
4. If $AC = 4t + 5$ and $XY = t + 40$, then $XY = \underline{\ ?\ }$.

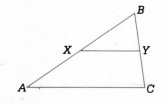

[5-8] $\overleftrightarrow{AX} \parallel \overleftrightarrow{BY} \parallel \overleftrightarrow{CZ} \parallel \overleftrightarrow{DW}$

5. If $\overline{AB} \cong \overline{BC} \cong \overline{CD}$ and $XY = 10$, then $ZW = \underline{\ ?\ }$.
6. If $AB = 17$ and $\overline{XY} \cong \overline{YZ} \cong \overline{ZW}$, then $CD = \underline{\ ?\ }$.
7. If $BC = 9$ and $\overline{WZ} \cong \overline{XY} \cong \overline{YZ}$, then $AB = CD = \underline{\ ?\ }$.
8. If $\overline{BC} \cong \overline{CD}$ and $WY = 21$, then $ZW = \underline{\ ?\ }$.

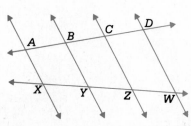

9. Mike is building a model plane. He must divide a strip of balsa wood into ten congruent pieces to glue onto the wings. Explain how Mike can use the ruled paper to mark congruent pieces on the balsa strip.

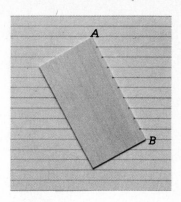

10. State the theorem which justifies your answer to exercise 10.

[11-17] In the diagram, X, Y, and Z are midpoints.

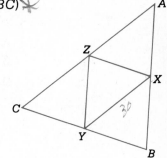

11. Prove: $XY + YZ + XZ = \frac{1}{2}(AC + AB + BC)$

12. If $AB + BC = 25$, find $ZY + XZ$.

13. If $XZ + XY = 30$, find $AC + BC$.

14. If $AB = 15$, $BC = 14$, and $AC = 21$, find $XY + YZ + XZ$.

15. If $XY + YZ + XZ = r + s$, find $AB + BC + AC$.

16. If $XY = 2u + 4$, $AZ = v$, and $ZC = 3u + v$, find AC, u, and v.

17. If $XY = u$, $AZ = 4v + 6$, and $ZC = u + 4v$, find AC, u, and v.

18. Prove Theorem 5.9.

19. Prove Theorem 5.10. Use three parallel lines.

20. Debbie needs to replace a panel on her garage door. She found a rectangular sheet of wood of the right size. She made a design by locating the midpoints of each side of the sheet and connecting the points. Use Theorem 5.9 to show that $WXYZ$ is a parallelogram. Why must $WXYZ$ also be a rhombus?

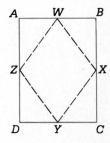

21. Prove: If the midpoints of the sides of any quadrilateral are connected in order, then the quadrilateral formed is a parallelogram.

22. Prove a second case of Theorem 5.10.
Given: $j \parallel k \parallel \ell$; transversals s
and t; $\overline{PQ} \cong \overline{QR}$
Prove: $\overline{XY} \cong \overline{YZ}$

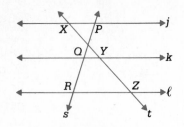

23. What other three cases need
to be considered in the proof of
Theorem 5.10?

24. Prove: If a line contains the midpoint of one side of a
triangle and is parallel to a second side, then it contains
the midpoint of the third side.

25. Given trapezoid $ABCD$ with $\overline{AB} \parallel \overline{CD}$. If X is the midpoint
of $\overline{AD}$ and Y is the midpoint of $\overline{BC}$, prove that $\overline{XY}$ bisects
$\overline{BD}$.

Construction Exercises

<u>Construction 9</u>   **Divide a segment into three congruent segments.**

Given $\overline{AB}$

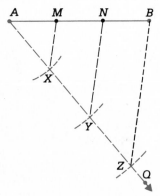

Construct   Points M and N such that $\overline{AM} \cong \overline{MN} \cong \overline{NB}$

Step 1: Draw $\overrightarrow{AQ}$ such that $\overrightarrow{AQ}$ is not
contained in $\overleftrightarrow{AB}$.

Step 2: On $\overrightarrow{AQ}$ mark off $\overline{AX} \cong \overline{XY} \cong \overline{YZ}$,
using any convenient length for AX.

Step 3: Draw $\overline{ZB}$. Through points X
and Y construct lines parallel to $\overline{ZB}$
that intersect $\overline{AB}$. Label the points
of intersection M and N, respectively.
Then $\overline{AM} \cong \overline{MN} \cong \overline{NB}$.

1. Write a plan for justifying Construction 9.

2. Divide a segment of 7 cm into three congruent segments.

3. Adapt the method of Construction 9 to divide a segment of
6 cm into five congruent segments.

4. Adapt the method of Construction 9 to divide a segment of
7 cm into four congruent segments.

5. Repeat exercise 4 using a different construction method.

Progress Check

Lesson 5.1
Page 218

[1-5] Define the term.

1. Parallelogram   3. Rhombus   5. Square
2. Rectangle   4. Trapezoid

Lesson 5.2
Page 223

[6-9] Is the statement always, sometimes, or never true?

6. The diagonals of a parallelogram are congruent.
7. The diagonals of a parallelogram bisect each other.
8. The distance between two parallel lines is constant.
9. Consecutive sides of a parallelogram are congruent.

[10-13] Given: $\square ABCD$

10. If $m\angle DAB = 56$, find $m\angle DCB$.
11. If $DO = 4.5$, then $DB = \underline{\ ?\ }$.
12. $\triangle BDA \cong \triangle \underline{\ ?\ }$.
13. If $m\angle DCB = 47$, find $m\angle CDA$.

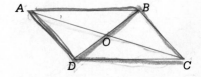

Lesson 5.3
Page 229

[14-17] Tell which theorem or definition justifies that $QRST$ is a parallelogram.

14. Given: $\overline{QR} \cong \overline{ST}$; $\overline{QR} \parallel \overline{ST}$
15. Given: $\overline{RT}$ and $\overline{QS}$ bisect each other.
16. Given: $\overline{QT} \cong \overline{RS}$; $\overline{QR} \cong \overline{ST}$
17. Given: $\overline{QR} \parallel \overline{ST}$; $\overline{QT} \parallel \overline{RS}$

Lesson 5.4
Page 234

[18-20] Given: X, Y, and Z are midpoints.

18. If $EF = 21$, find XY.
19. If $XY = 4.7$, find FZ.
20. If $XY + XZ = 14.5$, find $FG + EF$.

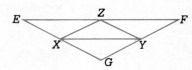

[21-22] Given: $\overleftrightarrow{AQ} \parallel \overleftrightarrow{BR} \parallel \overleftrightarrow{CS}$

21. If $AB = BC$, then $SR = \underline{\ ?\ }$.
22. If $AB = 5.5$, $AC = 11$, and $QS = 13$, then $RQ = \underline{\ ?\ }$.

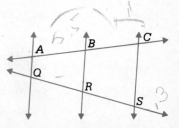

5.5   Rectangles and Rhombuses

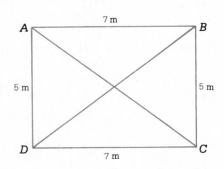

Dean Sagataw is a general contractor. When he builds a house or garage, he must be certain that the foundation is rectangular. Dean measures the sides of $ABCD$. He finds that $\overline{AB} \cong \overline{CD}$ and $\overline{AD} \cong \overline{BC}$, so he knows that $ABCD$ is a parallelogram. He next measures the diagonals and finds that $\overline{AC} \cong \overline{BD}$.

Theorem 5.11 guarantees that $\square ABCD$ is a rectangle. The two parts of the proof are exercises 25 and 26.

Theorem 5.11   A parallelogram is a rectangle if and only if its diagonals are congruent.

Part I   If $\overline{AC} \cong \overline{BD}$, then $\square ABCD$ is a rectangle.

Given $\square ABCD$ with $\overline{AC} \cong \overline{BD}$

Prove $ABCD$ is a rectangle.

Plan for Proof   Show $\triangle ADC \cong \triangle BCD$ by SSS.
Then $\angle BCD$ and $\angle CDA$ are supp. and $\cong$, so $\angle BCD$ and $\angle CDA$ are rt. $\angle$s.
Similarly $\angle DAB$ and $\angle ABC$ are rt. $\angle$s.

Part II   If $\square ABCD$ is a rectangle, then $\overline{AC} \cong \overline{BD}$.

Given $ABCD$ is a rectangle.

Prove $\overline{AC} \cong \overline{BD}$

Plan for Proof   Show $\overline{AD} \cong \overline{BC}$, $\overline{DC} \cong \overline{DC}$, and $\angle ADC \cong \angle BCD$.
Then $\triangle ADC \cong \triangle BCD$ by SAS, and $\overline{AC} \cong \overline{BD}$.

The diagonals of a rhombus have two properties given in Theorems 5.12 and 5.13. The proofs of these theorems are exercises 27-30.

Theorem 5.12	**A parallelogram is a rhombus if and only if its diagonals are perpendicular.**

Part I	If $\overline{AC} \perp \overline{BD}$, then $\square ABCD$ is a rhombus.
Given	$\square ABCD$ with $\overline{AC} \perp \overline{BD}$
Prove	$ABCD$ is a rhombus.
Plan for Proof	Show $\angle 1 \cong \angle 2$ and $\overline{AE} \cong \overline{EC}$. Then $\triangle AEB \cong \triangle CEB$, so $\overline{AB} \cong \overline{BC}$. Use Thm. 5.2 to show $\overline{CD} \cong \overline{AB} \cong \overline{BC} \cong \overline{AD}$.
Part II	If $\square ABCD$ is a rhombus, then $\overline{AC} \perp \overline{BD}$.
Given	$ABCD$ is a rhombus.
Prove	$\overline{AC} \perp \overline{BD}$
Plan for Proof	Show $\overline{AB} \cong \overline{BC}$ and $\overline{AE} \cong \overline{EC}$. $\triangle AEB \cong \triangle CEB$ by SSS and $\angle 1 \cong \angle 2$. Use Thm. 2.14 to get $\overline{AC} \perp \overline{BD}$.

Theorem 5.13	**A parallelogram is a rhombus if and only if each diagonal bisects a pair of opposite angles of the parallelogram.**

Part I	If $\overline{AC}$ bisects $\angle BAD$ and $\angle BCD$, and $\overline{BD}$ bisects $\angle ABC$ and $\angle CDA$, then $\square ABCD$ is a rhombus.
Given	$\square ABCD$; $\overline{AC}$ bisects $\angle BAD$ and $\angle BCD$; $\overline{BD}$ bisects $\angle ABC$ and $\angle CDA$.
Prove	$ABCD$ is a rhombus.
Part II	If $\square ABCD$ is a rhombus, then $\overline{AC}$ bisects $\angle BAD$ and $\angle BCD$, and $\overline{BD}$ bisects $\angle ABC$ and $\angle CDA$.
Given	$ABCD$ is a rhombus.
Prove	$\overline{AC}$ bisects $\angle BAD$ and $\angle BCD$; $\overline{BD}$ bisects $\angle ABC$ and $\angle CDA$.

Properties of Rectangles

1. All properties of parallelograms
2. All four angles are right angles.
3. The diagonals are congruent.

Properties of Rhombuses

1. All properties of parallelograms
2. All four sides are congruent.
3. The diagonals bisect the angles of the rhombus.
4. The diagonals are perpendicular.

Properties of Squares

1. All properties of parallelograms
2. All properties of rectangles
3. All properties of rhombuses

Class Exercises

[1-6] Given: Rhombus *ARMY*

1. Find $m\angle AXY$.
2. Why does $m\angle AYR = m\angle MYR$?
3. If $m\angle AYM = 70$, find $m\angle MYR$.
4. If $m\angle RAY = 124$, find $m\angle MYA$.
5. If $m\angle MRY = 30$, find $m\angle MYA$.
6. Is it possible for $m\angle AYR$ to be 35 and $m\angle MAY$ to be 56?

[7-11] Given: $\square NAVY$

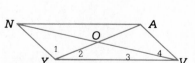

7. If $\overline{NY} \cong \overline{NA}$, then *NAVY* is a __?__ .
8. If $\overline{NV} \perp \overline{AY}$, then *NAVY* is a __?__ .
9. If $\overline{NO} \cong \overline{OA}$, then *NAVY* is a __?__ .
10. If $\angle 1 \cong \angle 2$ and $\angle 3 \cong \angle 4$, then *NAVY* is a __?__ .
11. If $\overline{NV} \perp \overline{AY}$ and $\overline{NV} \cong \overline{AY}$, then *NAVY* is a __?__ .

Written Exercises

[1-7] Given: Rectangle *ABCD* why

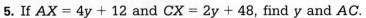

1. If $AC = 15$, then $BD = $ _?_ .
2. If $AC = 16.5$, then $DX = $ _?_ .
3. If $AX = 3.5$, then $BD = $ _?_ .
4. If $BD = 7.5$, then $XC = $ _?_ .
5. If $AX = 4y + 12$ and $CX = 2y + 48$, find y and AC.
6. If $AC = 9p - 35$ and $BD = 4p + 70$, then $p = $ _?_ .
7. If $DX = 7s + 11$ and $CX = 3s + 83$, then $AC = $ _?_ .

[8-19] Is the statement always, sometimes, or never true?

8. A square is a parallelogram.
9. A parallelogram is a rhombus.
10. A parallelogram with congruent diagonals is a square.
11. The diagonals of a rhombus are perpendicular.
12. A rectangle is a square.
13. A square is a rectangle.
14. A square is a rhombus.
15. A rhombus is a square.
16. The diagonals of a quadrilateral are perpendicular.
17. A diagonal of a rectangle bisects two angles of the rectangle.
18. The diagonals of a rectangle are congruent.
19. A trapezoid is a parallelogram.

[20-21] Given: Rhombus *ABCD*

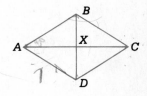

20. If $m\angle CAB = 30$ and $AD = 7$, find BD.
21. If $m\angle BAD = 64$, find $m\angle DCA$.

[22-24] Given: Rectangle *QRST*

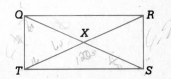

22. If $\overline{RX} \cong \overline{QT}$, find $m\angle TXS$.
23. If $m\angle RQS = 30$ and $QS = 13$, find SR.
24. If $m\angle QST = 45$ and $QT = 6.2$, find QR.

25. Prove Part I of Theorem 5.11.

26. Prove Part II of Theorem 5.11.

27. Prove Part I of Theorem 5.12.

28. Prove Part II of Theorem 5.12.

29. Prove Part I of Theorem 5.13.

30. Prove Part II of Theorem 5.13.

31. The rhombus-shaped mounting for a bearing has a perimeter of 12 in. and a width of 3 in. Find the measure of each angle of the rhombus.

32. The kite at the right is formed by creasing a rhombus along its shorter diagonal. The length of the shorter diagonal is 46 cm and $m\angle KIT = 2m\angle ITE$. Determine the amount of wood needed to frame the kite. (Note: Two pieces are needed along $\overline{IE}$.)

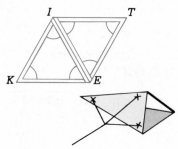

33. Given: Rectangle *HELP*; $\overline{OA} \perp \overline{PL}$
Prove: $\triangle HAE \cong \triangle POL$

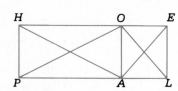

34. Given: Square *WREN*; $\square WORM$
Prove: *WORM* is a square.

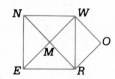

Set C

35. Given: Rectangle *ABCD*; $\overline{BC} \cong \overline{DX}$
Prove: $m\angle BXC = 60$

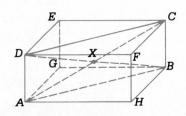

36. Prove: The length of the median to the hypotenuse of a right triangle is one-half the length of the hypotenuse.

244   Chapter 5   Using Congruent Triangles

Excursion   Nonperiodic Tessellations

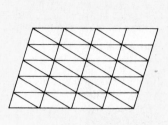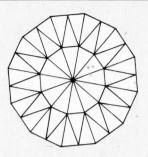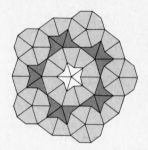

The first two tessellations, or tilings, above use the same isosceles triangle. Think of each tiling extended indefinitely to cover the plane.

A tiling that fits on itself when slid is called **periodic.** One that cannot fit onto itself is called **nonperiodic.** Which of the tessellations above are periodic? Which are nonperiodic?

Many polygonal shapes (like the triangles above) will tile both periodically and nonperiodically. Many shapes (such as squares) will tile *only* periodically, but a shape that tiles *only* nonperiodically has not been found.

There are two shapes that can be used together to tile only nonperiodically. The first example was discovered in 1974 by Roger Penrose, a British mathematician at the University of Oxford. The two shapes are obtained from a particular rhombus, shown at the right.

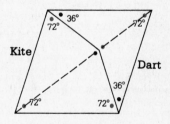

Of course the rhombus will tile periodically. However if the vertices are color coded and only vertices of the same color are allowed to meet, then the only way the pieces can tessellate is nonperiodically.

1. Make a set of darts and kites. To get elaborate patterns, you will need at least 100 kites and 60 darts.

2. One nonperiodic tessellation using darts and kites is shown at the top of the page. Create two others.

Trapezoids

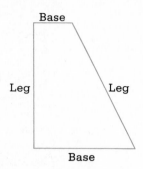

Base

Leg   Leg

Base

The buildings in the photo have sides shaped like trapezoids. In a trapezoid, the parallel sides are called **bases.** The nonparallel sides are called **legs.**

Can the bases of a trapezoid be congruent? Can the legs of a trapezoid be congruent?

Definition   An **isosceles trapezoid** is a trapezoid whose legs are congruent.

In isosceles trapezoid *ABCD,* ∠*A* and ∠*B* are called a pair of **base angles.** Another pair of base angles is ∠*C* and ∠*D.* What appears to be true about each pair of base angles?

Your answer should suggest Theorem 5.14.

Theorem 5.14   Each pair of base angles of an isosceles trapezoid is congruent.

Given   Isosceles trapezoid *ABCD* with $\overline{AD} \cong \overline{BC}$.

Prove   ∠*A* ≅ ∠*B*; ∠*C* ≅ ∠*D*

Plan for Proof   Draw $\overline{AX} \perp \overline{DC}$ and $\overline{BY} \perp \overline{DC}$.
Use Thm. 5.5 to show $\overline{AX} \cong \overline{BY}$.
Use HL to show △*DAX* ≅ △*CBY*.
Then ∠*D* ≅ ∠*C*.
Use Thms. 3.5 and 2.7 to show ∠*DAB* ≅ ∠*CBA*.

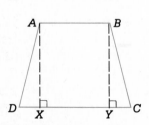

Theorem 5.15 is a corollary of Theorem 5.14. The proofs of these two theorems are exercises 13 and 14.

Theorem 5.15 The diagonals of an isosceles trapezoid are congruent.

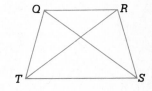

Given Isosceles trapezoid $QRST$; $\overline{TS} \| \overline{QR}$; $\overline{QT} \cong \overline{RS}$

Prove $\overline{QS} \cong \overline{RT}$

Plan for Proof Show $\angle TQR \cong \angle SRQ$ and $\overline{QT} \cong \overline{RS}$.
Show $\triangle TQR \cong \triangle SRQ$ by SAS.
Thus $\overline{QS} \cong \overline{RT}$.

Definition The **median** of a trapezoid is the segment joining the midpoints of the legs of the trapezoid.

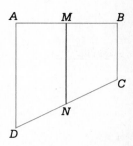

$\overline{MN}$ is the median of trapezoid $ABCD$.

The median of a trapezoid is related to the bases of the trapezoid by both position and length, as described in Theorem 5.16. The proof of Theorem 5.16 is exercise 15.

Theorem 5.16 The median of a trapezoid is parallel to the bases, and its length is one-half the sum of the lengths of the bases.

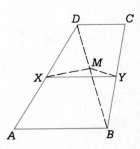

Given Trapezoid $ABCD$; $\overline{AB} \| \overline{CD}$; median $\overline{XY}$

Prove $\overline{XY} \| \overline{AB}$; $\overline{XY} \| \overline{CD}$; $XY = \frac{1}{2}(AB + CD)$

Plan for Proof Draw $\overline{BD}$ with midpoint M, $\overline{MX}$, and $\overline{MY}$.
Use Theorem 5.9 to show $\overline{MX} \| \overline{AB}$;
$\overline{MY} \| \overline{CD}$; $MX = \frac{1}{2}AB$ and $MY = \frac{1}{2}CD$.
Show $\overline{MY} \| \overline{AB}$ and X, Y, and M are collinear.
Then $\overline{XY} \| \overline{AB}$ and $\overline{XY} \| \overline{CD}$.
Use Seg. Add. Post. and Add. prop. of equality to show
$XY = XM + MY = \frac{1}{2}(AB + CD)$.

Class Exercises

[1-5] Given: Isosceles trapezoid $ABCD$ with $\overline{CD} \parallel \overline{AB}$; X and Y are midpoints.

1. Name the bases of trapezoid $ABCD$.
2. Name the legs of trapezoid $ABCD$.
3. Name two segments parallel to $\overline{XY}$.
4. Name the median of trapezoid $ABCD$.
5. Name a pair of congruent angles of trapezoid $ABCD$.

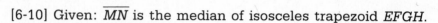

[6-10] Given: $\overline{MN}$ is the median of isosceles trapezoid $EFGH$.

6. $m \angle EHG = 135$. Find $m \angle FGH$.
7. $HE = 12.5$. Find FG.
8. $EG = 20.4$. Find FH.
9. $ME = 7.5$. Find FG.
10. $HG = 10$ and $EF = 22$. Find MN.

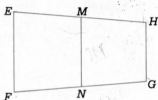

Written Exercises

Set A

[1-12] $\overline{XY}$ is the median of trapezoid $QRST$.

1. $TS = 8$ and $QR = 11$. Find XY.
2. $XY = 18$ and $TS = 7$. Find QR.
3. $XY = 16$. Find $TS + QR$.
4. $QR + TS = 42$. Find XY.
5. $TS = a$ and $QR = 6$. Find XY.
6. $QX = SY$ and $m \angle TXY = 45$. Find $m \angle R$.
7. $TX = \frac{1}{2}(SR)$ and $m \angle T = 130$. Find $m \angle R$.
8. $ST = a$ and $QR = 2b$. Find XY.
9. $XY = k$ and $ST = h$. Find QR.
10. $ST = 2c$, $QR = 4c$, and $XY = 12$. Find c.
11. $ST = 2c + 5$, $QR = 3c + 6$, and $XY = 33$. Find c.
12. A is the midpoint of $\overline{XT}$, B is the midpoint of $\overline{SY}$, $TS = 12$, and $QR = 28$. Find AB.

Set B

13. Prove Theorem 5.14.

14. Prove Theorem 5.15.

15. Prove Theorem 5.16.

[16-18] Given: Isosceles trapezoid $BROW$ with $\overline{BR} \parallel \overline{OW}$

16. Prove $\triangle BOW \cong \triangle RWO$.

17. Prove $\triangle BNW \cong \triangle RNO$.

18. Prove $\triangle WON$ is isosceles.

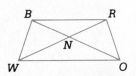

19. Dot James makes picture frames with a decorative line of trim between the edges of the inner and outer rectangles as shown. This trim joins the midpoints of $\overline{BX}$, $\overline{CY}$, $\overline{DZ}$, and $\overline{AW}$. The distance between the inner and outer rectangles is 3 in., $WZ = 8$ in. and $ZY = 10$ in. How much trim is needed for the frame?

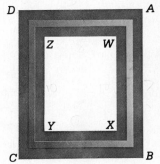

20. In the plan for a delta wing kite, a cross-stick is placed across a triangular piece of fabric. Cross-stick $\overline{AE}$ is parallel to the base of isosceles $\triangle DLT$. Prove that trapezoid $ELTA$ is isosceles.

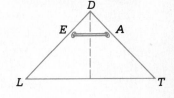

21. The ends of the weather kite shown are isosceles trapezoids. Each leg has length $5x$, and the bases have lengths $8x$ and $14x$. If the perimeter of each trapezoid is 192 cm, find the length of each side.

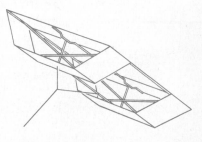

Set C

22. Prove: If two base angles of a trapezoid are congruent, then the trapezoid is isosceles.

23. In isosceles trapezoid $ABCD$, $\overline{AB} \parallel \overline{CD}$, $\overline{XY} \parallel \overline{CD}$, $AD = k$, $AB = s$, and $CD = t$. Find DX and CY such that the perimeter of $ABYX$ equals the perimeter of $XYCD$.

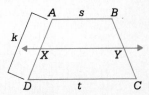

Locus

 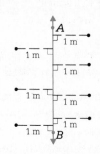 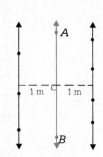

In a garden a rosebush is to be planted 1 m from the center line ($\overline{AB}$) of a path. What are all possible locations of the rosebush? In other words, in a plane, what is the set of all points 1 m from a given line?

To solve this problem, locate points that satisfy the condition. These points suggest a figure, called a locus.

Definition   A **locus** is the set of all points, and only those points, that satisfy a given condition.

In this problem, the suggested locus is a pair of parallel lines, each 1 m from the given line.

The following example illustrates the steps in answering a locus question.

Example 1   In a plane, what is the locus of points equidistant from two given points?

Solution   Sketch the given information.

Locate several points that satisfy the requirements. Find a pattern.

Describe the pattern of points.
The locus is the perpendicular bisector
of the segment joining the given points.

A description of a locus is correct if it describes all points that satisfy the conditions and only those points. If a locus problem is not restricted to a plane, always think in terms of three dimensions.

Example 2   What would the solution to example 1 be if the phrase *in a plane* were omitted?

Solution   The locus is a plane which contains the midpoint of the segment joining the given points and which is perpendicular to this segment.

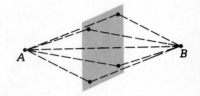

Definition   The **perpendicular bisecting plane** of a segment is the plane that is perpendicular to the segment at its midpoint.

Example 3   What is the locus of points in a plane at a distance of 1 cm from a given point P?

Solution   The locus is a circle of radius 1 cm whose center is P.

Class Exercises

[1-3] The diagram illustrates the locus of points 4 cm from a given line in a plane.

1. Explain why point Q which is 5 cm from the given line is not part of the locus.

2. Explain why the solution does not contain only one line.

3. Describe the locus.

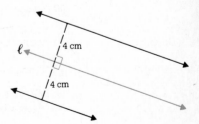

4. In a plane, what is the locus of points equidistant from two parallel lines?

5. What is the locus of all points 5 cm from a given line?

Written Exercises

[1-14] Draw a figure and describe the locus.

1. In a plane, the points between two given points

2. In space, the points between two given points

3. In a plane, the points equidistant from the sides of an angle

4. The points 10 cm from a given plane

5. In a plane, the points equidistant from two intersecting lines

6. In a plane, the points equidistant from two perpendicular lines

7. In a half-plane, the points 1 inch from the edge of the half-plane

8. In a half-plane, the points equidistant from the endpoints of $\overline{AB}$ if $\overline{AB}$ is contained in the edge of the half-plane

9. In a plane, the points equidistant from the four vertices of a square

10. In a plane, the midpoints of all segments joining point C to points of $\overline{AB}$, if C is not on $\overleftrightarrow{AB}$

11. The Park Commission wants to place a fountain in a rectangular play lot. The fountain is to be equidistant from the corners of the lot. What is the locus of points that satisfy these conditions?

12. The Jamisons want to install spotlights in their living room ceiling to highlight pictures on one wall. The lights are to be placed 18 inches from the wall. What is the locus of points where the lights may be placed?

13. The broadcasting range of a television station is 50 miles. What is the locus of points that can receive a signal from the station?

14. A heating contractor has two service centers. Each account is serviced by the center closer to it. What is the locus of points serviced by each center?

[15-20] Write a locus problem for which the figure in blue is the solution.

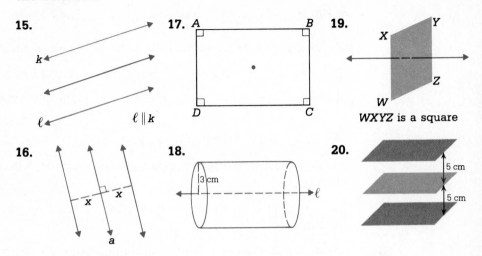

15. $\ell \parallel k$

16.

17.

18.

19. WXYZ is a square

20.

[21-26] Sketch each locus.

21. The points in a plane 3 cm from a given line

22. The points in a plane 1 inch from a given ray

23. The points in the exterior of an angle that are 2 cm from the angle

24. The points equidistant from two parallel planes

25. The positions for a telephone with a six-foot cord and an outlet in the center of a baseboard of a wall that is 15 feet long

26. The points that a dog can reach when it is tied 6 feet from the corner of a house with a 12-foot leash

[27-28] Given: $k \parallel \overleftrightarrow{AB}$; $n \parallel \overleftrightarrow{AB}$; k and n are 1 m from $\overleftrightarrow{AB}$.

27. Prove: If P is on k or n, then the distance from P to $\overleftrightarrow{AB}$ is 1 m.

28. If the distance from point Q to $\overleftrightarrow{AB}$ is 1 m, use an indirect proof to show that Q must be on either k or n.

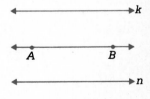

Locus Theorems

A bus company services two high schools in Wilmington. The company wants to build a garage that is equidistant from the two schools. Where should the company locate the garage?

Using the methods of lesson 5.7, you know that the garage should be built on the perpendicular bisector of the segment joining the two schools.

To prove this, you must show this locus contains all the points, and only those points, that satisfy the conditions.

Theorem 5.17

The locus of points in a plane equidistant from two given points is the perpendicular bisector of the segment joining the two points.

Part I

Any point on the perpendicular bisector of a segment is equidistant from the endpoints of the segment.

Given

ℓ is the $\perp$ bisector of $\overline{AB}$;
P is on ℓ.

Prove

$PA = PB$

Plan for Proof

Prove $\triangle AMP \cong \triangle BMP$ by SAS.
Then $PA = PB$.

Part II

Any point that is equidistant from two given points is on the perpendicular bisector of the segment joining these points.

Given

$QA = QB$; ℓ is the $\perp$ bisector of $\overline{AB}$.

Prove

Q is on ℓ.

Plan for Proof

Draw $\overline{QA}$, $\overline{QB}$, and $\overline{QM}$.
Show $\triangle QAM \cong \triangle QBM$ by SSS.
Then $\overline{QM} \perp \overline{AB}$ at M by Thm. 2.14,
and $\overleftrightarrow{QM}$ must be ℓ by Thm. 3.9.

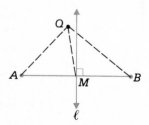

Theorem 5.18	The locus of points equidistant from two given points is the perpendicular bisecting plane of the segment joining the given points.
Part I	Any point in the perpendicular bisecting plane of the segment joining the given points is equidistant from the given points.
Part II	Any point that is equidistant from two given points must lie in the perpendicular bisecting plane of the segment joining the given points.
Theorem 5.19	In a plane, the locus of points equidistant from the sides of an angle is the bisecting ray of the angle, excluding its endpoint.

The proofs of Theorems 5.18 and 5.19 are exercises 11, 16, and 21. Theorem 5.20 shows how a locus theorem is used in a proof. The proof of Theorem 5.20 is exercise 19.

Theorem 5.20	If a line is perpendicular to each of two intersecting lines at their point of intersection, then it is perpendicular to the plane containing the two lines.

Given $\ell \perp m$; $\ell \perp n$; m and n lie in $\mathcal{E}$.

Prove $\ell \perp \mathcal{E}$

Plan for Proof

Draw any line k in $\mathcal{E}$ through X.
Choose A and B on ℓ such that
$AX = BX$.
Choose C on m and D on n.
Call Y the intersection of $\overline{CD}$ and k.
Then m and n are $\perp$ bisectors of $\overline{AB}$.

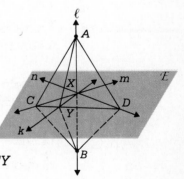

By Thm. 5.17, $AC = BC$ and $AD = BD$.
Then $\triangle ACD \cong \triangle BCD$ by SSS.
Show $\angle ACY \cong \angle BCY$ and $\triangle ACY \cong \triangle BCY$
by SAS.
Use corr. parts to show $\overline{AY} \cong \overline{BY}$.
Use Thm. 5.17 to show k is the
$\perp$ bisector of $\overline{AB}$.
Conclude that since $\ell \perp k$, then $\ell \perp \mathcal{E}$.

Class Exercises

1. If X and Y are each equidistant from A and B, use Theorem 5.17 to explain why $\overleftrightarrow{XY}$ is the perpendicular bisector of $\overline{AB}$.

2. State the two parts of Theorem 5.19 that must be proved.

3. Draw a diagram and state the Given and Prove for each part of Theorem 5.19.

[4-6] Use this statement: In a plane, the locus of points equidistant from two intersecting lines is two intersecting lines, excluding their point of intersection, that bisect each pair of vertical angles formed by the given lines.

4. Write the two parts of this statement that must be proved.

5. Draw a diagram and write the Given and Prove for each part.

6. Which locus theorem would be used in the proof?

Written Exercises

Set A

[1-3] Use this statement: In a plane, the locus of points equidistant from two parallel lines is another line parallel to the given lines and between the given lines at half the distance between them.

1. Write the two parts of this statement that must be proved.

2. Draw a diagram and write the Given and Prove for each part.

3. Describe the locus of all points equidistant from two parallel lines.

[4-7] State the line and plane that must be perpendicular.

4. Given: $\ell \perp m$; $\ell \perp p$
5. Given: $m \perp \ell$; $m \perp n$
6. Given: $m \perp n$; $\ell \perp n$
7. Given: $\ell \perp m$; $\ell \perp n$

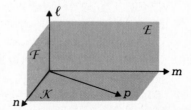

Chapter 5   Using Congruent Triangles

8. Draw a diagram and write the Given and Prove for Theorem 5.18, Part I.

9. Draw a diagram and write the Given and Prove for Theorem 5.18, Part II.

10. Prove Theorem 5.17, Part I.

11. Prove Theorem 5.18, Part I

12. In a plane what is the locus of points d cm from a given point? How can you justify this?

Set B

13. When an orbiting satellite crashed, three large pieces of debris of nearly the same size were found at positions A, B, and C. Copy the diagram at the right and determine the probable location of the impact.

A

C

B

14. George and Thelma Franklin are moving to Boston. George will work in Brookline, and Thelma will work in Cambridge. If they want to live equidistant from their jobs and along the Charles River, where should they look for a home?

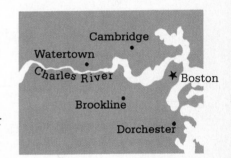

15. Prove Theorem 5.17, Part II.

16. Prove Theorem 5.19.

17. Prove: If the bisectors of two angles of a triangle intersect at a point P, then P is equidistant from the sides of the third angle.

18. Prove: If the perpendicular bisectors of two sides of a triangle intersect at a point Q, then Q is equidistant from the endpoints of the third side.

Set C

19. Prove Theorem 5.20.

20. Use an indirect proof to prove this statement: If a plane is perpendicular to a line at a point P, then the plane contains all the lines perpendicular to the given line at P.

21. Prove Theorem 5.18, Part II. Use the statement in exercise 20 as one of the reasons.

Using BASIC

Flow Charts

A flow chart is often used to describe a problem-solving procedure or *algorithm*. Often, it is very easy to translate each portion of the flow chart into statements in a computer program.

Below is a flow chart of a procedure for classifying △*ABC* as acute, right, or obtuse, given the measures of ∠*A* and ∠*B*. A BASIC program written from the flow chart is on the next page.

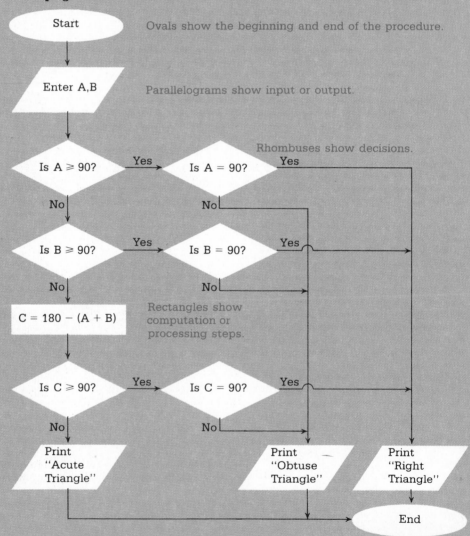

Ovals show the beginning and end of the procedure.

Parallelograms show input or output.

Rhombuses show decisions.

Rectangles show computation or processing steps.

```
100 REM CLASSIFYING TRIANGLES BY ANGLE MEASURE
110 PRINT "ENTER MEASURES OF ANGLE A"
120 PRINT "AND B, SEPARATED BY A COMMA."
130 INPUT A,B
140 IF A >= 90 THEN 200
150 IF B >= 90 THEN 220
160 LET C = 180 - (A + B)
170 IF C >= 90 THEN 240
180 PRINT "TRIANGLE ABC IS ACUTE."
190 GO TO 280
200 IF A = 90 THEN 270
210 GO TO 250
220 IF B = 90 THEN 270
230 GO TO 250
240 IF C = 90 THEN 270
250 PRINT "TRIANGLE ABC IS OBTUSE."
260 GO TO 280
270 PRINT "TRIANGLE ABC IS A RIGHT TRIANGLE."
280 END
```

1. RUN the program using these pairs as input for A and B.
   a. (27, 67) b. (38, 90) c. (42, 105) d. (212, 313)

★2. Make a change in the program so that it will give the message "NO SUCH TRIANGLE" for 1d. What change will be required in the flow chart for this check?

3. Write a flow chart of a procedure for classifying $\triangle ABC$ as scalene, isosceles but not equilateral, or equilateral, given side lengths a, b, and c.

4. Repeat exercise 3 with the measures of $\angle A$ and $\angle B$ as input instead of side lengths a, b, and c.

5. Write a flow chart of a procedure for deciding whether $\triangle ABC$ exists, given lengths for $\overline{AB}$, $\overline{BC}$, and $\overline{AC}$.

★6. Write a program for your flow chart in exercise 3.

★7. Write a program for your flow chart in exercise 4.

★8. Write a program for your flow chart in exercise 5.

★9. Write a flow chart and a program for deciding whether to prove $\triangle ABC \cong \triangle XYZ$ by SSS, ASA, SAS, or AAS. Ask if $\angle C \cong \angle Z$ and so on. The user should enter "1" if the parts are known to be congruent and "0" if not.

Chapter Summary

1. A quadrilateral is a parallelogram if and only if
   a. Both pairs of opposite sides are parallel. (page 218)
   b. Both pairs of opposite sides are congruent. (pages 223, 230)
   c. Both pairs of opposite angles are congruent. (page 224)
   d. One pair of sides is parallel and congruent. (page 229)
   e. The diagonals bisect each other. (pages 224, 230)

2. In a triangle, if a segment joins the midpoints of two sides, then it is parallel to the third side and its length is one-half the length of the third side. (page 234)

3. If three or more parallel lines cut off congruent segments on one transversal, then they cut off congruent segments on every transversal. (page 235)

4. A parallelogram is a rectangle if and only if its diagonals are congruent. (page 240)

5. A parallelogram is a rhombus if and only if
   a. The diagonals are perpendicular. (page 241)
   b. Each diagonal bisects a pair of opposite angles. (page 241)

6. In an isosceles trapezoid,
   a. The base angles are congruent. (page 246)
   b. The diagonals are congruent. (page 247)

7. The median of a trapezoid is parallel to the bases and its length is one-half the sum of the lengths of the bases. (page 247)

8. A locus is the set of all points, and only those points, that satisfy a given condition. (page 250)

9. In a plane, the locus of points equidistant from two given points is the perpendicular bisector of the segment joining the given points. In space, the locus is the perpendicular bisecting plane of the segment joining the given points. (pages 254, 255)

Chapter Review

Lesson 5.1
Page 218

[1-4] True or false

1. A parallelogram is a square.
2. A square is a rhombus.
3. A square is a rectangle.
4. A trapezoid can have two pairs of parallel sides.

Lesson 5.2
Page 223

[5-7] Given: $\square ABCD$

5. Name a pair of congruent triangles.
6. Name two pairs of congruent segments.
7. Name four pairs of congruent angles.

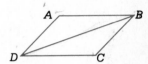

Lesson 5.3
Page 229

[8-11] State the definition or theorem needed to prove that quadrilateral *EFGH* is a parallelogram.

8. Given: $\overline{EF} \cong \overline{GH}$; $\overline{EH} \cong \overline{FG}$
9. Given: $\overline{FH}$ and $\overline{EG}$ bisect each other.
10. Given: $\overline{EF} \cong \overline{GH}$; $\overline{EF} \parallel \overline{GH}$
11. Given: $\overline{EF} \parallel \overline{GH}$; $\overline{EH} \parallel \overline{FG}$

Lesson 5.4
Page 234

[12-14] *M* and *N* are midpoints of $\overline{OJ}$ and $\overline{OK}$, respectively.

12. If $MN = 8$, find *JK*.
13. If $JK = 11$, find *MN*.
14. If $MN = x + 5$ and $JK = 4x - 15$, find *x*, *MN*, and *JK*.

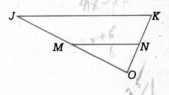

[15-17] Given: $\overline{PQ} \cong \overline{QR} \cong \overline{RS}$; $\overleftrightarrow{RT} \parallel \overleftrightarrow{QU} \parallel \overleftrightarrow{PV}$

15. If $ST = 6$, find *TU* and *UV*.
16. If $SV = 7.5$, find *ST*.
17. If $ST = 4a - 9$ and $UV = 2a + 10$, find *TU*.

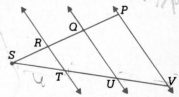

Lesson 5.5
Page 240

[18-21] Tell whether $\square ABCD$ is a rectangle, rhombus or square.

18. Given: $AC = 13$; $DB = 13$
19. Given: $m\angle A = 90$; $AB = BC$
20. Given: $\overline{AD} \cong \overline{DC}$
21. Given: $\overline{AC} \perp \overline{BD}$

[22-24] Given: $\overline{XY}$ is the median of trapezoid $MNOP$.

22. If $XY = 5k - 7$, $MN = k + 7$, and $PO = 3k + 3$, find k.

23. Prove: $\overline{XY}$ bisects each diagonal.

24. Prove: If $MNOP$ is isosceles, then $XYOP$ is an isosceles trapezoid.

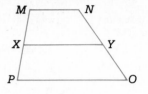

[25-28] Describe each locus.

25. In a plane, the points r cm from a given point

26. The points k cm from a given line

27. The points in a half-plane $\mathcal{H}$ that are 3 cm from a ray in $\mathcal{H}$ whose endpoint is on the edge of $\mathcal{H}$

28. In a plane, the points equidistant from a pair of opposite sides of a rectangle

29. Prove: The locus of points equidistant from two intersecting lines is two intersecting lines (excluding the point of intersection) that bisects each pair of vertical angles formed by the given lines.

Algebra Review Solving Quadratic Equations

Solve for x using the quadratic formula.

Example

$x^2 + 9x - 2 = 0$

Solution

$x = \dfrac{-b \pm \sqrt{b^2 - 4ac}}{2a}$; $a = 1$, $b = 9$, and $c = -2$

$x = \dfrac{-9 \pm \sqrt{9^2 - 4(1)(-2)}}{2(1)} = \dfrac{-9 \pm \sqrt{89}}{2}$

$x = \dfrac{-9 + \sqrt{89}}{2}$ or $x = \dfrac{-9 - \sqrt{89}}{2}$

1. $x^2 + 4x - 21 = 0$ **5.** $x^2 + x = 3$

2. $x^2 - 10x - 39 = 0$ **6.** $x^2 - 2x - 15 = 0$

3. $x^2 + 4x - 2 = 0$ **7.** $x^2 + 7x + 10 = 0$

4. $x^2 - 3x = 3$ **8.** $x^2 + 4x = -2$

Chapter Test

[1-5] Is the statement always, sometimes, or never true?

1. A rectangle is a parallelogram with four right angles.
2. If the diagonals of a quadrilateral are congruent, then it is a rectangle.
3. The diagonals of a rhombus bisect each other.
4. In $\triangle ABC$, if X and Y are the midpoints of $\overline{AC}$ and $\overline{BC}$, respectively, then $XY = AB$.
5. If the diagonals of $\square DEFG$ are perpendicular, then $DEFG$ is a square.

[6-7] Draw a figure and describe the locus.

6. In a plane, all points 6 cm from a given line
7. In a plane, all points equidistant from two parallel lines

8. List three proved properties of a parallelogram.
9. State the two parts of Theorem 5.19 that were proved: In a plane, the locus of points equidistant from the two sides of an angle is the bisecting ray of the angle, excluding its endpoint.

[10-12] Does the given information guarantee that $PQRS$ is a parallelogram?

10. $PQ = RS$; $QR = PS$
11. $\overline{PQ} \perp \overline{QR}$; $\overline{RS} \perp \overline{QR}$
12. $\angle 1 \cong \angle 2$; $PQ = RS$

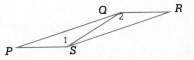

[13-15] X, Y, and Z are the midpoints of $\overline{AC}$, $\overline{BC}$, and $\overline{AB}$.

13. If $XY = 12$, find AB.
14. If $AC = 17$, find YZ.
15. If $AB = 14$, find the length of the median of trapezoid $ABYX$.

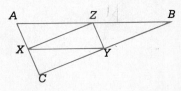

16. Given: Quadrilateral $ABCD$; $\overline{AC} \perp \overline{BD}$; $\overline{AC}$ and $\overline{BD}$ bisect each other.
    Prove: $ABCD$ is a rhombus.

Chapter 6

Similarity

When a car, boat, or plane is manufactured, a model of it is constructed first. *Columbia*, the space shuttle, is pictured to the left. A model of it is pictured above. The space shuttle and its model are similar to each other.

1. In general, what do actual structures and their models have in common? What are their differences?

2. The actual wing span of *Columbia* is 78.06 feet and its length is 122.2 feet. Suppose a model is to be built with a wing span equal to $\frac{1}{20}$ of the actual size. What should be its length? What can you say about the other dimensions of the model?

Similarity; Ratio and Proportion

In geometry, figures are called similar if they have the same shape but not necessarily the same size. The two flags shown below are similar rectangles.

Definition

Two convex polygons are **similar** if and only if there is a correspondence between their vertices such that the corresponding angles are congruent, and the ratios of the lengths of their corresponding sides are equal.

Polygons *ABCD* and *EFGH* are similar because their corresponding angles are congruent, and each side in polygon *ABCD* is twice as long as the corresponding side in polygon *EFGH*.

We write: polygon *ABCD* ~ polygon *EFGH*, naming corresponding vertices in order.

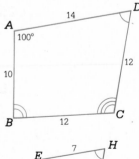

The ratio of the lengths of corresponding sides is 2:1. This relationship can be expressed by the proportion:

$$\frac{AB}{EF} = \frac{BC}{FG} = \frac{CD}{GH} = \frac{DA}{HE} = \frac{2}{1}.$$

A **proportion** is an equation which states that two or more ratios are equal. Thus, the second part of the definition of similar polygons can be restated as:

In similar polygons, the lengths of corresponding sides are proportional.

Since a proportion is an equation, the multiplication and addition properties of equality can be used to change the proportion to a more useful form.

For positive numbers a, b, c, and d, if $\dfrac{a}{b} = \dfrac{c}{d}$, then:

$ad = bc$ Multiplication Property of Equality

$\dfrac{a}{c} = \dfrac{b}{d}$ Multiplication Property of Equality

$\dfrac{b}{a} = \dfrac{d}{c}$ Multiplication Property of Equality

$\dfrac{a + b}{b} = \dfrac{c + d}{d}$ Addition Property of Equality

$\dfrac{a - b}{b} = \dfrac{c - d}{d}$ Addition Property of Equality

In a proof, if you change the form of a proportion in one of the five ways shown above, write either *Mult. prop. of equality* or *Add. prop. of equality* as the reason.

The properties of equality can be used to prove the *summation property of proportions:*

$$\text{If } \frac{a}{b} = \frac{c}{d}, \text{ then } \frac{a + c}{b + d} = \frac{a}{b}$$

This property can be applied repeatedly to any number of equal ratios. For example:

$$\text{If } \frac{a}{b} = \frac{c}{d} = \frac{e}{f}, \text{ then } \frac{a + c + e}{b + d + f} = \frac{a}{b}$$

Example 1   Given $\triangle MOJ \sim \triangle MKL$; $MK = 9$; $ML = 7$

Prove $\dfrac{LJ}{KO} = \dfrac{7}{9}$

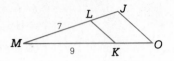

Statements	Reasons
1. $\triangle MOJ \sim \triangle MKL$	1. Given
2. $\dfrac{MJ}{ML} = \dfrac{MO}{MK}$	2. Def. of $\sim$ polygons [1]
3. $\dfrac{MJ - ML}{ML} = \dfrac{MO - MK}{MK}$	3. Add. prop. of equality [2]
4. $MJ = ML + LJ$ $MO = MK + KO$	4. Seg. Add. Post.
5. $MJ - ML = LJ$ $MO - MK = KO$	5. Add. prop. of equality [4]
6. $\dfrac{LJ}{ML} = \dfrac{KO}{MK}$	6. Substitution [3,5]
7. $MK = 9$; $ML = 7$	7. Given
8. $\dfrac{LJ}{7} = \dfrac{KO}{9}$	8. Substitution [6,7]
9. $\dfrac{LJ}{KO} = \dfrac{7}{9}$	9. Mult. prop. of equality [8]

Example 2   The floor plan below is a **scale drawing.**

Every figure in a scale drawing is similar to the object it represents. Thus, the dimensions of the rooms in the drawing are proportional to the actual room dimensions.

For example, $\dfrac{1}{\text{width of kitchen}} = \dfrac{1.5}{\text{length of kitchen}}$.

If you know that 1 centimeter in the scale drawing represents 3 meters in actual dimensions, what is the length of the kitchen?

Solution

$$\frac{1}{3} = \frac{1.5}{x}$$

$$(1)x = 3(1.5)$$

$$x = 4.5$$

The length of the kitchen is 4.5 meters.

The ratio of 1 centimeter to 3 meters is the scale of the drawing.

Find the perimeter of the kitchen using the drawing dimensions (centimeters). Find the actual perimeter of the kitchen (meters). What is the ratio of the perimeters?

Your answer should suggest Theorem 6.1. The proof of Theorem 6.1 for the case where the polygon is a pentagon is exercise 33.

Theorem 6.1   The ratio of the perimeters of two similar polygons is equal to the ratio of the lengths of any pair of corresponding sides.

Class Exercises

[1-10] Given: Pentagon $ABCDE \sim$ pentagon $FGHJK$

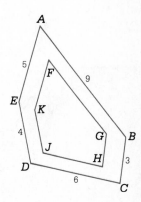

1. Name all pairs of corresponding vertices.

2. Write all ratios of corresponding sides.

[3-9] Given: $FG = 6$. Find each value.

3. GH 4. JK 5. HJ 6. KF

7. Perimeter of $FGHJK$

8. Perimeter of $ABCDE$

9. Ratio of the perimeters

10. If $m \angle K = 120$, find $m \angle E$.

11. If $\dfrac{a}{b} = \dfrac{c}{x}$, then $\dfrac{b}{x} = \underline{\ ?\ }$ and $bc = \underline{\ ?\ }$.

Written Exercises

Set A

[1-12] $\triangle ABC \sim \triangle ADE$

1. $AD = 8$; $AE = 6$; $AC = 15$; $AB = \underline{\ ?\ }$
2. $AE = 6$; $AD = 9$; $AB = 15$; $AC = \underline{\ ?\ }$
3. $AE = 6$; $EC = 4$; $AD = 8$; $DB = \underline{\ ?\ }$
4. $AD = 6$; $DB = 9$; $AE = 5$; $EC = \underline{\ ?\ }$
5. $AE = 4$; $AC = 5$; $AB = 10$; $AD = \underline{\ ?\ }$
6. $AD = 15$; $AB = 20$; $AC = 16$; $AE = \underline{\ ?\ }$
7. $AD = 5$; $DB = 3$; $AE = 2$; $AC = \underline{\ ?\ }$
8. $AE = 10$; $EC = 4$; $AD = 15$; $AB = \underline{\ ?\ }$
9. $AC = 4$; $EC = 1$; $AB = 6$; $AD = \underline{\ ?\ }$
10. $AB = 21$; $DB = 9$; $AC = 7$; $AE = \underline{\ ?\ }$
11. $AD = 6$; $AB = 10$; $BC = 5$; $DE = \underline{\ ?\ }$
12. $BD = 3$; $AD = 9$; $DE = 6$; $BC = \underline{\ ?\ }$

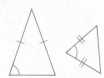

[13-16] Decide whether the given polygons are similar. Answer *yes*, *no*, or *not enough information*.

13.

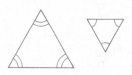

15.

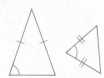

14.

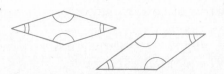

16.

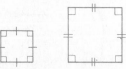

[17-22] Tell whether each statement is *always*, *sometimes*, or *never* true.

17. Two isosceles triangles are similar.
18. Two regular octagons are similar.
19. Two squares are similar.
20. A hexagon and an octagon are similar.
21. A parallelogram and a trapezoid are similar.
22. Two rectangles are similar.

23. If $\dfrac{x}{y} = \dfrac{p+q}{p}$, then $\dfrac{q}{p} = \dfrac{?}{y}$.

24. If $\dfrac{a+b}{a} = \dfrac{c-d}{c}$, then $\dfrac{ad}{bc} = \underline{\ ?\ }$.

In the floor plan at the right, the scale is
1 inch to 12 feet.

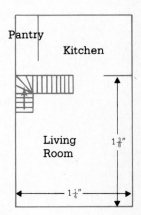

25. Find the actual dimensions of the living room.

26. If the actual dimensions of the pantry are 3 feet by 7.5 feet, what are its dimensions in the drawing?

27. In the drawing, the kitchen is $\frac{3}{8}$ inch longer than it is wide. By how much does its actual length exceed its actual width?

28. What should be the width of a rectangular card 12 centimeters long so that half the card is similar to the card?

29. In the figure at the right, $\triangle TRC \sim \triangle TQS$, and $TR = CS$. Find TR.

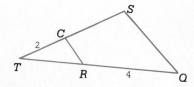

30. Two similar polygons have perimeters of 164 and 205. The length of one side in the larger polygon is 3 more than the length of the corresponding side in the smaller polygon. Find the length of the side of the smaller polygon.

31. Given: $\triangle ABC \sim \triangle CDA$
Prove: $ABCD$ is a parallelogram.

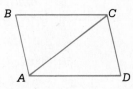

32. Given: $\triangle PQR \sim \triangle TSR$
Prove: $\overline{PQ} \parallel \overline{ST}$

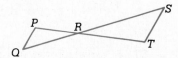

33. A yearbook company can reduce photos to fit a page, but the photo must first be cropped in proportion to the reduced size. If an original football candid measures 8″ × 10″, give three sets of possible cropped dimensions to fit a 2″ × 3″ layout block.

34. Prove the summation property of proportions: If $\dfrac{a}{b} = \dfrac{c}{d}$, then $\dfrac{a+c}{b+d} = \dfrac{a}{b}$.

35. Prove Theorem 6.1 for two pentagons.

Construction Exercises

1. Draw $\triangle ABC$ with $AB = \frac{3}{4}$ in; $BC = \frac{5}{8}$ in; $CA = \frac{1}{2}$ in.

2. Construct a segment, $\overline{DE}$, such that $DE = 3(AB)$.

3. Construct $\angle EDT \cong \angle A$.

4. On $\overrightarrow{DT}$, construct $\overline{DF}$ such that $DF = 3(AC)$. Draw $\overline{EF}$.

5. Using a protractor and a ruler, compare $m\angle E$ and $m\angle B$, $m\angle F$ and $m\angle C$, and BC and EF.

6. How is $\triangle DEF$ related to $\triangle ABC$?

7. Draw $\triangle PQR$ with $PQ = 3$ cm, $QR = 2$ cm, and $PR = 2.5$ cm.

8. Construct a segment, $\overline{XY}$, such that $XY = 2(PQ)$.

9. With X as center and compass radius $2(PR)$, make an arc on one side of $\overleftrightarrow{XY}$.

10. With Y as center and compass radius $2(QR)$, make an arc intersecting the first arc at Z. Draw $\overline{XZ}$ and $\overline{YZ}$.

11. Using a protractor, compare $m\angle P$ and $m\angle X$, $m\angle Q$ and $m\angle Y$, and $m\angle R$ and $m\angle Z$.

12. How is $\triangle XYZ$ related to $\triangle PQR$?

13. State two possible triangle similarity theorems suggested by your answers to exercises 6 and 12.

Similar Triangles

Using the definition of similar polygons, we can define similar triangles as follows:

$\triangle ABC \sim \triangle DEF$ if and only if $\angle A \cong \angle D$, $\angle B \cong \angle E$, $\angle C \cong \angle F$, and $\dfrac{AB}{DE} = \dfrac{BC}{EF} = \dfrac{CA}{FD}$.

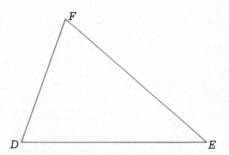
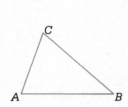

As with proving two triangles congruent, you do not need to know the measures of all the sides and angles of two triangles to conclude they are similar.

Postulate 19

AA Postulate

If two angles of one triangle are congruent to two angles of another, the triangles are similar.

Given that $\angle A \cong \angle D$ and $\angle B \cong \angle E$, verify $\triangle ABC \sim \triangle DEF$ by using a protractor and ruler.

Compare the definitions of similar triangles and congruent triangles. Both require that corresponding angles be congruent. In similar triangles, lengths of corresponding sides must be proportional, and in congruent triangles these lengths must be equal.

Suppose $\triangle ABC \cong \triangle DEF$. Then you know $\angle A \cong \angle D$, $\angle B \cong \angle E$, $\angle C \cong \angle F$; and $AB = DE$, $BC = EF$, $CA = FD$. The last three equations can be written as a proportion: $\dfrac{AB}{DE} = \dfrac{BC}{EF} = \dfrac{CA}{FD} = 1$. Since the corresponding angles of congruent triangles are congruent, and the ratios of the lengths of the corresponding sides are equal to 1, congruent triangles are always similar.

The definition of similar triangles or the AA Postulate shows that two triangles are similar. Theorems 6.2 and 6.3 also allow you to conclude that two triangles are similar.

Theorem 6.2

SAS Similarity Theorem

If an angle of one triangle is congruent to an angle of a second triangle, and if the lengths of the sides including these angles are proportional, then the triangles are similar.

Given

$\triangle ABC$ and $\triangle A'B'C'$; $\angle A \cong \angle A'$;
$$\frac{AB}{A'B'} = \frac{AC}{A'C'}$$

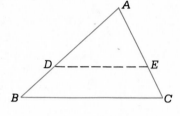

Prove

$\triangle ABC \sim \triangle A'B'C'$

Plan for Proof

Case I $AB = A'B'$
Prove $\triangle ABC \cong \triangle A'B'$
Then $\triangle ABC \sim \triangle A'B'C'$ by AA Post.

Case II $AB \neq A'B'$
Locate D on $\overrightarrow{AB}$ so that $AD = A'B'$.
Locate E on $\overrightarrow{AC}$ so that $\overline{DE} \parallel \overline{BC}$.
Show $\triangle ADE \sim \triangle ABC$ and $\triangle ADE \cong \triangle A'B'C'$.
Then use AA Post.

Proof

Case II

Statements	Reasons
1. Draw D on $\overrightarrow{AB}$ so that $AD = A'B'$.	1. Seg. Const. Post.
2. Draw $\overline{DE} \parallel \overline{BC}$, E on $\overleftrightarrow{AC}$.	2. Through a point not on a given line, _?_.
3. $\angle A \cong \angle A$	3. _?_
4. $\angle B \cong \angle ADE$	4. _?_ [2]
5. $\triangle ADE \sim \triangle ABC$	5. AA Postulate [3,4]
6. $\dfrac{AB}{AD} = \dfrac{AC}{AE}$	6. In $\sim$ polygons, _?_. [5]
7. $\dfrac{AB}{A'B'} = \dfrac{AC}{AE}$	7. Substitution principle [1,6]
8. $\dfrac{AB}{A'B'} = \dfrac{AC}{A'C'}$	8. _?_
9. $\dfrac{AC}{AE} = \dfrac{AC}{A'C'}$	9. Substitution principle [7,8]

Statements	Reasons
10. $(AE)(AC) = (AC)(A'C')$	10. ?
11. $AE = A'C'$	11. ?
12. $\overline{AD} \cong \overline{A'B'}$; $\overline{AE} \cong \overline{A'C'}$	12. Def. of $\cong$ seg. [1,11]
13. $\angle A \cong \angle A'$	13. ?
14. $\triangle A'B'C' \cong \triangle ADE$	14. ? [12,13]
15. $\angle ADE \cong \angle B'$	15. ? [14]
16. $\angle B \cong \angle B'$	16. Transitive prop. of equality [4,15]
17. $\triangle ABC \sim \triangle A'B'C'$	17. AA Post. [13,16]

The proof of Case I for Theorem 6.2 is exercise 24. The proof of Theorem 6.3 is exercise 40. Its proof is similar to the proof of the SAS $\sim$ Theorem.

Theorem 6.3

SSS Similarity Theorem

If the lengths of the sides of one triangle are proportional to the lengths of the sides of a second triangle, the triangles are similar.

Given

$\triangle ABC$ and $\triangle A'B'C'$;

$$\frac{AB}{A'B'} = \frac{BC}{B'C'} = \frac{CA}{C'A'}$$

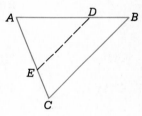

Prove

$\triangle ABC \sim \triangle A'B'C'$

Plan for Proof

Locate D on $\overrightarrow{AB}$ and E on $\overrightarrow{AC}$ so that $AD = A'B'$ and $AE = A'C'$.
Show $\triangle ADE \sim \triangle ABC$ by SAS $\sim$ Theorem.
Then show $\triangle ADE \cong \triangle A'B'C'$ by SSS Post.
Therefore, $\triangle ABC \sim \triangle A'B'C'$ by the SAS $\sim$ Theorem.

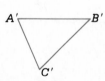

The AA Postulate, SAS $\sim$ Theorem, and SSS $\sim$ Theorem give you three ways to establish that two triangles are similar. Theorem 6.4 offers another possibility. Its proof is exercise 39.

Theorem 6.4

Similarity of polygons is reflexive, symmetric, and transitive.

Ways to Prove Triangles Similar

Two triangles are similar when:

All pairs of corresponding angles are congruent, and all
   pairs of corresponding sides are proportional.
Two pairs of corresponding angles are congruent. (AA)
Two pairs of corresponding sides are proportional, and
   the included angles are congruent. (SAS~)
All pairs of corresponding sides are proportional. (SSS~)
The triangles are similar to the same triangle.

Class Exercises

[1-6] Determine whether the given pair of triangles are
similar. If so, state the theorem or postulate that applies.
If not, explain why not.

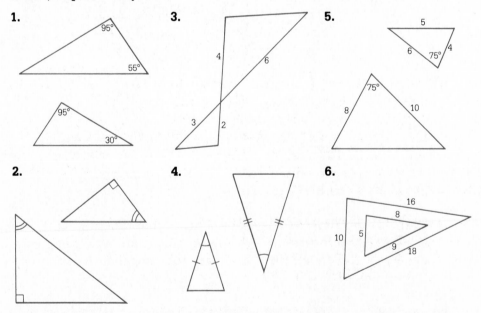

1.

2.

3.

4.

5.

6.

[7-10] Which of the following could be sides of similar
triangles?

7. 3, 5, 7 and 6, 10, 14

8. 2.4, 3.6, 4.8 and 8, 12, 15

9. $1\frac{1}{2}$, $2\frac{1}{2}$, 4 and 6, 10, 12

10. 5, 10, 12 and $2\frac{1}{2}$, 5, 6

[11-15] In the diagram, $\triangle RST \sim \triangle FGH$.
Find each measure.

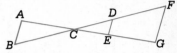
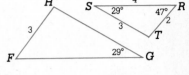

11. FG   **13.** $m\angle T$ **15.** $m\angle H$

12. GH   **14.** $m\angle F$

16. In the figure at the right,
$\triangle ABC \sim \triangle GFC$ and $\triangle GFC \sim \triangle EDC$.
Explain why $\triangle ABC \sim \triangle EDC$.

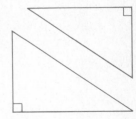

Written Exercises

Set A

[1-12] Decide whether the given triangles are similar.
Answer *yes*, *no*, or *not enough information*.

1.

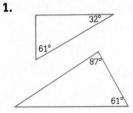

4.

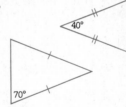

7.

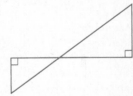

2.

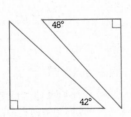

5.

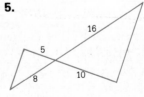

8.

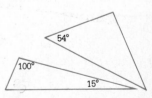

3.

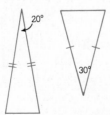

6.

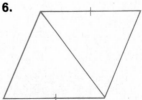

9.

10.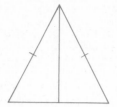

11.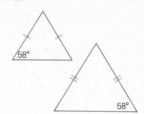

12.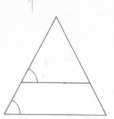

[13-16] Given: $\angle A \cong \angle D$; $\angle B \cong \angle E$

13. $\dfrac{AB}{DE} = \dfrac{BC}{?}$

14. $\dfrac{AC}{DF} = \dfrac{?}{FE}$

15. $\dfrac{EF}{BC} = \dfrac{DF}{?}$

16. $\dfrac{DE}{AB} = \dfrac{DF}{?}$

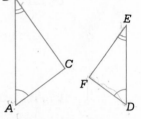

17. Prove that either diagonal of a parallelogram separates the parallelogram into two similar triangles.

18. Given: Trapezoid $RSTV$; $\overline{RS} \parallel \overline{VT}$
Prove: $\triangle ROS \sim \triangle TOV$

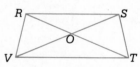

[19-20] Use the figure at the right.

19. Given: $\triangle ABC \sim \triangle ADE$
Prove: $\overline{BC} \parallel \overline{DE}$

20. Given: $\triangle ABC$; $\overline{BC} \parallel \overline{DE}$
Prove: $\triangle ABC \sim \triangle ADE$

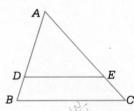

21. In the diagram, $\overline{XY} \parallel \overline{MN}$, $MO = 20$ m, $YO = 70$ m, and $MN = 25$ m. Find XY, the distance across the lake.

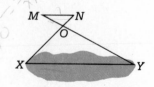

22. Frank stands so that his shadow and that of the flagpole are in line and have the same tip. Frank's height is 178 cm and his shadow is 267 cm long when the pole's shadow is 921 cm long. How tall is the flagpole?

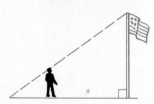

23. Prove: Any two equilateral triangles are similar.

24. Prove Case I of Theorem 6.2.

25. A quick test for similarity of two rectangles is used by engravers and photographers. Place one rectangle on top of the other so that two right angles coincide and the longer side of one lies on the longer side of the second. Explain why rectangle *ABCD* ~ rectangle *EFGD* but rectangle *WXYZ* is not similar to rectangle *PQRZ*.

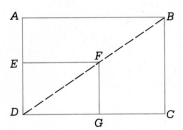 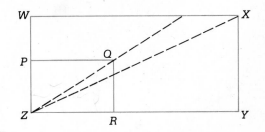

[26-31] Use a ruler and the *diagonal test* to determine if the rectangles are similar.

26. 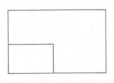 **28.** 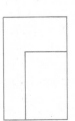 **30.**

27. 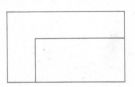 **29.** 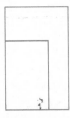 **31.**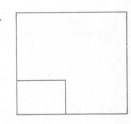

Set B

32. Proportional dividers are used to construct segments with proportional lengths. The legs $\overline{AD}$ and $\overline{BC}$ are of equal length, joined by a thumbscrew at *X*. The screw slides along the legs so that *AX* and *BX* remain equal. Describe where the screw should be located so that $CD = 2(AB)$.

33. Prove: Two right triangles with a pair of congruent acute angles are similar.

34. Prove: Two isosceles triangles with congruent vertex angles are similar.

35. Find the width of the Mink River.

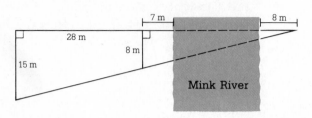

36. Given: $\overline{AB} \parallel \overline{DE}$; $\overline{BC} \parallel \overline{EF}$

Prove: $\dfrac{AB}{DE} = \dfrac{AC}{DF}$

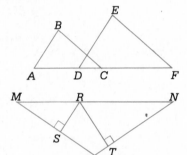

37. Given: $\triangle MNP$; $\overline{MP} \cong \overline{NP}$; $\overline{RT} \perp \overline{PN}$; $\overline{RS} \perp \overline{PM}$

Prove: $(RT)(RM) = (NR)(RS)$

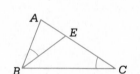

38. Given: $\triangle ABC$; $\angle C \cong \angle ABE$

Prove: $(AE)(BC) = (AB)(BE)$

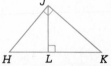

39. Prove Theorem 6.4.

Set C

40. Prove Theorem 6.3.

41. Given: Rt. $\triangle HJK$ with right angle at J; $\overline{JL} \perp \overline{HK}$

Prove: $\triangle HJK \sim \triangle JLK$

42. Given: Plane $\mathcal{K} \parallel$ plane $\mathcal{H}$; $FP = 2(PC)$; $EP = 2(PB)$; $DP = 2(PA)$

Prove: $\triangle ABC \sim \triangle DEF$

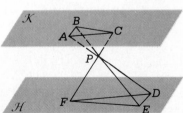

6.3 Segments Divided Proportionally

If T is a point on $\overline{AB}$ and S is a point on $\overline{CD}$ such that $\dfrac{AT}{TB} = \dfrac{CS}{SD}$, then $\overline{AB}$ and $\overline{CD}$ are divided proportionally by T and S.

A	T	B	C	S	D

Theorem 6.5   If a line parallel to one side of a triangle intersects the other two sides, it divides them proportionally.

Given $\triangle ABC$; D on $\overline{AB}$; E on $\overline{AC}$; $\overline{DE} \parallel \overline{BC}$

Prove $\dfrac{AD}{DB} = \dfrac{AE}{EC}$

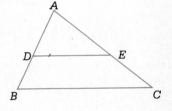

Plan for Proof   Show $\triangle ADE \sim \triangle ABC$ by AA Post.
Then use proportional parts.

The proof of Theorem 6.5 is exercise 19.

Example 1   The map below shows a section of some Chicago suburbs. The north-south street and the slanted street are divided proportionally by the east-west streets. Using the distances on the map, find the distance x from Willow Road to Euclid Avenue along Rand Road.

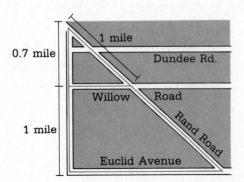

Solution   Write the proportion $\dfrac{0.7}{1} = \dfrac{1}{x}$. Therefore, $x \doteq 1.4$ miles.

Theorem 6.6   On any two transversals, parallel lines cut off segments whose lengths are proportional.

Given $\overleftrightarrow{AD} \parallel \overleftrightarrow{BE} \parallel \overleftrightarrow{CF}$

Prove $\dfrac{AB}{BC} = \dfrac{DE}{EF}$

Plan for Proof   Draw $\overleftrightarrow{AF}$ cutting $\overleftrightarrow{BE}$ at G.
                 Use Thm. 6.5 on $\triangle ACF$ and $\triangle FDA$.
                 Then use proportions.

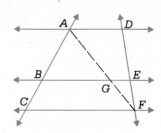

Proof

Statements	Reasons
1. $\overleftrightarrow{AD} \parallel \overleftrightarrow{BE} \parallel \overleftrightarrow{CF}$	1. Given
2. Draw $\overleftrightarrow{AF}$ cutting $\overleftrightarrow{BE}$ in G.	2. Line Postulate
3. $\dfrac{AB}{BC} = \dfrac{AG}{GF}$; $\dfrac{DE}{EF} = \dfrac{AG}{GF}$	3. If a line parallel to one side __?__ . [1]
4. $\dfrac{AB}{BC} = \dfrac{DE}{EF}$	4. Substitution principle [3]

Note that $\overline{AC}$ and $\overline{DF}$ are divided proportionally by $\overleftrightarrow{BE}$.

Example 2   A *pantograph* enlarges or reduces plane figures. The rods are hinged so that $ABCD$ is always a parallelogram with P, C, and C' collinear. The instrument lies flat, fastened down with a pivot at P. As a stylus at C moves from R to S along $\overline{RS}$, a pencil at C' will move from R' to a point collinear with P and S, say S'. As the stylus moves from S to T, the pencil will move from S' to a point collinear with P and T, say T'. Explain why $\triangle RST \sim \triangle R'S'T'$.

Solution   In each position, $\triangle PBC \sim \triangle PAC'$ by the AA Post. So $\dfrac{PR}{PR'} = \dfrac{PB}{PA} = \dfrac{PS}{PS'}$.
                 Then $\triangle PRS \sim \triangle PR'S'$ by SAS $\sim$.
                 Therefore, $\dfrac{RS}{R'S'} = \dfrac{PB}{PA}$.
                 Similarly, $\dfrac{ST}{S'T'} = \dfrac{PB}{PA} = \dfrac{RT}{R'T'}$.
                 Thus $\triangle RST \sim \triangle R'S'T'$ by SSS $\sim$.
                 To reduce a figure, interchange the pencil and the stylus.

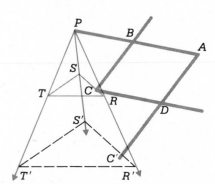

Class Exercises

[1-4] In △MON, $\overline{RS} \parallel \overline{MN}$.

1. $\dfrac{OS}{SN} = \dfrac{OR}{?}$ **3.** $\dfrac{OR}{OS} = \dfrac{RM}{?}$

2. $\dfrac{OR}{OM} = \dfrac{?}{ON}$ **4.** $\dfrac{OS}{ON} = \dfrac{?}{MN}$

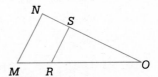

[5-8] State the proportion guaranteed by Theorem 6.6.

5. Given: $\overleftrightarrow{PQ} \parallel \overleftrightarrow{RS} \parallel \overleftrightarrow{TV}$

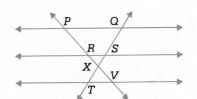

7. Given: $\overleftrightarrow{HJ} \parallel \overleftrightarrow{KL} \parallel \overleftrightarrow{MN}$

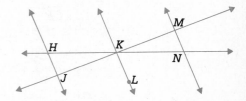

6. Given: $\overleftrightarrow{TV} \parallel \overleftrightarrow{WX} \parallel \overleftrightarrow{YZ}$

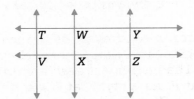

8. Given: $\overleftrightarrow{AB} \parallel \overleftrightarrow{CD} \parallel \overleftrightarrow{EF} \parallel \overleftrightarrow{GH}$

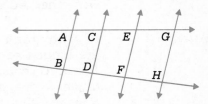

9. Is $\overline{AT} \parallel \overline{UB}$? Explain.

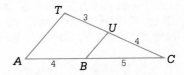

Written Exercises

Set A

[1-2] Avenues A, B, C, and K run parallel.

1. How far is it from Avenue A to Avenue B along D Street?

2. How far is it from Avenue C to Avenue K along E Street?

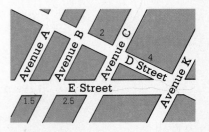

6.3 Segments Divided Proportionally

283

[3-6] Given $\overleftrightarrow{AB} \parallel \overleftrightarrow{CD} \parallel \overleftrightarrow{EF}$

3. $AC = 3$; $CE = 9$; $BD = 4$; $DF = $ __?__ .

4. $BD = 5$; $DF = 4$; $CE = 12$; $AC = $ __?__ .

5. $BF = 13$; $BD = 4$; $AE = 52$; $CE = $ __?__ .

6. $CE = 2$; $AE = 10$; $BD = 6$; $BF = $ __?__ .

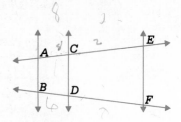

[7-12] Given $\overline{OP} \parallel \overline{AD}$. Which proportions are correct?

7. $\dfrac{x}{y} = \dfrac{z}{w}$

8. $\dfrac{w}{z} = \dfrac{t}{v}$

9. $\dfrac{x+y}{y} = \dfrac{z+w}{z}$

10. $\dfrac{x+y}{x} = \dfrac{y}{t}$

11. $\dfrac{z}{z+w} = \dfrac{t}{v}$

12. $\dfrac{z+w}{w} = \dfrac{y}{t}$

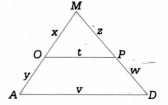

[13-16] Find x.

13.

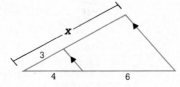

15.

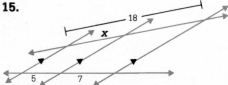

14.

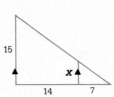

16.

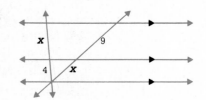

17. Given: $\square ABCD$; $\overline{EF} \parallel \overline{DC}$; $\overline{GH} \parallel \overline{BC}$

Prove: $\dfrac{AG}{GB} = \dfrac{AE}{ED}$

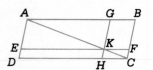

18. Given: $\overline{MN} \parallel \overline{TR}$; $\overline{MN} \parallel \overline{SV}$

Prove: $\dfrac{TS}{SM} = \dfrac{RV}{VN}$

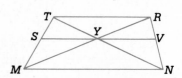

19. Prove Theorem 6.5.

20. State and prove the converse of Theorem 6.5.

21. Is the converse of Theorem 6.6 true?
Prove the converse or give a counterexample.

22. A half-mile ramp begins 2596 feet west of a bridge.
There is a pillar under the toll plaza which is located
1500 feet up the ramp. How far is the base of the
pillar from the west end of the bridge?

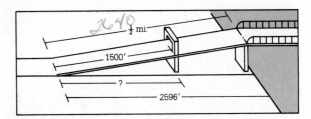

23. Residents are to pay for new curbing in proportion to
the footage their lots have on Monroe Street. What
part of the total cost must be paid by each resident?

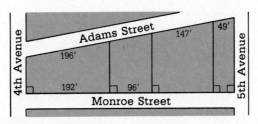

24. Given: △ABC; $\overline{FE} \parallel \overline{BC}$; $\overline{FD} \parallel \overline{AC}$; $\overline{ED} \parallel \overline{AB}$
Prove: D, E, and F are the midpoints
of $\overline{BC}$, $\overline{AC}$, and $\overline{AB}$, respectively.

25. Given: △ABC; D, E, and F are the
midpoints of $\overline{BC}$, $\overline{AC}$, and $\overline{AB}$,
respectively.
Prove: △ABC ~ △DEF

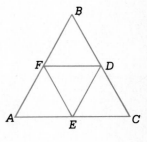

Set C

26. Given: △PQR; $\overline{PM}$ and $\overline{QN}$ are medians.
Prove: $\dfrac{PX}{XM} = \dfrac{2}{1}$ and $\dfrac{QX}{XN} = \dfrac{2}{1}$

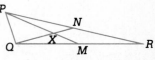

27. Given: Plane $\mathcal{K} \parallel$ plane $\mathcal{H} \parallel$ plane $\mathcal{E}$;
transversals ℓ and m
Prove: $\dfrac{AB}{BC} = \dfrac{DN}{NF}$

Hint Draw $\overleftrightarrow{AF}$ intersecting plane $\mathcal{H}$
at G. Then draw $\overline{AD}$, $\overline{BG}$, $\overline{GN}$, $\overline{CF}$.

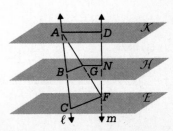

Construction Exercises

Construction 10 Separate a given segment into segments whose lengths are proportional to those of three other given segments.

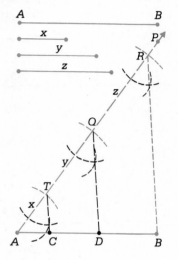

Given $\overline{AB}$; segments with lengths x, y, and z

Construct   Points C and D on $\overline{AB}$ such that
$$\frac{AC}{x} = \frac{CD}{y} = \frac{DB}{z}$$

Method   Step 1: Choose P not on $\overline{AB}$. Draw $\overrightarrow{AP}$.
Step 2: On $\overrightarrow{AP}$, mark off successive lengths $AT = x$, $TQ = y$, and $QR = z$. Draw $\overline{RB}$.
Step 3: Through T and Q, construct lines parallel to $\overline{RB}$ cutting $\overline{AB}$ at C and D, respectively.
Then $\dfrac{AC}{x} = \dfrac{CD}{y} = \dfrac{DB}{z}$.

1. Explain why Construction 10 works.

2. Draw a segment. Separate it into segments whose lengths are proportional to 1, 2, and 3.

3. How should the construction be modified to separate $\overline{AB}$ into segments whose lengths are proportional to x and y? To x, y, z, and w?

4. Draw a segment. Separate it into segments whose lengths are proportional to 1, 2, 4, and 5.

5. Separate the hypotenuse, $\overline{AB}$, of right $\triangle ABC$ into segments, $\overline{AD}$ and $\overline{DB}$, such that $\dfrac{AC}{AD} = \dfrac{CB}{DB}$.

Construction 11 Given segments of lengths a, b, and c, construct a segment of length t such that $\dfrac{a}{b} = \dfrac{c}{t}$. The number t is called the *fourth proportional* of a, b, and c.

Given   Segments of lengths a, b, and c.

Construct   A segment of length t such that $\dfrac{a}{b} = \dfrac{c}{t}$.

Method	Step 1: Draw $\angle DEF$. On $\overrightarrow{ED}$, mark off successive lengths $EG = a$ and $GH = b$ Step 2: On $\overrightarrow{EF}$, mark $EK = c$. Draw $\overline{KG}$. Step 3: Through H, construct a line parallel to $\overline{KG}$ cutting $\overrightarrow{EF}$ at J. Let $KJ = t$. Then $\dfrac{a}{b} = \dfrac{c}{t}$.

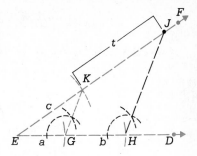

6. Explain why Construction 11 works.

7. Construct a segment of length t such that $\dfrac{2}{5} = \dfrac{1}{t}$.

8. Construct a segment of length r such that $\dfrac{1}{2} = \dfrac{r}{3}$.

Algebra Review   Simplifying Radicals

To write a radical in *simplest form*, factor out all perfect-square factors.

Example 1	Write $\sqrt{72}$ in simplest form.
Solution	$\sqrt{72} = \sqrt{36(2)} = \sqrt{36}\sqrt{2} = 6\sqrt{2}$

[1-8] Write each radical in simplest form.

1. $\sqrt{32}$ **3.** $\sqrt{300}$ **5.** $\sqrt{216}$ **7.** $\sqrt{128}$

2. $\sqrt{245}$ **4.** $\sqrt{28}$ **6.** $\sqrt{1000}$ **8.** $\sqrt{44}$

If an expression contains a radical in the denominator, the expression can be simplified by *rationalizing the denominator*.

Example 2	Simplify $\dfrac{12}{\sqrt{3}}$.
Solution	$\dfrac{12}{\sqrt{3}} = \dfrac{12}{\sqrt{3}}\left(\dfrac{\sqrt{3}}{\sqrt{3}}\right) = \dfrac{12(\sqrt{3})}{\sqrt{3}(\sqrt{3})} = \dfrac{12\sqrt{3}}{3} = 4\sqrt{3}.$

[9-16] Simplify each expression.

9. $\dfrac{6}{\sqrt{2}}$ **10.** $\dfrac{10}{\sqrt{5}}$ **11.** $\dfrac{9}{2\sqrt{2}}$ **12.** $\dfrac{\sqrt{6}}{\sqrt{12}}$

Progress Check

Lesson 6.1
Page 266

[1-7] Given $\triangle BAC \sim \triangle GEF$. Is the statement true or false?

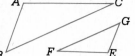

1. $\dfrac{AB}{EF} = \dfrac{AC}{EG}$ 3. $\dfrac{AB}{AC} = \dfrac{EG}{EF}$ 5. $\angle B \cong \angle F$

2. $\dfrac{AB}{EG} = \dfrac{AC}{EF}$ 4. $\dfrac{AB}{EG} = \dfrac{FG}{BC}$ 6. $\angle A \cong \angle E$

7. $AB = 9$; $AC = 12$; $FG = 5$; $EF = 4$; $BC = \underline{\ ?\ }$; $EG = \underline{\ ?\ }$.

8. If $\dfrac{m}{n} = \dfrac{p}{q}$, then $mq = \underline{\ ?\ }$ and $\dfrac{m}{m+n} = \dfrac{?}{p+q}$.

Lesson 6.2
Page 273

[9-11] Name the similar triangles; explain why they are similar; then find the value of x.

9.
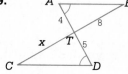

10.
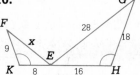

11.

12. Write a Plan for Proof to prove $\triangle I \sim \triangle III$.

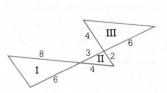

13. Find TY.

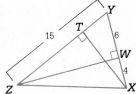

Lesson 6.3
Page 281

[14-17] Given $\overline{DE} \parallel \overline{AB}$. Is the statement true or false?

14. $\dfrac{CD}{CE} = \dfrac{DA}{EB}$ 15. $\dfrac{CD}{DA} = \dfrac{DE}{EB}$ 16. $\dfrac{CA}{CD} = \dfrac{CB}{CE}$

17. $CD = 20$; $AD = 12$; $CB = 24$; $CE = \underline{\ ?\ }$; $EB = \underline{\ ?\ }$.

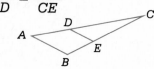

18. In trapezoid $SRTV$, $\overline{YZ} \parallel \overline{RS}$. If $RT = 10$, $SV = 15$, and $\dfrac{RP}{PV} = \dfrac{2}{3}$, find RY, YT, SZ, and ZV.

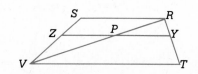

6.4 More Ratios in Similar Triangles

In any triangle, the bisector of each angle divides the opposite side into two segments. The following theorem shows how the lengths of these segments are related. The proof of Theorem 6.7 is exercise 11.

Theorem 6.7
The bisector of an angle of a triangle divides the opposite side into two segments whose lengths are proportional to the lengths of the other two sides.

Given
$\triangle ABC$; the bisector of $\angle B$ intersects $\overline{AC}$ at D.

Prove
$$\frac{AD}{AB} = \frac{CD}{CB}$$

Plan for Proof
Draw $\overline{EC} \parallel \overline{BD}$ with E on $\overleftrightarrow{AB}$.
Use corr. $\angle$s and alt. int. $\angle$s to show $\triangle BEC$ is isos. with $BE = BC$.
Then use Theorem 6.5.

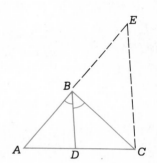

In similar triangles the ratios of the lengths of the corresponding sides are equal. The same ratio holds for their perimeters. The following theorems show this ratio also applies to their corresponding angle bisectors, altitudes, and medians. The proofs of Theorems 6.8, 6.9, and 6.10 are exercises 12, 17, and 18.

Theorem 6.8
In similar triangles, the lengths of bisectors of corresponding angles are in the same ratio as the lengths of corresponding sides.

Given
$\triangle ABC \sim \triangle A'B'C'$; $\overline{CD}$ bisects $\angle ACB$; $\overline{C'D'}$ bisects $\angle A'C'B'$

Prove
$$\frac{CD}{C'D'} = \frac{AC}{A'C'}$$

Plan for Proof
Show $\triangle ACD \sim \triangle A'C'D'$ by AA Post.

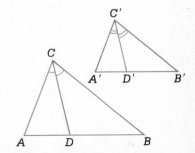

Theorem 6.9

In similar triangles, the lengths of the altitudes from corresponding vertices are in the same ratio as the lengths of corresponding sides.

Given $\triangle DEF \sim \triangle D'E'F'$; $\overline{FG} \perp \overline{DE}$; $\overline{F'G'} \perp \overline{D'E'}$

Prove $\dfrac{FG}{F'G'} = \dfrac{DF}{D'F'}$

Theorem 6.10

In similar triangles, the lengths of medians from corresponding vertices are in the same ratio as the lengths of corresponding sides.

Given $\triangle RST \sim \triangle R'S'T'$; $RM = MS$; $R'M' = M'S'$

Prove $\dfrac{TM}{T'M'} = \dfrac{RT}{R'T'}$

Class Exercises

[1-6] Given: $\triangle ABC \sim \triangle DEF$, $\overline{BG}$ bisects $\angle ABC$ and $\overline{EH}$ bisects $\angle DEF$.

1. $\dfrac{AG}{AB} = \dfrac{?}{BC}$

2. $\dfrac{HF}{EF} = \dfrac{DH}{?}$

3. $\dfrac{AC}{DF} = \dfrac{BG}{?}$

4. $\dfrac{DE}{AB} = \dfrac{?}{BG}$

5. $AB = 20$; $BC = 24$; $AC = 33$; $AG = \underline{\ ?\ }$.

6. $DH = 8$; $DF = 24$; $DE = 12$; $EF = \underline{\ ?\ }$.

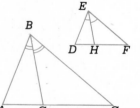

[7-12] Given: $\triangle RST \sim \triangle XYZ$; $\overline{SU}$ and $\overline{YP}$ are altitudes; $\overline{RW}$ and $\overline{XV}$ are medians.

7. $\dfrac{XZ}{RT} = \dfrac{?}{SU}$

8. $\dfrac{RS}{XY} = \dfrac{?}{YP}$

9. $\dfrac{RS}{XY} = \dfrac{RW}{?}$

10. $\dfrac{YZ}{ST} = \dfrac{XV}{?}$

11. $\dfrac{XV}{YP} = \dfrac{?}{SU}$

12. $\dfrac{SU}{YP} = \dfrac{RW}{?}$

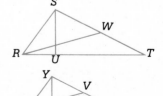

Written Exercises

[1-10] Given: $\triangle ABC \sim \triangle DEF$; $\overline{AH} \perp \overline{BC}$; $\overline{DK} \perp \overline{EF}$; $CM = MA$; $FN = ND$; $\angle BCJ \cong \angle ACJ$; $\angle DFL \cong \angle EFL$

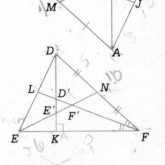

1. $\dfrac{AH}{BC} = \dfrac{DK}{?}$

2. $\dfrac{CJ}{AB} = \dfrac{?}{DE}$

3. $\dfrac{AH}{DK} = \dfrac{MB}{?}$

4. $\dfrac{FL}{CJ} = \dfrac{?}{MB}$

5. $\dfrac{EN}{FL} = \dfrac{?}{CJ}$

6. $\dfrac{MB}{AH} = \dfrac{EN}{?}$

7. $AH = 6$; $DK = 9$; $MC = 4$; $NF = \underline{\ ?\ }$.

8. $DN = 5$; $AM = 6$; $AB = 12$; $DE = \underline{\ ?\ }$.

9. $BC = 12$; $EF = 20$; $AJ = 8$; $DL = \underline{\ ?\ }$.

10. $AC = 4$; $DF = 10$; $EK = 6$; $BH = \underline{\ ?\ }$.

11. Prove Theorem 6.7.

12. Prove Theorem 6.8.

[13-14] Use a theorem from this lesson in each proof.

13. Given: $\triangle ABC$; $\angle A \cong \angle C$;
$\overline{BD}$ bisects $\angle ABC$
Prove: $AD = DC$

14. Given: $\triangle ABC$; $AD = DC$;
$\overline{BD}$ bisects $\angle ABC$
Prove: $\angle A \cong \angle C$

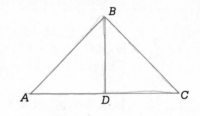

15. Given: $\triangle PWT \sim \triangle SQR$;
$\overline{PX}$ bisects $\angle TPW$;
$\overline{SY}$ bisects $\angle RSQ$;
Prove: $\dfrac{TX}{XW} = \dfrac{RY}{YQ}$

16. Given: $\triangle EFG$; $\overline{HJ} \parallel \overline{FG}$;
$\overline{EK}$ bisects $\angle GEF$
Prove: $\dfrac{JL}{LH} = \dfrac{GK}{KF}$

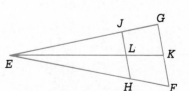

17. Prove Theorem 6.9.

18. Prove Theorem 6.10.

[19-22] Express x in terms of a, b, and c.

19. 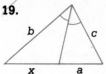   **20.**   **21.** 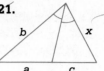   **22.**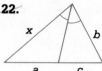

23. Given: $\triangle ABC \sim \triangle DEF$; $AJ = JB$;
$DK = KE$; $\overline{CG} \perp \overline{AB}$; $\overline{FH} \perp \overline{DE}$
Prove: $\triangle CGJ \sim \triangle FHK$

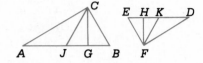

24. Given: $\triangle RST \sim \triangle MNP$; $RX = XS$;
$MY = YN$; $\angle RSV \cong \angle TSV$;
$\angle MNZ \cong \angle PNZ$
Prove: $\dfrac{VX}{ZY} = \dfrac{TS}{PN}$

Set C

25. Using the diagram and Given for Written Exercises 1-10,
prove $\triangle A'B'C' \sim \triangle D'E'F'$.

Algebra Review   Equations with Perfect Squares

If $x^2 = a^2$, then $x^2 - a^2 = 0$ or $(x + a)(x - a) = 0$.
So either $x + a = 0$ and $x = -a$ or $x - a = 0$ and $x = a$.
Thus if $x^2 = a^2$ then $x = \pm a$.

Examples

Solutions

1. Solve: $x^2 = 9a^2$ **2.** Solve: $x^2 = c^2 + 6c + 9$

$$x^2 = 9a^2$$
$$x^2 = (3a)^2$$
$$x = \pm 3a$$

$$x^2 = c^2 + 6c + 9$$
$$x^2 = (c + 3)^2$$
$$x = \pm(c + 3)$$

Solve each equation for x.

1. $x^2 = 49$

2. $x^2 = 441$

3. $x^2 = 64b^2$

4. $x^2 = 100d^4$

5. $x^2 = 169a^4b^2c^8$

6. $x^2 = 196e^{20}$

7. $x^2 = (c - 7)^2$

8. $x^2 = a^2 + 10a + 25$

9. $x^2 = 9b^2 + 24bd + 16d^2$

10. $x^2 = (a^2 + b^2)^2 - (2ab)^2$

11. $x^2 - 3e - 1 = e^2 - 5e$

12. $x^2 - c^2 + c = 4 - 3c$

6.5   Similarity in Right Triangles

Consider $\triangle ABC$ and $\triangle ACD$ at the right.
Both triangles contain the acute
angle A and a right angle. Therefore, by
the AA Postulate, $\triangle ACD \sim \triangle ABC$.

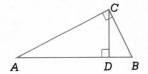

There are two other pairs of similar triangles in the figure
above: $\triangle CBD \sim \triangle ABC$ and $\triangle ACD \sim \triangle CBD$. Theorem 6.11
summarizes this information. Its proof is exercise 6.

Theorem 6.11

If an altitude is drawn to the hypotenuse of a right triangle, the
new triangles formed are similar to each other and to the given
triangle.

Given

$\triangle ABC$ with rt. $\angle C$; $\overline{CD} \perp \overline{AB}$

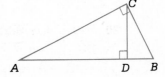

Prove

Part I: $\triangle ACD \sim \triangle ABC$
Part II: $\triangle CBD \sim \triangle ABC$
Part III: $\triangle ACD \sim \triangle CBD$

Plan for Proof

Part I: Use the AA Postulate with the rt. $\angle$s and $\angle A$.
Part II: Use the AA Postulate with the rt. $\angle$s and $\angle B$.
Part III: Use symmetry and transitivity with Parts I and II.

Since $\triangle ACD \sim \triangle CBD$, then $\dfrac{AD}{CD} = \dfrac{CD}{BD}$. Notice that CD
appears twice in this proportion. The length of $\overline{CD}$ is the
geometric mean of the lengths of $\overline{AD}$ and $\overline{BD}$.

Definition

The **geometric mean** of two positive real numbers a and b is the
positive number x such that $\dfrac{a}{x} = \dfrac{x}{b}$.

If $\dfrac{a}{x} = \dfrac{x}{b}$, then $x^2 = ab$, or $x = \sqrt{ab}$. Thus, the geometric
mean of two positive real numbers is the square root of
their product. For example, the geometric mean of 9 and 4
is $\sqrt{36}$ or 6, and the geometric mean of 5 and 7 is $\sqrt{35}$.

The next two theorems involve geometric means. Their
proofs are exercises 7 and 26.

Theorem 6.12	The length of the altitude to the hypotenuse of a right triangle is the geometric mean of the lengths of the segments into which the altitude separates the hypotenuse.

Given $\triangle ABC$ with rt. $\angle C$; $\overline{CD} \perp \overline{AB}$

Prove $\dfrac{AD}{CD} = \dfrac{CD}{DB}$

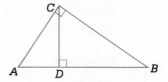

Theorem 6.13	If the altitude to the hypotenuse is drawn in a right triangle, the length of either leg is the geometric mean of the lengths of the hypotenuse and the segment on the hypotenuse which is adjacent to that leg.

Given $\triangle ABC$ with rt. $\angle C$; $\overline{CD} \perp \overline{AB}$

Prove $\dfrac{AB}{AC} = \dfrac{AC}{AD}$ and $\dfrac{BA}{BC} = \dfrac{BC}{BD}$

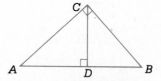

Thus, if $\triangle ABC$ is a right triangle and $\overline{CD}$ is the altitude to the hypotenuse $\overline{AB}$, then:

$\triangle ACD \sim \triangle ABC$, so $\dfrac{c}{b} = \dfrac{b}{n}$ and $b^2 = cn$.

$\triangle CBD \sim \triangle ABC$, so $\dfrac{c}{a} = \dfrac{a}{m}$ and $a^2 = cm$.

$\triangle ACD \sim \triangle CBD$, so $\dfrac{n}{h} = \dfrac{h}{m}$ and $h^2 = nm$.

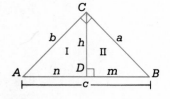

Examples

1. Find b.

$b^2 = 54(54 - 48)$
$b^2 = 324$
$b\ \ = 18$

2. Find c.

$15^2 = 9(c - 9)$
$225 = 9c - 81$
$306 = 9c$
$34 = c$

3. Find h.

$h^2 = 9(4)$
$h^2 = 36$
$h = 6$

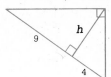

4. Find n.

$8^2 = 16n$
$64 = 16n$
$4 = n$

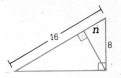

Class Exercises

[1-3] Name all triangles that are similar to $\triangle ABC$.

1.

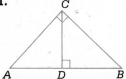

2.

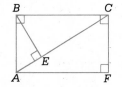

3.

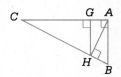

[4-12] Refer to the diagram at the right.

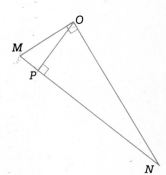

4. $\dfrac{?}{PO} = \dfrac{PO}{?}$

5. $\dfrac{?}{MO} = \dfrac{MO}{?}$

6. $\dfrac{?}{NO} = \dfrac{NO}{?}$

7. $\dfrac{MP}{PO} = \dfrac{?}{PN}$

8. $\dfrac{MN}{MO} = \dfrac{?}{MP}$

9. $\dfrac{MN}{NO} = \dfrac{?}{PN}$

10. $(MO)^2 = (\underline{\ ?\ })(\underline{\ ?\ })$

11. $(OP)^2 = (\underline{\ ?\ })(\underline{\ ?\ })$

12. $(NO)^2 = (\underline{\ ?\ })(\underline{\ ?\ })$

[13-21] Use the diagram at the right.

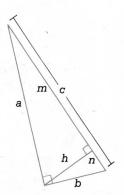

13. $m = 3$; $c = 12$; $a = \underline{\ ?\ }$

14. $n = 4$; $c = 9$; $b = \underline{\ ?\ }$

15. $m = 28$; $n = 7$; $h = \underline{\ ?\ }$

16. $n = 4$; $m = 25$; $h = \underline{\ ?\ }$

17. $c = 12$; $m = 4$; $h = \underline{\ ?\ }$

18. $c = 16$, $m = 7$; $b = \underline{\ ?\ }$

19. $c = 18$; $n = 10$; $a = \underline{\ ?\ }$

20. $h = 12$; $m = 4$; $c = \underline{\ ?\ }$

21. $m = 15$; $n = 3$; $b = \underline{\ ?\ }$

Written Exercises

[1-5] Refer to the diagram at the right.

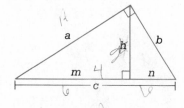

1. $c = 12$; $m = 6$; $a = $ __?__
2. $c = 8$; $n = 6$; $b = $ __?__
3. $m = 4$; $h = 25$; $n = $ __?__
4. $n = 4$; $h = 64$; $m = $ __?__
5. $c = 24$; $n = 6$; $h = $ __?__

6. Prove Theorem 6.11.

7. Prove Theorem 6.12.

8. Given: Rectangle $ABCD$; $\overline{BE} \perp \overline{AC}$
   Prove: $(CD)^2 = (AE)(AC)$

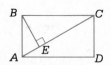

9. Given: $\triangle ABC$; $\overline{AB} \perp \overline{BC}$; $\overline{BD} \perp \overline{AC}$;
   $\overline{AB} \parallel \overline{DE}$
   Prove: $\triangle ABD \sim \triangle DCE$

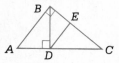

[10-17] Write your answers in terms of $x (x > 0)$.

10. $CD = x$; $BD = 4x$; $AD = $ __?__
11. $BC = x^2 + 9$; $BD = 9$; $AD = $ __?__
12. $CD = 2x$; $BD = 6x$; $AC = $ __?__
13. $CD = 5x$; $BD = 4x$; $AB = $ __?__
14. $BC = x^2 + 2x + 10$; $CD = 9$; $AD = $ __?__
15. $BD = 16$; $CD = x^2 + 6x - 7$; $AB = $ __?__
16. $AC = 8x$; $CD = 4x$; $BD = $ __?__ **Hint** Find BC first.
17. $BA = 12x$; $CB = 16x$; $CD = $ __?__ **Hint** Find BD first.

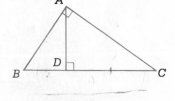

18. Find the length of the path
    from the corner of Elm and
    Oak streets to the river.

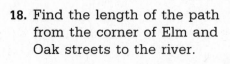

19. A carpenter's square with a plumb bob can serve as a level. On a level plane, if $\overline{DB} \perp \overline{AC}$, $AC = 26$ cm, and $DB = 12$ cm, find AB.

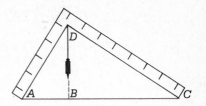

Set B

[20-25] Use the diagram at the right.

20. $a = 30$; $c = 50$; $h = $ _?_
21. $h = 12$, $m = 9$; $b = $ _?_
22. $a = 24$; $m = 4$; $b = $ _?_
23. $b = 45$; $n = 5$; $a = $ _?_
24. $b = 8$; $m = 12$; $c = $ _?_
25. $h = 14$; $c = 35$; $n = $ _?_

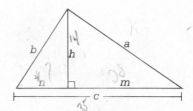

26. Prove Theorem 6.13.

27. Given: $\angle ACB$ is a right angle. $WXYZ$ is a square.
Prove: $(WX)^2 = (AW)(XB)$

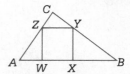

28. Find d.

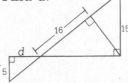

29. Find e.

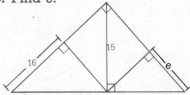

Set C

[30-31] Use the diagram for written exercises 20-25.

30. $a = 7\sqrt{5}$; $h = 14$; $c = $ _?_ ; $n = $ _?_
31. $a = 6\sqrt{5}$; $b = 3\sqrt{5}$; $m = $ _?_ ; $h = $ _?_

32. A right triangle has legs of lengths a and b. The altitude to the hypotenuse has length h; it divides the hypotenuse into segments of lengths m and n.

a. Prove: $h(m + n) = ab$

b. Prove: $a^2 + b^2 = (m + n)^2$

33. A carpenter's square is laid on the ground to find the width of a crater. Find AP if $BQ = 20.4$ meters and $QA = 3.4$ meters.

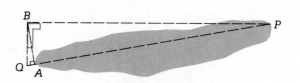

34. Given: $\triangle ABC$; $m\angle BAC = 2m\angle C$; $\overline{AF}$ bisects $\angle BAC$
Prove: AB is the geometric mean of CB and BF.

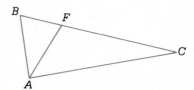

35. Given: $\triangle ABC$ with altitudes $\overline{AY}$, $\overline{BZ}$, and $\overline{CX}$ intersecting at P
Prove: $\left(\dfrac{AX}{XB}\right)\left(\dfrac{BY}{YC}\right)\left(\dfrac{CZ}{ZA}\right) = 1$

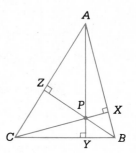

Geometry Maintenance

[1-2] Given: $AD = 7$; $AC = 5$; $BC = 3$

1. $\underline{\quad?\quad} < CD < \underline{\quad?\quad}$

2. $\underline{\quad?\quad} < AB < \underline{\quad?\quad}$

[3-5] Given: $m\angle 1 < m\angle 2 < m\angle 3$; $m\angle 5 < m\angle 4 < m\angle 6$

3. List the sides of $\triangle ACD$ in order from largest to smallest.

4. List the sides of $\triangle ABC$ in order from largest to smallest.

5. Name the shortest segment in the diagram. Explain.

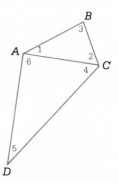

Excursion   The Golden Ratio

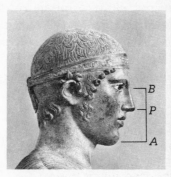
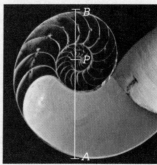

For centuries mathematicians have been fascinated by the *golden ratio*. Sometimes referred to as the divine proportion, the golden ratio appears frequently in nature and in art.

If a point, P, divides a segment, $\overline{AB}$, into segments $\overline{AP}$ and $\overline{PB}$ such that $\dfrac{AB}{AP} = \dfrac{AP}{PB}$, then this division is called the **golden section** of $\overline{AB}$. The ratio $\dfrac{AB}{AP}$ is called the **golden ratio.** The value of the golden ratio is $\frac{1}{2}(1 + \sqrt{5}) = 1.618$.

A **golden rectangle** is a rectangle in which the ratio of the longer side to the shorter one is the golden ratio. The Greeks realized the pleasing proportions of this figure and used it in much of their architecture.

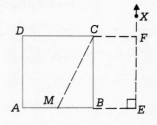

To construct a golden rectangle, begin with square $ABCD$, and locate M, the midpoint of $\overline{AB}$. Draw $\overline{CM}$. Locate E on $\overrightarrow{AB}$ so that $MC = ME$. Construct $\overrightarrow{EX} \perp \overline{AE}$. Extend $\overrightarrow{DC}$ to intersect $\overrightarrow{EX}$ at F. Then $AEFD$ is a golden rectangle.

Applications of Similarity

Some distances are not easy to measure directly. Such distances are often found indirectly by making other measurements and then using similar figures.

Example 1

Find the distance across a river from the shore at B to the rock at A.

Solution

Points C, D, and E are located by direct measurement so that $\overline{BC} \perp \overline{AB}$; $\overline{DE} \perp \overline{AD}$; $BC = 40$ m; $DE = 60$ m; and $DB = 30$ m.

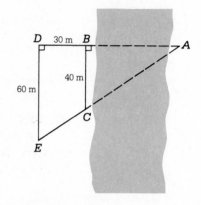

By the AA Postulate, $\triangle ABC \sim \triangle ADE$.

Therefore, $\dfrac{DA}{BA} = \dfrac{DE}{BC}$.

$$\frac{30 + BA}{BA} = \frac{60}{40} = \frac{3}{2}$$

$$2(30 + BA) = 3(BA)$$

$$60 = BA$$

Answer

The distance across the river from B to A is 60 meters.

Example 2

Estimate the height of Chicago's *Bat Column*, a sculpture by Claes Oldenburg.

Solution

A mirror is placed on the ground so that the viewer sees the top of the sculpture reflected in it. By direct measurement, $EO = 30$ cm, $BO = 5$ m, and $DE = 180$ cm.

A law of physics tells us that $m\angle DOE = m\angle AOB$. Then $\triangle DOE \sim \triangle AOB$ and $\dfrac{AB}{DE} = \dfrac{BO}{EO}$.

Substituting, $\dfrac{AB}{180} = \dfrac{500}{30}$.

$$30(AB) = 180(500)$$

$$AB = 3000 \text{ cm} = 30 \text{ m}$$

Answer

Taking the rounded top into account, the *Bat Column* is slightly taller than 30 meters.

Example 3	Find the mirror of minimum length that will permit Tony, who is 5 feet 8 inches tall, to see a full view of himself.
Solution	In the diagram, $\overline{DE} \perp \overline{AB}$, $\overline{BC} \perp \overline{AB}$ and $AD = DB$. Thus, $\triangle ADE \sim \triangle ABC$ and $\dfrac{AD}{AB} = \dfrac{DE}{BC}$. Since $\dfrac{AD}{AB} = \dfrac{1}{2}$, then $\dfrac{DE}{BC} = \dfrac{1}{2}$. Therefore, $DE = \dfrac{1}{2}(BC) = \dfrac{1}{2}(5'8'')$.
Answer	The minimum length mirror is $2'10''$.

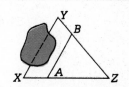

Class Exercises

1. How can this diagram be used to find the distance from X to Y if there is a rock between them? What measurements are needed?

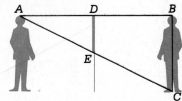

2. In the diagram, $AO = BO$ and $CO = DO$. Explain why the ironing board is parallel to the floor.

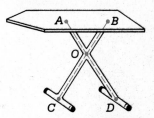

3. In the diagram, $\overline{XY} \parallel \overline{WZ}$, $XY = 40$ m, $YO = 30$ m, and $WO = 60$ m. Find WZ, the distance across the lake.

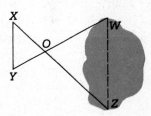

4. A 12-centimeter rod is held between a flashlight and a wall. Find the length of the shadow the rod casts.

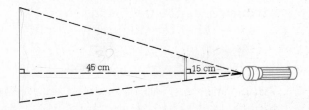

Written Exercises

1. Find the length of the shadow of the rod in class exercise 4 if the rod is 30 cm from the wall and the flashlight is 75 cm from the wall.

2. A 4"-deep camera is held so that the image is parallel to the subject, who is 6' tall and 10' from the camera. Find the height of the image.

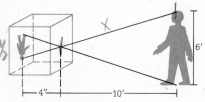

3. Find the distance between the subject and the camera in exercise 2 so that the image will just fit on $2\frac{1}{2}$" film.

4. A hiker begins walking up a hill at a spot where the elevation is 0.9 km. After she has walked 3 km, she sees a sign giving the elevation as 0.95 km. How far will she have walked when she reaches an elevation of 1.1 km?

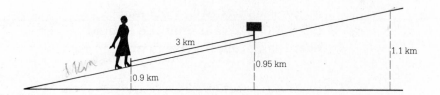

5. The cheerleaders at City High make their own megaphones by cutting off the small end of cones made from heavy paper. If the small end of each megaphone is to have a radius of 2.5 cm, what should be the height of the cone that is cut off?

6. Using similar triangles, an archaeologist can determine the original height of a pyramid, though its top has been worn away. Find the original height of the pyramid in the diagram.

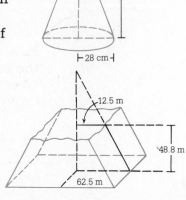

7. How many meters of lake frontage are on the Smith's lot? How many are on the park lot?

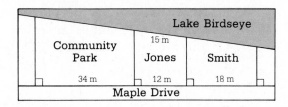

Set B

8. A tourist on the observation deck of a 400′ building looks west, facing another building 320′ high and two blocks from the first building. Her car is parked five blocks west of the second building. If no other buildings intervene, can she see her car?

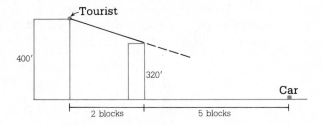

9. Refer to example 3 on page 301. If the top of the mirror is at *D*, Tony will not be able to see his feet. Where should the mirror be hung so that he can see a full view of himself?

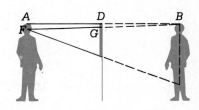

Set C

10. Two poles are braced as shown. How high above the ground do the braces cross if the braces are 24 m apart?

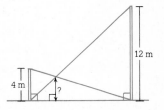

11. In exercise 10, how high above the ground do the braces cross if the distance between the poles is 36 m? What can you conclude about the distance between the poles and the height at which the braces cross?

Chapter Summary

1. In similar polygons
   a. corresponding angles are congruent and the lengths of corresponding sides are proportional. (page 266)
   b. the ratio of the perimeters is equal to the ratio of the lengths of corresponding sides. (page 269)

2. Two triangles can be shown to be similar by using the AA Postulate, the SAS ~ Theorem, or the SSS ~ Theorem. (pages 273–275)

3. Similarity of polygons is reflexive, symmetric, and transitive. (page 275)

4. If a line parallel to one side of a triangle intersects the other two sides, it divides them proportionally. (page 281)

5. On any two transversals, parallel lines cut off segments whose lengths are proportional. (page 282)

6. The bisector of an angle in a triangle divides the opposite side into two segments whose lengths are proportional to the lengths of the other two sides. (page 289)

7. In similar triangles, the ratio of the lengths of corresponding sides is equal to the ratio of the lengths of corresponding
   a. angle bisectors. (page 289)
   b. altitudes. (page 290)
   c. medians. (page 290)

8. The geometric mean of two positive real numbers, a and b, is equal to $\sqrt{ab}$. (page 293)

9. In a right triangle, the altitude to the hypotenuse
   a. divides the triangle into two triangles that are similar to each other and to the original triangle. (page 293)
   b. is the geometric mean of the lengths of the segments into which it separates the hypotenuse. (page 294)
   c. separates the hypotenuse into two segments such that each leg is the geometric mean of the lengths of the hypotenuse and the segment on the hypotenuse adjacent to that leg. (page 294)

Chapter Review

Lesson 6.1
Page 266

[1-2] Given: $\triangle STV \sim \triangle CFR$

1. Name all pairs of congruent angles.

2. Write all ratios of corresponding sides.

[3-4] Use the diagram at the right.

3. If $\triangle ABD \sim \triangle KED$, $AK = 3$, $KD = 6$, and the perimeter of $\triangle ABD$ is 24, find the perimeter of $\triangle KED$.

4. Given: $\triangle ABD \sim \triangle KED$; $AK = 5$; $KD = 10$
Prove: $BD = 3(BE)$

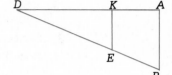

Lesson 6.2
Page 273

5. Given: $\square ABCD$
Prove: $\triangle BOE \sim \triangle DOC$

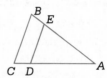

6. Given: $\dfrac{AE}{AC} = \dfrac{AD}{AB}$
Prove: $\angle AED \cong \angle ACB$

[7-8] Can these lengths be the sides of similar triangles?

7. 12, 28, 32 and 30, 20, 50

8. 12, 28, 32 and 35, 15, 45

9. If $\triangle I \sim \triangle II$, $\triangle II \sim \triangle III$, and $\triangle IV \sim \triangle III$, prove that $\triangle IV \sim \triangle I$.

Lesson 6.3
Page 281

[10-12] Given: $\overline{DE} \parallel \overline{BC}$

10. $AD = 20$; $AB = 24$; $AE = 15$; $AC = \underline{\ ?\ }$

11. $AD = 12$; $DB = 8$; $AE = 18$; $EC = \underline{\ ?\ }$

12. $AB = 24$; $DB = 4$; $AC = 20$; $AE = \underline{\ ?\ }$

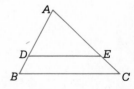

13. In $\square ABCD$, $BD = 16$, $AE = 2$, $EG = 4$, $CK = 2$, and $\overline{AD} \parallel \overline{EJ} \parallel \overline{GK}$.
Find DF, FH, and HB.

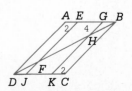

14. In $\triangle ABC$, $\overline{AX}$ bisects $\angle BAC$. If $AB = 18$, $AC = 10$, and $CX = 5$, find BX.

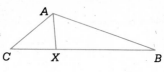

15. Given: $\triangle CNB \sim \triangle EMA$; $\overline{NO}$ bisects $\angle CNB$; $\overline{MD}$ bisects $\angle EMA$

Prove: $\dfrac{NO}{CO} = \dfrac{MD}{ED}$

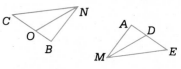

16. Given: $\triangle PTR \sim \triangle XYZ$; $\overline{TQ} \perp \overline{PR}$; $\overline{YV} \perp \overline{XZ}$; $TS = SR$; $YW = WZ$

Prove: $\dfrac{TQ}{YV} = \dfrac{PS}{XW}$

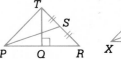

17. Given: $\overline{CD} \perp \overline{AB}$; $\overline{CD} \parallel \overline{EF}$; $m\angle ACB = 90$

Prove: $\triangle ACD \sim \triangle EBF$

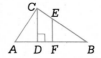

[18-20] Use the diagram at the right.

18. $m = 9$; $c = 25$; $a = $ ___?___

19. $m = 16$; $c = 20$; $h = $ ___?___

20. $a = 6$; $c = 9$; $n = $ ___?___

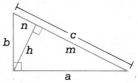

21. At a ground distance of 1.5 miles from takeoff, a plane's altitude is 1000 yards. Assuming a constant angle of ascent, find its altitude 5 miles from takeoff.

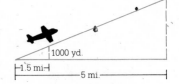

22. Use the information in the diagram to find the width of the river.

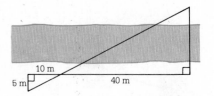

23. The diagram at the right shows a cross section of the strongest rectangular beam that can be cut from a log with diameter AC. If $AE = EF = FC$, find the ratio of AB to BC.

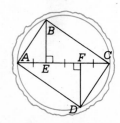

Chapter Test

[1-3] Name the postulate or theorem that guarantees the specified triangles are similar.

1. $\triangle AOB \sim \triangle COD$ **2.** $\triangle MOP \sim \triangle BAD$ **3.** $\triangle I \sim \triangle II$

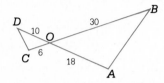

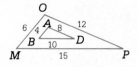

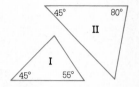

[4-5] Given: Polygon $SRVT \sim$ polygon $KPQJ$

4. Find the missing lengths.

5. Find the ratio of the perimeters.

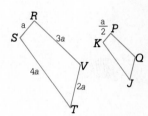

[6-7] Given: $\overline{BC} \parallel \overline{DE}$; $AC = 10$

6. Find AE.

7. Find DE.

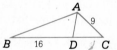

8. In the diagram at the right, $BC = 24$ and $\overline{AD}$ bisects $\angle BAC$. Find AB.

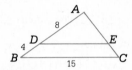

[9-11] Refer to the diagram at the right.

9. $a = 12$; $m = 6$; $c = \underline{\ ?\ }$

10. $m = 4$; $h = 10$; $c = \underline{\ ?\ }$

11. $c = 26$; $n = 8$; $h = \underline{\ ?\ }$

12. Given: $AC = 3(CD)$; $BC = 3(EC)$
Prove: $AB = 3(DE)$

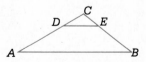

13. A man standing 16′ from an 18′ pole casts an 8′ shadow. How tall is he?

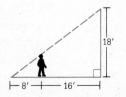

Cumulative Test   Chapters 1-6

Select the best answer for each item.

1. Points __?__ are collinear.

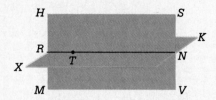

   a. *N*, *R*, and *T*   **c.** *S*, *T*, and *V*

   b. *H*, *M*, and *N*   **d.** *K*, *R*, and *X*

2. Name a ray shown here.

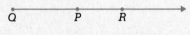

   a. $\overrightarrow{PQ}$ **b.** $\overrightarrow{RQ}$ **c.** $\overrightarrow{RP}$ **d.** $\overrightarrow{QP}$

3. Exactly one plane contains points *R*, *S*, and *T*. Therefore __?__.

   a. *R*, *S*, and *T* are collinear.

   b. $\overleftrightarrow{RS} \perp \overleftrightarrow{ST}$

   c. *S* is the midpoint of $\overline{RT}$.

   d. *R*, *S*, and *T* are noncollinear.

4. *S* is between *R* and *T*; $RT = 2ST = 12$. Find *RS*.

   a. 14   **b.** 6   **c.** 8   **d.** 14

5. $\angle 1$ and $\angle 2$ are complementary. Therefore __?__.

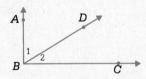

   a. $\angle 1 \cong \angle 2$ **c.** $\overrightarrow{BD}$ bisects $\angle ABC$

   b. $\overleftrightarrow{AB} \perp \overleftrightarrow{BC}$ **d.** $m\angle 1 + m\angle 2 = 180$

6. *P* lies in the interior of $\angle RST$; $m\angle RSP = 50$; $m\angle RST = 70$. Find $m\angle TSP$.

   a. 120   **b.** 60   **c.** 40   **d.** 20

7. Given: $RS = 6$ and $XY = 6$. Then $RS = XY$ because of the __?__.

   a. Reflexive property of equality

   b. Definition of congruent segments

   c. Symmetric and transitive properties of equality

   d. Distributive property

8. $\overleftrightarrow{AB}$ and $\overleftrightarrow{CD}$ intersect in point *E*. Therefore __?__.

   a. $\overleftrightarrow{AB} \perp \overleftrightarrow{CD}$

   b. *A*, *B*, *C*, and *E* are collinear.

   c. *A*, *B*, *C*, *D*, and *E* are coplanar.

   d. *E* is between *A* and *B*.

9. The hypothesis of the theorem "Vertical angles are congruent." is "If __?__."

   a. Two angles are congruent.

   b. Vertical angles are congruent.

   c. Congruent angles are vertical angles.

   d. Two angles are vertical angles.

10. Statement __?__ has a true converse.

   a. If it is the weekend, then school is closed.

   b. If $a = b$ and $c = d$, then $a + c = b + d$.

   c. If *B* is the midpoint of $\overline{AC}$, then *B* is between *A* and *C*.

   d. If two segments are congruent then their lengths are equal.

11. Give the Prove statement of this theorem: If a transversal is perpendicular to two lines in a plane, then the lines are parallel.

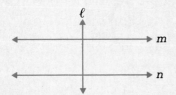

    a. $m \parallel n$ b. $\ell \perp m$ c. $m \perp n$ d. $\ell \perp n$

12. A triangle cannot be both __?__ .

    a. Obtuse and isosceles

    b. Acute and equilateral

    c. Scalene and isosceles

    d. Isosceles and equilateral

13. A statement in a proof is "$\angle 1 \cong \angle 2$." Which statement could not justify this step?

    a. If two angles are congruent, then they have equal measures.

    b. Definition of congruent angles

    c. Vertical angles are congruent.

    d. Right angles are congruent.

Items 14-15

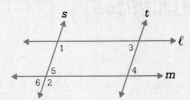

14. Given $\ell \parallel m$, $m\angle 1 = 3x + 30$ and $m\angle 5 = 6x - 60$. Find $m\angle 6$.

    a. 23.3   b. 70   c. 80   d. 100

15. Given $\angle 1 \cong \angle 2$. Then __?__ .

    a. $\angle 3 \cong \angle 4$ c. $\angle 1 \cong \angle 4$

    b. $s \parallel t$ d. $\angle 1$ and $\angle 3$ are supplementary.

16. Point R is on $\overleftrightarrow{ST}$. Through R there is (are) __?__ lines perpendicular to $\overleftrightarrow{ST}$.

    a. 0   c. 2

    b. 1   d. infinitely many

17. $m\angle 1 = 100$ and $\angle 1$ is an acute angle. This statement contradicts:

    a. Definition of degree measure

    b. Definition of acute angle

    c. Definition of right angle

    d. Protractor Postulate

18. Given $\ell \perp j$ at P and $j \perp k$ at Q. Then __?__ .

    a. $\ell \perp k$ c. ℓ and k are skew.

    b. $\ell \parallel k$ d. $\ell \parallel k$ or ℓ and k are skew.

19. In the triangle below, $x = $ __?__ .

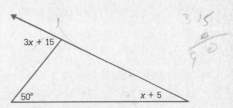

    a. 75   b. 25   c. 20   d. 18

20. A regular hexagon has sides of length 15. Its perimeter is __?__ .

    a. 75   b. 90   c. 105   d. 225

21. Given $\overline{VT}$ and $\overline{RU}$ bisect each other. $\triangle VSR \cong \triangle TSU$ by the __?__ Postulate.

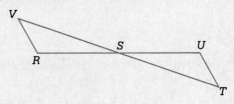

    a. SSS   b. SAS   c. ASA   d. AAS

22. The sum of the measures of the interior angles of a polygon is 1080. The polygon has __?__ sides.

   a. 6   **b.** 10   **c.** 4   **d.** 8

23. Given: $\triangle PQR \cong \triangle XYZ$. Name the side corresponding to $\overline{QR}$.

   a. $\overline{YZ}$ **b.** $\overline{XY}$ **c.** $\overline{PQ}$ **d.** $\overline{XZ}$

Items 24-25

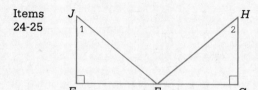

24. To prove $\triangle EFJ \cong \triangle GFH$ by the LL Theorem, show $\overline{EF} \cong \overline{FG}$ and __?__.

   a. $\overline{JF} \cong \overline{HF}$ **c.** $\angle 1 \cong \angle 2$

   b. $\angle J \cong \angle H$ **d.** $\overline{EJ} \cong \overline{GH}$

25. Given: $\triangle JFE \cong \triangle HFG$ and $JE = 4x$, $EF = 2x + 2$, and $HG = 20$. Then $FG = $ __?__.

   a. 20   **b.** 12   **c.** 10   **d.** 5

26. The lengths of two sides of a triangle are 7 and 16. The length of the third side is between __?__.

   a. 7 and 16   **c.** 9 and 23

   b. 7 and 23   **d.** 9 and 16

27. Given: $\triangle ACD \cong \triangle BCD$. Which statement need not be true?

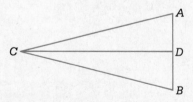

   a. $\overline{AB} \perp \overline{CD}$ **b.** $m\angle A > m\angle ACB$

   c. $\triangle ABC$ is isosceles.

   d. $\overline{CD}$ is a median.

28. According to the Hinge Theorem, if __?__, then $ST > NP$.

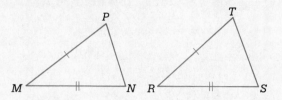

   a. $m\angle P > m\angle T$ **c.** $m\angle R > m\angle M$

   b. $m\angle N > m\angle S$ **d.** $m\angle R > m\angle S$

29. Which statement need not be true?

   a. A trapezoid is a quadrilateral.

   b. A rhombus is a parallelogram.

   c. A rectangle is a parallelogram.

   d. A rectangle is a square.

30. Given: $\square RSTU$. Then $m\angle S = $ __?__.

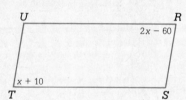

   a. 70   **b.** 80   **c.** 100   **d.** 110

31. Given: $\overline{XY}$ is the median of trapezoid $MNOP$, and X is the midpoint of $\overline{MP}$. Then __?__.

   a. $XY = \frac{1}{2}(MN + OP)$ **c.** $\overleftrightarrow{MP} \parallel \overleftrightarrow{NO}$

   b. $\overline{MX} \cong \overline{YN}$ **d.** $\overleftrightarrow{XY} \parallel \overleftrightarrow{NO}$

32. P is a point on $\overleftrightarrow{AB}$; $\overleftrightarrow{DP} \perp \overleftrightarrow{AB}$, and $\overleftrightarrow{EP} \perp \overleftrightarrow{AB}$. If D, P, and E are not collinear, which statement must be true?

   a. D is on $\overleftrightarrow{AB}$.

   b. $\overleftrightarrow{DP} \parallel \overleftrightarrow{EP}$

   c. $\overleftrightarrow{AB}$ is perpendicular to the plane containing $\overleftrightarrow{DP}$ and $\overleftrightarrow{EP}$.

   d. $\overleftrightarrow{DP}$ is perpendicular to the plane containing $\overleftrightarrow{AB}$ and $\overleftrightarrow{EP}$.

Items
33-34

33. If ___?___ , then WXYZ is a
parallelogram.
   a. $\overline{ZV} \cong \overline{VY}$ and $\overline{WV} \cong \overline{VX}$
   b. $\overline{WX} \parallel \overline{ZY}$ and $\overline{WZ} \cong \overline{XY}$
   c. $\overline{XY} \cong \overline{WZ}$ and $\overline{WX} \cong \overline{ZY}$
   d. $\overline{WY} \perp \overline{ZX}$

34. Given: WXYZ is a rhombus. To
prove it is a square, show that:
   a. $\overline{WZ} \cong \overline{ZY}$ **c.** $\overline{WY} \cong \overline{ZX}$
   b. $\overline{ZV} \cong \overline{XV}$ **d.** $\angle 1 \cong \angle 2$

35. Given: $\overleftrightarrow{KE} \parallel \overleftrightarrow{FJ} \parallel \overleftrightarrow{GH}$, $\overline{EF} \cong \overline{FG}$, and
$KH = 12$. Then $KJ = $ ___?___ .

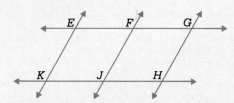

   a. 12   **b.** 24   **c.** 6   **d.** 8

36. The locus of points equidistant
from points A and B is the ___?___ .
   a. perpendicular bisecting plane of
      $\overline{AB}$
   b. perpendicular bisector of $\overline{AB}$
   c. midpoint M of $\overline{AB}$
   d. $\overleftrightarrow{AB}$

37. To prove $\triangle PQR \sim \triangle STU$ by the SAS
Similarity Theorem, given $\angle Q \cong \angle T$,
first show that ___?___ .
   a. $PQ = ST$ and
      $QR = TU$ **c.** $\dfrac{PQ}{ST} = \dfrac{PR}{SU}$
   b. $\angle P \cong \angle S$ or
      $\angle R \cong \angle U$ **d.** $\dfrac{QR}{TU} = \dfrac{PQ}{ST}$

38. If $EFGH \sim KLMN$, then the
perimeter of $KLMN$ is ___?___ .

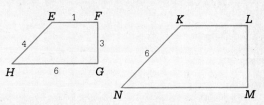

   a. 14   **b.** 21   **c.** 28   **d.** 32

39. If $\overline{ST} \parallel \overline{PQ}$ and $RQ = 12$, then
$SP = $ ___?___ .

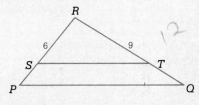

   a. 9   **b.** 6   **c.** 3   **d.** 2

40. The medians of two equilateral
triangles are in the ratio of 3 to 4.
If a side of the larger triangle is 12,
then the perimeter of the smaller
is ___?___ .
   a. 36   **b.** 27   **c.** 24   **d.** 9

41. Given: $\triangle RST \sim \triangle MNP$; $RT = x + 1$;
and $PM = 3x - 2$. Then $x = $ ___?___ .

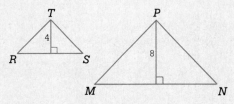

   a. 1.5   **b.** 2   **c.** 4   **d.** 9

42. A flagpole is 40 feet tall. It casts a
25-foot shadow at the same time
that a post casts a 5-foot shadow.
The post is ___?___ feet tall.
   a. 5   **b.** 7   **c.** 8   **d.** 10

Right Triangles

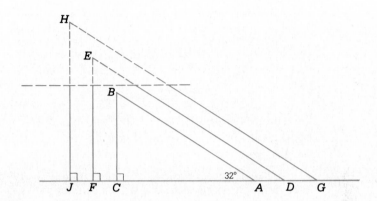

The three right triangles above are based on the photo of Kitt Peak National Observatory. In the diagram $\overline{AB} \parallel \overline{DE} \parallel \overline{GH}$, $BC = 90$ feet, and $AC = 144$ feet. Notice that the ratio $\dfrac{BC}{AC}$ can be expressed as $\dfrac{90}{144}$ or 0.625.

1. Name two triangles similar to $\triangle ABC$. Which similarity postulate did you use?

2. Name two pairs of segments whose ratios equal $\dfrac{BC}{AC}$.

3. If $EF = 115$, the proportion needed to solve for DF is $\dfrac{EF}{DF} = \dfrac{BC}{AC}$. Substitute for EF and $\dfrac{BC}{AC}$, and solve the proportion.

4. If $HJ = 140$, write a proportion and solve it for GJ.

In any right triangle with a 32° angle, the ratio of the shorter leg to the longer leg is always 0.625. The triangle does not need to be compared to a similar triangle to find the ratio of the legs.

In this chapter you will learn how to use a table of ratios to solve for parts of a right triangle.

7.1　The Pythagorean Theorem

The right-triangle relationship shown here is called the Pythagorean Theorem. It is named for the Greek mathematician Pythagoras (582–500? B.C.) who is credited with the first proof.

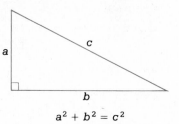

$$a^2 + b^2 = c^2$$

Notice that c is the length of the hypotenuse and a and b are the lengths of the legs.

Two illustrations of this theorem are shown below. The area of each square represents the square of the length of a side of the triangle.

The first example shows an isosceles right triangle. The square on each leg has been divided into triangular tiles.

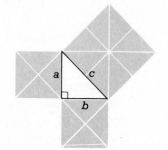

4 tiles show a^2
4 tiles show b^2
8 tiles show c^2
Since $4 + 4 = 8$, $a^2 + b^2 = c^2$.

In the second example, each square is divided into 1-by-1 tiles.

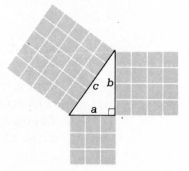

$a^2 = 3^2 = 9$
$b^2 = 4^2 = 16$
$c^2 = 5^2 = 25$
Since $9 + 16 = 25$, $a^2 + b^2 = c^2$.

This important relationship is true in all right triangles and is Theorem 7.1.

Theorem 7.1

Pythagorean Theorem

In a right triangle, the square of the length of the hypotenuse equals the sum of the squares of the lengths of the legs.

Given

Right $\triangle ABC$ with rt. $\angle C$; legs of lengths a and b; hypotenuse of length c

Prove

$c^2 = a^2 + b^2$

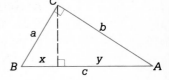

Plan for Proof

Draw the altitude from C to $\overline{AB}$.
Use Thm 6.13 to show that $a^2 = xc$ and $b^2 = yc$.
Then use Add. prop. of equality.

Proof

Statements	Reasons
1. Rt. $\triangle ABC$ with rt. $\angle C$; legs of lengths a and b; hypotenuse of length c	1. Given
2. Draw the altitude from C, so that $c = x + y$.	2. Through a point not on a given line __?__
3. $a^2 = xc$ and $b^2 = yc$	3. If an altitude is drawn to the hypotenuse of a right triangle, __?__ [1, 2]
4. $a^2 + b^2 = xc + yc$	4. Add. prop. of equality [3]
5. $a^2 + b^2 = (x + y)c$	5. Distributive property [4]
6. $a^2 + b^2 = c^2$	6. Substitution [2, 5]

To form a right angle, the Egyptian "rope stretchers" formed a triangle with sides of lengths 3, 4, and 5, using equally spaced knots on a rope. They decided that $\angle C$ was then a right angle. The converse of the Pythagorean Theorem, Theorem 7.2, justifies this procedure. The proof of Theorem 7.2 is exercise 13.

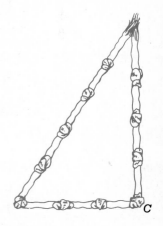

Theorem 7.2	If the sum of the squares of the lengths of two sides of a triangle is equal to the square of the length of the third side, then the triangle is a right triangle.

Given $\triangle ABC$; sides of lengths a, b, and c; $a^2 + b^2 = c^2$

Prove $\triangle ABC$ is a right triangle.

Plan for Proof Draw $\ell \perp m$ at point F.
Locate D on ℓ and E on m so that
$DF = b$ and $EF = a$.
Draw $\overline{DE}$.
Use the Pythagorean Thm. to show
$f = c$.
Show $\triangle ABC \cong \triangle DEF$ by SSS, and
$\angle C$ is a rt. $\angle$.

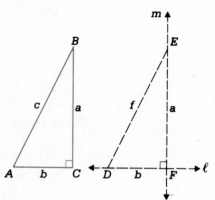

Class Exercises

[1-3] Write the equation that results from applying the Pythagorean Theorem.

1.
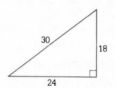

2.
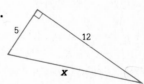

3.
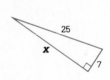

[4-6] Use the Pythagorean Theorem to find x.

4.
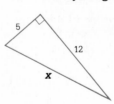

5.
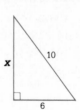

6.
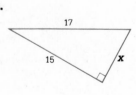

[7-10] Which of the following number triples can be lengths of sides of a right triangle?

7. 4, 5, and 7

8. 20, 21, and 29

9. 9, 40, and 41

10. 9, 12, and 16

Written Exercises

[1-6] Given: $\triangle ABC$ with right $\angle C$

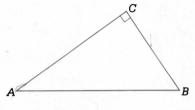

1. $AC = 1$; $BC = 3$; $AB =$ _?_
2. $AC = 2$; $BC = 5$; $AB =$ _?_
3. $AC = 2$; $AB = 4$; $BC =$ _?_
4. $AC = 3$; $AB = 6$; $BC =$ _?_
5. $AB = 8\sqrt{2}$; $BC = 8$; $AC =$ _?_
6. $AB = 8\sqrt{3}$; $BC = 4\sqrt{3}$; $AC =$ _?_

7. Find the length of the diagonal of a square with side of length 10.

8. Find the length of the diagonal of a rectangle with sides of lengths 8 and 20.

[9-12] Given: Equilateral $\triangle ABC$ with altitude $\overline{AD}$

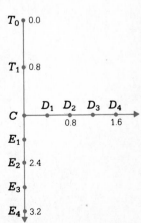

9. If $AB = 12$, find AD.   11. If $AD = 7$, find AB.
10. If $BC = 18$, find AD.   12. If $AD = 4\sqrt{3}$, find AC.

13. Prove Theorem 7.2.

[14-18] Two cars are at point C when a tornado is sighted at T_0, 1.6 km away. Car D drives along $\overrightarrow{CD_1}$ at a right angle to the path of the tornado. Car E drives along $\overrightarrow{CE_1}$ directly away from the tornado at the same speed as Car D. The tornado is moving along $\overrightarrow{T_0C}$ at twice the speed of the cars. Complete the table.

	Position			Distance from Tornado	
	Tornado	Car D	Car E	Car D	Car E
	T_0	C	C	1.6	1.6
14.	T_1	D_1	E_1	?	1.2
15.	C	D_2	E_2	?	?
16.	?	D_3	E_3	?	?
17.	?	D_4	E_4	?	?

18. Which path is the safer course?

T_0 • 0.0

T_1 • 0.8

D_1 D_2 D_3 D_4
C 0.8   1.6

E_1 •

E_2 • 2.4

E_3 •

E_4 • 3.2

19. Given: $\triangle ABC$ with altitude $\overline{CD}$
Prove: $a^2 - y^2 = b^2 - x^2$

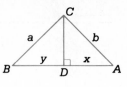

20. Given: $\triangle BTE$ with rt. $\angle T$
Prove: $ET^2 + BS^2 = BE^2 + ST^2$

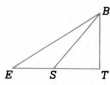

Set C

21. Given: P is in the interior of rectangle $QRST$.
Prove: $x^2 + z^2 = w^2 + y^2$

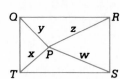

22. Given: Right $\angle C$; $\overrightarrow{DC} \perp \overline{AB}$
Prove: $\dfrac{1}{a^2} + \dfrac{1}{b^2} = \dfrac{1}{h^2}$

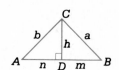

Construction Exercises

Construction 12 Construct a segment of length $\sqrt{5}$ times a given length.

Given $\overline{XY}$ of length a

Construct $\overline{AC}$ of length $a\sqrt{5}$

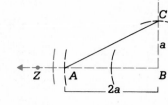

Step 1: Draw ray $\overrightarrow{BZ}$. Construct $\overrightarrow{BW} \perp \overrightarrow{BZ}$.

Step 2: On $\overrightarrow{BZ}$, construct $\overline{AB}$ of length $2a$. On $\overrightarrow{BW}$, construct $\overline{BC}$ of length a.

Step 3: Draw $\overline{AC}$.
Then $AC = a\sqrt{5}$.

1. Write a plan for justifying Construction 12.

[2-7] Construct segments of the given lengths. The length of the given segment $\overline{XY}$ is a.

2. $a\sqrt{10}$ **4.** $a\sqrt{7}$ **6.** $a\sqrt{6}$

3. $a\sqrt{17}$ **5.** $a\sqrt{15}$ **7.** $a\sqrt{8}$

7.2 Special Right Triangles

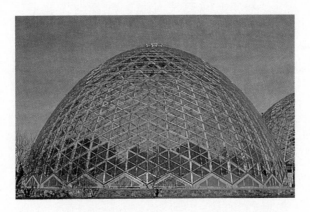

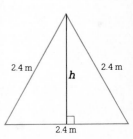

A glass panel of height h must be ordered for an equilateral triangle in this geodesic dome. Theorem 7.3 gives a property of 30-60-90 triangles that can be used to find h. The proof of Theorem 7.3 is exercise 30.

Theorem 7.3	In a 30-60-90 triangle, the length of the hypotenuse is twice the length of the shorter leg, and the length of the longer leg is $\sqrt{3}$ times the length of the shorter leg.

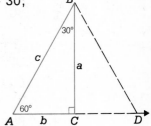

Given — Right $\triangle ABC$ with $m\angle A = 60$ and $m\angle ABC = 30$; $AC = b$; $AB = c$; $BC = a$

Prove — $c = 2b$ and $a = b\sqrt{3}$

Plan for Proof — Draw $\overleftrightarrow{AC}$.
Label D on $\overleftrightarrow{AC}$ so that $CA = CD$.
Draw $\overline{BD}$.
Show $\triangle ABC \cong \triangle DBC$ by SAS.
Then $\triangle ABD$ is equilateral and $c = 2b$.
Apply the Pythagorean Theorem, using $2b$ for c, to show $a = b\sqrt{3}$.

In the triangle from the dome, the altitude forms a 30-60-90 triangle. By Theorem 7.3, the length of the shorter leg is $\frac{1}{2}(2.4)$ or 1.2 meters, and $h = 1.2\sqrt{3} \doteq 2.1$ m.

The proof of the following corollary to Theorem 7.3 is exercise 28.

<u>Theorem 7.4</u> **The length of the altitude of an equilateral triangle with sides of length s is $\frac{1}{2}s\sqrt{3}$.**

A baseball diamond is a square with sides that are 90 feet long. To find the distance d from home plate to second base, use the following property of a 45-45-90 triangle. Its proof is exercise 29.

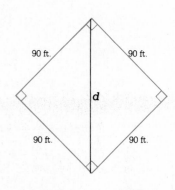

90 ft.   90 ft.

d

90 ft.   90 ft.

<u>Theorem 7.5</u> **In a 45-45-90 triangle, the length of the hypotenuse is $\sqrt{2}$ times the length of a leg.**

Given   Right $\triangle ABC$; $m\angle A = m\angle B = 45$;
         $AB = c$; $AC = a$

Prove $c = a\sqrt{2}$

Plan for Proof   Show that $BC = a$.
         Use the Pythagorean Theorem
         to show $c = a\sqrt{2}$.

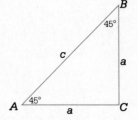

To find the distance from home plate to second base, first show that a 45-45-90 triangle is formed. Why is this true? Then apply Theorem 7.5, so that $d = 90\sqrt{2} \doteq 127$ feet.

Class Exercises

Find *x*, *y*, or both.

1.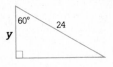

2.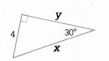

3.

4.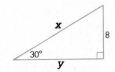

5.

6.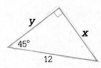

7.

8.

9.

Written Exercises

Set A   **[1-16]**

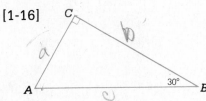

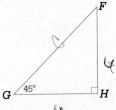

1. $AC = 6\sqrt{6}$; $BC =$ __?__

2. $AC = 8\sqrt{15}$; $BC =$ __?__

3. $AB = 4\sqrt{3}$; $BC =$ __?__

4. $AB = 6\sqrt{3}$; $BC =$ __?__

5. $BC = 6\sqrt{3}$; $AC =$ __?__

6. $BC = 12$; $AB =$ __?__

7. $FG = 6$; $GH =$ __?__

8. $FG = 12$; $FH =$ __?__

9. $FH = 14$; $FG =$ __?__

10. $GH = 9$; $FG =$ __?__

11. $FG = 18$; $GH =$ __?__

12. $FG = 20$; $FH =$ __?__

13. $FG = 3\sqrt{2}$; $FH =$ __?__

14. $FG = 5\sqrt{2}$; $GH =$ __?__

15. $GH = 9\sqrt{2}$; $FG =$ __?__

16. $FH = 15\sqrt{2}$; $FG =$ __?__

17. Find *HG*, *FH*, and *EG* in the square at the right.

[18-23] Find the perimeter of each polygon.

18.

20.

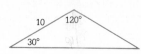

22.

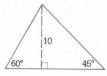

19.

21.

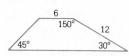

23.

[24-26] Find the lengths of the other two sides of each triangle in terms of x.

24.

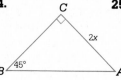

25.

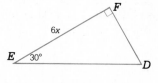

26.

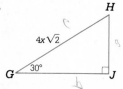

27. In $\triangle PQR$, find QR. Is $\angle PQR$ a right angle? Explain.

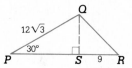

28. Prove Theorem 7.4.

29. Prove Theorem 7.5.

30. Prove Theorem 7.3.

31. Find the dimensions of the square sheet of metal from which the stop sign was cut.

32. Find the diameter of the smallest iron rod from which the regular hexagonal nut at the right can be cut.

33. Three pipes are stacked as shown. Find the height h of the stack if the diameter of each pipe is 8 inches.

7.3   Applications of the Pythagorean Theorem

Three practical applications of the Pythagorean Theorem are worked in detail in this lesson. Other applications are given in the exercises.

Example 1

The Moylans bought a 6-foot-square sheet of plywood as a base for their electric train. Will the plywood fit in the back of their van? The opening in the van is 44 inches high and 60 inches wide.

Solution

Use the Pythagorean Theorem to find the diagonal of the van opening.
$d^2 = 44^2 + 60^2 = 1936 + 3600 = 5536$
$d = \sqrt{5536} \doteq 74.4$

Since 74.4 inches is greater than 6 feet, the plywood will fit in the van.

Example 2

The Martinellis are installing a wide-screen television with a 60-inch diagonal in a paneled wall. The screen is 48 inches wide. If they cut a 36-inch by 48-inch opening in the paneling, is the opening the right size and shape?

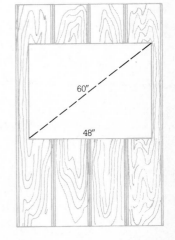

Solution

Use the converse of the Pythagorean Theorem.
$60^2 \overset{?}{=} 48^2 + 36^2$
$3600 \overset{?}{=} 2304 + 1296$
$3600 = 3600$

Since a 36-inch by 48-inch rectangle has a 60-inch diagonal, the opening is the right size and shape.

| Example 3 | The frame for this trellis is made with two pieces of wood each 1.5 m long. D is the midpoint of $\overline{AB}$. Wire is strung from A to C to B. How much wire is needed? | 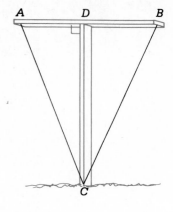 |

Solution

$\triangle ADC \cong \triangle BDC$ by SAS and $AC = BC$. Since $AB = 1.5$, $AD = 0.75$. Then,

$$AC^2 = AD^2 + DC^2$$
$$= (0.75)^2 + (1.5)^2$$
$$= 0.5625 + 2.25$$
$$= 2.8125$$

Thus $AC \doteq 1.7$ and $AC + BC \doteq 3.4$. About 3.4 m of wire are needed.

Class Exercises

[1-9] Given a square with side length s, or a rectangle with dimensions l and w. Find the length of a diagonal.

1. $s = 12$ **4.** $s = 8\sqrt{3}$ **7.** $l = 12; w = 9$

2. $s = 40$ **5.** $s = 5\sqrt{10}$ **8.** $l = 24; w = 8$

3. $s = 4\sqrt{2}$ **6.** $s = 4\sqrt{6}$ **9.** $l = w = 6\sqrt{2}$

10. The bottom of a 17-foot ramp is 15 feet from a building. How high above the ground is the top of the ramp?

Written Exercises

Set A

[1-3] The ladder is 15 feet long.

1. How high will the ladder reach if $m \angle A = 60$?

2. How high will the ladder reach if $m \angle A = 45$?

3. If the top of the ladder reaches a window sill 12 feet above the ground, how far from the house is the foot of the ladder?

4. Find the total length of wire needed to brace the two poles.

5. Find the ground distance between the two poles.

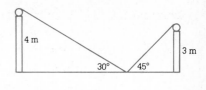

Set B

6. Find $\overline{AB}$.

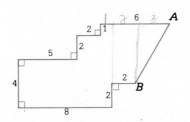

7. Find *XY*.

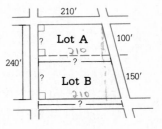

8. A carpenter built the stairs at the right. How high and how deep is each step?

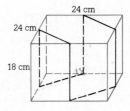

9. Find the dimensions not given in the drawing of the two lots at the right.

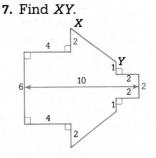

10. How much ribbon is needed for the package if each diagonal piece of ribbon passes through the midpoint of an edge?

Set C

11. $\triangle ABC$ is equilateral; $AB = 24$; $\overline{XA}$ is perpendicular to the plane of $\triangle ABC$; $m \angle XBA = 30$; and M is the midpoint of $\overline{BC}$. Find *XM*.

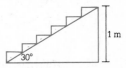

12. Find the length of wire needed to brace the two poles shown if the angles made by the wire with the ground are congruent.

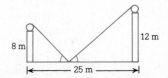

Excursion   The Pythagorean Theorem in Space

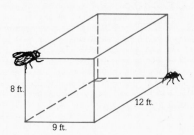

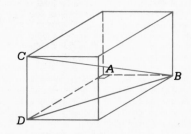

The room above is formed from six rectangles. If the fly at *C* were to fly in a straight path directly to the spider at *B*, how far would it travel?

1. Why is $\angle DAB$ a right angle?

2. Why is $\angle CDB$ a right angle?

3. Why is $BD^2 = AB^2 + AD^2$? Why is $BC^2 = BD^2 + CD^2$?

4. Why is $BC^2 = AB^2 + AD^2 + CD^2$?

5. How far would the fly travel in going from *C* to *B* in a straight path?

6. The dimensions of another room are 5 m by 4 m by 3 m. How far would the fly travel from *C* to *B* in this room?

7. A closet measures 4 feet by 8 feet by 5 feet. Will a 12-foot curtain rod fit inside?

8. A suitcase measures 24 inches by 18 inches by 10 inches. Will a 32-inch umbrella fit inside?

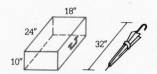

9. Assume that in the diagram at the top of the page the spider cannot fly. Find the shortest distance the spider could crawl to reach the fly. **Hint** Think of unfolding a model of the room along the lines where the walls meet.

The Coordinate Plane

Each location on this map can be described with a horizontal and vertical coordinate.

Downtown Chicago	6-G
O'Hare Airport	2-D

What are the coordinates of Glencoe? Of Evanston? Of Cicero?

Recall how a coordinate system is constructed and used. The x-axis and y-axis are perpendicular number lines. They meet at the origin, a point corresponding to 0 on both lines.

A point A is located by an ordered pair of real numbers $(-2, 3)$. The x-coordinate, -2, shows that A is two units to the left of the y-axis. The y-coordinate, 3, shows that A is three units above the x-axis.

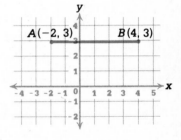

If B has coordinates $(4, 3)$, then $AB = |4 - (-2)| = 6$.

Postulate 20 allows us to place such a coordinate system on any plane.

Postulate 20

Coordinate Plane Postulate

There is a one-to-one correspondence between points in a plane and ordered pairs of real numbers such that:

1. If P and Q have coordinates (x_1, a) and (x_2, a), then $PQ = |x_2 - x_1|$, and
2. If R and S have coordinates (b, y_1) and (b, y_2), then $RS = |y_2 - y_1|$.

All points on the same horizontal line satisfy the equation $y = h$, where h is the y-coordinate of each point on the line. Similarly, all points on the same vertical line satisfy the equation $x = k$, where k is the x-coordinate of each point on the line.

Example 1	Given $A(-2, 2)$, $B(-2, -4)$, and $C(3, -4)$, find AB and BC.
Solution	Using part 2 of Postulate 20, $AB = \|-4 - 2\| = \|-6\| = 6$. Using part 1 of Postulate 20, $BC = \|3 - (-2)\| = \|5\| = 5$.

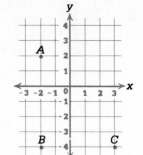

Example 2	Write equations to describe $\overleftrightarrow{AB}$ and $\overleftrightarrow{BC}$.
Solution	All points on $\overleftrightarrow{AB}$ have x-coordinate -2. Thus, the equation $x = -2$ describes $\overleftrightarrow{AB}$. Similarly, all points on $\overleftrightarrow{BC}$ have y-coordinate -4. Thus, the equation $y = -4$ describes $\overleftrightarrow{BC}$.

Class Exercises

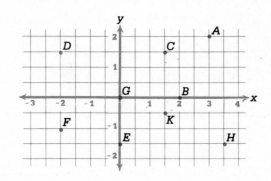

[1-6] Give the coordinates of each point.

   1. A **2.** B **3.** D **4.** E **5.** F **6.** G

[7-10] Give an equation of each line.

   7. $\overleftrightarrow{CD}$ **8.** $\overleftrightarrow{EG}$ **9.** $\overleftrightarrow{BG}$ **10.** $\overleftrightarrow{CK}$

[11-14] Find the length of each segment.

   11. $\overline{EG}$ **12.** $\overline{BG}$ **13.** $\overline{HE}$ **14.** $\overline{DF}$

Written Exercises

Set A

[1-8] Graph the following points.

1. $A(6, -2)$ **3.** $C(0, 4)$ **5.** $E(5, 5)$ **7.** $G(2.5, -2)$

2. $B(-3, 5)$ **4.** $D(-6, 0)$ **6.** $F(-3, -7)$ **8.** $H(2, -4.5)$

[9-16] Find the length of $\overline{XY}$.

9. $X(3, -1)$; $Y(-2, -1)$ **13.** $X(-5, 3.5)$; $Y(-7, 3.5)$

10. $X(6, 0)$; $Y(6, -5)$ **14.** $X(0, 17.5)$; $Y(0, 0)$

11. $X(-1, 8)$; $Y(-8, 8)$ **15.** $X(6.5, -3.5)$; $Y(-2.5, -3.5)$

12. $X(2, -7)$; $Y(2, 0)$ **16.** $X(8.5, -5)$; $Y(8.5, 2)$

Set B

[17-24] Write an equation for $\overleftrightarrow{XY}$, given the points in:

17. Exercise 9 **20.** Exercise 12 **23.** Exercise 15

18. Exercise 10 **21.** Exercise 13 **24.** Exercise 16

19. Exercise 11 **22.** Exercise 14

[25-30] Give the coordinates of the midpoint of each segment.

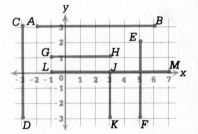

25. $\overline{AB}$ **28.** $\overline{GH}$

26. $\overline{CD}$ **29.** $\overline{JK}$

27. $\overline{EF}$ **30.** $\overline{LM}$

31. If $A(4, 1)$ is one endpoint of a segment and $M(4, -5)$ is the midpoint, find the coordinates of B, the other endpoint.

Set C

32. Study your results for exercises 25-30. Describe a way to find the coordinates of the midpoint of any vertical and any horizontal segment.

33. What is the length of the horizontal segment with endpoints $A(x_1, y_1)$ and $B(x_2, y_1)$?

34. What is the length of the vertical segment with endpoints $A(x_1, y_1)$ and $C(x_1, y_2)$?

35. Use the results of exercises 33-34 and the Pythagorean Theorem to find the distance between points B and C.

The Distance and Midpoint Formulas

The Pythagorean Theorem can be used to find the length of a segment that is neither vertical nor horizontal.

To find AB, draw a vertical line through B and a horizontal line through A to form right $\triangle ABC$. The coordinates of C are $(4, -3)$.

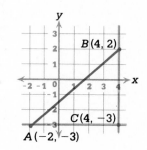

By the Pythagorean Theorem,

$$AB^2 = AC^2 + BC^2$$
$$= |{-2} - 4|^2 + |{-3} - 2|^2$$
$$= 61$$
$$AB = \sqrt{61}$$

This suggests a formula for the length of any segment.

$$AB^2 = AC^2 + BC^2$$
$$= |x_2 - x_1|^2 + |y_2 - y_1|^2$$
$$= (x_2 - x_1)^2 + (y_2 - y_1)^2$$
$$AB = \sqrt{(x_2 - x_1)^2 + (y_2 - y_1)^2}$$

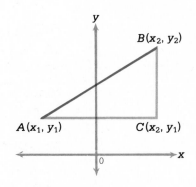

Theorem 7.6

Distance Formula

If the coordinates of P and Q are (x_1, y_1) and (x_2, y_2), respectively, then the distance between them is given by the formula

$$PQ = \sqrt{(x_2 - x_1)^2 + (y_2 - y_1)^2}.$$

Example 1

Find GH for $G(-5, 4)$ and $H(3, -2)$.

Solution

$$GH = \sqrt{(x_2 - x_1)^2 + (y_2 - y_1)^2}$$
$$= \sqrt{[3 - (-5)]^2 + (-2 - 4)^2}$$
$$= \sqrt{64 + 36}$$
$$= \sqrt{100}$$
$$= 10$$

Another useful formula gives the coordinates of the midpoint M of any segment $\overline{PQ}$.

If $\overline{PQ}$ is horizontal and $x_1 < x_2$, then the x-coordinate of

$$
\begin{aligned}
M &= x_1 + PM \\
&= x_1 + \tfrac{1}{2}PQ \\
&= x_1 + \tfrac{1}{2}(x_2 - x_1) \\
&= \tfrac{1}{2}x_1 + \tfrac{1}{2}x_2 \\
&= \frac{x_1 + x_2}{2}
\end{aligned}
$$

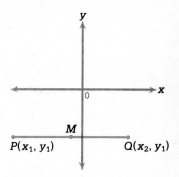

By a similar argument, if $\overline{PQ}$ is a vertical segment, then the y-coordinate of M is $\dfrac{y_1 + y_2}{2}$.

If $\overline{PQ}$ is neither vertical nor horizontal, to find the coordinates of the midpoint M, draw the horizontal and vertical segments shown at the right.

Since $\overline{MR} \parallel \overline{QT}$, $\triangle PMR \sim \triangle PQT$ and R is the midpoint of $\overline{PT}$. Similarly $\triangle QSM \sim \triangle QTP$ and S is the midpoint of $\overline{TQ}$.

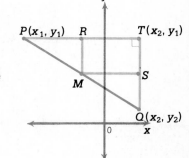

Then find the x-coordinate of R and the y-coordinate of S and use these to get:

$$
M\left(\frac{x_1 + x_2}{2}, \frac{y_1 + y_2}{2} \right)
$$

This suggests a proof for Theorem 7.7.

Theorem 7.7

Midpoint Formula

If the coordinates of P and Q are (x_1, y_1) and (x_2, y_2), respectively, then the midpoint of $\overline{PQ}$ has coordinates

$$
\left(\frac{x_1 + x_2}{2}, \frac{y_1 + y_2}{2} \right)
$$

Example 2

Find the coordinates of the midpoint M of $\overline{GH}$ for $G(-7, 5)$ and $H(3, 7)$.

Solution

The coordinates are $\left(\dfrac{-7 + 3}{2}, \dfrac{5 + 7}{2} \right)$ or $(-2, 6)$.

Class Exercises

[1-6] Find the distance between the given points.

1. $A(3, 4)$; $B(3, -2)$ **4.** $J(-1, -1)$; $K(6, 2)$

2. $C(-6, 7)$; $D(-1, 7)$ **5.** $L(3, -3)$; $M(-2, 5)$

3. $E(0, 0)$; $F(1, -3)$ **6.** $P(-3, -6)$; $Q(2, -1)$

[7-12] Find the coordinates of the midpoint of $\overline{AB}$.

7. $A(-2, 4)$; $B(-8, 4)$ **10.** $A(3, 0)$; $B(9, 12)$

8. $A(1, 5)$; $B(1, -9)$ **11.** $A(-2, -2)$; $B(2, 2)$

9. $A(2, 3)$; $B(4, 0)$ **12.** $A(5, -5)$; $B(-7, 7)$

Written Exercises

Set A

[1-4] Find the distance between the given points.

1. $A(-1, 2)$; $B(-9, 10)$ **3.** $E(-4, 7)$; $F(10, 0)$

2. $C(2, 1)$; $D(7, -11)$ **4.** $G(6, 1)$; $H(-2, 7)$

[5-8] Find the coordinates of the midpoint of $\overline{PQ}$.

5. $P(0, 2)$; $Q(4, 10)$ **7.** $P(4, 7)$; $Q(-2, -5)$

6. $P(-5, -4)$; $Q(-3, -6)$ **8.** $P(-5, -1)$; $Q(1, 1)$

[9-12] Find point B so that M is the midpoint of $\overline{AB}$.

9. $A(3, -2)$; $M(0, -1)$ **11.** $A(0, -1)$; $M(4, 3)$

10. $A(-4, 1)$; $M(-2, -3)$ **12.** $A(0, 4)$; $M(3, 1)$

[13-18] Show that $\triangle ABC$ is the type of triangle indicated.

13. $A(-2, 2)$; $B(6, 6)$; $C(2, -2)$; isosceles

14. $A(-2, 3)$; $B(6, -1)$; $C(4, 5)$; isosceles

15. $A(-7, 1)$; $B(-3, 5)$; $C(4, -2)$; right

16. $A(-2, -3)$; $B(4, 1)$; $C(2, 4)$; right

17. $A(-1, -1)$; $B(-5, 7)$; $C(7, 3)$; isosceles and right

18. $A(-3, 4)$; $B(-5, 0)$; $C(1, 2)$; isosceles and right

Chapter 7   Right Triangles

[19-20] Recall that if both pairs of opposite sides of a quadrilateral are congruent, then it is a parallelogram. Show that $ABCD$ is a parallelogram.

19. $A(-5, -2)$; $B(4, -2)$; $C(6, 4)$; $D(-3, 4)$
20. $A(-4, -4)$; $B(2, -2)$; $C(4, 3)$; $D(-2, 1)$

[21-22] Show that $\square$ $PQRS$ is a rectangle.

21. $P(0, 0)$; $Q(-6, -8)$; $R(-10, -5)$; $S(-4, 3)$
22. $P(-3, 2)$; $Q(2, 1)$; $R(0, -9)$; $S(-5, -8)$

[23-26] Find the midpoint of $\overline{JK}$.

23. $J(2a, 0)$; $K(0, 4a)$ **25.** $J(10, -4u)$; $K(2v, 6)$
24. $J(3t, 5)$; $K(-t, 3)$ **26.** $J(-7e, 4f)$; $K(e, -6f)$

[27-28] Right $\triangle SUN$ has vertices $S(-1, 2)$, $U(-3, 6)$, and $N(3, 4)$.

27. Find the coordinates of the midpoint of the hypotenuse.
28. Show that the length of the median to the hypotenuse is half the length of the hypotenuse.

[29-30] $\triangle SEA$ has vertices $S(6, 8)$, $E(-2, 8)$, and $A(4, 0)$.

29. Find X and Y, the midpoints of $\overline{SA}$ and $\overline{EA}$, respectively.
30. Show that $XY = \frac{1}{2} SE$.

31. Show that the quadrilateral with vertices $S(0, 0)$, $T(b, 0)$, $A(b + c, d)$, and $R(c, d)$ is a parallelogram.

Geometry Maintenance

1. Give four ways of proving that two triangles are similar.
2. Given: $\triangle ABC \sim \triangle DEF$. Name five pairs of corresponding segments that are proportional and have an endpoint at B or E.
3. Given: Right $\triangle PQR$ with hypotenuse $\overline{PR}$, and altitude to the hypotenuse $\overline{QS}$. Name two triangles similar to $\triangle PQR$.

Using BASIC

Distances Between Points

This program finds distances on a coordinate plane.

```
100 REM FINDING TOTAL DISTANCE TO 3 GIVEN POINTS
110 LET B = 1000    The variable B will hold "best total" distance.
120 FOR I = 1 TO 3
130 READ X(I),Y(I)     Read in coordinates of three given points.
140 NEXT I
150 INPUT "POINT TO TEST? ";TX,TY
160 LET S = 0    S holds total for current test point.
170 FOR I = 1 TO 3
180 LET D = SQR((TX-X(I))^2+(TY-Y(I))^2)
190 LET S = S + D
200 NEXT I
210 IF S>=B THEN 260    Change nothing if current total is
220 LET B = S                larger than previous best total;
230 LET BX = TX              otherwise change "best total" (B),
240 LET BY = TY              "best X" (BX), and "best Y" (BY).
250 PRINT " X";TAB(7);" Y","SUM OF DIST."    Table headings
260 PRINT TX;TAB(7);TY,S
270 INPUT "TEST ANOTHER POINT (YES OR NO)? ";C$
280 IF C$ = "YES" THEN 150
290 PRINT "LOWEST SUM OF DISTANCES IS ";B
300 PRINT "AT POINT (";BX;",";BY;")"
310 DATA 0,0,1,2,4,0
320 END
```

1. A retailer has three stores at (0, 0), (1, 2), and (4, 0). Four possible locations for a warehouse are (0, 1), (2, 0), (1.67, .333), and (1.5, .333). Which location has the least total distance to the three stores?

2. Do any other locations have smaller total distances?

3. Revise the program with these lines and RUN:

```
150 PRINT " X";TAB(7);" Y","SUM OF DIST."
155 FOR TX = 0 TO 4 STEP .2
158 FOR TY = 0 TO 2 STEP .5
250
270 NEXT TY
280 NEXT TX
```

Progress Check

Lesson 7.1
Page 314

Can the following lengths be sides of a right triangle?

1. 5, 7, 10 **2.** 11, 60, 61 **3.** 7, 24, 25

[4-5] Given: Right $\triangle ABC$ with hypotenuse c

4. $b = 2$, $a = 4$, $c =$ __?__ **5.** $c = 37$, $a = 35$, $b =$ __?__

Lesson 7.2
Page 319

[6-9] Given: $\triangle CAT$

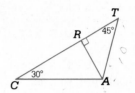

6. $AT = 10$; $RA =$ __?__

7. $AR = 25$; $AT =$ __?__

8. $CA = 10\sqrt{3}$; $AR =$ __?__

9. $CR = 8\sqrt{3}$; $CA =$ __?__

Lesson 7.3
Page 323

10. How far from the base of a building must a 12-foot ladder be placed to make an angle of 60° with the ground?

11. What is the height of the roof?

12. If a car is driven 12 km due north and 10 km due east, to the nearest kilometer, how far is the car from its starting point?

Lesson 7.4
Page 327

Give the coordinates of the points.

13. A **14.** B **15.** C

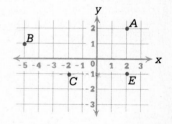

16. Find the coordinates of the midpoint of $\overline{CE}$.

17. Write an equation for $\overleftrightarrow{AE}$.

Lesson 7.5
Page 330

18. Find XY, given $X(-2, 3)$ and $Y(4, -5)$.

19. Find the coordinates of the midpoint of $\overline{RS}$, given $R(6, -9)$ and $S(-4, -2)$.

20. The vertices of $\triangle ABC$ are $A(4, -2)$, $B(2, 4)$ and $C(0, -3)$. Is $\triangle ABC$ a right triangle?

Right Triangle Trigonometry

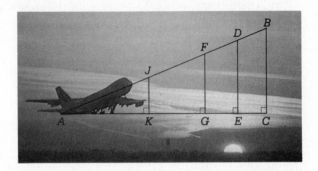

Similar triangles and the Pythagorean Theorem can be combined to produce new and useful relations. In right $\triangle ABC$ above, $\overline{DE}$, $\overline{FG}$, and $\overline{JK}$ have been constructed perpendicular to leg $\overline{AC}$ from hypotenuse $\overline{AB}$. By the AA Postulate, $\triangle AJK \sim \triangle AFG \sim \triangle ADE \sim \triangle ABC$.

This means that $\dfrac{BC}{AC} = \dfrac{DE}{AE} = \dfrac{FG}{AG} = \dfrac{JK}{AK}$. This common ratio is the **tangent ratio** for $\angle A$.

Also by similar triangles, $\dfrac{BC}{AB} = \dfrac{DE}{AD} = \dfrac{FG}{AF} = \dfrac{JK}{AJ}$. This common ratio is the **sine ratio** for $\angle A$.

Again, by similar triangles, $\dfrac{AC}{AB} = \dfrac{AE}{AD} = \dfrac{AG}{AF} = \dfrac{AK}{AJ}$. This common ratio is the **cosine ratio** for $\angle A$.

Definition

In a right $\triangle ABC$ with acute $\angle A$:

$$\tan A = \frac{\text{length of side opposite } \angle A}{\text{length of side adjacent to } \angle A}$$

$$\sin A = \frac{\text{length of side opposite } \angle A}{\text{length of hypotenuse}}$$

$$\cos A = \frac{\text{length of side adjacent } \angle A}{\text{length of hypotenuse}}$$

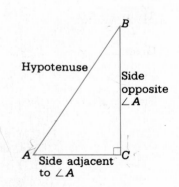

If an acute angle of one right triangle is congruent to the corresponding acute angle of another right triangle, then the triangles are similar. Hence, for a given acute angle, each of the three **trigonometric ratios** is constant.

Thus, for any right triangle ABC with acute $\angle A$,

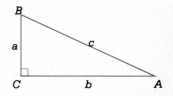

$$\tan A = \frac{a}{b}, \ \sin A = \frac{a}{c}, \text{ and } \cos A = \frac{b}{c}.$$

Example

Give the tangent, sine, and cosine ratios for $\angle P$ in $\triangle PQR$. Give the three ratios of $\angle Q$ in $\triangle PQR$.

Solution

Since $\triangle PQR$ is a 30-60-90 triangle, $QR = 2$ and $PR = 2\sqrt{3}$. Thus,

TOA
SOH
CAH

$$\tan P = \frac{2}{2\sqrt{3}} = \frac{1}{\sqrt{3}} = \frac{\sqrt{3}}{3};$$

$$\sin P = \frac{2}{4} = \frac{1}{2}; \text{ and } \cos P = \frac{2\sqrt{3}}{4} = \frac{\sqrt{3}}{2}.$$

Also, $\tan Q = \frac{2\sqrt{3}}{2} = \sqrt{3}$;

$$\sin Q = \frac{2\sqrt{3}}{4} = \frac{\sqrt{3}}{2}; \text{ and } \cos Q = \frac{2}{4} = \frac{1}{2}.$$

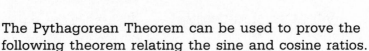

The Pythagorean Theorem can be used to prove the following theorem relating the sine and cosine ratios.

Theorem 7.8 In a right triangle ABC with right $\angle C$, $(\sin A)^2 + (\cos A)^2 = 1$.

Given Right $\triangle ABC$ with rt. $\angle C$

Prove $(\sin A)^2 + (\cos A)^2 = 1$.

Plan for Proof Use the Pythagorean Theorem to show $a^2 + b^2 = c^2$.
Divide through by c^2.
Then use the def. of sine and cosine.

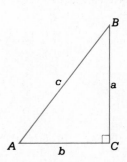

Class Exercises

[1-5] Name each of the following segments in right △*PQR*.

1. Hypotenuse of △*PQR*
2. Side opposite ∠*P*
3. Side adjacent to ∠*P*
4. Side opposite ∠*Q*
5. Side adjacent to ∠*Q*

[6-8] Name each ratio with respect to ∠*P*.

6. $\dfrac{p}{r}$ 7. $\dfrac{q}{r}$ 8. $\dfrac{p}{q}$

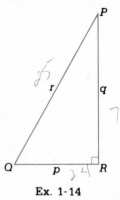
Ex. 1-14

[9-11] Name each ratio with respect to ∠*Q*.

9. $\dfrac{p}{r}$ 10. $\dfrac{q}{r}$ 11. $\dfrac{q}{p}$

[12-14] Given: $p = 24$, $q = 7$, $r = 25$; find each ratio.

12. $\cos Q$ 13. $\sin P$ 14. $\tan Q$

Written Exercises

Set A

Write each ratio in simplest form.

1. $\tan X$ 3. $\sin X$ 5. $\cos X$
2. $\tan Y$ 4. $\sin Y$ 6. $\cos Y$

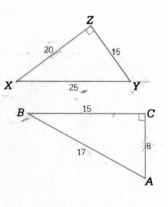

In right △*ABC*, name the trigonometric ratio represented for the given angle.

7. $\dfrac{15}{8}$; ∠*A*   9. $\dfrac{15}{17}$; ∠*A*   11. $\dfrac{8}{15}$; ∠*B*

8. $\dfrac{8}{17}$; ∠*A*   10. $\dfrac{8}{17}$; ∠*B*   12. $\dfrac{15}{17}$; ∠*B*

13. Use the dimensions of △*XYZ* in exercises 1-6 to verify that $(\sin X)^2 + (\cos X)^2 = 1$.

14. Use the dimensions of $\triangle ABC$ in exercises 7-12 to verify that $(\sin B)^2 + (\cos B)^2 = 1$.

[15-17] Draw square $PQRS$ with diagonal $\overline{PR}$ and $PQ = 4$ cm.

15. What kind of triangle is $\triangle PQR$?
16. How long is $\overline{PR}$?
17. Find $\sin 45°$, $\cos 45°$, and $\tan 45°$.

Set B

Given: $\triangle UVW$ with rt. $\angle W$, $\sin U = \dfrac{3}{5}$, $\cos U = \dfrac{4}{5}$, $\tan U = \dfrac{3}{4}$

18. If $VW = 9$, then $UW = \underline{\ ?\ }$ and $UV = \underline{\ ?\ }$.
19. If $UW = 6$, then $VW = \underline{\ ?\ }$ and $UV = \underline{\ ?\ }$.

Draw $\triangle ABC$ with right $\angle C$, $AC = 7$ cm, and $BC = 24$ cm.

20. $AB = \underline{\ ?\ }$.
21. Evaluate $\sin A$, $\cos A$, and $\tan A$.
22. Evaluate $\sin B$, $\cos B$, and $\tan B$.
23. What is the relationship between $\sin A$ and $\cos B$?
24. What is the value of $(\tan A)(\tan B)$?

Draw $\triangle HJK$ with right $\angle K$, $m\angle H = 40$, and $HK = 10$ cm.

25. Give a ratio of lengths of segments to represent $\tan H$.
26. Measure $\overline{JK}$.
27. Use this measurement to find $\tan 40°$.
28. Repeat exercises 25-27 for $m\angle H = 50$.

Set C

29. Prove Theorem 7.8.

30. If $\sin 53° = \dfrac{4}{5}$, how high is the kite?

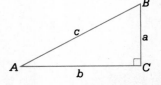

Prove in any right $\triangle ABC$ with right $\angle C$:

31. $\sin A = \cos B$
32. $(\tan A)(\tan B) = 1$

33. $\dfrac{\sin A}{\cos A} = \tan A$

Trigonometric Ratios

A surveyor uses trigonometric ratios to determine exact locations and distances.

Trigonometric ratios can be used to find the measures of sides or angles in a right triangle. Decimal values of these ratios can be found by using calculators or tables like the one on page 343. Each ratio is expressed as a decimal. Since many of these ratios involve irrational numbers, most of the decimals are approximations. A portion of the table is shown.

$m \angle A$ in degrees	tan A	sin A	cos A
20	.3640	.3420	.9397
21	.3839	.3584	.9336
22	.4040	.3746	.9272
23	.4245	.3907	.9205
24	.4452	.4067	.9135
25	.4663	.4226	.9063
26	.4877	.4384	.8988

Example 1   Find tan 23° from the table.

Solution   First find the angle measure in the column at the left. In the same row and in the second column is an approximate value for tan 23°. Thus, tan 23° ≐ 0.4245.

From the same portion of the table:
sin 20° ≐ 0.3420, cos 25° ≐ 0.9063, and tan 24° ≐ 0.4452.

The table can also be used to find the measure of an angle to the nearest degree, given one of its trigonometric ratios.

Example 2	If $\sin A = 0.4226$, find $m\angle A$.

Solution

First find .4226 in the "sin A" column. Then in the same row, read the entry in the "angle" column. Thus $m\angle A = 25$.

At times you may compute a value for a trigonometric ratio that does not match any entry in the table.

Example 3

Find the measure of the angle of the sun's rays, $\angle A$ in the diagram, when a 4-meter pole casts a 3-meter shadow.

Solution

$\tan A = \dfrac{4}{3} \doteq 1.3333$

This value is not in the table. But it lies between 1.3270 and 1.3764, which are $\tan 53°$ and $\tan 54°$. Since 1.3333 is closer to 1.3270, $m\angle A \doteq 53$. So the measure of the angle of the sun's rays is about 53°.

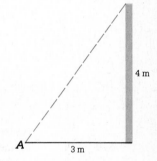

Class Exercises

Use the table on page 343.

1. As you read down the column entitled $m\angle A$, do the values increase or decrease?
2. As $m\angle A$ increases, does $\sin A$ increase or decrease?
3. As $m\angle A$ increases, does $\tan A$ increase or decrease?
4. As $m\angle A$ increases, does $\cos A$ increase or decrease?
5. For what values of $\angle A$ does $\sin A = \cos A$?
6. For what values of $\angle A$ is $\tan A = 1$? $\tan A > 1$? $\tan A < 1$?
7. For what values of $\angle A$ is $\sin A > \cos A$? $\sin A < \cos A$?
8. For what values of $\angle A$ is $\sin A > 1$? $\cos A > 1$?
9. For what values of $\angle A$ and $\angle B$ does $\sin A = \cos B$? How are these angles related?
10. For what values of $\angle A$ is $\tan A > \sin A$? $\tan A < \sin A$?

Written Exercises

Use a calculator or the table on page 343 as needed.

Use a calculator or the table on page 343 as needed.

Set A

Give a decimal value for each ratio.

   1. $\sin 29°$ **3.** $\tan 35°$ **5.** $\cos 17°$ **7.** $\sin 73°$

   2. $\sin 41°$ **4.** $\tan 15°$ **6.** $\cos 32°$ **8.** $\cos 54°$

Find $m\angle A$ to the nearest degree.

   9. $\sin A = 0.1564$ **12.** $\cos A = 0.6157$

  10. $\sin A = 0.8988$ **13.** $\tan A = 2.9042$

  11. $\cos A = 0.8910$ **14.** $\tan A = 0.8098$

Set B

Determine, to the nearest degree, the measures of the acute angles of a right triangle given the lengths of the legs.

  15. 7 and 24   **16.** 8 and 15

17. If the base of an isosceles triangle has length 16 and the measure of the vertex angle is 72°, what is the length of each leg?

18. If the length of each leg of an isosceles triangle is 24 and a base angle has measure 55°, how long is the base?

19. How tall is the tree?   **20.** How wide is the river?

76°

5 m

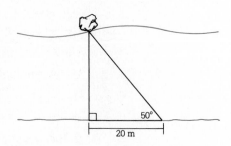

50°

20 m

Set C

21. Prove that $\tan A > \sin A$. Why does the table show some values for which $\tan A = \sin A$?

22. Prove that $\sin A > \cos A$ for $m\angle A > 45$ and that $\sin A < \cos A$ for $m\angle A < 45$.

Chapter 7   Right Triangles

Tangents, Sines, and Cosines

m∠A in degrees	tan A	sin A	cos A	m∠A in degrees	tan A	sin A	cos A
1	.0175	.0175	.9998	46	1.0355	.7193	.6947
2	.0349	.0349	.9994	47	1.0724	.7314	.6820
3	.0524	.0523	.9986	48	1.1106	.7431	.6691
4	.0699	.0698	.9976	49	1.1504	.7547	.6561
5	.0875	.0872	.9962	50	1.1918	.7660	.6428
6	.1051	.1045	.9945	51	1.2349	.7771	.6293
7	.1228	.1219	.9925	52	1.2799	.7880	.6157
8	.1405	.1392	.9903	53	1.3270	.7986	.6018
9	.1584	.1564	.9877	54	1.3764	.8090	.5878
10	.1763	.1736	.9848	55	1.4281	.8192	.5736
11	.1944	.1908	.9816	56	1.4826	.8290	.5592
12	.2126	.2079	.9781	57	1.5399	.8387	.5446
13	.2309	.2250	.9744	58	1.6003	.8480	.5299
14	.2493	.2419	.9703	59	1.6643	.8572	.5150
15	.2679	.2588	.9659	60	1.7321	.8660	.5000
16	.2867	.2756	.9613	61	1.8040	.8746	.4848
17	.3057	.2924	.9563	62	1.8807	.8829	.4695
18	.3249	.3090	.9511	63	1.9626	.8910	.4540
19	.3443	.3256	.9455	64	2.0503	.8988	.4384
20	.3640	.3420	.9397	65	2.1445	.9063	.4226
21	.3839	.3584	.9336	66	2.2460	.9135	.4067
22	.4040	.3746	.9272	67	2.3559	.9205	.3907
23	.4245	.3907	.9205	68	2.4751	.9272	.3746
24	.4452	.4067	.9135	69	2.6051	.9336	.3584
25	.4663	.4226	.9063	70	2.7475	.9397	.3420
26	.4877	.4384	.8988	71	2.9042	.9455	.3256
27	.5095	.4540	.8910	72	3.0777	.9511	.3090
28	.5317	.4695	.8829	73	3.2709	.9563	.2924
29	.5543	.4848	.8746	74	3.4874	.9613	.2756
30	.5774	.5000	.8660	75	3.7321	.9659	.2588
31	.6009	.5150	.8572	76	4.0108	.9703	.2419
32	.6249	.5299	.8480	77	4.3315	.9744	.2250
33	.6494	.5446	.8387	78	4.7046	.9781	.2079
34	.6745	.5592	.8290	79	5.1446	.9816	.1908
35	.7002	.5736	.8192	80	5.6713	.9848	.1736
36	.7265	.5878	.8090	81	6.3138	.9877	.1564
37	.7536	.6018	.7986	82	7.1154	.9903	.1392
38	.7813	.6157	.7880	83	8.1443	.9925	.1219
39	.8098	.6293	.7771	84	9.5144	.9945	.1045
40	.8391	.6428	.7660	85	11.4301	.9962	.0872
41	.8693	.6561	.7547	86	14.3007	.9976	.0698
42	.9004	.6691	.7431	87	19.0811	.9986	.0523
43	.9325	.6820	.7314	88	28.6363	.9994	.0349
44	.9657	.6947	.7193	89	57.2900	.9998	.0175
45	1.0000	.7071	.7071				

Applications of Trigonometric Ratios

Trigonometric ratios can be used to solve many practical problems. Two special angles often occur in these problems. The angle between a horizontal line and the line of sight to a point above the observer is the **angle of elevation.** The angle between a horizontal line and the line of sight to a point below the observer is the **angle of depression.**

In the diagram below $\angle BAC$ is an angle of depression and $\angle ACD$ is an angle of elevation. Since the horizontal lines are parallel lines cut by a transversal, $\angle BAC$ and $\angle ACD$ are alternate interior angles. Therefore the angle of depression and the angle of elevation are congruent.

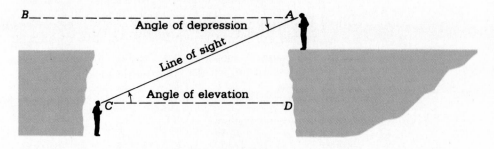

Example 1

An observer stands atop a building 25 m above the ground, and the angle of depression to a car on the ground is 27°. How far is the car from the building?

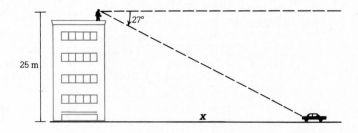

Solution

$$\tan 27° = \frac{25}{x}$$

$$x = \frac{25}{\tan 27°} \doteq \frac{25}{.5095} \doteq 49$$

The car is about 49 m from the building.

Example 2   A ladder is mounted on a firetruck, six
feet above the ground. If the maximum
length of the ladder is 120 feet, and the
maximum angle to which it can be safely
raised is 75°, how high will it reach?

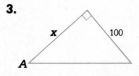

Solution $\sin 75° = \dfrac{x}{120}$

$x = 120(\sin 75°) \doteq 120(.9659) \doteq 115.9$
Then, $h = 115.9 + 6 \doteq 121.9$
The ladder can reach about 122 feet above the ground.

Class Exercises

[1-3] Give the trigonometric ratio which relates 100 and x to
$\angle A$. Write an equation to represent the relationship.

1.   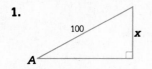   **2.**   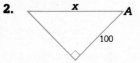   **3.**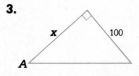

[4-7] (a) Identify the indicated angle as an angle of elevation
or of depression. (b) Tell which trigonometric ratio you would
use to find x. (c) Find x.

4.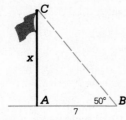

6.

5.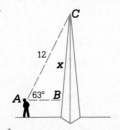

7.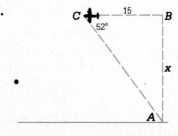

Written Exercises

1. How tall is the building?

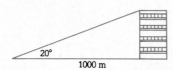

3. How high will the ladder reach?

2. How wide is the river?

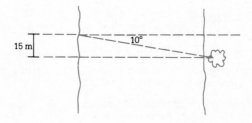

4. How tall is the San Jacinto Monument?

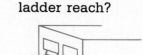

5. A rock dropped from the top of the Leaning Tower of Pisa lands 14 feet from the base of the tower. If the tower is 182 feet tall, at what angle does it lean from the vertical?

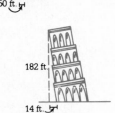

6. Sonar on a destroyer detects a submarine 400 m away. If the angle is 31°, what is the depth of the submarine?

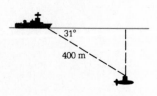

7. A car drives up a slope of 6° for 150 m and drives another 100 m at a slope of 9°. How far has the car climbed vertically?

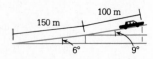

8. The angle of depression to the near and far banks of a river are 49° and 11°, respectively. If the observer is 1.8 m tall, how wide is the river?

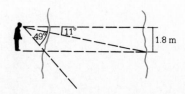

Career   Landscape Architect

Violeta Conti is a landscape architect. She is planning several gardens for a shopping mall. One flower bed has the shape of a regular polygon with 18 sides.

To position the stakes at the vertices of the polygon, Violeta first places a stake at point C, the center of the polygon. Then she uses a rope 2.5 m long to measure the distance from C to each vertex. She uses trigonometry to determine the distance between the stakes for the vertices.

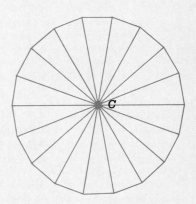

Exercises

$\triangle ACB$ is part of the plan above. The distance between the stakes is AB, and $\overline{CD}$ bisects $\angle ACB$.

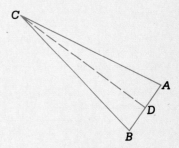

1. What kind of triangle is $\triangle ACB$?
2. What is $m\angle ACB$? $m\angle CBA$? $m\angle CDB$?
3. Find DB.
4. What is the distance between the stakes for the vertices?

Chapter Summary

1. A triangle is a right triangle if and only if the square of the length of the hypotenuse is equal to the sum of the squares of the lengths of the legs. (pages 315, 316)

2. In a 30-60-90 triangle with a shorter leg of length b:
   a. the length of the hypotenuse is $2b$, and
   b. the length of the longer leg is $b\sqrt{3}$. (page 319)

3. In a 45-45-90 triangle with legs of length a, the length of the hypotenuse is $a\sqrt{2}$. (page 320)

4. There is a one-to-one correspondence between points in a plane and ordered pairs of real numbers such that:
   a. If P and Q have coordinates (x_1, a) and (x_2, a), then $PQ = |x_2 - x_1|$, and
   b. If R and S have coordinates (b, y_1) and (b, y_2), then $RS = |y_2 - y_1|$. (page 327)

5. All points on the same horizontal line satisfy the equation $y = h$, where h is the y-coordinate of each point on the line. Similarly, all points on the same vertical line satisfy the equation $x = k$, where k is the x-coordinate of each point on the line. (page 327)

6. Given the points $P(x_1, y_1)$ and $Q(x_2, y_2)$:
   a. The distance PQ is $\sqrt{(x_2 - x_1)^2 + (y_2 - y_1)^2}$. (page 330)
   b. The midpoint of $\overline{PQ}$ is $M\left(\dfrac{x_1 + x_2}{2}, \dfrac{y_1 + y_2}{2}\right)$. (page 331)

7. The trigonometric ratios in a right triangle are:
   a. $\sin A = \dfrac{a}{c}$
   b. $\cos A = \dfrac{b}{c}$
   c. $\tan A = \dfrac{a}{b}$ (page 336)

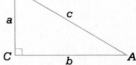

8. For any acute $\angle A$, $(\sin A)^2 + (\cos A)^2 = 1$. (page 337)

Chapter Review

Lesson 7.1
Page 314

[1-2] In $\triangle ABC$, $\angle C$ is a right angle.

1. $AC = 15$; $BC = 20$; $AB = \underline{\ ?\ }$.
2. $AB = 36$; $AC = 4$; $BC = \underline{\ ?\ }$.

3. Find the length of the diagonal of a rectangle that is 9 cm by 18 cm.

Lesson 7.2
Page 319

4. $AB = 8\sqrt{2}$; $AC = \underline{\ ?\ }$.   5. $YZ = 36$; $XZ = \underline{\ ?\ }$.

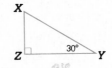

6. Find the length of a diagonal of a square with sides of length 64 cm.

7. Find the length of an altitude of an equilateral triangle with sides of length 20 cm.

Lesson 7.3
Page 323

[8-10] Give answers to the nearest unit.

8. The dimensions of a football field are 160 ft. by 300 ft. What is the distance between opposite corners of the field?

9. If the sun's rays make an angle of 60° with the ground, how long is the shadow of a person who is 180 cm tall?

10. The tower is 10.5 m high, and each wire brace is attached 4.5 m from the center of the base of the tower. Find the total length of wire needed for the three braces.

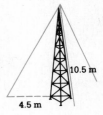

Lesson 7.4
Page 327

[11-14] $A(-1, 6)$, $B(7, -3)$, and $C(-1, -3)$

11. Graph points A, B, and C.
12. Find AC.
13. Find the coordinates of the midpoint of $\overline{BC}$.
14. Write an equation for $\overleftrightarrow{AC}$.

Lesson 7.5
Page 330

[15-17] $X(2, 7)$, $Y(-4, -1)$, and $A(3, 0)$

15. Find XY.

16. Find the coordinates of the midpoint of $\overline{XY}$.

17. Show that $\triangle XYA$ is a right triangle.

Lesson 7.6
Page 336

[18-21] Write each ratio.

18. $\tan A$ **20.** $\sin B$

19. $\tan B$ **21.** $\cos B$

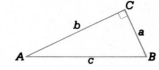

[22-23] In $\triangle XYZ$, identify the trigonometric ratio for the given angle.

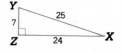

22. $\dfrac{24}{25}$; $\angle X$ **23.** $\dfrac{24}{7}$; $\angle Y$

[24-31] Use a calculator or the table on page 343.

Lesson 7.7
Page 340

[24-26] Give each ratio as a decimal.

24. $\sin 39°$ **25.** $\cos 85°$ **26.** $\tan 52°$

[27-28] Find $m\angle A$ to the nearest degree.

27. $\cos A = 0.3746$ **28.** $\tan A = 0.5310$

Lesson 7.8
Page 344

[29-31] Give each answer to the nearest degree or unit.

29. How long is the wire brace?

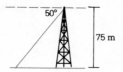

30. How far is the boat from the base of the cliff?

31. A treasure chest is buried 150 ft. under a building. If the entrance to a tunnel is begun 850 ft. from the building, at what angle must the tunnel slope to reach the treasure?

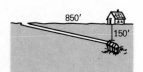

Chapter Test

[1-5] Given: Right $\triangle ABC$ with right $\angle C$

1. $AC = 14$; $BC = 48$; $AB = $ ___?___.
2. $AB = 9$; $AC = 7$; $BC = $ ___?___.
3. $AB = 18$; $m\angle A = 45°$; $AC = $ ___?___.
4. $BC = 24$; $m\angle A = 30°$; $AC = $ ___?___.
5. $BC = 20\sqrt{3}$; $m\angle A = 60°$; $AB = $ ___?___.

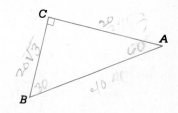

[6-10] Given: $X(3, 8)$, $Y(3, -7)$, and $Z(-6, -4)$

6. Graph points X, Y, and Z.
7. Find YZ.
8. Find the coordinates of the midpoints of $\overline{XZ}$.
9. Write an equation for $\overleftrightarrow{XY}$.
10. Show that $\triangle XYZ$ is isosceles.

11. Write a ratio that represents $\tan P$.
12. What trigonometric ratio does $\dfrac{20}{29}$ represent with respect to $\angle Q$?

[13-17] Use a calculator or the table on page 343. In items 14-17, give answer correct to the nearest degree or unit.

13. Give a decimal approximation for $\sin 48°$.
14. If $\tan A = 4.0108$, find $m\angle A$.
15. A rectangular enclosure is 75 m by 100 m. How much fencing is needed to divide the enclosure diagonally?

16. If 250 m of string have been let out as the kite passes over a point 150 m away, how high is the kite?

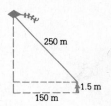

17. The golf ball was driven 300 yd. How long must the putt be to reach the hole?

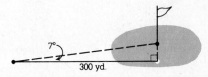

Chapter 8

Circles

As a ship nears the coastline, it must avoid dangerous rocks and shoals. Based on sailors' observations, the hazardous waters are charted. Then the region is represented by a circle, as shown below. The circle passes through lighthouses *A* and *B*. Point *C* is any other point on the part of the circle which passes through the water.

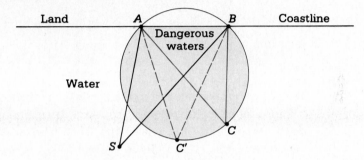

1. ∠*C* is called the *horizontal danger angle.* Use your protractor to find the measure of ∠*C*.

2. Do you think the measure of ∠*C* is the same for all locations of *C*? For example, does *m*∠*C'* = *m*∠*C*?

3. Let *S* be the location of the ship. Instruments mounted on the ship can determine the measure of ∠*ASB*. Measure ∠*ASB*. How does its measure compare with the measure of ∠*C*?

4. Trace the diagram above. Choose a point, *S'*, inside the circle to represent the ship sailing in dangerous waters. Measure ∠*AS'B*. How does its measure compare with the measure of ∠*C*?

5. Let *S"* be another location of the ship. Where is the ship if *m*∠*AS"B* = *m*∠*AS'B*?

6. Explain how sailors use the horizontal danger angle to keep out of dangerous water. **Hint** Consider your answers to exercises 3, 4, and 5.

Circles and Spheres

The photograph above shows *center point irrigation.* The circular field is irrigated by dozens of sprinkler outlets positioned on a pipe that runs from the center of the field to its outer edge. The pipe is mounted on wheels and is driven by electrical power. It sweeps around the entire field. As it does, each sprinkler outlet travels the path of a circle.

Definition

A **circle** is the set of coplanar points at a given distance from a given point in the plane. The given point is called the **center.**

A **radius** of a circle is a segment determined by the center and a point on the circle. *Radius* is also used to mean the length of this segment.

A **diameter** of a circle is a segment that contains the center and has its endpoints on the circle. *Diameter* is also used to mean the length of this segment.

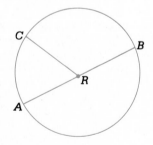

The diagram shows a circle with center R. It is called circle R (written $\odot R$). $\overline{RA}$, $\overline{RB}$, and $\overline{RC}$ are radii. $\overline{AB}$ is a diameter.

| **Definition** | In a plane, **the interior of a circle** is the set of points whose distance from the center is less than the radius. The **exterior of a circle** is the set of points in the plane whose distance from the center is greater than the radius. |

Point E is in the interior of $\odot S$.
Point D is in the exterior of $\odot S$.
If $ST = 5$, then $SD > 5$ and $SE < 5$.

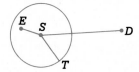

| **Definition** | A **secant** is a line that intersects a circle in two points. |

A **chord** is a segment whose endpoints lie on a circle.

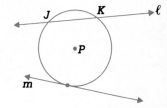

Line ℓ is a secant. $\overline{JK}$ is a chord.

| **Theorem 8.1** | A line that lies in the plane of a circle and contains an interior point of the circle is a secant. |

The proof of Theorem 8.1 is exercise 35.

Line m intersects $\odot P$ above in exactly one point. Such a line is called a tangent.

| **Definition** | A **tangent** to a circle is a line in the plane of the circle that intersects the circle in exactly one point. The point of intersection is called the **point of tangency**. |

In the diagram, $\overleftrightarrow{AB}$ is a tangent.
Point A is the point of tangency.

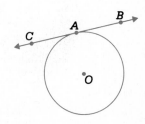

A ray or segment is tangent to a circle if and only if it is a subset of a tangent line and contains the point of tangency.
Thus, $\overrightarrow{AB}$ and $\overrightarrow{BC}$ are **tangent rays** and $\overline{BC}$, $\overline{AB}$, and $\overline{AC}$ are **tangent segments**.

In space, the counterpart of a circle is a sphere. Spheres are suggested by these tennis balls.

Definition   A **sphere** is the set of all points in space that are a given distance from a given point. The given point is called the **center** of the sphere.

A **radius of a sphere** is a segment determined by the center and a point on the sphere.

A **diameter of a sphere** is a segment that contains the center and has its endpoints on the sphere.

Radius and *diameter* are also used to mean the lengths of these segments.

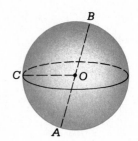

The diagram above shows sphere O. $\overline{OA}$, $\overline{OB}$, and $\overline{OC}$ are radii. $\overline{AB}$ is a diameter.

The intersection of a sphere and a plane containing the center of the sphere is a **great circle** of the sphere. At the right, $\odot P$ is a great circle of sphere P.

The intersection of a sphere and a plane containing an interior point of the sphere, but not containing the center, is a **small circle** of the sphere. $\odot D$ is a small circle of sphere O in the diagram at the right.

A line or a plane containing exactly one point of a sphere is **tangent to the sphere**. At the right, line ℓ is tangent to sphere T at point M. Also, plane $\mathcal{E}$ is tangent to sphere T at point M.

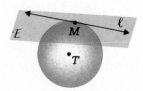

Class Exercises

1. A circle separates the plane into three sets of points. Describe the three sets.

2. Name three radii of ⊙O.
3. Name a diameter of ⊙O.
4. Name a secant of ⊙O.
5. Name a chord of ⊙O.
6. If $OA = 12$, then $BC = \underline{\ ?\ }$.
7. How are OW and OA related?
8. How are OX and OW related?
9. If line t is tangent to the circle, what is the point of tangency?
10. Name a tangent ray.
11. Is $\overleftrightarrow{CW}$ a secant or a tangent? Why?

[12-16] Use the diagram at the right.

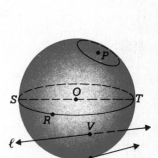

12. Name three radii of the sphere.
13. Name a diameter of the sphere.
14. Name a small circle of the sphere.
15. Name a great circle of the sphere.
16. Which line appears to be tangent to the sphere?

Written Exercises

Set A

[1-6] Draw ⊙P and label the following.

1. A radius, $\overline{PX}$
2. A diameter, $\overline{YZ}$
3. A secant, $\overleftrightarrow{YQ}$
4. A chord, $\overline{UY}$
5. A tangent, $\overleftrightarrow{WY}$
6. A tangent segment, $\overline{VX}$

[7-12] Find the radius of a circle with the given diameter.

7. 10   8. 7   9. 9.4   10. $\frac{1}{3}$ 11. $4x$ 12. $x + 1$

[13-18] Find the diameter of a sphere with the given radius.

13. 6   **14.** $\frac{1}{2}$ **15.** 8.6   **16.** $4\frac{3}{4}$ **17.** $x - 5$ **18.** $3x$

[19-25] Tell whether the statement is always, sometimes, or never true.

19. The longest chord of a circle is a diameter.

20. A chord of a circle can be a radius.

21. A tangent of a circle contains a chord.

22. A secant of a circle contains a chord.

23. A secant of a circle contains a diameter.

24. A diameter of a great circle is a diameter of the sphere.

25. The diameters of two small circles are congruent.

26. Write a definition for a segment that is a **chord of a sphere.**

27. Write a definition for a line that is a **secant of a sphere.**

Set B

[28-31] Circle R contains point A. Use the distance formula to decide whether point B is an interior point, an exterior point, or on the circle.

28. $R(4, 1)$; $A(3, 7)$; $B(2, -5)$

29. $R(2, 4)$; $A(9, 3)$; $B(6, -1)$

30. $R(-3, -2)$; $A(-9, -2)$; $B(-3, 4)$

31. $R(-3, 3)$; $A(0, -4)$; $B(5, 2)$

[32-33] Points C and D are on $\odot P$. Use the distance formula to decide whether $\overline{CD}$ is a diameter.

32. $P(5, 5)$; $C(8, 9)$; $D(2, 1)$

33. $P(-1, -2)$; $C(-2, 6)$; $D(3, -9)$

34. The sphere shown has small circle R and great circle O. $\overline{OR} \perp \overline{RQ}$, $OS = 2$, and $RQ = 1$. $OR = \underline{\ ?\ }$.

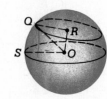

Set C

35. Prove Theorem 8.1.

8.2   Tangents

This picture of a train wheel on a track suggests a circle and a line. How does the line appear to be related to the circle? What appears to be the relationship between the radius of the circle and the line?

Your answers should be consistent with the following theorem.

Theorem 8.2   In a plane, a line is tangent to a circle if and only if it is perpendicular to a radius at a point on the circle.

Part I   If a line is tangent to a circle, then it is perpendicular to a radius at a point on the circle.

Given   Line m is tangent to $\odot P$ at Q.

Prove $\overline{PQ} \perp m$

Plan for Proof   Use indirect proof. Suppose $\overline{PQ} \not\perp m$. Draw $\overline{PR} \perp m$. By Thm. 4.15, $PQ > PR$ and R is in the interior of $\odot P$. So m is a secant. This contradicts the Given.

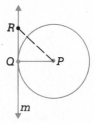

Part II   In a plane, if a line is perpendicular to a radius of a circle at a point on the circle, then the line is tangent to the circle.

Given   Line m and $\odot P$ are coplanar; $m \perp \overline{PQ}$ at Q.

Prove m is tangent to $\odot P$.

Plan for Proof   Let R be any other point on m. Use Thm. 4.15 to show $PR > PQ$.

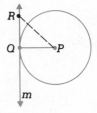

The proof of Theorem 8.2 is exercises 18 and 19.

Theorem 8.3 on the next page is a corollary to Theorem 8.2. Its proof is exercise 20.

Theorem 8.3 Tangent segments drawn from an exterior point to points on the circle are congruent.

Given $\overline{QA}$ and $\overline{QB}$ tangent to $\odot O$ at A and B, respectively

Prove $\overline{QA} \cong \overline{QB}$

Plan for Proof   Draw $\overline{QO}$, $\overline{OA}$, and $\overline{OB}$.
Show $\triangle QOA \cong \triangle QOB$.
Use corresponding parts.

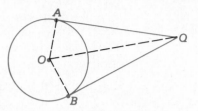

This artist's sketch shows the path of the moon during a lunar eclipse. The moon appears the darkest when it is in the earth's umbra. Notice that the umbra and penumbra, regions in the earth's shadow, are bounded by lines that are tangent to both the sun and the earth.

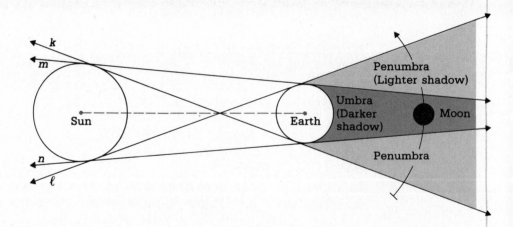

Definition A **common tangent** is a line that is tangent to each of two coplanar circles.

Common external tangents do not intersect the segment joining the centers of the circles. Lines m and n in the sketch above are common external tangents.

Common internal tangents intersect the segment joining the centers of the circles. Lines k and ℓ above are common internal tangents.

Definition

Tangent circles are two coplanar circles that are tangent to the same line at the same point.

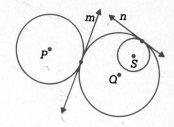

$\odot P$ and $\odot Q$ are **externally tangent circles**. $\odot S$ and $\odot Q$ are **internally tangent circles**.

Class Exercises

[1–3] Line t is tangent to $\odot O$ at point B.

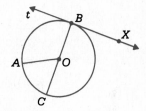

1. What is $m\angle XBO$? Explain.
2. Why is $\overline{BX}$ tangent to $\odot O$?
3. If line k is drawn in the plane of $\odot O$ such that it intersects $\odot O$ in point A and is perpendicular to $\overline{OA}$, what name is given to line k?

4. How many common tangents can be drawn to two internally tangent circles?
5. How many common tangents can be drawn to two externally tangent circles?

Written Exercises

Set A

1. Draw two circles having one common external tangent.
2. Draw two circles having two common external tangents and no common internal tangents.
3. Draw two circles having two common external tangents and one common internal tangent.
4. Draw two circles having two common external tangents and two common internal tangents.
5. Draw two circles having no common tangents.

6. Given: ⊙O; diameter $\overline{AB}$; ℓ and k
   tangent to ⊙O at A and B,
   respectively
   Prove: ℓ ∥ k

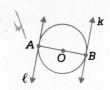

[7-10] $\overline{AC}$ is tangent to ⊙P.

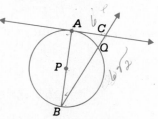

7. $BC = 13$; $AC = 5$; $AB = $ __?__
8. $BC = 20$; $AC = 16$; $AB = $ __?__
9. $BC = 12$; $AC = 6$; $PB = $ __?__
10. $BC = 6\sqrt{2}$; $AC = 6$; $AP = $ __?__

[11-14] Use the Pythagorean Theorem to find the indicated
lengths so that line t is a tangent. Lines ℓ and t are in the
plane of ⊙P.

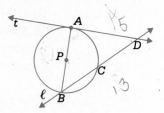

11. $PB = 4$; $AD = 6$; $BD = $ __?__
12. $BD = 13$; $AD = 5$; $AP = $ __?__
13. $CD = BC$; $BP = 4$; $AD = 8$; $CD = $ __?__
14. $CD = BC + 2$; $AP = 2\sqrt{7}$; $AD = 12$;
    $CD = $ __?__

Set B

15. Refer to the diagram and the Given in Theorem 8.3.
    Prove that $\overrightarrow{OQ}$ bisects ∠AOB.

[16-17] $\overleftrightarrow{AB}$ is a common external tangent.

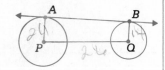

16. $AP = 24$; $BQ = 14$; $PQ = 26$; $AB = $ __?__
17. $AB = 16$; $PQ = 20$; $AP = 18$; $BQ = $ __?__

18. Prove Theorem 8.2, Part I.
19. Prove Theorem 8.2, Part II.
20. Prove Theorem 8.3.

21. How many tangent lines can be drawn to a sphere at a
    point on the sphere?

Set C

[22-23] $\overline{UR}$ and $\overline{ST}$ are common internal
tangents of ⊙P and ⊙Q.

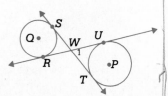

22. Prove: $\overline{UR} \cong \overline{ST}$.
23. $PU = 6$; $QS = 5$; $m\angle 1 = 60$; $PQ = $ __?__

8.3 Chords of a Circle

Sally Jepson designs barbecue grills. She wants to modify the grill shown by inserting support wires $\overline{AD}$ and $\overline{BC}$.

1. How long are the support wires ($\overline{AD}$ and $\overline{BC}$)?

2. How long are the rest of the wires?

To answer these questions, some properties of a circle are needed.

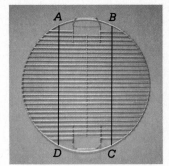

Definition   **Congruent circles** are circles with congruent radii.

If $\overline{PA} \cong \overline{OB}$, then $\odot P \cong \odot O$.
Conversely, if $\odot P \cong \odot O$, then $\overline{PA} \cong \overline{OB}$.

Clearly, a circle is congruent to itself.

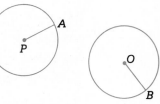

The lengths of the wires of the grill can be found by using Theorem 8.4. Its proof is exercise 15.

Theorem 8.4   If a line through the center of a circle is perpendicular to a chord, it bisects the chord.

Given $\odot P$; line ℓ contains P; chord $\overline{AB}$; $\overline{PC} \perp \overline{AB}$.

Prove ℓ bisects $\overline{AB}$.

Plan for Proof   Draw $\overline{PA}$ and $\overline{PB}$.
Use HL to show that $\triangle PAC \cong \triangle PBC$.
Thus, $AC = CB$.

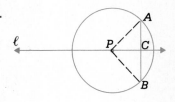

If the radius of the grill above and the distance from the center to a support wire were known, how could Theorem 8.4 be used to find the length of that support wire?

Theorem 8.5 explains why two support wires that are the same distance from the center of the grill have equal length. The proof of the theorem is exercises 16 and 17.

Theorem 8.5	In the same circle or in congruent circles, two chords are congruent if and only if they are the same distance from the center(s) of the circle(s).

Part I — In the same circle or in congruent circles, if two chords are the same distance from the center, then the chords are congruent.

Given — $\odot P \cong \odot Q$; chords $\overline{AB}$ and $\overline{CD}$; $\overline{PX} \perp \overline{AB}$; $\overline{QY} \perp \overline{CD}$; $PX = QY$

Prove — $\overline{AB} \cong \overline{CD}$

Plan for Proof — Draw $\overline{PB}$ and $\overline{QD}$.
Show $\triangle QDY \cong \triangle PBX$.
Thus, $XB = YD$.
Use Thm. 8.4 to show $AB = 2(XB)$ and $CD = 2(YD)$.
Thus, $AB = CD$.

Part II — In the same circle or in congruent circles, if two chords are congruent, then they are the same distance from the center.

Class Exercises

1. Under what conditions are two circles congruent?

[2-6] $\overline{PX} \perp \overline{AB}$ and $\overline{PY} \perp \overline{CD}$.

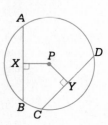

2. $CY = \underline{\quad ? \quad}$
3. If $PY = PX$, then $\overline{AB} \cong \underline{\quad ? \quad}$.
4. If $\overline{CD} \cong \overline{BA}$, then $\overline{PX} \cong \underline{\quad ? \quad}$.
5. If $\overline{PX} \cong \overline{PY}$, why is $\overline{BX} \cong \overline{YD}$?
6. If $PX = PY$ and $YD = 7$, then $AB = \underline{\quad ? \quad}$.

Written Exercises

Set A

[1-4] $\overline{AC}$ is a diameter of $\odot P$, $\overline{AB}$ is a chord, and $\overline{PD} \perp \overline{AB}$.

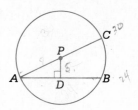

1. $AP = 10$; $PD = 6$; $AB = $ _?_
2. $AC = 12$; $PD = 3$; $AB = $ _?_
3. $AB = 24$; $PD = 5$; $AP = $ _?_
4. $AC = 30$; $AB = 24$; $PD = $ _?_

[5-10] Is each statement always, sometimes, or never true?

5. Two circles with congruent radii are congruent.
6. Two circles with congruent chords are congruent.
7. A circle is congruent to itself.
8. A line perpendicular to a chord bisects the chord.
9. If a radius of a circle is perpendicular to a chord of the circle, then the radius bisects the chord.
10. In a circle, two chords the same distance from the center are congruent.

[11-14] In $\odot P$, $\overline{PX} \perp \overline{AB}$.

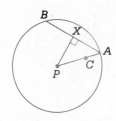

11. $AB = 56$; $PA = 35$; $PX = $ _?_
12. $PX = 10$; $AB = 48$; $PA = $ _?_
13. $PA = 2(PX)$; $AB = 16\sqrt{3}$; $PA = $ _?_
14. $PX = PC$; $AB = 2(PX)$; $PA = 14\sqrt{2}$; $AC = $ _?_

15. Prove Theorem 8.4.

Set B

16. Prove Theorem 8.5, Part I.
17. Prove Theorem 8.5, Part II.
18. Prove: In a plane, if a line through the center of a circle bisects a chord which is not a diameter, it is perpendicular to the chord.
19. Prove: In a plane, the perpendicular bisector of a chord passes through the center of the circle.
20. In a circle, what is the locus of midpoints of all chords congruent to a given chord? Explain.

8.3   Chords of a Circle

21. Pictured at the right is a portion of a circular plate. Describe a method for finding the diameter of the plate. (See exercise 19.)

[22-24] A circular grill 22″ in diameter has 28 horizontal wires. The distance from the center to the first wire is $\frac{1}{4}$″. Thereafter, the distance between any two consecutive horizontal wires is $\frac{3}{4}$″. The distance between the two vertical support wires is 6″.

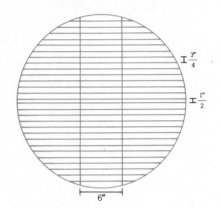

22. Find the length of a support wire.

23. Find the length of the shortest horizontal wire.

24. How could the total amount of wire for all 30 wires be found?

25. Write a definition for congruent spheres.

[26-27] $\odot P$ is a great circle and $\odot Q$ is a small circle of sphere P. Point X and $\odot Q$ are coplanar. $\overline{AB}$ is a chord of both circles. $\overline{PQ} \perp \overline{AB}$; $\overline{QX} \perp \overline{AB}$; $\overline{PQ} \perp \overline{QX}$.

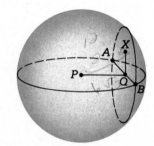

26. $AB = 24$; $PA = 20$; $XA = 13$; $PX =$ _?_

27. $XA = 10$; $PX = 12$; $PQ = 6\sqrt{3}$; $PA =$ _?_

Set C

28. Prove: If two chords of a circle have unequal lengths, then the shorter chord is a greater distance from the center of the circle.

[29-30] $\overline{AB}$ is a chord of coplanar circles P and Q; $\overline{QP} \perp \overline{AB}$.

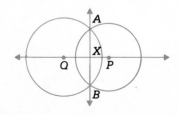

29. Prove: If $QX = PX$, then $QA = PA$.

30. Prove: If $QX > PX$, then $QA > PA$.

8.4 Circumscribed and Inscribed Circles

Decorative designs are often made by combining circles and polygons. In some of the designs, each side of a polygon is a chord of a circle.

Definition

A **polygon inscribed in a circle** is a polygon whose vertices lie on the circle. The circle is **circumscribed about the polygon**.

In other types of designs, each side of the polygon is tangent to a circle.

Definition

A **polygon circumscribed about a circle** is a polygon whose sides are tangent to the circle. The circle is **inscribed in the polygon**.

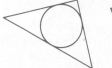

The diagrams below suggest that if the circle is drawn first, a triangle of any shape can be inscribed in or circumscribed about the circle.

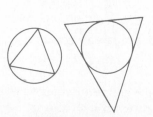

Acute triangle

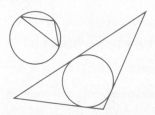

Obtuse triangle

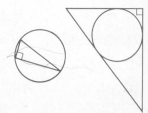

Right triangle

If the triangle is drawn first, exactly one circle can be circumscribed about it. The following definition and Theorem 8.6 help to explain how to circumscribe a circle about a given triangle. The proofs of Theorems 8.6 and 8.7 are exercises 18 and 19.

Definition	Two or more lines that intersect in a single point are **concurrent**. The point is called the **point of concurrency**.

Theorem 8.6	The perpendicular bisectors of the sides of a triangle are concurrent in a point equidistant from the vertices of the triangle.

Given
$\triangle ABC$ with ℓ_1, ℓ_2, and ℓ_3 the perpendicular bisectors of $\overline{AB}$, $\overline{AC}$, and $\overline{BC}$, respectively

Prove
ℓ_1, ℓ_2, and ℓ_3 are concurrent at P and $PA = PB = PC$.

Plan for Proof
Use indirect proof to show that ℓ_1 and ℓ_2 intersect. Suppose $\ell_1 \| \ell_2$. Since $\ell_1 \perp \overline{AB}$, $\ell_2 \perp \overline{AB}$. But $\ell_2 \perp \overline{AC}$. So $\overline{AB} \| \overline{AC}$. This contradicts the fact that A is on $\overline{AB}$ and $\overline{AC}$.

Let ℓ_1 and ℓ_2 intersect at P.
Use Thm. 5.17 to show $PB = PA$ and $PA = PC$.
Therefore, $PB = PC$ and P is on ℓ_3.

The plan for proof of Theorem 8.6 shows that points A, B, and C are equidistant from P. Thus, A, B, and C all lie on the same circle with center P. This suggests the following corollary and definition.

Theorem 8.7	A circle can be circumscribed about any triangle.

Definition	The point of concurrency of the perpendicular bisectors of the sides of a triangle is the **circumcenter** of the triangle.

Given a triangle, exactly one circle can be inscribed in it.
Theorems 8.8 and 8.9 help to explain how to inscribe a circle
in a triangle. Their proofs are exercises 20 and 21.

Theorem 8.8   The angle bisectors of a triangle are concurrent in a point
equidistant from the sides of the triangle.

Given $\triangle ABC$; $\overline{AX}$, $\overline{BY}$, and $\overline{CZ}$ the bisectors
of $\angle A$, $\angle B$, and $\angle C$, respectively

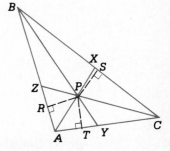

Prove $\overline{AX}$, $\overline{BY}$, and $\overline{CZ}$ are concurrent at P;
P is equidistant from $\overline{AB}$, $\overline{BC}$, and $\overline{AC}$.

Plan for Proof   Use indirect proof to show $\overline{AX}$ and
$\overline{BY}$ intersect. Suppose $\overline{AX} \parallel \overline{BY}$.
Then $m\angle ABY + m\angle BAX = 180$.
So $m\angle ABC + m\angle BAC = 360$.
But this contradicts Thm. 3.14.

Let $\overline{AX}$ intersect $\overline{BY}$ at P.
Use Thm. 5.19 to show $PR = PS = PT$.
Thus, P is on $\overrightarrow{CZ}$.

Since $PR = PS = PT$, points R, S, and T all lie on the same
circle with center P. This suggests the following corollary and
definition.

Theorem 8.9   A circle can be inscribed in any triangle.

Definition   The point of concurrency of the angle bisectors of a triangle is
the **incenter** of the triangle.

Other sets of concurrent lines also can be identified.
The lines containing the altitudes of a triangle are concurrent
in a point called the **orthocenter** of the triangle.
The medians of a triangle are concurrent in a point called the
centroid of the triangle.

Class Exercises

1. If a circle is circumscribed about a pentagon, how many points of the pentagon lie on the circle? Describe them.

2. If a circle is inscribed in a pentagon, how many points of the pentagon lie on the circle? Describe them.

[3-6] Tell whether the polygon appears to be inscribed in the circle, circumscribed about the circle, or neither.

3.   **4.**   **5.**   **6.**

7. If a circle is drawn first, how many triangles can be inscribed in it? Circumscribed about it?

8. If a triangle is drawn first, how many circles can be inscribed in it? Circumscribed about it?

9. What are concurrent lines?

10. Which set of concurrent lines determines the center of a circle inscribed in a triangle?

11. Which set of concurrent lines determines the center of a circle circumscribed about a triangle?

Written Exercises

Set A

[1-4] $\triangle ABC$ is circumscribed about $\odot P$. X, Y, and Z are the points of tangency.

1. $XC = 12$; $BC = 21$; $BY = $ __?__

2. $AX = 8$; $AB = 24$; $BZ = $ __?__

3. $BZ = 2m$; $CY = 3m + 5$; $BC = 35$; $m = $ __?__

4. $CY = n + 3$; $AX = 2n - 1$; $AC = 23$; $n = $ __?__

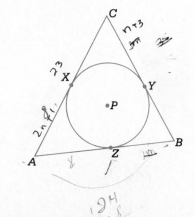

5. Amy is making a geometric mobile. She plans to draw circles with radius 2 cm in a rectangular array on a sheet of paper 36 cm by 48 cm. How many nonoverlapping circles can she draw?

6. Given: $\triangle ABC$ inscribed in $\odot P$;
$\overline{PY} \perp \overline{AC}$; $\overline{PX} \perp \overline{AB}$; $XD = EY$
Prove: $\triangle ABC$ is isosceles.

[7-10] Identify each point of concurrency pictured below.

7.   **8.** 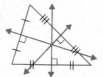   **9.**   **10.**

Set B

[11-16] Equilateral triangle ABC is inscribed in $\odot P$.

11. If $AB = 12$, then $PA = \underline{\ ?\ }$.

12. If $PB = 10$; then $BC = \underline{\ ?\ }$.

13. What is the relationship between the circumcenter and incenter of $\triangle ABC$?

14. Find $m\angle APB$.

15. If $PC = x$, find the length of the radius of a circle inscribed in $\triangle ABC$.

16. What is the relationship between the circumcenter, incenter, orthocenter, and centroid of $\triangle ABC$?

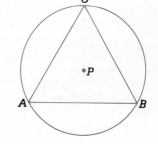

17. Art is a glass cutter. He needs to cut a circle from a square piece of glass. Describe a method of finding the center of the inscribed circle.

Set C

18. Prove Theorem 8.6.   **20.** Prove Theorem 8.8.

19. Prove Theorem 8.7.   **21.** Prove Theorem 8.9.

22. Show that the ratio of the radius of the inscribed circle to the radius of the circle circumscribed about a square is $\sqrt{2}$ to 2.

Construction Exercises

Construction 13 Construct a line tangent to a circle at a given point on the circle.

Given   Point Q on $\odot P$

Construct   A tangent to $\odot P$ at point Q

Method   Step 1: Draw $\overleftrightarrow{PQ}$.

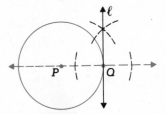

Step 2: Construct $\ell \perp \overleftrightarrow{PQ}$ at Q.

Then ℓ is tangent to $\odot P$ at point Q.

1. Draw a large circle and mark a point on the circle. Construct a tangent at the given point.

2. Write a plan for justification of your construction in exercise 1. **Hint** Use Thm. 8.2.

3. Draw a circle. Construct a triangle circumscribing the circle.

4. Draw a circle. Construct a quadrilateral circumscribing the circle.

5. Draw a large acute triangle. Use Theorem 8.6 to construct the circle circumscribing the triangle.

6. Draw a large acute triangle. Use the plan for proof for Theorem 8.8 to construct the circle inscribed in the triangle.

7. Draw a large obtuse triangle. Construct both the inscribed and circumscribed circles.

8. Draw a large right triangle. Construct the circumscribed circle.

9. Repeat exercise 8 using a different right triangle. What is the relationship between the hypotenuse of the triangle and the circumscribed circle?

10. Draw a triangle with sides of length 4″, 5″, and 7″. By methods of construction, locate the circumcenter, P, the orthocenter, O, and the centroid, C. These three points should be collinear. They lie on a line called the *Euler Line*.

Progress Check

Lesson 8.1
Page 354

1. Name a radius of ⊙P.
2. Name a secant of ⊙P.
3. Name a chord of ⊙P.
4. Name a diameter of ⊙P.
5. Name a tangent of ⊙P.
6. Name an interior point of ⊙P.

7. Name a small circle of sphere O.
8. Name a great circle of sphere O.

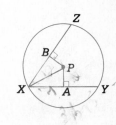

Lesson 8.2
Page 359

[9-12] True or false

9. A tangent of a circle is perpendicular to the radius drawn to the point of tangency.
10. Tangent circles have at least two points in common.
11. Externally tangent circles are tangent to the same line at the same point.
12. Tangent segments drawn from an exterior point to points on the circle are congruent.

Lesson 8.3
Page 363

[13-16] $\overline{PA} \perp \overline{XY}$ and $\overline{PB} \perp \overline{XZ}$

13. $XY = 24$; $PA = 10$; $PX =$ __?__
14. $PX = 12$; $XY = 12\sqrt{3}$; $PA =$ __?__
15. $AX = 7$; $\overline{PA} \cong \overline{PB}$; $XZ =$ __?__
16. $PA = 2$; $\overline{XA} \cong \overline{XB}$; $PB =$ __?__

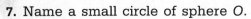

Lesson 8.4
Page 367

[17-20] True or false

17. A polygon is circumscribed about a circle if its sides are tangent to the circle.
18. The circumcenter of a triangle is equidistant from the sides of the triangle.
19. The angle bisectors of a triangle are concurrent at the incenter of the triangle.
20. A triangle has infinitely many circumscribed circles.

8.5   Arcs of a Circle

This *circle graph* describes the membership of the Lincoln School Band.

How could you determine which class has the most band members even if the percents were not shown on the graph?

Notice that each angle of the graph has its vertex at the center of the circle. In geometry, such an angle is called a central angle.

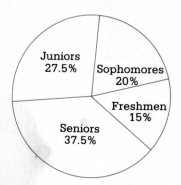

Definition   A **central angle** of a circle is an angle in the plane of the circle whose vertex is the center of the circle.

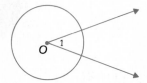

Angle 1 is a central angle of $\odot O$.

Definition   A **minor arc** of a circle is the set of points on the circle that lie on a central angle or in the interior of the central angle.

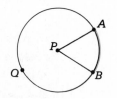

In $\odot P$, arc AB (written $\overarc{AB}$ or $\overarc{BA}$) is a minor arc.

The arc formed by A and B and the points of the circle in the exterior of $\angle APB$ is called a **major arc.**

$\overarc{AB}$ will mean minor arc. To avoid confusion, three letters will always be used to name a major arc. $\overarc{AQB}$ (or $\overarc{BQA}$) is a major arc. Three letters may also be used to name minor arcs or semicircles.

Definition   A **semicircle** is the union of the endpoints of a diameter and the points of the circle in a given half-plane formed by the line containing the diameter.

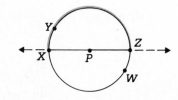

$\overarc{XYZ}$ and $\overarc{ZWX}$ are semicircles of $\odot P$.

Definition	The **degree measure of a minor arc** is the measure of its central angle.

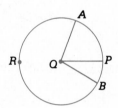

Definition	The **degree measure of a major arc**, $\widehat{ACB}$, is $360 - m\widehat{AB}$.

If $m\angle APB = 50$, then $m\widehat{AB} = 50$ and $m\widehat{ACB} = 310$.

Definition	The **degree measure of a semicircle** is 180.

Just as there is an Angle Addition Postulate, there is also an Arc Addition Postulate.

Postulate 21 Arc Addition Postulate	If P is on $\widehat{AB}$, then $m\widehat{AP} + m\widehat{PB} = m\widehat{APB}$.

If $m\widehat{AP} = 70$ and $m\widehat{PB} = 30$, then $m\widehat{APB} = 100$.

Are all arcs with the same measure congruent? Consider the concentric circles at the right. **Concentric circles** are coplanar circles with the same center.

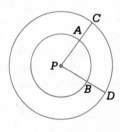

$\widehat{AB}$ and $\widehat{CD}$ have the same central angle, $\angle P$, so $m\widehat{AB} = m\widehat{CD}$. Why? But $\widehat{AB}$ and $\widehat{CD}$ are not congruent. What other condition must be included in the definition of congruent arcs?

Definition	**Congruent arcs** are arcs that have the same measure and lie on the same or on congruent circles.

Properties of chords of congruent arcs are given in Theorem 8.10. Its proof is exercises 23 and 24.

| **Theorem 8.10** | In the same circle or in congruent circles, two minor arcs are congruent if and only if their corresponding chords are congruent. |

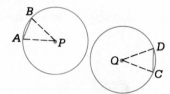

Part I If $\odot P \cong \odot Q$ and $\overarc{AB} \cong \overarc{CD}$,
then $\overline{AB} \cong \overline{CD}$.

Part II If $\odot P \cong \odot Q$ and $\overline{AB} \cong \overline{CD}$,
then $\overarc{AB} \cong \overarc{CD}$.

Class Exercises

[1-14] $\overline{AB}$ is a diameter of $\odot P$.

1. Name four central angles of $\odot P$.
2. Name three minor arcs of $\odot P$.
3. Name two major arcs of $\odot P$.
4. Name a semicircle of $\odot P$.
5. Name a pair of congruent arcs.
6. Name a pair of congruent chords.

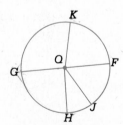

7. $m\overarc{BC} = $ _?_
8. $m\overarc{BD} = $ _?_
9. $m\overarc{BFD} = $ _?_
10. $m\overarc{CEA} = $ _?_
11. $m\overarc{FA} + $ _?_ $= m\overarc{FE}$
12. $m\overarc{AD} + m\overarc{DG} = $ _?_
13. $m\overarc{BD} + m\overarc{BFD} = $ _?_
14. $m\overarc{AE} + m\overarc{ECA} = $ _?_

Written Exercises

Set A

[1-6] Tell whether the figure is a central angle, a major arc, a minor arc, a semicircle, or none of these. $\overline{FG}$ is a diameter of $\odot Q$.

1. $\overarc{FK}$
2. $\overarc{GKF}$
3. $\angle GQJ$
4. $\angle QJK$
5. $\overarc{GFK}$
6. $\overarc{GHJ}$

[7-14] $\overline{AC}$ is a diameter of $\odot P$. Find the measure of each arc.

7. $\overparen{AE}$ **9.** $\overparen{BC}$ **11.** $\overparen{CE}$ **13.** $\overparen{ADC}$

8. $\overparen{CD}$ **10.** $\overparen{DE}$ **12.** $\overparen{BCE}$ **14.** $\overparen{CBE}$

[15-18] Mary and Dan are making a quilt. The instructions show a quarter of the design for the center circle. The letters indicate the colors of the fabrics to be used. The red and blue triangles are all cut from the same pattern.

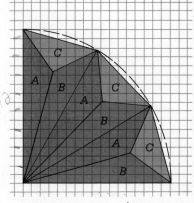

Scale: 1 square = $\frac{1}{2}''$

15. What is the measure of each central angle? Explain.

16. Find the diameter of the center circle in the finished quilt.

17. How many patterns are needed to make the green triangles? Explain.

18. Mary wants to change the design by making the red and blue triangles isosceles. She will not change the size of the central angle. What effect will the changes have on the green triangles? Explain.

[19-20] Points A, B, C, and D are on $\odot P$ as shown.

19. If $\overparen{AC} \cong \overparen{BD}$, prove $\overparen{AB} \cong \overparen{CD}$.

20. If $\overparen{AB} \cong \overparen{CD}$, prove $\overparen{AC} \cong \overparen{BD}$.

21. Prove: In the same circle or in congruent circles, if two minor arcs are congruent, then their central angles are congruent.

22. Prove: In the same circle or in congruent circles, if two central angles are congruent, then their minor arcs are congruent.

23. Prove Theorem 8.10, Part I.

24. Prove Theorem 8.10, Part II.

[25-28] Find the measure of each arc.

25. $\overset{\frown}{DE}$ 27. $\overset{\frown}{EF}$

26. $\overset{\frown}{DEF}$ 28. $\overset{\frown}{GDE}$

[29-31] Refer to the circle graph on page 374. The measure of the central angle of the sophomore region is 20% of 360, or 72. Find the measure of the central angle of the indicated region.

29. Freshman 30. Junior 31. Senior

[32-37] $\overline{AB}$ is a diameter of $\odot P$.

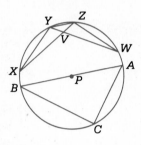

32. If $\overline{XZ} \cong \overline{YW}$, prove $\overset{\frown}{XY} \cong \overset{\frown}{ZW}$.

33. If $\overset{\frown}{XY} \cong \overset{\frown}{ZW}$, prove $\overline{XZ} \cong \overline{YW}$.

34. If $\overline{BC} \cong \overline{AC}$, prove $m\angle ACB = 90$.

35. If $m\overset{\frown}{BC} = 2(m\overset{\frown}{AC})$, prove that $\angle A$ and $\angle B$ are complementary.

36. Prove that $\angle BCA$ is a right angle.
    Hint Let $m\overset{\frown}{BC} = 2x$.

37. If $\overset{\frown}{XY} \cong \overset{\frown}{WZ}$, prove $\angle XYV \cong \angle WZV$.

[38-43] $m\overset{\frown}{AD} = 3(m\overset{\frown}{AB})$, $m\overset{\frown}{AC} = 90$, $m\overset{\frown}{DC} = 3(m\overset{\frown}{BC})$, and $m\overset{\frown}{BCD} = 5(m\overset{\frown}{AB})$. Find the measure of each arc or angle.

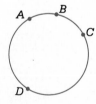

38. $\overset{\frown}{AB}$ 40. $\overset{\frown}{CD}$ 42. $\angle DAC$

39. $\overset{\frown}{BC}$ 41. $\overset{\frown}{AD}$ 43. $\angle ACD$

Geometry Maintenance

1. How many acute angles are in an obtuse triangle?

2. Opposite angles of a parallelogram are __?__ .

3. $\overline{YW}$ is the altitude drawn to the hypotenuse of right triangle XYZ. Name three similar triangles.

Inscribed Angles

The beginning of a string design is shown. The angle suggested in black is not a central angle. Why?

In geometry, such an angle is called an inscribed angle.

Definition   An **angle inscribed in a circle** is an angle whose sides contain the endpoints of an arc and whose vertex is a point on the arc other than the endpoints.

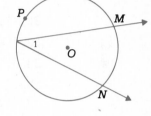

∠1 is inscribed in ⊙O. It also is said that ∠1 is inscribed in $\overset{\frown}{MPN}$. $\overset{\frown}{MN}$ is called the intercepted arc.

Definition   An **intercepted arc** is an arc whose endpoints lie on different sides of an angle and whose other points lie in the interior of the angle.

In these diagrams, $\overset{\frown}{AB}$ and $\overset{\frown}{CD}$ are arcs intercepted by ∠2.

  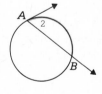 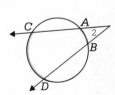

At the right, $\overset{\frown}{GE}$ is intercepted by inscribed angle GFE and, also, by central angle GOE. How do you think m∠GFE compares with $m\overset{\frown}{GE}$?

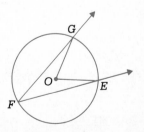

The relationship between these measures is explained in Theorem 8.11. Its proof is exercises 29-31.

Theorem 8.11   The measure of an inscribed angle is one-half the measure of its intercepted arc.

Given $\odot P$; $\angle ACB$ is an inscribed angle.

Prove $m\angle ACB = \frac{1}{2}(m\widehat{AB})$

Plan for Proof

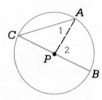

Case I P lies on $\angle ACB$:
Draw $\overline{AP}$ and show $\angle ACB \cong \angle 1$.
Show $m\angle ACB + m\angle 1 = m\angle 2$.
Since $m\angle 2 = m\widehat{AB}$, $2(m\angle ACB) = m\widehat{AB}$.

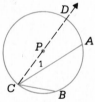

Case II P is in the interior of $\angle ACB$:
Draw $\overrightarrow{CP}$ and use Case I to show
$m\angle 1 = \frac{1}{2}(m\widehat{AD})$ and $m\angle 2 = \frac{1}{2}(m\widehat{BD})$.
Show $m\angle ACB = m\angle 1 + m\angle 2$.
$m\angle ACB = \frac{1}{2}(m\widehat{AD}) + \frac{1}{2}(m\widehat{BD}) = \frac{1}{2}(m\widehat{AD} + m\widehat{BD})$.
Show $m\widehat{AD} + m\widehat{DB} = m\widehat{AB}$.
Use substitution.

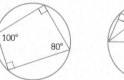

Case III P is in the exterior of $\angle ACB$:
Draw $\overrightarrow{CP}$ and show
$m\angle ACB = m\angle DCB - m\angle 1$.
Use Case I to show $m\angle DCB = \frac{1}{2}(m\widehat{DB})$
and $m\angle 1 = \frac{1}{2}(m\widehat{DA})$.
Show $m\angle ACB = \frac{1}{2}(m\widehat{DB}) - \frac{1}{2}(m\widehat{DA}) = \frac{1}{2}(m\widehat{DB} - m\widehat{DA})$.
Show $m\widehat{AB} = m\widehat{DB} - m\widehat{DA}$.
Use substitution.

These diagrams suggest the following three corollaries to Theorem 8.11. Their proofs are exercises 17, 18, and 32.

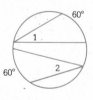

$\angle 1 \cong \angle 2$

$\angle 1 \cong \angle 2$

Theorem 8.12   If two inscribed angles intercept the same arc or congruent arcs, then the angles are congruent.

Theorem 8.13   If a quadrilateral is inscribed in a circle, then its opposite angles are supplementary.

Theorem 8.14   If an angle is inscribed in a semicircle, then it is a right angle.

Class Exercises

[1-11] $\overline{DB}$ is a diameter of $\odot P$.

1. Name four inscribed angles.
2. Name three angles that intercept $\overset{\frown}{DC}$.
3. Name the inscribed angles that intercept $\overset{\frown}{DC}$.
4. Name the angle inscribed in $\overset{\frown}{DAB}$.
5. Name two congruent inscribed angles.
6. Name a right angle.
7. Name two inscribed angles that are supplementary.
8. If $m\overset{\frown}{AB} = 60$, then $m\angle ADB = \underline{\ ?\ }$.
9. If $m\angle DAE = 75$, then $m\overset{\frown}{DC} = \underline{\ ?\ }$.
10. If $m\angle ACB = 35$, then $m\angle ADB = \underline{\ ?\ }$.
11. If $m\overset{\frown}{BC} = 30$, then $m\angle DAE = \underline{\ ?\ }$.

Written Exercises

Set A

[1-6] $\overline{HF}$ is a diameter of $\odot O$.

1. If $m\overset{\frown}{EH} = 65$, then $m\angle 1 = \underline{\ ?\ }$.
2. If $m\overset{\frown}{GF} = 144$, then $m\angle 4 = \underline{\ ?\ }$.
3. If $m\angle 3 = 15$, then $m\overset{\frown}{EH} = \underline{\ ?\ }$.
4. If $m\angle 5 = 45$, then $m\overset{\frown}{EF} = \underline{\ ?\ }$.
5. If $m\overset{\frown}{HG} = 44$, then $m\angle 2 = \underline{\ ?\ }$.
6. If $m\overset{\frown}{EF} = 124$, then $m\angle 3 = \underline{\ ?\ }$.

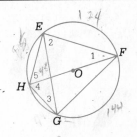

[7-10] $\overline{ED}$ is tangent to $\odot P$ at A;
$\overline{AB}$ is a diameter; $m\overset{\frown}{BC} = 20$

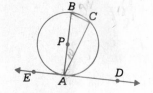

7. $m\angle BAC =$ ___?___   **9.** $m\angle ACB =$ ___?___

8. $m\angle CAD =$ ___?___   **10.** $m\angle ABC =$ ___?___

[11-12] $\overline{KH}$ is a diameter of $\odot Q$.

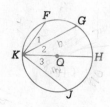

11. $m\overset{\frown}{HJ} = 70$, $m\overset{\frown}{FG} = 20$, and $m\overset{\frown}{FK} = 100$.
Find $m\angle 1$, $m\angle 2$, and $m\angle 3$.

12. $m\angle 2 = 37$, $m\angle 3 = 42$, and $m\overset{\frown}{FK} = 86$.
Find $m\overset{\frown}{FG}$, $m\overset{\frown}{KJ}$, and $m\angle FKH$.

[13-16] $ABCD$ is inscribed in $\odot P$.

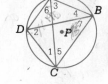

13. $m\angle DAB = 95$; $m\angle DCB =$ ___?___

14. $m\angle ADC = 70$; $m\angle 7 = 75$; $m\angle 4 =$ ___?___

15. $m\angle DAB = 110$; $m\angle 2 = 35$; $m\angle 6 =$ ___?___

16. Prove: $m\angle 1 + m\angle 2 = m\angle 3 + m\angle 4$

17. Prove Theorem 8.12.

18. Prove Theorem 8.14.

Set B

19. Joan has a drawing of a circle whose center is not marked. How can she draw a diameter of this circle using only the corner of a 3 × 5 index card?

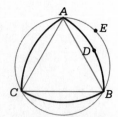

20. The Wankel engine is designed around a curve called a *Reuleaux triangle*. The curve is formed by drawing $\overset{\frown}{AB}$, $\overset{\frown}{BC}$, and $\overset{\frown}{AC}$ with centers at C, A, and B, respectively. Find $m\overset{\frown}{ADB}$ of the Reuleaux triangle. Find $m\overset{\frown}{AEB}$ of the circle that circumscribes $\triangle ABC$.

Equilateral $\triangle ABC$

[21-22] A, B, C, and D are on a circle.

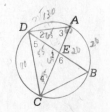

21. $m\overset{\frown}{AD} = 100$, $m\overset{\frown}{AB} = 60$, and $m\overset{\frown}{BC} = 80$.
Find $m\angle 2$, $m\angle 3$, and $m\angle 1$.

22. $m\overset{\frown}{AD} = 130$, $m\overset{\frown}{AB} = 20$, and $m\overset{\frown}{DC} = 110$.
Find $m\angle 4$, $m\angle 5$, and $m\angle 6$.

[23-26] *QRST* is inscribed in a circle.

23. $m\angle Q = 2x + 12$ and $m\angle S = 3x + 18$.
Find $m\angle Q$.

24. $m\angle R = 2x + 15$ and $m\angle T = 8x - 5$.
Find $m\angle T$.

25. $m\angle Q = 4x + 5$, $m\angle R = 7x + 2$, and
$m\angle T = 5x - 2$. Find $m\angle S$.

26. $m\angle Q = 6x - 5$, $m\angle R = 2x + 30$, and
$m\angle S = 9x - 10$. Find $m\angle T$.

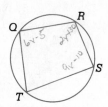

[27-28] Refer to $\odot O$ at the right.

27. $m\widehat{KF} = 60$ and $m\widehat{GH} = 30$. Show that
$m\angle J = 15$. **Hint** Draw $\overline{GK}$.

28. $m\widehat{KF} = 80$ and $m\widehat{GH} = 20$. Find $m\angle J$.

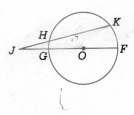

29. Prove Theorem 8.11, Case I.

30. Prove Theorem 8.11, Case II.

31. Prove Theorem 8.11, Case III.

32. Prove Theorem 8.13.

33. Prove: If two chords in a circle are
parallel, then they cut off congruent
arcs. **Hint** Draw $\overline{BC}$ and use
Thm. 8.11.

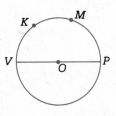

[34-35] Draw a figure and write a
description of the locus.

34. In $\odot O$, what is the locus of
vertices of inscribed angles that
intercept $\widehat{KM}$?

35. In a plane, what is the locus of
the vertices of right triangles
with hypotenuse $\overline{VP}$?

Set C

[36-37] *QRST* is inscribed in $\odot P$.

36. $m\angle QTS = x^2 + 2x + 115$ and
$m\angle QRS = 3x + 71$. Find $m\angle QTS$.

37. If $m\angle QRS = m\angle TSR - k$, prove that
$m\angle TQR = m\angle QTS - k$.

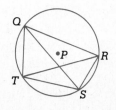

8.6   Inscribed Angles

383

Construction Exercises

Construction 14 Construct the tangents to a circle from a given exterior point.

Given   ⊙P and point R in its exterior

Construct   Tangents to ⊙P from R

Method   Step 1: Draw $\overline{PR}$. Construct ℓ, the perpendicular bisector of $\overline{PR}$. Let O be the point of intersection of ℓ and $\overline{PR}$.

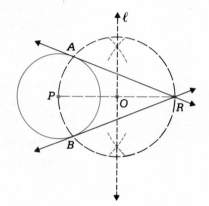

Step 2: Using OP as the radius, draw ⊙O. Let A and B be the points of intersection of ⊙O and ⊙P.

Step 3: Draw $\overleftrightarrow{RA}$ and $\overleftrightarrow{RB}$.

Then $\overleftrightarrow{RA}$ and $\overleftrightarrow{RB}$ are tangents to ⊙P from point R.

1. Draw a circle and mark a point in its exterior. Construct tangents to the circle from the exterior point.

2. Write a plan for justification of your construction in exercise 1. **Hint** In the given circle, draw a radius to a point of tangency.

3. Draw ⊙T and $\overline{AB}$, a diameter. Construct a 30-60-90 triangle whose hypotenuse is $\overline{AB}$. **Hint** Use Thm. 7.3.

4. Write a plan for justification of your construction in exercise 3.

5. Draw two segments, $\overline{AB}$ and $\overline{CD}$. Construct a segment whose length is the geometric mean of AB and CD. **Hint** Construct a circle with diameter equal to $AB + CD$. Use Thm. 6.12 to construct $\overline{MN}$, such that $MN = \sqrt{(AB)(CD)}$.

6. Draw two segments, $\overline{PQ}$ and $\overline{RS}$. Construct a segment of length $\sqrt{3(PQ)(RS)}$.

7. Draw a segment, $\overline{VW}$. Assume $VW = 1$. Construct a segment of length $\sqrt{7}$.

8. Draw a segment, $\overline{XY}$. Assume $XY = 1$. Construct a right triangle such that the hypotenuse is 5 and the altitude to the hypotenuse is $\sqrt{3}$.

8.7

Angles Formed by Secants and Tangents

The angles shown are formed by two intersecting secants. Recall that a secant is a line which intersects a circle in two points.

What is the relationship between the measure of $\angle 1$ and the measures of the two intercepted arcs?

Your answer should suggest the next theorem. Its proof is exercise 27.

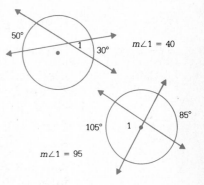

Theorem 8.15

The measure of an angle formed by two secants which intersect in the interior of a circle is one-half the sum of the measures of the arcs intercepted by the angle and its vertical angle.

Given

$\overleftrightarrow{QS}$ and $\overleftrightarrow{RT}$ intersect in the interior of the circle.

Prove

$m\angle 1 = \frac{1}{2}(m\widehat{QT} + m\widehat{RS})$

Plan for Proof

Draw $\overline{TS}$.
Show $m\angle 1 = m\angle 2 + m\angle 3$.
Use Thm. 8.11 to show $m\angle 2 = \frac{1}{2}(m\widehat{RS})$ and $m\angle 3 = \frac{1}{2}(m\widehat{QT})$.
Use substitution.

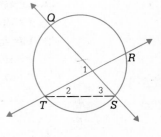

Is there a similar relationship for the measure of an angle formed by secants that intersect in the exterior of a circle? Consider the following diagrams and try to find a relationship.

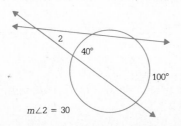

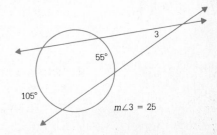

Theorem 8.16   The measure of an angle formed by two secants that intersect in the exterior of a circle is one-half the difference of the measures of the intercepted arcs.

Given $\overleftrightarrow{BC}$ and $\overleftrightarrow{ED}$ intersect in the exterior of the circle.

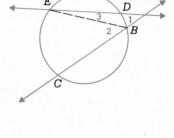

Prove $m\angle 1 = \frac{1}{2}(m\widehat{CE} - m\widehat{BD})$

Plan for Proof   Draw $\overline{BE}$.
Show $m\angle 1 = m\angle 2 - m\angle 3$.
Show $m\angle 2 = \frac{1}{2}(m\widehat{CE})$ and $m\angle 3 = \frac{1}{2}(m\widehat{BD})$.
Use substitution.

The proof of Theorem 8.16 is exercise 28.

Similar results can be proved for angles formed by tangents and secants.

Theorem 8.17   The measure of an angle formed by a tangent and a secant that intersect at the point of tangency is one-half the measure of the intercepted arc.

Given $\odot P$ with tangent $\overleftrightarrow{BC}$ and secant $\overleftrightarrow{AC}$; C is the point of tangency.

Prove $m\angle ACB = \frac{1}{2}(m\widehat{AXC})$

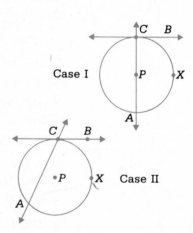

Plan for Proof   **Case I** P lies on $\angle ACB$:
Show $\angle ACB$ is a rt. $\angle$.
Since $\widehat{AXC}$ is a semicircle, $m\widehat{AXC} = 180$.
Thus, $m\angle ACB = \frac{1}{2}(m\widehat{AXC})$.

Case II P lies in the interior of $\angle ACB$:
Use a method similar to the plan for proof of Thm. 8.11, Case II.

Case III P lies in the exterior of $\angle ACB$:
Use a method similar to the plan for proof of Thm. 8.11, Case III.

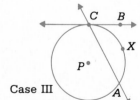

Chapter 8   Circles

Theorem 8.18   The measure of an angle formed by a secant and a tangent that intersect in the exterior of a circle is one-half the difference of the measures of the intercepted arcs.

Given $\overleftrightarrow{CQ}$ is tangent to the circle at Q;
$\overleftrightarrow{BC}$ is a secant.

Prove $m\angle 1 = \frac{1}{2}(m\overarc{BQ} - m\overarc{AQ})$

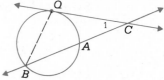

Theorem 8.19   The measure of an angle formed by two intersecting tangents is one-half the difference of the measures of the intercepted arcs.

Given $\overleftrightarrow{BC}$ and $\overleftrightarrow{AC}$ are tangent to the circle at B and A, respectively.

Prove $m\angle 1 = \frac{1}{2}(m\overarc{BYA} - m\overarc{BA})$

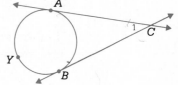

The proofs of these three theorems are exercises 29-33.

The following chart summarizes the relationships between the measures of certain angles and the measures of the intercepted arcs.

Position of vertex of angle	Measure of angle	Definition or Theorem(s)
Center of circle	Equal to measure of the intercepted arc	Def. of measure of minor arc
On circle	One-half the measure of the intercepted arc	Thm. 8.11 Thm. 8.17
In the interior of the circle	One-half the sum of the measures of the intercepted arcs	Thm. 8.15
In the exterior of the circle	One-half the difference of the measures of the intercepted arcs	Thm. 8.16 Thm. 8.18 Thm. 8.19

Class Exercises

[1-9] Find *x*.

1.

110°

4.

50°   *x*°   75°

7.

65°   *x*°

80°

2.

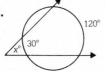

120°

30°

x°

5.

134°

x°

8.

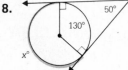

130°   50°

x°

3.

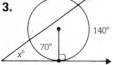

140°

70°

x°

6.

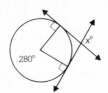

280°

x°

9.

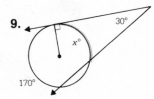

30°

x°

170°

Written Exercises

Set A

[1-6] $\overrightarrow{MN}$ and $\overrightarrow{MR}$ are tangents and $\overline{KN}$ is a diameter of $\odot P$. $m\widehat{ON} = 150$, $m\widehat{KR} = 60$, $m\widehat{RL} = 50$, and $m\widehat{LQ} = 10$. Find the measure of each angle.

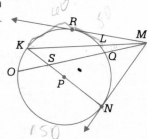

1. $\angle KSO$ **3.** $\angle OMN$ **5.** $\angle KNM$

2. $\angle KMO$ **4.** $\angle MKN$ **6.** $\angle RMN$

[7-12] $\overleftrightarrow{AD}$ and $\overleftrightarrow{AE}$ are tangents, $\overleftrightarrow{AC}$ is a secant, and $\overline{GD}$ and $\overline{FE}$ are chords.

7. $m\widehat{DC} = 110$; $m\widehat{DB} = 43$; $m\angle 2 = $ _?_

8. $m\widehat{FD} = 70$; $m\widehat{GE} = 50$; $m\angle 1 = $ _?_

9. $m\widehat{DCE} = 300$; $m\angle DAE = $ _?_

10. $m\angle DAE = 60$; $m\widehat{DE} = $ _?_

11. $m\widehat{FD} = 65$; $m\angle 1 = 60$; $m\widehat{GE} = $ _?_

12. $m\widehat{BD} = 50$; $m\angle 2 = 20$; $m\widehat{CD} = $ _?_

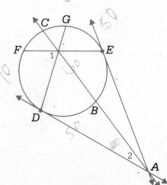

[13-24] $\overleftrightarrow{QV}$ is a tangent, $\overline{UR}$ is a
diameter, $m\widehat{SR} = 40$, $m\angle UPT = 100$, and
$m\widehat{UQ} = 70$. Find the measure of each
angle.

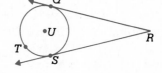

13. $\angle TWQ$ 17. $\angle RQY$ 21. $\angle RUQ$

14. $\angle URQ$ 18. $\angle UQV$ 22. $\angle TUP$

15. $\angle SPR$ 19. $\angle UQW$ 23. $\angle SQY$

16. $\angle SXR$ 20. $\angle RQU$ 24. $\angle UPS$

Set B

[25-26] $\overrightarrow{RQ}$ and $\overrightarrow{RS}$ are tangent to $\odot U$.

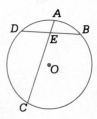

25. Prove that $m\widehat{QS} + m\angle R = 180$.

26. Prove that $m\widehat{STQ} = 180 + m\angle R$.

27. Prove Theorem 8.15.

28. Prove Theorem 8.16.

29. Prove Theorem 8.17, Case I.

30. Prove Theorem 8.17, Case II.

31. Prove Theorem 8.17, Case III.

32. Prove Theorem 8.18.

33. Prove Theorem 8.19.

34. In $\odot O$, $m\widehat{AD} = 3x$, $m\widehat{BC} = 2x + 5$, and
$m\angle AED = 2x + 11$. Find $m\angle AED$.

35. In $\odot O$, $m\widehat{AB} = 2x$, $m\widehat{DC} = x + 55$, and
$m\angle DEC = x + 33$. Find $m\angle DEC$.

36. In $\odot O$, $m\widehat{DC} = 7x + 4$, $m\widehat{AB} = x^2$, and
$m\angle DEC = 3x + 5$. Find $m\angle DEC$.

37. In $\odot O$, $m\widehat{AD} = x^2 + 4$, $m\widehat{BC} = x^2 - 2x$,
and $m\angle AED = \frac{1}{2}x + 12$. Find $m\angle AED$.

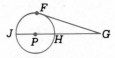

Set C

38. $\overline{FG}$ is tangent to $\odot P$. $\overline{JH}$ is a
diameter. If $FG = 12$ and $GH = 8$,
then $m\widehat{FH} = \underline{\quad ? \quad}$.

39. In $\odot T$, $\overrightarrow{RQ}$ and $\overrightarrow{RS}$ are tangent rays.
$m\angle R = 120$ and $TQ = x$. Show that the
radius of the circle circumscribed
about $\triangle TQR$ is $\frac{1}{3}(x\sqrt{3})$.

8.8 Segments Formed by Chords, Secants, and Tangents

Each of these circles contains two chords that intersect at point P. The lengths of the segments formed are given.

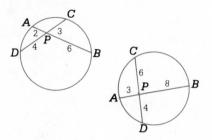

In each circle, compare $(AP)(PB)$ with $(DP)(PC)$. What appears to be true?

Theorem 8.20 If two chords intersect in a circle, then the product of the lengths of the segments on one chord is equal to the product of the lengths of the segments on the other.

Given   In $\odot P$, chords $\overline{AB}$ and $\overline{CD}$ intersect at O.

Prove $(AO)(OB) = (DO)(OC)$

Plan for Proof   Draw $\overline{AD}$ and $\overline{BC}$.
Use AA Post. to show $\triangle AOD \sim \triangle COB$.
Thus, $\dfrac{AO}{OC} = \dfrac{DO}{OB}$.

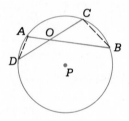

The proof of Theorem 8.20 is exercise 14.

A similar result can be proved for secants.

At the right, $\overleftrightarrow{AC}$ is a secant of $\odot P$. $\overline{AC}$ and $\overline{AB}$ are subsets of $\overleftrightarrow{AC}$. $\overline{AC}$ is a **secant segment**, and its **external secant segment** is $\overline{AB}$.

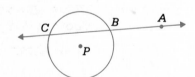

In the diagrams at the right, the measures of secant segments and their external secant segments are given.

In each circle, compare $(PA)(PB)$ with $(PC)(PD)$. Your computations should suggest Theorem 8.21. Its proof is exercise 18.

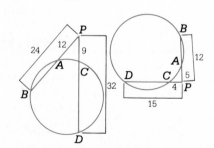

Theorem 8.21   If two secants are drawn to a circle from an exterior point, the product of the lengths of one secant segment and its external secant segment is equal to the product of the lengths of the other secant segment and its external secant segment.

Given

In ⊙O, secants $\overleftrightarrow{BA}$ and $\overleftrightarrow{DC}$ intersect at P.

Prove

$(PA)(PB) = (PC)(PD)$

Plan for Proof

Draw $\overline{DA}$ and $\overline{BC}$.
Use AA Post. to show $\triangle PBC \sim \triangle PDA$.
Then show $\dfrac{PB}{PD} = \dfrac{PC}{PA}$.

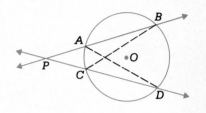

The following theorem establishes the relationship between the lengths of a secant segment, its external secant segment, and a tangent segment. Its proof is exercise 19.

Theorem 8.22   If a tangent and a secant are drawn to a circle from an exterior point, the square of the length of the tangent segment is equal to the product of the lengths of the secant segment and its external secant segment.

Given

⊙O with tangent $\overleftrightarrow{PQ}$ and secant $\overleftrightarrow{PT}$

Prove

$(QP)^2 = (PS)(PT)$

Plan for Proof

Draw $\overline{QS}$ and $\overline{QT}$.
Show $\triangle PQS \sim \triangle PTQ$.
Then show $\dfrac{QP}{PT} = \dfrac{PS}{QP}$.

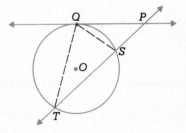

Class Exercises

[1-3] $\overleftrightarrow{RQ}$ is tangent to the circle.

1. Name a secant segment.
2. Name an external secant segment.
3. Name a tangent segment.

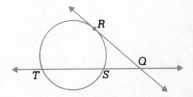

$\frac{8x-24}{8}$

[4-9] Find x.

4.

6.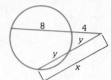

8.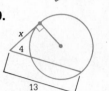

5.

7.

9.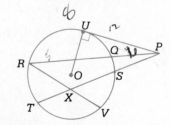

Written Exercises

Set A

[1-6] Find x.

1.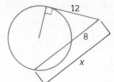

3.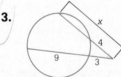

5.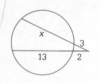

2.

4.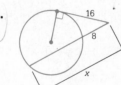

6.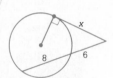

[7-8] Refer to the diagram at the right.

7. If $\overline{AB} \cong \overline{AD}$, prove that $\overline{AC} \cong \overline{AE}$.

8. If $\overline{AC} \cong \overline{AE}$, prove that $\overline{AB} \cong \overline{AD}$.

[9-13] $\overline{PU}$ is tangent to $\odot O$.

9. $PQ = 3$; $PR = 8$; $PT = 12$; $PS = $ ___?___

10. $PU = 12$; $PQ = 6$; $PR = $ ___?___

11. $RX = 9$; $XV = 2$; $TX = 6$; $SX = $ ___?___

12. $RX = 14$; $ST = 11$; $SX = 4$; $XV = $ ___?___

13. $RQ = 10$; $PT = 13$; $PQ = 4$; $ST = $ ___?___

14. Prove Theorem 8.20.

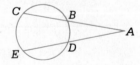
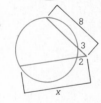

15. Find the radius of the circle used in making the stars on a flag of the United States. $EF = 5.51$, $DF = 6.47$, and $CF = 10.47$.

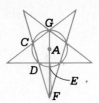

[16-17] Two concentric circles have center O. $\overline{VZ}$ is a tangent and $\overline{VY}$ is a diameter.

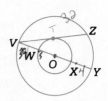

16. $VW = 5$; $VZ = 30$; $WX =$ __?__

17. $XY = 4$; $VZ = 32$; $WO =$ __?__

Set B

18. Prove Theorem 8.21.

19. Prove Theorem 8.22.

[20-21] $\odot P$ and $\odot Q$ are internally tangent at J. $\overrightarrow{FG}$ is tangent to $\odot P$ at Q.

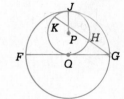

20. $\dfrac{GH}{HK} = \dfrac{2}{7}$; $GK = 18$; $PJ =$ __?__

21. $HK = 4(GH)$; $GK = 25$; $PJ =$ __?__

[22-25] $\overline{AB}$ and $\overline{CD}$ intersect at E.

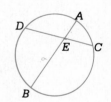

22. $BE = 9$; $AE = 4$; $DC = 12$; $EC =$ __?__

23. $DE = 3$; $EC = 16$; $AB = 14$; $BE =$ __?__

24. $CE = c + b$; $DE = b$; $EB = a$; $AE =$ __?__

25. $AE = 2x$; $EB = x + 9$; $DE = x$; $CE = 3x + 3$; $AE =$ __?__

26. Observation towers are to be built in a national forest. In order to observe the entire forest, the distance from the top of each tower to the horizon must be 25 miles. How tall must each tower be? (Use 8000 miles for the earth's diameter.)

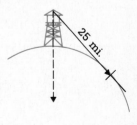

Set C

27. Given: Coplanar circles P and O intersect in Q and R. $\overline{DE}$ is a common external tangent.
Prove: $\overrightarrow{RQ}$ bisects $\overline{DE}$.

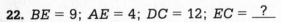

Chapter Summary

1. Points of a circle are those points in a plane that are a given distance from a given point. (page 354)

2. Points of a sphere are those points in space that are a given distance from a given point. (page 356)

3. A tangent to a circle is perpendicular to the radius drawn to the point of tangency. (page 359)

4. Congruent circles are circles with congruent radii. (page 363)

5. A line through the center of a circle and perpendicular to a chord bisects the chord. (page 363)

6. The perpendicular bisectors of the sides of a triangle are concurrent, as are the angle bisectors. (pages 368-369)

7. A central angle of a circle has the center as its vertex. (page 374)

8. The sides of an inscribed angle contain endpoints of an arc and the vertex is any other point of the arc. (page 379)

9. If X is on $\widehat{AB}$, then $m\widehat{AX} + m\widehat{XB} = m\widehat{AXB}$. (page 375)

Position of vertex	Diagrams	Arc-Angle Relationships	Segment Relationships
Interior of circle	**a.** **b.**	**a.** $m\angle 1 = m\widehat{AB}$ **b.** $m\angle 2 = \frac{1}{2}(m\widehat{AB} + m\widehat{CD})$	**b.** $wx = yz$
On circle	**c.** **d.**	**c.** $m\angle 1 = \frac{1}{2}(m\widehat{AB})$ **d.** $m\angle 2 = \frac{1}{2}(m\widehat{AB})$	
Exterior of circle	**e.** **f.** **g.**	**e.** $m\angle 1 = \frac{1}{2}(m\widehat{CD} - m\widehat{AB})$ **f.** $m\angle 2 = \frac{1}{2}(m\widehat{CB} - m\widehat{AB})$ **g.** $m\angle 3 = \frac{1}{2}(m\widehat{ACB} - m\widehat{AB})$	**e.** $wx = yz$ **f.** $z^2 = xy$ **g.** $x = y$

Chapter Review

Lesson 8.1
Page 354

[1-6] Identify each of the following.

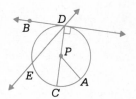

1. $\overleftrightarrow{BD}$ is a __?__ .
2. $\overleftrightarrow{ED}$ is a __?__ .
3. $\overline{ED}$ is a __?__ .
4. $\overline{PA}$ is a __?__ .
5. $\overline{CD}$ is a __?__ .
6. Point D is a __?__ .

[7-8] True or false

7. In a sphere, the center of a small circle is the center of the sphere.

8. A line containing exactly one point of a sphere is tangent to the sphere.

Lesson 8.2
Page 359

[9-12] Give the number of common tangents that could be drawn in each diagram.

9. 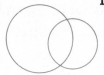   10. 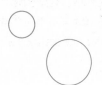   11.   12.

Lesson 8.3
Page 363

[13-15] $\overline{AB}$ and $\overline{CD}$ are chords of $\odot P$.

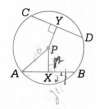

13. $AP = 10$; $PX = 5$; $AB =$ __?__
14. $AB = 24$; $PX = 12$; $PA =$ __?__
15. If $\overline{PX} \cong \overline{PY}$, then $\overline{AB} \cong$ __?__ .

Lesson 8.4
Page 367

[16-19] Decide whether each statement is always, sometimes, or never true.

16. The vertices of a polygon inscribed in a circle are in the interior of the circle.

17. Given $\triangle ABC$, there exists a circle that can be circumscribed about it.

18. The circumcenter and incenter of a triangle are in its interior.

19. The center of the circle circumscribed about a triangle is the point of concurrency of the perpendicular bisectors of the sides.

Lesson 8.5
Page 374

[20-25] Find the indicated measure.

20. $m\overset{\frown}{QR}$ **22.** $m\overset{\frown}{STU}$ **24.** $m\angle UPQ$

21. $m\angle SPT$ **23.** $m\overset{\frown}{UR}$ **25.** $m\overset{\frown}{URS}$

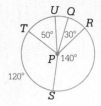

Lesson 8.6
Page 379

[26-29] Refer to the diagram at the right.

26. If $m\angle CDE = 110$, then $m\overset{\frown}{CAE} = $? .

27. Name two congruent inscribed angles.

28. Name a supplement of $\angle EAC$.

29. If $\overline{AC}$ is a diameter, then ? is a right angle.

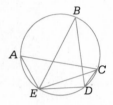

30. Given: $\overline{FG} \cong \overline{JK}$
Prove: $\triangle FGH \cong \triangle JKH$

Lesson 8.7
Page 385

[31-37] $\overline{WS}$ and $\overline{WV}$ are tangents.

31. $m\overset{\frown}{VU} = 40$; $m\overset{\frown}{QR} = 75$; $m\angle 1 = $?

32. $m\overset{\frown}{QR} = 70$; $m\overset{\frown}{UT} = 32$; $m\angle 2 = $?

33. $m\overset{\frown}{UT} = 15$; $m\overset{\frown}{TS} = 43$; $m\overset{\frown}{UVQ} = 155$;
$m\angle QWS = $?

34. $m\overset{\frown}{VR} = 120$; $m\angle 3 = $?

35. $m\overset{\frown}{STV} = 130$; $m\angle VWS = $?

36. $m\angle 1 = 50$; $m\overset{\frown}{QR} = 55$; $m\overset{\frown}{VU} = $?

37. $m\angle VWS = 42$; $m\overset{\frown}{SRV} = $?

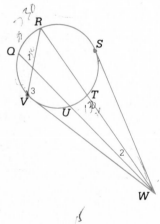

Lesson 8.8
Page 390

[38-41] $\overrightarrow{PB}$ is a tangent.

38. $BX = 3$; $XE = 12$; $AX = 2$; $DX = $?

39. $PE = 28$; $PD = 16$; $PC = 14$; $PF = $?

40. $PC = 6$; $CF = 9$; $PD = 2$; $DE = $?

41. $PD = 4$; $PE = 12$; $PB = $?

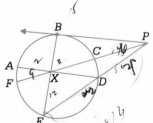

Chapter Test

[1-9] True or false. If false, explain.

1. If $\overline{PA}$ is a radius of $\odot P$ and point Q is in the exterior of $\odot P$, then $PA < PQ$.

2. A secant is a line that contains a chord of a circle.

3. A line that is tangent to a great circle of a sphere is tangent to the sphere.

4. If $\angle A$ is inscribed in a semicircle, then $m\angle A = 180$.

5. Two externally tangent circles have exactly two common tangents.

6. Two circles are congruent if their radii are congruent.

7. All arcs having equal measures are congruent.

8. If X is on $\overarc{AB}$, then $m\overarc{AX} + m\overarc{XB} = m\overarc{AXB}$.

9. The opposite angles of an inscribed quadrilateral are supplementary.

[10-15] $\overline{AB}$ is a tangent segment.

10. $m\overarc{DE} = 25$; $m\overarc{CF} = 45$; $m\angle 1 = $ __?__

11. $m\overarc{AC} = 100$; $m\overarc{AD} = 65$; $m\angle 3 = $ __?__

12. $m\overarc{CF} = 85$; $m\overarc{DE} = 37$; $m\angle 2 = $ __?__

13. $m\angle 1 = 43$; $m\overarc{DE} = 15$; $m\overarc{CF} = $ __?__

14. $m\overarc{AC} = 80$; $m\angle 4 = $ __?__

15. If $\overline{CD}$ is a diameter, then __?__ is a right angle.

[16-19] Find x.

16.

17.

18.

19.

20. Given: $\overline{XZ} \cong \overline{WY}$
    Prove: $\overline{XW} \parallel \overline{ZY}$

Chapter 9

Area of Polygons and Circles

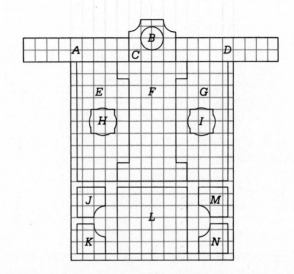

The photograph on the opposite page shows the formal garden of the chateau Vaux-le-Vicomte in France. The diagram above shows one portion of the garden.

1. Name three regions that appear to be rectangular. Name five regions that do not appear to be polygonal.

2. Which region appears to be larger, *A* or *L*? How many squares does each region contain? What is the perimeter of each region?

3. If you were told the area of region *H*, how would you find the area of region *E*?

4. On a grid draw a 3-by-5 rectangular region and a 6-by-10 rectangular region. How many times will the smaller region fit into the larger one?

5. On a grid sketch a circle whose radius is 3 units and another whose radius is 6 units. About how many square units are contained in each circle? How do these numbers seem to compare?

9.1   Area of Polygonal Regions

A triangle separates the plane into
three sets of points: the triangle, its
interior, and its exterior.

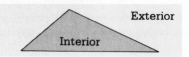

Definition   A **triangular region** consists of a triangle and its interior.

If the interiors of two coplanar triangles intersect, the two
triangular regions *overlap*. *Nonoverlapping* regions do not
intersect or intersect only at vertices or sides.

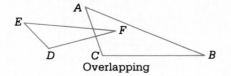
Overlapping

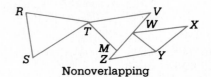
Nonoverlapping

Definition   A **polygonal region** is a plane figure that is the union of a finite
number of coplanar, nonoverlapping triangular regions.

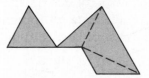 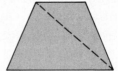 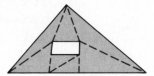

To compare the sizes of polygonal regions, we can associate
a number with each region.

Postulate 22

Area Postulate

To every polygonal region there corresponds a unique positive
number, called the **area** of the region.

For simplicity, we call the area of a triangular region the area
of the triangle, the area of a circular region the area of the
circle, and so on.

Postulate 23

Area Postulate
for Congruent
Triangles

If two triangles are congruent, then the triangles have equal
areas.

Since the first shaded rectangular region below is composed of 15 congruent square regions, each with an area of 1 square unit, the area of the rectangle is 15. Similarly, the area of any polygonal region may be thought of as the number of square units (squares with sides of length 1) that fill it exactly.

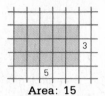 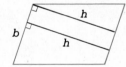 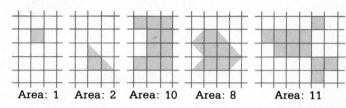

Area: 15   Area: 1   Area: 2   Area: 10   Area: 8   Area: 11

Postulate 24

Area Addition Postulate

The area of the union of two or more nonoverlapping polygonal regions is the sum of the areas of these polygonal regions.

Any side of a parallelogram may be selected as its **base**. An **altitude** corresponding to that base is a segment perpendicular to the base, with endpoints on the base and the opposite side (or on the lines containing them). The length of an altitude is called the **height** for that base.

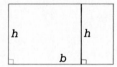 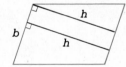 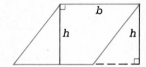

Postulate 25

Area Postulate for Rectangles

The area, *A*, of a rectangle is equal to the product of the length, *b*, of a base and the corresponding height, *h*. $A = bh$

If the rectangle is a square with side length *s*, then $b = h = s$.

Theorem 9.1

The area, *A*, of a square is equal to the square of the length, *s*, of a side. $A = s^2$

The proof of Theorem 9.1 is exercise 21.

Class Exercises

1. Use the definition of polygonal region to determine whether each figure is or is not a polygonal region.

a. 　b. 　c. 　d.

2. Find the area of rectangle $ABCD$ if $AB = 5$ and $BC = 8$.

3. If $RS = 5$ cm, find the area of square $PQRS$.

4. Give possible dimensions of a rectangle with area 48.

5. Find the length of a side of a square with area 48 cm².

6. The area of a rectangle is 72 and a base has a length of 12. What is the corresponding height?

7. The area of a square is $64s^2$. Find its perimeter.

8. The lengths of the base and altitude of a rectangle are doubled. By what factor is the area multiplied?

Find the area of each shaded region.

9. 　　10. 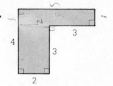　　11.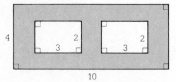

Written Exercises

Set A

Find the area of each rectangle.

1. $b = 3$ cm
   $h = 25$ cm

2. $b = 36$ cm
   $h = 4$ cm

3. $b = 0.25$ m
   $h = 2$ m

4. $b = 5$
   $h = 18.7$

5. $b = 3\sqrt{2}$
   $h = 5\sqrt{2}$

6. $b = 4\sqrt{3}$
   $h = 2\sqrt{3}$

7. $b = r + 2$
   $h = r - 2$

8. $b = 6k$
   $h = k$

Find the area of each square.

9. $s = 11$　　10. $s = 2.7$　　11. $s = 4\sqrt{5}$　　12. $s = r\sqrt{3b}$

13. Find the length of the base of a rectangle with area 186 sq. yd. and height 13 yd.

14. A rectangular table is 76 cm wide. If its area is 8664 cm^2, find its length.

15. How many 4-inch square tiles are needed to cover a rectangular floor 12 ft. 8 in. long and 8 ft. wide?

16. How many 6-inch square glass bricks are needed to fill a square window frame whose area is 900 sq. in.?

Find the area of each shaded region.

17.   18.   19.   20.

21. Prove Theorem 9.1.

Set B

22. Find the area of a rectangle with a base length of 15 meters and a diagonal length of 17 meters.

23. Find the area of a rectangle if the length of a base is 5 in. and the length of a diagonal is 13 in.

24. Find the area of rectangle *FIVE* for $F(1, 3)$, $I(4, 3)$, $V(4, 0)$, and $E(1, 0)$.

25. Find the area of square *FOUR* for $F(0, 5)$, $O(5, 0)$, $U(0, -5)$, and $R(-5, 0)$.

26. In the diagram, which area is larger, rectangle *FECD* or $\square ABCD$?

27. Find a relationship between the areas of $\triangle ADC$ and $\square ABCD$.

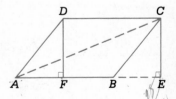

28. The area of a rectangle is 28 cm^2 and its perimeter is 22 cm. Find the dimensions of the rectangle.

29. The area of a rectangle is 75 sq. in. and the length is 3 times the width. Find the length and the width.

Set C

30. Prove: If a diagonal of a square has length d, then the area of the square is $\frac{1}{2}d^2$.

Area of Parallelograms and Triangles

The Area Addition Postulate and the area postulates for rectangles and congruent triangles can be used to develop a formula for the area of a parallelogram.

Theorem 9.2

The area, A, of a parallelogram is equal to the product of the length, b, of a base and the corresponding height, h. $A = bh$

Given

$\square ABCD$; base $\overline{AB}$ with length b; altitude $\overline{DE}$ with length h

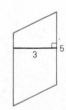

Prove

Area $\square ABCD = bh$

Plan for Proof

Draw a segment from C perpendicular to $\overleftrightarrow{AB}$; label the intersection F.
Quadrilateral $EFCD$ is a rectangle.
By the HL Thm., $\triangle AED \cong \triangle BFC$.
Show $EF = AB = b$.
Using the Area Addition Post., show area $\square ABCD$ = area rectangle $EFCD = bh$.

The proof of Theorem 9.2 is exercise 37.

Example 1

Find the area of each parallelogram.

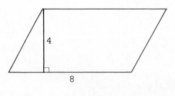

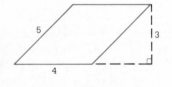

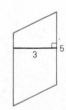

Solution

$A = bh$
$\quad = 8(4)$
$\quad = 32$

$A = bh$
$\quad = 4(3)$
$\quad = 12$

$A = bh$
$\quad = 5(3)$
$\quad = 15$

Example 2

Find the area of $\square PQRS$ for $P(0, 0)$ $Q(5, 0)$, $R(7, 3)$, $S(2, 3)$.

Solution

Graph the parallelogram and draw in an altitude. $ST = 3$ and $PQ = 5$, so
$A = bh = 5(3) = 15$.

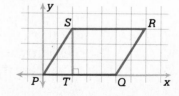

Postulate 23 and Theorem 9.2 can be used to develop a formula for the area of a triangle. Recall that an altitude of a triangle is a segment from a vertex perpendicular to the line that contains the opposite side. The length of the altitude is called the **height**.

Theorem 9.3   The area, A, of a triangle is equal to one-half the product of the length, b, of any side and the corresponding height, h. $A = \frac{1}{2}bh$

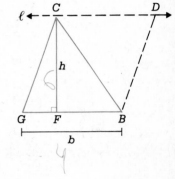

Given $\triangle GBC$; base $\overline{GB}$ of length b; altitude $\overline{CF}$ of length h

Prove   Area $\triangle GBC = \frac{1}{2}bh$

Plan for Proof   Through C, draw $\ell \parallel \overline{GB}$.
Choose D on ℓ on the B-side of $\overleftrightarrow{GC}$ with $GB = CD$.
Draw $\overline{BD}$ to form $\square GBDC$ with $A = bh$.
Show $\triangle GBC \cong \triangle DCB$ by Theorem 5.1.
Then area $\square GBDC = bh = 2(\text{area } \triangle GBC)$.
Thus area $\triangle GBC = \frac{1}{2}bh$.

The proof of Theorem 9.3 is exercise 38.

The following corollary applies Theorem 9.3 to the special case of an equilateral triangle.

Theorem 9.4   The area, A, of an equilateral triangle with side length, s, is equal to $\frac{s^2}{4}\sqrt{3}$. $A = \frac{s^2}{4}\sqrt{3}$

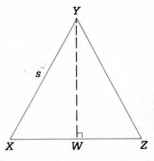

Given   Equilateral $\triangle XYZ$ with side length s

Prove   Area $\triangle XYZ = \frac{s^2}{4}\sqrt{3}$

Plan for Proof   Draw altitude $\overline{YW}$.

$\triangle YWX$ is a 30-60-90 $\triangle$, so $YW = \frac{s}{2}\sqrt{3}$.

Use $A = \frac{1}{2}bh$.

The proof of Theorem 9.4 is exercise 39.

Example 2   Find the area of each triangle.

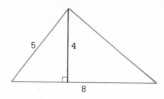 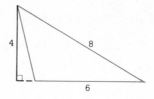

Solution

$$A = \tfrac{1}{2}bh$$
$$= \tfrac{1}{2}(8)(4)$$
$$= 16$$

$$A = \tfrac{1}{2}bh$$
$$= \tfrac{1}{2}(6)(4)$$
$$= 12$$

$$A = \frac{s^2}{4}\sqrt{3}$$
$$= \frac{4^2}{4}\sqrt{3}$$
$$= 4\sqrt{3}$$

Class Exercises

In $\square ABCD$, find an altitude
corresponding to the given base.

1. $\overline{AD}$ **2.** $\overline{DC}$ **3.** $\overline{BC}$

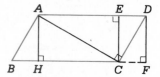

4. Is it possible to find the area of a parallelogram given the
length of one pair of opposite sides?

[5-6] Find the area of each parallelogram.

5. $b = 8$ ft.; $h = 4$ ft.   **6.** $b = 10$ cm; $h = 5$ cm

[7-8] Find the area of each triangle.

7. $b = 20$ mm; $h = 12$ mm   **8.** $b = 22$ in.; $h = 8$ in.

9. Find the area of a right triangular sail. The lengths of its
legs are 6 feet and 8 feet.

10. What is the area of an equilateral triangle with side
length 6 cm?

11. Find the areas of $\triangle ACD$, $\triangle DBC$,
and $\triangle ACB$.

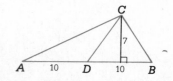

Written Exercises

[1-8] Find the area of $\square ABCD$.

1. $DC = 18$ in.; $DE = 15$ in.
2. $AB = 13$; $DE = 7$
3. $AB = 12$; $m\angle A = 30$; $AD = 8$
4. $AB = 16$; $m\angle A = 30$; $CB = 10$
5. $AB = 15$; $AD = 6\sqrt{2}$; $m\angle A = 45$
6. $AB = 6.5$ cm; $AD = 3\sqrt{2}$ cm; $m\angle A = 45$
7. $AB = 2x - 4$; $DE = x - 2$
8. $AB = 3x + 9$; $DE = x - 3$

[9-16] Find the area of $\triangle ABC$.

9. $AB = 24$; $CD = 9$
10. $AB = 13$; $CD = 7$
11. $AB = 3x - 5$; $CD = x + 5$
12. $AB = 2x + 7$; $CD = x - 9$
13. $AB = 18$ cm; $AC = 10$ cm; $m\angle A = 30$
14. $AB = 28$; $AC = 19$; $m\angle A = 30$
15. $AB = 36$; $AC = 12\sqrt{2}$; $m\angle A = 45$
16. $AB = 34$; $AC = 10\sqrt{2}$; $m\angle A = 45$

Find the missing measure for $\square ABCD$ if its area is 152.

17. $b = 38$; $h =$ __?__   18. $h = 10$; $b =$ __?__

Find the area of right $\triangle ABC$ with legs $\overline{AB}$ and $\overline{AC}$.

19. $AB = 12$; $AC = 17$ 20. $AC = 11$; $AB = 16$

Find the area of equilateral $\triangle ABC$ with side lengths:

21. 11 cm   22. 7 ft.   23. $2\sqrt{2}$ yd.   24. $3\sqrt{3}$ m

[25-28] Find the area of each figure.

25. $\triangle ABC$ with $A(1, 3)$, $B(7, 3)$, and $C(4, -1)$
26. $\triangle DEF$ with $D(1, -1)$, $E(1, -5)$, and $F(7, 2)$

27. □*PQRS* with *P*(0, 1), *Q*(0, 5), *R*(−5, 7), and *S*(−5, 3)

28. □*XYZW* with *X*(−6, 0), *Y*(0, 0), *Z*(3, 4), and *W*(−3, 4)

Set B

In each equilateral triangle, find the missing measure.

29. Perimeter = 8; *A* = __?__   **30.** *A* = √3; perimeter = __?__

Find the area and perimeter of each parallelogram.

31. 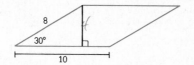   **32.**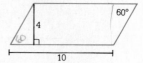

33. A pennant in the shape of an
isosceles triangle is cut from a 24-cm
by 16-cm rectangle as shown. How
much material is wasted?

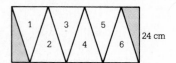

34. Six pennants like the one in
exercise 33 are cut from a 24-cm
wide rectangle as shown. Find the
rectangle length and the waste.

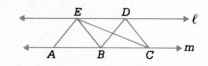

35. Given: ℓ ∥ *m*; *AB* = *BC*. Compare
the areas of triangles *ABE*, *BCE*,
and *ACE*.

36. *P* is the midpoint of $\overline{RE}$. Show
that the area of trapezoid *ROVE*
is equal to the area of △*VOS*.

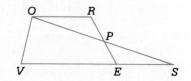

37. Prove Theorem 9.2.

38. Prove Theorem 9.3.

39. Prove Theorem 9.4.

Set C

40. Prove: The area of an equilateral triangle constructed on
the hypotenuse of a right triangle is equal to the sum of
the areas of the equilateral triangles constructed on the
legs.

Excursion Heron's Theorem

To find the area of a triangular sail given only the lengths of its sides, you can use a formula developed nineteen centuries ago by the Greek mathematician Heron of Alexandria.

Heron's Theorem The area of $\triangle ABC$ with side lengths a, b, c, is
$$\sqrt{s(s-a)(s-b)(s-c)},$$
where s is $\frac{1}{2}(a+b+c)$.

Example

Find the area of a triangular sail with sides 5 meters, 8 meters, and 11 meters long.

Solution

$$s = \frac{1}{2}(a+b+c)$$
$$s = \frac{1}{2}(5+8+11) = 12$$
$$\begin{aligned}\text{Area} &= \sqrt{s(s-a)(s-b)(s-c)}\\ &= \sqrt{12(12-5)(12-8)(12-11)}\\ &= \sqrt{12(7)(4)(1)}\\ &= \sqrt{336}, \text{ or about } 18.33 \text{ m}^2\end{aligned}$$

Find the area of a triangle with the given side lengths.

1. 6, 8, 10   **2.** 5, 12, 13   **3.** 5, 9, 13   **4.** 9, 17, 21

5. Use Heron's Theorem to find the area of an equilateral triangle with sides of length x.

6. Prove Heron's Theorem. **Hint** Draw altitude $\overline{CD}$ with length h. Use

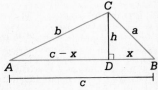

$$h^2 = a^2 - x^2 = b^2 - (c-x)^2$$

to solve for x in terms of a, b, c. Use this value of x in $h^2 = (a-x)(a+x)$ and factor so that

$$h^2 = \frac{(a+b+c)(-a+b+c)(a-b+c)(a+b-c)}{4c^2}$$

Let $2s = a + b + c$; solve for h. Substitute this value into $\frac{1}{2}ch$.

Area of Other Quadrilaterals

The area of a trapezoid can be found by considering two triangles and finding the sum of their areas. Recall that the bases of a trapezoid are the parallel sides.

Definition An **altitude of a trapezoid** is a perpendicular segment from any point in one base to a point on the line containing the other base. Its length is the **height** of the trapezoid.

Theorem 9.5 The area, A, of a trapezoid is equal to one-half the product of the height, h, and the sum of the lengths, b_1 and b_2, of the bases.
$A = \frac{1}{2}h(b_1 + b_2)$

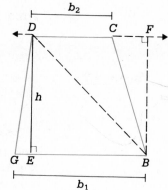

Given Trapezoid $GBCD$; bases $\overline{GB}$ and $\overline{CD}$ of lengths b_1 and b_2; altitude $\overline{DE}$ of length h

Prove $A = \frac{1}{2}h(b_1 + b_2)$

Plan for Proof Draw $\overline{BD}$ to form $\triangle GBD$ and $\triangle DCB$. From B, draw a segment perpendicular to $\overleftrightarrow{DC}$; label the intersection F. Show $BF = DE = h$. Then show area $\triangle GBD = \frac{1}{2}(DE)(GB) = \frac{1}{2}hb_1$ and area $\triangle DCB = \frac{1}{2}(BF)(DC) = \frac{1}{2}hb_2$. Use the Area Addition Postulate.

The proof of Theorem 9.5 is exercise 37.

Example 1 Ms. Craig wants to rent a space in a shopping center to open a boutique. According to her real estate agent, shop C has 3200 sq. ft. of floor space. To check this, she measures the width, h, of the shop. What should h be?

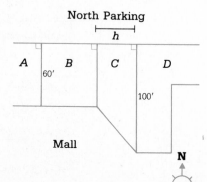

Solution
$$A = \tfrac{1}{2}h(b_1 + b_2)$$
$$3200 = \tfrac{1}{2}h(60 + 100)$$
$$3200 = 80h$$
$$h = 40 \text{ feet}$$

Example 2	Find the area of a trapezoid that has a height of 5 cm and bases 10 cm and 6 cm long.
Solution	$A = \frac{1}{2}h(b_1 + b_2)$
	$ = \frac{1}{2}(5)(10 + 6)$
	$ = 40 \text{ cm}^2$

Recall that sides of a rhombus are congruent and that the diagonals are perpendicular bisectors of each other.

In rhombus $ABCD$ with diagonal $\overline{AC}$, congruent triangles ADC and ABC each have base $\overline{AC}$ of length d_2 and an altitude of length $\frac{1}{2}d_1$.

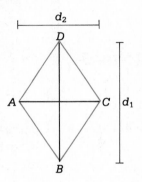

Area $\triangle ABC =$ area $\triangle ADC$

$ = \frac{1}{2}d_2\left(\frac{1}{2}d_1\right)$

Area rhombus $ABCD = 2\left[\frac{1}{2}d_2\left(\frac{1}{2}d_1\right)\right]$

$ = \frac{1}{2}d_1d_2$

Theorem 9.6 The area, A, of a rhombus is equal to one-half the product of the lengths, d_1 and d_2, of its diagonals. $A = \frac{1}{2}d_1d_2$

If exactly one diagonal of a quadrilateral is a perpendicular bisector of the other, the figure is called a *kite*.

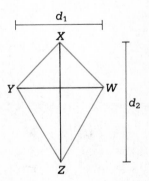

The diagonal $\overline{XZ}$ of the kite separates it into two congruent triangles, each with base $\overline{ZX}$ of length d_2 and height $\frac{1}{2}d_1$. The proof that the area of a kite is $A = \frac{1}{2}d_1d_2$ is the same as the proof for the area of a rhombus.

Area Formulas for Quadrilaterals

Rectangle: $A = bh$ Trapezoid: $A = \frac{1}{2}h(b_1 + b_2)$
Square: $A = s^2$ Kite: $A = \frac{1}{2}d_1d_2$
Parallelogram: $A = bh$ Rhombus: $A = \frac{1}{2}d_1d_2$

Class Exercises

Find the area of each figure.

1.

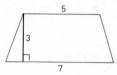

4.

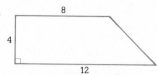

2. $BD = 6$; $AC = 10$

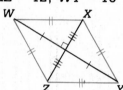

5. $AC = 12$; $BD = 7$

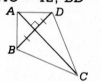

3. $XZ = 12$; $WY = 16$

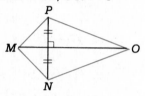

6. $MO = 18$; $PN = 9$

7. Some cub scouts made a kite with diagonals of 3.5 ft. and 4 ft. How much tissue is on the kite's surface?

8. Find the length of the median of a trapezoid if $b_1 = 8$ and $b_2 = 9$.

9. Is it possible to find the area of a trapezoid given the height and the length of the median?

10. Find the area of a trapezoid if the lengths of its median and altitude are 20 and 15, respectively.

11. Find the area of trapezoid $BAND$ for $B(-2, 0)$, $A(2, 0)$, $N(5, 4)$, and $D(-2, 4)$.

Written Exercises

Set A

[1-6] Given a trapezoid with base lengths b_1 and b_2, height h, and area A, supply the missing item.

1. $b_1 = 6$; $b_2 = 8$; $h = 4$; $A = $ __?__

2. $b_1 = 10$; $b_2 = 15$; $h = 10$; $A = $ __?__

3. $b_1 = 28$; $h = 14$; $A = 364$; $b_2 = \underline{\ ?\ }$

4. $b_2 = 3$; $h = 40$; $A = 260$; $b_1 = \underline{\ ?\ }$

5. $b_1 = 8t$; $b_2 = 12t$; $A = 60t^2$; $h = \underline{\ ?\ }$

6. $b_1 = \sqrt{2x}$; $b_2 = 5\sqrt{2x}$; $A = 10\sqrt{2x}$; $h = \underline{\ ?\ }$

[7-10] The lengths of the diagonals of a rhombus are given. Find the area of each rhombus.

7. 7.4 cm; 4.3 cm   **9.** $x + 6$; $2x - 1$

8. $2\sqrt{6}$; $3\sqrt{6}$ **10.** $8 - y$; $8 + y$

[11-14] Identify each quadrilateral and give its area.

11. $G(-2, 0)$, $I(0, 4)$, $V(5, 4)$, and $E(17, 0)$

12. $T(5, 0)$, $A(8, 6)$, $K(5, 8)$, and $E(2, 6)$

13. $Z(3, -1)$, $E(5, 4)$, $U(3, 9)$, and $S(1, 4)$

14. $H(-2, -1)$, $E(3, 2)$, $R(-2, 5)$, and $A(-7, 2)$

15. Estimate the area of North Dakota if its northern and southern borders are 310 and 360 miles long, respectively, and are 210 miles apart.

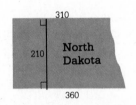

16. Assume Wyoming is shaped like a trapezoid. Its northern and southern borders are 345 and 365 miles long, and they are 275 miles apart. Estimate its area.

17. The area of a rhombus is 2352 sq. in. and a diagonal length is 56 in. How long is the other diagonal?

18. Given: Kite $ABCD$; $AC = 36$; area $= 99$. Find BD.

Set B

Find the area of each trapezoid.

19.

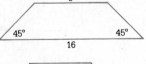

21.

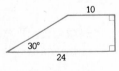

20.

22.

Find the area of each figure.

23. Kite *STUV*

24. Rhombus *PQRS*

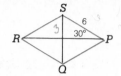

25. Nevada is roughly the shape of a trapezoid, but the Colorado River cuts off a trapezoidal region at the southern tip. Estimate the area of Nevada.

26. Estimate the area of Texas.

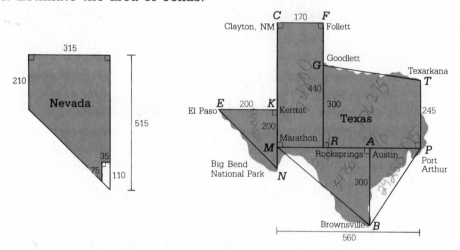

27. A hang glider is formed by two isosceles triangles with 45° vertex angles. Find the area (also called the sail area) of the glider.

28. If the hang glider in exercise 27 weighs 35 lbs. and the total weight it can carry (including its own) is 1 lb. per sq. ft. of sail area, how much can the user weigh?

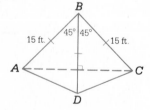

29. The lengths of the diagonals of a rhombus are 10 and 24. Find the height of the rhombus.

30. A rhombus has sides of length 10 and one diagonal of length 16. Find the area of the rhombus.

31. Find the area of $\triangle DEC$, $\triangle ABC$, and trapezoid $DEBA$. Find the ratio of the area of $\triangle DEC$ to that of $\triangle ABC$.

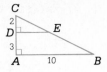

32. Given: Trapezoid $ABCD$
Prove: Area $\triangle ADE$ = area $\triangle BCE$

33. The area of a trapezoid is 168 cm^2. The height is 8 cm. If the length of the longer base is 12 cm more than twice the shorter, what are the base lengths?

34. Prove: The area of a trapezoid is equal to the product of its height and its median.

35. Find the area of the tent floor at the right.

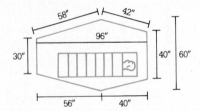

36. One way to approximate the area of an irregularly shaped region is to divide it into trapezoidal and rectangular regions, all with the same height h. For example, to estimate the area of Tennessee, divide it into twelve regions and find the height and the lengths of the bases of each region. Estimate the area of Tennessee as shown below.

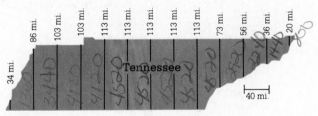

Set C

37. Prove Theorem 9.5.

38. Prove Theorem 9.6.

39. Prove: The segment joining the midpoints of the parallel sides of a trapezoid separates it into two trapezoids that have equal areas.

Area of Similar Triangles

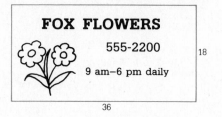

18

12

36   24

Mrs. Fox owns a flower store. She is deciding which size ad to place in the newspaper. The larger ad covers more area so has more visibility but the smaller ad is cheaper.

The ads can be represented by similar rectangles. The ratio of the lengths of corresponding sides is 2 to 3.

Find the area of each ad. What is the ratio of the areas? How is this ratio related to the ratio of the lengths of a pair of corresponding sides?

The relationship suggested by your answer is also true for pairs of similar triangles.

Theorem 9.7	If two triangles are similar, then the ratio of their areas is equal to the square of the ratio of the lengths of any two corresponding sides.

Given $\triangle ABC \sim \triangle XYZ$

Prove $\dfrac{\text{Area } \triangle ABC}{\text{Area } \triangle XYZ} = \left(\dfrac{AB}{XY}\right)^2 = \left(\dfrac{BC}{YZ}\right)^2 = \left(\dfrac{CA}{ZX}\right)^2$

Plan for Proof Draw altitudes $\overline{BD}$ and $\overline{YW}$.
Express the areas of $\triangle ABC$ and $\triangle XYZ$.
Use Theorem 6.9: In similar triangles, the lengths of the altitudes from corresponding vertices are in the same ratio as the lengths of corresponding sides.

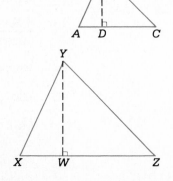

The proof of Theorem 9.7 is exercise 20.

Example

Show that the triangles are similar and find the ratio of their areas.

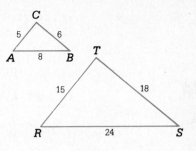

Solution

$$\frac{AB}{RS} = \frac{8}{24}; \frac{BC}{ST} = \frac{6}{18}; \frac{CA}{TR} = \frac{5}{15}$$

Since each ratio is equivalent to $\frac{1}{3}$, $\triangle ABC \sim \triangle RST$.

$$\frac{\text{Area } \triangle ABC}{\text{Area } \triangle RST} = \left(\frac{1}{3}\right)^2 = \frac{1}{9}$$

Theorem 9.7 can be applied to similar polygons that are composed of nonoverlapping triangles. For example, you can show that two regular pentagons with sides of lengths 2 and 3 have areas that are in the ratio $\left(\frac{2}{3}\right)^2$, or $\frac{4}{9}$.

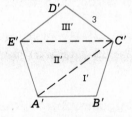
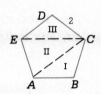

From vertices C and C' draw diagonals $\overline{CE}, \overline{CA}, \overline{C'E'}$, and $\overline{C'A'}$ to separate the pentagons into triangular regions. By the SAS Similarity Theorem, I $\sim$ I' and III $\sim$ III'.

$$\frac{AC}{A'C'} = \frac{BC}{B'C'} = \frac{2}{3} \text{ and } \frac{EC}{E'C'} = \frac{DC}{D'C'} = \frac{2}{3}, \text{ so II} \sim \text{II' by}$$
the SSS Similarity Theorem.

$$\frac{\text{Area I}}{\text{Area I'}} = \frac{\text{area II}}{\text{area II'}} = \frac{\text{area III}}{\text{area III'}} = \left(\frac{2}{3}\right)^2 \text{ by Theorem 9.7.}$$

$$\frac{\text{Area I} + \text{area II} + \text{area III}}{\text{Area I'} + \text{area II'} + \text{area III'}} = \left(\frac{2}{3}\right)^2 \text{ by the summation}$$

property of proportions, so $\dfrac{\text{area } ABCDE}{\text{area } A'B'C'D'E'} = \left(\dfrac{2}{3}\right)^2$ by the Area Addition Postulate.

This analysis suggests the general result in Theorem 9.8.

Theorem 9.8   If two polygons are similar, the ratio of their areas is equal to the square of the ratio of the lengths of any two corresponding sides.

Class Exercises

1. The lengths of the corresponding sides of two similar triangles are 3 and 7. What is the ratio of the areas?

2. What is the ratio of the areas of the two similar triangles at the right?

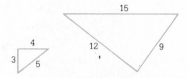

3. Find the ratio of the areas of the two photographs at the right.

4. The areas of two similar triangles are 64 cm^2 and 100 cm^2. What is the ratio of the lengths of their corresponding sides?

Written Exercises

Set A

1. The area of a given triangle is 9 times that of a similar triangle. Find the ratio of the lengths of the corresponding sides of the two triangles.

2. The area of a rectangle is 16 times that of a similar one. Find the ratio of corresponding side lengths.

3. The length of each side of a triangle is doubled. What is the effect on the perimeter? The area?

4. The lengths of the sides of a square are doubled. What is the effect on the perimeter? On the area?

5. Given: $\triangle ABC \sim \triangle DEF$ with $AB = 18$ in., $DE = 3$ in. and area $\triangle ABC = 72$ sq. in. Find the area of $\triangle DEF$.

6. Two similar triangles have corresponding sides with lengths 8 and 4. If the area of the first triangle is 52, what is the area of the second triangle?

7. Find the length of a side of a square whose area is five times the area of a square with side length 6 cm.

8. Find the side length of equilateral $\triangle ABC$ that has twice the area of equilateral $\triangle DEF$ if $DE = 8$ ft.

9. The area of a triangle is 9 and its perimeter is $4x - 4$. The area of a similar triangle is 4 and its perimeter is $2x + 6$. Find the perimeter of each.

10. A rectangle with area 60 has perimeter $12x + 8$. A similar rectangle has perimeter $20x + 8$ and area 135. Find the perimeter of each rectangle.

11. What is the ratio of the areas of two triangles with corresponding sides of lengths $2\sqrt{3}$ and $6\sqrt{3}$?

12. A sign painter is copying a corporate symbol. The area of a triangle on the letterhead logo is 30 mm^2 and the length of a side is 6 mm. The length of the corresponding side of the triangle on the sign logo is 75 cm. What is the area of the triangle on the sign?

Set B

13. Two similar triangles have areas of 121 cm^2 and 81 cm^2. If a side length of the larger is 22 cm, find the length of the corresponding side of the smaller.

14. The area of one equilateral triangle is 16 times that of another. What is the ratio of their perimeters?

Assume that the television screens described below are shaped like similar rectangular regions.

15. What is the ratio of the areas of 12-in. and 19-in. diagonal screens?

16. Find the ratio of the areas of a 6-ft. diagonal projection TV screen to a 10-in. diagonal TV screen.

17. The area of the rectangular design on a tablecloth is 2.25 times its area on a matching napkin. What is the ratio of the lengths of a pair of corresponding sides?

18. A scale drawing of a convention hall is 11 cm × 30 cm. The actual dimensions are 67.0 m × 182.7 m. Find the ratio of the area of the drawing to that of the hall.

19. A fountain is drawn to the same scale as the hall in exercise 18. The drawing of the fountain has an area of 3.1 cm². What is the actual area of the fountain?

20. Prove Theorem 9.7.

21. Without using Theorem 9.8, show that the ratio of the areas of two regular hexagons is equal to the square of the ratio of the lengths of their corresponding sides. **Hint** Draw diagonals.

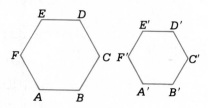

22. Given: $\triangle PQR \sim \triangle TUV$ with altitudes $\overline{RS}$ and $\overline{VW}$

Prove: $\dfrac{\text{area } \triangle PQR}{\text{area } \triangle TUV} = \left(\dfrac{RS}{VW} \right)^2$

Set C

23. The midpoints of the sides of squares are joined by segments as shown. Find the ratio of the areas of square *WXYZ* and square *ABCD*.

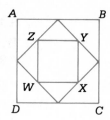

24. In $\triangle ABC$, the height CF is 8, AB is 16, and $\overline{DE} \parallel \overline{AB}$. Find DE and GC such that $\triangle CDE$ and trapezoid *ABED* have equal areas.

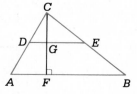

Geometry Maintenance

[1-3] In $\odot P$, $AP = 60$ cm.

1. If $\overline{AB}$ is 36 cm from P, find AB.

2. If $m\angle APQ = 60$, find AB.

3. If $m\angle APQ = 45$, find AB.

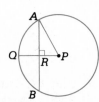

Progress Check

Lesson 9.1
Page 400

1. The length of a base and the corresponding height of a rectangle are 15 and 22, respectively. Find the area of the rectangle.

2. Find the length of a side of a square with area 169 m^2.

3. Given $\triangle ABC \cong \triangle DEF$. What is the ratio of the areas of the two congruent triangles?

Lesson 9.2
Page 404

Find the area of each polygon.

4. A parallelogram with base length 14 and height 24.

5. $\square ABCD$; $m\angle A = 30$; $AB = 17$; $AD = 12$

6. A triangle with base length 18 in. and height 12 in.

7. A right triangle with leg lengths 5 cm and 12 cm

8. An equilateral triangle with side length 10 cm

Lesson 9.3
Page 410

Find the area of each polygon.

9. A trapezoid with height 15 and base lengths 9 and 13

10. Trapezoid $ABCD$; bases $\overline{AB}$ and $\overline{CD}$; $m\angle A = 60$; $AD = 16$; $AB = 20$; $CD = 10$

11. A rhombus with diagonal lengths 8 cm and 6 cm

12. A kite with diagonal lengths 14 in. and 18 in.

13. Find the area of the flat trapezoidal roof.

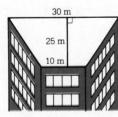

14. Find the area of the game table.

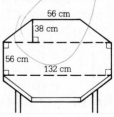

Lesson 9.4
Page 416

15. $\triangle ABC \sim \triangle DEF$; $\dfrac{AB}{DE} = \dfrac{4}{9}$. What is the ratio of the areas of the triangles?

16. The ratio of the areas of two similar polygons is 36 to 48. Find the ratio of the lengths of two corresponding sides.

9.5 Regular Polygons and Circles

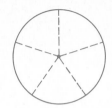

A graphic designer plans to use a regular pentagon in a company logo. She draws a circle and pencils in a radius. Then she draws five congruent, adjacent central angles (72° each) and marks off five congruent arcs. Finally, she draws in the chord for each arc.

Using a similar procedure, a regular polygon with any number of sides can be inscribed in a given circle. Conversely, for any given regular polygon, there is a circle through its vertices.

Theorem 9.9	A circle can be circumscribed about any regular polygon.
Given	Regular n-gon with vertices P_1, P_2, P_3, . . . , P_n
Prove	A circle can be circumscribed about $P_1P_2P_3$ . . . P_n.
Plan for Proof	Draw $\odot O$ through P_1, P_2, and P_3 by applying Theorem 8.7.

Draw $\overline{OP_4}$ and radii $\overline{OP_1}$, $\overline{OP_2}$, and $\overline{OP_3}$.
Use $\angle P_1P_2P_3 \cong \angle P_2P_3P_4$ and $\angle 2 \cong \angle 3$ to show $\angle 1 \cong \angle 4$.
Show $\triangle P_2OP_1 \cong \triangle P_3OP_4$ by SAS.
Since $OP_1 = OP_4$, P_4 lies on $\odot O$.
Likewise, show that the remaining vertices P_5, P_6, . . . , P_n lie on $\odot O$.

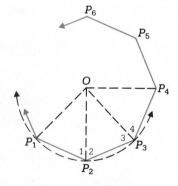

If a circle is circumscribed about a regular polygon, its sides are congruent chords of the circle. By Theorem 8.5, the sides of the polygon are equidistant from the center. Thus we have the following definitions and Theorem 9.10.

Definition	For a regular polygon:

For a regular polygon:

the **center** is the center of the circumscribed circle;

a **radius** is a segment from the center to a vertex, or the segment's length;

a **central angle** is an angle formed by two radii drawn to the endpoints of one side;

and the **apothem** is the distance from the center to each side.

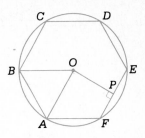

Center: O
Radii: $\overline{OA}, \overline{OB}$
Central $\angle$: $\angle AOB$
Apothem: OP

Theorem 9.10	A circle can be inscribed in any regular polygon.

Theorem 9.11	The area, A, of a regular polygon is equal to one-half the product of the apothem, a, and the perimeter, p. $\quad A = \frac{1}{2}ap$

Given

Regular n-gon $P_1P_2P_3 \ldots P_n$, each side of length s; apothem a; perimeter p.

Prove

$A = \frac{1}{2}ap$

Plan for Proof

Draw all radii of the polygon to form n congruent triangles.
Express the area of each triangle: $\frac{1}{2}as$.
Show the area of the polygon equal to $n\left(\frac{1}{2}as\right) = \frac{1}{2}a(ns) = \frac{1}{2}ap$.

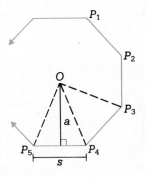

The proof of Theorem 9.11 is exercise 29.

Example

The roof of the arena at the right has the shape of a regular hexagon. Find the area of the roof.

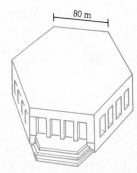

Solution

$A = \frac{1}{2}ap$
$A = \frac{1}{2}[\frac{1}{2}(80)(\sqrt{3})][(6)(80)]$
$A = \frac{1}{2}(40\sqrt{3})(480)$
$A = 9600\sqrt{3}$, or about 16,628 m^2

Class Exercises

1. Draw a regular octagon.

2. Can a circle be inscribed in any regular polygon? Can any regular polygon be circumscribed about a circle?

3. Sketch a nonregular polygon inscribed in a circle.

Find the area of a regular n-gon with perimeter p and apothem a.

4. $n = 6$; $p = 24$; $a = 2\sqrt{3}$ 5. $n = 8$; $p = 24$; $a = 4$

Find the measure of a central angle of a regular polygon with the given number of sides.

6. 3	**8.** 5	**10.** 8	**12.** m	**14.** $n + 1$
7. 4	**9.** 6	**11.** 12	**13.** $7n$	**15.** $n - 2$

16. For a regular polygon, is the length of a radius always, sometimes, or never greater than the apothem?

Written Exercises

Set A

Find the area of a regular hexagon with apothem a, perimeter p, radius r, and side length s.

1. $s = 12$	**3.** $a = 6$	**5.** $p = 60$	**7.** $r = 2\sqrt{3}$
2. $s = 8$	**4.** $a = 10$	**6.** $p = 84$	**8.** $r = 5\sqrt{3}$

9. Draw a regular decagon.   10. Draw a regular hexagon.

Find the area of a square inscribed in a circle of radius r.

11. $r = 8$ 12. $r = 10$

For each regular polygon with n sides of length s, find the apothem, a; perimeter, p; radius, r; and area, A.

13. $n = 4$; $s = 18$	**15.** $n = 6$; $s = 9$	**17.** $n = 3$; $s = y$
14. $n = 3$; $s = 18$	**16.** $n = 4$; $s = x$	**18.** $n = 6$; $s = z$

19. The ratio of the lengths of two corresponding sides of two similar polygons is 2:5. Find the ratio of the apothems.

20. Given: A regular polygon with center at O; side $\overline{AB}$; $\overline{OC} \perp \overline{AB}$ at C
Prove: OC is the apothem; $\overrightarrow{OC}$ bisects $\angle AOB$; $\overline{OC}$ bisects $\overline{AB}$.

21. Given: Two similar regular polygons
Prove: The ratio of the apothems is equal to the ratio of the lengths of any two corresponding sides.

22. Prove: The ratio of the areas of two similar regular polygons is the square of the ratio of their apothems.

A square and a regular hexagon are inscribed in the same circle. Which polygon has:

23. the greater apothem?   **25.** the greater area?

24. the longer side?   **26.** the greater perimeter?

27. Circle O has an inscribed equilateral $\triangle ABC$ and a circumscribed equilateral $\triangle XYZ$. Find the ratio of AB to XY and the ratio of the areas of the triangles.

28. Find the ratio of the areas of an equilateral triangle and a regular hexagon that have the same perimeter.

29. Prove Theorem 9.11.

30. Prove: The area of a regular hexagon with side length s is $\frac{3}{2}s^2 \sqrt{3}$.

31. Join the midpoints of the sides of a regular hexagon to form another hexagon. Find the ratio of the areas of the two hexagons.

32. Construct a circle inscribed in a rhombus.

33. Prove: The area of a regular hexagon constructed on the hypotenuse of right $\triangle ABC$ is the sum of the areas of the regular hexagons constructed on the legs.

Using BASIC

Perimeters of Regular Polygons

Given the length of a side of a regular polygon of n sides, it is possible to find the length of a side of a polygon of the same radius with $2n$ sides.

$\overline{AB}$ is a side of length s of a regular n-gon inscribed in a circle of radius r, and $\overline{AC}$ is a side of a regular $2n$-gon inscribed in the same circle.

$$(DO)^2 + (AD)^2 = (OA)^2$$
$$(DO)^2 + (\tfrac{1}{2}s)^2 = r^2$$
$$DO = \sqrt{r^2 - (\tfrac{1}{2}s)^2}$$
$$(AD)^2 + (CD)^2 = (AC)^2$$
$$(\tfrac{1}{2}s)^2 + (r - \sqrt{r^2 - (\tfrac{1}{2}s)^2})^2 = (AC)^2$$
$$2r^2 - r\sqrt{4r^2 - s^2} = (AC)^2$$

The program below uses the final equation to compute perimeters of regular polygons, given an initial regular polygon with N sides, radius R, and sides of length S.

```
100 REM COMPUTING PERIMETER OF REGULAR POLYGONS
110 PRINT "WHAT ARE N, R, AND S (SEPARATED BY COMMAS)";
120 INPUT N,R,S
130 PRINT "R = ";R
140 PRINT "N","PERIMETER"
150 PRINT N,N*S
160 LET S = SQR( 2*R*R-(R*SQR( 4*R*R-S*S )))
170 LET S = INT( S*100000000 + .5 )/100000000
180 LET N = 2*N
190 IF N < 2000 THEN 150
200 END
```

1. A square inscribed in a circle of radius 4 has a side length of $4\sqrt{2}$, or about 5.65685425. RUN the program for $N = 4$, $R = 4$, and $S = 5.65685425$.

2. RUN the program for a square of side length 0.707106781 inscribed in a circle of radius 0.5.

3. What is the length of a side of a regular hexagon inscribed in a circle of radius 4? Of radius 0.5? RUN the program for these initial regular polygons.

Area and Circumference of a Circle

The distance around a polygon is called its perimeter. The distance around a circle is called its *circumference*. One way to estimate the circumference of a circle is to inscribe regular polygons in the circle.

As we increase the number of sides of the polygon:

the apothem approaches the radius of the circle;

the perimeter of the polygon becomes a better approximation of the circumference of the circle;

the area of the polygon approaches the area of the circle.

By increasing the number of sides, we can make the apothem, perimeter, and area of the polygon as close as we want to the radius, circumference, and area of the circle.

The **circumference of a circle** is the *limit* of the perimeters of the inscribed regular polygons.

The **area of a circle** is the *limit* of the areas of the inscribed regular polygons.

Consider two circles with circumferences C and C', radii r and r', diameters d and d', and with regular n-gons inscribed in each circle with side lengths s and s', respectively. The limit descriptions given above show that ns approaches C and ns' approaches C' as n gets larger. But all regular n-gons for a given n are similar, and their central angles are parts of similar triangles. Hence:

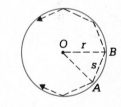

$$\frac{ns}{ns'} = \frac{s}{s'} = \frac{r}{r'} = \frac{\frac{1}{2}d}{\frac{1}{2}d'} = \frac{d}{d'}$$

For large values of n, $ns \doteq C$, $ns' \doteq C'$. It can be shown that $\dfrac{C}{C'} = \dfrac{d}{d'}$ so $\dfrac{C}{d} = \dfrac{C'}{d'}$.

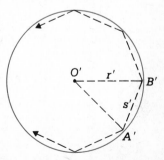

Theorem 9.12	The ratio of the circumference to the diameter is the same for all circles.

Definition	The ratio of the circumference, C, of a circle to the diameter, d, is denoted by π. $\dfrac{C}{d} = \pi$

Theorem 9.13 is an immediate consequence of the definition of π. Since π is not a rational number, approximations such as 3.14 and 3.1416 are commonly used in computation.

Theorem 9.13	The circumference, C, of a circle, is equal to the product of π and the diameter, d. $C = \pi d$ or $C = 2\pi r$

Suppose a regular n-gon is inscribed in circle O. If the perimeter of the polygon is p and the apothem is a, the area of the polygon is $\frac{1}{2}ap$. As the number of sides increases, a approaches r and p approaches C. For large values of n, $\frac{1}{2}ap \doteq \frac{1}{2}rC = \frac{1}{2}r(2\pi r)$, or πr^2. As the area of the polygon approaches the area of the circle, it gets close to πr^2.

Theorem 9.14	The area, A, of a circle is equal to the product of π and the square of the radius, r, of the circle. $A = \pi r^2$

Class Exercises

[1-8] These exercises refer to a circle of radius r, area A, circumference C, and diameter d. For each given measure, find the other three measures. Give answers in terms of π.

1. $d = 4$ 3. $r = 7$ 5. $C = 10\pi$ 7. $A = 4\pi$
2. $d = 6$ 4. $r = 11$ 6. $C = 18\pi$ 8. $A = 16\pi$

9. If the radius of a circle is doubled, by what factors are the circumference and the area multiplied?

Written Exercises

[1-35] Use $\pi \doteq 3.14$.

Set A

1. Find the circumference of a bicycle tire with a 26-inch diameter.

2. Find the circumference of a basketball hoop with an 18-inch diameter.

3. Find the area of a circular stove-top burner with a 24-centimeter diameter.

4. Find the cooking area of a barbeque grill rack that is circular and has a 40-centimeter diameter.

5. Find the area of a circular rug with a 1.2-m radius.

6. Find the area of a circular window with a 30-cm radius.

7. By what factor must the radius of a circle be multiplied to make its area 9 times as large?

8. By what factor must the radius of a circle be multiplied to make its area 25 times as large?

9. The area of a circular skating rink is 1257 m². Find the length of its diameter.

10. The area of a circular reading glass is 63.6 cm². Find the length of its diameter.

Find the missing measure for each circle.

11. $C = 27$; $d = \underline{\ ?\ }$ 12. $C = 43$; $d = \underline{\ ?\ }$

13. Which has the greater area, a 10-inch square griddle or a 10-inch diameter round griddle? How much greater?

14. Which has the greater area, the bottom of a 20-cm square baking dish or a 20-cm diameter round baking dish? How much greater?

Set B

15. Find the ratio of the areas of the two containers in exercise 13. In exercise 14.

Find the ratio of the circumferences of circles with the given radii. Find the ratio of their areas.

16. $r_1 = 1$, $r_2 = 4$ 17. $r_1 = 2$, $r_2 = 5$

18. Estimate the length of a cable if it lies in five 3-ft. diameter coils.

19. A caterer charges $10.95 for a 9-inch diameter quiche and $15.95 for a 12-inch diameter quiche. Which is the better buy (lower price per square inch)?

20. If the air moved by a fan depends only on the area covered by its blades, how many fans with 12-inch diameter blades move as much air as a 30-in. blade fan?

Find the area of each shaded region.

21.

23.

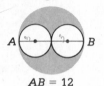

$AB = 12$

25.

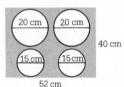

22.

24.

26.

27. Which has the greater area, a square with perimeter 20 or a circle with circumference 20?

28. Prove: The ratio of the areas of two circles is equal to the square of the ratio of their radii.

29. The areas of two circles are 18 cm² and 16 cm². What is the ratio of their radii?

30. Find the area and perimeter of a regular hexagon inscribed in a circle with circumference 20π.

[31-33] Find the circumference of a circle circumscribed about a regular polygon with n sides of length s.

31. $n = 4$, $s = 16$ **32.** $n = 3$, $s = 8$ **33.** $n = 6$, $s = 20$

Set C

34. Find the circumference of a circle inscribed in a rhombus with diagonal lengths 12 and 16.

35. Given a square, prove that the area of the inscribed circle is half the area of the circumscribed circle.

36. Find the circumference of a circle inscribed in an isosceles trapezoid with base lengths 8 and 20.

Career   Plumber

Peg Bennett is a plumber. She knows that the amount of water a pipe can carry depends on the area of its opening. The opening of a pipe is referred to as its cross section.

The cross-sectional area of a 4-inch pipe is more than four times the cross-sectional area of a 1-inch pipe. How many times greater is the area of a cross section of 4-inch pipe than that of a 1-inch pipe?

$$\frac{\text{area of 4-inch pipe cross section}}{\text{area of 1-inch pipe cross section}} = \frac{\pi(2)^2}{\pi(0.5)^2} = \frac{4}{0.25} = \frac{16}{1}$$

Thus, it will take sixteen 1-inch pipes to carry the same amount of water as one 4-inch pipe.

1. How many 2-inch pipes are needed to carry the amount of water carried by a 4-inch pipe?

2. How many 4-inch branch pipes should Peg install to carry the same amount of water as a 16-inch main pipe?

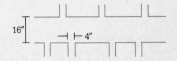

3. Eleven 4-inch branch pipes and some 2-inch branch pipes are being installed to feed into a 16-inch main pipe. How many 2-inch pipes are needed if the smaller pipes are to carry as much water as the 16-inch main pipe?

Area of Sectors and Segments of Circles

$\widehat{AB}$ can be divided into n arcs of equal measure. If chords are drawn in these n arcs, we say that the **length of** $\widehat{AB}$ is the limit of the sum of the lengths of the n chords as n gets very large.

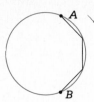

Theorem 9.15 In a circle of radius r, the ratio of the length, s, of an arc to the circumference, C, of the circle is the same as the ratio of the arc measure, m, to 360. $\dfrac{s}{C} = \dfrac{m}{360}$ or $s = \dfrac{m}{360}(2\pi r)$

Example 1 Chicago and Paris lie on a circle as shown. ($r = 4000$ mi.) The measure of the arc from Chicago to Paris is 60°. Find the distance between the two cities.

Solution

$$s = \frac{m}{360}(2\pi r)$$
$$= \frac{60}{360}(2\pi)(4000)$$
$$= \frac{1}{6}(8000\pi), \text{ or about } 4189 \text{ miles}$$

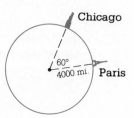

Definition A **sector of a circle** is a region bounded by two radii and either the major arc or the minor arc that is intercepted.

The sector formed with $\widehat{ACB}$ is shaded. The sector formed with $\widehat{AKB}$ is unshaded.

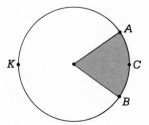

Theorem 9.16 In a circle of radius r, the ratio of the area, A_s, of a sector to the area, A_c, of the circle is the same as the ratio of the arc measure, m, to 360. $\dfrac{A_s}{A_c} = \dfrac{m}{360}$ or $A_s = \dfrac{m}{360}(\pi r^2)$

| Example 2 | A lawn sprinkler waters a lawn as shown. Find the area of the watered sector. |

Solution

$$A = \frac{m}{360}(\pi r^2)$$
$$= \frac{120}{360}[\pi(15)^2]$$
$$= \frac{1}{3}[\pi(225)], \text{ or about } 236 \text{ m}^2$$

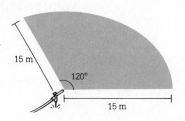

| Definition | A **segment of a circle** is a region bounded by a chord and either the major arc or the minor arc that is intercepted. |

The area of the shaded segment formed by minor arc $\overset{\frown}{ACB}$ is found by subtracting the area of $\triangle AOB$ from the area of the sector with $\overset{\frown}{ACB}$. How would you find the area of the unshaded major arc segment?

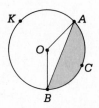

Example 3

Find the area of a drop leaf of a round table with a 120-cm diameter. Each drop leaf has an arc measure of 90.

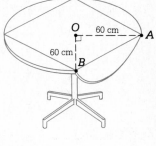

Solution

Since the diameter is 120 cm, $r = 60$ cm.

Area of sector $= \dfrac{90}{360}\pi(60)^2 \doteq 2827$

Area of $\triangle AOB = \frac{1}{2}(60)(60) = 1800$

Area of drop leaf $\doteq 2827 - 1800$
$$\doteq 1027 \text{ cm}^2$$

Class Exercises

[1-8] What fraction of the area of a circle is the area of a sector with the given arc measure:

1. 20	**3.** 90	**5.** 135	**7.** 240
2. 60	**4.** 120	**6.** 150	**8.** 320

9. Find the area of the segment of a circle if the arc measure is 60 and the radius is 15.

10. Find the segment area in exercise 9 if the radius is 4.

[11-20] Given: An arc of measure m and length s in a circle with radius r forming a sector with area A. Give areas and arc lengths in terms of π.

11. $r = 8$, $m = 30$; find s.   **15.** $s = 3\pi$, $m = 45$; find r.

12. $r = 5$, $m = 60$; find s.   **16.** $s = 2.5\pi$, $m = 30$; find r.

13. $r = 7$, $m = 120$; find A.   **17.** $A = 8.5\pi$, $r = 15$; find m.

14. $r = 10$, $m = 90$; find A.   **18.** $A = 13.5\pi$, $r = 9$; find m.

19. $r = 12$, $m = 60$; find the area of the segment.

20. $r = 8$; $m = 90$; find the area of the segment.

Written Exercises

Set A

[1-26] Given: An arc of measure m and length s in a circle with radius r forming a sector with area A. Give arc lengths and sector areas in terms of π.

1. $r = 12$, $m = 150$; find s.   **5.** $r = 9$, $m = 120$; find A.

2. $r = 15$, $m = 75$; find s.   **6.** $r = 13$, $m = 135$; find A.

3. $r = 20$, $m = 45$; find s.   **7.** $r = 6$, $m = 270$; find A.

4. $r = 14$, $m = 135$; find s.   **8.** $r = 16$, $m = 75$; find A.

[9-16] Find the two missing measures.

9. $s = 25.1$, $r = 16$ **13.** $m = 30$, $A = 3\pi$

10. $s = 5.76$, $r = 11$ **14.** $m = 120$, $A = 27\pi$

11. $s = 20.9$, $r = 10$ **15.** $s = 47.1$, $m = 135$

12. $s = 18.8$, $r = 8$ **16.** $s = 19.6$, $m = 75$

[17-26] Find the area of the segment. Use $\pi \doteq 3.14$.

17. $r = 10$, $m = 60$ **21.** $m = 120$, $r = 6$

18. $r = 8.5$, $m = 60$ **22.** $m = 120$, $r = 14$

19. $r = 11$, $m = 90$ **23.** $m = 90$, $r = 7$

20. $r = 17$, $m = 90$ **24.** $m = 90$, $r = 15$

25. Find the segment area with arc length 4π and $r = 8$ cm.

26. Find the segment area with arc length 10π and $r = 15$.

Set B

27. Find the area of the free-throw key.

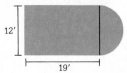

28. Find the area of the ice rink. $m\overarc{AC} = 90$.

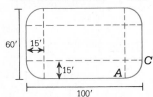

Find the area of each shaded region.

29.

30.

$\triangle ABC$ is equilateral; $r = 8$.

31.

$PQRSTU$ is a regular hexagon; $r = 8$.

Find the length of $\overarc{AEC}$.

32.

33.

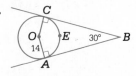

34.

35. Equilateral $\triangle ABC$ with apothem 5 is inscribed in circle O. Find the area of the shaded segment.

36. The shaded area is 36 cm^2. $OC = 6$. Find OA.

Set C

37. $\triangle ABC$ is inscribed in a semicircle and semicircles are drawn on its legs. Show that the area of $\triangle ABC$ is equal to the sum of the areas of the two shaded regions.

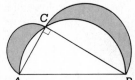

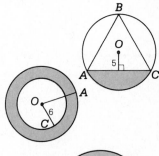

Chapter Summary

1. A polygonal region may be separated into a finite number of nonoverlapping triangular regions. (page 400)

2. If two triangles are congruent, they have equal areas. (page 400)

3. Areas of nonoverlapping polygonal regions may be added to find the area of the union of the regions. (page 401)

4. Area formulas for polygons:

   Rectangle: $A = bh$ (page 401)
   Square: $A = s^2$ (page 401)
   Parallelogram: $A = bh$ (page 404)
   Triangle: $A = \frac{1}{2}bh$ (page 405)
   Equilateral triangle: $A = \frac{s^2}{4}\sqrt{3}$ (page 405)
   Trapezoid: $A = \frac{1}{2}h(b_1 + b_2)$ (page 410)
   Rhombus: $A = \frac{1}{2}d_1 d_2$ (page 411)
   Kite: $A = \frac{1}{2}d_1 d_2$ (page 411)
   Regular polygon: $A = \frac{1}{2}ap$ (page 423)

5. Formulas for circles:

   Circumference: $C = 2\pi r$ (page 428)
   Area: $A = \pi r^2$ (page 428)
   Arc length: $s = \frac{m}{360}(2\pi r)$ (page 432)
   Area of sector: $A = \frac{m}{360}(\pi r^2)$ (page 432)

   Area of a segment bounded by a minor arc:
   $A =$ area of the sector $-$ area of the triangle (page 433)

6. The ratio of the areas of two similar polygons is the square of the ratio of the lengths of any two corresponding sides. (page 418)

7. For any circle, the ratio of the circumference to the diameter is the constant π. (page 428)

Chapter Review

Lesson 9.1
Page 400

1. Find the area of a rectangle with base length 15 and height 13.
2. Find the area of a square with side length $2\sqrt{3}$.
3. Find the area of a square with diagonal length $8\sqrt{2}$.

Lesson 9.2
Page 404

Find the area of each triangle.

4.

5.

6.

Find the area of each parallelogram.

7.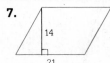

8.

9.

10. Find the area of a right triangle whose legs have lengths 20 and 25.
11. Find the area of a parallelogram with base length 35 and corresponding altitude of length 10.

Lesson 9.3
Page 410

[12-19] Find the area of each polygon.

12.

13.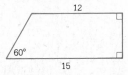

14.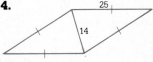

15. A kite whose diagonals have lengths 12 and 24
16. A rhombus with diagonal lengths 10 and 17
17. A trapezoid with a median of length 25 and height 14
18. Trapezoid $XYZW$ with bases $\overline{XY}$ and $\overline{ZW}$; $m\angle X = 30$; $XW = 30$; $XY = 35$; $ZW = 10$
19. A trapezoid with height 2 and base lengths 3 and 4

Lesson 9.4
Page 416

20. Two similar regular pentagons have side lengths in the ratio of 7 to 10. What is the ratio of their perimeters? What is the ratio of their areas?

21. The ratio of the areas of two similar polygons is 81 to 25. A side length of the larger is 14. Find the corresponding side length of the smaller.

22. $\triangle ABC \sim \triangle XYZ$, area $\triangle ABC = 2$(area $\triangle XYZ$), and $XY = 10$. Find AB.

Lesson 9.5
Page 422

Find the area of each regular polygon.

23.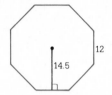

24.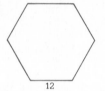

25.

26. Find the apothem of a regular pentagon with area 690 and side length 20.

Lesson 9.6
Page 427

27. Find the radius and area of a circle with a circumference of 12π.

28. Find area and circumference of a circle with radius 5.

29. Find the area of a circle circumscribed about a square with side length 8.

30. Find the area of the region bounded by concentric circles with radii of 9 and 11.

31. The area of a circle is 289π. Find the radius and the circumference.

Lesson 9.7
Page 432

Find the area of each shaded region.

32.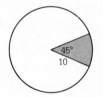

33.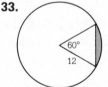

34.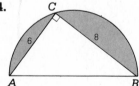

35. Find the arc length and area of a sector of a circle if the arc measure is 80 and the radius is 6.

Chapter Test

Find the area of each figure.

1.

6.5
7

4.
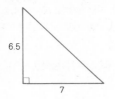
8
10

7.
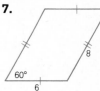
60°
6
8

2.
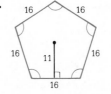
17
17   17
17   17
17

5.

16   16
16   11   16
16

8.
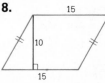
15
10
15

3.

12
6
18

6.
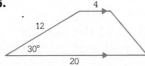
4
12
30°
20

9.

28

[10-15] Find the area of each polygon.

10. A kite with diagonals of lengths 12 and 16

11. A rhombus with diagonals of lengths 10 and 15

12. A square with diagonal length $9\sqrt{2}$

13. An equilateral triangle with side length 10

14. A trapezoid with median of length 30 and height 12

15. A rectangle with side length 7 and diagonal length 25

16. Find the radius of a regular hexagon of side length 9.

17. Find the area of a regular hexagon of side length 15.

18. Two similar polygons have areas of 36 cm² and 121 cm². Find the ratio of the lengths of corresponding sides.

19. Find the circumference and area for a circle of radius 12.

20. A and B are on $\odot O$; $OA = 8$; $m\overarc{AB} = 60$. Find the length of $\overarc{AB}$, the area of its sector, and the area of its segment.

21. Find the height of a rectangle with an area of 221 cm² and a base length of 13 cm.

Cumulative Test Chapters 7-9

In each item select the best answer.

1. If $RT = 12$ and $RS = 4$, then $ST = $ __?__ .

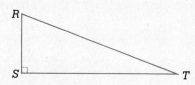

  a. 6   **b.** $6\sqrt{3}$ **c.** 8   **d.** $8\sqrt{2}$

2. The length of the median of an equilateral triangle is $10\sqrt{3}$. The length of a side is __?__ .

  a. 5   **b.** 20   **c.** $20\sqrt{3}$ **d.** 10

3. An equation which describes the line containing points $R(5, -3)$ and $S(5, 8)$ is __?__ .

  a. $y = 5$ **c.** $y = 8$

  b. $y = -3$ **d.** $x = 5$

4. M is the midpoint of $\overline{RS}$. If the coordinates of S are $(-1, 4)$ and the coordinates of M are $(2, 1)$, then the coordinates of R are __?__ .

  a. $\left(\frac{1}{2}, 2\frac{1}{2}\right)$ **c.** $(5, -2)$

  b. $\left(\frac{3}{2}, -\frac{3}{2}\right)$ **d.** $(-5, 2)$

5. $\tan J = $ __?__ .

  a. $\dfrac{5}{13}$ **c.** $\dfrac{5}{12}$

  b. $\dfrac{12}{13}$ **d.** $\dfrac{12}{5}$

6. If the coordinates of E are $(8, -2)$ and those of F are $(3, 10)$, then $EF = $ __?__ .

  a. $\sqrt{119}$ **c.** 8

  b. $\sqrt{185}$ **d.** 13

7. If $\sin 40° \doteq .6428$ and $\cos 40° \doteq .7660$, then $BD \doteq$ __?__ .

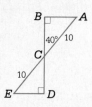

  a. 7.66   **c.** 6.428

  b. 15.32   **d.** 12.856

8. If $\sin 28° \doteq .4695$, $\cos 28° \doteq .8829$, and $\tan 28° \doteq .5317$, then $PQ \doteq$ __?__ .

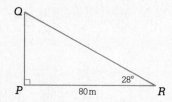

  a. 37.56 m   **c.** 42.536 m

  b. 70.632 m   **d.** 75.12 m

9. Point $P(3, 1)$ is on a circle centered at $R(1, 0)$. Point $S(-3, 1)$ is __?__ .

  a. On $\odot R$

  b. In the interior of $\odot R$

  c. In the exterior of $\odot R$

  d. More information is needed.

10. If $\overleftrightarrow{CP}$ is tangent to circle O and $AB = 10$, then $OP = $ __?__ .

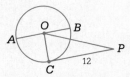

  a. 15   **b.** 10   **c.** 14   **d.** 13

11. Given $\overline{AB} \cong \overline{CD}$ and $CF = 4$.
$AB = \underline{\quad?\quad}$.

a. 5   b. 8   c. 6   d. 12

12. The length of a side of a square is 6. The length of the radius of a circle circumscribed about the square is $\underline{\quad?\quad}$.

a. $6\sqrt{2}$ b. $3\sqrt{2}$ c. 6   d. 3

13. In $\odot O$, if $m\overset{\frown}{RS} = 80$, then $m\overset{\frown}{RU} + m\overset{\frown}{SV} = \underline{\quad?\quad}$.

a. 40   b. 80   c. 100   d. 140

14. In the circle, $m\angle 1 = \underline{\quad?\quad}$.

a. 30   b. 50   c. 60   d. 130

15. If $BC = CD = 4$ and $CE = 14$, then $AB = \underline{\quad?\quad}$.

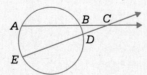

a. 14   b. $4\sqrt{5}$ c. 10   d. $4\sqrt{3}$

16. The area of a rectangle is 40 and the perimeter is 26. The lengths of the sides are $\underline{\quad?\quad}$.

a. 4 and 10   c. 5 and 8

b. 13 and 2   d. 6 and 8

17. This garden is in the shape of a trapezoid. Its area is $\underline{\quad?\quad}$ m^2.

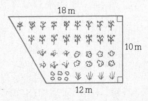

a. 120   b. 150   c. 180   d. 300

18. Given: $\triangle EFG \sim \triangle KLM$; area of $\triangle EFG = 36$; area of $\triangle KLM = 16$.
$x = \underline{\quad?\quad}$.

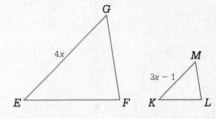

a. $\frac{9}{11}$ b. 3   c. $\frac{7}{11}$ d. 4

19. The apothem of a regular hexagon is $4\sqrt{3}$. Its area is $\underline{\quad?\quad}$.

a. $12\sqrt{3}$ c. $48\sqrt{3}$

b. $24\sqrt{3}$ d. $96\sqrt{3}$

20. The area of a circle is 36π. The circumference is $\underline{\quad?\quad}$.

a. 36π b. 18π c. 12π d. 6π

21. The radius of a circle is 12 and the measure of the arc of a sector is 30. Find the area of the sector.

a. 3π b. 6π c. 12π d. 24π

Solids

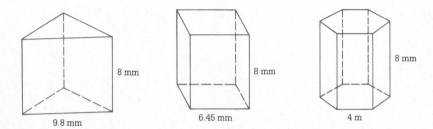

8 mm

8 mm

8 mm

9.8 mm

6.45 mm

4 m

The photo on page 442 shows the hexagonal openings of honeycomb cells. A cell with either an equilateral triangle or square opening would also fill the same space. But would cells of either shape fill the space as efficiently?

1. Complete the chart below using the cell patterns above. To find the volume, or cubic millimeters of honey each cell will hold, multiply the area of the opening by the height (8 mm).

Cell shape	Triangular	Square	Hexagonal
Area of opening	?	?	?
Volume	?	?	?
Area of one wall	?	?	?
Area of all walls	?	?	?

2. How are the volumes of the three cells related?

3. Which cell has the least wall surface? Which cell would require the least amount of material to build?

10.1 Polyhedrons and Prisms

A polyhedron is suggested by the photo below.

Definition

A **polyhedron** is a union of polygons, not all coplanar, with their interiors, which encloses a region of space. The enclosed space is the **interior** of the polyhedron. A **solid polyhedron** is the union of a polyhedron and its interior.

Polygonal region *KMNP* is a **face** of polyhedron *KLMNOP*. An intersection of two faces, such as $\overline{KP}$, is an **edge**. A **vertex,** such as point *K* or point *O*, is the intersection of three or more edges.

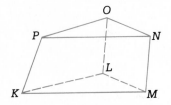

Definition

A **prism** is a polyhedron with two congruent polygonal faces contained in parallel planes. These faces are called the **bases** of the prism. The other faces, called **lateral faces,** are parallelograms.

In the prism at the right, *ABCDE* and *A'B'C'D'E'* are **bases.** Parallelograms *ABB'A'* and *BCC'B'* are **lateral faces.** $\overline{AA'}$ and $\overline{BB'}$ are **lateral edges.**

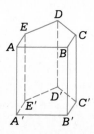

Two properties of prisms are given in Theorems 10.1 and 10.2. Their proofs are omitted.

Theorem 10.1 The bases of a prism have corresponding sides and corresponding angles congruent.

Theorem 10.2 The bases of a prism have equal area.

A segment from a point in one base perpendicular to the plane of the other base is an **altitude of the prism.** The length of the altitude is the **height** of the prism.

A prism is a **right prism** if the lateral edges are perpendicular to the planes of the bases. Otherwise, the prism is an **oblique prism.**

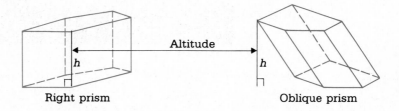

Right prism   Oblique prism

Prisms are named by the shape of their bases.

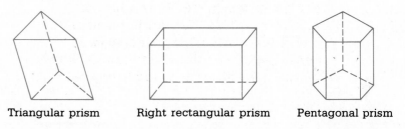

Triangular prism   Right rectangular prism   Pentagonal prism

A **regular prism** is a right prism whose bases are regular polygons. A **cube** is a prism in which all faces are squares. A **parallelepiped** is a prism in which all faces are parallelograms.

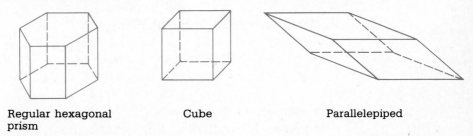

Regular hexagonal   Cube   Parallelepiped
prism

Class Exercises

1. How many faces does a pentagonal prism have?
2. What is the least number of faces a prism can have?
3. How many faces does an octagonal prism have?
4. How many faces does a triangular prism have?
5. How many faces does a hexagonal prism have?
6. A prism has nine faces. Each of its bases has how many sides?
7. The lateral edge of a regular triangular prism is 14 cm long. A side of its base is 20 cm long. How long is the altitude of the prism?
8. How many edges does an octagonal prism have?
9. Each base of a prism has ten sides. How many edges does the prism have?
10. How many edges intersect to form each vertex of a prism?

Written Exercises

Set A

[1-8] Each prism has *e* edges, *f* faces, *v* vertices, and each base has *s* sides. Find the missing items.

1. $s = 5$	**3.** $v = 18$	**5.** $e = 30$	**7.** $f = 14$
2. $s = 7$	**4.** $v = 24$	**6.** $e = 42$	**8.** $f = 16$

9. Given: Right prism with bases $PQRSTU$ and $P'Q'R'S'T'U'$
   Prove: $\overline{QU} \cong \overline{Q'U'}$

10. Given: Right prism with bases $PQRSTU$ and $P'Q'R'S'T'U'$
    Prove: $\overline{TT'} \parallel \overline{UU'}$

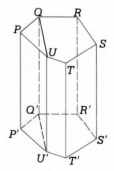

11. Given: Right rectangular prism
    with bases $ABCD$ and $A'B'C'D'$
    Prove: $\overline{A'B} \cong \overline{D'C}$

12. Given: Right rectangular prism
    with bases $ABCD$ and $A'B'C'D'$
    Prove: $\triangle BDC \cong \triangle D'B'A'$

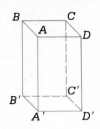

Set B

13. Given: Right prism with bases
    $WXYZ$ and $W'X'Y'Z'$
    Prove: $\overline{W'Y} \cong \overline{WY'}$

14. Given: Right prism with
    bases $WXYZ$ and $W'X'Y'Z'$,
    which are rhombuses
    Prove: $\overline{WY'}$ bisects $\overline{W'Y}$.

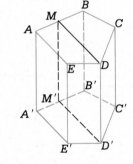

15. Given: Right prism with bases
    $ABCDE$ and $A'B'C'D'E'$; M is the
    midpoint of $\overline{AB}$; M' is the midpoint
    of $\overline{A'B'}$; $\overline{MM'} \parallel \overline{DD'}$
    Prove: $\overline{MD} \cong \overline{M'D'}$

16. Given: Right prism with bases
    $ABCDE$ and $A'B'C'D'E'$; $\overline{MD} \parallel \overline{M'D'}$;
    $\overline{MM'} \perp$ base $ABCDE$
    Prove: $\overline{MD} \cong \overline{M'D'}$

17. If the base of a prism has n sides, find the number of
    faces, edges, and vertices of the prism.

18. How many sides does each base of a prism have if the
    prism has m vertices?

19. Given: Parallelepiped with $\overline{AD} \parallel \overline{B'C'}$
    Prove: $\overline{AB'} \cong \overline{DC'}$

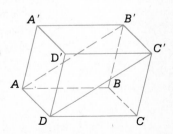

10.2   Area of Prisms

The pattern below can be folded to form a pentagonal prism. To find the area of the prism, we must find the area of the lateral faces and the area of the bases.

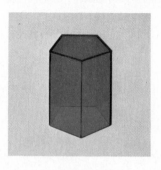

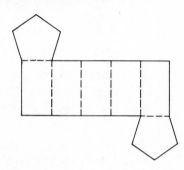

Definition   The **lateral area, L.A.,** of a prism is the sum of the areas of its lateral faces. The **total area, T.A.,** of a prism is the sum of its lateral area and the areas of its two bases.

The following theorem gives a formula for computing lateral area. A paragraph proof is given for a right pentagonal prism. Notice that paragraph proofs have a less rigid structure than two-column proofs. They should include enough steps to present a persuasive argument.

Theorem 10.3   The lateral area, L.A., of a right prism is the product of the length of a lateral edge, h, and the perimeter, p, of the base.   L.A. $= hp$

Given   A right pentagonal prism with the length of a lateral edge $\overline{AA'} = h$; and perimeter p

Prove   L.A. $= hp$

Proof   Since all lateral faces of a prism are parallelograms, each lateral face of a right prism is a rectangle. The area of rectangle $AA'B'B$ is $h(AB)$. The area of each of the other lateral faces can be represented similarly. Thus, L.A. $= h(AB + BC + CD + DE + EA)$ and L.A. $= hp$.

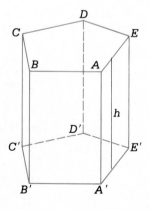

Example   Find the lateral area and the total area of a regular hexagonal prism with the length of a lateral side 3 m, the length of one side of the hexagon 2 m, and the apothem $\sqrt{3}$ m.

Solution   Perimeter of the hexagon is 12 m.

L.A. $= hp$
$= 3(12)$
$= 36$ m^2

$B =$ area of base
$= \frac{1}{2}ap$
$= \frac{1}{2}\sqrt{3}(12)$
$= 6\sqrt{3}$ m^2

T.A. $=$ L.A. $+ 2B$
$= 36 + 2(6\sqrt{3})$
$\doteq 56.4$ m^2

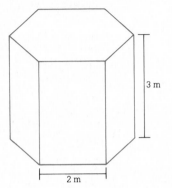

Class Exercises

Find the L.A. of each right prism.

1.

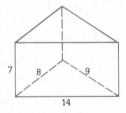

2.

3.

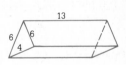

4. The total area of a right prism is 2500 cm^2, and its lateral area is 2000 cm^2. What is the area of a base of the prism?

5. A right prism has a square base with a perimeter of 48 cm and a height of 10 cm. Find the L.A. and the T.A. of the prism.

6. A right prism has a rectangular base with dimensions 7 cm by 12 cm and its height is 5 cm. Find the L.A. and the T.A. of the prism.

Written Exercises

Set A

Find the lateral area and the total area for each right rectangular prism.

1.

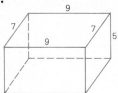

2.

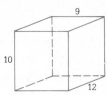

3.

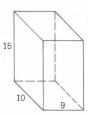

4. The perimeter of the base of a right prism is 12 cm and its height is 6 cm. Find the L.A.

5. A right prism has a height of 3 m and a base with a perimeter of 8 m. Find the L.A.

[6-11] Find the L.A. and T.A. of each cube.

6. An edge is 5 m.

7. An edge is 7 m.

8. An edge has length e.

9. The perimeter of a base is 16 cm.

10. The perimeter of a base is 24 cm.

11. The perimeter of a base is 8x.

12. Find the L.A. and T.A. of a right prism whose base is a square 15 cm on a side and whose height is 24 cm.

13. Find the L.A. and T.A. of a right prism whose base is a square 8 m on a side and whose height is 10 m.

14. Find the T.A. of a rectangular darkroom 8 m long and 5 m wide if the ceiling is 3 m above the floor.

15. A dining room has the shape of a hexagonal prism. The walls of the room are to be painted. Allowing 76 ft.^{2} for doors and windows, find the area to be painted.

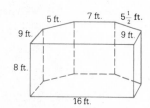

Set B

16. The T.A. of a cube is 150 cm^2. How long is an edge?

17. The L.A. of a cube is 196 cm^2. How long is an edge?

18. The base of a regular prism is a pentagon with sides of 8 m. The altitude measures 16 m. Find the L.A.

19. The base of a regular prism is a pentagon with sides of 15 cm. The height is 18 cm. Find the L.A.

20. Find the amount of glass needed to build a regular octagonal terrarium. Each edge of the octagon is 10 cm, the apothem is 12 cm, and the height is 30 cm.

21. The base of a right prism is a rhombus with diagonals measuring 10 cm and 24 cm. The height of the prism is 15 cm. Find the L.A.

22. The T.A. of a right prism is 210 cm². Each base of the prism is a square 5 cm on a side. Find the height of the prism.

23. Find the L.A. and the T.A. of the right prism shown. Its bases are isosceles trapezoids.

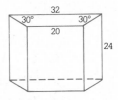

Set C

24. The base of a regular prism is a hexagon having sides of 7 cm. The height of the prism is 16 cm. Find the T.A. of the prism.

25. The ratio of the lengths of the edges of two cubes is 3 to 1. What is the ratio of their total areas?

Geometry Maintenance

Given: $\odot P$ with diameter $AB = 6$; ℓ and m tangent to $\odot P$ at A and B, respectively; $\overrightarrow{PQ} \perp \overline{AB}$ at P

1. Find $m\widehat{AQ}$.

2. Why is $\ell \perp \overline{AB}$?

3. Why is $\overleftrightarrow{PQ} \parallel \ell$?

4. Name two isosceles triangles.

5. Find $m\angle ACB$ and QC.

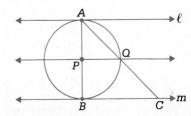

10.3   Volume of Prisms

To compare the capacities of the freezers pictured below, we can associate a number with each.

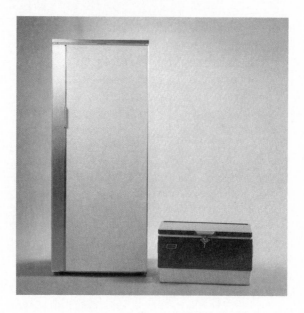

Postulate 26
Volume
Postulate

To every solid polyhedron there corresponds a unique positive real number, called the volume of the solid polyhedron.

A solid cube whose edge is one unit long is used as the unit of volume. Volume is the number of these cubes that exactly fill the interior of the polyhedron.

We will refer to the volume of a solid polyhedron simply as the volume of the solid or the volume of the polyhedron.

This rectangular solid contains 5 horizontal layers of unit cubes. Each layer contains 3 rows of 4 cubes each. Thus there are 12 cubes in each layer, so the volume of the solid is 60 cubic units.

The volume, *V*, of a rectangular solid is equal to the product of its length, *l*, width, *w*, and height, *h*. $V = lwh$

Restatement $V = Bh$ where *B* is the area of one base.

Definition   A **cross section** of a solid is the intersection of the solid and a plane parallel to a base of the solid.

Theorem 10.4   All cross sections of a prism have equal area.

The proof of Theorem 10.4 is omitted.

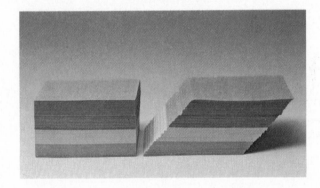

Two matching stacks of paper are shown. Do the solids suggested by the two stacks have the same volume? If we let a single sheet of paper represent a cross section of each stack, then at every level, the cross sections have the same area. Bonaventura Cavalieri (1598–1647), an Italian mathematician, used this idea to compare the volumes of two solids.

Postulate 28   Given a plane and two solids. If every plane that is parallel to
Cavalieri's   the given plane and intersects one of the solids also intersects
Principle   the second solid, and if the cross sections formed have the same area, then the solids have the same volume.

Using Cavalieri's Principle, the volume of a given solid can be compared with that of a solid whose volume is known.

| Theorem 10.5 | The volume, V, of a prism is equal to the product of the height, h, and the area of a base, B. $V = Bh$ |

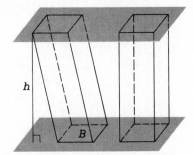

Given

A prism with base area B; and height h.

Prove

$V = Bh$

Proof

Consider a rectangular solid that has bases in the same planes as the bases of the given prism, and has base area B. The volume of the rectangular solid is Bh. By Cavalieri's Principle the two solids have the same volume. Thus, the volume of the given prism is Bh.

Example

Find the volume of the regular pentagonal prism shown.

Solution

$B = \frac{1}{2}ap$
$ = \frac{1}{2}(5.5)(40)$
$ = 110 \text{ cm}^2$

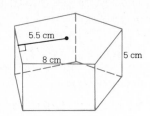

$V = Bh$
$ = 110(5)$
$ = 550 \text{ cm}^3$

Class Exercises

[1-4] Find the volume of each prism.

1. $B = 20 \text{ cm}^2$; $h = 6$ cm

2. $B = 16$ sq. ft.; $h = 3$ ft.

3. $B = 11$ sq. in.; $h = 14$ in.

4. $B = 72$ sq. yd.; $h = 24$ yd.

5. Find the volume of a prism with a square base 6 cm on a side and a height of 10 cm.

6. The area of the base of a prism is 12 m^2, and its volume is 156 m^3. What is its height?

Written Exercises

Set A

[1-6] Find the volume of each right rectangular prism.

1. **2.** **3.** **4.**

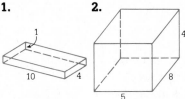 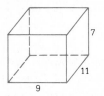 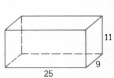

5. A pentagonal prism has a base with an area of 3.5 sq. yd. and a height of 9 yd.

6. A rectangular prism has a height of 8 cm and a base with an area of 24 cm².

7. How many cubic yards of sand can be placed in the pickup truck shown?

8. How many cubic meters of concrete will be needed for a patio 12 m long, 10 m wide, and 10 cm deep?

Set B

[9-11] Find the volume of each right prism.

9. **10.** **11.**

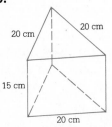 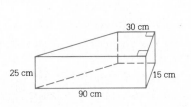 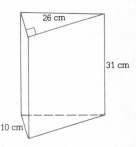

12. Find the weight of a wooden beam 4 in. by 12 in. by 8 ft., if the wood weighs 46 lb. per cu. ft.

13. What is the effect on the volume of a cube when the length of each edge is doubled?

14. What is the effect on the volume of a cube when each of its dimensions is tripled?

[15-16] Use the right prism with square base shown.

15. How long is the side of a base if the volume of the prism is 588 cm^3 and its height is 12 cm?

16. How long is a side of a base if the volume is 576 cm^3 and the height is 9 cm?

17. Find the weight of an iron post shaped like a square prism. Each side of a square base is 10 cm and the height is 1.3 m. The iron weighs 7 g/cm^3.

18. A water tank shaped like a right rectangular prism measures 6 ft. by 8 ft. by 10 ft. How many gallons will it hold? (1 cu. ft. ≐ 7.5 gal.)

19. A board foot is a piece of lumber 1 ft. by 1 ft. by 1 in. How many board feet are there in a board 8 in. by $\frac{3}{4}$ in. by 10 ft.?

20. The container shown is a right square prism half filled with water. What volume of water is in the container?

21. A stone is placed in the container of water. The water level rises 2 cm. What is the volume of the water and the stone? What is the volume of the stone?

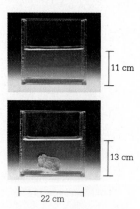

11 cm

13 cm

22 cm

Set C

22. Prove that the volume of a cube with edge e is equal to e^3.

23. If the number of cubic inches in the volume of a cube equals the number of square inches in its T.A., what is the length of an edge of the cube?

24. A tinsmith wishes to make a rectangular tank to contain 16 cu. ft. of water. How many square feet of material will it take if the base is a square and the height of the tank is 2 ft.? No cover is used.

25. A cube measures 2 in. on each side. By what number must the length of a side be multiplied to double the volume of the cube?

10.4   Area and Volume of Cylinders

Tin cans, silos, hot water heaters, and refinery storage tanks all suggest cylinders.

Definition   A **cylinder** is the union of (1) two congruent circles and their interiors, lying in parallel planes and (2) all segments that have one endpoint on each circle and that are parallel to the line joining the centers of the circles.

The circular regions of a cylinder are its **bases.** The segment joining the centers of the circles is the **axis** of the cylinder.

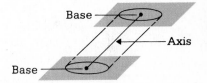

Prisms and cylinders differ in the shape of their bases. But the terms *altitude, height,* and *cross section* are defined similarly for both. If the axis of a cylinder is perpendicular to the bases, the cylinder is a **right cylinder.** Otherwise, it is an **oblique cylinder.**

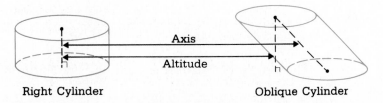

Right Cylinder   Oblique Cylinder

In the following model of a right cylinder, suppose the bases are removed and the model is cut along the dotted line and flattened out.

The lateral area of the model is the area of the rectangle.

Theorem 10.6

The lateral area, L.A., of a right cylinder is equal to the product of the circumference, C, of a base and the height, h. L.A. = Ch or L.A. = $2\pi rh$

The total area, T.A., of a cylinder is the sum of the lateral area, L.A., and the area, B, of each base. T.A. = L.A. + 2B or T.A. = $2\pi rh + 2\pi r^2$

Cavalieri's Principle can be applied to give a formula for the volume of a cylinder.

Theorem 10.7

The volume, V, of a cylinder is equal to the product of the height, h, and the area, B, of a base. $V = Bh$ or $V = \pi r^2 h$

The proofs of Theorems 10.6 and 10.7 are omitted.

Example   Find the L.A., T.A., and volume of a tennis-ball can 19.05 cm high whose base has a radius of 3.18 cm.

Solution

$$L.A. = 2\pi rh$$
$$\doteq 2(3.14)(3.18)(19.05)$$
$$\doteq 380.4 \text{ cm}^2$$

$$B = \pi r^2$$
$$\doteq 3.14(3.18)^2$$
$$\doteq 31.8 \text{ cm}^2$$

$$T.A. = L.A. + 2B$$
$$\doteq 380.4 + 2(31.8)$$
$$\doteq 444.0 \text{ cm}^2$$

$$V = Bh$$
$$\doteq 31.8(19.05)$$
$$\doteq 605.8 \text{ cm}^3$$

Class Exercises

[1-3] Find the area of the base, the L.A., T.A., and volume of each right cylinder. Leave answers in terms of π.

1. Radius = 6 cm; height = 8 cm
2. Circumference = 18π; height = 7
3. $C = 9\pi$; $h = 10$

4. Find the height of a cylinder whose volume is 72 cm^3 and whose base has a radius of 3 cm.
5. Find the height of a cylinder whose volume is 200 cm^3 and whose base has a diameter of 12 cm.

Written Exercises

Set A

[1-8] Leave each answer in terms of π.

1. Find the volume and total area of the storage tank shown.

4 ft   8 ft

2. Find the volume and total area of the can shown.

[3-8] Each figure is a right cylinder.

3. L.A. = _?_

4. T.A. = _?_

5. V = _?_

5 cm

8 cm

6. L.A. = _?_

7. T.A. = _?_

8. V = _?_

8 cm

15 cm

[9-15] Use $\pi \doteq 3.14$.

9. How many cubic feet of water can be held in 144 ft. of pipe whose internal diameter is 2 in.?

10. How many cubic feet of gas will a pipeline hold if it is 1000 miles long with a diameter of 2 feet?

11. How many gallons of water can be contained in a cylindrical tank that is 5.25 ft. in diameter and 8 ft. deep? (1 cu. ft. $\doteq$ 7.5 gal.)

Set B

12. A cylindrical tank with horizontal bases has a diameter of 18 in. It is half filled with water. What volume of water will raise the water level 8 in.?

13. How many square meters of tin will be used to make 50 stovepipes, each 18 cm in diameter and 90 cm long?

14. Find the weight of a cylindrical marble column 27 ft. high and 2.5 ft. in diameter. (1 cu. ft. $\doteq$ 154 lb.)

Set C

15. A regular triangular prism with a height of 25 cm and a base with a perimeter of $6\sqrt{3}$ cm is "inscribed" in a right cylinder. Find the T.A. of the cylinder.

Progress Check

Lesson 10.1
Page 444

1. A prism has 11 lateral faces. How many sides does each base of the prism have?

2. How many vertices does a pentagonal prism have?

3. A base of a prism has nine sides. How many edges does the prism have?

4. A lateral face of an oblique prism makes a dihedral angle of 30° with the plane of a base. A lateral edge is 18 cm. What is the height of the prism?

Lesson 10.2
Page 448

5. Find the L.A. of a right triangular prism if the height is 24 in. and the sides of a base are 6 in., 14 in., and 18 in.

6. Find the T.A. of a cube whose edges are 8 cm long.

7. A right prism has a height of 12 cm and a lateral area of 240 cm^2. What is the perimeter of a base?

8. A base of a regular hexagonal prism has a perimeter of 90 cm. What is the total area of the prism if the height is 25 cm?

Lesson 10.3
Page 452

9. Find the volume of a rectangular prism whose dimensions are 6 cm by 4 cm by 8 cm.

10. The volumes of two cubes are in the ratio of 8 to 27. What is the ratio of the lengths of their edges?

11. Find the volume of a prism having a height of 7 in. and whose bases each have an area of 35 sq. in.

12. A prism has a height of 16 cm and a volume of 3584 cm^3. What is the area of a base?

Lesson 10.4
Page 457

13. A cylindrical container has a height of 14 cm. If a base has an area of 135 cm^2, what is the volume of the container?

14. An oblique cylinder has a height of 28 cm. Each base has a radius of 8 cm. What is the volume?

15. A right cylinder has a lateral area of 2480 cm^2. If the height of the cylinder is 16 cm, what is the radius of a base?

Using BASIC

Optimization and Container Design

A container manufacturing company has been contracted to design and manufacture cylindrical cans for lawn mower motor oil. The capacity of each can is to be 236 ml. In order to minimize production costs, they wish to design a can that requires the smallest amount of metal possible. What should the dimensions of the can be?

The cans will be made using a layout similar to this one.

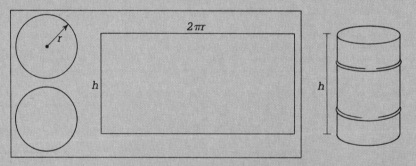

Since a 236-cm^3 can is needed to hold 236 ml, $V = 236 = \pi r^2 h$, so $h = 236/[(3.1416)r^2]$.

The height of a 236-cm^3 can depends only on its radius, and its T.A. depends only on the height and radius (T.A. $= 2\pi rh + 2\pi r^2$). So you can test various values of the radius to find which corresponding T.A. is smallest. To use systematic trial and error and to look for a pattern, use the following program. It lets you choose where to begin a table and what size step or increment to use in the table. The sample run shows the results for an initial radius of 1 cm and an increment of 1 cm.

```
100 REM   MINIMIZING T.A. OF A CLOSED CAN
110 PRINT "WHAT ARE INITIAL RADIUS AND INCREMENT"
120 PRINT "SEPARATED BY A COMMA";
130 INPUT R,I
140 PRINT "RADIUS";TAB(9);"HEIGHT";
150 PRINT TAB(27);"T.A."
160 FOR J=1 TO 10
170 LET H=236/(3.1416*R^2)
180 LET TA=2*3.1416*R*H+2*3.1416*R^2
190 PRINT R;TAB(7);H;TAB(25);TA
200 LET R=R+I
210 NEXT J
220 END


]RUN
WHAT ARE INITIAL RADIUS AND INCREMENT
SEPARATED BY A COMMA?1,1
RADIUS  HEIGHT               T.A.
1        75.1209575          478.2832
2        18.7802394          261.1328
3        8.34677306          213.882133
4        4.69505984          218.5312
5        3.0048383           251.48
6        2.08669326          304.861867
7        1.53308076          375.305372
8        1.17376496          461.1248
9        .927419228          561.383645
10       .751209575          675.52
```

1. What is the optimal length for the radius?

2. RUN the program with different values to find the ideal radius of a can to the nearest millimeter (0.1 cm).

3. Change one number in one line of the program so that you can use it to find optimal dimensions for a can of automotive motor oil ($V = 946$ ml).

★ 4. Change the original program so that the user can input the volume of the can whose total area is to be minimized. What are the optimal dimensions for 1000-ml and 500-ml cans?

★ 5. Write a program that will help determine the dimensions of a cylindrical can that will yield the greatest possible volume for 354 cm^2 of metal (total area).

10.5   Area and Volume of Pyramids

A prism has two polygonal bases. A pyramid has only one.

Definition

A **pyramid** is a polyhedron with all but one vertex, *V*, contained in a plane, *E*. The polygonal region determined by the vertices in plane *E* is the **base** of the pyramid. The lateral faces of a pyramid are triangles.

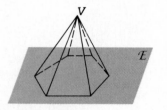

The **altitude of a pyramid** is the segment from the vertex perpendicular to the plane of the base. The length of the altitude is the **height** of the pyramid. As with a prism, a pyramid is named by the shape of its base.

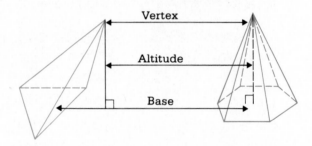

A **regular pyramid** has a regular polygon for a base, and lateral edges that are congruent. The **slant height** of a regular pyramid is the length of the altitude of any lateral face from the vertex of the pyramid.

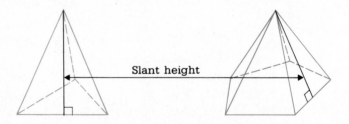

Theorem 10.8

The lateral faces of a regular pyramid are congruent isosceles triangles.

Theorem 10.9	The lateral area, L.A., of a regular pyramid is equal to one-half the product of the perimeter, p, of the base and the slant height, s. L.A. $= \frac{1}{2}sp$

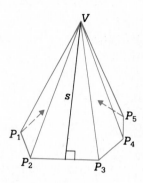

Given	A regular pyramid with vertex V and base $P_1 P_2 \ldots P_n$; slant height s and perimeter p.
Prove	L.A. $= \frac{1}{2}sp$
Proof	By definition all lateral faces of a pyramid are triangles. In a regular pyramid the triangles are all congruent. The area of $\triangle VP_1 P_2$ is $\frac{1}{2}s\,(P_1 P_2)$. Thus, L.A. $= \frac{1}{2}s(P_1 P_2 + P_2 P_3 + \cdots + P_n P_1) = \frac{1}{2}sp$.

The total area, T.A., of a pyramid is the sum of the lateral area, L.A., and the area of the base B. T.A. $=$ L.A. $+ B$

The volume of a pyramid can be found by relating it to a prism with the same base and height.

Theorem 10.10	The volume, V, of a pyramid is equal to one-third the product of the area, B, of the base and the height h. $V = \frac{1}{3}Bh$

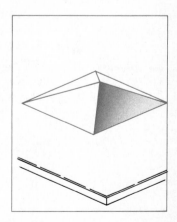

Example	The skylight has the shape of a regular square pyramid. Each side of the square is 2 m. The height of the pyramid is 0.5 m, and the slant height is 1.1 m. Find the lateral area and the volume of the skylight.
Solution	L.A. $= \frac{1}{2}sp$ $\quad = \frac{1}{2}(1.1)(8)$ $\quad = 4.4 \text{ m}^2$ $V = \frac{1}{3}Bh$ $\quad = \frac{1}{3}(4)(0.5)$ $\quad = \frac{2}{3}\text{m}^3$

Class Exercises

[1-3] Find the L.A., T.A., and volume for each regular pyramid.

1.

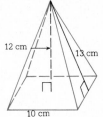

12 cm   13 cm

10 cm

2.

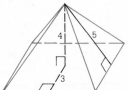

4   5

3

3.

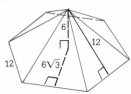

6

12

12   6√3

Written Exercises

Set A

[1-3] The figure is a regular pyramid.

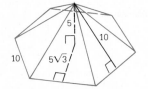

5   10

10   5√3

1. L.A. = ?

2. T.A. = ?

3. V = ?

4. Find the L.A. and T.A. for a square pyramid if each side of the base is 36 m and each lateral edge is 30 m.

5. Find the L.A. and T.A. of a regular hexagonal pyramid if each side of the base is 20 cm and each lateral edge is 26 cm.

6. Find the volume of a square pyramid with sides 15 cm long and height 45 cm.

7. Find the volume of a pyramid whose base is a square with sides 24 cm long and whose altitude is 36 cm.

8. Find the perimeter of the base of a regular pyramid with a slant height of 9 cm and L.A. of 94.5 cm^2.

9. Find the perimeter of the base of a regular pyramid with a slant height of 15 cm and L.A. of 270 cm^2.

10. The L.A. of a regular pyramid is 644 cm^2 and the perimeter of the base is 56 cm. Find the slant height.

11. Find the slant height of a regular pyramid whose base is a pentagon with each side 6 cm and whose L.A. is 120 cm^2.

10.6   Area and Volume of Cones

A prism and a cylinder differ in the shapes of their base. A similar relationship exists between a pyramid and a cone.

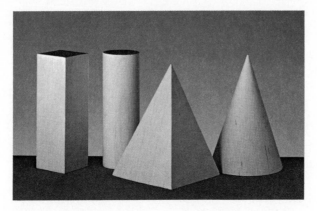

Definition   A **cone** is a figure containing a **vertex**, *V*, not in a plane *E*, a circular region in plane *E*, and all segments joining a point of the circle to *V*.

The circular region in plane *E* is the **base** of the cone. The points of the cone not in the base form the **lateral** surface of the cone.

The **altitude of a cone** is the segment from the vertex perpendicular to the plane of the base. The length of the altitude is the height of the cone. The segment from the vertex to the center of the base is the **axis of the cone.** If the axis is perpendicular to the base, the cone is a **right cone.** Otherwise, it is an **oblique cone.** The **slant height** of a right cone is the length of a segment from the vertex to a point of the circle.

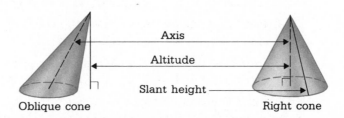

Oblique cone   Right cone

Theorems 10.11 and 10.12 give formulas for the area and volume of a right cone. They are similar to those for a pyramid, except that circumference replaces perimeter.

Theorem 10.11   The lateral area, L.A., of a right cone is equal to one-half the product of its slant height, *s*, and the circumference, *C*, of its base.   L.A. = $\frac{1}{2}sC$ or L.A. = πrs

The total area, T.A., of a right cone is the sum of its lateral area and the area of its base. T.A. = $\pi rs + \pi r^2$

Theorem 10.12   The volume, *V*, of a cone is equal to one-third the product of its height, *h*, and the area of its base, *B*. $V = \frac{1}{3}Bh$

Example

The funnel shown has the shape of a right cone. Its diameter is 9 m and its height is 4 m. Find the slant height, L.A., and *V*.

Solution

Use the Pythagorean Theorem.
$s^2 = r^2 + h^2$
$s^2 = (4.5)^2 + (4)^2$
$s^2 = 36.25$
$s \doteq 6.02$ m

L.A. = πrs
$\doteq (3.14)(4.5)(6.02)$
$\doteq 85.06$ m^2

$V = \frac{1}{3}\pi r^2 h$
$\doteq \frac{1}{3}(3.14)(4.5)^2(4)$
$\doteq 84.78$ m^3

Class Exercises

Leave answers in terms of π.

1. L.A. = _?_
2. T.A. = _?_
3. *V* = _?_

4. L.A. = ___?___

5. T.A. = ___?___

6. V = ___?___

Written Exercises

Set A

[1-6] Find L.A., T.A., and V. Give answers in terms of π.

1.
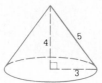

2.

3.

4.

5.

6.

[7-12] Given a right cone with radius r, slant height s, height h, lateral area L.A., total area T.A., and volume V. Find the four measures not given. Use $\pi \doteq 3.14$.

7. $r = 4;\ s = 12$ **10.** $r = 12;\ h = 30$

8. $r = 11;\ s = 20$ **11.** $r = 12a;\ h = 20a$

9. $r = 5;\ h = 12$ **12.** $r = 24y;\ h = 26y$

Set B

13. How many square meters of material will it take to make a conical tent 5 m in diameter and 2.5 m high? The tent is made without a floor. Use $\pi \doteq 3.14$.

14. The area of the base of a right cone is 144π cm^2 and the height is 5 cm. Find the L.A. Use $\pi \doteq 3.14$.

15. The L.A. of a right cone is 135π m^2 and the slant height is 15 m. Find the height of the cone.

10.6   Area and Volume of Cones

Excursion   Regular Polyhedrons

In nature, when certain liquids evaporate, they form crystals shaped like regular polyhedrons.

A polyhedron is **regular** if each pair of its dihedral angles is congruent, and if all the polygons in its faces are congruent regular polygons. In addition note:

1. The same number of faces meet at each vertex.
2. The sum of the measures of the face angles at each vertex must be less than 360.

Since the sum of the measures of the face angles at each vertex must be less than 360, a regular polyhedron can be made up only of faces that are equilateral triangles, squares, and regular pentagons. Why? The possible regular polyhedrons are shown below.

Tetrahedron   Hexahedron   Octahedron   Dodecahedron   Icosahedron
(Cube)

These five regular polyhedrons are known as **Platonic solids,** because Plato (429–348 B.C.) described them so fully in his writings.

Here are patterns for models of the regular polyhedrons.

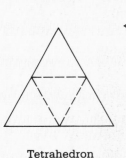

Tetrahedron

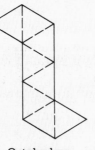

Octahedron

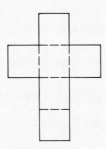

Hexahedron
(Cube)

Dodecahedron

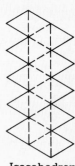

Icosahedron

	Faces (F)	Vertices (V)	Edges (E)
Tetrahedron	4	4	6
Hexahedron	6	8	12
Octahedron	8	6	12
Dodecahedron	12	20	30
Icosahedron	20	12	30

Do you see the relationship between F, V, and E in the table above? In the 18th century, the Swiss mathematician Leonhard Euler (1707−1783) stated the relationship for all polyhedrons in the following theorem.

Euler's Theorem: In any polyhedron, $F + V = E + 2$, where F, V, and E are the number of faces, vertices, and edges.

[1-3] Verify Euler's Theorem for each polyhedron.

1.

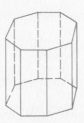

2.

3.

4. Verify Euler's Theorem for a prism whose bases are n-sided polygons.

5. Verify Euler's Theorem for a pyramid whose base is an n-sided polygon.

10.7   Area and Volume of Spheres

In space the counterpart of a circle is a sphere.
Theorems 10.13 and 10.14 give formulas for computing the
volume and area of spheres. The following argument
suggests how Theorem 10.13 could be proved.

Consider the volumes of a solid sphere of radius r, and of a
solid cylinder with radius r and height $2r$. Suppose two solid
right cones each with radius r, height r, and vertex V, have
been carved out of the cylinder, as shown.

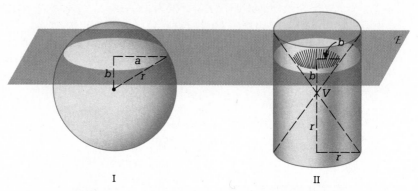

I   II

Each plane that is parallel to the base of the cylinder and
intersects the cylinder will intersect it in a circle. Each of
these planes will also intersect the sphere in either a great
or small circle. Let plane $\mathcal{E}$ be one of these planes,
intersecting the solids at a distance b from the center of the
sphere. By the Pythagorean Theorem, $a^2 = r^2 - b^2$. Thus the
cross sections shown below have the same area at every
level.

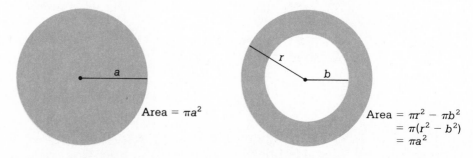

$$\text{Area} = \pi a^2$$

$$\begin{aligned}\text{Area} &= \pi r^2 - \pi b^2 \\ &= \pi(r^2 - b^2) \\ &= \pi a^2\end{aligned}$$

By Cavalieri's Principle, the volume of solid I is equal to the
volume of solid II.

The volume of solid II is equal to the volume of the cylinder minus the volumes of the two cones.

$$\text{Volume of solid II} = Bh - 2\left(\tfrac{1}{3}Bh\right)$$
$$= \pi r^2(2r) - 2\left[\tfrac{1}{3}(\pi r^2)(r)\right]$$
$$= 2\pi r^3 - \tfrac{2}{3}\pi r^3$$
$$= \tfrac{4}{3}\pi r^3$$

Theorem 10.13 The volume, V, of a sphere of radius, r, is $\tfrac{4}{3}\pi r^3$. $V = \tfrac{4}{3}\pi r^3$

To find the formula for the area of a sphere, use the formula for its volume. Consider a solid sphere with center Q and radius r. Imagine that the sphere is made up of solids resembling pyramids. Each "pyramid" has vertex Q and height r. One such pyramid is shown.

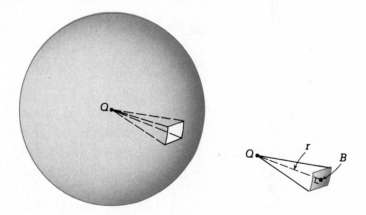

The volume of each "pyramid" is $\tfrac{1}{3}Br$, where B is the area of the base.

Since the volume of the sphere equals the sum of the volumes of the "pyramids,"

$$\tfrac{4}{3}\pi r^3 = \tfrac{1}{3}r(B_1 + B_2 + B_3 + \cdots + B_n)$$
$$4\pi r^2 = (B_1 + B_2 + B_3 + \cdots + B_n)$$
$$= \text{Area of the sphere}$$

Theorem 10.14 The area, A, of a sphere of radius, r, is $4\pi r^2$. $A = 4\pi r^2$

Example   Echo I, the first communications
satellite, was a large plastic balloon
with a thin metal coating. If its
diameter was 30 m, find its area and
volume.

Solution

$A = 4\pi r^2$
$= 4\pi(15)^2$
$\doteq 4(3.14)(225)$
$\doteq 2826 \text{ m}^2$

$V = \frac{4}{3}\pi(15)^3$
$\doteq \frac{4}{3}(3.14)(3375)$
$\doteq 14,130 \text{ m}^3$

Class Exercises

[1-6] Leave answers in terms of π.

1. Find the volume of a sphere whose radius is 5 m.
2. Find the volume of a sphere whose diameter is 12 cm.
3. Find the area of a sphere whose diameter is 20 cm.
4. Find the area of a sphere whose radius is 7 m.
5. Find the volume and area of a sphere whose radius is 9 m.
6. Find the volume and area of a sphere whose diameter is 32 cm.

[7-10] Tell whether the statement is always, sometimes, or never true.

7. If a plane intersects a sphere, the intersection is a great circle of the sphere.
8. Two great circles of the same sphere intersect.
9. A diameter of a great circle of a sphere is a diameter of the sphere.
10. A radius of a small circle of a sphere is a radius of the sphere.

Written Exercises

Leave answers in terms of π.

[1-8] Find the area and volume of the sphere.

1. $d = 8$ m   **5.** $d = 60$ cm

2. $r = 70$ cm   **6.** $d = 22$ m

3. $r = 9$ m   **7.** $r = 5t$

4. $d = 1.2$ m   **8.** $r = 3k$

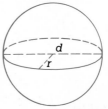

9. A soccer ball has a diameter of 8.6 in. Find its area and volume.

10. The kettle shown has a diameter of 58 cm. Find its area and volume.

[11-20] Given a sphere with radius r, diameter d, area A, volume V, and a great circle of circumference C. Find the four items not given.

11. $A = 2916\pi$ **16.** $A = 1296\pi$

12. $A = 784\pi$ **17.** $C = 28\pi$

13. $V = 288\pi$ **18.** $C = 172\pi$

14. $V = 4500\pi$ **19.** $V = 24\pi$

15. $A = 1936\pi$ **20.** $V = \frac{4}{3}\pi$

21. Consider the earth to be a sphere with a radius of 4000 miles. Find its area and volume. Use $\pi \doteq 3.14$.

22. The area of a great circle of a sphere is 6900 cm^2. What is the area of the sphere? Use $\pi \doteq 3.14$.

23. The area of a great circle of a sphere is 1 m². What is the area of the sphere?

24. The area of a sphere is 476 m². What is the area of a great circle of the sphere?

25. The area of a sphere is 1516 cm². What is the area of a great circle of the sphere?

26. Two spheres have radii of 5 m and 8 m, respectively. What is the ratio of their areas?

27. Two spheres have radii of 6 m and 11 m, respectively. What is the ratio of their areas?

Set B

[28-36] Use $\pi \doteq 3.14$.

28. Find the volume of a sphere whose area is 180 m².

29. Find the area of a sphere whose volume is 3052.08 cm³.

30. The areas of two spheres are in the ratio of 81 to 4. Find the ratio of their diameters.

31. The ratio of the volumes of two spheres is 8 to 27. What is the ratio of their radii?

32. Prove: The volumes of two spheres are to each other as the cubes of their radii.

33. Prove: The areas of two spheres are to each other as the squares of their radii.

34. The diameters of the two balls are 4 cm and 7 cm. What is the ratio of their volumes?

Set C

35. An inflated balloon has a radius of 15 cm. If more air is added and the radius increases 3 cm, what will be the increase in volume?

36. The radius of a sphere is increased 3 cm. This causes the area to become 4 times as great. Find the radius of the original sphere.

37. Prove: The area of a sphere with radius r is $\frac{2}{3}$ the T.A. of a right cylinder with radius r and height $2r$.

Career   Sheet-Metal Worker

Tony Hall is a sheet-metal worker. He makes metal products such as ducts for ventilating systems, metal framework for neon signs, and stainless steel kitchen equipment. He lays out an object from a drawing, and calculates dimensions, areas, and volumes.

A mailbox and its layout pattern are shown below. The dashed lines on the layout indicate where the metal is to be bent. The base of the mailbox is rectangular and the vertical edges are perpendicular to the base.

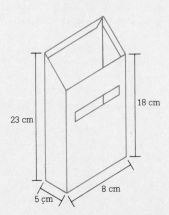

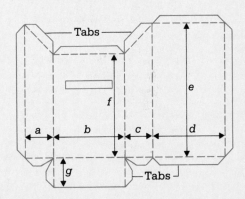

1. Give the dimensions a, b, c, d, e, f, and g.
2. Find the area of the base of the mailbox without tabs.
3. Find the total area of the mailbox without tabs.
4. The tabs are 1 cm wide. Give the dimensions of the rectangular sheet of metal needed for the box.
5. Give the area of this sheet of metal.

Chapter Summary

1. A polyhedron is a union of noncoplanar regions which encloses a region of space. (page 444)

2. Formulas for lateral area
   Right prism: L.A. = ph (page 448)
   Right cylinder: L.A. = $2\pi rh$ (page 458)
   Regular pyramid: L.A. = $\frac{1}{2}sp$ (page 465)
   Right cone: L.A. = πrs (page 468)

3. Formulas for total area
   Prism: T.A. = L.A. + $2B$ (page 448)
   Cylinder: T.A. = $2\pi rh + 2\pi r^2$ or T.A. = L.A. + $2B$ (page 458)
   Pyramid: T.A. = L.A. + B (page 465)
   Right cone: T.A. = $\pi rs + \pi r^2$ or T.A. = L.A. + B (page 468)

4. Formulas for volume
   Rectangular solid: $V = lwh$ (page 453)
   Prism: $V = Bh$ (page 454)
   Cylinder: $V = \pi r^2 h$ (page 458)
   Pyramid: $V = \frac{1}{3}Bh$ (page 465)
   Cone: $V = \frac{1}{3}Bh$ (page 468)

5. Formulas for a sphere (page 473)
   $A = 4\pi r^2$
   $V = \frac{4}{3}\pi r^3$

Chapter Review

Lesson 10.1
Page 444

1. Each base of an oblique prism has nine sides. How many faces of the prism are parallelograms?

2. A prism has 22 vertices. How many sides does each base of the prism have?

3. A prism has 16 faces. How many edges does it have?

4. How many faces of a regular hexagonal prism are rectangles?

Lesson 10.2
Page 448

5. Find the lateral area and the total area of the right rectangular prism.

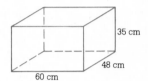

6. Find the L.A. and the T.A. of the regular hexagonal prism shown.

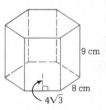

7. The perimeter of a base of a right prism is 3 m. The length of a lateral edge is 4 m. Find the L.A.

8. Find the T.A. of a cube whose base has a perimeter of 28 cm.

9. The T.A. of a prism is 592 cm^2 and the L.A. is 352 cm^2. What is the area of a base of the prism?

Lesson 10.3
Page 452

10. Find the volume of a rectangular solid if each base is a rectangle 12 cm by 8 cm and the height is 18 cm.

[11-13] Find the volume of each regular prism.

11.
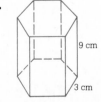

12.
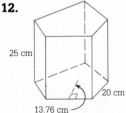

13.
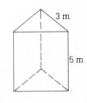

Lesson 10.4
Page 457

[14-16] Use the right cylinder shown.

14. L.A. = __?__

15. T.A. = __?__

16. V = __?__

2 m

10 cm

17. The circumference of a base of a right cylinder is 55 cm. Its height is 10 cm. What is its L.A.?

Lesson 10.5
Page 464

[18-20] Find the L.A., T.A., and volume for each regular pyramid.

18.

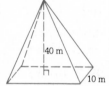

40 m

10 m

19.

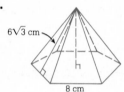

6√3 cm

h

8 cm

20.

12 cm 12 cm

12 cm

12 cm

Lesson 10.6
Page 467

[21-26] Each cone is right.

21. L.A. = __?__

22. T.A. = __?__

23. V = __?__

40 cm

18 cm

24. L.A. = __?__

25. T.A. = __?__

26. V = __?__

17 cm

12 cm

h

Lesson 10.7
Page 472

27. Find the height of a right cone whose volume is 924 cm³ and whose base has a radius of 14 cm. Use $\pi \doteq 3.14$.

28. Find the area and volume of a sphere whose radius is 7 cm. Use $\pi \doteq 3.14$.

29. The circumference of a great circle of a sphere is 16π m. Find the area and volume of the sphere. Leave answer in terms of π.

Chapter Test

[1-3] Find the lateral area, total area, and volume. Leave answers in terms of π.

1.

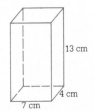

13 cm
4 cm
7 cm

2.

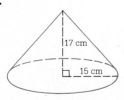

17 cm
15 cm

3.

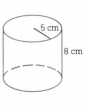

5 cm
8 cm

4. How many faces does a pentagonal prism have?

5. The dimensions of a rectangular solid are 8 cm, 10 cm, and 12 cm. Find its T.A. and volume.

6. Find the volume of a regular triangular prism whose height is 6 m and whose bases have sides of 9 m.

7. The T.A. of a cube is 216 cm^2. Find the volume.

[8-13] Find the L.A., T.A., and volume of each right cone, right cylinder, or regular pyramid.

8.

13 cm
8 cm

10.

12 cm
4 cm

12.

13 cm
5 cm

9.

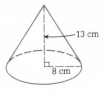

10 cm
8 cm
12 cm
12 cm

11.

10 cm
6 cm

13.

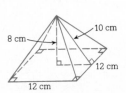

16 cm
16 cm

14. Find the area and volume of a sphere whose radius is 4 cm. Use $\pi \doteq 3.14$.

15. The area of a sphere is 832 cm^2. What is the area of a great circle of the sphere?

16. A right cone has a volume of 4500 cm^3. If the radius of its base is 12 cm, find its height. Use $\pi \doteq 3.14$.

17. A sphere has an area of 9850 cm^2. What is its radius? Use $\pi \doteq 3.14$.

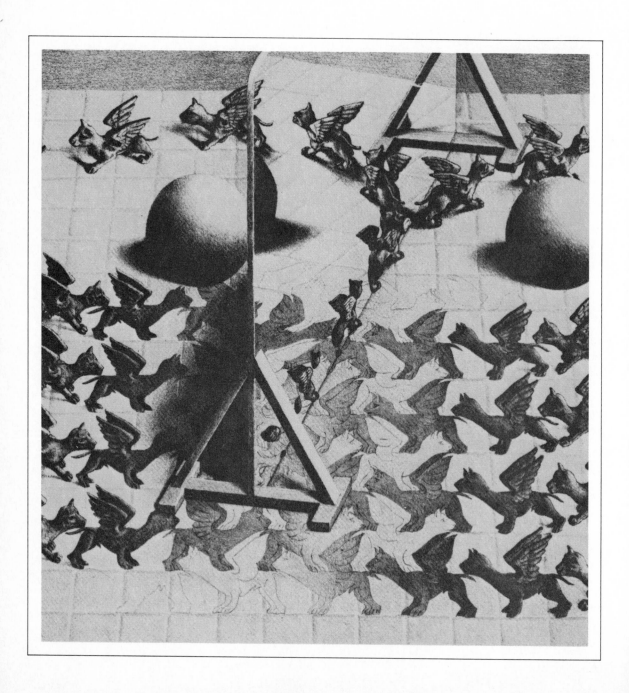

Using Transformations in Geometry

Escher's *Magic Mirror,* shown on page 482, suggests that reflections in a mirror assume an existence of their own behind the mirror.

Similar results can be obtained using a piece of tinted Plexiglas.

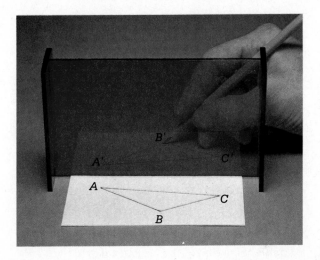

Suppose that the reflection of △*ABC* is drawn and labeled as shown.

1. What point is the reflection of *A*? Of *B*?
2. Where are the reflections of points between *A* and *B*?
3. The reflection of $\overline{AB}$ is __?__ .
4. The reflection of ∠*BAC* is __?__ .
5. The reflection of △*ABC* is __?__ .
6. How do a triangle and its reflection appear to be related?
7. If you looked through the other side of the Plexiglas mirror, what point would you see as the reflection of *A'*? Of *B'*?

11.1   Reflections

Suppose rectangle *ABCD* is traced from a plane onto a transparent sheet of rubber, which is then stretched as shown. The "stretched" vertices are marked on the plane as *A'*, *B'*, *C'*, and *D'*.

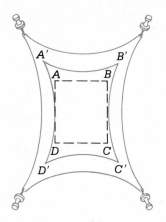

In this way each point *P* of the plane is associated with a unique point *P'*. Such a correspondence is a transformation.

Definition — A **transformation** of a plane is a one-to-one correspondence between the points of the plane and themselves.

A transformation is also called a **mapping;** above, *A* is mapped onto *A'*. *A'* is called the **image** of *A*. *A* is the **preimage** of *A'*.

The Plexiglas mirror pictured at the right provides another example of a transformation. The mirror can be used to pair points with their reflected images.

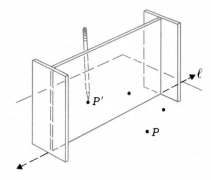

Suppose the mirror is placed along a line *ℓ*. The images of *A* and *B* are *A'* and *B'*, respectively.

How is *ℓ* related to the segments $\overline{AA'}$ and $\overline{BB'}$?

What is the image of a point on *ℓ*?

Your observations should suggest the next definition.

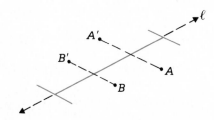

Definition	In a plane, a **reflection over line** ℓ is a transformation that maps each point P of the plane onto a point P' as follows:

If P is not on ℓ, then ℓ is the perpendicular bisector of $\overline{PP'}$.

If P is on ℓ, then P' coincides with P (written $P' = P$). |

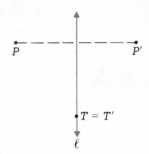

ℓ is called the **line of reflection**. P' is called the **reflection image** of P. What is the reflection image of P'? Why?

A transformation *preserves* distance if and only if the distance between two points is the same as the distance between their images.

Do you think the "stretch" transformation on page 484 preserves distance? For example, does $AD = A'D'$?

Does reflection over a line preserve distance? In each case of a line reflection below, does $PQ = P'Q'$?

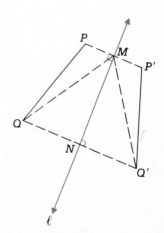

Case I   Case II   Case III   Case IV

Definition	A transformation that preserves distance is called an **isometry**.

Theorem 11.1	A line reflection is an isometry.

Given	P' and Q' are the reflection images over ℓ of P and Q, respectively.
Prove	$PQ = P'Q'$
Plan for Proof	**Case I** P and Q on the same side of ℓ: Draw $\overline{PP'}$ and $\overline{QQ'}$ intersecting ℓ in M and N as shown. Draw $\overline{MQ}$ and $\overline{MQ'}$. Show $\triangle MNQ \cong \triangle MNQ'$. Show $\triangle PQM \cong \triangle P'Q'M'$.

The proof of Theorem 11.1, Cases I-IV, is exercises 18-21.

Another transformation is a point reflection. Its definition is similar to that of a line reflection.

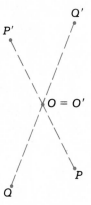

Definition

In a plane, a **reflection through point** O is a transformation that maps each point P of the plane onto a point P' as follows:

If P does not coincide with O, then O is the midpoint of $\overline{PP'}$.

If P coincides with O, then $P' = P$.

In the diagram, P' and Q' are the images of P and Q, respectively, under a reflection through point O. What is the image of P'? Why?

Suppose points P and Q above were traced onto a sheet of paper pinned at point O. If the paper were then turned halfway around, the tracing of points P and Q would coincide with P' and Q', respectively. For this reason, a point reflection is also called a **half-turn.** Point O is called the **center** of the half-turn.

In the diagram, $PO = OP'$ and $QO = OQ'$ by definition of midpoint. How could you show that $PQ = P'Q'$?

Theorem 11.2

A point reflection is an isometry.

The proof of Theorem 11.2 is exercises 22-24.

Class Exercises

[1-4] A transformation maps A onto B and E onto F.

1. Name the image of A.

2. Name the preimage of B.

3. Name the image of E.

4. Does $AE = BF$?

[5-9] What appears to be the reflection image over ℓ of each of these points?

5. D   6. C   7. X   8. S   9. Y

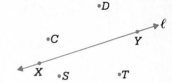

[10-11] Given only P and its image P', tell how to find the line of reflection for the given condition.

10. $P \neq P'$ 11. $P = P'$

[12-15] What appears to be the reflection image through point O of each of these points?

12. H   13. G   14. O   15. F

[16-17] Given only P and its image P', tell how to find the center of a half-turn for the given condition.

16. $P \neq P'$ 17. $P = P'$

Written Exercises

Set A

[1-4] Trace line ℓ and points A, B, C, and D. Find the reflection images of A, B, C, and D over ℓ.

1. Are A, B, C, and D collinear?
2. What appears to be true about the images of these points?
3. If E is a point on $\overline{AD}$, where do you think the image of E would be?
4. If F is between C and D, where do you think the image of F would be?

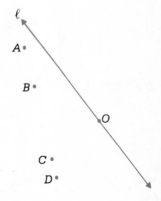

[5-8] Trace points O, A, B, C, and D from the diagram above. Find the images of A, B, C, and D under a half-turn about O. With respect to this half-turn, answer the questions in exercises 1-4.

9. Trace line ℓ and $\angle PQR$. Draw the reflection image of $\angle PQR$ over ℓ. Compare the measures of the angles.

10. Trace point O and $\angle PQR$. Draw the image of $\angle PQR$ under a half-turn about O. Compare the measures of the angles.

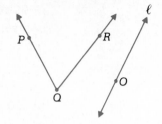

[11-13] For each exercise, graph points $A(5, 0)$, $B(0, -4)$, and $C(-3, 4)$. Draw A', B', and C', the images of A, B, and C, respectively, under the reflection described. State the coordinates of A', B', and C'.

11. Over the x-axis

12. Over the y-axis

13. Through the origin, $O(0, 0)$

Set B

[14-17] Trace points X and Y for each exercise.

14. Use a protractor to find line ℓ so that Y is the reflection image of X over ℓ.

15. How can you do exercise 14 by folding your paper?

16. Use a ruler to find point O so that X is the image of Y under a half-turn about O.

17. How can you do exercise 16 by folding your paper?

[18-21] Use the Given, Prove, and appropriate diagram from page 485 to prove Theorem 11.1 for each case.

18. Case I   19. Case II   20. Case III   21. Case IV

[22-24] Prove Theorem 11.2 for each case shown.

22.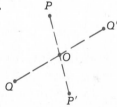

23.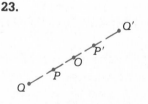

24.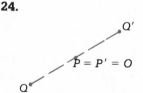

Case I   Case II   Case III

[25-26] m is a line in a plane. A correspondence between points of the plane is defined as follows:

If point A is not on m, its image, A', is the intersection of m and the line perpendicular to m through A.

If point A is on m, then $A' = A$.

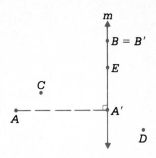

25. Trace the diagram. Find C', D', and E'.

26. Is this correspondence a transformation? An isometry?

[27-28] O is a point in a plane. A correspondence between points of the plane is defined as follows:

If point X does not coincide with O, its image, X', is the midpoint of $\overline{OX}$.

If X coincides with O, then $X = X'$.

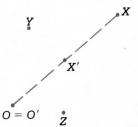

27. Trace the diagram and find Y' and Z'.

28. Is this correspondence a transformation? An isometry?

Set C

[29-31] Determine the coordinates of the reflection image of any point $P(x, y)$ over the indicated line.

29. y-axis   **30.** x-axis   **31.** Line with equation $y = 4$

[32-34] Determine the coordinates of the reflection image of any point $P(x, y)$ through the indicated point.

32. $O(0, 0)$ **33.** $A(3, 0)$ **34.** $B(3, 4)$

Geometry Maintenance

[1-4] Given: A cone of height 2, diameter of the base 2. Find each measure.

1. Slant height   **3.** Total area

2. Lateral area   **4.** Volume

11.2   Properties of Isometries

The reflection image of △*TUV* is marked behind a Plexiglas mirror.

Are *T*, *S*, and *V* collinear? Are the reflection images of *T*, *S*, and *V* collinear? Your answers should indicate that a mirror reflection *preserves* collinearity of points.

Is *S* between *T* and *V*? What is the position of *S'*? A mirror reflection also preserves betweenness of points.

These properties hold for all line reflections and point reflections. In fact, they hold for any isometry.

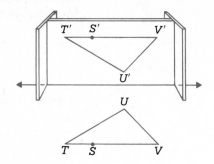

Theorem 11.3   **An isometry preserves collinearity and betweenness of points.**

Given   Collinear points *A*, *B*, and *C*, with *A'*, *B'*, and *C'*, their respective images under an isometry; *B* is between *A* and *C*.

Prove   *A'*, *B'*, and *C'* are collinear; *B'* is between *A'* and *C'*.

Statements	Reasons
1. *A'*, *B'*, and *C'* are the images of *A*, *B*, and *C* under an isometry.	1. Given
2. $AB = A'B'$; $BC = B'C'$; $AC = A'C'$	2. Def. of isometry [1]
3. *B* is between *A* and *C*.	3. Given
4. $AB + BC = AC$	4. Segment Addition Post. [3]
5. $A'B' + B'C' = A'C'$	5. Substitution [2, 4]
6. *A'*, *B'*, and *C'* are collinear and *B'* is between *A'* and *C'*.	6. Points *A*, *B*, and *C* are collinear and *B* is between *A* and *C* if $AB + BC = AC$. [5]

Theorem 11.3 suggests that isometries map lines onto lines, rays onto rays, and segments onto segments. This is formalized in Theorem 11.4.

Theorem 11.4   If an isometry maps A onto A' and B onto B', then the image of $\overleftrightarrow{AB}$ is $\overleftrightarrow{A'B'}$, the image of $\overrightarrow{AB}$ is $\overrightarrow{A'B'}$, and the image of $\overline{AB}$ is $\overline{A'B'}$.

Since an angle is defined in terms of rays, the image of an angle under an isometry is another angle. It can be proven that the angle and its image have the same measure. It can also be proven for any isometry that a triangle and its image are congruent.

These properties are given in Theorems 11.5 and 11.6. Their proofs are exercises 20 and 21.

Theorem 11.5   **An isometry preserves angle measure.**

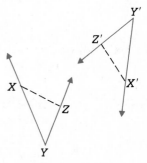

Given X', Y', and Z' are the images under an isometry of X, Y, and Z, respectively.

Prove $m\angle XYZ = m\angle X'Y'Z'$

Plan for Proof   Draw $\overline{XZ}$ and $\overline{X'Z'}$.
Show $\triangle XYZ \cong \triangle X'Y'Z'$.
Use corresponding parts.

Theorem 11.6   **Under an isometry, a triangle and its image are congruent.**

These properties of isometries hold for all reflections. (Why?) Thus, the reflection image of any polygon can be drawn by joining the images of consecutive vertices.

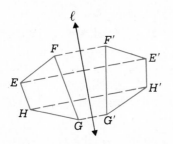 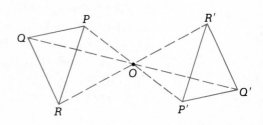

One basic property of a set of points is not preserved by a line reflection. Observe that for quadrilateral *EFGH* on page 491, the *orientation* from *E* to *F* to *G* to *H* is clockwise. However, the orientation from *E′* to *F′* to *G′* to *H′* is counterclockwise. A line reflection *reverses* orientation. A point reflection preserves orientation.

Class Exercises

[1-6] Name the reflection image over line ℓ of each figure.

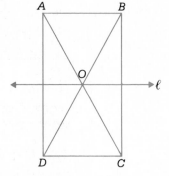

1. Point *A*   3. $\overline{DC}$ 5. $\angle ADC$
2. Point *C*   4. $\overline{AC}$ 6. $\triangle ABC$

[7-12] Name the reflection image through point *O* of each figure.

7. Point *A*   9. $\overline{AB}$ 11. $\angle BOC$
8. Point *D*   10. $\overline{AC}$ 12. $\triangle ABC$

[13-18] Describe the points that must be reflected to find the reflection image of each figure.

13. Line   15. Segment   17. Convex quadrilateral
14. Ray   16. Angle   18. Convex hexagon

Written Exercises

Set A

[1-7] An isometry maps *P* onto *P′*, *Q* onto *Q′*, and *R* onto *R′*.

1. What is the orientation of $\triangle PQR$?
2. What is the orientation of $\triangle P'Q'R'$?
3. Can $\triangle P'Q'R'$ be the image of $\triangle PQR$ under a line reflection? Explain.

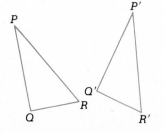

[4-7] Which theorem or definition justifies each statement?

4. $PR = P'R'$ **5.** $\angle P \cong \angle P'$ **6.** $\triangle PQR \cong \triangle P'Q'R'$

7. If X is on $\overleftrightarrow{PQ}$, then the image of X is on $\overleftrightarrow{P'Q'}$.

[8-11] A reflection over line ℓ maps
A, B, C, and D onto A', B', C', and
D', respectively. Explain why each
statement is true.

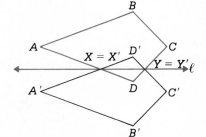

8. $BD = B'D'$

9. The image of $\overrightarrow{AD}$ is $\overrightarrow{A'D'}$.

10. $\angle CDA \cong \angle C'D'A'$

11. $\triangle XDY \cong \triangle XD'Y$

[12-15] A reflection through point O
maps P onto S and Q onto R. Explain
why each statement is true.

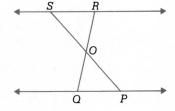

12. $PO = OS$ **14.** $\angle PQR \cong \angle SRQ$

13. $\overline{PQ} \cong \overline{SR}$ **15.** $\overleftrightarrow{PQ} \parallel \overleftrightarrow{RS}$

Set B

[16-19] For each exercise, draw $\triangle ABC$ with coordinates
$A(2, 4)$, $B(4, -1)$, and $C(0, 2)$. Draw the image of $\triangle ABC$ under
the reflection described.

16. Over the x-axis   **17.** Over the y-axis

18. Over the line with equation $x = 2$

19. Through the origin, $O(0, 0)$

20. Prove Theorem 11.5.   **21.** Prove Theorem 11.6.

[22-23] An isometry maps ℓ onto ℓ' and m onto m'. Explain
why each statement is true.

22. If $\ell \perp m$, then $\ell' \perp m'$.   **23.** If $\ell \parallel m$, then $\ell' \parallel m'$.

Set C

24. Trace this diagram in which A' is
the reflection image of A over n.
Using only a straightedge, locate
the reflection image of B.

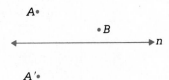

Applications of Reflections

Reflections have useful applications in art, engineering, science, and sports.

Example 1

Two farms, located at A and B, are to be connected by separate wires to a transformer on a main power line ℓ. Where should the power company locate the transformer so that the minimum amount of wire will be needed?

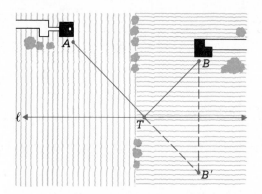 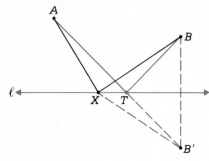

Solution

Find B', the reflection image of B over ℓ. Locate the transformer T at the intersection of $\overline{AB'}$ and ℓ. Then $AT + TB$ is the minimum amount of wire needed.

To see why, suppose the transformer were located at some other point X on ℓ. Use Theorem 11.1 and the Triangle Inequality Theorem to show that $AX + XB > AT + TB$.

Example 2

Where should you aim to make a hole-in-one on the miniature golf green shown?

Solution

Visualize H', the reflection image of H over k. Aim for the point P where $\overline{BH'}$ intersects k.

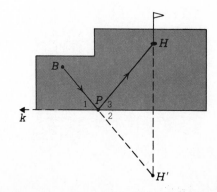

Since the ball hits the side and *rebounds* at the same angle, P must be located so that $\angle 1 \cong \angle 3$.

We can show that $\angle 1 \cong \angle 2$. (How?) Also, $\angle 2 \cong \angle 3$. (Why?) Thus, we have $\angle 1 \cong \angle 3$, as desired.

Example 3	On the billiard table shown, where should you aim so that the cue ball at C hits three sides and then hits the ball at R?	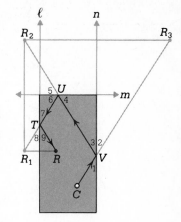
Solution	Let R_1 be the reflection image of R over ℓ; R_2, the reflection image of R_1 over m; and R_3, the reflection image of R_2 over n. Aim the cue ball for V, the point where $\overline{CR_3}$ intersects n.	

Reasoning as in example 2, you can show $\angle 1 \cong \angle 3$; $\angle 4 \cong \angle 6$; and $\angle 7 \cong \angle 9$.

Class Exercises

[1-7] Refer to example 3 above. Explain why each statement is true.

1. $\angle 1 \cong \angle 2$ **3.** $\angle 4 \cong \angle 6$ **5.** $TR_1 = TR$

2. $\angle 1 \cong \angle 3$ **4.** $\angle 7 \cong \angle 9$ **6.** $UR_1 = UR_2$

7. The distance the cue ball travels is equal to CR_3.

[8-10] Tell how to find each point on $\overleftrightarrow{AB}$.

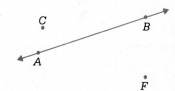

8. Point P, such that $CP + PF$ is as small as possible

9. Point Q, such that $CQ + QD$ is as small as possible

10. Point R, such that $\angle CRA \cong \angle DRB$

Written Exercises

Set A

1. A pumping station P is to be built to pipe water to towns S and T with a minimum amount of pipe. Trace the diagram. Locate P on the river.

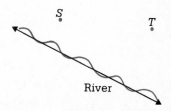

[2-6] For each exercise, trace the diagram at the right. Show how to determine the path of a cue ball at *C*, so that it bounces off the given sides and then hits the ball at *R*.

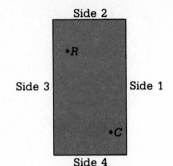

Side 2

•*R*

Side 3   Side 1

•*C*

Side 4

2. Side 1

3. Side 4

4. Side 1, then side 2

5. Side 1, then side 2, then side 3

6. Side 3, then side 1, then side 2

[7-9] For each exercise trace the diagram at the right. Show how to determine the path of a ball at *B*, so that a hole-in-one is made after the ball bounces off the given number of sides.

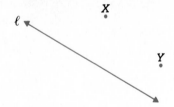

•*B*

H•

7. 1 side   8. 2 sides   9. 3 sides

10. A laser beam emitted from point *X* is to be received by a measuring device *Y* upon reflection from a flat surface ℓ. Trace the diagram. At what point on ℓ should the beam be aimed? Explain.

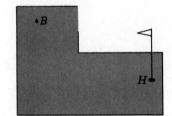

X

ℓ

Y

[11-12] Strip or *frieze* patterns, as shown below, are used in architecture and interior decorating.

11. Trace and complete this frieze pattern by finding images of the flag under repeated reflections over the given lines.

12. Trace and complete this frieze pattern by finding images of the flag under repeated reflections through the given points.

13. Commercial artists use a device similar to that shown for drawing mirror images. $AP = PB = BP' = P'A$. The joints pivot freely as A and B slide along ℓ. As P traces out a figure, P' traces out its reflection image. Why does this work?

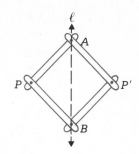

Set B

[14-15] For a canoe race, contestants begin at A, paddle to any point on the shoreline, and end at B. Trace the diagram.

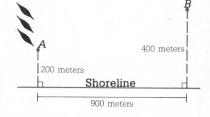

14. Show how to determine the point on the shore to which you should paddle.

15. Find the length of the shortest route to the nearest ten meters.

16. In a vacuum tube, an electron sent from E is to be aimed at ℓ so that it reflects from ℓ to m and finally to F. Trace the diagram and show how to determine the path of the electron.

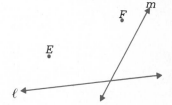

Set C

[17-19] Given: P_1 is the reflection image of P over $\overline{AC}$, and P_2 is the reflection image of P over $\overline{AB}$.

17. Why is the perimeter of $\triangle PQR$ smaller than the perimeter of any other triangle with vertex P and other vertices on $\overline{AB}$ and $\overline{AC}$? **Hint** Compare the perimeters to P_1P_2.

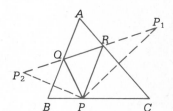

18. Find the triangle with minimum perimeter having one vertex on each side of $\triangle ABC$.

19. Formulate a real-world problem that can be solved using exercise 18.

11.4   Translations and Rotations

This photograph shows two parallel mirrors generating a repeating pattern.

Figure 1 is the mirror reflection of a cardboard triangle placed between the mirrors. Note the orientation of the curved arrow.

Figure 2 is the reflection image of Figure 1. Observe the orientation.

The result of two successive mirror reflections is called the composite of the reflections.

This idea can be applied to any two transformations.

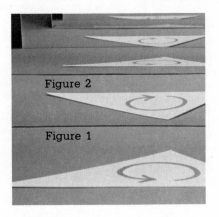

Figure 2

Figure 1

Definition   Let F and G be transformations. The **composite** of F and G is the transformation which maps each point P onto a point P' as follows:

First P is mapped onto P_1 under F.

Then P_1 is mapped onto P' under G.

The diagram shows the image of $\triangle ABC$ under a composite of two line reflections; first over ℓ and then over m, with $\ell \parallel m$. In this case, it appears that $\triangle ABC$ "slides" onto $\triangle A'B'C'$. The definition below gives a mathematical description of this physical motion of sliding.

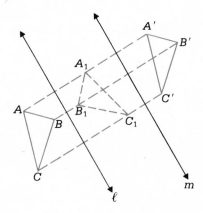

Definition   A **translation** is a composite of two reflections over two parallel lines.

In the diagram above, $AB = A_1B_1$ and $A_1B_1 = A'B'$ since line reflections are isometries. Thus, $AB = A'B'$. This suggests Theorem 11.7. Its proof is exercise 51.

Theorem 11.7   A translation is an isometry.

It follows that translations share all the properties of isometries, as summarized on page 502.

Other properties of translations are suggested by the diagram at the right.

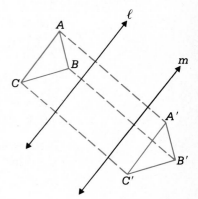

How do $\overleftrightarrow{AC}$ and $\overleftrightarrow{A'C'}$ seem to be related? $\overleftrightarrow{AB}$ and $\overleftrightarrow{A'B'}$?

What appears to be true about $\overline{AA'}$, $\overline{BB'}$, and $\overline{CC'}$?

Your observations should suggest the next two theorems. The proof of Theorem 11.8 is exercise 53.

For the rest of this chapter, in order to simplify the statements of theorems, we will extend our definition of parallel lines to include: Every line is parallel to itself.

Theorem 11.8   Under a translation, a line and its image are parallel.

Theorem 11.9   If a translation maps A onto A' and B onto B', then $\overline{AA'} \parallel \overline{BB'}$ and $\overline{AA'} \cong \overline{BB'}$.

Theorem 11.9 suggests that the translation image of any point is determined by just one point and its image. Example 1 gives a method for finding the translation image of a point.

Example 1   A translation maps A onto A'. Find the image of P.

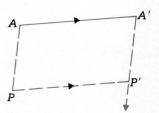

Solution   Draw the parallelogram having P, A, and A' as three of its vertices, and $\overline{AA'}$ as a side. P' is the fourth vertex.

Consider now the composite of two reflections over intersecting lines.

In the diagram, a reflection over ℓ maps $\triangle ABC$ onto $\triangle A_1 B_1 C_1$ and a reflection over m maps $\triangle A_1 B_1 C_1$ onto $\triangle A'B'C'$.

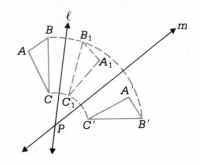

Since $\triangle ABC$ and $\triangle A'B'C'$ have the same orientation, the composite mapping cannot be equivalent to a single reflection. Nor does it appear to be a translation. Why?

However, if the triangles were on a turntable with center at P, $\triangle ABC$ could be rotated to the position of $\triangle A'B'C'$.

Definition
A **rotation** is the composite of two reflections over two intersecting lines.

The point of intersection of the two lines is called the **center of the rotation.** The direction of the rotation can be either clockwise or counterclockwise. $\triangle ABC$ above was rotated in a clockwise direction about center P.

Since line reflections are isometries, $AB = A_1 B_1$ and $A_1 B_1 = A'B'$ in the diagram above. Therefore, $AB = A'B'$. This suggests Theorem 11.10. Its proof is exercise 52.

Theorem 11.10
A rotation is an isometry.

Since rotations are isometries, they have all the properties of isometries, as summarized on page 502.

A counterclockwise rotation with center P is shown at the right.

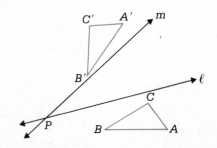

Trace the diagram. Draw and measure $\angle APA'$, $\angle BPB'$, and $\angle CPC'$. How do these measures compare?

This should suggest the next theorem.

Chapter 11 Using Transformations in Geometry

Theorem 11.11   If a rotation with center P maps A onto A' and B onto B' (and P is not on $\overline{AA'}$ or $\overline{BB'}$), then $m\angle APA' = m\angle BPB'$.

The measure of $\angle APA'$ is called the *magnitude* of the rotation. If P lies on $\overline{AA'}$, the magnitude is 180. In this case, the rotation is simply a half-turn.

While a line is parallel to its image under a translation, the same is true for a rotation only when the rotation is a half-turn.

Theorem 11.12   Under a half-turn, a line and its image are parallel.

The proof of Theorem 11.12 is exercise 54.

Any rotation can be specified by giving its center, the magnitude of the rotation, and its direction.

Example 2   Find the image of A under a rotation with center P, magnitude 135, and clockwise direction.

Solution   Draw $\overrightarrow{PA}$ and then, in a clockwise direction, a ray that forms a 135° angle with $\overrightarrow{PA}$. Locate A' on this new ray so that $PA' = PA$.

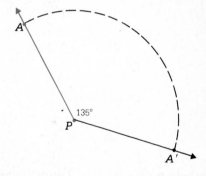

Then A' is the rotation image of A.

Now consider the composite of two reflections over two lines that coincide. Again, this composite is an isometry. It simply maps every point of the plane onto itself.

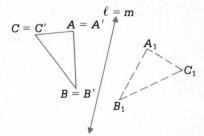

Definition   The **identity transformation** is the transformation that maps each point of the plane onto itself.

The isometries studied in this chapter are line reflections, point reflections (half-turns), translations, rotations, and the identity transformation. It should be noted that the composite of *any* number of line reflections is an isometry. (Why is this true?) The basic properties of isometries are summarized below.

Isometries preserve	Isometries map
Distance	A line onto a line
Collinearity	A ray onto a ray
Betweenness	A segment onto a segment
Angle measure	A triangle onto a congruent triangle

Class Exercises

[1-4] Name the image of each figure under the composite: reflection over ℓ and then reflection over m.

1. A **2.** $\overline{AB}$ **3.** $\angle BAC$ **4.** $\triangle ABC$

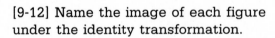

[5-8] Name the image of each figure under the composite: reflection over m and then reflection over ℓ.

5. X **6.** $\overline{YZ}$ **7.** $\angle XZY$ **8.** $\triangle XYZ$

[9-12] Name the image of each figure under the identity transformation.

9. A **10.** $\overline{PB}$ **11.** $\angle ABC$ **12.** $\triangle XYZ$

[13-15] Under what condition is the composite of two line reflections the given transformation?

13. A translation   **14.** A rotation

15. The identity transformation

16. Which isometries preserve orientation? Explain.

Written Exercises

[1-18] Refer to the tessellation below.

[1-6] A translation maps *A* onto *B*. Find the image of:

1. *E*   **2.** *K*   **3.** *B*   **4.** $\overline{AE}$ **5.** $\angle EJK$ **6.** $\square BCGF$

[7-12] Find the image of each figure in exercises 1-6 under a translation that maps *A* onto *F*.

[13-18] Find the image of each figure in exercises 1-6 under a half-turn with center *F*.

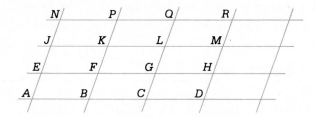

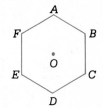

[19-35] Refer to the regular hexagon above.

[19-23] A rotation with center *O* maps *A* onto *C*. Find the image of:

19. *B*   **20.** *C*   **21.** $\overline{DE}$ **22.** $\angle EFA$

23. What are the magnitude and direction of this rotation?

[24-28] Repeat exercises 19-23 for a rotation that maps *E* onto *D*.

[29-33] Repeat exercises 19-23 for a rotation that maps *F* onto *C*.

34. A transformation maps *F* onto *B*, *E* onto *C*, and *A* onto itself. Is this transformation a rotation or a line reflection?

35. A transformation maps *B* onto *E* and *A* onto *D*. Is this transformation a rotation or a line reflection?

[36-38] For each exercise, trace the diagram below.

36. Draw $\overline{AB}$. Find its image under a clockwise rotation about P with magnitude 90.

37. Draw $\overline{AB}$. Find its image under a counterclockwise rotation about P with magnitude 120.

38. Find the image of P under a translation that maps A onto B.

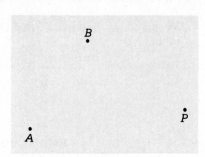

Set B

39. Graph points $A(2, 2)$, $B(-2, 3)$, $C(0, -2)$ and $D(3, -4)$. Find the images of A, B, C, and D under a translation that maps $Q(-4, -3)$ onto $Q'(-2, -2)$.

40. Graph points A, B, C, and D given in exercise 39. Find the images of A, B, C, and D under a clockwise rotation with center $O(0, 0)$ and magnitude 90.

[41-48] Refer to this tessellation with isosceles right triangles. Name an isometry that maps the first triangle onto the second triangle.

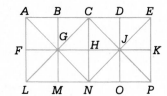

41. $\triangle LFG$, $\triangle ABG$ **45.** $\triangle HJN$, $\triangle HJN$

42. $\triangle ABG$, $\triangle CDJ$ **46.** $\triangle CHG$, $\triangle NHJ$

43. $\triangle LFG$, $\triangle AFG$ **47.** $\triangle NHJ$, $\triangle EKJ$

44. $\triangle LFG$, $\triangle GFA$ **48.** $\triangle CHG$, $\triangle EKJ$

49. Give an example of two translations whose composite is the identity transformation.

50. Give an example of two rotations whose composite is the identity transformation.

51. Prove Theorem 11.7.   **52.** Prove Theorem 11.10.

Set C

53. Prove Theorem 11.8.   **54.** Prove Theorem 11.12.

55. Prove: The composite of two reflections over two perpendicular lines is a half-turn.

56. Find the coordinates of the image of $P(x, y)$ under a translation that maps $O(0, 0)$ onto $A(a, b)$.

57. Find the coordinates of the image of $P(x, y)$ under a clockwise rotation with center $O(0, 0)$, magnitude 90.

Progress Check

Lesson 11.1
Page 484

1. Can two points have the same image under a transformation?

2. If X is the reflection image of Y over line ℓ, how are ℓ and $\overline{XY}$ related?

3. If A is the image of B under a half-turn about point O, how are A, B, and O related?

4. A transformation that preserves distance is called a(n) __?__ .

Lesson 11.2
Page 490

[5–9] An isometry maps A, B, C, D, and E onto A', B', C', D', and E', respectively. Why is each statement true?

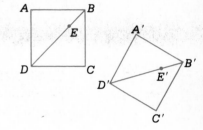

5. $AD = A'D'$

6. $m\angle B'C'D' = m\angle BCD$

7. $\triangle BDC \cong \triangle B'D'C'$

8. The image of $\overleftrightarrow{CD}$ is $\overleftrightarrow{C'D'}$.

9. If E is between B and D, then E' is between B' and D'.

10. Line reflections __?__ orientation.

Lesson 11.3
Page 494

11. Explain how to find point P on $\overleftrightarrow{VW}$ such that $\angle TPV \cong \angle UPW$.

12. Explain how to find point Q on $\overleftrightarrow{VW}$ such that $TQ + QU$ is minimal.

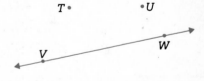

Lesson 11.4
Page 498

13. The composite of two reflections over two parallel lines is called a(n) __?__ .

14. The composite of two reflections over two intersecting lines is called a(n) __?__ .

15. Name four properties preserved by all isometries.

16. Trace X, Y, and R. A translation maps X onto Y. Draw the image of R.

17. Trace X and R. Draw the image of X under a counterclockwise rotation with center R and magnitude 90.

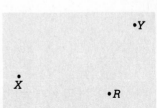

11.5   Symmetry

The symmetry of the figures below is important to biologists. Observe that each figure coincides roughly with its reflection image over ℓ.

Definition

A plane figure has **line symmetry** if and only if there is a line ℓ such that the figure coincides with its reflection image over ℓ. Line ℓ is called a **line of symmetry** or a **symmetry line** for the figure.

For an isosceles triangle, the perpendicular bisector of the base is a line of symmetry.

Since $AB = AC$, A is on the perpendicular bisector of $\overline{BC}$. Reflection over $\overleftrightarrow{AD}$ maps A onto A and B and C onto each other. Thus, $\triangle ABC$ is its own image under a reflection over $\overleftrightarrow{AD}$. So $\overleftrightarrow{AD}$ is a symmetry line.

Observe that a rectangle has two lines of symmetry—the perpendicular bisectors of the sides.

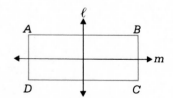

How many symmetry lines do you think a circle has? Describe them.

Designs and symbols frequently exhibit symmetry. Only the first two symbols above have line symmetry. The third one exhibits point symmetry.

Definition   A plane figure has **point symmetry** if and only if there is a point P such that the figure and its image coincide under a reflection through P.

A parallelogram has point symmetry about the point of intersection of its diagonals.

The diagonals of $\square ABCD$ bisect each other at P. Therefore, A and C are the images of each other, as are B and D under a reflection through P. Hence, the images of $\overline{AB}$, $\overline{BC}$, $\overline{CD}$, and $\overline{DA}$ are $\overline{CD}$, $\overline{DA}$, $\overline{AB}$, and $\overline{BC}$, respectively.

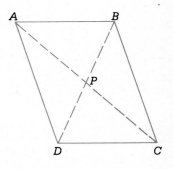

Thus, reflection through P maps $\square ABCD$ onto itself. Therefore, $\square ABCD$ has point symmetry.

Point symmetry is a special case of rotational symmetry.

Definition   A plane figure has **rotational symmetry** if and only if there is a rotation such that the figure and its image coincide under the rotation.

Each design at the right has rotational symmetry. A rotation of magnitude 120, either clockwise or counterclockwise, maps each figure onto itself.

Which figure also has line symmetry? How many symmetry lines does it have?

Class Exercises

[1-4] Refer to these pictures of *diatoms*. Diatoms are single-celled sea plants.

a.   b. 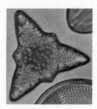   c.    d.

1. Which pictures exhibit line symmetry?
2. Which pictures exhibit point symmetry?
3. Which pictures exhibit rotational symmetry?
4. Which pictures have more than one line of symmetry?

5. If a figure has two or more lines of symmetry, must it have rotational symmetry? Explain.

Written Exercises

Set A

[1-12] For each figure:
a. Determine the number of symmetry lines.
b. Determine if the figure has point symmetry.
c. Determine if the figure has rotational symmetry. If it does, state the magnitude and direction of all rotations that map the figure onto itself.

1.   3.   5.   7.

2.   4.   6.   8.

9. _____

10. (figure)

11. (figure)

12. (figure)

[13-15] Refer to the alphabet below.

A B C D E F G H I J K L M N O P Q R S T U V W X Y Z

13. The letter A has a *vertical* symmetry line. List the other letters that have vertical symmetry lines.

14. The letter E has a *horizontal* symmetry line. List the other letters that have horizontal symmetry lines.

15. List the letters that have point symmetry.

Set B

[16-21] Draw a figure that satisfies the given conditions. If impossible, so state.

16. A triangle with line symmetry and rotational symmetry

17. A triangle with line symmetry but no rotational symmetry

18. A quadrilateral with four lines of symmetry

19. A quadrilateral with line symmetry but no rotational symmetry

20. An angle with no lines of symmetry

21. A pentagon with no rotational symmetry

22. Prove that the perpendicular bisector of a side of a rectangle is a symmetry line for the rectangle.

Set C

[23-25] A figure contains the point $P(a, b)$. State the coordinates of another point on the figure if the figure has the symmetry described below.

23. The y-axis as a line of symmetry

24. The x-axis as a line of symmetry

25. Point symmetry about $O(0, 0)$

26. How many lines of symmetry does a regular n-gon have?

27. How many different rotations will map a regular n-gon onto itself?

11.5 Symmetry

509

Dilations

Cartographers (map makers) often need to alter the size but not the shape of a map. They sometimes use a *pantograph* like the one shown below. The rods are hinged so that *PQRS* is always a parallelogram, and *C*, *P*, and *P'* are always collinear.

The pantograph is fastened down at *C*. A stylus and a pencil may be used interchangeably at *P* and *P'*.

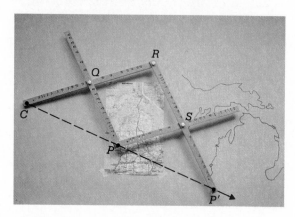

In every position of the pantograph, $\triangle CPQ \sim \triangle CP'R$, so $\dfrac{CR}{CQ} = \dfrac{CP'}{CP}$. If $\dfrac{CR}{CQ} = 2$, then $\dfrac{CP'}{CP} = 2$ and $CP' = 2(CP)$.

Thus the pantograph can be used to set up a one-to-one correspondence which pairs any point *P* on the plane with an image point *P'*.

This correspondence can be interpreted in mathematical terms as a transformation of the plane.

Definition

Let *C* be a point and *k*, a positive real number. A **dilation** is a transformation that maps each point of the plane onto an image point as follows:

C is its own image.

For any point *P* other than *C*, the image of *P* is the point *P'* on $\overrightarrow{CP}$ for which $CP' = k(CP)$.

C is called the **center** and *k* the **scale factor** of the dilation.

Two different dilations are illustrated below.

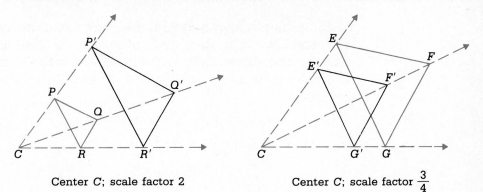

Center C; scale factor 2   Center C; scale factor $\dfrac{3}{4}$

The diagrams suggest that a dilation preserves shape.

If $k > 1$, the dilation is an **enlargement.**

If $k < 1$, the dilation is a **reduction.**

If $k = 1$, the dilation is simply the identity transformation.

The diagram at the right illustrates an enlargement with center C and scale factor 3.

By definition, $CA' = 3(CA)$ and $CB' = 3(CB)$. Thus $\dfrac{CA'}{CA} = 3 = \dfrac{CB'}{CB}$.

Since $\angle ACB \cong \angle A'CB'$, it follows that $\triangle ACB \sim \triangle A'CB'$.

So $\dfrac{A'B'}{AB} = 3$ or $A'B' = 3(AB)$.

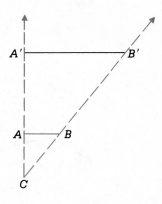

This idea is generalized in the next theorem. Its proof is exercise 13.

Theorem 11.13   If a dilation with center C and scale factor k maps A onto A' and B onto B', then $A'B' = k(AB)$.

Clearly, a dilation is an isometry only if $k = 1$.

Class Exercises

[1-8] Name the image of A under a dilation with center O and scale factor k. Then state whether the dilation is an enlargement, a reduction, or the identity transformation.

$$\begin{array}{c} P\ Q\ R\ A\ S\ T\ U\ V\ W\ X\ Y\ Z \\ \vdash\!+\!\!+\!\!+\!\!+\!\!+\!\!+\!\!+\!\!+\!\!+\!\!+\!\!+\!\!\rightarrow \\ 0\quad 1\quad 2\quad 3\quad 4\quad 5\quad 6 \end{array}$$

1. $k = 2$ **3.** $k = 1$ **5.** $k = \frac{3}{4}$ **7.** $k = \frac{5}{2}$

2. $k = \frac{1}{2}$ **4.** $k = 3$ **6.** $k = \frac{3}{2}$ **8.** $k = \frac{5}{4}$

Written Exercises

Set A

[1-6] For each exercise, trace the diagram at the right. Draw the image of each point under a dilation with center C and scale factor k.

1. $k = 2$ **3.** $k = 3$ **5.** $k = \frac{1}{3}$

2. $k = \frac{1}{2}$ **4.** $k = \frac{1}{4}$ **6.** $k = 1$

7. Under a(n) __?__ the image is further from the center than is the preimage.

8. Under a(n) __?__ the image is closer to the center than is the preimage.

Set B

[9-12] A dilation with center C and scale factor k maps A onto A' and B onto B'. For each exercise, draw a sketch and find the missing value.

9. $CB = 12$; $CB' = 4$; $k = $ __?__

10. $CB = 7$; $CB' = 7$; $k = $ __?__

11. $CA = 3$; $AA' = 9$; $k = $ __?__

12. $A'B' = 14$; $k = 2$; $AB = $ __?__

Set C

13. Prove Theorem 11.13.

14. Find the coordinates of the image of $P(x, y)$ under a dilation with center $O(0, 0)$ and scale factor k.

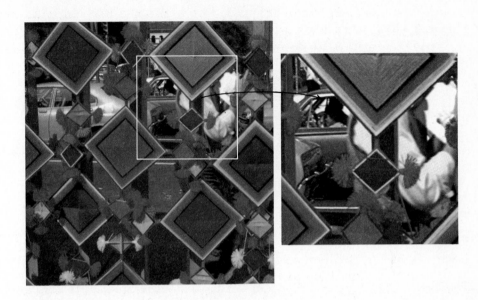

A photographic enlargement can be viewed geometrically as a dilation with $k > 1$. Does the enlargement above appear to preserve collinearity? Betweenness? Angle measure?

Theorem 11.14   A dilation preserves collinearity and betweenness of points.

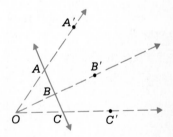

Given   Collinear points A, B, and C with B between A and C; A', B', and C' the images of A, B, and C, respectively, under a dilation with center O and scale factor k

Prove A', B', and C' are collinear; B' is between A' and C'.

Plan for Proof   Use Segment Addition Post. and Mult. prop. of equality to get $k(AB) + k(BC) = k(AC)$.
Using Thm. 11.13, substitute to get $A'B' + B'C' = A'C'$.
Show that this implies collinearity and betweenness, using Thm. 4.14.

The next theorem is a corollary of Theorem 11.14.

Theorem 11.15 If a dilation maps A onto A' and B onto B', then the image of $\overleftrightarrow{AB}$ is $\overleftrightarrow{A'B'}$, the image of $\overrightarrow{AB}$ is $\overrightarrow{A'B'}$, and the image of $\overline{AB}$ is $\overline{A'B'}$.

Note that while a dilation maps a segment onto a segment, the image and preimage are not congruent unless the scale factor is 1.

Exercises 17 and 18 ask for a Plan for Proof of each of the next two theorems. These theorems and their proofs are similar to Theorems 11.5 and 11.6 about isometries.

Theorem 11.16 A dilation preserves angle measure.

Theorem 11.17 Under a dilation, a triangle and its image are similar.

Recall that under a translation or a half-turn, a line is parallel to its image. This is also true for dilations.

Theorem 11.18 Under a dilation, a line and its image are parallel.

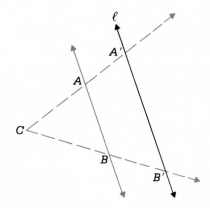

Given $\overleftrightarrow{AB}$; ℓ, the image of $\overleftrightarrow{AB}$ under a dilation with center C and scale factor k

Prove $\overleftrightarrow{AB} \parallel \ell$

Plan for Proof Let A' and B' be the images of A and B, respectively, under the dilation.
Use Thm. 11.15 to show that A' and B' are on ℓ.
Show from the def. of dilation that C is the intersection of $\overleftrightarrow{AA'}$ and $\overleftrightarrow{BB'}$.
Then use Thm. 11.16 and corr. ∠s to show $\overleftrightarrow{AB} \parallel \ell$.

Class Exercises

[1-14] A dilation with center C and scale factor 5 maps P onto P', Q onto Q', and R onto R'.

1. $CP = 3$; $CP' = $ _?_

3. $QR = 6$; $Q'R' = $ _?_

2. $CR' = 25$; $CR = $ _?_

4. $P'R' = 20$; $PR = $ _?_

5. If Q is between P and R, then _?_ is between _?_ and _?_ .

[6-10] State the image of each figure named below.

6. $\overline{PQ}$ **7.** $\overrightarrow{RP}$ **8.** $\overleftrightarrow{QR}$ **9.** $\angle RPQ$ **10.** $\triangle PQR$

11. If $m\angle PQR = 70$, then $m\angle P'Q'R' = $ _?_ .

12. $\triangle QRP$ _?_ $\triangle Q'R'P'$

13. $\overline{PR} \parallel$ _?_ and $\overline{QR} \parallel$ _?_

14. Explain how to find the image of any polygon under this dilation.

Written Exercises

Set A

[1-4] For each exercise, trace the diagram at the right. Draw the image of $\triangle ABC$ under the indicated dilation.

1. Center O and scale factor 2

2. Center O and scale factor $\frac{1}{2}$

3. Center A and scale factor $\frac{1}{3}$

4. Center A and scale factor 3

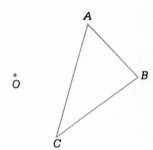

[5-8] For each exercise, trace the diagram at the right. Draw the image of $DEFGH$ under the indicated dilation.

5. Center Q and scale factor $\frac{3}{2}$

6. Center Q and scale factor $\frac{5}{2}$

7. Center P and scale factor $\frac{1}{2}$

8. Center P and scale factor 2

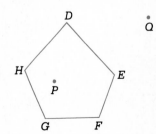

[9-12] For each exercise, graph $\triangle ABC$ with vertices $A(4, 4)$, $B(-2, 6)$, and $C(-2, 2)$. Find the image of $\triangle ABC$ under a dilation with center $O(0, 0)$ and scale factor k.

9. $k = 2$ **10.** $k = 3$ **11.** $k = \frac{1}{2}$ **12.** $k = 1$

Set B

[13-15] Trace this diagram.

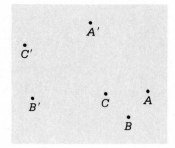

13. Find the center of the dilation that maps A onto A' and B onto B'.

14. Find the scale factor of the dilation described in exercise 13.

15. Is there a dilation that maps A onto A' and C onto C'? Explain.

16. Copy the diagram at the right. A dilation that maps A onto A' has its center on m. Find the image of B under this dilation.

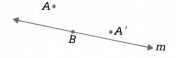

17. Write a Plan for Proof for Theorem 11.16.

18. Write a Plan for Proof for Theorem 11.17.

19. Does a dilation preserve orientation?

[20-21] Given: $\overline{QR} \parallel \overline{ST}$

20. Find the center and scale factor of the dilation that maps $\triangle PQR$ onto $\triangle PST$.

21. Find the center and scale factor of the dilation that maps $\triangle PST$ onto $\triangle PQR$.

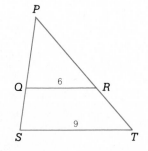

22. Prove that a dilation preserves perpendicularity of lines.

23. Prove that a dilation preserves parallelism of lines.

24. Prove that under the composite of a dilation followed by an isometry, a triangle and its image are similar.

Set C

25. In $\triangle ABC$, $\overline{AM}$ is a median and $\overline{EF} \parallel \overline{BC}$. Use a dilation to prove that $\overline{AM}$ bisects $\overline{EF}$.

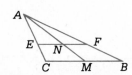

11.8   Congruence and Similarity Revisited

Theorem 11.6 states that under an isometry a triangle and its image are congruent. Do you think that the converse of Theorem 11.6 is also true?

Consider the congruent triangles shown at the right. A composite of line reflections that maps $\triangle ABC$ onto $\triangle A'B'C'$ can be specified as follows.

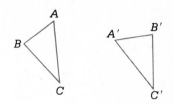

Let ℓ_1 be the perpendicular bisector of $\overline{AA'}$. $\triangle A'B_1C_1$ is the reflection image of $\triangle ABC$ over ℓ_1.

If $B_1 = B'$ and $C_1 = C'$, then ℓ_1 is the only line of reflection needed. If $B_1 \neq B'$, find a second line.

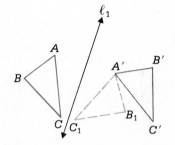

Let ℓ_2 be the perpendicular bisector of $\overline{B_1B'}$. $\triangle A'B'C_2$ is the reflection image of $\triangle A'B_1C_1$ over ℓ_2.

If $C_2 = C'$, then ℓ_1 and ℓ_2 are the only lines of reflection needed. If not, find a third line.

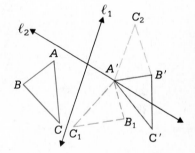

Let ℓ_3 be the perpendicular bisector of $\overline{C_2C'}$. $\triangle A'B'C'$ is the reflection image of $\triangle A'B'C_2$ over ℓ_3.

Thus, the composite of reflections over ℓ_1, ℓ_2, and ℓ_3, in that order, maps $\triangle ABC$ onto $\triangle A'B'C'$. This suggests Theorem 11.19, the converse of Theorem 11.6.

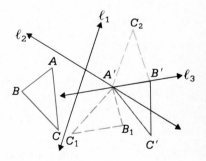

Theorem 11.19   In a plane, if $\triangle ABC \cong \triangle A'B'C'$, then there is a unique isometry that maps $\triangle ABC$ onto $\triangle A'B'C'$.

We can now give a definition of congruence which applies not only to triangles, but to all geometric figures in a plane.

Definition   Two plane figures are **congruent** if and only if there is an isometry that maps one figure onto the other.

In the Escher drawing below, figures 2 and 3 are point reflection images of each other. Hence, they are congruent.

Also, figures 1 and 3 are congruent because a translation maps one figure onto the other.

Theorem 11.19 guarantees that if two plane figures are congruent, there is a unique isometry that maps one figure onto the other. The method for specifying this isometry, as shown on page 517, suggests the following striking result.

Theorem 11.20   Every isometry can be expressed as a composite of at most three line reflections.

In the Escher print on page 519, some of the reptiles are congruent. Others are similarly shaped, but vary in size.

Figure 1 can be mapped onto figure 2 by a dilation with center C.

Figure 1 cannot be mapped onto figure 3 by a dilation alone. However, a dilation with center C followed by a clockwise rotation about C does map figure 1 onto figure 3. The dilation maps figure 1 onto figure 2; then the rotation maps figure 2 onto figure 3.

Definition	A **similarity transformation** is a composite of a dilation and an isometry.

Here are some examples of similarity transformations. The figures referred to are in the Escher print above.

Figures being mapped	Similarity Transformation
1 onto 2	Dilation, then identity transformation
1 onto 3	Dilation, then rotation
2 onto 3	Identity transformation (dilation with $k = 1$), then rotation

A composite of the identity and a second transformation is the second transformation. Thus, any isometry or dilation is itself a similarity transformation. Compare the next theorem with Theorem 11.19.

Theorem 11.21 In a plane, if $\triangle ABC \sim \triangle A'B'C'$, then there is a unique similarity transformation that maps $\triangle ABC$ onto $\triangle A'B'C'$.

Given $\triangle ABC \sim \triangle A'B'C'$

Prove   **Part I** There is a similarity transformation that maps $\triangle ABC$ onto $\triangle A'B'C'$.
Part II This transformation is unique.

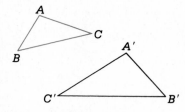

Plan for Proof   **Part I** Show that under a composite of a dilation and an isometry, $\triangle ABC$ can be mapped onto $\triangle A'B'C'$.

Let $\dfrac{A'B'}{AB} = \dfrac{B'C'}{BC} = \dfrac{A'C'}{AC} = k$.

Let the image of $\triangle ABC$ under a dilation with center A and scale factor k be $\triangle AB_1C_1$.
Show $\triangle AB_1C_1 \cong \triangle A'B'C'$.
Use Thm. 11.19 to show there is an isometry that maps $\triangle AB_1C_1$ onto $\triangle A'B'C'$.
Finally, show that the composite of these two mappings is a similarity transformation that maps $\triangle ABC$ onto $\triangle A'B'C'$.

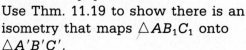

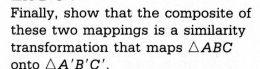

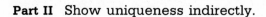

Part II Show uniqueness indirectly.

We can now give a general definition of similarity.

Definition   Two plane figures are **similar** if and only if there is a similarity transformation that maps one figure onto the other.

Class Exercises

1. If $\triangle ABC \cong \triangle DEF$ by the definition in Chapter 4, are they also congruent by the new definition? Explain.

2. If $\triangle ABC \cong \triangle DEF$ by the new definition, are they also congruent by the definition in Chapter 4? Explain.

3. If $\triangle ABC \sim \triangle DEF$ by the definition in Chapter 6, are they also similar by the new definition? Explain.

4. If $\triangle ABC \sim \triangle DEF$ by the new definition, are they also similar by the definition in Chapter 6? Explain.

[5-10] Explain why each transformation is a similarity transformation.

5. Line reflection   **8.** Enlargement

6. Translation   **9.** Reduction

7. Rotation   **10.** Identity transformation

[11-16] Is each property preserved by all similarity transformations? Explain.

11. Distance   **14.** Angle measure

12. Collinearity   **15.** Parallelism

13. Betweenness   **16.** Orientation

Written Exercises

Set A

[1-6] For each pair of congruent figures, name an isometry that appears to map one figure onto the other.

1.

3.

5.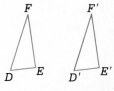

2.

4.

6.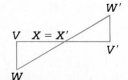

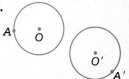

[7-8] For each pair of similar figures, find the scale factor of a dilation that will map figure I onto a figure congruent to figure II.

7.

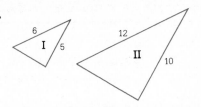

8.

[9-10] Suppose a tailor uses the pattern at the right to cut two front coat panels from the same bolt of fabric.

9. Will both panels be congruent? Why?

10. Suppose one panel is for the right side and the other is for the left side of the same coat. What must the tailor do with the pattern in cutting the second panel? Are the two panels still congruent?

11. Why is every similarity transformation equivalent to the composite of a dilation and at most three line reflections?

12. $\triangle ABC \sim \triangle A'B'C'$ and the triangles have the same orientation. Explain why the composite of a dilation and one line reflection will not map $\triangle ABC$ onto $\triangle A'B'C'$.

Set B

[13-18] Specify a similarity transformation that will map

13. $\triangle$I onto $\triangle$II

14. $\triangle$I onto $\triangle$III

15. $\triangle$II onto $\triangle$IV

16. $\triangle$I onto $\triangle$IV

17. $\triangle$V onto $\triangle$IV

18. $\triangle$V onto $\triangle$II

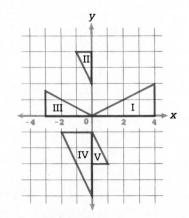

19. Explain why ⊙P with radius 7 is similar to ⊙Q with radius 15.

20. In a plane, suppose △ABC ~ △A'B'C'. Under what condition(s) will there be a unique dilation that maps △ABC onto △A'B'C'?

[21-22] A transformation maps each point A(x, y) of the coordinate plane onto B(x + 2y, y). For example, S(2, 3) is mapped onto T(8, 3).

21. Graph the rectangle with vertices O(0, 0), P(3, 0), Q(3, 2), and R(0, 2). Draw the image of OPQR.

22. Explain why this transformation is *not* a similarity transformation.

[23-24] At the right, the concentric circles are inscribed in squares. Assume the innermost circle has radius 1. Specify a similarity transformation that maps square ABCD onto square WXYZ so that the given conditions are met.

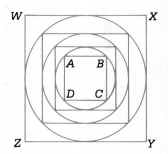

23. The image of A is W and the image of B is X.

24. The image of A is X and the image of B is Y.

Set C

25. Prove indirectly that the isometry in Theorem 11.19 is unique.

Construction Exercises

1. An isometry maps △ABC onto △PQR. Trace the diagram. Using only a compass, find the image of X under this isometry.

2. Trace the diagram. Construct appropriate lines so that △ABC is mapped onto △PQR under a composite of reflections over these lines.

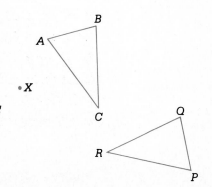

Chapter Summary

1. A transformation is a one-to-one correspondence between the points of a plane and themselves. (page 484)

2. Isometries are transformations that preserve distance. (page 485)

3. All isometries preserve distance, collinearity, betweenness, and angle measure. (pages 490-491)

4. Two plane figures are congruent if and only if there is an isometry that maps one figure onto the other. (page 518)

5. A figure may have line symmetry, point symmetry, rotational symmetry, or combinations of these. (page 507)

6. A dilation with scale factor k is an enlargement if $k > 1$, a reduction if $k < 1$, or the identity transformation if $k = 1$. (page 511)

7. Enlargements and reductions preserve collinearity, betweenness, and angle measure, but not distance. (pages 513-514)

8. The composite of a dilation and an isometry is called a similarity transformation. (page 519)

9. Two plane figures are similar if and only if there is a similarity transformation that maps one figure onto the other. (page 520)

The chart below shows the subset relationships for the transformations studied in this chapter.

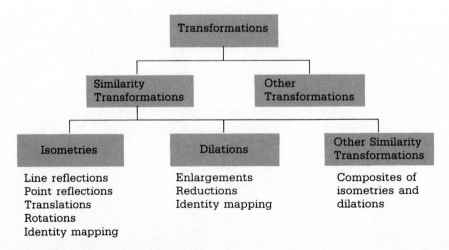

Chapter Review

Lesson 11.1
Page 484

[1-2] A' and B' are the reflection images of A and B, respectively, over line ℓ.

1. Name the reflection image of B'.

2. How is ℓ related to $\overline{AA'}$?

[3-4] A' and B' are the reflection images of A and B, respectively, through point O.

3. Name the point reflection image of A'.

4. How is O related to $\overline{BB'}$?

5. Under a line or point reflection which maps A onto A' and B onto B', which distances below are equal?

　a. AA'　　**b.** AB　　**c.** $A'B'$　　**d.** BB'

Lesson 11.2
Page 490

[6-8] An isometry maps X, Y, and Z onto X', Y', and Z', respectively.

6. If $XY = 11$, then $X'Y' = $ _?_ .

7. If Z is between X and Y, then _?_ is between _?_ and _?_ .

8. If $m \angle XZY = 32$, then $m \angle X'Z'Y' = $ _?_ .

Lesson 11.3
Page 494

9. A hockey player at A passes the puck to his teammate at B, first bouncing it off $\overline{FG}$. Find the path of the puck. Explain your solution.

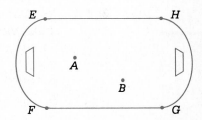

Lesson 11.4
Page 498

[10-17] Refer to the tessellation at the right. A translation maps A onto F. Name the image of:

10. B　　　**13.** $\overleftrightarrow{BF}$　　　**16.** $\triangle FGC$

11. E　　　**14.** $\angle FBC$　　　**17.** $\square BCGF$

12. $\overline{AB}$　　**15.** $\angle BGC$

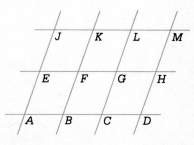

[18-23] Refer to this regular pentagon. A rotation about P maps A onto C. Name the image of:

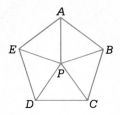

18. B **20.** $\overline{PB}$ **22.** $\angle EAP$

19. E **21.** $\overline{CD}$ **23.** $\triangle CPD$

24. What are the magnitude and direction of the rotation in exercises 18-23?

Lesson 11.5
Page 506

[25-27] Refer to the figures named below.

a. Segment   **d.** Equilateral triangle
b. Isosceles trapezoid   **e.** Parallelogram
c. Regular pentagon   **f.** Regular hexagon

25. How many lines of symmetry has each figure?

26. Which figures have point symmetry?

27. Which figures have rotational symmetry?

Lesson 11.6
Page 510

[28-29] X' and Y' are the images of X and Y, respectively, under a dilation with center C and scale factor $\frac{3}{2}$.

28. If $CX = 8$, then $CX' = \underline{\ ?\ }$.

29. If $X'Y' = 18$, then $XY = \underline{\ ?\ }$.

Lesson 11.7
Page 513

30. A triangle and its image under a dilation are $\underline{\ ?\ }$.

[31-32] Given: $\overline{DE} \parallel \overline{BC}$. Specify the center and scale factor of a dilation that maps:

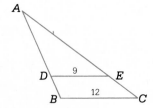

31. $\triangle ADE$ onto $\triangle ABC$

32. $\triangle ABC$ onto $\triangle ADE$

Lesson 11.8
Page 517

33. No more than $\underline{\ ?\ }$ line reflections are needed to express any isometry.

34. Name three properties preserved by all similarity transformations.

35. At the right, $\triangle ABC$ and $\triangle CDE$ are equilateral. Specify a similarity transformation that maps $\triangle ACB$ onto $\triangle DCE$.

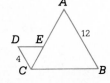

Chapter Test

[1-5] Tell whether each statement is true or false. If false, explain.

1. Isometries preserve angle measure.

2. If A' and B' are the images of A and B, respectively, under an isometry, then $AA' = BB'$.

3. The image of a square under a dilation is a square.

4. The composite of a dilation and a rotation is a similarity transformation.

5. A figure with rotational symmetry has line symmetry.

[6-11] Refer to this tessellation with equilateral triangles.

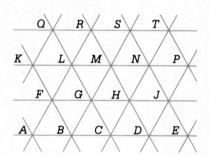

6. Name the reflection image of $\overline{FG}$ over $\overleftrightarrow{FB}$.

7. A translation maps A onto F. Name the image of $\angle LGM$.

8. State the magnitude and direction of a rotation about M that maps N onto G.

9. Name the image of $\triangle LMG$ under a half-turn about G.

10. Name the image of $\triangle QCT$ under a dilation with center C and scale factor $\frac{2}{3}$.

11. Specify a similarity transformation that maps $\triangle ABF$ onto $\triangle BES$.

12. Jim, at point J, needs to get water at the river on the way to his campsite at C. Trace this diagram and draw the shortest route possible.

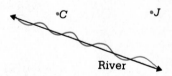

[13-14] Draw the figure described. If impossible, so state.

13. A quadrilateral with rotational symmetry but no line symmetry

14. A triangle with exactly two lines of symmetry

Using Coordinates in Geometry

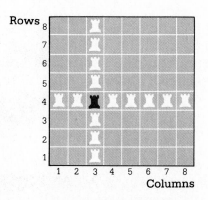

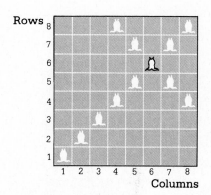

Coordinates can be assigned to a chessboard and used to record moves in a game and the position of each piece. For example, the black *rook* in column 3, row 4 is at square (3, 4).

A rook can be moved horizontally or vertically any number of squares. If we use variables to represent the column *c* and row *r* of a square (c, r), we can describe every square in the same column as the rook with the equation $c = 3$.

1. List every square in the same row as the rook.

2. What equation would you use to describe the squares in the same row as the rook?

A *bishop* can be moved diagonally any number of squares. The diagram at the right above shows how the white bishop in the photograph might be moved.

3. List all the squares shown on the long diagonal (from the lower left to the upper right) to which the bishop can be moved. Write an equation using *c* and *r* to describe all of these squares.

4. List all the squares shown on the shorter diagonal to which the bishop can be moved. Can you write an equation to describe these squares?

12.1   Slopes of Lines

The *grade* of a road is a measure of its steepness. It is the ratio, expressed as a percent, of the vertical distance (rise) between two points to the horizontal distance (run). For example, a car driven up the ramp above moves 4 feet up and 50 feet to the right.

$$\frac{\text{rise}}{\text{run}} = \frac{4}{50} = 0.08$$

Thus, the ramp has a grade of 8%.

The ratio of the rise to the run is also used to measure the steepness of a line or segment in the coordinate plane.

Definition

The **slope** m of a nonvertical line that contains two points $P(x_1, y_1)$ and $Q(x_2, y_2)$ is

$$m = \frac{y_2 - y_1}{x_2 - x_1}.$$

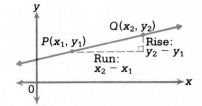

Example 1

Find the slope of the line that contains $A(-2, 1)$ and $B(2, 3)$.

Solution

$$m = \frac{y_2 - y_1}{x_2 - x_1} = \frac{3 - 1}{2 - (-2)} = \frac{1}{2}$$

What would the slope be if you reversed the choices for (x_1, y_1) and (x_2, y_2) in this example?

Point $C(4, 4)$ also lies on $\overleftrightarrow{AB}$ in example 1. What would the slope be if you used A and C to compute it? B and C? Your answers should suggest that the slope of a given line is the same regardless of which two points on the line are used to compute the slope.

The general orientation of a line is indicated by the
sign of its slope.

A line such as $\overleftrightarrow{AB}$ that
slants upward to the right
has positive slope.

A line such as $\overleftrightarrow{CD}$ that
slants downward to the
right has negative slope.

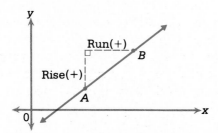

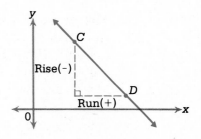

A horizontal line such as
$\overleftrightarrow{EF}$ has a slope of zero:

$y_1 = y_2$, so $\dfrac{y_2 - y_1}{x_2 - x_1} = 0.$

The slope of a vertical
line such as $\overleftrightarrow{GH}$ is
undefined. Why?

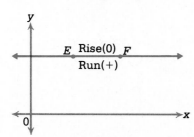

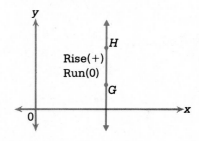

Example 2

Given: $O(0, 0)$, $P(6, 0)$, $Q(9, 5)$, and $R(3, 5)$. Compute
the slope of each side of $\square OPQR$.

Solution

Slope of $\overline{OP} = \dfrac{0 - 0}{6 - 0} = 0$

Slope of $\overline{PQ} = \dfrac{5 - 0}{9 - 6} = \dfrac{5}{3}$

Slope of $\overline{QR} = \dfrac{5 - 5}{3 - 9} = 0$

Slope of $\overline{RO} = \dfrac{0 - 5}{0 - 3} = \dfrac{5}{3}$

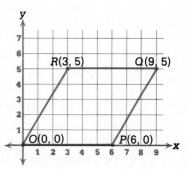

Note that the opposite sides of $OPQR$, which are parallel
to each other, have the same slope. This should suggest
Theorems 12.1 and 12.2 which follow.

12.1 Slopes of Lines

If two nonvertical lines are parallel, then they have equal slopes.

Given   Nonvertical lines h and j with slopes m_1 and m_2, respectively; $h \parallel j$

Prove $m_1 = m_2$

Proof   **Case I** h and j are parallel to the x-axis. Then each line has slope zero and $m_1 = m_2$.

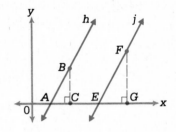

Case II h and j intersect the x-axis and have positive slopes. Let A and E, respectively, be the points of intersection with the x-axis. Let B and F be points on each line on the same side of the x-axis. Draw $\overline{BC}$ and $\overline{FG}$ so that each is perpendicular to the x-axis. Since $\triangle ACB \sim \triangle EGF$, by the AA Postulate,
$$\frac{BC}{FG} = \frac{AC}{EG}, \text{ so } \frac{BC}{AC} = \frac{FG}{EG}.$$
$\dfrac{BC}{AC} = m_1$, $\dfrac{FG}{EG} = m_2$. Thus, $m_1 = m_2$.

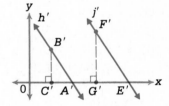

Case III h' and j' intersect the x-axis and have negative slopes. Then by an argument as in Case II,
$$m_1 = -\frac{B'C'}{A'C'} \text{ and } m_2 = -\frac{F'G'}{E'G'},$$
so $m_1 = m_2$.

Theorem 12.2   If two nonvertical lines have equal slopes, then they are parallel.

Given   Nonvertical lines s and t with slopes m_1 and m_2, respectively; $m_1 = m_2$

Prove $s \parallel t$

Proof   **Case I** $m_1 = m_2 = 0$. Then the lines are both parallel to the x-axis and thus are parallel to each other.

Case II $m_1 = m_2 \neq 0$. Choose A, B, C, E, F, and G as in Theorem 12.1.

Then $\dfrac{BC}{AC} = \dfrac{FG}{EG}$. By the SAS $\sim$ Theorem, $\triangle ACB \sim \triangle EGF$ and $\angle BAC \cong \angle FEG$. Then $s \parallel t$ by the Parallel Lines Postulate.

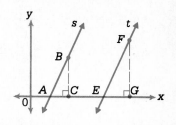

Example 3

Given: $M(8, 4)$, $N(3, 4)$, $O(0, 0)$, and $P(5, 0)$. Show that $MNOP$ is a rhombus and compute the slopes of the diagonals.

Solution

Use the distance formula to compute the length of each side.

$$MN = \sqrt{(8-3)^2 + (4-4)^2} = \sqrt{25} = 5$$
$$NO = \sqrt{(3-0)^2 + (4-0)^2} = \sqrt{9+16} = 5$$
$$OP = \sqrt{(0-5)^2 + (0-0)^2} = \sqrt{25} = 5$$
$$PM = \sqrt{(5-8)^2 + (0-4)^2} = \sqrt{9+16} = 5$$

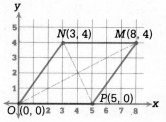

Since all four sides are congruent, $MNOP$ is both a parallelogram and a rhombus.

Slope of $\overline{MO} = \dfrac{4-0}{8-0} = \dfrac{1}{2}$ Slope of $\overline{NP} = \dfrac{4-0}{3-5} = -\dfrac{2}{1}$

Note that the product of the slopes of the diagonals is -1; that is, the two slopes are negative reciprocals of each other. Recall that the diagonals of a rhombus are perpendicular to each other. This relationship between slopes of perpendicular lines is true in general.

Theorem 12.3

Two nonvertical lines are perpendicular if and only if the slope m_1 of one line is the negative reciprocal of the slope m_2 of the other line.

$$m_1 = -\frac{1}{m_2}, \text{ or } m_1 m_2 = -1$$

The proof of Theorem 12.3 is omitted. Why is the word *nonvertical* needed?

Class Exercises

Classify the slope of the given line as positive, negative, zero, or undefined.

1.

2.

3.

4.

Find the slope of the line containing the given points.

5. $A(3, 7)$, $B(5, -2)$ **6.** $C(4, -3)$, $D(6, -2)$

Write the negative reciprocal.

7. $-\frac{4}{7}$ **8.** $\frac{21}{3}$ **9.** $\frac{c}{d}$ **10.** $-r$

Given: $J(-3, 5)$, $K(-1, 2)$, $L(4, 1)$, and $M(2, 4)$

11. Show that $\overleftrightarrow{JK} \parallel \overleftrightarrow{ML}$.

12. Show that $\overleftrightarrow{JK} \perp \overleftrightarrow{KM}$.

13. Show that the diagonals of $\square JKLM$ bisect each other.

Written Exercises

Set A

Find the slope of the line containing the given points.

1. $A(-1, 1)$, $B(7, 4)$ **3.** $E(-7, -3)$, $F(-7, 10)$

2. $C(4, -3)$, $D(8, -3)$ **4.** $G(-2, -5)$, $Q(-5, -4)$

Give the slope of a line parallel to $\overleftrightarrow{AB}$.

5. $A(7, 12)$, $B(-1, -4)$ **7.** $A(c, d)$, $B(e, f)$

6. $A(-5, -8)$, $B(4, 9)$ **8.** $A(r, s)$, $B(u, v)$

Give the slope of a line perpendicular to $\overleftrightarrow{CD}$.

9. $C(5, 3)$, $D(2, 7)$ **11.** $C(a, 0)$, $D(b, 0)$

10. $C(-3, -5)$, $D(-2, -7)$ **12.** $C(0, a)$, $D(0, b)$

    Chapter 12 Using Coordinates in Geometry

13. One turn of the Daytona International Speedway is banked so that it rises 3 feet vertically for each 5 feet of horizontal distance. What is the grade of this bank?

14. The Federal Highway Commission recommends a maximum grade of 12% for a road. What is the maximum vertical rise for a section of road covering 100 ft. of horizontal distance?

Set B

Given: $P(-6, 1)$, $Q(-2, 0)$, $R(1, 1)$, $S(5, 0)$, $T(-1, -2)$, and $U(0, -3)$

15. Show that $\overleftrightarrow{PQ} \parallel \overleftrightarrow{RS}$.   **17.** Show that $\overleftrightarrow{PQ} \perp \overleftrightarrow{RU}$.

16. Show that $\overleftrightarrow{QR} \parallel \overleftrightarrow{ST}$.   **18.** Show that $\overleftrightarrow{RS} \perp \overleftrightarrow{RU}$.

Given: $S(-5, 5)$, $E(0, 8)$, $N(6, -2)$, and $D(1, -5)$

19. Show that $SEND$ is a parallelogram.

20. Show that $\triangle END$ is a right triangle.

21. Show that the sides of $\square SEND$ are perpendicular.

22. Show that the diagonals of $\square SEND$ are congruent.

Given: $T(1, 3)$, $A(5, 0)$, $K(2, -4)$, and $E(-2, -1)$

23. Show that $\triangle TEA$ is isosceles.

24. Show that $TAKE$ is a parallelogram.

25. Show that $\square TAKE$ has four congruent sides.

26. Show that the diagonals of $\square TAKE$ are perpendicular bisectors of each other.

27. The vertical height of a ski hill is 50 meters. Find d, the distance down the hill, if its slope is $\frac{1}{8}$.

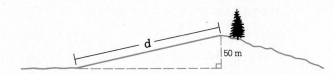

28. A driveway from a street to a garage has a grade of 30%. The end of the driveway is 1.5 meters higher than the street level. How long is the driveway?

29. For points $P(3, 5)$ and $Q(a, b)$, what is the slope of a line parallel to $\overleftrightarrow{PQ}$? Perpendicular to $\overleftrightarrow{PQ}$?

30. Show that $\overleftrightarrow{EF} \perp \overleftrightarrow{GH}$ for points $E(a, b)$, $F(c, d)$, $G(b, c)$, and $H(d, a)$.

Find n so that $\overleftrightarrow{AB}$ has the given slope.

31. $A(5, -2)$, $B(-4, n)$; slope 0

32. $A(3, n)$, $B(8, 1)$; slope -2

33. $A(n + 1, n)$, $B(n - 1, 1)$; slope $\frac{1}{2}$

34. $A(-1, n - 1)$, $B(n - 1, n)$; slope $\frac{1}{3}$

The point $P(4, 7)$ is on a line. Give the coordinates of another point on the line with the given slope.

35. $-\frac{5}{3}$ **36.** $\frac{4}{3}$ **37.** 0 **38.** Undefined

Given: $P(x_1, y_1)$, $Q(x_2, y_2)$, $R(x_3, y_3)$, and $S(x_4, y_4)$, all on line k; $\overline{PT}$ and $\overline{RU}$ horizontal; $\overline{QT}$ and $\overline{SU}$ vertical

39. Why is $\angle QPT \cong \angle SRU$?

40. Why is $\triangle PTQ \sim \triangle RUS$?

41. $\dfrac{QT}{PT} = \dfrac{?}{?}$

42. Write the distances in exercise 41 using the coordinates of the points. Rewrite the proportion.

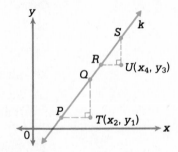

Set C

43. A line with slope 4 contains $A(3, 2)$. Is $B(5, 10)$ on this line?

44. Given: $J(0, 8)$, $K(-2, -9)$, and $L(3, y)$ are collinear. Find y.

45. Are $X(4, 3)$, $Y(-2, -9)$, and $Z(7, 9)$ collinear?

46. Given: $A(-2, -6)$, $B(4, -3)$, $C(7, 1)$, and $D(2, 4)$. Show that the segments joining the midpoints of consecutive sides of $ABCD$ form a parallelogram.

Through $A(3, 2)$, there is exactly one line with slope $\frac{1}{2}$. Call the line j. If (x, y) is another point on j, then

$$\frac{1}{2} = \frac{y - 2}{x - 3}, \text{ or } y - 2 = \frac{1}{2}(x - 3)$$

The second equation describes every point on j; if a point is on j, then its coordinates satisfy the equation. Conversely, a point must be on j if its coordinates satisfy the equation. These facts suggest Theorem 12.4.

Theorem 12.4
The graph of the equation $y - y_1 = m(x - x_1)$ is the nonvertical line ℓ that has slope m and contains $P(x_1, y_1)$.

Part I
All points on ℓ satisfy the equation.

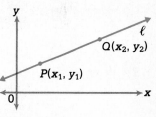

Given
Nonvertical line ℓ through $P(x_1, y_1)$ with slope m; $Q(x_2, y_2)$ is on ℓ.

Prove
The coordinates of Q satisfy the equation $y - y_1 = m(x - x_1)$.

Proof
Case I P and Q coincide. Then $x_1 = x_2$ and $y_1 = y_2$, so $x_2 - x_1 = 0$ and $y_2 - y_1 = 0$. Thus $y_2 - y_1 = m(x_2 - x_1)$.

Case II P and Q are distinct. Then $x_1 \neq x_2$. By definition, $m = \dfrac{y_2 - y_1}{x_2 - x_1}$. So $y_2 - y_1 = m(x_2 - x_1)$.

Part II
All points that satisfy the equation are on ℓ.

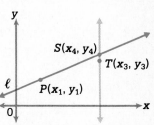

Given
Any point T whose coordinates satisfy $y - y_1 = m(x - x_1)$

Prove
T is on the nonvertical line ℓ through $P(x_1, y_1)$ with slope m.

Proof
Let (x_3, y_3) be the coordinates of T. Suppose T is *not* on ℓ. Then a vertical line through T will intersect ℓ in a point $S(x_4, y_4)$, where $x_3 = x_4$, but $y_3 \neq y_4$. $m = \dfrac{y_4 - y_1}{x_4 - x_1}$, so $y_4 = m(x_4 - x_1) + y_1$. Substitution gives $y_4 = m(x_3 - x_1) + y_1$ and $y_3 \neq m(x_3 - x_1) + y_1$. But this contradicts the Given. We conclude that T is on ℓ.

An equation of a line in the form $y - y_1 = m(x - x_1)$ is said to be in **point-slope** form.

Example 1

Write an equation in point-slope form of the line with slope $\frac{2}{3}$ that contains the point $P(3, 4)$.

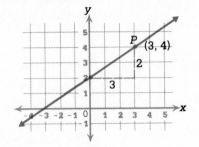

Solution

$y - y_1 = m(x - x_1)$
$y - 4 = \frac{2}{3}(x - 3)$

This equation may also be written as $y = \frac{2}{3}x + 2$. If we let $x = 0$, then $y = 2$. The point $Q(0, 2)$ is where the line intersects the y-axis. The y-coordinate of this point is called the **y-intercept** of the line. The equation $y = \frac{2}{3}x + 2$ is an instance of the general form $y = mx + b$, where m is the slope of the line and b is the y-intercept.

Theorem 12.5

The graph of the equation $y = mx + b$ is the nonvertical line with slope m and y-intercept b.

If line ℓ has slope m and y-intercept b, then by Theorem 12.4, its equation is $y - b = m(x - 0)$, or $y = mx + b$. So Theorem 12.5 is a corollary of Theorem 12.4.

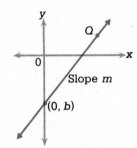

An equation of a line in the form $y = mx + b$ is said to be in **slope-intercept** form.

Example 2

Write an equation of the line with y-intercept 3 and slope 2. Graph the line.

Solution

Use $y = mx + b$ to write the equation.

$$y = 2x + 3$$

To graph the line, find two or more points on the line.

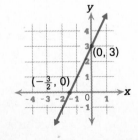

If $x = 0$, then $y = 3$.
If $y = 0$, then $2x + 3 = 0$, or $x = -\frac{3}{2}$.

In example 2, it was convenient to let $x = 0$ to find the y-intercept 3. Another point with easily computed coordinates is the intersection of the line with the x-axis. The x-coordinate of this point is called the **x-intercept** of the line; its y-coordinate is zero.

Example 3   Write an equation of the line which contains the two points $S(3, -5)$ and $T(5, 7)$. Give the y-intercept of the line.

Solution   Find the slope of the line: $m = \dfrac{y_2 - y_1}{x_2 - x_1} = \dfrac{7 - (-5)}{5 - 3} = 6.$

Now use the point-slope form of an equation of a line and the coordinates of either S or T.

Using T: $y - 7 = 6(x - 5)$. This is one solution for the first part.

To find the y-intercept, either (a) write the equation in slope-intercept form, or (b) let $x = 0$ in the equation and solve for y.

Using method (a): $\quad y - 7 = 6x - 30$
$$y = 6x - 23$$

The y-intercept is -23.

Class Exercises

1. Write an equation of the line in example 3 in point-slope form using point S. Then solve for the y-intercept by letting $x = 0$ in this equation.

Give the slope and the coordinates of one point on the line described by the given equation.

2. $y - 1 = \frac{2}{3}(x + 4)$ 3. $y - 5 = 3x$ 4. $y = 2(x - 6)$

Write an equation for each line described. Give the x- and y-intercepts and graph the equation.

5. The line that contains $P(5, -4)$ and has slope $-\frac{2}{5}$
6. The line that contains $A(-2, 5)$ and $B(4, -1)$

Written Exercises

Set A

Graph each equation.

1. $y - 2 = \frac{1}{3}(x + 6)$ **2.** $y + 1 = \frac{1}{2}(x - 2)$

Graph the three given equations on one set of axes.

3. a. $y = 2x$ **b.** $y = 2x + 1$ **c.** $y = 2x - 3$

4. a. $y = -\frac{1}{3}x + 2$ **b.** $y = 2x + 2$ **c.** $y = -2x + 2$

Write an equation of the line containing P with slope m.

5. $P(1, 4);\ m = \frac{1}{2}$ **8.** $P(3, 0);\ m = -\frac{5}{4}$

6. $P(6, 2);\ m = \frac{3}{4}$ **9.** $P(0, 5);\ m = -\frac{3}{4}$

7. $P(4, -3);\ m = 0$ **10.** $P(-2, 1);\ m = -2$

Write an equation of the line with slope m and y-intercept b.

11. $m = \frac{2}{3};\ b = 8$ **13.** $m = \frac{4}{3};\ b = \frac{2}{3}$

12. $m = -2;\ b = -3$ **14.** $m = 0;\ b = \frac{1}{2}$

Write an equation of the line through the given points.

15. $A(3, 2);\ B(5, 1)$ **18.** $G(-5, 8);\ H(-5, -6)$

16. $D(3, 5);\ C(2, 3)$ **19.** $J(0, 3);\ K(4, 0)$

17. $E(-6, -3);\ F(2, -3)$ **20.** $L(0, -2);\ M(-6, 0)$

21. Write an equation of the vertical line through $S(50, 25)$.

22. Write an equation of the horizontal line through $B(-6, 4)$.

Set B

[23-30] Write an equation of the line that:

23. Contains the origin and is parallel to the line whose equation is $y = \frac{2}{3}x + 6$.

24. Contains the origin and is perpendicular to the line whose equation is $y = -5x - 9$.

25. Contains $B(-2, 4)$ and is perpendicular to the line whose equation is $y - 1 = -\frac{3}{5}(x + 6)$.

26. Contains $D(7, -6)$ and is parallel to the line whose equation is $y + 7 = 9(x - 4)$.

27. Has y-intercept -4 and is parallel to the line whose equation is $y = -\frac{4}{3}x - 6$.

28. Has x-intercept 6 and is perpendicular to the line whose equation is $y - 4 = -\frac{3}{4}(x + 4)$.

29. Has slope 5 and contains the midpoint of the segment joining $A(3, 8)$ and $B(-5, -2)$.

30. Is the perpendicular bisector of $\overline{CD}$ with $C(0, 6)$ and $D(10, -8)$.

During a submarine's test dive, a ship followed directly above it on the surface. The submarine was 25 m deep when the ship had gone 300 m from the point of submergence, and 75 m deep when the ship had gone 900 m.

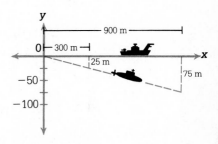

31. Write an equation for the path of the submarine.

32. How deep was the submarine when the ship had gone 1140 m from the point of submergence?

Set C

[33-34] Equations of lines and other curves are important tools for programming computer graphics. The display below shows the graph $\overline{OP}$ of $y = 8x$ for $0 \le x \le 1$.

33. Draw $\overline{OP_1}$, the reflection image of $\overline{OP}$ over the y-axis. Write an equation for $\overline{OP_1}$. Do $\overline{OP}$ and $\overline{OP_1}$ form a symmetric figure?

34. A translation maps $O(0, 0)$ onto $Q(-4, 5)$. Draw $\overline{QP_2}$, the image of $\overline{OP}$ under this translation. Write an equation for $\overline{QP_2}$. Do $\overline{OP}$ and $\overline{QP_2}$ form a symmetric figure?

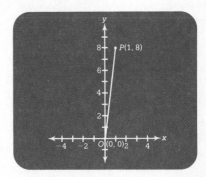

35. Given: $\triangle DEF$; $D(-2, -5)$, $E(4, -3)$, $F(2, 7)$. Write an equation of the line passing through the midpoints of $\overline{DE}$ and $\overline{DF}$. Show that this line is parallel to $\overleftrightarrow{EF}$.

12.3 Standard Form for Equations of Lines and Circles

An equation of a line such as $y + 5 = 6(x - 3)$ is in point-slope form. The equation can also be written $6x - y = 23$. This is in the **standard form** $Ax + By = C$, where A, B, and C are integers. In this case, $A = 6$, $B = -1$, and $C = 23$.

Definition

A **linear equation in x and y** is an equation that can be written in the form $Ax + By = C$, with A and B not both zero.

Theorem 12.6

The graph of an equation in x and y is a line if and only if the equation is a linear equation.

Part I Any line can be described with a linear equation.

Given Any line ℓ

Prove There is an equation for ℓ of the form $Ax + By = C$ with A and B not both zero.

Proof **Case I** ℓ is vertical. Then it has an equation $x = C$, which is of the form $(1)x + (0)y = C$.

Case II ℓ is nonvertical. Then it has slope m and intersects the y-axis in some point $(0, b)$. By Thm. 12.5, ℓ has an equation $y = mx + b$, or $(m)x + (-1)y = -b$.

Part II The graph of any linear equation is a line.

Given An equation $Ax + By = C$ with A and B not both zero.

Prove The graph of $Ax + By = C$ is a line ℓ.

Proof **Case I** $B = 0$. Then $Ax = C$, or $x = \dfrac{C}{A}$.
The graph of this equation is a vertical line.

Case II $B \neq 0$. Then solving $Ax + By = C$ for y gives

$$y = -\frac{A}{B}x + \frac{C}{B}.$$ By Theorem 12.5, the graph of this equation

is a line ℓ with slope $-\dfrac{A}{B}$ and y-intercept $\dfrac{C}{B}$.

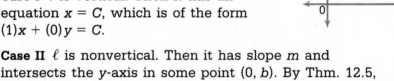

Example 1   Write an equation in standard form for the line with slope $-\frac{3}{2}$ and y-intercept 3. Graph the equation.

Solution   Begin with point-slope form, $y = mx + b$.

$$y = -\frac{3}{2}x + 3$$
$$2y = -3x + 6$$
$$3x + 2y = 6$$

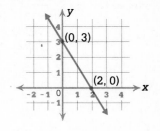

Example 2   Graph the linear equations:

a. $2x - 3y = 6$ **b.** $2x - 3y = -3$ **c.** $2x - 3y = -9.$

Solution   Find the intercepts and use them to graph the lines.

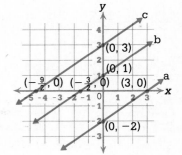

	x-intercept: if $y = 0$, then	y-intercept: if $x = 0$, then
a.	$x = 3$	$y = -2$
b.	$x = -\frac{3}{2}$	$y = 1$
c.	$x = -\frac{9}{2}$	$y = 3$

The equations in example 2 can be written in slope-intercept form. What is true of the slopes of the three lines?

The photo at the right is a radar image of a hurricane. The radius of the innermost circle is 25 km. The distance formula can be used to write an equation of the circle. Let $P(x, y)$ be any point on the circle. Since $OP = 25$,

$$\sqrt{(x - 0)^2 + (y - 0)^2} = 25$$
$$\sqrt{x^2 + y^2} = 25$$
$$x^2 + y^2 = 625$$

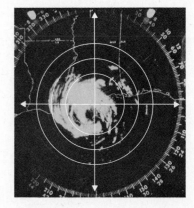

This is the equation of the circle. That is, *all* points on this circle and *only* these points have coordinates that satisfy the equation.

The distance formula can also be used to derive an equation of a circle with radius r and center $A(h, k)$.

Let $P(x, y)$ be any point on the circle. The distance from A to P is $AP = \sqrt{(x - h)^2 + (y - k)^2}$.

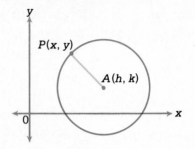

Since $AP = r$,

$$\sqrt{(x - h)^2 + (y - k)^2} = r$$
$$(x - h)^2 + (y - k)^2 = r^2$$

This establishes Theorem 12.7.

Theorem 12.7   The equation of a circle with center (h, k) and radius r is $(x - h)^2 + (y - k)^2 = r^2$.

Example 3   Graph the equations:
a. $x^2 + y^2 = 4$,

b. $[x - (-4)]^2 + (y - 2)^2 = 9$.

Solution   a. Since $r^2 = 4$, $r = 2$. The center is $(0, 0)$.

b. Since $r^2 = 9$, $r = 3$. The center is $(-4, 2)$.

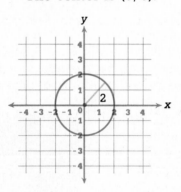

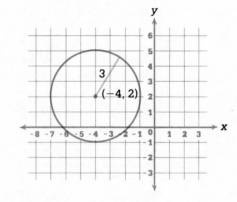

Class Exercises

Find the slope and y-intercept of the line with the given equation.

1. $x - y = 6$ 3. $3x + 2y = 8$

2. $2x - 3y = 9$ 4. $y = 7$

Find the x- and y-intercepts of the line with equation:

5. $x + 2y = -6$ **6.** $-4x + y = 8$ **7.** $x = -5$

Find the radius and center of the circle with the given equation.

8. $x^2 + y^2 = 9$ **9.** $(x + 1)^2 + y^2 = 16$

10. Write an equation of a circle with center (1, 3) and radius 2. Graph the equation.

Written Exercises

Set A

Find the slope and y-intercept of the line with the given equation. Graph the equations in exercises 2 and 3.

1. $3x - 5y = 10$ **2.** $-2x + y = -8$ **3.** $7x + 3y = 3$

Find the x- and y-intercepts of the line with the given equation. Graph the equations in exercises 5 and 6.

4. $x + 3y = -12$ **5.** $30x + 10y = 30$ **6.** $-4x + 3y = -24$

Write an equation in standard form for each line described.

7. The line that contains $P(3, 2)$ and is parallel to the line whose equation is $-x + 2y = 6$.

8. The line that has y-intercept 4 and is perpendicular to the line whose equation is $-8x + 9y = -2$.

Find the radius and center of the circle with the given equation. Graph the equations in exercises 9 and 10.

9. $x^2 + y^2 = 36$ **11.** $(x + 11)^2 + (y - 2)^2 = a^2$

10. $(x - 2)^2 + (y + 3)^2 = 25$ **12.** $x^2 + y^2 = \frac{1}{4}$

Tell whether the given point is on the circle whose equation is $x^2 + y^2 = 25$.

13. $A(-3, 4)$ **15.** $C(16, 9)$ **17.** $E(0, 5)$

14. $B(-3, -4)$ **16.** $D(11, 14)$ **18.** $F(0, 25)$

19. Graph the following equations on one set of axes.
   a. $x - 2y = -4$
   b. $3x - y = 3$
   c. The equation which results from adding the equations in parts **a** and **b**

20. Graph the following equations on one set of axes.
   a. The equation obtained by multiplying each term of $x - 2y = -4$ by 5
   b. The equation obtained by multiplying each term of $3x - y = 3$ by -3
   c. The equation which results from adding the equations in parts **a** and **b**

21. Write an equation of the circle with center $A(5, 8)$ and radius 7.

22. Write an equation of the circle with center $B(-2, 8)$ and radius 5.

Write an equation of the circle whose center is the origin and which passes through the given point.

23. $A(8, 15)$ **24.** $B(5, 12)$ **25.** $C(0, -t)$ **26.** $D(4a, 3a)$

27. Does the point $O(0, 0)$ lie on the circle whose radius is 17 and whose center is $A(8, 15)$? Explain.

28. Does the point $P(4, -3)$ lie on the circle with center $A(-4, 3)$ and radius 7? Explain.

[29-31] Given: $A(-4, 0)$, $B(4, 8)$, and $C(6, -3)$. Write an equation in standard form for each line described.

29. Each line containing a median of $\triangle ABC$

30. Each line containing an altitude of $\triangle ABC$

31. The perpendicular bisector of each side of $\triangle ABC$

32. Graph the circle with equation $x^2 - 10x + y^2 - 6y = 30$.

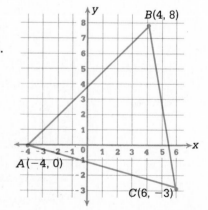

Progress Check

Lesson 12.1
Page 530

1. Given: $A(3, 8)$ and $B(-7, -4)$. Find the slope of $\overleftrightarrow{AB}$.
2. Find n so that the line through $(-3, n - 2)$ and $(n, 1)$ has a slope of $-\frac{1}{3}$.
3. What is the slope of a line parallel to the x-axis?

Given: $C(1, 2)$, $D(-4, 5)$, $E(-4, 7)$, and $F(5, 4)$

4. Find the slope of a line parallel to $\overleftrightarrow{CD}$.
5. Find the slope of a line perpendicular to $\overleftrightarrow{EF}$.

Given: $H(6, -3)$, $J(4, 1)$, $K(p, 4)$, and $L(-5, 6)$

6. Find p so that $\overleftrightarrow{HJ} \| \overleftrightarrow{KL}$.
7. Find p so that $\overleftrightarrow{HJ} \perp \overleftrightarrow{KL}$.

8. Given: $N(3, -1)$, $O(0, 0)$, and $P(2, 6)$. Show that $\triangle NOP$ is a right triangle.

Lesson 12.2
Page 537

[9-11] Write an equation of the line described.

9. The line that contains $A(-7, 9)$ and has slope $\frac{2}{3}$
10. The line that has slope $-\frac{5}{6}$ and y-intercept -4
11. The line that contains $C(-3, 5)$ and $D(7, -4)$

12. Graph the equation of the line in exercise 9.
13. Graph the equation of the line in exercise 10.

14. What is the x-intercept of the line with slope 3 through the point $P(-1, 6)$?

Lesson 12.3
Page 542

15. Find the slope and y-intercept of the line whose equation is $2x + 3y = 9$. Graph the equation.
16. Find the x- and y-intercepts of the line with equation $-3x + 5y = 15$. Graph the equation.
17. Write an equation in standard form of the line that contains $E(5, -3)$ and is perpendicular to the line whose equation is $-2x + 9y = 18$.
18. Find the center and radius of a circle whose equation is $(x - 3)^2 + (y + 4)^2 = 25$. Graph the equation.

12.4   Intersection of Lines

You know that if two distinct lines intersect, they intersect in one and only one point. So you would expect the coordinates of only one point to satisfy the equations of the two intersecting lines. These coordinates can be estimated by graphing the two lines. Exact values can be found algebraically.

Example 1

Graph the following pair of equations and estimate the coordinates of the point of intersection:

$$x + 2y = 6$$
$$3x - y = 3$$

Solution

Find the intercepts to graph the lines.

$x + 2y = 6$:
    if $x = 0$, then $y = 3$;
    if $y = 0$, then $x = 6$.

$3x - y = 3$:
    if $x = 0$, then $y = -3$;
    if $y = 0$, then $x = 1$.

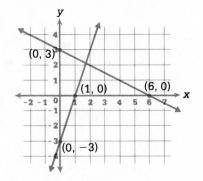

Answer

The approximate coordinates of the point of intersection are $(2, 2)$.

Example 2

Find the exact values of the coordinates of the point of intersection of the two lines in example 1.

Solution

(1) $x + 2y = 6$
(2) $3x - y = 3$

(3) $-3x - 6y = -18$ Multiply both sides of equation (1)
(2) $\underline{3x - y = 3}$ by -3. Copy equation (2).

$-7y = -15$ Add equations (3) and (2).

$y = \frac{15}{7}$

$x + 2\left(\frac{15}{7}\right) = 6$ Substitute $\frac{15}{7}$ for y in equation (1)

$x = \frac{12}{7}$ or (2), then solve for x.

Answer

The coordinates of the point of intersection are $\left(\frac{12}{7}, \frac{15}{7}\right)$.

Example 3   Find the coordinates of the point of intersection of
             lines s and t if s contains $A(-1, 0)$ and has slope $-\frac{1}{3}$,
             and t contains $B(4, -4)$ and has slope 2.

Solution   Write an equation for s; begin with point-slope form and
             rewrite the equation in standard form.

$$y - 0 = -\tfrac{1}{3}[x - (-1)]$$
$$y = -\tfrac{1}{3}x - \tfrac{1}{3}$$
$$3y = -x - 1$$
$$x + 3y = -1$$

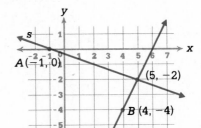

Write an equation for t.

$$y - (-4) = 2(x - 4)$$
$$y + 4 = 2x - 8$$
$$2x - y = 12$$

Solve the two equations simultaneously, using the addition
method of example 2 or the substitution method shown below.

(1) $x + 3y = -1$
(2) $2x - y = 12$

(3) $x = -1 - 3y$ Solve equation (1) for x.
(2) $2x - y = 12$ Copy equation (2).

$2(-1 - 3y) - y = 12$ Substitute $-1 - 3y$ for x in
$\quad -2 - 7y = 12$ equation (2); then solve for y.
$\quad\quad\quad y = -2$

$x + 3(-2) = -1$ Substitute -2 for y in equation (1)
$\quad\quad x = 5$ or (2); then solve for x.

Answer   The coordinates of the point of intersection are $(5, -2)$.

             You should check to see that the coordinates $(5, -2)$
             satisfy the equations of both s and t.

Example 4   Do the lines with the following equations intersect?

$$2x + 3y = 5$$
$$2x + 3y = 7$$

Solution   Note that the slope of each line is $-\frac{2}{3}$ and the
             y-intercepts are $\frac{5}{3}$ and $\frac{7}{3}$. So the lines are parallel,
             and thus do not intersect.

Class Exercises

Graph each pair of equations and estimate the coordinates of the point of intersection of the lines.

1. $2x + y = 0$
   $x + 2y = 3$

2. $x + y = 6$
   $3x = y$

Find the exact coordinates of the point of intersection of the graphs of the given equations.

3. $x + y = -1$
   $-x + y = 5$

4. $3x + 2y = 14$
   $5x - 2y = 2$

5. $x + 3y = 3$
   $1 = y - 3x$

Written Exercises

Set A

Graph each pair of equations and estimate the coordinates of the point of intersection of the lines.

1. $x - 4y = -11$
   $5x + 2y = 0$

2. $3x + y = 3$
   $x - 5y = 9$

Find the exact coordinates of the point of intersection of the graphs of the given equations.

3. $4x + 2y = 5$
   $-4x - 14y = 5$

5. $2x + 2y = 0$
   $6x + y = 6$

7. $2x - 7y = 11$
   $3x + 5y = 1$

4. $2x + 8y = 7$
   $2x - 8y = -13$

6. $x + 7y = -3$
   $3x - y = 2$

8. $x + 3y = -3$
   $3y - x = 2$

Set B

9. Find the intersection of the line through $A(-2, 1)$ with slope $\frac{1}{2}$ and the line through $B(2, 2)$ with slope $-\frac{3}{2}$.

10. Find the intersection of the line through $P(-1, -5)$ with slope 3 and the line through $Q(-2, 6)$ with slope $-\frac{1}{2}$.

11. Find the coordinates of the intersection of $\overleftrightarrow{AB}$ and $\overleftrightarrow{CD}$ for $A(-4, -1)$, $B(2, 3)$, $C(-5, 5)$, and $D(0, 0)$.

12. Find the coordinates of the intersection of $\overleftrightarrow{EF}$ and $\overleftrightarrow{GH}$ for $E(1, -3)$, $F(4, 6)$, $G(4, -6)$, and $H(1, 9)$.

Tell whether the graphs of the given equations intersect. Explain.

13. $2x + 4y = 16$
$x + 2y = 8$

15. $9x + 2y = -4$
$2x - 9y = -4$

14. $3x + y = 7$
$9x + 3y = -21$

16. $2y - 5x = 8$
$4y - 10x = 16$

Find the coordinates of the point of intersection of the graphs of the given equations.

17. $2x - y = 7;\ x = k$

19. $kx - 3y = 5;\ y = 3$

18. $x + 5y = 4;\ y = k$

20. $3x + ky = 7;\ x = 9$

Graph the line and the circle with the given equations. Show that the given point is a point of intersection.

21. $x - y = 1;\ x^2 + y^2 = 25;\ S(4, 3)$

22. $x + y = 17;\ x^2 + y^2 = 169;\ T(12, 5)$

For exercises 23-26, use the same set of axes.
Equation A is $y - 3x = -2$. Equation B is $2y + x = 10$.

23. Graph equations A and B.

24. Add equations A and B. Graph this equation, "$A + B$."

25. Multiply both sides of equation B by 3. Add the result to equation A. Graph this equation, "$A + 3B$."

26. Multiply both sides of equation A by -2. Add the result to equation B. Graph this equation, "$-2A + B$."

Set C

Are the graphs of the three given lines concurrent?

27. $x - 2y = -8;\ 3x - y = -9;\ 5x + y = -7$

28. $5x - 6y = -1;\ x + y = 2;\ 2x + y = 4$

Given: $A(-4, 0)$, $B(4, 8)$, and $C(6, -3)$. Find the point of concurrence of the lines containing the given segments.

29. The medians of $\triangle ABC$

30. The altitudes of $\triangle ABC$

31. The perpendicular bisectors of the sides of $\triangle ABC$

12.5   Coordinate Proofs

Given $W(1, 0)$, $X(4, 0)$, $Y(4, 4)$ and $Z(1, 4)$, you can prove that rectangle $WXYZ$ has congruent diagonals. By using variables for the coordinates, you can prove that *any* rectangle has congruent diagonals.

Example 1

Given: Rectangle $OPQR$; $O(0, 0)$, $P(a, 0)$, $Q(a, b)$, $R(0, b)$
Prove: The diagonals of $OPQR$ are congruent.

Solution

Use the distance formula.

$$OQ = \sqrt{(a - 0)^2 + (b - 0)^2}$$
$$= \sqrt{a^2 + b^2}$$

$$PR = \sqrt{(0 - a)^2 + (b - 0)^2}$$
$$= \sqrt{a^2 + b^2}$$

Therefore, $\overline{OQ}$ and $\overline{PR}$ have the same length and are congruent.

In example 1, the description of rectangle $OPQR$ applies to *any* rectangle. You can set a equal to the length and b equal to the width of any given rectangle so that $OPQR$ is congruent to it. This proves part of Theorem 5.11.

Note that you could have chosen other coordinates for the rectangle in example 1, but not all choices would have been as convenient. Below, $ABCD$ looks like a rectangle, but its coordinates do not show its right angles or its congruent sides. The coordinates for $EFGH$ are harder to use in the distance formula than those for $OPQR$.

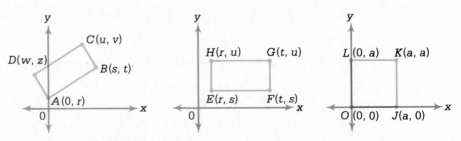

The coordinates of $OJKL$ show that it is a square. You cannot use $OJKL$ to prove that the diagonals of *any* rectangle are congruent.

Example 2	Locate an isosceles triangle in a convenient position on a set of coordinate axes.
Solution	In $\triangle DOG$, choose $2a$ for the x-coordinate of D to avoid fractions in computation. The x-coordinate of G is a since G has the same x-coordinate as M, the midpoint of $\overline{DO}$.

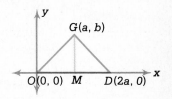

In $\triangle PET$, use the symmetry of the isosceles triangle to place each vertex on one of the axes.

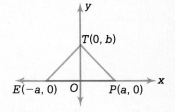

Example 3	Prove: If the diagonals of a rhombus are congruent, then the rhombus is a square.
Solution	Given: Rhombus $OPQR$ with $\overline{OQ} \cong \overline{PR}$. Place $OPQR$ so that three vertices are $O(0, 0)$, $P(c, 0)$, and $R(a, b)$. Since $\overline{OP} \parallel \overline{QR}$ and $\overline{OP} \cong \overline{QR}$, the fourth vertex must be $Q(a + c, b)$. Since $\overline{OQ} \cong \overline{PR}$,

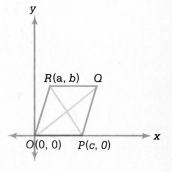

$$\sqrt{(a + c)^2 + b^2} = \sqrt{(a - c)^2 + b^2}.$$

Simplifying this equation gives $4ac = 0$. Since P is not the origin, $c \neq 0$, so a must be zero. Then R is on the y-axis, $\overline{OP} \perp \overline{OR}$, and rhombus $OPQR$ is a square.

Hints for Placing Polygons on Coordinate Planes

Place a vertex at the origin and let the nonnegative portion of the x-axis contain a side of the polygon.

If the polygon has a right angle, let the sides of the right angle lie on the x- and y-axes.

Place any axis of symmetry along the x- or y-axis.

Use an expression such as $2a$ instead of a simple variable a if symmetry or midpoints are involved.

Coordinate methods are especially helpful in proofs dealing with distances and lengths of segments.

Example 4

Prove the medians of a triangle are concurrent in a point whose distance from each vertex is two-thirds the length of the median containing that vertex.

Given

$\triangle MNO$; A, B, and C are the midpoints of $\overline{MN}$, $\overline{NO}$, and $\overline{OM}$, respectively.

Prove

Part I: There is a point D which lies on $\overleftrightarrow{AO}$, $\overleftrightarrow{BM}$, and $\overleftrightarrow{CN}$.

Part II: $\dfrac{DO}{AO} = \dfrac{DM}{BM} = \dfrac{DN}{CN} = \dfrac{2}{3}$

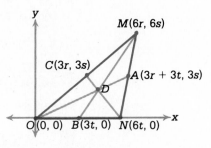

Proof of Part I

Let the vertices have coordinates $M(6r, 6s)$, $N(6t, 0)$, and $O(0, 0)$. So the midpoints are $A(3r + 3t, 3s)$, $B(3t, 0)$, and $C(3r, 3s)$. Write an equation for each median.

Line	Slope	Equation (point-slope form)
$\overleftrightarrow{AO}$	$\dfrac{s}{r + t}$	$y - 0 = \left(\dfrac{s}{r + t}\right)(x)$
$\overleftrightarrow{BM}$	$\dfrac{2s}{2r - t}$	$y - 0 = \left(\dfrac{2s}{2r - t}\right)(x - 3t)$
$\overleftrightarrow{CN}$	$\dfrac{s}{r - 2t}$	$y - 0 = \left(\dfrac{s}{r - 2t}\right)(x - 6t)$

Find the intersection of $\overleftrightarrow{AO}$ and $\overleftrightarrow{BM}$ by substitution.

$$\left(\frac{s}{r + t}\right)(x) = \left(\frac{2s}{2r - t}\right)(x - 3t)$$

$$\left(\frac{s}{r + t}\right)(x) = \left(\frac{2s}{2r - t}\right)(x) - \left(\frac{2s}{2r - t}\right)(3t)$$

$$x\left(\frac{s}{r + t} - \frac{2s}{2r - t}\right) = \frac{-6st}{2r - t}$$

$$x\left[\frac{2rs - st - 2rs - 2st}{(r + t)(2r - t)}\right] = \frac{-6st}{2r - t}$$

$$x = \frac{(r + t)(2r - t)}{-3st} \cdot \frac{-6st}{2r - t}$$

$$x = 2(r + t), \text{ or } 2r + 2t$$

Substitute this value for x in the equation for $\overleftrightarrow{AO}$ to find y.

$y = \left(\dfrac{s}{r + t}\right)(2r + 2t)$, or $2s$. So $D(2r + 2t, 2s)$ lies on $\overleftrightarrow{AO}$ and $\overleftrightarrow{BM}$. Substitute the coordinates of D in the equation for $\overleftrightarrow{CN}$.

$$(2s) = \frac{s}{r - 2t}[(2r + 2t) - 6t]$$

$$= \frac{s}{r - 2t}(2r - 4t) = 2s$$

Since the coordinates satisfy the equation, D lies on $\overleftrightarrow{CN}$.

The proof of Part II is exercise 11.

Class Exercises

[1-4] Find the coordinates of each point whose coordinates are not given.

1. Square $ABCD$, $AO = BO$

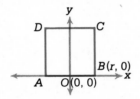

3. Equilateral $\triangle MNO$

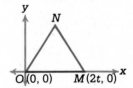

2. Rectangle $EFGO$

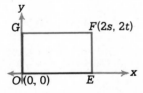

4. Isosceles trapezoid $DEFG$; $DO = EO$

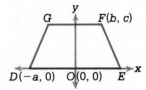

[5-7] $OPQR$ is a parallelogram.

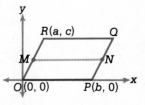

5. What are the coordinates of Q?

6. What are the slopes of $\overleftrightarrow{RO}$ and of $\overleftrightarrow{PQ}$?

7. If M and N are midpoints of $\overline{PQ}$ and $\overline{RO}$, what is the slope of $\overleftrightarrow{MN}$?

8. Given: Isosceles trapezoid *MNOP* with *P*(2*a*, 0), *O*(0, 0), *N*(2*b*, 2*c*), and $\overline{OP} \parallel \overline{MN}$. Find the coordinates of *M*.

[9-12] In trapezoid *ROCK*, *R*(2, 3), *O*(0, 0), *C*(6, 0), and *K*(5, 3).

9. Find the coordinates of the midpoints of the sides.
10. Find the slope of the median of trapezoid *ROCK*.
11. Write the equation of the line joining the midpoints of the bases.
12. Compare the length of the median with the lengths of the bases.

Written Exercises

Set A

Find the coordinates of each point whose coordinates are not given.

1. Square *OFGH*

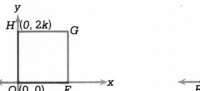

3. Equilateral △*RST*

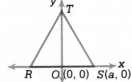

2. *CE* = *DE*, *GC* = *GE*, *FD* = *FE*, *CO* = *DO*

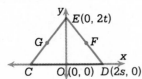

4. Rectangle *DEFG*; *DO* = *EO*

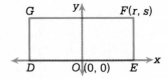

5. Square *ABCD* is placed so that the y-axis bisects $\overline{AB}$ and $\overline{CD}$, and the x-axis bisects $\overline{BC}$ and $\overline{DA}$. Assign coordinates to *A*, *B*, *C*, and *D*.

6. Rectangle *DEFG* is placed so that the midpoint of $\overline{EF}$ is on the x-axis and the midpoint of $\overline{FG}$ is on the y-axis. Assign coordinates to *D*, *E*, *F*, and *G*.

Given: Isosceles $\triangle PQR$ with $R(0, b)$, $\overline{PQ}$ on the x-axis

7. If $PR = RQ$, assign coordinates to P and Q.

8. If $m \angle RPQ = 90$, find the coordinates of P and Q.

9. Given: $\square OBCD$; $O(0, 0)$, $B(s, 0)$, $C(t, u)$. Find the coordinates of D.

10. Given: $\square EFGH$ with $\overline{EF}$ parallel to the x-axis and diagonals that intersect at the origin; $F(c, -b)$, $G(a, b)$. Find the coordinates of E and H.

11. Prove Part II of example 4.

[12-19] Prove each statement by coordinate methods.

12. The diagonals of an isosceles trapezoid are congruent. **Hint** Use class exercise 8.

Set B

13. If the diagonals of a parallelogram are congruent, then the parallelogram is a rectangle.

14. The segments joining the midpoints of consecutive sides of a rectangle form a rhombus.

15. The lines containing the altitudes of a triangle are concurrent.

16. The perpendicular bisectors of the sides of a triangle are concurrent.

Set C

17. The diagonals of a rhombus are perpendicular.

18. If the diagonals of a quadrilateral bisect each other, then the quadrilateral is a parallelogram.

19. The segments joining the midpoints of consecutive sides of a rhombus form a rectangle.

Geometry Maintenance

1. A __?__ is a line that intersects a circle in two points.

2. How many circles can be inscribed in a given triangle? Circumscribed about it?

3. Are all arcs with the same measure congruent? Explain.

12.6 Coordinates in Space

A point in space is described by an ordered triple of real numbers, (x_1, y_1, z_1). The x-, y-, and z-axes in a three-dimensional coordinate system are perpendicular to each other at the origin. The axes determine the xy-, xz-, and yz-coordinate planes. The x-coordinate of a point is its directed distance from the yz-plane, the y-coordinate its directed distance from the xz-plane, and the z-coordinate its directed distance from the xy-plane.

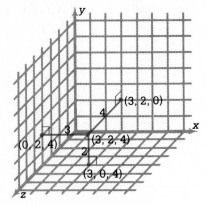

The midpoint formula for three-dimensional coordinates is analogous to the midpoint formula for two dimensions. If the coordinates of P and Q are (x_1, y_1, z_1) and (x_2, y_2, z_2), respectively, then the midpoint of $\overline{PQ}$ has coordinates

$$\left(\frac{x_1 + x_2}{2}, \frac{y_1 + y_2}{2}, \frac{z_1 + z_2}{2} \right).$$

The distance formula also resembles its two-dimensional counterpart. For points $P(x_1, y_1, z_1)$ and $Q(x_2, y_2, z_2)$,
$$PQ = \sqrt{(x_2 - x_1)^2 + (y_2 - y_1)^2 + (z_2 - z_1)^2}.$$

Example

Given: $A(5, -1, 6)$ and $C(9, 7, -2)$. Find B, the midpoint of $\overline{AC}$. Then find AB and BC.

Solution

The coordinates of B are $\left(\dfrac{9 + 5}{2}, \dfrac{7 + (-1)}{2}, \dfrac{-2 + 6}{2} \right)$, or $(7, 3, 2)$. Use the distance formula to find AB and BC.

$$\begin{aligned} AB &= \sqrt{(5 - 7)^2 + (-1 - 3)^2 + (6 - 2)^2} \\ &= \sqrt{2^2 + 4^2 + 4^2} \\ &= 6 \end{aligned}$$

$$\begin{aligned} BC &= \sqrt{(9 - 7)^2 + (7 - 3)^2 + (-2 - 2)^2} \\ &= \sqrt{2^2 + 4^2 + 4^2} \\ &= 6 \end{aligned}$$

This verifies that the midpoint formula gives a point equidistant from the endpoints of this segment.

Class Exercises

1. Given: $A(6, -6, 1)$ and $B(2, 10, 1)$. Find the length and the midpoint of $\overline{AB}$.

Each move in a three-dimensional tic-tac-toe game can be recorded as an ordered triple. For example, the yellow marble is at (4, 1, 2) since it is in the fourth column and first row of the second level.

2. What are the coordinates of the orange marble?

3. Would marbles at (2, 4, 1), (2, 3, 2), and (2, 1, 4) be collinear?

Written Exercises

Set A

For a segment with the given endpoints, find the length of the segment and the coordinates of its midpoint.

1. $A(3, 4, 2)$; $B(6, -2, 8)$ 3. $E(2, 4, 1)$; $F(5, -3, 7)$
2. $C(-1, -4, -8)$; $D(1, 4, 8)$ 4. $G(6, 2, 8)$; $H(-3, 4, -2)$

Set B

In a two-dimensional coordinate plane, you are given four points: $A(-5, 7)$, $B(-2, 3)$, $C(3, -3)$, and $D(7, -9)$.

5. Compute AB, BD, and AD. Are A, B, and D collinear?
6. Compute AC, CD, and AD. Are A, C, and D collinear?
7. Are $P(1, 1, 1)$, $Q(2, -3, -7)$, and $R(-1, 9, 17)$ collinear?

Set C

8. a. Give four examples of points in a coordinate plane whose x- and y-coordinates are in the ratio 2:3; that is, points with coordinates of the form $(2t, 3t)$. Graph these points.
   b. Write an equation for the points in part a.
   c. Give four examples of points in space whose x-, y-, and z-coordinates are in the ratio 2:1:2; that is, points with coordinates of the form $(2t, t, 2t)$.
   d. Are the points in part c collinear?

Using BASIC

Perpendiculars to Lines

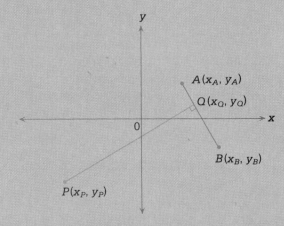

If the coordinates of three points $A(x_A, y_A)$, $B(x_B, y_B)$, and $P(x_P, y_P)$ are known, then the program on page 561 can be used to locate the perpendicular from P to $\overleftrightarrow{AB}$. Let $Q(x_Q, y_Q)$ be the intersection of $\overleftrightarrow{AB}$ and the perpendicular through P, and let m_{AB} and m_{PQ} be the slopes of $\overleftrightarrow{AB}$ and $\overleftrightarrow{PQ}$, respectively.

The slopes and equations of $\overleftrightarrow{AB}$ and $\overleftrightarrow{PQ}$ are, respectively,

Line.	Slope	Equation (from point-slope form)
$\overleftrightarrow{AB}$	$m_{AB} = \dfrac{y_A - y_B}{x_A - x_B}$	$y = (m_{AB})(x - x_A) + y_A$
$\overleftrightarrow{PQ}$	$m_{PQ} = -\dfrac{1}{m_{AB}}$	$y = (m_{PQ})(x - x_P) + y_P$

To find their intersection, point Q, substitute one equation into the other and solve for x. This gives the formula for x_Q used in line 180. The y-coordinate of Q, y_Q, can be computed by using x_Q in one of the original equations. This gives the formula used in line 190.

Chapter 12   Using Coordinates in Geometry

```
100 REM FINDING PERPENDICULAR FROM P NOT ON LINE AB
110 PRINT "ENTER X,Y COORDINATES OF A, B, AND P"
120 PRINT "IN THAT ORDER, WITH COMMAS."
130 INPUT XA,YA,XB,YB,XP,YP
140 IF XA = XB THEN 210
150 IF YA = YB THEN 270
160 LET MAB = (YA-YB)/(XA-XB)
170 LET MPQ = -1/MAB
180 LET XQ = (MAB*XA-YA-MPQ*XP+YP)/(MAB-MPQ)
190 LET YQ = MAB*(XQ-XA)+YA
200 GO TO 290
210 IF YA<>YB THEN 240
220 PRINT "A AND B MUST BE DISTINCT POINTS."
230 GO TO 110
240 LET XQ=XA
250 LET YQ=YP
260 GO TO 290
270 LET XQ=XP
280 LET YQ=YA
290 PRINT "FOOT OF THE PERPENDICULAR"
300 PRINT "FROM P TO LINE AB IS (";XQ;",";YQ;")."
310 END
```

[1-6] Given a triangle with vertices $X(6, 8)$, $Y(4, 2)$, and $Z(11, 4)$.

1. Find W so that $\overline{WX}$ is an altitude of $\triangle XYZ$.

2. Use the distance formula to find the length of $\overline{WX}$.

3. Compute the area of $\triangle XYZ$.

4. Find V so that $\overline{VY}$ is an altitude of $\triangle XYZ$.

5. Write equations in slope-intercept form for $\overleftrightarrow{WX}$ and $\overleftrightarrow{VY}$.

6. Graph $\triangle XYZ$, $\overline{WX}$, and $\overline{VY}$ and calculate the coordinates of the intersection of $\overleftrightarrow{WX}$ and $\overleftrightarrow{VY}$.

7. Repeat exercises 1-4 for $X(0, 3)$, $Y(-12, 0)$, and $Z(4, -2)$.

⋆ **8.** Revise the program to compute the distance from P to $\overleftrightarrow{AB}$.

⋆ **9.** Revise the program to compute the area of $\triangle XYZ$.

Chapter Summary

1. The slope m of a nonvertical line that contains points $P(x_1, y_1)$ and $Q(x_2, y_2)$ is $m = \dfrac{y_2 - y_1}{x_2 - x_1}$. (page 530)

2. The slope of a horizontal line is zero. The slope of a vertical line is undefined. (page 531)

3. Two nonvertical lines are parallel if and only if they have equal slopes. (page 532)

4. Two nonvertical lines are perpendicular if and only if the slope m_1 of one line is the negative reciprocal of the slope m_2 of the other line. That is, $m_1 m_2 = -1$, or $m_1 = -\dfrac{1}{m_2}$. (page 533)

5. **Point-slope form** An equation of the line containing $P(x_1, y_1)$ with slope m is $y - y_1 = m(x - x_1)$. A point is on the line if and only if its coordinates satisfy the equation. (page 537)

6. **Slope-intercept form** An equation of the line with slope m and y-intercept b is $y = mx + b$. (page 538)

7. **Standard form** The graph of an equation is a line if and only if the equation can be written in the form $Ax + By = C$ with A and B not both zero. (page 542)

8. The equation of a circle with center (h, k) and radius r is $(x - h)^2 + (y - k)^2 = r^2$. (page 544)

9. The coordinates of the point of intersection of two lines can be found algebraically. (page 548)

10. To prove a theorem by coordinate methods, place the given geometric figure on coordinate axes in a position which simplifies the work. (page 553)

11. The midpoint of $\overline{PQ}$ for $P(x_1, y_1, z_1)$ and $Q(x_2, y_2, z_2)$ has coordinates $\left(\dfrac{x_1 + x_2}{2}, \dfrac{y_1 + y_2}{2}, \dfrac{z_1 + z_2}{2} \right)$. (page 558)

12. The distance between points $P(x_1, y_1, z_1)$ and $Q(x_2, y_2, z_2)$ is $PQ = \sqrt{(x_2 - x_1)^2 + (y_2 - y_1)^2 + (z_2 - z_1)^2}$. (page 558)

Chapter Review

Lesson 12.1
Page 530

Find the slope of the line through the given points.

1. $A(-2, -4)$; $B(5, 3)$ **2.** $P(3, 8)$; $Q(3, 11)$

3. What is the slope of a line perpendicular to the *y*-axis?

The slope of line *m* is $\frac{2}{3}$. Find the slope of line *n*.

4. $m \parallel n$ **5.** $m \perp n$

Are $\overleftrightarrow{AB}$ and $\overleftrightarrow{CD}$ parallel, perpendicular, or neither?

6. $A(8, 6)$, $B(0, 3)$, $C(5, 3)$, $D(2, 11)$
7. $A(4, 7)$, $B(-5, 0)$, $C(-16, 4)$, $D(-7, 11)$

Given: $P(3, 0)$, $Q(7, 2)$, $R(6, -3)$, and $S(x, -2)$

8. Find x if $\overleftrightarrow{PQ} \parallel \overleftrightarrow{RS}$.   **9.** Find x if $\overleftrightarrow{PQ} \perp \overleftrightarrow{RS}$.

10. Given: $E(3, 2)$, $F(5, 5)$, $G(11, 7)$, $H(9, 4)$. Show that *EFGH* is a parallelogram.

Lesson 12.2
Page 537

Write an equation of the line described. Graph items 11 and 12.

11. The line that contains $P(-1, 2)$ and has slope -3
12. The line that has *y*-intercept 4 and slope $-\frac{3}{4}$
13. The line that contains $A(-1, 6)$ and $B(3, -2)$
14. The line that contains $E(5, -4)$ and is parallel to the *x*-axis
15. The line that contains $D(3, -2)$ and is parallel to the graph of $y = \frac{2}{3}x - 5$
16. The line that has *y*-intercept -2 and is perpendicular to the line whose equation is $y - 4 = -2(x + 5)$

Lesson 12.3
Page 542

17. Find the slope and *y*-intercept of the line whose equation is $3x - 5y = 15$. Graph the equation.

Write an equation in standard form of the line that:

18. Contains $K(-3, 2)$ and is perpendicular to the line whose equation is $5x + 3y = 9$.

19. Contains $G(6, -3)$ and is parallel to the graph of $3y - 4x = 9$.

20. Has x-intercept 3 and is perpendicular to the line whose equation is $-4x - 2y = 3$.

21. Find the center and radius of the circle whose equation is $(x + 2)^2 + (y - 3)^2 = 121$.

22. Write an equation for the circle with center $(3, -1)$ and radius 9.

Lesson 12.4
Page 548

Find the coordinates of the point of intersection of the lines with the given equations.

23. $2x + 3y = 6$
$x - 2y = 10$

24. $3x - 2y = 1$
$2y - x = 5$

25. $4x + y = -8$
$x + 2y = -2$

Lesson 12.5
Page 552

Given: Equilateral $\triangle FGH$

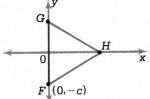

26. Find the coordinates of G and H.

27. Find the slope of a line that is perpendicular to $\overleftrightarrow{GH}$.

Given: $\square OPQR$; $O(0, 0)$, $P(2t, 0)$, $R(2s, 2z)$

28. Find the slope of $\overline{OR}$.

29. Find the coordinates of point Q.

30. Find the coordinates of the midpoint of $\overline{PQ}$.

31. Prove: The diagonals of a parallelogram bisect each other.

32. Prove: The medians of an equilateral triangle are congruent.

Lesson 12.6
Page 558

33. Find the distance between $G(-1, 0, 1)$ and $H(3, -2, 7)$.

34. Show that $C(2, 3, 3)$ is equidistant from $B(1, 1, 5)$ and $D(4, 4, 1)$. Is C the midpoint of $\overline{DB}$?

Chapter 12 Using Coordinates in Geometry

Chapter Test

1. Find the slope of $\overleftrightarrow{PQ}$ for $P(-2, 7)$ and $Q(3, -5)$.

2. Find the value of x such that the line through $U(x, 0)$ and $V(-3, 5)$ will have slope $\frac{2}{5}$.

3. Given: $A(2, 3)$, $B(1, 5)$, $C(6, 5)$, $D(4, 8)$. Are $\overleftrightarrow{AB}$ and $\overleftrightarrow{CD}$ parallel, perpendicular, or neither?

4. Given: $E(2, 1)$, $F(7, 3)$, $G(6, 7)$, $H(1, 5)$. Show that $EFGH$ is a parallelogram.

5. Are the graphs of $4y + 6x = 5$ and $-3y + 2x = 12$ parallel, perpendicular, or neither?

6. Write an equation in point-slope form of the line through $P(-3, 4)$ with slope $-\frac{3}{5}$.

7. Write an equation in slope-intercept form of the line containing $A(-2, 3)$ and $B(4, -1)$.

8. Graph the equations $y + 1 = \frac{2}{5}(x - 1)$ and $2x - 5y = -8$ on a single set of coordinate axes.

9. Write an equation in standard form of the line through $P(2, -1)$ that is perpendicular to the line whose equation is $2x + 3y = 7$.

10. Find the coordinates of the point of intersection of the lines whose equations are $x - 3y = 5$ and $x + 2y = -5$.

11. What is the center and radius of the circle whose equation is $(x - 9)^2 + (y + 16)^2 = 64$?

[12-14] $\overline{OB} \parallel \overline{CD}$ and $\overline{OB} \cong \overline{CD}$

12. What are the coordinates of C?

13. What is the slope of a line perpendicular to $\overleftrightarrow{BC}$?

14. Prove: $\overline{BC} \parallel \overline{DO}$ and $\overline{BC} \cong \overline{DO}$

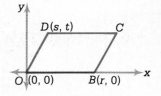

15. Prove: The segments joining the midpoints of consecutive sides of a quadrilateral form a parallelogram.

16. Given: $P(-4, 3, 0)$ and $Q(4, -5, 4)$. Find the length and the midpoint of $\overline{PQ}$.

Cumulative Test Chapters 7-12

In each item select the best answer.

1. *ABCD* is a rectangle. *BD* = __?__.

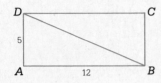

   a. $\sqrt{109}$ **b.** 13   **c.** 17   **d.** 15

2. The hypotenuse of an isosceles right triangle has length 6. The perimeter of the triangle is __?__.

  a. $3\sqrt{2}$ **c.** $12\sqrt{2}$

  b. $6\sqrt{2}$ **d.** $6\sqrt{2} + 6$

3. The length of guy wire $\overline{PG}$ is __?__.

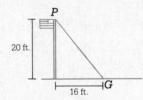

  a. 24   **c.** $16\sqrt{3}$

  b. $4\sqrt{41}$ **d.** 12

4. The coordinates of *A* are __?__.

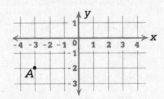

  a. $(3, -2)$ **c.** $(-2, -3)$

  b. $(-3, 2)$ **d.** $(-3, -2)$

5. Given: $A(7, -3)$ and $B(-1, -3)$
    AB = __?__.

  a. $6\sqrt{2}$ **b.** 10   **c.** 100   **d.** 8

6. If $\cos B = \frac{3}{5}$, then $\sin B =$ __?__.

  a. $\frac{4}{5}$ **b.** $\frac{5}{3}$ **c.** $\frac{3}{4}$ **d.** $\frac{5}{4}$

7. If $\sin 40 = .6428$ and $\cos 40 = .7660$, then *EF* = __?__.

  a. 15.320   **c.** 7.660

  b. 12.856   **d.** 6.428

8. In $\odot O$, $\overline{AB}$ is called a __?__.

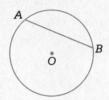

  a. Tangent   **c.** Chord

  b. Diameter   **d.** Secant

9. Circles *P* and *Q* are externally tangent. If the radius of $\odot P$ is 6 and $PQ = 10$, then the radius of $\odot Q$ is __?__.

  a. 16   **c.** $2\sqrt{34}$

  b. Not enough   **d.** 4
     information

10. If $OI = OJ$ and $EF = 8$, find JH.

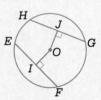

  a. 4   **b.** 6   **c.** 8   **d.** 16

11. A circle of radius 6 is circumscribed about an equilateral triangle. The length of a side of the triangle is:

a. 3   **b.** $3\sqrt{3}$ **c.** 6   **d.** $6\sqrt{3}$

12. In $\odot P$, $\overline{EF} \cong \overline{FG}$. If $m\widehat{EF} = 140$, then $m\widehat{EG} = \underline{}$.

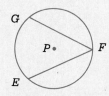

a. 80   **c.** 120
b. 110   **d.** 140

13. If $m\widehat{AB} = 80$ and $m\angle 1 = 75$, then $m\widehat{CD} = \underline{}$.

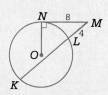

a. 230   **b.** 70   **c.** 75   **d.** 80

14. In $\odot O$, $KL = \underline{}$.

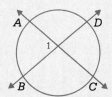

a. 10   **b.** 12   **c.** 14   **d.** 16

15. The area of a rectangle is 72 cm², and the perimeter is 34 cm. The lengths of the sides are $\underline{}$ and $\underline{}$.

a. 4, 18   **c.** 9, 8
b. 7, 10   **d.** 6, 12

16. The area of $\square ABCD$ is $\underline{}$.

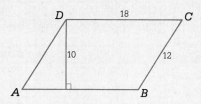

a. 180   **c.** 120
b. 216   **d.** 90

17. The lengths of the diagonals of a rhombus are 6 and 8. The area of the rhombus is $\underline{}$.

a. 48   **b.** 28   **c.** $24\sqrt{3}$ **d.** 24

18. The perimeter of $\triangle EFG$ is 9 and that of $\triangle HIJ$ is 4. If $\triangle EFG \sim \triangle HIJ$, then the ratio of the area of $\triangle EFG$ to that of $\triangle HIJ$ is $\underline{}$.

a. 3 to 2   **c.** 3 to 4
b. 9 to 4   **d.** 81 to 16

19. The apothem of a regular hexagon is $4\sqrt{3}$. Its perimeter is $\underline{}$.

a. 8   **b.** 24   **c.** 36   **d.** 48

20. The circumference of a circle is 16π. The area is $\underline{}$.

a. 8π **c.** 64π
b. 16π **d.** 256π

21. The radius of a circle is 4. If the arc of a segment has measure 90, then the area of the segment is $\underline{}$.

a. 4π **c.** $4\pi - 8$
b. $4\pi - 16$ **d.** $16\pi - 8$

22. Isometries do not necessarily preserve $\underline{}$.

a. distance   **b.** angle measure
c. betweenness of points
d. orientation of points

23. A right prism has a square base. The perimeter of the base is 24 m and the height is 10 m. The total area is __?__ m².

  a. 240   **c.** 120

  b. 312   **d.** 288

24. The volume of the prism in item 23 is __?__ m³.

  a. 80   **c.** 240

  b. 120   **d.** 360

25. The total area of this right circular cylinder is __?__ .

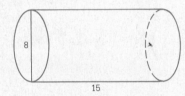

  a. 120π **c.** 152π

  b. 136π **d.** 240π

26. A regular pyramid has a square base 6 inches on a side. Its slant height is 5 inches. Its lateral area is __?__ square inches.

  a. 120   **b.** 60   **c.** 48   **d.** 40

27. The height of a right circular cone is 12 cm and the radius of the base is 5 cm. The lateral area of the cone is __?__ cm.

  a. 100π **c.** 65π

  b. 90π **d.** 60π

28. The area of a great circle of a sphere is 324π m². The area of the sphere is __?__ m².

  a. 7776π **c.** 648π

  b. 1296π **d.** 81π

29. P' is the reflection image of P over line $\overleftrightarrow{AB}$ provided __?__ .

  a. $\overleftrightarrow{PP'}$ is the perpendicular bisector of $\overline{AB}$.

  b. $\overleftrightarrow{AB}$ is the perpendicular bisector of $\overline{PP'}$.

  c. $AP' = AP$

  d. P and P' are on opposite sides of $\overleftrightarrow{AB}$.

30. Each lateral face of a prism is a:

  a. Rectangle   **c.** Triangle

  b. Parallelogram   **d.** Trapezoid

31. The shortest path from R to S via line ℓ is __?__ .

  a.   **c.**

  b. 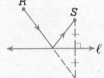   **d.**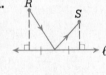

32. If $\ell \perp m$, then the composite of the reflections over ℓ and then m is:

  a. a translation

  b. another reflection

  c. a rotation

  d. the identity transformation

33. A figure which has exactly one line of symmetry is __?__ .

  a. a rectangle

  b. a rhombus

  c. a square

  d. an isosceles triangle

34. A dilation centered at P maps S onto S' and T onto T'. If $PS = 8$, $PS' = 12$, and $PT' = 18$, then $PT = \underline{}$.

   a. 27   **b.** 16   **c.** 14   **d.** 12

35. The image of square $EFGH$ under a dilation is $\underline{}$.

   a. a square congruent to $EFGH$

   b. a square that is not necessarily congruent to $EFGH$

   c. not necessarily a square

   d. a smaller square

36. An isometry which maps $\triangle ACD$ onto $\triangle BCD$ is $\underline{}$.

   a. a rotation about C of magnitude 20

   b. a rotation about C of magnitude 40

   c. a reflection over $\overleftrightarrow{CD}$

   d. a translation that maps A to B

37. $\overleftrightarrow{EF}$ contains points $E(2, -3)$ and $F(1, 4)$. The slope of a line perpendicular to $\overleftrightarrow{EF}$ is $\underline{}$.

   a. $\frac{1}{7}$ **b.** 7   **c.** $-\frac{1}{7}$ **d.** -7

38. The y-intercept of a line is 6 and it is perpendicular to the line whose equation is $y = 2x + 7$. An equation of the line is $\underline{}$.

   a. $y = -\frac{1}{2}x + 6$ **c.** $y = 2x - 6$

   b. $y = 2x + 6$ **d.** $y = -\frac{1}{2}x - 6$

39. An equation of line ℓ is $6x - 4y = 6$. An equation of a line parallel to ℓ is $\underline{}$.

   a. $2x - 3y = 3$ **c.** $3x - 2y = 8$

   b. $6x + 4y = 6$ **d.** $4y + 6x = 10$

40. The equations of two lines are:
$$3x - y = 5$$
$$x + 2y = 4$$
The coordinates of the point of intersection of these lines are $\underline{}$.

   a. $\left(\frac{9}{2}, \frac{1}{4}\right)$ **c.** $(2, 1)$

   b. $(3, 4)$ **d.** $(0, 2)$

41. If $ABCD$ is an isosceles trapezoid, $\sqrt{d^2 + c^2} = \sqrt{(b - a)^2 + c^2}$ because:

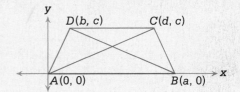

   a. Of the definition of isosceles trapezoid

   b. The bases of a trapezoid are parallel.

   c. The diagonals of an isosceles trapezoid are perpendicular.

   d. The diagonals of an isosceles trapezoid are congruent.

42. In three-space, the coordinates of A and B are $(3, -2, 2)$ and $(-3, 0, 5)$, respectively. $AB = \underline{}$.

   a. 7   **b.** $2\sqrt{10}$ **c.** $\sqrt{53}$ **d.** 6

43. The lengths of the altitude and median of a trapezoid are 24 and 30, respectively. The area of the trapezoid is $\underline{}$.

   a. 720   **c.** 360

   b. 405   **d.** 210

Squares and Square Roots

n	n^2	$\sqrt{n}$	n	n^2	$\sqrt{n}$	n	n^2	$\sqrt{n}$	n	n^2	$\sqrt{n}$
1	1	1.000	51	2601	7.141	101	10,201	10.050	151	22,801	12.288
2	4	1.414	52	2704	7.211	102	10,404	10.100	152	23,104	12.329
3	9	1.732	53	2809	7.280	103	10,609	10.149	153	23,409	12.369
4	16	2.000	54	2916	7.348	104	10,816	10.198	154	23,716	12.410
5	25	2.236	55	3025	7.416	105	11,025	10.247	155	24,025	12.450
6	36	2.449	56	3136	7.483	106	11,236	10.296	156	24,336	12.490
7	49	2.646	57	3249	7.550	107	11,449	10.344	157	24,649	12.530
8	64	2.828	58	3364	7.616	108	11,664	10.392	158	24,964	12.570
9	81	3.000	59	3481	7.681	109	11,881	10.440	159	25,281	12.610
10	100	3.162	60	3600	7.746	110	12,100	10.488	160	25,600	12.649
11	121	3.317	61	3721	7.810	111	12,321	10.536	161	25,921	12.689
12	144	3.464	62	3844	7.874	112	12,544	10.583	162	26,244	12.728
13	169	3.606	63	3969	7.937	113	12,769	10.630	163	26,569	12.767
14	196	3.742	64	4096	8.000	114	12,996	10.677	164	26,896	12.806
15	225	3.873	65	4225	8.062	115	13,225	10.724	165	27,225	12.845
16	256	4.000	66	4356	8.124	116	13,456	10.770	166	27,556	12.884
17	289	4.123	67	4489	8.185	117	13,689	10.817	167	27,889	12.923
18	324	4.243	68	4624	8.246	118	13,924	10.863	168	28,224	12.961
19	361	4.359	69	4761	8.307	119	14,161	10.909	169	28,561	13.000
20	400	4.472	70	4900	8.367	120	14,400	10.954	170	28,900	13.038
21	441	4.583	71	5041	8.426	121	14,641	11.000	171	29,241	13.077
22	484	4.690	72	5184	8.485	122	14,884	11.045	172	29,584	13.115
23	529	4.796	73	5329	8.544	123	15,129	11.091	173	29,929	13.153
24	576	4.899	74	5476	8.602	124	15,376	11.136	174	30,276	13.191
25	625	5.000	75	5625	8.660	125	15,625	11.180	175	30,625	13.229
26	676	5.099	76	5776	8.718	126	15,876	11.225	176	30,976	13.266
27	729	5.196	77	5929	8.775	127	16,129	11.269	177	31,329	13.304
28	784	5.292	78	6084	8.832	128	16,384	11.314	178	31,684	13.342
29	841	5.385	79	6241	8.888	129	16,641	11.358	179	32,041	13.379
30	900	5.477	80	6400	8.944	130	16,900	11.402	180	32,400	13.416
31	961	5.568	81	6561	9.000	131	17,161	11.446	181	32,761	13.454
32	1024	5.657	82	6724	9.055	132	17,424	11.489	182	33,124	13.491
33	1089	5.745	83	6889	9.110	133	17,689	11.533	183	33,489	13.528
34	1156	5.831	84	7056	9.165	134	17,956	11.576	184	33,856	13.565
35	1225	5.916	85	7225	9.220	135	18,225	11.619	185	34,225	13.601
36	1296	6.000	86	7396	9.274	136	18,496	11.662	186	34,596	13.638
37	1369	6.083	87	7569	9.327	137	18,769	11.705	187	34,969	13.675
38	1444	6.164	88	7744	9.381	138	19,044	11.747	188	35,344	13.711
39	1521	6.245	89	7921	9.434	139	19,321	11.790	189	35,721	13.748
40	1600	6.325	90	8100	9.487	140	19,600	11.832	190	36,100	13.784
41	1681	6.403	91	8281	9.539	141	19,881	11.874	191	36,481	13.820
42	1764	6.481	92	8464	9.592	142	20,164	11.916	192	36,864	13.856
43	1849	6.557	93	8649	9.644	143	20,449	11.958	193	37,249	13.892
44	1936	6.633	94	8836	9.695	144	20,736	12.000	194	37,636	13.928
45	2025	6.708	95	9025	9.747	145	21,025	12.042	195	38,025	13.964
46	2116	6.782	96	9216	9.798	146	21,316	12.083	196	38,416	14.000
47	2209	6.856	97	9409	9.849	147	21,609	12.124	197	38,809	14.036
48	2304	6.928	98	9604	9.899	148	21,904	12.166	198	39,204	14.071
49	2401	7.000	99	9801	9.950	149	22,201	12.207	199	39,601	14.107
50	2500	7.071	100	10,000	10.000	150	22,500	12.247	200	40,000	14.142

Selected Answers to Odd-Numbered Exercises

Chapter 1

Pages 5-7
Class Exercises **1.** c; sphere **3.** b; pentagram
Written Exercises **1.** f; octagon **3.** e; square
5. c; circle **7.** Slanted parking places are easier
to enter/leave than perpendicular ones.
9. Measure the distances between the lines.
11. Yes

Pages 11-13
Class Exercises **1.** B **3.** ℓ **5.** D or E **7.** A, B, C
9. B **Written Exercises** **1.** Typical answer: F,
G, D **3.** G **5.** Typical answer: A, F, B, D **7.** B
9. Plane **11.** Point **13.** Line **15.** a. Infinitely
many b. One c. If the 3 points are collinear,
they lie in infinitely many planes. If they are
noncollinear, they lie in only one. **25.** Ray AB is
the set of points formed by segment AB and all
points P such that B is between A and P.

Pages 15-17
Class Exercises **1.** Exactly one; Line Post.
Two pts. determine a line. **3.** Yes; Flat Plane
Post. If 2 pts. are contained in a plane, the line
through them is contained in the same plane.
5. $\overleftrightarrow{AB}$; Plane Intersection Post. If 2 planes
intersect, they intersect in a line. **Written
Exercises** **1.** Line **3.** Plane **5.** $\overleftrightarrow{PQ}$ **7.** Plane
Post. Three noncollinear pts. determine a
plane. **9.** Plane Intersection Post. If 2 planes
intersect, they intersect in a line. **11.** Flat Plane
Post. If 2 pts. are contained in a plane, the line
through them is contained in the same plane.
13. Sometimes **15.** Always **17.** Flat Plane Post.
If 2 pts. lie in a plane, the line through them
lies in the same plane. **19.** Plane Intersection
Post. If 2 planes intersect, they intersect in a
line. **21.** Points Post. A plane contains at least
3 noncoll. pts. **23.** Line Post. 2 pts. are
contained in one and only one line. **25.** Line
Post. 2 pts. are contained in one and only one

line. Flat Plane Post. If 2 pts. lie in a plane, the
line through them lies in the same plane. Plane
Intersection Post. If 2 planes intersect, they
intersect in a line. **27.** Ten

Pages 20-22
Class Exercises **1.** Two **3.** None **5.** Yes. The
segment consists of points A and B and all
points between A and B. **7.** P **9.** No; only if P
is between Q and R. **11.** Two **Written
Exercises** **1.** Typical answers: $\overrightarrow{AB}$, $\overrightarrow{BC}$ **3.** $\overrightarrow{BC}$,
$\overrightarrow{BD}$ **7.** $\overrightarrow{DE}$ and one of $\overrightarrow{DC}$, $\overrightarrow{DB}$, $\overrightarrow{DA}$ **9.** $\overrightarrow{CA}$ **11.** $\mathcal{H}_1$
and $\mathcal{H}_2$ **13.** ℓ **23.** Ray **25.** Line **27.** They are on
the same side of line m. **31.** d **33.** 28 **35.** 378

Pages 28-30
Class Exercises **1.** Ruler Post. For every pair
of points, there is a unique, positive, real
number called the distance between them.
3. Seg. Add. Post. If point P is between points
A and B, then $AP + PB = AB$. **5.** Def. of
midpoint **7.** Compass and straightedge
Written Exercises **1.** 6 **3.** 12 **5.** 9 **7.** Starting
at the free end of the ribbon, measure along
the edge of the ribbon. There is one and only
one point on the edge which represents the
length of ribbon wanted. **9.** a. 35 yd. b. Seg.
Add. Post. **11.** Def. of congruent seg. **13.** Def.
of bisector of a segment **15.** Def. of congruent
seg. **21.** 6 **23.** Seg. Construction Post.

Pages 34-37
Class Exercises **1.** F **3.** P **5.** 40 **7.** 100 **9.** 165
11. 140 **13.** $\overrightarrow{PC}$ **15.** $\angle BPD$ **Written Exercises**
1. $\angle DEG$, $\angle GED$ **3.** $\angle 1$, $\angle 2$, $\angle 3$, $\angle DEH$, $\angle GEF$
5. D or F **7.** No; the rays are collinear
9. $m\angle 1 = m\angle 2$ **11.** $\angle APC$ **13.** $\angle BPC$ **15.** 28
17. 115 **19.** 150; Angle Add. Post.
31. 1600; 2400

Pages 43-45
Class Exercises **1.** $\angle APB$ **3.** $\angle APE$, $\angle EPD$,
$\angle BPF$, $\angle FPC$ **7.** $\angle EPD$ and $\angle BPF$ **9.** $\angle APE$ and

$\angle FPC$; $\angle EPD$ and $\angle FPB$; $\angle APD$ and $\angle BPC$; $\angle APB$ and $\angle DPC$; $\angle FPA$ and $\angle EPC$; $\angle FPD$ and $\angle BPE$ **11.** $\overleftrightarrow{AC}$; $\overline{BD}$ **13.** 170 **Written Exercises** **9.** 85 **11.** 45 **13.** 52 **15.** 149 **17.** 137 **19.** 105 **21.** Not adjacent; no common vertex. **23.** Not adjacent; no common side **25.** 140 **27.** 50 **29.** Right angle **31.** Right angle **33.** 4 **35.** Complementary **37.** $m\angle B = 18$; $m\angle A = 72$ **41.** $\angle 1$ is a rt. $\angle$ since $m\angle 1 = 180 - m\angle 2 = 180 - 90 = 90$. **43.** 65

Pages 50-52

Class Exercises **3.** 8 **5.** 10, $2n$ **Written Exercises** **7.** 31 **9.** $E + 2 = V + R$

Chapter 2

Pages 62-65

Class Exercises **1.** Jim has a physical education class. **3.** I will learn to play better **5.** Trans. prop. of eq. **7.** Mult. prop. of ineq. **9.** Add. prop. of eq. **11.** Reflex. prop. of eq. **Written Exercises** **1.** 2 pounds **3.** repaired or replaced the clock. **5.** Add. prop. of eq. **7.** Trans. prop. of eq. or substitution **9.** Mult. prop. of eq. **11.** Dist. prop. **13.** Substitution principle **15.** Seg. Add. Post. **17.** Def. of midpoint **19.** Def. of supp. angles **21.** Def. of angle bisector **23.** bisects; midpoint **25.** Supplement; def. of supp. angles **27.** Since B is the midpt. of $\overline{AC}$, $AB = BC$. (Def. of midpt.) Since $AB = BC$, $\overline{AB} \cong \overline{BC}$. (Def. of $\cong$ segs.) **29.** Since B is in the int. of $\angle XYZ$, $m\angle XYZ = m\angle XYB + m\angle BYZ$. ($\angle$ Add. Post.) Since $m\angle XYZ = m\angle XYB + m\angle BYZ$, $m\angle XYZ - m\angle BYZ = m\angle XYB$. (Subtr. prop. of eq.) **31.** Since $\angle TON$ and $\angle NOP$ are comp., $m\angle TON + m\angle NOP = 90$. (Def. of comp. $\angle$s) Since $\overrightarrow{ON}$ is in the interior of $\angle TOP$, $m\angle TOP = m\angle TON + m\angle NOP$. ($\angle$ Add. Post.) Thus $m\angle TOP = 90$. (Trans. prop. of eq.) **33.** Since N is the midpt. of $\overline{JS}$, $JN = NS$ and N is between J and S. (Def. of midpt.) Since N is between J and S, $JN + NS = JS$. (Seg. Add. Post.) Since $JN + NS = JS$ and $JN = NS$, $JN + JN = JS$. (Subst. prin.) Since $JN + JN = JS$, $2(JN) = JS$. (Dist. prop.) And since $2(JN) = JS$, $JN = 0.5(JS)$. (Mult. prop. of eq.)

Pages 68-70

Class Exercises **1.** Given **3.** Def. of rt. $\angle$ [1] **5.** Def. of $\cong \angle$s **Written Exercises** **1.** Given; Seg. Add. Post.; Reflex. prop. of eq.; Subtr. prop. of eq. **3.** Given; Def. of rt. $\angle$; Def. of $\perp$ lines **5.** Given; Def. of bisects; Def. of midpt. **7.** $\overline{AB} \cong \overline{XY}$; Def. of $\cong$ segs.; Symmetric prop. of eq.; Def. of $\cong$ segs. **9.** $\overleftrightarrow{MA}$ and $\overleftrightarrow{TH}$ intersect at A; a linear pair; $\angle MAT$ and $\angle MAH$ are Supplementary

Pages 73-75

Class Exercises **1.** c **3.** Yes **5.** No **7.** Yes **9.** False **11.** False **Written Exercises** **1.** Def. of adj. $\angle$s **3.** Supp. Post. **5.** Angle Add. Post. **13.** Not possible. An angle bisector is a ray whose endpoint is the vertex of the angle. The endpoint of $\overrightarrow{AB}$ is A, but the vertex of $\angle CDA$ is D. **19.** Thm. 2.5: A line and a point not on the line are contained in one and only one plane. **27.** True **29.** True **31.** True **33.** False **35.** True **37.** False

Pages 80-82

Written Exercises **1.** Hyp: $AB = CD$; concl: $\overline{AB}$ and $\overline{CD}$ are collinear. **3.** Hyp: ab is even and b is odd; concl: a is even. **5.** If $\overleftrightarrow{CD}$ bisects $\overline{AB}$ at E, then E is the midpoint of $\overline{AB}$. **7.** If two planes intersect, then their intersection is a line. **9.** If two angles form a linear pair, then they are supp. **11.** If two angles are comps. of congruent angles, then the two angles are congruent. **13.** They are a linear pair. **15.** 30; $\angle APD$ and $\angle APC$ form a linear pair, so $m\angle APD + m\angle APC = 180$. Thus 150 + $m\angle APC = 180$. **17.** No **19.** If C, D, and M are collinear and $\overline{CM} \cong \overline{DM}$, then M is the midpt. of $\overline{CD}$. **21.** If 3 pts. are noncollinear, then they are contained in one and only one plane. **23.** If two angles form a linear pair, then they are supp. **25.** $p \Rightarrow q$; q No conclusion. There are many factors that might explain the congruence. **27.** If two lines intersect, then they lie in a plane. $p \Rightarrow q$; p; Conclude: q is true; $\overleftrightarrow{AB}$ and $\overleftrightarrow{OR}$ lie in a plane.

Pages 86-90

Class Exercises **1.** Postulates, theorems, definitions, properties of real numbers **5.** Typical ans.: $\angle WOX \cong \angle ZOY$; $\angle WOZ \cong$

$\angle XOY$; $\overline{OW} \cong \overline{OY}$; $\overline{OZ} \cong \overline{OX}$ **7.** Typical ans.:
$m\angle 1 = m\angle 2$; $m\angle HMN = m\angle HNM$; $GM = NI$;
$\overline{GM} \cong \overline{NI}$ **Written Exercises 1.** a. 70 b. 70
c. 110 **3.** $k \perp \ell$ **5.** a. Inc. by 10 b. Dec. by 10
c. Dec. by 10 **7.** $x = 8$ **9.** a, b **11.** c, a, b, d
13. Use the given and the Add. prop. of eq. to
show that $JK + KL = KL + LM$. Use the Seg.
Add. Post. to show $JK + KL = JL$ and
$KL + LM = KM$. Then substitute to get
$JL = KM$. **15.** Use def. of linear pair and Thm.
2.12 to show that $\angle 3$ is a rt. $\angle$. Then use Thm.
2.1. **17.** Use the Supp. Post. to show that $\angle 1$
and $\angle 2$ are supp., and $\angle 3$ and $\angle 4$ are supp.
Then use the given and "Supps. of $\cong$ $\angle$s are
$\cong$" to show $\angle 2 \cong \angle 3$. **19.** Use the def. of linear
pair and Thm. 2.12 to show $\angle ABE$ is a rt. $\angle$.
Then use def. of angle bisector, Angle Add.
Post., def. of comp. angles, and Thm. 2.9.
23. $x = 94$; $y = 8$

Pages 94-95

Class Exercises 1. Use the fact that vert. $\angle$s
are $\cong$ to show $\angle 1 \cong \angle 3$ and $\angle 2 \cong \angle 4$. Then use
trans. of angle $\cong$ to show $\angle 3 \cong \angle 4$. **3.** Use the
def. of $\perp$ and the def. of rt. $\angle$ to show that
$m\angle ABC = 90$. Use the Angle Add. Post. to
show that $m\angle 5 + m\angle 6 = m\angle ABC$. Use
transitivity to show $m\angle 5 + m\angle 6 = 90$. **5.** Use
the def. of midpt. to show that $PM = MQ$ and
$PN = NR$. Then use the given and transitivity to
show $PM = PN$. **Written Exercises 1.** 1. $\angle A$
is any angle. (Given) 2. $m\angle A = m\angle A$ (Reflex.
prop. of eq.) 3. $\angle A \cong \angle A$ (Def. of $\cong$ $\angle$s) **3.** 1.
$\angle D \cong \angle E$; $\angle E \cong \angle F$ (Given) 2. $m\angle D = m\angle E$;
$m\angle E = m\angle F$ (Def. of $\cong$ $\angle$s) 3. $m\angle D = m\angle F$
(Trans. prop. of eq. [2]) 4. $\angle D \cong \angle F$ (Def. of $\cong$
$\angle$s) **5.** 1. $\angle 1$ and $\angle 2$ are supp. (Given) 2. $\angle 2$
and $\angle 3$ are supp. (Supp. Post.) 3. $\angle 1 \cong \angle 3$
(Supp. of same $\angle$ are $\cong$.) **7.** 1. $\angle 1 \cong \angle 4$ (Given)
2. $\angle 1$ and $\angle 2$ are supp.; $\angle 3$ and $\angle 4$ are supp.
(Supp. Post.) 3. $\angle 2 \cong \angle 3$ (Supps. of $\cong$ $\angle$s are
$\cong$.) **11.** Given: $\angle 1$ and $\angle 2$ are supp.; $\angle 1 \cong \angle 2$.
Prove: $\angle 1$ and $\angle 2$ are rt. $\angle$s. 1. $\angle 1$ and $\angle 2$ are
supp.; $\angle 1 \cong \angle 2$ (Given) 2. $m\angle 1 + m\angle 2 = 180$
(Def. of supp.) 3. $m\angle 1 = m\angle 2$ (Def. of $\cong$ $\angle$s
[1]) 4. $m\angle 1 + m\angle 1 = 180$ (Subst. [2, 3]) 5.
$2(m\angle 1) = 180$ (Dist. prop.) 6. $m\angle 1 = 90$ (Mult.
prop. of eq.) 7. $m\angle 2 = 90$ (Subst. [3, 6]) 8. $\angle 1$
and $\angle 2$ are rt. $\angle$s (Def. of rt. $\angle$s [6, 7])
13. Given: Line ℓ and point P not on ℓ. Prove: ℓ

and P lie in a plane. 1. P is not on line ℓ.
(Given) 2. Let A and B be any two pts. on ℓ. (A
line contains at least 2 pts.) 3. ℓ is the only line
that contains both A and B. (2 pts. are
contained in exactly one line.) 4. A, B, and P
are noncollinear. (Def. of noncoll.) 5. A, B, and P
are contained in exactly one plane, say $\mathcal{K}$. (3
noncoll. pts. determine a plane.) 6. ℓ is
contained in $\mathcal{K}$. (Flat Plane Post.) 7. P and ℓ are
contained in one and only one plane $\mathcal{K}$. (Steps
5 and 6)

Pages 98-99

Class Exercises 1. If $2x + 5 = 11$, then $x = 3$.
True **3.** If I get sick, then I have eaten too
much candy. False **5.** If r, then q. **7.** If h, then
k. **9.** If two segments are congruent, then they
have the same length. **11.** Two segments are
congruent if and only if they have the same
length. **Written Exercises 1.** False **3.** True
5. True **7.** If three angles of a triangle are
congruent, then the three sides are congruent.
True **9.** If a figure is a rectangle, then it is a
square. False **11.** If two angles are congruent,
then they are right angles. False **13.** If the sum
of the measures of two angles is 90, then the
angles are complementary. True **15.** If two
angles have a common ray, then they are
adjacent. False **17.** If $\overrightarrow{OA}$ bisects $\angle XOY$, then
$m\angle XOA = m\angle AOY$. If $m\angle XOA = m\angle AOY$,
then $\overrightarrow{OA}$ bisects $\angle XOY$. **19.** If $\angle E \cong \angle F$, then
$m\angle E = m\angle F$. If $m\angle E = m\angle F$, then $\angle E \cong \angle F$.
21. Two lines are perpendicular if and only if
they intersect to form a right angle. **23.** An
angle is a right angle if and only if its measure
is 90. **25.** Given: $\angle 1$ and $\angle 2$ form a lin. pr.;
$\ell \perp k$. Prove: $\angle 1 \cong \angle 2$ 1. $\angle 1$ and $\angle 2$ are a lin.
pr.; $\ell \perp k$ (Given) 2. $\angle 1$ and $\angle 2$ are rt. $\angle$s. (2 $\perp$
lines form 4 rt. $\angle$s) 3. $\angle 1 \cong \angle 2$ (All rt. $\angle$s are
$\cong$.) **27.** Part I: Given: $\angle A$ and $\angle B$ are rt. $\angle$s.
Prove: $\angle A \cong \angle B$ 1. $\angle A$ and $\angle B$ are rt. $\angle$s.
(Given) 2. $\angle A \cong \angle B$ (All rt. $\angle$s are $\cong$.) Part II:
Given: $\angle A \cong \angle B$; $\angle B$ is a rt. $\angle$. Prove: $\angle A$ is a
rt. $\angle$. 1. $\angle A \cong \angle B$; $\angle B$ is a rt. $\angle$. (Given) 2.
$m\angle B = 90$ (Def. of rt. $\angle$) 3. $m\angle A = m\angle B$ (Def.
of $\cong$ $\angle$s [1]) 4. $m\angle A = 90$ (Trans. prop. of eq.
[2, 3]) 5. $\angle A$ is a rt. $\angle$ (Def. of rt. $\angle$)

Chapter 3

Pages 110-111

Class Exercises **5.** $\overleftrightarrow{RS}$ or $\overleftrightarrow{WV}$ **7.** t **9.** $\angle 1$ and $\angle 3$; $\angle 2$ and $\angle 4$; $\angle 5$ and $\angle 7$; $\angle 6$ and $\angle 8$ **11.** $m\angle 2 = 80$; $m\angle 6 = 110$; $m\angle 3 = 100$; $m\angle 4 = 80$; $m\angle 7 = 70$; $m\angle 8 = 110$ **Written Exercises** **3.** Alt. int. $\angle$s **5.** Corres. $\angle$s **7.** Alt. int. $\angle$s **9.** $\angle APQ$ and $\angle PQB$ **11.** A, E, F, H, M, N, W, Z **13.** E, F, H, M, N, W, Z **15.** True

Pages 114-115

Class Exercises **1.** Parallel Lines Post: 2 lines $\parallel \Rightarrow$ corr. $\angle$s $\cong$. **3.** Parallel Lines Post: Corr. $\angle$s $\cong \Rightarrow$ 2 lines $\parallel$. **Written Exercises** **3.** 102 **5.** 78 **7.** 102 **9.** $k \parallel j$ **11.** $m \parallel n$ **13.** $k \parallel j$ **15.** In a plane, 2 lines $\perp$ to the same line are parallel. **17.** Given: Coplanar lines n, m, and t; $n \perp t$; $m \perp t$ Prove: $n \parallel m$ 1. Lines n, m, t are coplanar; $n \perp t$; $m \perp t$ (Given) 2. $\angle 1$ is a rt. $\angle$; $\angle 2$ is a rt. $\angle$. (2 $\perp$ lines form 4 rt. $\angle$s) 3. $\angle 1 \cong \angle 2$ (All rt. $\angle$s are $\cong$. [2]) 4. $n \parallel m$ (Corres. $\angle$s $\cong \Rightarrow$ 2 lines $\parallel$. [3]) **19.** Given: $\overleftrightarrow{BC} \parallel \overleftrightarrow{DE}$; $\angle 1 \cong \angle 2$ Prove: $\angle 2 \cong \angle 3$ 1. $\overleftrightarrow{BC} \parallel \overleftrightarrow{DE}$; $\angle 1 \cong \angle 2$ (Given) 2. $\angle 3 \cong \angle 1$ (2 lines $\parallel \Rightarrow$ corres. $\angle$s $\cong$. [1]) 3. $\angle 2 \cong \angle 3$ ($\cong$ of angles is trans. [1, 2]) **21.** $x = 40$; $m\angle 1 = 110$; $m\angle 2 = 110$ **23.** $x = 250$; $m\angle 1 = m\angle 2 = 160$ **27.** If two lines are parallel, then the alternate interior angles formed by any transversal are congruent. **29.** $\ell \parallel m$; Plan for proof: Use the Supp. Post. and the def. of supp. to show $m\angle 1 = 180 - m\angle 3 = 180 - 115 = 65$. Then use Parallel Lines Post. to show $\ell \parallel m$.

Pages 118-120

Class Exercises **1.** 100 **3.** 104 **5.** 107 **7.** 75 **9.** 75 **Written Exercises** **1.** 75 **3.** 68 **5.** 72 **7.** Yes; corres. $\angle$s $\cong \Rightarrow$ 2 lines $\parallel$. **9.** Yes; in a plane, 2 lines $\perp$ to the same line are $\parallel$. **11.** No **13.** $\ell \parallel m$ **15.** $k \parallel j$ **17.** None **19.** $m\angle 1 = m\angle 3$ **21.** $m\angle 2 + m\angle 3 = 180$ **23.** Yes; both sides of the ladder are $\perp$ to each rung. **25.** 1. $\ell \parallel m$; $\angle 2 \cong \angle 5$ (Given) 2. $\angle 3 \cong \angle 2$ (2 lines $\parallel \Rightarrow$ alt. int. $\angle$s $\cong$. [1]) 3. $\angle 3 \cong \angle 5$ ($\cong$ of $\angle$s is trans. [1, 2]) 4. $n \parallel t$ (Corres. $\angle$s $\cong \Rightarrow$ 2 lines $\parallel$. [3]) **27.** 1. $\ell \parallel m$; $n \parallel t$ (Given) 2. $\angle 1 \cong \angle 3$; $\angle 3 \cong \angle 5$ (2 lines $\parallel \Rightarrow$ corres. $\angle$s $\cong$. [1]) 3. $\angle 1 \cong \angle 5$ ($\cong$ of $\angle$s is trans. [2]) **31.** 1. $\overleftrightarrow{BC} \parallel \overleftrightarrow{EF}$; $m\angle 1 + m\angle 4 = 180$ (Given) 2. $\angle 2 \cong \angle 4$ (2 lines $\parallel \Rightarrow$ corres. $\angle$s $\cong$ [1]) 3. $m\angle 2 = m\angle 4$ (Def. of $\cong \angle$s)

4. $m\angle 1 + m\angle 2 = 180$ (Subst. [1, 3]) **5.** $\angle 1$ and $\angle 2$ are supp. (Def. of supp. $\angle$s [4]) **6.** $\overleftrightarrow{BA} \parallel \overleftrightarrow{ED}$ (Int. $\angle$s on same side supp. $\Rightarrow$ 2 lines $\parallel$. [5]) **35.** 4 **37.** 24 **39.** -9 or 8

Pages 123-125

Class Exercises **1.** $\angle A$ is not congruent to $\angle B$. **3.** ℓ is not perpendicular to m. **5.** $\ell \parallel m$ **Written Exercises** **5.** Two intersecting lines lie in one and only one plane. **7.** A segment has exactly one midpoint. **9.** P and ℓ lie in only one plane. **11.** $\mathcal{E}$ and $\mathcal{K}$; Line; P, Q, R **13.** P and ℓ lie in two or more planes; false **15.** Either $\angle 1 \cong \angle 4$ or $\angle 1 \not\cong \angle 4$. Suppose $\angle 1 \cong \angle 4$. Then since $\cong$ corr. $\angle$s $\Rightarrow$ 2 lines $\parallel$, $\ell \parallel m$. This contradicts the hypothesis. Thus $\angle 1 \cong \angle 4$ is false. We conclude $\angle 1 \not\cong \angle 4$. **17.** Either $\ell \parallel m$ or $\ell \not\parallel m$. Suppose $\ell \parallel m$. Then $m\angle 2 + m\angle 4 = 180$ (two lines $\parallel \Rightarrow$ int. $\angle$s on same side supp.) This contradicts the hypothesis. Thus $\ell \parallel m$ is false. We conclude $\ell \not\parallel m$. **19.** Yes **21.** Yes

Pages 129-131

Class Exercises **1.** True **3.** False **Written Exercises** **1.** Points Post. **3.** Def. of rt. $\angle$ **5.** Two points lie in one and only one line. **7.** A segment has exactly one midpoint. **9.** Through a pt. not on a given line, there is exactly one line perpendicular to the given line. **13.** Lines in $\mathcal{K}$ through P perpendicular to ℓ. **15.** 90; 90 **17.** that there are 2 or more lines in $\mathcal{K}$ through P perpendicular to ℓ is false. **19.** Align the square along $\overleftrightarrow{AB}$ as shown, but so that P is on the other edge of the tool. Draw $\overleftrightarrow{PC}$ perpendicular to $\overleftrightarrow{AB}$ at C. Then align the tool along $\overleftrightarrow{PC}$ so that the corner of the tool rests at P. Draw $\overleftrightarrow{PD}$ perpendicular to $\overleftrightarrow{PC}$ at P. Then $\overleftrightarrow{PD} \parallel \overleftrightarrow{AB}$. (In a plane, 2 lines $\perp$ the same line are $\parallel$.) **21.** Not necessarily; there is no assurance that the $\perp$ bisector of $\overline{AB}$ would contain C. **23.** Yes; through a pt. not on a given line, there is exactly one line $\perp$ the given line. **27.** Given: t, ℓ, and m are coplanar; t intersects ℓ at A; $\ell \parallel m$ Prove: t intersects m Proof: Since t and m are coplanar, either $t \parallel m$ or t intersects m. Suppose $t \parallel m$. Then t and ℓ both contain A and t and ℓ are both parallel to m. This contradicts the fact that through a pt. not on a given line, there is one and only one line $\parallel$ the given line. So the assumption that $t \parallel m$ is false. We conclude that t and m intersect. **29.** 90

Pages 135-136

Class Exercises **1.** Yes **3.** $m \perp \mathcal{K}$, $m \perp \mathcal{E}$, and $\mathcal{E} \parallel \mathcal{K}$ **Written Exercises** **1.** $j \parallel k$ **3.** $j \parallel k$ **5.** $m \perp n$; $j \perp n$; $j \parallel k$; $k \perp n$; $\ell \perp n$ **7.** Sometimes **9.** Never **11.** Sometimes **13.** Always

Pages 140-141

Class Exercises **1.** $\triangle ABC$, $\triangle ABD$, $\triangle ABE$, $\triangle ACD$, $\triangle ACE$, $\triangle ADE$ **3.** $\triangle TRP$ **5.** $\triangle TRP$ **7.** $\overline{BC}$ **9.** $\triangle ABC$ **Written Exercises** **7.** Rt. triangle **9.** Isosceles **11.** Base: $\overline{FH}$; legs: $\overline{GF}$ and $\overline{GH}$ **17.** 4; 10

Pages 144-146

Class Exercises **1.** 50 **3.** 130 **5.** 45 **7.** 50 **Written Exercises** **1.** $m \angle R = 30$ **3.** $m \angle P = 50$; $m \angle Q = 70$; $m \angle R = 60$ **5.** $m \angle Q = 55$; $m \angle R = 30$; $m \angle P = 95$ **7.** If 2 $\angle$s of a $\triangle$ are $\cong$ to 2 $\angle$s of another $\triangle$, the third $\angle$s are $\cong$. **11.** Given: $\triangle ABC$ is equiangular Prove: $m \angle A = 60$; $m \angle B = 60$; $m \angle C = 60$ 1. $\triangle ABC$ is equiangular. (Given) 2. $\angle A \cong \angle B \cong \angle C$ (Def. of equiangular $\triangle$) 3. $m \angle A = m \angle B = m \angle C$ (Def. of $\cong$ $\angle$s) 4. $m \angle A + m \angle B + m \angle C = 180$ (Sum of meas. of $\angle$s of $\triangle = 180$.) 5. $3(m \angle A) = 180$ (Subst. [3, 4]) 6. $m \angle A = 60$ (Mult. prop. of eq. [5]) 7. $m \angle B = 60$; $m \angle C = 60$ (Subst. [3, 6]) **13.** $m \angle 2 = 155$ **15.** Given: $m \angle 4 = 41$; $m \angle 2 = 27$ Prove: $m \angle 1 = 68$ 1. $m \angle 1 = m \angle 2 + m \angle 3$ (Meas. of ext. $\angle$ of $\triangle$ = sum of meas. of 2 remote int. $\angle$s) 2. $\angle 4 \cong \angle 3$ (Vert. $\angle$s are $\cong$.) 3. $m \angle 4 = m \angle 3$ (Def. of $\cong$ $\angle$s) 4. $m \angle 4 = 41$; $m \angle 2 = 27$ (Given) 5. $m \angle 1 = 27 + 41 = 68$ (Subst. [1, 3, 4]) **19.** 1. $\overline{CD} \perp \overline{AB}$; $\angle A \cong \angle B$ (Given) 2. $\angle ADC$ is a rt. $\angle$; $\angle BDC$ is a rt. $\angle$. (2 $\perp$ lines form 4 rt. $\angle$s.) 3. $\angle ADC \cong \angle BDC$ (All rt. $\angle$s are $\cong$.) 4. $\angle ACD \cong \angle BCD$ (If 2 $\angle$s of a $\triangle$ are $\cong$ 2 $\angle$s of another $\triangle$, the third $\angle$s are $\cong$.) 5. $m \angle ACD = m \angle BCD$ (Def. of $\cong$ $\angle$s) 6. $\overrightarrow{CD}$ bisects $\angle ACB$ (Def. of $\angle$ bisector) **23.** 1. In $\triangle MAY$, $\angle M \cong \angle Y$ (Given) 2. $m \angle M = m \angle Y$ (Def. of $\cong$ $\angle$s) 3. $m \angle NAM = m \angle M + m \angle Y$ (Meas. of ext. $\angle$ of $\triangle$ = sum of meas. of remote int. $\angle$s.) 4. $m \angle NAM = m \angle M + m \angle M$ (Subst. [2, 3]) 5. $m \angle NAM = 2(m \angle M)$ (Dist. prop.)

Pages 149-151

Class Exercises **1.** Convex quadrilateral **3.** Not a polygon; $\overline{WX}$ and $\overline{QP}$ each intersect only one other segment **5.** $\overline{GA}$, $\overline{AD}$, $\overline{DC}$, $\overline{CB}$, $\overline{BF}$, $\overline{FE}$, $\overline{EG}$ **7.** Answers may vary. Examples: $\angle C$ and $\angle B$ **9.** Answers may vary. Examples: $\overline{GE}$ and $\overline{FB}$ **Written Exercises** **1.** A, B, C, D, E, and F **3.** $\angle A$, $\angle B$, $\angle C$, $\angle D$, $\angle E$, $\angle F$ **5.** Answers may vary. Examples: $\angle A$ and $\angle B$ **7.** Convex, equiangular **9.** Nonconvex, equilateral **11.** 16 **13.** $x = 2$; sides: 4, 5, 3, 6 **15.** 7.02 **19.** a. $n - 3$ b. $0.5n(n - 3)$ **21.** 42 matches; 14 weeks **23.** 1 $EFGHJ$ has diags. $\overline{EG}$, $\overline{EH}$ (Given) 2. $m \angle J + m \angle 5 + m \angle 11 = 180$; $m \angle 10 + m \angle 6 + m \angle 7 = 180$; $m \angle 8 + m \angle 9 + m \angle F = 180$ (Sum of meas. of $\angle$s of $\triangle = 180$) 3. $m \angle J + m \angle 5 + m \angle 6 + m \angle 7 + m \angle 8 + m \angle F + m \angle 9 + m \angle 10 + m \angle 11 = 540$ (Add. prop. of eq. [2]) 4. $m \angle 11 + m \angle 10 = m \angle JEG$ (Angle Add. Post.) 5. $m \angle JEG + m \angle 9 = m \angle JEF$ (Angle Add. Post.) 6. $m \angle 9 + m \angle 11 + m \angle 10 = m \angle JEF$ (Subst. [4, 5]) 7. $m \angle 5 + m \angle 6 = m \angle JHG$; $m \angle 7 + m \angle 8 = m \angle HGF$ (Angle Add. Post.) 8. $m \angle J + m \angle JHG + m \angle HGF + m \angle JEF + m \angle F = 540$ (Subst. [3, 6, 7])

Pages 154-155

Class Exercises **1.** False; the sum of the measures of the int. angles is $(5 - 2)180 = 540$. **3.** True **5.** False; $(5 - 2)180 = 540$, but the sum of the measures of the exterior angles is 360. **Written Exercises** **1.** 360 **3.** 720 **5.** 1080 **7.** 6840 **9.** 90 **11.** 144 **13.** 8 **15.** $360/r$ **17.** 7 **19.** 9 **21.** The 60° angle is an exterior angle of the hexagon. Each angle of a reg. hex. has measure 120. So each ext. angle has measure 60. **23.** 45-45-90 triangle **25.** 10 **27.** 24 **29.** Given: Any convex hexagon $ABCDEF$ Prove: At least one angle of $ABCDEF$ has a measure of 120 or more. Proof: Suppose every angle of $ABCDEF$ has a measure less than 120. Then the sum of the measures of the six angles of the hexagon will be less than $6(120)$ or 720, by the Add. prop. of $\neq$. This contradicts the fact that the sum of the measures of the angles of any convex hexagon is $(6 - 2)180 = 720$. Thus the assumption is false. We conclude that at least one angle of $ABCDEF$ has a measure of 120 or more.

Chapter 4

Pages 168-169

Class Exercises   1. Two marks **3.** Three marks
5. $\overline{YZ}$ **7.** $\triangle RST$; $\triangle TRS$; $\triangle TSR$; $\triangle SRT$; $\triangle STR$
9. True **11.** False **13.** True   **Written**
Exercises   1. $\overline{PA} \cong \overline{TE}$, $\overline{PS} \cong \overline{TL}$, $\overline{AS} \cong \overline{EL}$
3. True **5.** True **7.** True **9.** False **11.** $\overline{AB} \cong \overline{CB}$,
$\overline{AE} \cong \overline{CD}$, $\overline{BE} \cong \overline{BD}$, $\angle A \cong \angle C$, $\angle ABE \cong \angle CBD$,
$\angle AEB \cong \angle CDB$ **13.** $\overline{EB} \cong \overline{DB}$, $\overline{ED} \cong \overline{DE}$, $\overline{BD} \cong$
$\overline{BE}$, $\angle DEB \cong \angle EDB$, $\angle EBD \cong \angle DBE$, $\angle EDB \cong$
$\angle DEB$ **15. a.** Yes; segs. are $\cong$ if lengths $=$.
b. Vert. lines are $\perp$ to horizontal lines; $\overline{PD} \perp \overline{CD}$
and $\overline{TB} \perp \overline{AB}$. Thus, $\angle D$ and $\angle B$ are rt. $\angle$s and
$\angle B \cong \angle D$. **c.** Yes **d.** Heights appear to be $=$.
17. Given: $\triangle ABC$ Prove: $\triangle ABC \cong \triangle ABC$ Proof:
1. $\overline{AB} \cong \overline{AB}$; $\overline{AC} \cong \overline{AC}$; $\overline{BC} \cong \overline{BC}$ ($\cong$ of segs. is
reflex.) 2. $\angle A \cong \angle A$; $\angle B \cong \angle B$; $\angle C \cong \angle C$ ($\cong$ of
$\angle$s is reflex.) 3. $\triangle ABC \cong \triangle ABC$ (Def. of $\cong \triangle$s
[1, 2]) **19.** Given: $\triangle ABC \cong \triangle DEF$, $\triangle DEF \cong$
$\triangle GHK$. Prove: $\triangle ABC \cong \triangle GHK$ Proof:
1. $\triangle ABC \cong \triangle DEF$ (Given) 2. $\overline{AB} \cong \overline{DE}$, $\overline{AC} \cong$
$\overline{DF}$, $\overline{BC} \cong \overline{EF}$, $\angle A \cong \angle D$, $\angle B \cong \angle E$, $\angle C \cong \angle F$
(Corres. parts of $\cong \triangle$s are $\cong$.) 3. $\triangle DEF \cong$
$\triangle GHK$ (Given) 4. $\overline{DE} \cong \overline{GH}$, $\overline{DF} \cong \overline{GK}$, $\overline{EF} \cong \overline{HK}$,
$\angle D \cong \angle G$, $\angle E \cong \angle H$, $\angle F \cong \angle K$ (Corres. parts of
$\cong \triangle$s are $\cong$.) 5. $\overline{AB} \cong \overline{GH}$, $\overline{AC} \cong \overline{GK}$, $\overline{BC} \cong \overline{HK}$
($\cong$ of segs. is trans. [2, 4]) 6. $\angle A \cong \angle G$, $\angle B \cong$
$\angle H$, $\angle C \cong \angle K$ ($\cong$ of $\angle$s is trans. [2, 4])
7. $\triangle ABC \cong \triangle GHK$ (Def. of $\cong \triangle$s)
21. 1. $\triangle ABC \cong \triangle ACB$ (Given) 2. $\overline{AB} \cong \overline{AC}$
(Corres. parts of $\cong \triangle$s are $\cong$.) 3. $\triangle ABC \cong$
$\triangle CBA$ (Given) 4. $\overline{AB} \cong \overline{BC}$ (Corres. parts of $\cong$
$\triangle$s are $\cong$.) 5. $\overline{AC} \cong \overline{BC}$ ($\cong$ of segs. is trans.
[2, 4]) 6. $\triangle ABC$ is equilateral (Def. of equilateral
$\triangle$s [2, 4, 5]) **23.** Two convex n-gons are $\cong$ if and
only if there is a correspondence between the
vertices such that each side and each angle $\cong$
to its corres. side or angle.

Pages 174-176

Class Exercises   1. SSS **3.** ASA **5.** $\triangle OLD \cong$
$\triangle NEW$ by SAS **7.** $\triangle APE \cong \triangle NUT$ by SSS
Written Exercises   1. $\overline{AR}$; $\overline{RT}$; $\overline{AT}$
3. $\angle O \cong \angle R$; $\angle W \cong \angle T$ **5.** $\overline{OW}$; $\overline{NW}$ **7.** 1. Given
2. Given 3. $\cong$ of segs. is reflex. 4. SAS Post.
[1, 2, 3] **9.** 1. $\overline{AD} \cong \overline{CB}$ (Given) 2. $\overline{AB} \cong \overline{CD}$
(Given) 3. $\overline{AC} \cong \overline{AC}$ ($\cong$ of segs. is reflex.)
4. $\triangle ABC \cong \triangle CDA$ (SSS Post. [1, 2, 3])

11. 1. $\overline{AB} \cong \overline{CD}$ (Given) 2. $\overline{AB} \parallel \overline{CD}$ (Given)
3. $\angle CAB \cong \angle ACD$ (2 lines $\parallel \Rightarrow$ alt. int. $\angle$s $\cong$.)
4. $\overline{AC} \cong \overline{AC}$ ($\cong$ of segs. is reflex.) 5. $\triangle ABC \cong$
$\triangle CDA$ (SAS Post. [1, 4, 3]) **13.** $\angle M \cong \angle F$;
$\angle N \cong \angle G$; $\angle P \cong \angle H$ **15.** $\angle X \cong \angle D$; $\overline{XZ} \cong \overline{DF}$;
$\overline{YZ} \cong \overline{EF}$ **17.** 1. $\angle A \cong \angle D$; (Given) 2. B is
midpt. of $\overline{AD}$. (Given) 3. $AB = BD$ (Def. of
midpt.) 4. $\overline{AB} \cong \overline{BD}$ (Def. of $\cong$ segs.)
5. $\angle ABC \cong \angle DBE$ (Vert. $\angle$s are $\cong$.)
6. $\triangle ABC \cong \triangle DBE$ (ASA Post. [1, 4, 5])
19. 1. $\overline{AC} \parallel \overline{DE}$; $\overline{AC} \cong \overline{DE}$ (Given) 2. $\angle A \cong \angle D$
(2 lines $\parallel \Rightarrow$ alt. int. $\angle$s $\cong$.) 3. $\angle ABC \cong \angle DBE$
(Vert. $\angle$s are $\cong$.) 4. $\angle C \cong \angle E$ (If 2 $\angle$s of two
$\triangle$s are $\cong$, their third $\angle$s are $\cong$. [2, 3])
5. $\triangle ABC \cong \triangle DBE$ (ASA Post. [1, 2, 4]) **21.** By
construction, $\angle PRO \cong \angle SRO$ and $\overline{RS} \cong \overline{RP}$. Since
$\cong$ of segs. is reflex., $\overline{RO} \cong \overline{RO}$. Therefore,
$\triangle PRO \cong \triangle SRO$ by the SAS Post. Thus, $\overline{OP} \cong \overline{OS}$
and $OP = OS$, because corres. parts of $\cong \triangle$s are
$\cong$. **23.** 1. $\overline{PR} \perp \overline{MN}$ (Given) 2. $\angle MRP$ and $\angle NRP$
are rt. $\angle$s. (2 $\perp$ lines form 4 rt. $\angle$s.)
3. $\angle MRP \cong \angle NRP$ (All rt. $\angle$s are $\cong$.) 4. R is the
midpt. of $\overline{MN}$. (Given) 5. $MR = RN$ (Def. of
midpt.) 6. $\overline{MR} \cong \overline{RN}$ (Def. of $\cong$ segs.) 7. $\overline{PR} \cong \overline{PR}$
($\cong$ of segs. is reflex.) 8. $\triangle MRP \cong \triangle NRP$ (SAS
Post. [3, 6, 7])

Pages 179-182

Class Exercises   1. ASA Post. **3.** LA Thm.
5. $\triangle ANJ \cong \triangle EBF$ by HA Thm. **7.** $\triangle WIN \cong$
$\triangle BYE$ by LL Thm.   **Written Exercises   1.** N; D
3. $\overline{TN}$; $\overline{RD}$ **5.** 1. Given 2. 2 $\perp$ lines form 4 rt.
$\angle$s. 3. Def. of rt. $\triangle$ 4. $\cong$ of segs. is reflex.
5. Given 6. LA Thm. [3, 4, 5] **7.** 1. $\angle A \cong \angle D$
(Given) 2. $\angle AOB \cong \angle DOC$ (Vert. $\angle$s are $\cong$.)
3. $\overline{AB} \cong \overline{DC}$ (Given) 4. $\triangle AOB \cong \triangle DOC$ (AAS
Thm. [1, 2, 3]) **9.** 1. $\overline{AB} \perp \overline{BC}$, $\overline{DC} \perp \overline{BC}$ (Given)
2. $\angle ABO$ and $\angle DCO$ are rt. $\angle$s (2 $\perp$ lines form
4 rt. $\angle$s.) 3. $\triangle AOB$ and $\triangle DOC$ are rt. $\triangle$s. (Def.
of rt. $\triangle$) 4. O is the midpt. of $\overline{AD}$. (Given)
5. $AO = OD$ (Def. of midpt.) 6. $\overline{AO} \cong \overline{OD}$ (Def. of
$\cong$ segs.) 7. $\angle BOA \cong \angle DOC$ (Vert. $\angle$s are $\cong$.)
8. $\triangle AOB \cong \triangle DOC$ (HA Thm. [3, 6, 7])
11. 1. $\overline{PT} \perp \overline{IO}$ (Given) 2. $\angle PTI$ and $\angle PTO$ are
rt. $\angle$s. (2 $\perp$ lines form 4 rt. $\angle$s.) 3. $\triangle TIP$ and
$\triangle TOP$ are rt. $\triangle$s. (Def. of rt. $\triangle$) 4. $\overline{IP} \cong \overline{OP}$;
$\angle I \cong \angle O$ (Given) 5. $\triangle TIP \cong \triangle TOP$ (HA Thm.
[3, 4]) **13.** 1. $\overline{IP} \cong \overline{OP}$ (Given) 2. $\overline{PT} \cong \overline{PT}$ ($\cong$ of
segs. is reflex.) 3. T is midpt. of $\overline{IO}$. (Given)

4. $TI = TO$ (Def. of midpt.) 5. $\overline{TI} \cong \overline{TO}$ (Def. of $\cong$ segs.) 6. $\triangle TIP \cong \triangle TOP$ (SSS Post. [1, 2, 5])
15. $\angle Q \cong \angle T$; $\overline{QR} \cong \overline{TU}$; $\angle P \cong \angle S$ (Given) 2. $\angle R \cong \angle U$ (If 2 $\angle$s of 2 $\triangle$s are $\cong$, their third $\angle$s are $\cong$.) 3. $\triangle PQR \cong \triangle STU$ (ASA Post. [1, 2])
17. Given: Rt. $\triangle ABC$ with hypotenuse $\overline{AB}$; rt. $\triangle DEF$ with hypotenuse $\overline{DE}$; $\overline{AB} \cong \overline{DE}$; $\angle A \cong \angle D$ Prove: $\triangle ABC \cong \triangle DEF$ 1. $\overline{AB} \cong \overline{DE}$ (Given) 2. $\angle A \cong \angle D$ (Given) 3. $\angle C$ and $\angle F$ are rt. $\angle$s. (Def. of hypotenuse) 4. $\angle C \cong \angle F$ (All rt. $\angle$s are $\cong$.) 5. $\triangle ABC \cong \triangle DEF$ (AAS Thm. [1, 2, 4])
19. 1. $\overrightarrow{RT}$ bis. $\angle SRW$ (Given) 2. $m\angle SRT = m\angle TRW$ (Def. of $\angle$ bis.) 3. $\angle SRT \cong \angle TRW$ (Def. of $\cong$ $\angle$s) 4. $\overline{RT} \cong \overline{RT}$ ($\cong$ of segs. is reflex.) 5. $\overrightarrow{RT}$ bisects $\angle STW$ (Given) 6. $m\angle STR = m\angle RTW$ (Def. of $\angle$ bis.) 7. $\angle STR \cong \angle RTW$ (Def. of $\cong$ $\angle$s) 8. $\triangle RST \cong \triangle RWT$ (ASA Post. [3, 4, 7])
23. 1. $\overline{WT} \| \overline{RS}$ (Given) 2. $\angle RSW \cong \angle TWS$ (2 lines $\|$ $\Rightarrow$ alt. int. $\angle$s $\cong$.) 3. $\overline{SW} \cong \overline{WS}$ ($\cong$ of segs. is reflex.) 4. $\overline{RW} \| \overline{ST}$ (Given) 5. $\angle RWS \cong \angle TSW$ (2 lines $\|$ $\Rightarrow$ alt. int. $\angle$s $\cong$.) 6. $\triangle RSW \cong \triangle TWS$ (ASA Post. [2, 3, 5]) **25.** 1. $\angle RSP$ and $\angle RSQ$ are rt. $\angle$s. (Given) 2. $\triangle PSR$ and $\triangle QSR$ are rt. $\triangle$s (Def. of rt. $\triangle$) 3. $\overline{PS} \cong \overline{SQ}$ (Given) 4. $\overline{SR} \cong \overline{SR}$ ($\cong$ of segs. is reflex.) 5. $\triangle PSR \cong \triangle QSR$ (LL Thm. [2, 3, 4]) **27.** 1. $\angle QSP$ and $\angle RSP$ are rt. $\angle$s. (Given) 2. $\triangle PQS$ and $\triangle PRS$ are rt. $\triangle$s. (Def. of rt. $\triangle$) 3. $\overline{PS} \cong \overline{PS}$ ($\cong$ of segs. is reflex.) 4. $\angle PQS \cong \angle PRS$ (Given) 5. $\triangle PQS \cong \triangle PRS$ (LA Thm. [2, 3, 4]) **29.** Locate A and C so that $RA = SC$. Since $RB = SB$, $\triangle ARB \cong \triangle CSB$ by LL Thm. **31.** $\triangle ABC \cong \triangle ABD$ by LA Thm. since $\overline{AB} \cong \overline{AB}$ and $\angle ABC \cong \angle ABD$. The surveyor could then measure $\overline{AD}$ to get the height of the pole, because $\overline{AD} \cong \overline{AC}$.

Pages 185-186

Class Exercises **1.** $\angle 1$ and $\angle 2$ **3.** $\triangle CDA$ **5.** $\triangle SUR$ and $\triangle SUT$, or $\triangle RVS$ and $\triangle TVS$ **7.** $\triangle RUS$ and $\triangle TUS$ **9.** $\triangle SVR$ and $\triangle SVT$, or $\triangle RUV$ and $\triangle TUV$ **Written Exercises** **1.** 1. $\overline{WZ} \cong \overline{YZ}$; $\angle 1 \cong \angle 2$ (Given) 2. $\overline{XZ} \cong \overline{XZ}$ ($\cong$ of segs. is reflex.) 3. $\triangle WXZ \cong \triangle YXZ$ (SAS Post. [1, 2]) 4. $\angle 3 \cong \angle 4$ (Corres. parts of $\cong$ $\triangle$s are $\cong$.) **3.** 1. $\angle 1 \cong \angle 2$ (Given) 2. $\overline{XZ} \cong \overline{XZ}$ ($\cong$ of segs. is reflex.) 3. $\angle 3 \cong \angle 4$ (Given) 4. $\triangle WXZ \cong \triangle YXZ$ (ASA Post. [1, 2, 3]) 5. $\overline{WZ} \cong \overline{YZ}$ (Corres. parts of $\cong$ $\triangle$s are $\cong$.) **5.** 1. $\angle P \cong \angle N$; $\angle 1 \cong \angle 2$;

$\overline{PK} \cong \overline{NM}$ (Given) 2. $\triangle PKL \cong \triangle NML$ (AAS Thm. [1]) 3. $\angle K \cong \angle M$ (Corres. parts of $\cong$ $\triangle$s are $\cong$.)
7. 1. $\overline{AC} \cong \overline{BC}$; $\overline{CM}$ bisects $\angle ACB$ (Given) 2. $m\angle ACM = m\angle BCM$ (Def. of $\angle$ bis.) 3. $\angle ACM \cong \angle BCM$ (Def. of $\cong$ $\angle$s) 4. $\overline{CM} \cong \overline{CM}$ ($\cong$ of segs. is reflex.) 5. $\triangle ACM \cong \triangle BCM$ (SAS Post. [1, 3, 4]) 6. $\angle AMC \cong \angle BMC$ (Corres. parts of $\cong$ $\triangle$s are $\cong$.) 7. $\overline{CM} \perp \overline{AB}$ (If $\angle$s in a lin. pr. are $\cong$, sides are $\perp$.) **9.** 1. $\overline{AB} \cong \overline{CD}$; $\angle 2 \cong \angle 3$ (Given) 2. $\overline{AC} \cong \overline{CA}$ ($\cong$ of segs. is reflex.) 3. $\triangle ACD \cong \triangle CAB$ (SAS Post. [1, 2]) 4. $\angle 1 \cong \angle 4$ (Corres. parts of $\cong$ $\triangle$s are $\cong$.) 5. $\overline{AD} \| \overline{CB}$ (Alt. int. $\angle$s $\Rightarrow$ 2 lines $\|$.) **11.** 1. $\overline{AD} \cong \overline{BC}$ (Given) 2. $\angle 1 \cong \angle 4$ (Given) 3. $\overline{AC} \cong \overline{AC}$ ($\cong$ of segs. is reflex.) 4. $\triangle ABC \cong \triangle CDA$ (SAS Post. [1, 2, 3]) 5. $\angle D \cong \angle B$ (Corres. parts of $\cong$ $\triangle$s are $\cong$.) 6. $m\angle D = m\angle B$ (Def. of $\cong$ $\angle$s) 7. $\overline{AB} \perp \overline{BC}$ (Given) 8. $\angle B$ is a rt. $\angle$. (2 $\perp$ lines form 4 rt. $\angle$s.) 9. $m\angle B = 90$ (Def. of rt. $\angle$) 10. $m\angle D = 90$ (Subst. [6, 9]) 11. $\angle D$ is a rt. $\angle$. (Def. of rt. $\angle$) 12. $\overline{AD} \perp \overline{DC}$ (Def. of $\perp$ lines) **13.** Since $PQ = PS$, $RQ = RS$, and $\overline{RP} \cong \overline{RP}$, it follows that $\triangle PQR \cong \triangle PSR$ by the SSS Post. Since corres. parts of $\cong$ $\triangle$s are $\cong$, $\angle Q \cong \angle S$ or $m\angle Q = m\angle S$.

Pages 188-191

Class Exercises **1.** $\overline{AB} \cong \overline{BA}$, $\overline{AD} \cong \overline{BC}$, $\overline{BD} \cong \overline{AC}$, $\angle BAD \cong \angle ABC$, $\angle ABD \cong \angle BAC$, $\angle ADB \cong \angle BCA$ **3.** $\overline{CA} \cong \overline{BD}$, $\overline{CB} \cong \overline{BC}$, $\overline{AB} \cong \overline{DC}$, $\angle ACB \cong \angle DBC$, $\angle CAB \cong \angle BDC$, $\angle CBA \cong \angle BCD$ **5.** $\angle 1 \cong \angle 2$; $\angle 2 \cong \angle 3$ **7.** $\overline{VY} \cong \overline{VY}$; $\angle XYV \cong \angle ZYV$ **9.** AAS Thm. **Written Exercises** **1.** Yes; by the ASA Post. **3.** Not nec. $\cong$; $\angle$ not included **5.** Yes; by the LL Thm. **7.** Yes, by the SAS Post. **9.** Yes; by the ASA Post. **11.** Not nec. $\cong$; cannot use "AAA" **13.** 1. $\overline{AD} \cong \overline{BC}$; $\angle DAB \cong \angle CBA$ (Given) 2. $\overline{AB} \cong \overline{BA}$ ($\cong$ of segs. is reflex.) 3. $\triangle ADB \cong \triangle BCA$ (SAS Post. [1, 2]) **15.** 1. $\angle D \cong \angle C$; $\angle 1 \cong \angle 2$ (Given) 2. $\overline{AB} \cong \overline{BA}$ ($\cong$ of segs. is reflex.) 3. $\triangle ADB \cong \triangle BCA$ (AAS Thm. [1, 2]) **17.** 1. $\angle TVR \cong \angle TUS$; $\overline{UT} \cong \overline{VT}$ (Given) 2. $\angle T \cong \angle T$ ($\cong$ of $\angle$s is reflex.) 3. $\triangle RTV \cong \triangle STU$ (ASA Post. [1, 2]) **19.** 1. $\angle TRV \cong \angle TSU$ (Given) 2. $\angle T \cong \angle T$ ($\cong$ of $\angle$s is reflex.) 3. $\overline{RV} \cong \overline{SU}$ (Given) 4. $\triangle RTV \cong \triangle STU$ (AAS Thm. [1, 2, 3]) **25.** $\triangle PTR \cong \triangle QTS$; $\triangle PSU \cong \triangle QRU$; $\triangle PRS \cong \triangle QSR$ **27.** $\angle U \cong \angle U$ since $\cong$ of

∡s is reflex. Hence △UPS ≅ △UQR by the SAS Post. **29. 1.** $\overline{NK} \cong \overline{MP}$; $\overline{PN} \cong \overline{KM}$ (Given) 2. $\overline{MN} \cong \overline{NM}$ (≅ of segs. is reflex.) 3. △KMN ≅ △PNM (SSS Post. [1, 2]) 4. ∡K ≅ ∡P (Corres. parts of ≅ △s are ≅.) 5. ∡KON ≅ ∡POM (Vert. ∡s are ≅.) 6. △KON ≅ △POM (AAS Thm. [4, 5, 6]) 7. $\overline{MO} \cong \overline{NO}$ (Corres. parts of ≅ △s are ≅.) **31. 1.** $\overline{AD} \cong \overline{BC}$; ∡ADC ≅ ∡BCD (Given) 2. $\overline{DC} \cong \overline{CD}$ (≅ of segs. is reflex.) 3. △ADC ≅ △BCD (SAS Post. [1, 2]) **35. 1.** $\overline{XU} \cong \overline{ZU}$; $\overline{XY} \cong \overline{ZY}$ (Given) 2. $\overline{UY} \cong \overline{UY}$ (≅ of segs. is reflex.) 3. △UXY ≅ △UZY (SSS Post. [1, 2]) 4. ∡XUV ≅ ∡ZUV (Corres. parts of ≅ △s are ≅.) 5. $\overline{VU} \cong \overline{VU}$ (≅ of segs. is reflex.) 6. △XUV ≅ △ZUV (SAS Post. [1, 4, 5]) 7. ∡XVU ≅ ∡ZVU (Corr. parts of ≅ △s are ≅.) 8. $\overline{UY} \perp \overline{XZ}$ (If ∡s of lin. pr. are ≅, lines are ⊥.) **37.** △CBA, △BCD, △DCB, △CDE, △EDC, △DEA, △AED, △EAB, △BAE **39.** △BCH, △CDJ, △DEK, △EAF, △BAK, △AEJ, △EDH, △DCG, △CBF **43. 1.** $\overline{RW} \cong \overline{RS}$; ∡1 ≅ ∡2 (Given) 2. $\overline{UR} \cong \overline{UR}$ (≅ of segs. is reflex.) 3. △URW ≅ △URS (SAS Post. [1, 2]) 4. ∡UWR ≅ ∡USR (Corres. parts of ≅ △s are ≅.) 5. ∡VWU and ∡UWR are supp.; ∡TSU and ∡USR are supp. (Supp. Post.) 6. ∡VWU ≅ ∡TSU (Supps. of ≅ ∡s are ≅. [4, 5]) 7. ∡VUW ≅ ∡TUS (Vert. ∡s are ≅.) 8. $\overline{WU} \cong \overline{SU}$ (Corres. parts of ≅ △s are ≅. [3]) 9. △VWU ≅ △TSU (ASA Thm. [6, 7, 8]) 10. $\overline{VU} \cong \overline{TU}$ (Corres. parts of ≅ △s are ≅.)

Pages 194-196

Class Exercises **1.** Altitude **3.** False **5.** True **7.** $BD = BE$ **9.** $QP = QR$ **11.** R, D, E **Written Exercises**

7.

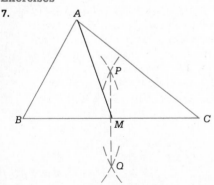

Pages 199-201

Class Exercises **1.** ∡A ≅ ∡B ≅ ∡C; m∡A = m∡B = m∡C = 60 **3.** 13 **5.** If a △ is equilateral, then it is equiangular. If a △ is equiangular, then it is equilateral. **Written Exercises** **1.** 65 **3.** 4 **5.** 6 **7.** 80 **9.** 120 **11.** 130 **13. 1.** ∡A ≅ ∡B (Given) 2. Draw $\overrightarrow{CE}$, the bisector of ∡ACB. (Angle Bis. Post.) 3. m∡ACD = m∡BCD (Def. of ∡ bis.) 4. ∡ACD ≅ ∡BCD (Def. of ≅ ∡s) 5. $\overline{CD} \cong \overline{CD}$ (≅ of segs. is reflex.) 6. △ACD ≅ △BCD (AAS Thm. [1, 4, 5]) 7. $\overline{AC} \cong \overline{BC}$ (Corres. parts of ≅ △s are ≅.) **15.** Given: Equiangular △ABC Prove: △ABC is equilateral. 1. ∡A ≅ ∡B ≅ ∡C (Def. of equiangular △) 2. $\overline{AC} \cong \overline{BC}$, $\overline{BC} \cong \overline{BA}$ (2 ∡s of a △ ≅ ⇒ the sides opp. those ∡s are ≅.) 3. $\overline{AC} \cong \overline{BA}$ (≅ of segs. is trans.) 4. △ABC is equilateral. (Def. of equilateral △) **17.** m∡P = 60; QR = 5 m **19. 1.** ∡YXZ ≅ ∡YZX (Given) 2. $\overline{YX} \cong \overline{YZ}$ (If 2 ∡s of a △ are ≅, then the sides opp. those ∡s are ≅.) 3. $\overline{XY} \perp \overline{TZ}$, $\overline{YZ} \perp \overline{XV}$ (Given) 4. ∡YTZ and ∡YVX are rt. ∡s. (2 ⊥ lines form 4 rt. ∡s.) 5. △TYZ and ∡VYX are rt. △s. (Def. of rt. △) 6. ∡Y ≅ ∡Y (≅ of ∡s is reflex.) 7. △TYZ ≅ △VYX (HA Thm. [2, 5, 6]) **21. 1.** $\overline{XY} \cong \overline{ZY}$ (Given) 2. ∡YXZ ≅ ∡YZX (Isos. △ Thm.) 3. $\overline{XZ} \cong \overline{ZX}$ (≅ of segs. is reflex.) 4. $\overline{XY} \perp \overline{TZ}$, $\overline{YZ} \perp \overline{XV}$ (Given) 5. ∡XTZ and ∡ZVX are rt. ∡s. (2 ⊥ lines form 4 rt. ∡s.) 6. △XTZ and △ZVX are rt. ∡s. (Def. of rt. △) 7. △XTZ ≅ △ZVX (HA Thm. [2, 3]) 8. ∡XZT ≅ ∡ZXV (Corres. parts of ≅ △s are ≅.) 9. $\overline{XW} \cong \overline{ZW}$ (2 ∡s of a △ ≅ ⇒ the sides opp. those ∡s are ≅.) **37.** To make shelf level, make $\overline{XY} \perp \overline{XZ}$ and $\overline{MN} \perp \overline{MO}$. Shelf width is constant, so $XY = MN$ and △s are ≅ by HL Thm. Thus, $XZ = MO$. **39. 1.** $\overline{AC} \cong \overline{BC}$ (Given) 2. ∡CAE ≅ ∡CBE (If 2 sides of △ are ≅, opp. ∡s are ≅.) 3. ∡1 ≅ ∡2 (Given) 4. △ACE ≅ △BCE (AAS Thm. [1, 2, 3]) 5. ∡ACD ≅ ∡BCD (Corres. parts of ≅ △s are ≅.) 6. $\overline{CD} \cong \overline{CD}$ (≅ of segs. is reflex.) 7. △ACD ≅ △BCD (SAS Post. [1, 5, 6]) 8. ∡CAD ≅ ∡CBD (Corres. parts of ≅ ∡s are ≅.) **41. 1.** $\overline{AB} \perp \overline{CD}$ (Given) 2. ∡1 and ∡2 are rt. ∡s (2 ⊥ lines form 4 rt. ∡s) 3. △ACE and △BCE are rt. △s. (Def. of rt. △) 4. $\overline{CE} \cong \overline{CE}$ (≅ of segs. is reflex.) 5. ∡CAB ≅ ∡CBA (Given) 6. △ACE ≅ △BCE (LA Thm. [3, 4, 5]) 7. ∡AED and ∡BED are rt. ∡s. (2 ⊥ lines form 4 rt. ∡s.)

8. $\triangle AED$ and $\triangle BED$ are rt. $\triangle$s. (Def. of rt. $\triangle$)
9. $\overline{AE} \cong \overline{BE}$ (Corres. parts of $\cong$ $\triangle$s are $\cong$. [6])
10. $\overline{ED} \cong \overline{ED}$ ($\cong$ of segs. is reflex.) 11. $\triangle AED \cong$ $\triangle BED$ (LL Thm. [8, 9, 10]) 12. $\angle DAB \cong \angle DBA$ (Corres. parts of $\cong$ $\triangle$s are $\cong$.)

Pages 204-206

Class Exercises 1. Yes 3. No 5. If $x > 1$, yes; otherwise, no. 7. $\overline{AC}$ is the longest; $\overline{AB}$ is the shortest side. 9. The lengths of two sides of a triangle are unequal in a certain order if and only if the measures of the angles opposite those sides are unequal in the same order.
Written Exercises 1. $2 < x < 12$ 3. $1.5 < x <$ 5.7 5. $5 < x < 10$ 7. $\overline{BC}$ is shortest; $\overline{AB}$ is longest. 9. $\overline{MN}$ is shortest; $\overline{NP}$ is longest.
11. $m\angle U$ smallest; $m\angle V$ largest. 13. 1. C is in int. of $\angle DAB$. (Given) 2. $m\angle BAC + m\angle CAD =$ $m\angle BAD$ (Angle Add. Post.) 3. $m\angle CAD > 0$ (Protractor Post.) 4. $m\angle BAC < m\angle BAD$ (Def. of $<$ [2, 3]) 15. 1. $\angle YXZ$ is a rt. $\angle$. (Given) 2. $m\angle YXZ = 90$ (Def. of rt. $\angle$) 3. $m\angle X +$ $m\angle Y + m\angle Z = 180$ (Sum of $\angle$ meas. of $\triangle =$ 180.) 4. $90 + m\angle Y + m\angle Z = 180$ (Subst. [2, 3]) 5. $m\angle Y + m\angle Z = 90$ (Subtr. prop. of eq.) 6. $m\angle Y > 0$; $m\angle Z > 0$ (Protractor Post.) 7. $90 > m\angle Y$; $90 > m\angle Z$ (Def. of $>$ [5, 6]) 8. $m\angle YXZ > m\angle Y$; $m\angle YXZ > m\angle Z$ (Subst. [2, 7]) 9. $YZ > XZ$; $YZ > XY$ (Meas. of 2 $\angle$s of a $\triangle \neq$ $\Rightarrow$ lengths of opp. sides $\neq$ in same order.) 17. See p. 204. 1. $\overline{PQ} \perp \overline{XY}$ (Given) 2. $\angle PQM$ is a rt. $\angle$. (2 $\perp$ lines form 4 rt. $\angle$s.) 3. $m\angle PQM = 90$ (Def. of rt. $\angle$) 4. $m\angle PMQ + m\angle P + m\angle PQM = 180$ (Sum of $\angle$ measures in a $\triangle$ is 180.) 5. $m\angle PMQ + m\angle P = 90$ (Subtr. prop. of eq. [3, 4]) 6. $90 > m\angle PMQ$ (Symm. prop. of eq. and def. of $>$) 7. $m\angle PQM > m\angle PMQ$ (Subst. [3, 6]) 8. $PM > PQ$ (Meas. of 2 $\angle$s of a $\triangle \neq$ $\Rightarrow$ lengths of sides opp. those $\angle$s are $\neq$ in the same order.) 19. 1. $m\angle B > m\angle A$; $m\angle E > m\angle D$ (Given) 2. $AC > BC$; $CD > CE$ (If 2 $\angle$s of $\triangle$ are $\neq$, opp. sides are $\neq$ in same order.) 3. $AD =$ $AC + CD$; $BE = BC + CE$ (Seg. Add. Post.) 4. $AC + CD > BC + CE$ (Add. prop. of $>$ [2]) 5. $AD > BE$ (Subst. [3, 4]) 23. 4 25. 1. $\overline{BC} \perp$ $\overline{AD}$; $\overline{AC} \perp \overline{AB}$ (Given) 2. $\angle ADB$ and $\angle BAC$ are rt. $\angle$s. (2 $\perp$ lines form 4 rt. $\angle$s) 3. $BC > AB$; $AB > AD$ (Ex. 15, above) 4. $BC > AD$ (Trans.

prop. of ineq. [3]) 29. By the $\triangle$ Ineq. Thm., $DQ + QB > DB$ and $QA + QC > AC$. Hence, $DQ + QB + QA + QC > DB + AC$. Since $DB =$ $DP + PB$ and $AC = AP + PC$, it follows by substitution that $DQ + QB + QA + QC > DP +$ $PB + AP + PC$.

Pages 210-211

Class Exercises 1. $BC > EF$ 3. $MN < NP$
5. $m\angle 2 > m\angle 1$ **Written Exercises** 1. $AC > BE$
3. $m\angle RWT > m\angle VWT$ 5. 1. $\overline{GH} \cong \overline{GJ}$ (Given)
2. $\overline{GK} \cong \overline{GK}$ ($\cong$ of segs. is reflex.)
3. $m\angle HGK > m\angle JGK$ (Given) 4. $HK > JK$ (Hinge Thm. [1, 2, 3]) 7. 1. $\overline{VW} \cong \overline{XY}$ (Given)
2. $\overline{WX} \cong \overline{WX}$ ($\cong$ of segs. is reflex.)
3. $m\angle WXY > m\angle VWX$ (Given) 4. $WY > VX$ (Hinge Thm. [1, 2, 3]) 9. 1. $\overline{VW} \cong \overline{XY}$; $\overline{WZ} \cong \overline{XZ}$ (Given) 2. $WZ = XZ$ (Def. of $\cong$ segs.) 3. $WY >$ VX (Given) 4. $WY - WZ > VX - XZ$ (Subtr. prop. of $>$ [2, 3]) 5. $WY = WZ + ZY$; $VX = VZ + XZ$ (Seg. Add. Post.) 6. $ZY = WY -$ WZ; $VZ = VX - XZ$ (Subtr. prop. of eq. [5]) 7. $ZY > VZ$ (Subst. [4, 6]) 8. $m\angle YXZ > m\angle VWX$ (Converse of Hinge Thm. [1, 7]) 11. 1. $\overline{AD} \cong \overline{BC}$ (Given) 2. $\overline{AB} \cong \overline{AB}$ ($\cong$ of segs. is reflex.)
3. $m\angle BAD < m\angle ABC$ (Given) 4. $BD < AC$ (Hinge Thm. [1, 2, 3]) 13. 1. $\overline{AD} \cong \overline{BC}$, $\overline{AD} \parallel \overline{BC}$, $\angle BAD$ is acute. (Given) 2. $m\angle BAD < 90$ (Def. of acute) 3. $m\angle BAD + m\angle ABC < 90 + m\angle ABC$ (Add. prop. of $\neq$) 4. $\angle BAD$ and $\angle ABC$ are supp. (2 lines $\parallel$ $\Rightarrow$ int. $\angle$s on same side of transv. are supp. [1]) 5. $m\angle BAD + m\angle ABC = 180$ (Def. of supp.) 6. $180 < 90 + m\angle ABC$ (Subst. [3, 5]) 7. $90 < m\angle ABC$ (Subtr. prop. of $\neq$) 8. $m\angle BAD < m\angle ABC$ (Trans. prop. of $\neq$ [2, 7]) 9. $\overline{AB} \cong \overline{AB}$ ($\cong$ of segs. is reflex.) 10. $BD < AC$ (Hinge Thm. [1, 8, 9]) 15. 1. $\overline{MQ} \cong \overline{NQ}$; $\overline{PN} \cong$ $\overline{RM}$; $PQ > QR$ (Given) 2. $m\angle N > m\angle M$ (Converse of Hinge Thm. [1]) 3. $SM > SN$ (If 2 $\angle$s of $\triangle$ are $\neq$, opp. sides are $\neq$ in same order.) 17. 1. $\overline{AD} \cong \overline{BD}$ (Given) 2. $\overline{DE} \cong \overline{DE}$ ($\cong$ of segs. is reflex.) 3. $m\angle ADE < m\angle BDE$ (Given) 4. $AE < BE$ (Hinge Thm. [1, 2, 3])

Chapter 5

Pages 219-222

Class Exercises **1.** A, B, K, L, M, O **3.** A, B, M, O **5.** M **7.** G, M **9.** O **Written Exercises**
1. True **3.** False; since a square has both prs. of opp. sides ∥, no square is a trap. **5.** True
7. False; all quadrilaterals are plane figures.
9. False; if the figure is a square, it is already a rectangle. **11.** $m\angle U = 75$ **13.** $m\angle MNT = 135$
15. $m\angle UMN = 105$ **17.** $\overline{AB}$, $\overline{XY}$ **19.** 65 **21.** 100
23. $18b$ **25.** $AB = BC = CD = DA = 20$
27. $m\angle E = 100.5$; $m\angle H = 79.5$ **29.** 1. $\square RUBY$
(Given) 2. $\overline{RU} \parallel \overline{YB}$; $\overline{RY} \parallel \overline{UB}$ (Def. of $\square$) 3. $\angle R$
and $\angle U$ are supp.; $\angle U$ and $\angle B$ are supp. (2
lines ∥ ⇒ int. $\angle$s on same side supp.)
35. 1. $\square ABCD$ (Given) 2. $\overline{AB} \parallel \overline{CD}$; $\overline{AD} \parallel \overline{BC}$ (Def.
of $\square$) 3. $\angle A$ and $\angle B$ are supp.; $\angle B$ and $\angle C$ are
supp. (2 lines ∥ ⇒ int. $\angle$s on same side supp.)
4. $\angle A \cong \angle C$ (Supps. of same $\angle$ are $\cong$.) 5. $\angle B$
and $\angle C$ are supp.; $\angle C$ and $\angle D$ are supp. (2
lines ∥ ⇒ int. $\angle$s on same side supp. [2])
6. $\angle B \cong \angle D$ (Supps. of same $\angle$ are $\cong$.) **37.** It
appears that $\overline{CX}$ and $\overline{BX'}$ are $\cong$ segs., so X and
X' would coincide if X is chosen to be the
midpt. of $\overline{BC}$.

Pages 225-228

Class Exercises **1.** $\overleftrightarrow{EL} \parallel \overleftrightarrow{FT}$ or $\overleftrightarrow{EF} \parallel \overleftrightarrow{LT}$ **3.** $\overline{EL} \cong$
$\overline{FT}$ or $\overline{EF} \cong \overline{LT}$ **5.** A diag. and the sides of a $\square$
form 2 $\cong$ $\triangle$s. **7.** 12 **9.** 11.5 **11.** 18 **13.** In a
plane, 2 lines ⊥ to same line are ∥. **Written**
Exercises **1.** 18 **3.** 20 **5.** 70 **7.** $\overline{OT}$; def. of $\square$
9. $\angle TUO$; 2 lines ∥ ⇒ alt. int. $\angle$s $\cong$. **11.** $\angle UTO$;
opp. $\angle$s of $\square$ are $\cong$. **13.** If a quad. is a $\square$, then
its opp. $\angle$s are $\cong$. **15.** If the opp. sides of a
quad. are $\cong$, then the quad. is a $\square$. (True)
17. If the diags. of a quad. bisect each other,
then the quad. is a $\square$. (True) **19.** $\square EFGH$; 2
pts. are contained in exactly one line; a diag.
and the sides of a $\square$ form 2 $\cong$ $\triangle$s. [1, 2];
$\angle EFG$; corr. parts of $\cong$ $\triangle$s are $\cong$; a diag. and
the sides of a $\square$ form 2 $\cong$ $\triangle$s. [1, 2]; $\angle HEF \cong$
$\angle HGF$; corr. parts of $\cong$ $\triangle$s are $\cong$. [5] **21.** 15
23. 15 **25.** 2.5 **27.** $y = -40$; $z = 60$ **31.** 1.
$\square GRIN$ and $\square GLAD$ (Given) 2. $\angle A \cong \angle G$;
$\angle G \cong \angle I$ (Opp. $\angle$s of a $\square$ are $\cong$.) 3. $\angle A \cong \angle I$
($\cong$ of $\angle$s is trans. [2]) **33.** 1. $\square EFGH$; $\overline{EG} \cong \overline{FH}$

(Given) 2. $\overline{EF} \parallel \overline{HG}$ (Def. of $\square$) 3. $\angle FEH$ and
$\angle GHE$ are supp. (2 lines ∥ ⇒ int. $\angle$s on same
side supp.) 4. $\overline{EF} \cong \overline{HG}$ (Opp. sides of $\square$ are $\cong$.
[1]) 5. $\overline{HE} \cong \overline{EH}$ ($\cong$ of segs. is reflex.)
6. $\triangle FEH \cong \triangle GHE$ (SSS Post. [1, 4, 5])
7. $\angle FEH \cong \angle GHE$ (Corr. parts of $\cong$ $\triangle$s are $\cong$.)
8. $\angle HEF$ is a rt. $\angle$. (If 2 $\angle$s are $\cong$ and supp.,
each is a rt. $\angle$. [3, 7])

Pages 231-233

Class Exercises **1.** Def. of seg. bisector; if
diags. of quad. bis. each other, quad. is $\square$.
3. Def. of $\square$ **5.** Alt. int. $\angle$s of ∥ lines are $\cong$;
vert. $\angle$s are $\cong$; ASA Post.; if a pr. of opp. sides
of quad. are both ∥ and $\cong$, quad. is a $\square$. **7.** Alt.
int. $\angle$s $\cong$ ⇒ 2 lines ∥; if pr. of opp. sides of
quad. are both ∥ and $\cong$, quad. is a $\square$. **Written**
Exercises **1.** If both prs. of opp. sides of a
quad. are $\cong$, the quad. is a $\square$; opp. sides of $\square$
are ∥. **3.** Support should be on 2nd and 3rd
pegs from the bottom. If opp. sides are both ∥
and $\cong$, quad. is a $\square$. Since opp. sides of a $\square$
are ∥, the shelves will then be ∥. **5.** 9; if diags.
of quad. bis. each other, quad. is $\square$. **7.** 50; def.
of $\square$ **9.** 115; def. of $\square$ **11.** 1. $\overline{ST} \parallel \overline{QR}$; $\overline{TX} \cong$
$\overline{RX}$ (Given) 2. $\angle QRX \cong \angle STX$; $\angle 1 \cong \angle 2$ (2 lines
∥ ⇒ alt. int. $\angle$s $\cong$.) 3. $\triangle QRX \cong \triangle STX$ (AAS Thm.
[1, 2]) 4. $\overline{ST} \cong \overline{QR}$ (Corr. parts of $\cong$ $\triangle$s are $\cong$.)
5. $QRST$ is a $\square$. (If pr. of opp. sides of quad.
are ∥ and $\cong$, quad. is $\square$. [1, 4]) **13.** 1. $\angle 1 \cong \angle 2$;
$\angle QTS \cong \angle SRQ$ (Given) 2. $\overline{QS} \cong \overline{QS}$ ($\cong$ of segs.
is reflex.) 3. $\triangle QST \cong \triangle SQR$ (AAS Thm. [1, 2])
4. $\overline{ST} \cong \overline{QR}$; $\overline{SR} \cong \overline{TQ}$ (Corr. parts of $\cong$ $\triangle$s are
$\cong$.) 5. $QRST$ is a $\square$. (If both prs. of opp. sides
of quad. are $\cong$, quad. is $\square$.) **15.** 1. $\angle 1 \cong \angle 2$;
$\angle 3 \cong \angle 4$ (Given) 2. $\overline{QR} \parallel \overline{TS}$; $\overline{RS} \parallel \overline{QT}$ (Alt. int.
$\angle$s $\cong$ ⇒ 2 lines ∥.) 3. $QRST$ is a $\square$. (Def. of $\square$)
17. It appears to be a $\square$. **21.** $x = 13$; $y = 6$
23. $x = 6$; $y = 3$ **25.** 1. $\square HIJK$; $\angle 1 \cong \angle 2$ (Given)
2. $\overline{HK} \cong \overline{JI}$ (Opp. sides of $\square$ are $\cong$.) 3. $\angle K \cong \angle I$
(Opp. $\angle$s of $\square$ are $\cong$. [1]) 4. $\triangle KXH \cong \triangle IYJ$
(ASA Post. [1, 2, 3]) 5. $\angle KXH \cong \angle IYJ$; $\overline{HX} \cong \overline{JY}$
(Corr. parts of $\cong$ $\triangle$s are $\cong$.) 6. $\overline{HI} \parallel \overline{KJ}$ (Def. of
$\square$) 7. $\angle IYJ \cong \angle KJY$ (2 lines ∥ ⇒ alt. int. $\angle$s $\cong$.)
8. $\angle KXH \cong \angle KJY$ ($\cong$ of $\angle$s is trans. [5, 7])
9. $\overline{HX} \parallel \overline{JY}$ (Corr. $\angle$s $\cong$ ⇒ 2 lines ∥.) 10. $HYJX$ is
a $\square$. (If 2 sides ∥ and $\cong$, quad. is $\square$. [5, 9])

Pages 236-238

Class Exercises **1.** 14 **3.** $4s + 2$ **5.** $0.5p$
7. Since $\overrightarrow{AM}$ is also a trans. of the 3 ∥ lines,
$\overline{AX} \cong \overline{XM}$. (3 ∥ lines cut off $\cong$ segs. on 1 trans.
⇒ lines cut off $\cong$ segs. on every trans.)
9. 6.5 **Written Exercises** **1.** 6.5 **3.** 30 **5.** 10
7. 9 **9.** Place the top right corner of the balsa
on a rule and rotate the balsa until the bottom
right corner is on the tenth rule below.
11. 1. X, Y, and Z are midpts. of $\overline{AB}$, $\overline{BC}$, and
$\overline{AC}$, resp. (Given) 2. $XY = \frac{1}{2}(AC)$; $YZ = \frac{1}{2}(AB)$;
$XZ = \frac{1}{2}(BC)$ (Length of seg. joining midpts. of 2
sides of △ is half length of third side.) 3. $XY +$
$YZ + XZ = \frac{1}{2}AC + \frac{1}{2}AB + \frac{1}{2}BC = \frac{1}{2}(AC + AB +$
$BC)$ (Add. prop. of eq.) **13.** 60 **15.** $2r + 2s$
17. $u = 6$; $v = 0$; $AC = 12$ **23.** s and t intersect
on k; $s \parallel t$; s and t intersect on j or on l.

Pages 242-244

Class Exercises **1.** 90 **3.** 35 **5.** 60
7. Rhombus **9.** Rectangle **11.** Square **Written**
Exercises **1.** 15 **3.** 7 **5.** $y = 18$; $AC = 168$
7. 274 **9.** Sometimes **11.** Always **13.** Always
15. Sometimes **17.** Sometimes **19.** Never **21.** 32
23. 6.5 **25.** 1. $\square ABCD$ with $\overline{AC} \cong \overline{BD}$ (Given)
2. $\overline{AD} \cong \overline{BC}$ (Opp. sides of $\square$ are $\cong$.) 3. $\overline{CD} \cong$
$\overline{CD}$ ($\cong$ of segs. is reflex.) 4. $\triangle ADC \cong \triangle BCD$
(SSS Post. [1, 2, 3]) 5. $\measuredangle ADC \cong \measuredangle BCD$ (Corr.
parts of $\cong$ △s are $\cong$.) 6. $\overline{AD} \parallel \overline{BC}$ (Def. of $\square$ [1])
7. $\measuredangle ADC$ and $\measuredangle BCD$ are supp. (2 lines ∥ ⇒ int.
$\measuredangle$s on same side supp.) 8. $\measuredangle ADC$ and $\measuredangle BCD$
are rt. $\measuredangle$s. (2 $\measuredangle$s $\cong$ and supp. ⇒ each is a rt. $\measuredangle$.
[5, 7]) 9. $m\measuredangle ADC = m\measuredangle BCD = 90$ (Def. of rt. $\measuredangle$)
10. $\measuredangle ADC \cong \measuredangle ABC$; $\measuredangle BCD \cong \measuredangle BAD$ (Opp. $\measuredangle$s
of $\square$ are $\cong$. [1]) 11. $m\measuredangle ADC = m\measuredangle ABC$;
$m\measuredangle BCD = m\measuredangle BAD$ (Def. of $\cong$ $\measuredangle$s)
12. $m\measuredangle ABC = m\measuredangle BAD = 90$ (Subst. [9, 11])
13. $\measuredangle ABC$ and $\measuredangle BAD$ are rt. $\measuredangle$s. (Def. of rt. $\measuredangle$)
14. $ABCD$ is a rectangle. (Def. of rectangle
[1, 8, 13]) **31.** 60; 120; 60; 120 **33.** 1. Rect.
$HELP$; $\overline{OA} \perp \overline{PL}$ (Given) 2. $HELP$ is a $\square$. (Def. of
rect.) 3. $\overline{HE} \parallel \overline{LP}$ (Def. of $\square$) 4. $\overline{AO} \perp \overline{HE}$ (In a
plane, a line $\perp$ to one of two ∥ lines is $\perp$ to the
other. [1, 3]) 5. $\measuredangle HPA$ and $\measuredangle ELA$ are rt. $\measuredangle$s.
(Def. of rect. [1]) 6. $\overline{HP} \perp \overline{PL}$; $\overline{EL} \perp \overline{PL}$ (Def. of $\perp$
lines) 7. $\overline{HP} \parallel \overline{OA}$; $\overline{OA} \parallel \overline{EL}$ (In a plane, 2 lines $\perp$
to same line are ∥. [1, 6]) 8. $\measuredangle HOA$, $\measuredangle OAP$,

$\measuredangle AOE$, and $\measuredangle OAL$ are rt. $\measuredangle$s. (Def. of $\perp$ lines)
9. $\measuredangle PHO$ and $\measuredangle HEL$ are rt. $\measuredangle$s. (Def. of rect. [1])
10. $HOAP$ and $OELA$ are $\square$s. (Def. of $\square$ [3, 7])
11. $HOAP$ and $OELA$ are rects. (Def. of rect.
[5, 8, 9, 10]) 12. $\overline{HA} \cong \overline{PO}$; $\overline{OL} \cong \overline{AE}$ (Diags. of
rect. are $\cong$.) 13. $\overline{HE} \cong \overline{PL}$ (Opp. sides of $\square$ are
$\cong$. [2]) 14. $\triangle HAE \cong \triangle POL$ (SSS [12, 13])

Pages 248-249

Class Exercises **1.** $\overline{AB}$ and $\overline{CD}$ **3.** $\overline{AB} \parallel \overline{XY}$ and
$\overline{CD} \parallel \overline{XY}$ **5.** $\measuredangle A \cong \measuredangle B$ or $\measuredangle C \cong \measuredangle D$ **7.** 12.5
9. 15 **Written Exercises** **1.** 9.5 **3.** 32
5. $\frac{1}{2}a + 3$ **7.** 50 **9.** $2k - h$ **11.** 11 **13.** 1. Isos.
trap. $ABCD$ with $\overline{AD} \cong \overline{BC}$ (Given) 2. Draw
$\overline{AX} \perp \overline{DC}$ and $\overline{BY} \perp \overline{DC}$ (Through a pt. not on a
line, there is exactly 1 line $\perp$ to the given line.)
3. $\measuredangle AXD$ and $\measuredangle BYC$ are rt. $\measuredangle$s. ($\perp$ lines form 4
rt. $\measuredangle$s.) 4. $\triangle AXD$ and $\triangle BYC$ are rt. △s. (Def. of
rt. △) 5. $\overline{AB} \parallel \overline{CD}$ (Def. of trap. [1]) 6. $\overline{AX} \cong \overline{BY}$
(Dist. between ∥ lines is constant.) 7. $\triangle AXD \cong$
$\triangle BYC$ (HL Thm. [1, 4, 6]) 8. $\measuredangle C \cong \measuredangle D$ (Corr.
parts of $\cong$ △s are $\cong$.) 9. $\measuredangle D$ and $\measuredangle BAD$ are
supp.; $\measuredangle C$ and $\measuredangle ABC$ are supp. (2 lines ∥ ⇒ int.
$\measuredangle$s on same side supp. [5]) 10. $\measuredangle BAD \cong \measuredangle ABC$
(Supps. of $\cong$ $\measuredangle$s are $\cong$. [8, 9]). **17.** 1. Isos. trap.
$BROW$ with $\overline{BR} \parallel \overline{OW}$ (Given) 2. $\overline{BW} \cong \overline{RO}$ (Legs
of isos. trap. are $\cong$.) 3. $\overline{BO} \cong \overline{RW}$ (Diags. of isos.
trap. are $\cong$. [1]) 4. $\overline{WO} \cong \overline{WO}$ ($\cong$ of segs. is
reflex.) 5. $\triangle BOW \cong \triangle RWO$ (SSS Post. [2, 3, 4])
6. $\measuredangle OBW \cong \measuredangle WRO$ (Corr. parts of $\cong$ △s are $\cong$.)
7. $\measuredangle BNW \cong \measuredangle RNO$ (Vert. $\measuredangle$s are $\cong$.)
8. $\triangle BNW \cong \triangle RNO$ (AAS Thm. [2, 6, 7])
19. 48 in. **21.** Bases, 48 cm and 84 cm; legs,
30 cm **23.** $DX = CY = \frac{1}{4}(2k + s - t)$

Pages 251-253

Class Exercises **1.** Locus is pts. 4 cm from l; Q
doesn't satisfy this prop., so it isn't in the
locus. **3.** Locus is 2 ∥ lines, each 4 cm from l.
5. In space, an infinitely long cylinder with
radius 5 cm **Written Exercises** **1.** The
segment joining the given points, excluding the
endpts. **3.** The bisector of the given angle,
excluding its vertex **5.** The pair of $\perp$ lines that
bisect the $\measuredangle$s formed by the given lines,
excluding their intersection pt. **7.** The line, in
the half-plane, that is ∥ to the edge and 1″ from

it **9.** The pt. at which the diags. intersect
11. The pt. at which the diags. intersect **13.** A
sphere of radius 50 miles and its interior,
excluding those points of the sphere and its
interior which are in the ground **15.** In a plane,
what is the locus of pts. equidistant from $\parallel$ lines
l and *k*? **17.** In a plane, what is the locus of
pts. equidistant from the sides (or vert.) of rect.
ABCD? **19.** What is the locus of pts.
equidistant from the sides (or vert.) of square
WXYZ?

Pages 256-257

Class Exercises 1. *X* and *Y* are equidistant
from *A* and *B*, so they are on the $\perp$ bis. of $\overline{AB}$.
$\overleftrightarrow{XY}$ is one way to name this bisector. **Written
Exercises 1.** In a plane, if a point is
equidistant from 2 $\parallel$ lines, then it lies on a line $\parallel$
to the given lines at half the distance between
them. If a pt. lies on a line $\parallel$ to 2 given lines at
half the distance between them, then the pt. is
equidistant from the given lines. **3.** A plane
halfway between the given lines which is $\perp$ to
a line that is $\perp$ to both lines. **5.** $m \perp \mathcal{F}$ **7.** $1 \perp \mathcal{K}$
11. See fig. on p. 255. Given: $\overline{AB} \perp \mathcal{E}$ at *X*;
$\overline{AX} \cong \overline{BX}$; *D* lies in $\mathcal{E}$. Prove: $AD = BD$. 1. $\overline{AB} \perp$
$\mathcal{E}$ at *X*; $\overline{AX} \cong \overline{BX}$; *D* lies in $\mathcal{E}$. (Given) 2. Draw
$\overline{DX}$, $\overline{DA}$, and $\overline{DB}$. (Line Post.) 3. $\overline{DX} \perp \overline{AB}$ (Def.
of line $\perp$ to plane) 4. $\angle DXA$ and $\angle DXB$ are rt.
$\angle$s. ($\perp$ lines form 4 rt. $\angle$s.) 5. $\triangle DXA$ and $\triangle DXB$
are rt. $\triangle$s. (Def. of rt. $\triangle$) 6. $\overline{DX} \cong \overline{DX}$ ($\cong$ of segs.
is reflex.) 7. $\triangle DXA \cong \triangle DXB$ (LL Thm. [1, 5, 6])
8. $\overline{AD} \cong \overline{BD}$ (Corres. parts of $\cong \triangle$s are $\cong$.)
9. $AD = BD$ (Def. of $\cong$ segs.) **15.** 1. $QA = QB$; *l*
is $\perp$ bis. of $\overline{AB}$ at *M*. (Given) 2. $\overline{QA} \cong \overline{QB}$ (Def.
of $\cong$ segs.) 3. Draw $\overline{QM}$. (2 pts. determine a
line.) 4. $\overline{QM} \cong \overline{QM}$ ($\cong$ of segs. is reflex.) 5. *M* is
midpt. of $\overline{AB}$. (Def. of $\perp$ bis. [1]) 6. $AM = MB$
(Def. of midpt.) 7. $\overline{AM} \cong \overline{MB}$ (Def. of $\cong$ seg.)
8. $\triangle QMA \cong \triangle QMB$ (SSS Post. [2, 4, 7])
9. $\angle QMA \cong \angle QMB$ (Corr. parts of $\cong \triangle$s are $\cong$.)
10. $\overleftrightarrow{QM} \perp \overline{AB}$ at *M* ($\angle$s of lin. pr. $\cong \Rightarrow$ lines $\perp$.)
11. $\overleftrightarrow{QM} = l$, so *Q* lies on *l*. (In a plane, through
a pt. on a line, there is exactly 1 line $\perp$ to the
given line. [1, 10])

Chapter 6

Pages 269-272

Class Exercises 1. *A* and *F*; *B* and *G*; *C* and
H; *D* and *J*; *E* and *K* **3.** 2 **5.** 4 **7.** 18 **9.** 3 to 2
11. $\dfrac{a}{c}$; *ax* **Written Exercises 1.** 20 **3.** $5\frac{1}{3}$ **5.** 8
7. 3.2 **9.** 4.5 **11.** 3 **13.** Yes **15.** Not enough info.
17. Sometimes **19.** Always **21.** Never **23.** $x - y$
25. 15 ft. by 16.5 ft. **27.** 54 in. **29.** $2\sqrt{2}$
31. 1. $\triangle ABC \sim \triangle CDA$ (Given) 2. $\angle BAC \cong$
$\angle DCA$; $\angle BCA \cong \angle DAC$ (Corres. $\angle$s of $\sim$ poly.
are $\cong$.) 3. $\overline{AB} \parallel \overline{CD}$; $\overline{AD} \parallel \overline{BC}$ (Alt. int. $\angle$s $\cong \Rightarrow$ 2
lines $\parallel$. [2]) 4. *ABCD* is a $\square$. (Def. of $\square$. [3])
33. 2 in. by 3 in.; 4 in. by 6 in.; 6 in. by 9 in.

Pages 276-280

Class Exercises 1. Yes; AA Post. **3.** Yes; SAS
$\sim$ Thm. **5.** No; the sides are not proportional:
$\frac{4}{8} \neq \frac{6}{10}$ **7.** Yes **9.** No **11.** 6 **13.** 104 **15.** 104
Written Exercises 1. Yes **3.** No **5.** Yes **7.** Yes
9. Not enough information **11.** Yes **13.** *EF*
15. *AC* **17.** Given: $\square ABCD$ Prove: $\triangle ABD \sim$
$\triangle CDB$; $\triangle ADC \sim \triangle CBA$ Proof: 1. *ABCD* is a $\square$.
(Given) 2. $\triangle ABD \cong \triangle CDB$; $\triangle ADC \cong \triangle CBA$ (A
diagonal and the sides of a $\square$ form 2 $\cong \triangle$s.)
3. $\angle BAD \cong \angle DCB$ and $\angle ABD \cong \angle CDB$;
$\angle ADC \cong \angle CBA$ and $\angle DAC \cong \angle BCA$ (Corres.
parts of $\cong \triangle$s are $\cong$. [2]) 4. $\triangle ABD \sim \triangle CDB$;
$\triangle ADC \sim \triangle CBA$ (AA Post. [3]) **19.** 1. $\triangle ABC \sim$
$\triangle ADE$ (Given) 2. $\angle ABC \cong \angle ADE$ (Corres. $\angle$s of
$\sim \triangle$s are $\cong$.) 3. $\overline{BC} \parallel \overline{DE}$ (Corres. $\angle$s $\cong \Rightarrow$ 2 lines
$\parallel$. [2]) **21.** 87.5 m **23.** Given: $\triangle ABC$ and $\triangle XYZ$
are equilateral. Prove: $\triangle ABC \sim \triangle XYZ$ Proof:
1. $\triangle ABC$ and $\triangle XYZ$ are equilateral. (Given)
2. $AB = BC = AC$; $XY = YZ = XZ$ (Def. of
equilateral $\triangle$s) 3. $\dfrac{AB}{XY} = \dfrac{BC}{YZ} = \dfrac{AC}{XZ}$
(Mult. prop. of eq. [2])
4. $\triangle ABC \sim \triangle XYZ$ (SSS $\sim$ Thm.) **25.** $\triangle DFG \sim$
$\triangle DBC$ and $\triangle DEF \sim \triangle DAB$, so rectangles *ABCD*
and *EFGD* are $\sim$. $\triangle ZQR$ and $\triangle ZXY$ are not $\sim$,
so rectangles *WXYZ* and *PQRZ* are not $\sim$.
27. No **29.** Yes **31.** No **33.** Given: $\triangle ABC$ and
$\triangle XYZ$ with rt. $\angle$s $\angle A$ and $\angle X$; $\angle B \cong \angle Y$ Prove:
$\triangle ABC \sim \triangle XYZ$ Proof: 1. $\triangle ABC$ and $\triangle XYZ$
have rt. $\angle$s $\angle A$ and $\angle X$; $\angle B \cong \angle Y$ (Given)
2. $\angle A \cong \angle X$ (All rt. $\angle$s are $\cong$. [1]) 3. $\triangle ABC \sim$
$\triangle XYZ$ (AA Post. [1, 2]) **35.** 17 m **37.** 1. In

$\triangle MNP$, $\overline{MP} \cong \overline{NP}$; $\overline{RT} \perp \overline{PN}$; $\overline{RS} \perp \overline{PM}$ (Given)
2. $\angle M \cong \angle N$ (Isos. $\triangle$ Thm. [1]) 3. $\angle RSM$ and $\angle RTN$ are rt. $\angle$s. (2 $\perp$ lines form 4 rt. $\angle$s. [1])
4. $\angle RSM \cong \angle RTN$ (All rt. $\angle$s are $\cong$.)
5. $\triangle RSM \sim \triangle RTN$ (AA Post. [2, 4]) 6. $\dfrac{RM}{RN} =$
$\dfrac{RS}{RT}$ (Corr. sides $\sim\triangle$s are prop.) 7. $(RT)(RM) = (RN)(RS)$ (Mult. prop. of eq.) **41.** 1. $\triangle HJK$ has rt. $\angle$ at J; $\overline{JL} \perp \overline{HK}$ (Given) 2. $\angle JLK$ is a rt. $\angle$. (2 $\perp$ lines form 4 rt. $\angle$s.) 3. $\angle HJK \cong \angle JLK$ (All rt. $\angle$s are $\cong$. [1, 2]) 4. $\angle K \cong \angle K$ ($\cong$ of $\angle$s is reflex.) 5. $\triangle HJK \sim \triangle JLK$ (AA Post. [3, 4])

Pages 283-285
Class Exercises 1. RM **3.** SN **5.** $\dfrac{VR}{RP} = \dfrac{TS}{SQ}$
7. $\dfrac{HK}{KN} = \dfrac{JK}{KM}$ **9.** No; if $\overline{AT} \parallel \overline{UB}$, $\dfrac{CU}{UT} = \dfrac{CB}{BA}$, but $\dfrac{4}{3} \neq \dfrac{5}{4}$. Thus, $\overline{AT} \nparallel \overline{UB}$. **Written Exercises 1.** 1.2 **3.** 12 **5.** 36 **7.** Correct **9.** Incorrect **11.** Correct **13.** 7.5 **15.** 7.5
17. 1. $\square ABCD$; $\overline{EF} \parallel \overline{DC}$; $\overline{GH} \parallel \overline{BC}$ (Given)
2. $\dfrac{AK}{KC} = \dfrac{AE}{ED}$; $\dfrac{AK}{KC} = \dfrac{AG}{GB}$ (If a line $\parallel$ to one side of $\triangle$ intersects the other 2 sides, it divides them proportionally. [1]) 3. $\dfrac{AG}{GB} = \dfrac{AE}{ED}$; (Subst. [2]) **19.** 1. $\triangle ABC$; D on $\overline{AB}$; E on $\overline{AC}$; $\overline{DE} \parallel \overline{BC}$ (Given) 2. $\angle A \cong \angle A$ ($\cong$ of $\angle$s is reflex.)
3. $\angle ADE \cong \angle ABC$ (2 lines $\parallel \Rightarrow$ corres. $\angle$s $\cong$. [1])
4. $\triangle ADE \sim \triangle ABC$ (AA Post. [2, 3]) 5. $\dfrac{AB}{AD} =$
$\dfrac{AC}{AE}$ (Corres. sides of $\sim \triangle$s are prop.) 6. $AB = AD + DB$; $AC = AE + EC$ (Seg. Add. Post.)
7. $\dfrac{AD + DB}{AD} = \dfrac{AE + EC}{AE}$ (Subst. [5, 6])
8. $\dfrac{DB}{AD} = \dfrac{EC}{AE}$ (Add. prop. of eq. [7]) 9. $\dfrac{AD}{DB} =$
$\dfrac{AE}{EC}$ (Mult. prop. of eq. [8]) **21.** No. Consider $\triangle ABC$ with D on $\overline{AB}$, E on $\overline{AC}$, and $\overline{DE} \parallel \overline{BC}$. Let l be a line through A, with $l \nparallel \overline{BC}$. Then $\dfrac{AD}{DB} = \dfrac{AE}{EC}$, but l is not $\parallel$ to $\overline{DE}$ or to $\overline{BC}$.
23. $\dfrac{4}{10}$, $\dfrac{2}{10}$, $\dfrac{3}{10}$, $\dfrac{1}{10}$ **25.** 1. In $\triangle ABC$, D, E, and F are midpts. of $\overline{BC}$, $\overline{AC}$, and $\overline{AB}$, resp. (Given)

2. $FD = \frac{1}{2}(AC)$; $DE = \frac{1}{2}(AB)$; $EF = \frac{1}{2}(BC)$ (Seg. joining midpts. of 2 sides of $\triangle$ is $\parallel$ to third side and its length is $\frac{1}{2}$ the length of third side.)
3. $\dfrac{FD}{AC} = \dfrac{1}{2}$; $\dfrac{DE}{AB} = \dfrac{1}{2}$; $\dfrac{EF}{BC} = \dfrac{1}{2}$
(Mult. prop. of eq.) 4. $\triangle ABC \sim \triangle DEF$ (SSS $\sim$ Thm. [3])

Pages 290-292
Class Exercises 1. GC **3.** EH **5.** 15 **7.** YP
9. XV **11.** RW **Written Exercises 1.** EF **3.** EN
5. MB **7.** 6 **9.** $13\frac{1}{3}$ **11.** 1. In $\triangle ABC$, the bisector of $\angle B$ intersects $\overline{AC}$ at D. (Given) 2. Draw $\overline{EC} \parallel \overline{BD}$ with E on $\overleftrightarrow{AB}$. (Through a pt. not on a given line, there is exactly one line $\parallel$ to the given line.) 3. $\angle ABD \cong \angle E$ (2 lines $\parallel \Rightarrow$ corr. $\angle$s $\cong$.) 4. $\angle DBC \cong \angle BCE$ (2 lines $\parallel \Rightarrow$ alt. int. $\angle$s $\cong$. [2]) 5. $m\angle ABD = m\angle DBC$ (Def. of $\angle$ bisector [1]) 6. $\angle ABD \cong \angle DBC$ (Def. of $\cong \angle$s)
7. $\angle BCE \cong \angle E$ ($\cong$ of $\angle$s is trans. [3, 4, 6])
8. $\overline{BE} \cong \overline{BC}$ (If 2 $\angle$s of $\triangle \cong$, sides opp. are $\cong$.)
9. $BE = BC$ (Def. of $\cong$ segs.) 10. $\dfrac{AD}{DC} = \dfrac{AB}{BE}$
(If a line $\parallel$ to one side of a $\triangle$ intersects the other 2 sides, it divides them prop. [2])
11. $\dfrac{AD}{DC} = \dfrac{AB}{BC}$ (Subst. [9, 10]) 12. $\dfrac{AD}{AB} = \dfrac{DC}{BC}$
(Mult. prop. of eq.)
13. 1. In $\triangle ABC$, $\angle A \cong \angle C$; $\overline{BD}$ bisects $\angle ABC$. (Given) 2. $\overline{AB} \cong \overline{BC}$ (If 2 $\angle$s of $\triangle$ are $\cong$, sides opp. are $\cong$.) 3. $AB = BC$ (Def. of $\cong$ segs.)
4. $\dfrac{AD}{AB} = \dfrac{DC}{BC}$ (Bis. of $\angle$ of $\triangle$ divides opp. side into 2 segs. whose lengths are prop. to lengths of other 2 sides. [1]) 5. $\dfrac{AD}{AB} = \dfrac{DC}{AB}$ (Subst. [3, 4]) 6. $AD = DC$ (Mult. prop. of eq.)
15. 1. $\triangle PWT \sim \triangle SQR$; $\overline{PX}$ bisects $\angle TPW$; $\overline{SY}$ bisects $\angle RSQ$ (Given) 2. $\dfrac{TX}{TP} = \dfrac{WX}{WP}$;
$\dfrac{YQ}{QS} = \dfrac{YR}{SR}$ (Bis. of $\angle$ of $\triangle$ divides opp. side into 2 segs. whose lengths are prop. to lengths of other 2 sides.) 3. $\dfrac{TX}{WX} = \dfrac{TP}{WP}$; $\dfrac{YR}{YQ} = \dfrac{SR}{QS}$
(Mult. prop. of eq.) 4. $\dfrac{TP}{RS} = \dfrac{WP}{QS}$ (Corres. sides of $\sim \triangle$s are prop. [1]) 5. $\dfrac{TP}{WP} = \dfrac{RS}{QS}$

(Mult. prop. of eq.) 6. $\dfrac{TX}{WX} = \dfrac{YR}{YQ}$ (Subst. [3, 5])

17. 1. $\triangle DEF \sim \triangle D'E'F'$; $\overline{FG} \perp \overline{DE}$; $\overline{F'G'} \perp \overline{D'E'}$ (Given) 2. $\angle D \cong \angle D'$ (Corres. $\angle$s of $\sim \triangle$s are $\cong$.) 3. $\angle FGD$ and $\angle F'G'D'$ are rt. $\angle$s. (2 $\perp$ lines form 4 rt. $\angle$s. [1]) 4. $\angle FGD \cong \angle F'G'D'$ (All rt. $\angle$s are $\cong$.) 5. $\triangle FGD \sim \triangle F'G'D'$ (AA Post. [2, 4])

6. $\dfrac{FG}{F'G'} = \dfrac{DF}{D'F'}$ (Corres. sides of $\sim \triangle$s are prop. [5]) **19.** $x = \dfrac{ab}{c}$ **21.** $x = \dfrac{cb}{a}$

23. 1. $\triangle ABC \sim \triangle DEF$ (Given) 2. $\angle A \cong \angle D$ (Corr. $\angle$s of $\sim \triangle$s are $\cong$. [1]) 3. $\dfrac{AC}{DF} = \dfrac{AB}{DE}$ (Corr. sides of $\sim \triangle$s are prop. [1]) 4. $AJ = JB$; $DK = KE$ (Given) 5. $AJ + JB = AB$; $DK + KE = DE$ (Seg. Add. Post.) 6. $AJ + AJ = 2AJ = AB$; $DK + DK = 2DK = DE$ (Subst. [4, 5]) 7. $\dfrac{AC}{DF} = \dfrac{2AJ}{2DK} = \dfrac{AJ}{DK}$ (Subst. [3, 6]) 8. $\triangle ACJ \sim \triangle DFK$ (SAS $\sim$ Thm. [2, 7]) 9. $\angle AJC \cong \angle DKF$ (Corr. $\angle$s of $\sim \triangle$s are $\cong$. [8]) 10. $\angle AJC$ and $\angle CJG$ are supp.; $\angle DKF$ and $\angle FKH$ are supp. (Supp. Post.) 11. $\angle CJG \cong \angle FKH$ (Supp. of $\cong \angle$s are $\cong$. [9, 10]) 12. $\overline{CG} \perp \overline{AB}$; $\overline{FH} \perp \overline{DE}$ (Given) 13. $\angle CGJ$ and $\angle FHK$ are rt. $\angle$s. (2 $\perp$ lines form 4 rt. $\angle$s. [12]) 14. $\angle CGJ \cong \angle FHK$ (All rt. $\angle$s are $\cong$. [13]) 15. $\triangle CGJ \sim \triangle FHK$ (AA $\sim$ Post. [11, 14])

Pages 295-298

Class Exercises **1.** $\triangle ACD$, $\triangle CBD$ **3.** $\triangle HBA$, $\triangle HAC$, $\triangle GHC$, $\triangle GAH$ **5.** MP; MN **7.** PO **9.** NO **11.** $(MP)(PN)$ **13.** 6 **15.** 14 **17.** $4\sqrt{2}$ **19.** 12 **21.** $3\sqrt{6}$ **Written Exercises** **1.** $6\sqrt{2}$ **3.** 156.25 **5.** $6\sqrt{3}$ **7.** 1. $\triangle ABC$ with rt. $\angle C$; $\overline{CD} \perp \overline{AB}$ (Given) 2. $\triangle ACD \sim \triangle CBD$ (If alt. is drawn to hyp. of rt. $\triangle$, the new $\triangle$s formed are $\sim$ to each other and to the given $\triangle$.) 3. $\dfrac{AD}{CD} = \dfrac{CD}{BD}$ (Corres. sides of $\sim \triangle$s are prop.) **9.** 1. $\triangle ABC$; $\overline{AB} \perp \overline{BC}$; $\overline{BD} \perp \overline{AC}$; $\overline{AB} \| \overline{DE}$ (Given) 2. $\angle EDC \cong \angle BAC$ (2 lines $\| \Rightarrow$ corres. $\angle$s $\cong$.) 3. $\angle C \cong \angle C$ ($\cong$ of $\angle$s is reflex.) 4. $\triangle DCE \sim \triangle ACB$ (AA Post. [2, 3]) 5. $\triangle ACB \sim \triangle ABD$ (If alt. to hyp. is drawn in rt. $\triangle$, the new $\triangle$s formed are $\sim$ to each other and to the given $\triangle$.)

6. $\triangle DCE \sim \triangle ABD$ ($\sim$ of $\triangle$s is transitive. [4, 5])
7. $\triangle ABD \sim \triangle DCE$ ($\sim$ of $\triangle$s is symmetric.)
11. $3x$ **13.** $6x$ **15.** $4(x + 3)$ **17.** $7x$ **19.** 8 cm or 18 cm **21.** 20 **23.** $180\sqrt{5}$ **25.** 28 or 7
27. 1. $\angle ACB$ is a rt. $\angle$; $WXYZ$ is a square. (Given) 2. $\angle A \cong \angle A$; $\angle B \cong \angle B$ ($\cong$ of $\angle$s is reflex.) 3. $\angle ZWX$ and $\angle YXW$ are rt. $\angle$s. (Def. of square) 4. $\overline{ZW} \perp \overline{AB}$; $\overline{YX} \perp \overline{AB}$ (Def. of $\perp$) 5. $\angle AWZ$ and $\angle YXB$ are rt. $\angle$s. (2 $\perp$ lines form 4 rt. $\angle$s.) 6. $\angle AWZ \cong \angle ACB$; $\angle YXB \cong \angle ACB$ (All rt. $\angle$s are $\cong$. [1, 5]) 7. $\triangle AWZ \sim \triangle ACB$; $\triangle BXY \sim \triangle BCA$ (AA Post. [2, 6]) 8. $\dfrac{AW}{AC} = \dfrac{WZ}{CB}$; $\dfrac{BX}{BC} = \dfrac{YX}{AC}$ (Corres. sides of $\sim \triangle$s are prop.)
9. $\dfrac{AW}{WZ} = \dfrac{AC}{CB}$; $\dfrac{BX}{YX} = \dfrac{BC}{AC}$ (Mult. prop. of eq.)
10. $\dfrac{AW}{WZ}\left(\dfrac{BX}{YX}\right) = \dfrac{AC}{CB}\left(\dfrac{BC}{AC}\right) = 1$ (Mult. prop. of eq.) 11. $(AW)(BX) = (WZ)(YX)$ (Mult. prop. of eq.) 12. $WZ = YX = WX$ (Def. of square) 13. $(AW)(BX) = (WX)(WX) = (WX)^2$ (Subst. [11, 12]) **29.** 6.75 **31.** $m = 12$; $h = 6$ **33.** 119 m **35.** 1. $\triangle ABC$ with alts. $\overline{AY}$, $\overline{BZ}$, $\overline{CX}$, intersecting at P (Given) 2. $\angle AZP$, $\angle CZP$, $\angle CYP$, $\angle BYP$, $\angle BXP$, $\angle AXP$ are rt. $\angle$s. (2 $\perp$ lines form 4 rt. $\angle$s.) 3. $\angle AZP \cong \angle CZP \cong \angle CYP \cong \angle BYP \cong \angle BXP \cong \angle AXP$ (All rt. $\angle$s are $\cong$.) 4. $\angle ZPA \cong \angle YPB$; $\angle XPA \cong \angle YPC$; $\angle XPB \cong \angle ZPC$ (Vert. $\angle$s are $\cong$.) 5. $\triangle ZPA \sim \triangle YPB$; $\triangle XPA \sim \triangle YPC$; $\triangle XPB \sim \triangle ZPC$ (AA Post. [3, 4])
6. $\dfrac{YB}{ZA} = \dfrac{YP}{ZP}$; $\dfrac{AX}{CY} = \dfrac{XP}{YP}$; $\dfrac{ZC}{XB} = \dfrac{ZP}{XP}$ (Corres. sides of $\sim \triangle$s are prop.)
7. $\left(\dfrac{YB}{ZA}\right)\left(\dfrac{AX}{CY}\right)\left(\dfrac{ZC}{XB}\right) = \left(\dfrac{YP}{ZP}\right)\left(\dfrac{XP}{YP}\right)\left(\dfrac{ZP}{XP}\right) = 1$ (Mult. prop. of eq.) 8. $\left(\dfrac{AX}{XB}\right)\left(\dfrac{YB}{CY}\right)\left(\dfrac{ZC}{ZA}\right) = 1$ (Comm. prop.)

Pages 301-303

Class Exercises **1.** If $\overline{AB} \| \overline{XY}$, then $\triangle ABZ \sim \triangle XYZ$; lengths of sides are prop. **3.** 80 m **Written Exercises** **1.** 20 cm **3.** 115.2 in. or 9.6 ft. **5.** About 5.4 cm **7.** 22.5 m; 42.5 m **9.** DG should be $\frac{1}{2}AF$. **11.** 3 m; the height is independent of the distance between the braces.

Chapter 7

Pages 316-318

Class Exercises **1.** $18^2 + 24^2 = 30^2$ **3.** $x^2 + 7^2 = 25^2$ **5.** 8 **7.** No **9.** Yes **Written Exercises** **1.** $\sqrt{10}$ **3.** $2\sqrt{3}$ **5.** 8 **7.** $10\sqrt{2}$ **9.** $6\sqrt{3}$ **11.** $\frac{14}{3}\sqrt{3}$ **13.** 1. $\triangle ABC$; sides a, b, c; $a^2 + b^2 = c^2$ (Given) 2. Draw $l \perp m$ through a pt. F on m. (Through a pt. on a line exactly one line $\perp$ to the given line can be drawn.) 3. Locate D on m and E on l so that $DF = b$ and $EF = a$. (Seg. Construction Post.) 4. Draw $\overline{DE}$. (2 pts. determine a line.) 5. $\angle EFD$ is a rt. $\angle$. (2 $\perp$ lines form 4 rt. $\angle$s. [2]) 6. $\triangle EFD$ is a rt. $\triangle$. (Def. of rt. $\triangle$) 7. $a^2 + b^2 = f^2$ (Pyth. Thm. [5, 6]) 8. $c^2 = f^2$, or $c = f$ (Subst. [1, 7]) 9. $\overline{DF} \cong \overline{AC}$; $\overline{EF} \cong \overline{BC}$; $\overline{DE} \cong \overline{AB}$ (Def. of $\cong$ segs. [3, 8]) 10. $\triangle ABC \cong \triangle DEF$ (SSS Post. [9]) 11. $\angle C \cong \angle F$ (Corr. parts of $\cong \triangle$s are $\cong$.) 12. $m\angle EFD = 90$ (Def. of rt. $\angle$ [5]) 13. $m\angle C = m\angle F$ (Def. of $\cong \angle$s [11]) 14. $m\angle C = 90$ (Subst. [12, 13]) 15. $\angle C$ is a rt. $\angle$. (Def. of rt. $\angle$) 16. $\triangle ABC$ is a rt. $\triangle$. (Def. of rt. $\triangle$) **15.** Car D: 0.8 km; Car E: 0.8 km **17.** Tornado: E_4; Car D: 2.3 km; Car E: 0 **19.** 1. Alt. $\overline{CD}$ in $\triangle ABC$ (Given) 2. $\overline{CD} \perp \overline{BA}$ (Def. of alt.) 3. $\angle CDB$ and $\angle CDA$ are rt. $\angle$s. (2 $\perp$ lines form 4 rt. $\angle$s.) 4. $\triangle CDB$ and $\triangle CDA$ are rt. $\triangle$s. (Def. of rt. $\triangle$) 5. $a^2 = y^2 + CD^2$; $b^2 = x^2 + CD^2$ (Pyth. Thm.) 6. $a^2 - y^2 = CD^2$; $b^2 - x^2 = CD^2$ (Add. prop. of eq.) 7. $a^2 - y^2 = b^2 - x^2$ (Subst. [6])

21.

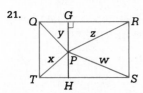

1. P is in int. of rect. QRST. (Given) 2. Through P, draw $\overline{GH} \perp \overline{QR}$ at G. (Through a pt. not on a line, there is exactly 1 line $\perp$ to the given line.) 3. QRST is a $\square$. (Def. of rect. [1]) 4. $\overline{QR} \parallel \overline{TS}$; $\overline{QT} \parallel \overline{RS}$ (Def. of $\square$) 5. $\overline{GH} \perp \overline{TS}$ at H. (If trans. $\perp$ to one of 2 $\parallel$ lines, it is $\perp$ to the other. [2, 4]) 6. $\angle QTS$ is a rt. $\angle$.

(Def. of rect. [1]) 7. $\overline{QT} \perp \overline{TS}$ (If 2 lines intersect to form a rt. $\angle$, the lines are $\perp$.) 8. $\overline{GH} \parallel \overline{QT}$ (In a plane, if 2 lines are $\perp$ to same line, they are $\parallel$. [5, 7]) 9. $\overline{GH} \parallel \overline{RS}$ (In a plane, if a line is $\parallel$ to one of 2 $\parallel$ lines, it is $\parallel$ to the other. [4, 8]) 10. QGHT and GRSH are $\square$s. (Def. of $\square$ [4, 8, 9]) 11. $\overline{GR} \cong \overline{HS}$; $\overline{QG} \cong \overline{TH}$ (Opp. sides of $\square$ are $\cong$.) 12. $GR = HS$; $QG = TH$ (Def. of $\cong$ segs.) 13. $\overline{PG}$ is alt. of $\triangle QPR$; $\overline{PH}$ is alt. of $\triangle TPS$. (Def. of alt. [2, 5]) 14. $x^2 - TH^2 = w^2 - HS^2$; $z^2 - GR^2 = y^2 - QG^2$ (Exer. 19. above) 15. $z^2 - HS^2 = y^2 - TH^2$ (Subst. [12, 14]) 16. $x^2 - TH^2 + z^2 - HS^2 = w^2 - HS^2 + y^2 - TH^2$ (Add. prop. of eq. [14, 15]) 17. $x^2 + z^2 = w^2 + y^2$ (Add. prop. of eq. [16])

Pages 321-322

Class Exercises **1.** 8 **3.** $x = 8$; $y = 4\sqrt{3}$ **5.** $x = y = 5\sqrt{2}$ **7.** $x = y = 8$ **9.** $x = 8\sqrt{2}$ **Written Exercises** **1.** $18\sqrt{2}$ **3.** 6 **5.** 6 **7.** $3\sqrt{2}$ **9.** $14\sqrt{2}$ **11.** $9\sqrt{2}$ **13.** 3 **15.** 18 **17.** $HG = 15$; $FH = 15\sqrt{2}$; $EG = 15\sqrt{2}$ **19.** 18 **21.** $30 + 6\sqrt{3} + 6\sqrt{2}$ **23.** $12 + 4\sqrt{3}$ **25.** $ED = 4x\sqrt{3}$; $FD = 2x\sqrt{3}$ **27.** $QS = 6\sqrt{3}$, $QR = 3\sqrt{21}$; no; $PR^2 = 729$; $QR^2 + PQ^2 = 621$ **29.** 1. Rt. $\triangle ABC$; $m\angle A = m\angle B = 45$; $AB = c$; $AC = a$ (Given) 2. $\angle A \cong \angle B$ (Def. of $\cong \angle$s) 3. $\overline{CB} \cong \overline{AC}$ (If 2 $\angle$s of $\triangle$ are $\cong$, sides opp. them are $\cong$.) 4. $CB = AC$ (Def. of $\cong$ segs.) 5. $CB = a$ (Trans. prop. of eq. [1, 4]) 6. $c^2 = a^2 + a^2 = 2a^2$ (Pyth. Thm. [1, 5]) 7. $c = a\sqrt{2}$ (Algebra) **31.** 72.4 cm by 72.4 cm **33.** About 14.9 in.

Pages 324-325

Class Exercises **1.** $12\sqrt{2}$ **3.** 8 **5.** $10\sqrt{5}$ **7.** 15 **9.** 12 **Written Exercises** **1.** $7.5\sqrt{3} \doteq 12.99$ **3.** 9 **5.** $3 + 4\sqrt{3} \doteq 9.93$ m **7.** 5 **9.** Lot A: 96 ft., 238 ft.; Lot B: 144 ft., 280 ft. **11.** $4\sqrt{39}$

Pages 328-329

Class Exercises **1.** (3, 2) **3.** (−2, 1.5) **5.** (−2, −1) **7.** $y = 1.5$ **9.** $y = 0$ **11.** 1.5 **13.** 3.5

Written Exercises

1-8.

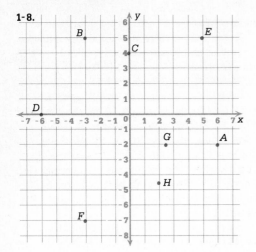

9. 5 **11.** 7 **13.** 2 **15.** 9 **17.** $y = -1$ **19.** $y = 8$
21. $y = 3.5$ **23.** $y = -3.5$ **25.** $(2, 3)$ **27.** $(5, -0.5)$
29. $(3, -1.5)$ **31.** $(4, -11)$ **33.** $|x_1 - x_2|$
35. $\sqrt{|x_1 - x_2|^2 + |y_1 - y_2|^2}$

Pages 332-333

Class Exercises **1.** 6 **3.** $\sqrt{10}$ **5.** $\sqrt{89}$
7. $(-5, 4)$ **9.** $(3, 1.5)$ **11.** $(0, 0)$ **Written**
Exercises **1.** $8\sqrt{2}$ **3.** $7\sqrt{5}$ **5.** $(2, 6)$ **7.** $(1, 1)$
9. $(-3, 0)$ **11.** $(8, 7)$ **13.** $AB = \sqrt{64 + 16} = \sqrt{80}$;
$BC = \sqrt{16 + 64} = \sqrt{80}$; $AB = BC = 4\sqrt{5}$
15. $AB = \sqrt{16 + 16} = \sqrt{32}$; $BC = \sqrt{49 + 49} = $
$\sqrt{98}$; $AC = \sqrt{121 + 9} = \sqrt{130}$; $AB^2 + BC^2 =$
$32 + 98 = 130 = AC^2$; B is a rt. $\angle$. **17.** $AB =$
$\sqrt{16 + 64} = \sqrt{80}$; $AC = \sqrt{64 + 16} = \sqrt{80}$;
$BC = \sqrt{144 + 16} = \sqrt{160}$; $AB^2 + AC^2 = 80 +$
$80 = 160 = BC^2$; A is a rt. $\angle$; $AB = AC = 4\sqrt{5}$
19. $AB = \sqrt{81} = 9$; $CD = \sqrt{81} = 9$; $BC =$
$\sqrt{4 + 36} = \sqrt{40}$; $AD = \sqrt{4 + 36} = \sqrt{40}$; $AB =$
$CD = 9$; $AD = BC = 2\sqrt{10}$ **21.** $PQ =$
$\sqrt{36 + 64} = 10$; $RS = \sqrt{36 + 64} = 10$; $QR =$
$\sqrt{16 + 9} = 5$; $PS = \sqrt{16 + 9} = 5$; $PR =$
$\sqrt{100 + 25} = \sqrt{125}$; $PS^2 + RS^2 = 25 + 100 =$
$125 = PR^2$; S is a rt. $\angle$; $RS = PQ = 10$;
$PS = QR = 5$ **23.** $(a, 2a)$ **25.** $(5 + v, 3 - 2u)$
27. $(0, 5)$ **29.** $X(5, 4)$; $Y(1, 4)$ **31.** $ST = \sqrt{b^2} = b$;
$AR = \sqrt{b^2} = b$; $SR = \sqrt{c^2 + d^2}$; $AT = \sqrt{c^2 + d^2}$;
$\overline{ST} \cong \overline{AR}$ and $\overline{SR} \cong \overline{AT}$, so $STAR$ is a $\square$.

Pages 338-339

Class Exercises **1.** $\overline{PQ}$ **3.** $\overline{PR}$ **5.** $\overline{QR}$ **7.** $\cos P$
9. $\cos Q$ **11.** $\tan Q$ **13.** $\frac{24}{25}$ **Written**
Exercises **1.** $\frac{3}{4}$ **3.** $\frac{3}{5}$ **5.** $\frac{4}{5}$ **7.** $\tan A$ **9.** $\sin A$
11. $\tan B$ **13.** $\left(\frac{20}{25}\right)^2 + \left(\frac{15}{25}\right)^2 = \frac{400}{625} + \frac{225}{625} = \frac{625}{625} = 1$
15. 45-45-90 triangle **17.** $\sin 45° = \frac{1}{2}\sqrt{2}$;
$\cos 45° = \frac{1}{2}\sqrt{2}$; $\tan 45° = 1$ **19.** $VW = 4.5$;
$UV = 7.5$ **21.** $\sin A = \frac{24}{25} = 0.96$;
$\cos A = \frac{7}{25} = 0.28$; $\tan A = \frac{24}{7} \doteq 3.43$
23. $\sin A = \cos B = \frac{24}{25}$

25. $\tan H = \dfrac{JK}{HK}$

27. 0.84

29. 1. Right $\triangle ABC$ with rt. $\angle C$ (Given) 2. $a^2 +$
$b^2 = c^2$ (Pyth. Thm.) 3. $\dfrac{a^2}{c^2} + \dfrac{b^2}{c^2} = \dfrac{c^2}{c^2}$
(Mult. prop. of eq.) 4. $\left(\dfrac{a}{c}\right)^2 + \left(\dfrac{b}{c}\right)^2 = 1$
(Algebra) 5. $\sin A = \dfrac{a}{c}$ (Def. of sine of an $\angle$ [1])
6. $\cos A = \dfrac{b}{c}$ (Def. of cosine of an $\angle$ [1])
7. $(\sin A)^2 + (\cos A)^2 = 1$ (Subst. [4, 5, 6])
31. Given: Rt. $\triangle ABC$ with rt. $\angle C$. Prove:
$\sin A = \cos B$ Proof: 1. Rt. $\triangle ABC$ has rt. $\angle C$.
(Given) 2. $\sin A = \dfrac{a}{c}$ (Def. of sine [1])
3. $\cos B = \dfrac{a}{c}$ (Def. of cosine [1]) 4. $\sin A = \cos B$
(Subst. [2, 3]) **33.** Given: Rt. $\triangle ABC$ with rt. $\angle C$.
Prove: $\dfrac{\sin A}{\cos A} = \tan A$ Proof: 1. Rt. $\triangle ABC$ has
rt. $\angle C$. (Given) 2. $\sin A = \dfrac{a}{c}$ (Def. of sine [1])
3. $\cos A = \dfrac{b}{c}$ (Def. of cosine [1]) 4. $\dfrac{\sin A}{\cos A} =$
$\dfrac{\frac{a}{c}}{\frac{b}{c}} = \dfrac{a}{b}$ (Mult. prop. of eq. [2, 3]) 5. $\tan A = \dfrac{a}{b}$
(Def. of tangent [1]) 6. $\dfrac{\sin A}{\cos A} = \tan A$ (Subst.
[4, 5])

Pages 341–342

Class Exercises **1.** Increase **3.** Increase **5.** 45
7. $m \angle A > 45$; $m \angle A < 45$ **9.** Comp. prs. of
angles **Written Exercises** **1.** 0.4848 **3.** 0.7002
5. 0.9563 **7.** 0.9563 **9.** 9 **11.** 27 **13.** 71
15. $m \angle A = 16$; $m \angle B = 74$ **17.** 13.6 **19.** 20.1 m
21. The table shows $\sin 1° = \tan 1°$ because the
entries are approximations. Given: Rt. $\triangle ABC$
with rt. $\angle C$. Prove: $\tan A > \sin A$ Proof: 1. Rt.
$\triangle ABC$ has rt. $\angle C$. (Given)
2. $\tan A = \dfrac{CB}{AC}$ (Def. of tan. [1]) 3. $\sin A = \dfrac{CB}{AB}$
(Def. of sine [1]) 4. $\overline{AB}$ is hyp. of $\triangle ABC$. (Def.
of hyp. [1]) 5. $AB > AC$ (The $\perp$ seg. from a pt.
to a line is the shortest seg. from that pt. to
the line.) 6. $(CB)(AB) > (CB)(AC)$ (Mult. prop. of
ineq. [5]) 7. $\dfrac{CB}{AC} > \dfrac{CB}{AB}$ (Mult. prop. of ineq. [6])
8. $\tan A > \sin A$ (Subst. [2, 3, 7])

Pages 345–346

Class Exercises **1.** $\sin A = \dfrac{x}{100}$ **3.** $\tan A = \dfrac{100}{x}$ **5. a.** Elevation **b.** $\sin 63°$ **c.** 10.7
7. a. Depression **b.** $\tan 52°$ **c.** 19.2 **Written Exercises** **1.** 364.0 m **3.** 11.3 m **5.** $= 4°$
7. 31.3 m

Chapter 8

Pages 357–358

Class Exercises **1.** The points on the circle,
the points in the interior, and the points in the
exterior of the circle **3.** $\overline{BC}$ **5.** $\overline{BD}$ or $\overline{BC}$
7. $OW < OA$ **9.** B **11.** Secant: $\overleftrightarrow{CW}$ contains an
interior pt., W, of the circle. **13.** $\overline{ST}$ **15.** $\odot O$
Written Exercises **7.** 5 **9.** 4.7 **11.** $2x$ **13.** 12
15. 17.2 **17.** $2x - 10$ **19.** Always **21.** Never
23. Sometimes **25.** Sometimes **27.** A secant of a
sphere is a line that intersects the sphere in
two points. **29.** Interior pt., since the radius is
$\sqrt{50}$ and $RB = \sqrt{41}$. **31.** Exterior pt., since the
radius is $\sqrt{58}$ and $RB = \sqrt{65}$. **33.** Not a
diameter

Pages 361–362

Class Exercises **1.** 90 **3.** Tangent **5.** Three
Written Exercises **7.** 12 **9.** $3\sqrt{3}$ **11.** 10
13. $4\sqrt{2}$ **15.** 1. $\overline{OA}$ and $\overline{QB}$ are tangent to $\odot O$
at A and B, resp. (Given) 2. $\overline{QA} \cong \overline{QB}$ (Tang.
segs. drawn from an ext. pt. to pts. on a $\odot$ are
$\cong$.) 3. $\overline{OA} \cong \overline{OB}$ (Radii of same circle are $\cong$.)
4. $\overline{OA} \perp \overline{AQ}$; $\overline{OB} \perp \overline{BQ}$ (In a plane, if a line is
tang. to a $\odot$, it is $\perp$ to a radius at a pt. on the
$\odot$.) 5. $\angle A$ and $\angle B$ are rt. $\angle$s. (2 $\perp$ lines form 4
rt. $\angle$s.) 6. $\triangle OAQ \cong \triangle OBQ$ (LL Thm. [2, 3, 5])
7. $\angle AOQ \cong \angle BOQ$ (Corres. parts of $\cong$ $\triangle$s are
$\cong$.) 8. $\overrightarrow{OQ}$ bisects $\angle AOB$ (Def. of bisects) **17.** 6
19. 1. Line m and $\odot P$ are coplanar;
$m \perp \overline{PQ}$ at Q (Given) 2. Let R be any other pt.
on m (A line contains at least 2 pts.) 3. Draw
$\overline{PR}$. (2 pts. determine a line.) 4. $PR > PQ$ (The $\perp$
seg. from a pt. to a line is the shortest seg.
from the pt. to the line. [1, 3]) 5. R lies in the
ext. of $\odot P$ (Def. of ext. of a $\odot$ [2, 4]) 6. m is
tang. to $\odot P$ (Def. of tang. [1, 2, 5])
21. Infinitely many **23.** 22

Pages 364–366

Class Exercises **1.** If their radii are $\cong$ **3.** $\overline{CD}$
5. If $\overline{PX} \cong \overline{PY}$, then $\overline{AB} \cong \overline{CD}$ by Thm. 8.5.
$AX = BX$ and $CY = YD$ by Thm. 8.4. So $BX = YD$
by def. of $\cong$ seg., Seg. Add. Post., and
substitution.

Written Exercises 1. 16 **3.** 13 **5.** Always
7. Always **9.** Always **11.** 21 **13.** 16
15. 1. $\odot P$; P is on ℓ; $\overline{AB}$ is a chord; $\overline{PC} \perp \overline{AB}$.
(Given) 2. Draw $\overline{PA}$ and $\overline{PB}$. (2 pts. determine a
line.) 3. $\overline{PA} \cong \overline{PB}$ (Def. of $\odot$ [1]) 4. $\overline{PC} \cong \overline{PC}$
(Congruence of segs. is reflexive.) 5. $\angle PCA$ and
$\angle PCB$ are rt. $\angle$s. (2 $\perp$ lines form 4 rt. $\angle$s. [1])
6. $\triangle PCA$ and $\triangle PCB$ are rt. $\triangle$. (Def. of rt. $\triangle$ [5])
7. $\triangle PAC \cong \triangle PBC$ (HL Thm. [3, 4, 6]) 8. $\overline{AC} \cong$
$\overline{BC}$ (Corr. parts of $\cong$ $\triangle$ are $\cong$. [7]) 9. $AC = BC$
(Def. of $\cong$ segs. [8]) 10. C is midpt. of $\overline{AB}$. (Def.
of midpt. [9]) 11. ℓ bisects $\overline{AB}$. (Def. of bisect
[1, 10])
17. 1. $\odot P \cong \odot Q$; chords $\overline{AB}$, $\overline{CD}$; $\overline{AB} \cong \overline{CD}$;
$\overline{PX} \perp \overline{AB}$; $\overline{QY} \perp \overline{CD}$ (Given) 2. Draw $\overline{PA}$, $\overline{PB}$, $\overline{QC}$,
$\overline{QD}$. (2 pts. determine a line.) 3. $\overline{PA} \cong \overline{QC}$;
$\overline{PB} \cong \overline{QD}$ (Radii of $\cong$ $\odot$'s are $\cong$. [1]) 4. $\triangle PAB \cong$
$\triangle QCD$ (SSS Post. [1, 3]) 5. $\angle PBX \cong \angle QDY$ (Corr.
parts of $\cong$ $\triangle$ are $\cong$. [4]) 6. $\angle PXB$ and $\angle QYD$ are
rt. $\angle$. (2 $\perp$ lines form 4 rt. $\angle$ [1]) 7. $\triangle PXB$ and
$\triangle QYD$ are rt. $\triangle$. (Def. of rt. $\triangle$ [6]) 8. $\triangle PXB \cong$
$\triangle QYD$ (HA Thm. [3, 5, 7]) 9. $\overline{PX} \cong \overline{QY}$ (Corr.
parts of $\cong$ $\triangle$ are $\cong$. [8]) 10. $PX = QY$ (Def. of $\cong$
segs. [9])
19. 1. ℓ is the $\perp$ bis. of chord $\overline{AB}$ of $\odot Q$. (Given)
2. $AQ = BQ$ (Def. of $\odot$) 3. Q is on ℓ (The locus
of pts. equidistant from 2 given pts. is the $\perp$
bis. of the segment joining the pts.)
21. Draw any 2 chords and construct their $\perp$
bisectors. The point of intersection of these
bisectors is the center of the circle. Use the
center to measure a radius and determine the
diameter. **23.** $2\sqrt{21}$ inches **25.** Spheres are $\cong$ if
their radii are $\cong$. **27.** $2\sqrt{43} \doteq 13.1$
29. 1. $\overline{AB}$ is chord of coplanar circles P and Q;
$\overline{QP} \perp \overline{AB}$; $QX = PX$ (Given) 2. $\overleftrightarrow{AB}$ is the $\perp$ bis.
of $\overline{QP}$. (Def. of $\perp$ bis.) 3. $QA = PA$ (The locus of
pts. equidistant from 2 given pts. is the $\perp$ bis.
of the segment joining the 2 pts.)

Pages 370-371

Class Exercises 1. Five; they are the vertices
of the pentagon. **3.** Inscribed **5.** Circumscribed
7. Infinitely many; infinitely many **9.** Two or
more lines that intersect in a single pt. **11.** The
$\perp$ bisectors of the sides of the $\triangle$.

Written Exercises 1. 9 **3.** 6 **5.** 108
7. Orthocenter **9.** Incenter **11.** $4\sqrt{3}$ **13.** They
are the same point: P. **15.** $0.5x$ **17.** Draw the
diagonals of the square. Their point of
intersection is the center of the circle.
19. Given: Any $\triangle ABC$ Prove: A circle can be
circumscribed about $\triangle ABC$. Proof: 1. $\triangle ABC$ is
any $\triangle$. (Given) 2. Let P be the point of
concurrency of the $\perp$ bisectors of the sides of
$\triangle ABC$, $PA = PC = PB = r$ (The $\perp$ bis. of the
sides of a $\triangle$ are concurrent in a pt. equidistant
from the vertices of the $\triangle$.) 3. The circle with
center P and radius r contains pts. A, B, and C.
(Def. of $\odot$) 4. $\odot P$ circumscribes $\triangle ABC$. (Def. of
circumscribes)

Pages 376-378

Class Exercises 5. $\overarc{GB}$, $\overarc{BC}$; $\overarc{AG}$, $\overarc{AC}$; or $\overarc{GBA}$,
$\overarc{CBA}$ **7.** 60 **9.** 280 **11.** $m\overarc{AE}$ **13.** 360
Written Exercises 1. Minor arc **3.** Central $\angle$
5. Major arc **7.** 35 **9.** 65 **11.** 145 **13.** 180
15. 15 **17.** One; the green triangles are $\cong$.
19. 1. $\overarc{AC} \cong \overarc{BD}$ on $\odot P$ (Given) 2. $m\overarc{AC} = m\overarc{BD}$
(Def. of $\cong$ arcs) 3. $m\overarc{AC} = m\overarc{AB} + m\overarc{BC}$;
$m\overarc{BD} = m\overarc{BC} + m\overarc{CD}$ (Arc. Add. Post.)
4. $m\overarc{AB} + m\overarc{BC} = m\overarc{CD} + m\overarc{BC}$ (Subst. [2, 3])
5. $m\overarc{AB} = m\overarc{CD}$ (Subtr. prop. of eq.) 6. $\overarc{AB} \cong \overarc{CD}$
(Def. of $\cong$ arcs [1, 5])
23. Given: $\odot P \cong \odot Q$: $\overarc{AB} \cong \overarc{CD}$ Prove: $\overline{AB} \cong \overline{CD}$
Proof: 1. $\odot P \cong \odot Q$; $\overarc{AB} \cong \overarc{CD}$ (Given)
2. $m\overarc{AB} = m\overarc{CD}$ (Def. of $\cong$ arcs) 3. $m\overarc{AB} =$
$m\angle APB$: $m\overarc{CD} = m\angle CQD$ (Def. of arc meas.)
4. $m\angle APB = m\angle CQD$ (Subst. [2, 3])
5. $\angle APB \cong \angle CQD$ (Def. of $\cong$ $\angle$s) 6. $\overline{AP} \cong \overline{BP} \cong$
$\overline{QD} \cong \overline{QC}$ (Radii of same or $\cong$ $\odot$s are $\cong$.)
7. $\triangle APB \cong \triangle DQC$ (SAS Post. [5, 6])
8. $\overline{AB} \cong \overline{DC}$ (Corres. parts of $\cong$ $\triangle$s are $\cong$.)
25. 95 **27.** 80 **29.** 54 **31.** 135 **39.** 50 **41.** 120
43. 60

Pages 381-383

Class Exercises Answers may vary. **1.** $\angle CAB$,
$\angle ABD$, $\angle ACB$, $\angle BCD$ **3.** $\angle DAC$, $\angle DBC$
5. $\angle DAC$, $\angle DBC$ **7.** $\angle DAB$, $\angle DCB$ **9.** 150
11. 75 **Written Exercises 1.** 32.5 **3.** 30
5. 68 **7.** 10 **9.** 90 **11.** 10; 30; 35 **13.** 85 **15.** 75

19. Place the corner of the card on the circle and mark the points on the circle where the edges of the card touch the circle. These two points are the endpoints of a diameter.
21. $m\angle 2 = 30$; $m\angle 3 = 60$; $m\angle 1 = 90$
23. 72 **25.** 115 **27.** Draw $\overline{GK}$, $m\angle KGF = 0.5(m\widehat{KF}) = 30$; $m\angle GKJ = 0.5(m\widehat{GH}) = 15$; $m\angle GKJ + m\angle J = m\angle KGF$; $15 + m\angle J = 30$; $m\angle J = 15$ **29. 1.** $\angle ACB$ is inscribed in $\odot P$; P lies on $\angle ACB$ (Given) **2.** Draw $\overline{AP}$. (2 pts. determine a line.) **3.** $\overline{AP} \cong \overline{CP}$ (Radii of same $\odot$ are $\cong$.) **4.** $\angle 1 \cong \angle ACB$ (Isos. $\triangle$ Thm.)
5. $m\angle 1 = m\angle ACB$ (Def. of $\cong \angle$s) **6.** $m\angle 2 = m\angle 1 + m\angle ACB$ (Meas. of ext. $\angle$ of $\triangle$ = sum of meas. of 2 remote int. $\angle$s.) **7.** $m\angle 2 = m\angle ACB + m\angle ACB = 2(m\angle ACB)$ (Subst. [5, 6]) **8.** $m\angle 2 = m\widehat{AB}$ (Def. of arc meas.) **9.** $2(m\angle ACB) = m\widehat{AB}$ (Subst. [7, 8]) **10.** $m\angle ACB = 0.5(m\widehat{AB})$ (Mult. prop. of eq.)
31. 1. $\angle ACB$ is inscribed in $\odot P$; P is in the ext. of $\angle ACB$ (Given) **2.** Draw $\overleftrightarrow{CP}$. (2 pts. determine a line.) **3.** $m\angle 1 + m\angle ACB = m\angle DCB$ (Angle Add. Post.) **4.** $m\angle ACB = m\angle DCB - m\angle 1$ (Subtr. prop. of eq.) **5.** $m\angle DCB = 0.5(m\widehat{DB})$; $m\angle 1 = 0.5(m\widehat{DA})$ (Case I above) **6.** $m\angle ACB = 0.5(m\widehat{DB} - m\widehat{DA})$ (Subst. [4, 5]) **7.** $m\widehat{DB} = m\widehat{DA} + m\widehat{AB}$ (Arc Add. Post.)
8. $m\widehat{AB} = m\widehat{DB} - m\widehat{DA}$ (Subtr. prop. of eq.)
9. $m\angle ACB = 0.5(m\widehat{AB})$ (Subst. [6, 8])
35. $\odot O$, excluding V and P

Pages 388-389
Class Exercises **1.** 55 **3.** 35 **5.** 67 **7.** 50
9. 110 **Written Exercises** **1.** 45 **3.** 45 **5.** 90
7. 33.5 **9.** 120 **11.** 55 **13.** 15 **15.** 40 **17.** 55
19. 70 **21.** 55 **23.** 75 **25. 1.** $\overrightarrow{RQ}$ and $\overrightarrow{RS}$ are tang. to $\odot U$ (Given) **2.** $m\angle R = 0.5(m\widehat{QTS} - m\widehat{QS})$ (Meas. of $\angle$ formed by 2 tangs. is 0.5 times the diff. of the meas. of the intercepted arcs.)
3. $m\widehat{QTS} = 360 - m\widehat{QS}$ (Def. of meas. of major arc) **4.** $m\angle R = 0.5(360 - m\widehat{QS} - m\widehat{QS})$ (Subst. [2, 3]) **5.** $m\angle R = 180 - m\widehat{QS}$ (Algebra)
6. $m\widehat{QS} + m\angle R = 180$ (Add. prop. of eq.)
27. 1. $\overleftrightarrow{QS}$ and $\overleftrightarrow{RT}$ intersect in the int. of the circle. (Given) **2.** Draw $\overline{TS}$. (2 pts. determine a line.) **3.** $m\angle 1 = m\angle 2 + m\angle 3$ (Meas. of ext. $\angle$ of $\triangle$ = sum of meas. of 2 remote int. $\angle$s.)
4. $m\angle 2 = 0.5(m\widehat{RS})$; $m\angle 3 = 0.5(m\widehat{QT})$ (Meas. of ins. $\angle$ = 0.5 times meas. of its intercepted arc.)

5. $m\angle 1 = 0.5(m\widehat{RS}) + 0.5(m\widehat{QT})$ (Sub. [3, 4])
6. $m\angle 1 = 0.5(m\widehat{RS} + m\widehat{QT})$ (Dist. prop.)
29. 1. $\odot P$ has tang. $\overleftrightarrow{BC}$ and sec. $\overleftrightarrow{AC}$; C is pt. of tang.; P lies on $\angle ACB$ (Given) **2.** $\overline{PC} \perp \overleftrightarrow{BC}$ (A line is tang. to a $\odot$ if and only if it is $\perp$ to a radius drawn to a pt. on the circle.) **3.** $\angle ACB$ is a rt. $\angle$. (2 $\perp$ lines form 4 rt. $\angle$s.) **4.** $m\angle ACB = 90$ (Def. of rt. $\angle$.) **5.** $\widehat{AXC}$ is a semicircle. (Def. of semicircle) **6.** $m\widehat{AXC} = 180$ (Def. of meas. of semicircle) **7.** $0.5(m\widehat{AXC}) = 90$ (Mult. prop. of eq.) **8.** $m\angle ACB = 0.5(m\widehat{AXC})$ (Subst. [4, 7])
35. 44 **37.** 10.75 or 14

Pages 391-393
Class Exercises **1.** $\overline{QT}$ **3.** $\overline{QR}$ **5.** 3 **7.** $\frac{12}{7}$
9. $2\sqrt{13}$ **Written Exercises** **1.** 25 **3.** 9
5. $2\sqrt{21}$ **7. 1.** $\overline{AB} \cong \overline{AD}$ (Given) **2.** $AB = AD$ (Def. of $\cong$ segs.) **3.** $(AB)(AC) = (AD)(AE)$ (If 2 secs. are drawn from ext. pt. of $\odot$, product of lengths of 1 sec. seg. and its ext. sec. seg. = product of lengths of other sec. seg. and its ext. sec. seg.) **4.** $AC = AE$ (Mult. prop. of eq. [2, 3])
5. $\overline{AC} \cong \overline{AE}$ (Def. of $\cong$ segs.) **9.** 2 **11.** 3 **13.** $8\frac{9}{13}$
15. About 3.39 **17.** 30 **19. 1.** $\odot O$ has tang. $\overleftrightarrow{PQ}$ and sec. $\overleftrightarrow{PT}$. (Given) **2.** Draw $\overline{QS}$ and $\overline{QT}$. (2 pts. determine a line.) **3.** $m\angle T = 0.5(m\widehat{QS})$ (Meas. of inscribed $\angle$ = 0.5 times meas. of its intercepted arc.) **4.** $m\angle SQP = 0.5(m\widehat{QS})$ (Meas. of angle formed by tang. and sec. that intersect at the pt. of tangency = 0.5 times the meas. of the intercepted arc.) **5.** $m\angle T = m\angle SQP$ (Subst. [3, 4]) **6.** $\angle T \cong \angle SQP$ (Def. of $\cong \angle$s) **7.** $\angle P \cong \angle P$ ($\cong$ of $\angle$s is reflex.) **8.** $\triangle PQT \sim \triangle PSQ$ (AA Post. [6, 7]) **9.** $\dfrac{PQ}{PS} = \dfrac{PT}{PQ}$ (Corres. parts of $\sim \triangle$s are prop.) **10.** $(PQ)^2 = (PS)(PT)$ (Mult. prop. of eq.)
21. $2.5\sqrt{5}$ **23.** 6 or 8 **25.** 30 **27. 1.** $\odot P$ and $\odot O$ are coplanar and intersect in Q and R; $\overline{DE}$ is common ext. tang. (Given) **2.** $(XE)^2 = (XR)(XQ)$; $(XD)^2 = (XR)(XQ)$ (If tang. and sec. are drawn to $\odot$ from ext. pt., the sq. of length of tang. seg. = product of lengths of sec. seg. and its ext. sec. seg.) **3.** $(XE)^2 = (XD)^2$ (Subst. [2]) **4.** $XE = XD$ (Algebra) **5.** X is midpt. of $\overline{DE}$. (Def. of midpt.) **6.** $\overleftrightarrow{RQ}$ bisects $\overline{DE}$ (Def. of bisects)

Chapter 9

Pages 402-403

Class Exercises **1.** a. Yes b. Yes c. No d. Yes
3. 25 **5.** $4\sqrt{3}$ cm **7.** $32s$ **9.** 14 **11.** 28 **Written Exercises** **1.** 75 cm^2 **3.** 0.5 m^2 **5.** 30 **7.** $r^2 - 4$
9. 121 **11.** 80 **13.** $14\frac{4}{13}$ yd. **15.** 912 **17.** 25 **19.** 8
21. Given: Square $ABCD$ with sides of length s
Prove: Area of $ABCD = s^2$ Proof: 1. $ABCD$ is a
square with $AB = s$ (Given) 2. $ABCD$ is a
rectangle; $AB = BC$ (Def. of square) 3. Area of
$ABCD = (AB)(BC)$ (Area Post. for Rectangles)
4. Area $= s(s) = s^2$ (Substitution [1, 2, 3])
23. 60 sq. in. **25.** 50 **27.** Area $\square ABCD = 2$(area
$\triangle ADC$) **29.** Length: 15; width: 5

Pages 406-408

Class Exercises **1.** $\overline{CE}$, $\overline{AH}$, or $\overline{DF}$ **3.** $\overline{DF}$, $\overline{CE}$,
or $\overline{AH}$ **5.** 32 sq. ft. **7.** 120 mm^2 **9.** 24 sq. ft.
11. Area $\triangle ACD = 35$; area $\triangle DBC = 35$; area
$\triangle ACB = 70$ **Written Exercises**
1. 270 sq. in. **3.** 48 **5.** 90 **7.** $2x^2 - 8x + 8$
9. 108 **11.** $0.5(3x^2 + 10x - 25)$ **13.** 45 cm^2
15. 216 **17.** 4 **19.** 102 **21.** $\frac{121}{4}\sqrt{3}$ cm^2
23. $2\sqrt{3}$ sq. yd. **25.** 12 **27.** 20 **29.** $\frac{16}{9}\sqrt{3}$
31. Perimeter $= 36$; area $= 40$ **33.** 192 cm^2
35. Area $\triangle ABE =$ area $\triangle BCE = 0.5$(area $\triangle ACE$)
37. 1. $\square ABCD$; base $\overline{AB}$ has length b; altitude
$\overline{DE}$ has length h. (Given) 2. Draw $\overrightarrow{CF} \perp \overrightarrow{AB}$ at F.
(Through a pt. not on a line there is exactly one
line $\perp$ to the given line.) 3. $\angle CFA$ is a rt. $\angle$. (2
$\perp$ lines form 4 rt. $\angle$s.) 4. $\overline{CF} \| \overline{DE}$ (In a plane,
lines $\perp$ to the same line are $\|$. [1, 2]) 5. $CDEF$ is
a $\square$. (Def. of $\square$ [1, 4]) 6. $\square CDEF$ is a rectangle.
(Def. of rectangle [3, 5]) 7. Area $\square CDEF =$
$(DE)(EF)$ (Area Post. for rectangles) 8. $\overline{DA} \cong \overline{CB}$;
$\overline{DE} \cong \overline{CF}$ (Opp. sides of $\square$ are $\cong$. [1, 5])
9. $\triangle DAE \cong \triangle CBF$ (HL Thm. [1, 3, 8]) 10. Area
$\triangle DAE =$ area $\triangle CBF$ ($\cong \triangle$s have $=$ area.)
11. $\overline{AE} \cong \overline{BF}$ (Corres. parts of $\cong \triangle$s are $\cong$.)
12. $AE = BF$ (Def. of $\cong$ segs.) 13. $AE + EB =$
$EB + BF$ (Add. prop. of eq.) 14. $AE + EB = AB$;
$EB + BF = EF$ (Seg. Add. Post.) 15. $AB = EF = b$
(Subst. [1, 13, 14]) 16. Area $\square CDEF =$
$(DE)(EF) = bh$ (Subst. [1, 7, 15]) 17. Area
$\square CDEF =$ area $EBCD +$ area $\triangle CBF$; area
$\square ABCD =$ area $EBCD +$ area $\triangle AED$ (Area Add.
Post.) 18. Area $\square ABCD =$ area $EBCD +$ area
$\triangle CBF$ (Subst. [10, 17]) 19. Area $\square ABCD =$ area
$\square CDEF = bh$ (Subst. [16, 17, 18])

39. 1. $\triangle XYZ$ is equilateral with side length s.
(Given) 2. $m\angle Z = 60$ (Each $\angle$ of equilateral $\triangle$
has meas. 60.) 3. Draw $\overline{YW} \perp \overline{XZ}$. (Through a
pt. not on a given line, there is exactly one
line $\perp$ to the given line.) 4. $\angle YWZ$ is a rt. $\angle$.
(2 $\perp$ lines form 4 rt. $\angle$s.) 5. $m\angle YWZ = 90$ (Def.
of rt. $\angle$) 6. $m\angle WYZ + m\angle YWZ + m\angle Z = 180$
(Sum of meas. of $\angle$s of $\triangle = 180$.)
7. $m\angle WYZ + 90 + 60 = 180$ (Subst. [2, 5, 6])
8. $m\angle WYZ = 30$ (Subtr. prop. of eq.) 9. $WZ =$
$\frac{1}{2}s$ and $YW = \frac{1}{2}s\sqrt{3}$ (In a 30-60-90 $\triangle$, the
length of leg opp. 30°$\angle$ is half the hyp. and the
length of leg opp. 60°$\angle$ is $\frac{1}{2}\sqrt{3}$ times the
hyp.) 10. Area $\triangle YXZ = \frac{1}{2}(XZ)(YW)$ (Area of $\triangle$
is half the product of lengths of a side and its
corres. alt.) 11. Area $\triangle XYZ = \frac{1}{2}(s)(\frac{1}{2}s\sqrt{3}) =$
$\frac{1}{4}s^2\sqrt{3}$ (Subst. [1, 9, 10])

Pages 412-415

Class Exercises **1.** 18 **3.** 96 **5.** 42 **7.** 7 sq. ft.
9. Yes; multiply **11.** 22 **Written Exercises**
1. 28 **3.** 24 **5.** $6t$ **7.** 15.91 cm^2 **9.** $x^2 + 5.5x - 3$
11. Trapezoid; 48 **13.** Rhombus; 20 **15.** About
70,350 sq. miles **17.** 84 in. **19.** 48 **21.** $\frac{238}{3}\sqrt{3}$
23. 168 **25.** About 110,950 sq. miles
27. $112.5\sqrt{2}$ sq. ft. **29.** $\frac{120}{13}$ **31.** 4; 25; 21; 4:25
33. 10 cm and 32 cm **35.** 4520 sq. in.
37. 1. Trap. $GBCD$ has bases $\overline{GB}$ and $\overline{CD}$ of
lengths b_1 and b_2, and alt. $\overline{DE}$ of length h.
(Given) 2. Draw $\overline{BD}$. (2 pts. determine a line.)
3. Construct $\overline{BF} \perp \overline{DC}$ at F. (Through a pt. not
on a given line, there is exactly 1 line $\perp$ to the
given line.) 4. $\overline{DC} \| \overline{GB}$ (Def. of trap. [1])
5. $DE = BF = h$ (Distance between $\|$ lines is
constant. [1, 4]) 6. Area $\triangle GBD = \frac{1}{2}(DE)(GB) =$
$\frac{1}{2}hb_1$; area $\triangle DCB = \frac{1}{2}(BF)(DC) = \frac{1}{2}hb_2$ (Area of
$\triangle = \frac{1}{2}$ product of length of side and its corres.
alt. [1, 5]) 7. Area $GBCD =$ area $\triangle GBD +$ area
$\triangle DCB$ (Area Add. Post.) 8. Area $GBCD =$
$\frac{1}{2}hb_1 + \frac{1}{2}hb_2$ (Subst. [6, 7]) 9. Area $GBCD =$
$\frac{1}{2}h(b_1 + b_2)$ (Dist. prop.)

Pages 418-420

Class Exercises 1. $\frac{9}{49}$ 3. $\frac{4}{9}$ **Written**
Exercises 1. 3:1 3. Perimeter is doubled. Area
is quadrupled. 5. 2 sq. in. 7. $6\sqrt{5}$ cm 9. 48; 32
11. $\frac{1}{9}$ 13. 18 cm 15. $\frac{144}{361}$ 17. $\frac{3}{2}$ 19. About 115.0 m²
21. Draw the six diagonals from A and A'.
Show that $\triangle ABC$, $\triangle ACD$, $\triangle ADE$, and $\triangle AEF$
are similar to the corr. $\triangle$s in the other hexagon
by the SAS $\sim$ Thm. Each $\triangle$ contains at least
one side of the hexagon, so use Thm. 9.7 to
show the ratios of areas of $\triangle$s = square of the
ratio of side lengths. Apply the Area Addition
Post. and the summation prop. of proportions.
23. $\frac{1}{4}$

Pages 424-425

Class Exercises 5. 48 7. 90 9. 60 11. 30
13. $\frac{360}{7n}$ 15. $\frac{360}{(n-2)}$ **Written Exercises**
1. $216\sqrt{3}$ 3. $72\sqrt{3}$ 5. $150\sqrt{3}$ 7. $18\sqrt{3}$ 11. 128
13. $a = 9$; $p = 72$; $r = 9\sqrt{2}$; $A = 324$ 15. $a =$
$\frac{9}{2}\sqrt{3}$; $p = 54$; $r = 9$; $A = \frac{243}{2}\sqrt{3}$ 17. $a = \frac{1}{6}y\sqrt{3}$;
$p = 3y$; $r = \frac{1}{3}y\sqrt{3}$; $A = \frac{1}{4}y^2\sqrt{3}$ 19. 2 to 5
23. Hexagon 25. Hexagon 27. 1:2; 1:4
29. 1. $P_1P_2P_3 \cdots P_n$ is a reg. n-gon with sides of
length s, apothem a, perimeter p, center O.
(Given) 2. Draw $\overline{OP_1}$, $\overline{OP_2}$, $\overline{OP_3}$, ..., $\overline{OP_n}$. (2 pts.
determine a line.) 3. $\overline{OP_1} \cong \overline{OP_2} \cong \overline{OP_3} \cong \cdots \cong$
$\overline{OP_n}$ (Radii of a reg. poly. are $\cong$. [1]) 4. $\overline{P_1P_2} \cong$
$\overline{P_2P_3} \cong \overline{P_3P_4} \cong \cdots \cong \overline{P_nP_1}$ (Def. of reg. poly. [1])
5. $\triangle P_1OP_2 \cong \triangle P_2OP_3 \cong \cdots \cong \triangle P_nOP_1$ (SSS [3, 4])
6. Area $\triangle P_1OP_2$ = area $\triangle P_2OP_3 = \cdots =$
Area $\triangle P_nOP_1$ (Areas of $\cong$ $\triangle$s are =.) 7. Area
$P_1P_2P_3 \cdots P_n$ = area $\triangle P_1OP_2$ + area $\triangle P_2OP_3 + \cdots$
+ area $\triangle P_nOP_1$ (Area Add. Post.) 8. Area
$P_1P_2P_3 \cdots P_n = n$(area $\triangle P_1OP_2$) (Subst.; algebra
[6, 7]) 9. Area $\triangle P_1OP_2 = \frac{1}{2}as$ (Area $\triangle = \frac{1}{2}$
product of lengths of alt. and corres. side.)
10. Area $P_1P_2P_3 \cdots P_n = n(\frac{1}{2}as)$ (Subst. [8, 9])
11. Area $P_1P_2P_3 \cdots P_n = \frac{1}{2}a(ns)$ (Algebra)
12. $p = ns$ (Def. of perimeter [1]) 13. Area
$P_1P_2P_3 \cdots P_n = \frac{1}{2}ap$ (Subst. [11, 12])
31. 4 to 3

33.

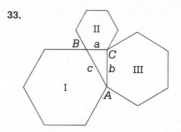

Given: $\triangle ABC$ with rt. $\angle C$; reg. hex. I, II,
and III with sides of lengths c, a, and b, resp.
Prove: Area I = area II + area III Proof:
1. $\triangle ABC$ has rt. $\angle C$; Reg. hex. I, II, III have
side lengths c, a, b, resp. (Given) 2. $c^2 = a^2 +$
b^2 (Pyth. Thm. [1]) 3. Area I $= \frac{3}{2}c^2\sqrt{3}$; area
II $= \frac{3}{2}a^2\sqrt{3}$; area III $= \frac{3}{2}b^2\sqrt{3}$ (Exer. 30, above)
4. Area II + area III $= \frac{3}{2}\sqrt{3}(a^2 + b^2)$ (Add. prop.
of eq.) 5. Area II + area III $= \frac{3}{2}\sqrt{3}(c^2)$ (Subst.
[2, 4]) 6. Area II + area III = area I (Subst. [3, 5])

Pages 428-430

Class Exercises 1. $r = 2$; $C = 4\pi$; $A = 4\pi$
3. $d = 14$; $C = 14\pi$; $A = 49\pi$ 5. $r = 5$; $d = 10$;
$A = 25\pi$ 7. $r = 2$; $C = 4\pi$; $d = 4$
9. Circumference is multiplied by 2; area is
multiplied by 4. **Written Exercises**
1. 81.64 in. 3. 452.16 cm² 5. 4.5216 m² 7. 3
9. 40 m 11. 8.6 13. Square; 21.5 sq. in.
15. 1.27:1; 1.27:1 17. 2 to 5; 4 to 25 19. 12-
inch 21. $12^2 - 36\pi \doteq 30.96$ 23. $18\pi \doteq 56.52$
25. $2080 - 312.5\pi \doteq 1098.75$ 27. Circle
29. $3\sqrt{2}$ to 4, or about 1.06 to 1
31. $16\pi\sqrt{2} \doteq 71.04$ 33. $40\pi \doteq 125.6$

Pages 433-435

Class Exercises 1. $\frac{1}{18}$ 3. $\frac{1}{4}$ 5. $\frac{3}{8}$ 7. $\frac{2}{3}$
9. $\frac{225}{6}\pi - \frac{225}{4}\sqrt{3} \doteq 20.33$ 11. $\frac{4}{3}\pi$ 13. $\frac{49}{3}\pi$
15. 12 17. 13.6 19. $24\pi - 36\sqrt{3}$ **Written**
Exercises 1. 10π 3. 5π 5. 27π 7. 27π 9. $A \doteq$
64π; $m = \frac{282.375}{\pi} \doteq 90$ 11. $m = \frac{376.2}{\pi} \doteq 120$; $A =$
$\frac{100}{3}\pi$ 13. $r = 6$; $s = \pi$ 15. $r = \frac{62.8}{\pi} \doteq 20$; $A \doteq 150\pi$
17. $\frac{50}{3}\pi - 25\sqrt{3} \doteq 9.03$ 19. $\frac{121}{4}\pi - \frac{121}{2} \doteq 34.49$

21. $12\pi - 9\sqrt{3} \doteq 22.09$ **23.** $12.25\pi - 24.5 \doteq$
13.97 **25.** $16\pi - 32 \doteq 18.24$ **27.** $228 + 18\pi \doteq$
284.52 sq. ft. **29.** $\frac{50}{3}\pi \doteq 52.3$ **31.** $64\pi - 96\sqrt{3} \doteq$
34.69 **33.** $\frac{35}{3}\pi \doteq 36.63$ **35.** $\frac{100}{3}\pi - 25\sqrt{3} \doteq 61.37$
37. Let $AB = 2c$, $BC = 2a$, and $CA = 2b$. Then
the area of the semicircle on $\overline{AB}$ is $(\frac{1}{2}\pi c^2)$; the
area of the semicircle on $\overline{AC}$ is $(\frac{1}{2}\pi b^2)$; and
the area of the semicircle on $\overline{BC}$ is $(\frac{1}{2}\pi a^2)$. The
area of the shaded regions is the area of the
semicircle on $\overline{AC}$ plus the area of the semicircle
on $\overline{BC}$ minus the difference of the area of the
semicircle on $\overline{AB}$ and the area of $\triangle ABC$. Since
area $\triangle ABC = \frac{1}{2}(AC)(BC) = \frac{1}{2}(2b)(2a) = 2ab$, the
area of the shaded regions is $\frac{1}{2}\pi b^2 + \frac{1}{2}\pi a^2 -$
$(\frac{1}{2}\pi c^2 - 2ab)$. Thus, the area of the shaded
regions is $\frac{1}{2}\pi(b^2 + a^2 - c^2) + 2ab$. But, by the
Pythagorean Theorem, $b^2 + a^2 = c^2$, so $b^2 +$
$a^2 - c^2 = 0$. So the area of the shaded regions
is $2ab =$ area $\triangle ABC$.

Chapter 10

Pages 446-447
Class Exercises 1. 7 **3.** 10 **5.** 8 **7.** 14 cm
9. 30 **Written Exercises 1.** $e = 15$; $f = 7$; $v =$
10 **3.** $s = 9$; $e = 27$; $f = 11$ **5.** $s = 10$; $f = 12$;
$v = 20$ **7.** $s = 12$; $e = 36$; $v = 24$ **11.** 1. Rt. rect.
prism has bases $ABCD$ and $A'B'C'D'$. (Given)
2. $ABCD$ is a rect. (Def. of rect. prism) 3. $ABCD$
is a $\square$. (Def. of rect.) 4. $AA'D'D$ is a $\square$. (Def. of
prisms) 5. $\overline{AB} \cong \overline{CD}$; $\overline{AA'} \cong \overline{DD'}$ (Opp. sides of
$\square$ are $\cong$. [3, 4]) 6. $\overline{AA'}$ and $\overline{DD'}$ are $\perp$ to the
plane of $\square ABCD$. (Def. of rt. prism) 7. $\overline{AA'} \perp$
$\overline{AB}$; $\overline{DD'} \perp \overline{DC}$ (Def. of line $\perp$ to plane.)
8. $\measuredangle BAA'$ and $\measuredangle CDD'$ are rt. $\measuredangle$s. (2 $\perp$ lines
form 4 rt. $\measuredangle$s.) 9. $\measuredangle BAA' \cong \measuredangle CDD'$ (All rt. $\measuredangle$s
are $\cong$.) 10. $\triangle BAA' \cong \triangle CDD'$ (SAS Post. [5, 9])
11. $\overline{A'B} \cong \overline{D'C}$ (Corres. parts of $\cong \triangle$s are $\cong$.)
13. 1. Rt. prism with bases $WXYZ$ and
$W'X'Y'Z'$ (Given) 2. $\overline{WW'}$ and $\overline{YY'}$ are $\perp$ to
$WXYZ$ and $W'X'Y'Z'$; $WW'Z'Z$ and $ZZ'Y'Y$ are
$\square$s (Def. of rt. prism) 3. $\overline{WW'} \perp \overline{WY}$; $\overline{YY'} \perp \overline{WY}$
(Def. of line $\perp$ to plane) 4. $\triangle W'WY$ and $\triangle Y'YW$
are rt. $\triangle$s ($\perp$ lines form 4 rt. $\angle$s; def. of rt. $\triangle$)
5. $\overline{WY} \cong \overline{YW}$ ($\cong$ of segs. is refl.)
6. $\overline{WW'} \cong \overline{ZZ'} \cong \overline{YY'}$ (Opp. sides of a $\square$ are $\cong$;
$\cong$ of segs. is trans. [2]) 7. $\triangle W'WY \cong \triangle Y'YW$
(LL Thm. [4, 5, 6]) 8. $\overline{W'Y} \cong \overline{WY'}$ (Corr. parts of
$\cong \triangle$s are $\cong$.)
15. 1. Rt. prism with bases $ABCDE$ and
$A'B'C'D'E'$; $\overline{MM'} \parallel \overline{DD'}$ (Given) 2. $\overline{DD'} \perp$
planes of $ABCDE$ and $A'B'C'D'E'$ (Def. of rt.
prism) 3. $\overline{DD'} \perp \overline{MD}$ and $\overline{DD'} \perp \overline{M'D'}$ (Def. of
line $\perp$ to plane) 4. M, D, D', and M' are
coplanar (Def. of $\parallel$ lines [1]) 5. $\overline{MD}$, $\overline{DD'}$, and
$\overline{M'D'}$ are coplanar (Flat Plane Post.)
6. $\overline{MD} \parallel \overline{M'D'}$ (In a plane, if 2 lines $\perp$ to same
line, they are $\parallel$. [3, 5]) 7. $MDD'M'$ is a $\square$. (Def.
of $\square$ [1, 6]) 8. $\overline{MD} \cong \overline{M'D'}$ (Opp. sides of a $\square$
are $\cong$.)
17. $f = n + 2$; $e = 3n$; $v = 2n$
19. 1. Parallelepiped with $\overline{AD} \parallel \overline{B'C'}$ (Given)
2. $\overline{AD} \cong \overline{BC}$ (Opp. sides of $\square$ are $\cong$.) 3. $\overline{BC} \cong$
$\overline{B'C'}$ (Bases of prism have corres. sides and
corres. $\measuredangle$s $\cong$. [1]) 4. $\overline{AD} \cong \overline{B'C'}$ ($\cong$ of segs. is
trans. [2, 3]) 5. A, D, B', and C' are coplanar.
(Def. of $\parallel$ [1]) 6. $ADC'B'$ is a $\square$. (If opp. sides of
quad. are $\parallel$ and $\cong$, quad. is a $\square$. [1, 4, 5])
7. $\overline{AB'} \cong \overline{DC'}$ (Opp. sides of $\square$ are $\cong$.)

Pages 449-451

Class Exercises **1.** 217 **3.** 208 **5.** L.A. = 480 cm^2; T.A. = 768 cm^2 **Written Exercises** **1.** L.A. = 160; T.A. = 286 **3.** L.A. = 570; T.A. = 750 **5.** 24 m^2 **7.** L.A. = 196 m^2; T.A. = 294 m^2 **9.** L.A. = 64 cm^2; T.A. = 96 cm^2 **11.** L.A. = 16x^2; T.A. = 24x^2 **13.** L.A. = 320 m^2; T.A. = 448 m^2 **15.** 336 sq. ft. **17.** 7 cm **19.** 1350 cm^2 **21.** 780 cm^2 **23.** L.A. = 1248 + 192$\sqrt{3}$ $\doteq$ 1580.55; T.A. = 1248 + 296$\sqrt{3}$ $\doteq$ 1760.69 **25.** 9 to 1

Pages 454-456

Class Exercises **1.** 120 cm^3 **3.** 154 cu. in. **5.** 360 cm^3 **Written Exercises** **1.** 40 **3.** 693 **5.** 31.5 cu. yd. **7.** 9 cu. yd. **9.** 1500$\sqrt{3}$ cm^3 or about 2598.08 cm^3 **11.** 3720 cm^3 **13.** Multiplied by 8 **15.** 7 cm **17.** 91,000 g or 91 kg **19.** 5 board feet **21.** 6292 cm^3; 968 cm^3 **23.** 6 in. **25.** $\sqrt[3]{2}$ $\doteq$ 1.26

Pages 459-460

Class Exercises **1.** B = 36π cm^2; L.A. = 96π cm^2; T.A. = 168π cm^2; V = 288π cm^3 **3.** B = 20.25π; L.A. = 90π; T.A. = 130.5π; V = 202.5π **5.** $\frac{50}{9\pi}$ $\doteq$ 1.77 cm **Written Exercises** **1.** T.A. = 40π sq. ft.; V = 32π cu. ft. **3.** 80π cm^2 **5.** 200π cm^3 **7.** 152π cm^2 **9.** π cu. ft. $\doteq$ 3.14 cu. ft. **11.** 1298.1 gal. **13.** 25.4 m^2 **15.** 108π $\doteq$ 339.12 cm^2

Page 466

Class Exercises **1.** L.A. = 260 cm^2; T.A. = 360 cm^2; V = 400 cm^3 **3.** L.A. = 432; T.A. = 432 + 216$\sqrt{3}$ $\doteq$ 806.12; V = 432$\sqrt{3}$ $\doteq$ 748.25 **Written Exercises** **1.** 300 **3.** 250$\sqrt{3}$ $\doteq$ 433.01 **5.** L.A. = 1440 cm^2; T.A. = 600$\sqrt{3}$ + 1440 $\doteq$ 2479.2 cm^2 **7.** 6912 cm^3 **9.** 36 cm **11.** 8 cm

Pages 468-469

Class Exercises **1.** 65π **3.** 100π **5.** 200π **Written Exercises** **1.** L.A. = 15π; T.A. = 24π; V = 12π **3.** L.A. = 135π; T.A. = 216π; V = 324π **5.** L.A. = 3$\pi\sqrt{17}$; T.A. = 3$\pi\sqrt{17}$ + 3π; V = 4$\pi\sqrt{3}$ **7.** h = 8$\sqrt{2}$ $\doteq$ 11.31; L.A. = 48π $\doteq$ 150.72; T.A. = 64π $\doteq$ 200.96 V = $\frac{128}{3}\pi\sqrt{2}$ $\doteq$ 189.44 **9.** s = 13; L.A. = 65π $\doteq$ 204.1; T.A. = 90π $\doteq$ 282.6; V = 100π $\doteq$ 314 **11.** s = 4$a\sqrt{34}$ $\doteq$ 23.32a; L.A. = 48$a^2\pi\sqrt{34}$ $\doteq$ 878.84a^2; T.A. = 48$a^2\pi\sqrt{34}$ + 144$a^2\pi$ $\doteq$ 1331a^2; V = 960$a^3\pi$ $\doteq$ 3014a^3 **13.** 6.25$\pi\sqrt{2}$ $\doteq$ 27.75 m^2 **15.** 12 m

Pages 474-476

Class Exercises **1.** $\frac{500}{3}\pi$ m^3 **3.** 400π cm^2 **5.** V = 972π m^3; A = 324π m^2 **7.** Sometimes **9.** Always **Written Exercises** **1.** V = $\frac{256}{3}\pi$ m^3; A = 64π m^2 **3.** V = 972π m^3; A = 324π m^2 **5.** V = 36,000π cm^3; A = 3600π cm^2 **7.** V = $\frac{500}{3}\pi t^3$; A = 100πt^2 **9.** A $\doteq$ 73.96π sq. in.; V $\doteq$ 106.01π cu. in. **11.** r = 27; d = 54; C = 54π; V = 26,244π **13.** r = 6; d = 12; C = 12π; A = 144π **15.** r = 22; d = 44; C = 44π; V = $\frac{42,592}{3}\pi$ **17.** d = 28; r = 14; A = 784π; V = $\frac{10,976}{3}\pi$ **19.** r = $\sqrt[3]{18}$; d = 2$\sqrt[3]{18}$; C = 2$\pi\sqrt[3]{18}$; A = 12$\pi\sqrt[3]{12}$ **21.** A = 64,000,000π $\doteq$ 200,960,000 sq. mi.; V = $\frac{1}{3}$(256,000,000,000π) $\doteq$ 267,950,000,000 cu. mi. **23.** 4 m^2 **25.** 379 cm^2 **27.** 36 to 121 **29.** 324π $\doteq$ 1017.36 cm^2 **31.** 2 to 3 **33.** $\dfrac{\text{Area sphere I}}{\text{Area sphere II}} = \dfrac{4\pi(r_1)^2}{4\pi(r_2)^2} = \dfrac{(r_1)^2}{(r_2)^2}$ by Thm. 10.14 and mult. prop. of equality **35.** 3276π $\doteq$ 10,286.64 cm^3

Chapter 11

Pages 486-489

Class Exercises **1.** B **3.** F **5.** T **7.** X **9.** Y
11. A unique line of reflection cannot be found. There are infinitely many lines containing P.
13. F **15.** G **17.** Center is point P. **Written Exercises** **1.** Yes **3.** On the image of $\overline{AD}$
5. Yes **7.** On the image of $\overline{AD}$ **9.** The meas. are equal. **11.** $A'(5, 0)$; $B'(0, 4)$; $C'(-3, -4)$
13. $A'(-5, 0)$; $B'(0, 4)$; $C'(3, -4)$ **15.** Fold X onto Y and crease the paper. The crease line is ℓ. **17.** Fold paper along $\overleftrightarrow{XY}$ and crease. Next fold Y onto X and crease the paper. The intersection of the two crease lines is point O.
19. 1. P' and Q' are refl. images over ℓ of P and Q, resp.; P and Q are on opp. sides of ℓ; M is pt. of intersect. of $\overline{PQ}$ and $\overline{P'Q'}$; M is on ℓ. (Given) 2. ℓ is $\perp$ bis. of $\overline{PP'}$ and $\overline{QQ'}$. (Def. of line refl.) 3. $PM = P'M$; $QM = Q'M$ (In a plane, locus of pts. equidist. from 2 given pts. is $\perp$ bis. of seg. joining the 2 pts.)
4. $PM + MQ = P'M + MQ'$ (Add. prop. of eq. [2]) 5. $PM + MQ = PQ$; $P'M + MQ' = P'Q'$ (Seg. Add. Post.) 6. $PQ = P'Q'$ (Subst. [4, 5]) **21.** 1. P' and Q' are refl. images of P and Q over ℓ; $P = P'$; $Q = Q'$ (Given) 2. $PQ = P'Q'$ (Reflex. prop. of eq.) **23.** Given: P' and Q' are the refl. images through O of P and Q, resp.; P and P' are on $\overline{QQ'}$. Prove: $PQ = P'Q'$ 1. P' and Q' are the refl. images through O of P and Q, resp.; P and P' are on $\overline{QQ'}$. (Given) 2. O is midpt. of $\overline{PP'}$ and $\overline{QQ'}$. (Def. of pt. refl. [1]) 3. $PO = OP'$; $QO = OQ'$ (Def. of midpt. [2]) 4. $OP + PQ = OQ$; $OP' + P'Q' = OQ'$ (Seg. Add. Post.) 5. $OP + PQ = OP' + P'Q'$ (Subst. [3, 4]) 6. $PQ = P'Q'$ (Subtr. prop. of eq. [3, 5]) **29.** $(-x, y)$
31. $(x, 8 - y)$ **33.** $(6 - x, -y)$

Pages 492-493

Class Exercises **1.** D **3.** $\overline{AB}$ **5.** $\angle DAB$ **7.** C
9. $\overline{CD}$ **11.** $\angle DOA$ **13.** Any 2 pts. on the line
15. Endpoints **17.** Vertices **Written Exercises** **1.** Counterclockwise **3.** No; line refl. reverse orientation. **5.** Isometry preserves $\angle$ meas.; def. of $\cong$ $\angle$s. **7.** Isometry preserves coll. and betweenness. **9.** If isom. maps A onto A' and D onto D', then image of $\overrightarrow{AD}$ is $\overrightarrow{A'D'}$; line

refl. is isom. **11.** Line refl. is isom.; under isom., $\triangle$ and its image are $\cong$. **13.** Pt. refl. is isom.; def. of isom.; def. of $\cong$ segs. **15.** Exercise 14 and alt. int. $\angle$s $\cong$ $\Rightarrow$ 2 lines $\parallel$.
17. $A'(-2, 4)$; $B'(-4, -1)$; $C'(0, 2)$
19. $A'(-2, -4)$; $B'(-4, 1)$; $C'(0, -2)$
21. Use fig. for Thm. 11.5. Given: X', Y', and Z' are the images under an isom. of X, Y, and Z, resp. Prove: $\triangle XYZ \cong \triangle X'Y'Z'$ 1. X', Y', and Z' are the images under an isom. of X, Y, and Z, resp. (Given) 2. $XY = X'Y'$; $YZ = Y'Z'$; $XZ = X'Z'$ (Def. of isom. [1]) 3. $\overline{XY} \cong \overline{X'Y'}$; $\overline{YZ} \cong \overline{Y'Z'}$; $\overline{XZ} \cong \overline{X'Z'}$ (Def. of $\cong$ segs. [2])
4. $\triangle XYZ \cong \triangle X'Y'Z'$ (SSS Post. [3]) **23.** Suppose ℓ' and m' intersect in a pt. X. Then there is a pt. A on ℓ and a pt. B on m, each of which maps onto X. Since $\ell \parallel m$, $A \neq B$. But this contradicts the fact that an isometry is a 1 to 1 correspondence. Thus $\ell' \parallel m'$.

Pages 495-497

Class Exercises **1.** Vert. $\angle$s are $\cong$. **3.** $\angle 4 \cong \angle 5$ (Vert. $\angle$s are $\cong$.); $\angle 5 \cong \angle 6$ ($\angle 5$ is refl. image of $\angle 6$ over m); thus $\angle 4 \cong \angle 6$ ($\cong$ of $\angle$s is trans.)
5. T and R_1 are refl. images of T and R over ℓ; line refl. is an isom. **7.** Let d be distance traveled by ball. $d = CV + VU + UT + TR$; $d = CV + VU + UT + TR_1$ (Ex. 5, above); $d = CV + VU + UR_1$ (Seg. Add. Post.); $d = CV + VU + UR_2$ (Ex. 6, above); $d = CV + VR_2$ (Seg. Add. Post.); $d = CV + VR_3$ (Line refl. is isom.; V and R_3 are images of V and R_2 over n.); $d = CR_3$ (Seg. Add. Post.) **9.** Draw D', the refl. image of D over $\overleftrightarrow{AB}$. Draw $\overline{CD'}$. Q is pt. of intersection of $\overline{CD'}$ and $\overleftrightarrow{AB}$. **Written Exercises**

1.   **3.**

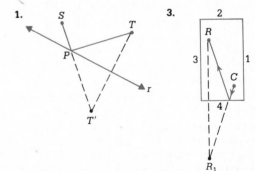

5.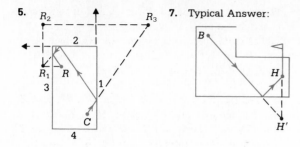

7. Typical Answer:

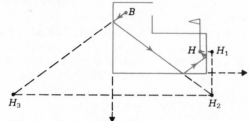

9. Typical Answer:

11.

13. $APBP'$ is a rhombus. Since the diags. of a rhombus are $\perp$ bis. of each other, P' is refl. image of P over ℓ for any position of P. **15.** 1080 m **17.** Perimeter of $\triangle PQR = P_1P_2$. For other pts. R' and Q' on $\overline{AB}$ and $\overline{AC}$, perimeter of $\triangle PQ'R' = PQ' + Q'R' + R'P = P_2Q' + Q'R' + R'P_1$, which must be greater than P_1P_2 by Thm. 4.13.

Pages 502–504

Class Exercises 1. X **3.** $\angle YXZ$ **5.** A **7.** $\angle ACB$ **9.** A **11.** $\angle ABC$ **13.** The lines of refl. are $\parallel$. **15.** The lines of refl. coincide. **Written Exercises 1.** F **3.** C **5.** $\angle FKL$ **7.** K **9.** G **11.** $\angle KPQ$ **13.** G **15.** K **17.** $\angle GCB$ **19.** D **21.** $\overline{FA}$ **23.** 120, clockwise **25.** B **27.** $\angle DEF$ **29.** E **31.** $\overline{AB}$ **33.** 180° either direction **35.** Rotation **39.** $A'(4, 3)$; $B'(0, 4)$; $C'(2, -1)$; $D'(5, -3)$ **41.** 90° clockwise rotation about G **43.** Reflection over $\overleftrightarrow{FG}$ **45.** Identity transformation **47.** Half-turn about J **49.** Typical answer: A translation that maps A onto B, a translation that maps B onto A

51. Given: P' and Q' are the images of P and Q under a translation which is the comp. of 2 refl., first over ℓ and then over m, $\ell \parallel m$. Prove: $PQ = P'Q'$. 1. P' and Q' are the images of P and Q under a translation which is the comp. of 2 refl., first over ℓ and then over m, $\ell \parallel m$. (Given) 2. Let P_1 and Q_1 be the refl. images of P and Q over ℓ. (Def. of line refl. [1]) 3. $PQ = P_1Q_1$ (A line refl. is an isom. [2]) 4. P' and Q' are the refl. images of P_1 and Q_1 over m. (Def. of translation [1]) 5. $P_1Q_1 = P'Q'$ (A line refl. is an isom. [4]) 6. $PQ = P'Q'$ (Trans. prop. of eq. [3, 5])

53. Given: A' and B' are the images of A and B, resp., under a translation that is a composite of reflections over ℓ and then over m. (There are several cases to consider. For this plan, see fig. on p. 498.) Prove: $\overleftrightarrow{AB} \parallel \overleftrightarrow{A'B'}$. Plan: Let A_1 and B_1 be the refl. images over ℓ of A and B, resp. Draw $\overleftrightarrow{BB_1}$ and $\overleftrightarrow{B_1B'}$. Show ℓ is $\perp$ bis. of $\overline{BB_1}$ and m is $\perp$ bis. of $\overline{B_1B'}$. Since $\ell \parallel m$, use Thm. 3.1 to show $\overrightarrow{BB_1} \perp m$. Show B' is on $\overrightarrow{BB_1}$ by Thm. 3.11. Show $m\angle ABB_1 = m\angle A_1B_1B$; $m\angle A_1B_1B' = m\angle A'B'B_1$. Show $\angle A_1B_1B$ and $\angle A_1B_1B'$ are supp. Thus, $\angle ABB_1$ and $\angle A'B'B_1$ are supp. Finally, use Thm. 3.6.

55. Given: A_1 is the refl. image of A over ℓ; A' is the refl. image of A_1 over m; $\ell \perp m$ at O. Prove: A' is the image of A under a half-turn. Proof: Case I: A lies on ℓ or m. Then O is midpoint of $\overline{AA'}$ (Def. line refl.) and A' is the image of A under a half-turn about pt. O. Case II: A does not lie on ℓ or m. Let P and Q be midpts. of $\overline{AA_1}$ and $\overline{A_1A'}$, resp. Since ℓ is the $\perp$ bis. of $\overline{AA_1}$ and m is the $\perp$ bis. of $\overline{A_1A'}$ (Def. of line refl.), $\triangle APO$ and $\triangle A'QO$ are rt. $\triangle$s. Since ℓ and $\overline{A_1A'}$ are both $\perp$ to m and since m and $\overline{AA_1}$ are both $\perp$ to ℓ, $POQA_1$ is a $\square$ and a rectangle. Thus, $\triangle AA_1A'$ is also a rt. $\triangle$. Let $x = AP$ and $y = A'Q$. By midpts. and rect., $A_1P = OQ = x$ and $A_1Q = PO = y$. By Pythagorean Thm., $AO = \sqrt{x^2 + y^2}$, $OA' = \sqrt{x^2 + y^2}$, and $AA' = \sqrt{(2x)^2 + (2y)^2} = 2\sqrt{x^2 + y^2}$. Since $AA' = AO + OA'$, O, A, and A' are collinear. (Thm. 4.14) Since $AO = OA'$, O is the midpt. of $\overline{AA'}$. So A' is the image of A under a half-turn about pt. O. (Def. of half-turn)

57. $(y, -x)$

Pages 508-509

Class Exercises **1.** a, b, c, d **3.** a, b, c, d
5. Yes; composite of refl. over 2 of the
intersecting lines is a rotation; each refl. maps
the figure onto itself; so will the composite.
Written Exercises **1. a.** 1 **b.** No **c.** No **3. a.** 0
b. No **c.** Yes; 120° either direction **5. a.** 1
b. No **c.** No **7. a.** 8 **b.** Yes **c.** Yes; 45° either
direction, 90° either direction, 135° either
direction, or 180° either direction **9. a.** 2 **b.** Yes
c. Yes; 180° either direction **11. a.** Infinitely
many **b.** Yes **c.** Yes; 180° either direction
13. H, I, M, O, T, U, V, W, X, Y
15. H, I, N, O, S, X, Z
17. A nonequilateral isos. $\triangle$ **19.** An isos.
trapezoid, or a quadrilateral with 2 distinct
pairs of adjacent sides $\cong$ **21.** A nonregular
pentagon **23.** $(-a, b)$ **25.** $(-a, -b)$ **27.** $n - 1$

Page 512

Class Exercises **1.** V; enlargement **3.** A;
identity transf. **5.** R; reduction **7.** X;
enlargement **Written Exercises**
7. Enlargement **9.** $\frac{1}{3}$ **11.** 4
13. Use fig. on page 511. Given: A dilation with
center C and scale factor k maps A onto A' and
B onto B'. Prove: $A'B' = k(AB)$ 1. A dilation
with center C and scale factor k maps A onto
A' and B onto B'. (Given) 2. $CA' = k(CA)$;
$CB' = k(CB)$ (Def. of dilation [1]) 3. $\dfrac{CA'}{CA} = k$;
$\dfrac{CB'}{CB} = k$ (Mult. prop. of eq. [2]) 4. $\dfrac{CA'}{CA} = \dfrac{CB'}{CB}$
(Subst. [3]) 5. $\angle C \cong \angle C$ ($\cong$ of $\angle$s is reflexive.)
6. $\triangle A'CB' \sim \triangle ACB$ (SAS $\sim$ Thm. [4, 5])
7. $\dfrac{A'B'}{AB} = \dfrac{CA'}{CA} = \dfrac{CB'}{CB}$ (In $\sim$ polygons, the
lengths of corr. sides are proportional. [6])
8. $\dfrac{A'B'}{AB} = k$ (Subst. [3, 7]) 9. $A'B' = k(AB)$
(Mult. prop. of eq. [8])

Pages 515-516

Class Exercises **1.** 15 **3.** 30 **5.** Q'; P'; R'
7. $\overrightarrow{R'P'}$ **9.** $\angle R'P'Q'$ **11.** 70 **13.** $\overline{P'R'}$; $\overline{Q'R'}$

1. 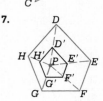 **3.**

5. 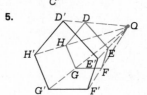 **7.**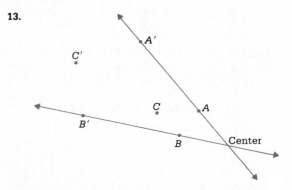

9. $A'(8, 8)$; $B'(-4, 12)$; $C'(-4, 4)$
11. $A'(2, 2)$; $B'(-1, 3)$; $C'(-1, 1)$

13.

15. No; under a dilation, a line is $\parallel$ to its image,
but $\overleftrightarrow{AC}$ is not $\parallel$ to $\overleftrightarrow{A'C'}$.
17. Given: A', B', and C' are the images of A, B,
and C, resp., under a dilation with center O and
scale factor k. (A, B, and C are noncollinear.)
Prove: $m\angle ABC = m\angle A'B'C'$ Plan for Proof:
Draw $\overleftrightarrow{AC}$ and $\overleftrightarrow{A'C'}$. Use Thm. 11.13 and mult.
prop. of eq. to show $\dfrac{A'B'}{AB} = \dfrac{B'C'}{BC} = \dfrac{A'C'}{AC}$.
Use SSS $\sim$ Thm. to show $\triangle ABC \sim \triangle A'B'C'$.
$\angle ABC \cong \angle A'B'C'$ because in $\sim$ polygons corr.
$\angle$s are $\cong$. Then use def. of $\cong$ $\angle$s.
19. Yes **21.** P; $\frac{2}{3}$
23. Given: $\overleftrightarrow{AB} \parallel \overleftrightarrow{CD}$; A', B', C', and D' are the
images of A, B, C, and D, resp., under a
dilation. Prove: $\overleftrightarrow{A'B'} \parallel \overleftrightarrow{C'D'}$ 1. A', B', C', and D'
are the images of A, B, C, and D, resp., under a

dilation. (Given) 2. $\overleftrightarrow{A'B'}$ is the image of $\overleftrightarrow{AB}$; $\overleftrightarrow{C'D'}$ is the image of $\overleftrightarrow{CD}$. (If a dilation maps A onto A' and B onto B', then the image of $\overleftrightarrow{AB}$ is $\overleftrightarrow{A'B'}$. [1]) 3. $\overleftrightarrow{AB} \| \overleftrightarrow{A'B'}$; $\overleftrightarrow{CD} \| \overleftrightarrow{C'D'}$ (Under a dilation, a line and its image are $\|$. [2]) 4. $\overleftrightarrow{AB} \| \overleftrightarrow{CD}$ (Given) 5. $\overleftrightarrow{A'B'} \| \overleftrightarrow{CD}$ (In a plane, if 2 lines are $\|$ to the same line, they are $\|$ to each other. [3, 4]) 6. $\overleftrightarrow{A'B'} \| \overleftrightarrow{C'D'}$ (In a plane, if 2 lines are $\|$ to the same line, they are $\|$ to each other. [3, 5])

Pages 521-523

Class Exercises **1.** Yes; if $\triangle ABC \cong \triangle DEF$, then there is an isom. that maps $\triangle ABC$ onto $\triangle DEF$. So $\triangle ABC \cong \triangle DEF$ by the new def. **3.** Yes; if $\triangle ABC \sim \triangle DEF$, then there is a sim. transf. that maps $\triangle ABC$ onto $\triangle DEF$. So $\triangle ABC \sim \triangle DEF$ by the new def. **5.** It is the composite of a dilation (scale factor 1) and an isom. (the line refl.) **7.** It is the composite of a dilation (scale factor 1) and an isom. (the rotation). **9.** It is the composite of a dilation (the reduction) and an isom. (identity transf.). **11.** No; distance is preserved only if the scale factor of the dilation is 1. **13.** Yes; all dilations and all isom. preserve betweenness. **15.** Yes: all dilations and all isom. preserve $\|$s. **Written Exercises** **1.** Line reflection **3.** Half-turn or rotation **5.** Translation **7.** 2 **9.** Yes; each panel is $\cong$ to the pattern since each is the image of the pattern under an isom. **11.** Thm. 11.20 **13.** Typical answer: dilation with center (4, 0) and scale factor $\frac{1}{2}$ followed by 90° counterclockwise rotation about the origin **15.** Typical answer: dilation with center (0, 4) and scale factor 2 followed by translation 5 units down the y-axis **17.** Typical answer: dilation with center $(0, -1)$ and scale factor 2 followed by a half-turn about $(0, -3)$ **19.** A sim. transf. maps $\odot P$ onto $\odot Q$: dilation with center P and scale factor $\frac{15}{7}$ followed by translation mapping P onto Q. **21.** $O'(0, 0)$; $P'(3, 0)$; $Q'(7, 2)$; $R'(4, 2)$ **23.** Dilation with center at center of concentric circles and scale factor $2\sqrt{2}$ followed by the identity transf.

Chapter 12

Pages 534-536

Class Exercises **1.** Zero **3.** Positive **5.** $-\frac{9}{2}$ **7.** $\frac{7}{4}$ **9.** $\frac{-d}{c}$ **11.** Slope $\overleftrightarrow{JK} = \frac{3}{-2}$; Slope $\overleftrightarrow{ML} = \frac{-3}{2}$; the slopes are equal, so the lines are $\|$. **13.** Midpt. $\overline{JL} = (\frac{1}{2}, 3)$; midpt. $\overline{KM} = (\frac{1}{2}, 3)$ **Written Exercises** **1.** $\frac{3}{8}$ **3.** Undefined **5.** $\frac{2}{1}$ **7.** $\frac{f - d}{e - c}$ **9.** $\frac{3}{4}$ **11.** Undefined **13.** 60% **15.** Slope $\overleftrightarrow{PQ} = \frac{-1}{4}$; slope $\overleftrightarrow{RS} = \frac{-1}{4}$; so $\overleftrightarrow{PQ} \| \overleftrightarrow{RS}$ **17.** Slope $\overleftrightarrow{PQ} = \frac{-1}{4}$; slope $\overleftrightarrow{RU} = \frac{4}{1}$; so $\overleftrightarrow{PQ} \perp \overleftrightarrow{RU}$ **19.** Slope $\overleftrightarrow{SE} = \frac{3}{5}$; slope $\overleftrightarrow{DN} = \frac{3}{5}$; so $\overleftrightarrow{SE} \| \overleftrightarrow{DN}$; slope $\overleftrightarrow{EN} = \frac{-5}{3}$; slope $\overleftrightarrow{DS} = \frac{-5}{3}$; so $\overleftrightarrow{EN} \| \overleftrightarrow{DS}$; thus $SEND$ is a $\square$. **21.** Slope $\overline{SE} = \frac{3}{5}$; slope $\overline{EN} = \frac{-5}{3}$; slope $\overline{ND} = \frac{3}{5}$; slope $\overline{DS} = \frac{-5}{3}$; thus $\overline{SE} \perp \overline{EN}$; $\overline{EN} \perp \overline{ND}$; $\overline{ND} \perp \overline{DS}$; and $\overline{DS} \perp \overline{SE}$ **23.** $TA = 5$; $TE = 5$; $\overline{TA} \cong \overline{TE}$, so $\triangle TEA$ is isos. **25.** $TA = TE = 5$; (Ex. 23); $EK = 5$; $KA = 5$; thus $\overline{TA} \cong \overline{TE} \cong \overline{EK} \cong \overline{KA}$ **27.** 403.1 m **29.** $\frac{b - 5}{a - 3}$; $\frac{a - 3}{5 - b}$ **31.** -2 **33.** 2 **35.** Typical answer: (7, 2) **37.** Typical answer: (5, 7), or $(k, 7)$ for any $k \neq 4$ **39.** $\overleftrightarrow{PT} \| \overleftrightarrow{RU}$; $\angle QPT$ and $\angle SRU$ are corres. $\angle$s. **41.** $\frac{SU}{RU}$ **43.** Yes **45.** Yes

Pages 539-541

Class Exercises **1.** $y + 5 = 6(x - 3)$; -23 **3.** 3; typical answer: (0, 5) **5.** $y + 4 = -\frac{2}{5}(x - 5)$; -5; -2

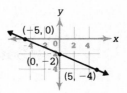

Written Exercises

1.

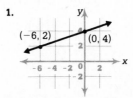

3.

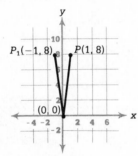

5. $y - 4 = \frac{1}{2}(x - 1)$ **7.** $y = -3$ **9.** $y = -\frac{3}{4}x + 5$
11. $y = \frac{2}{3}x + 8$ **13.** $y = \frac{4}{3}x + \frac{2}{3}$ **15.** $y - 2 =$
$-\frac{1}{2}(x - 3)$ **17.** $y = -3$ **19.** $y = \frac{-3}{4}x + 3$
21. $x = 50$ **23.** $y = \frac{2}{3}x$ **25.** $y - 4 = \frac{5}{3}(x + 2)$
27. $y = -\frac{4}{3}x - 4$ **29.** $y - 3 = 5(x + 1)$ **31.** $y =$
$-\frac{1}{12}x$ **33.** $y = -8x$ for
$-1 \leq x \leq 0$; yes

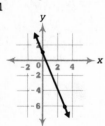

35. Midpt. $\overline{DE} = M_1(1, -4)$; midpt. $\overline{DF} =$
$M_2(0, 1)$ slope $\overleftrightarrow{M_1M_2} = -5$; slope $\overleftrightarrow{EF} = -5$;
$y + 4 = -5(x - 1)$; slope $\overleftrightarrow{M_1M_2} =$ slope $\overleftrightarrow{EF} = -5$

Pages 544-546

Class Exercises **1.** 1; −6 **3.** $-\frac{3}{2}$; 4 **5.** −6; −3
7. −5; no y-intercept **9.** 4; $(-1, 0)$ **Written**
Exercises **1.** $\frac{3}{5}$; −2
3. $-\frac{7}{3}$; 1   **5.** 1; 3

7. $x - 2y = -1$
9. 6; $(0, 0)$

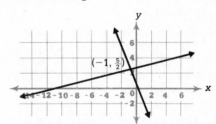

11. $|a|$; $(-11, 2)$ **13.** Yes **15.** No **17.** Yes
21. $(x - 5)^2 + (y - 8)^2 = 49$ **23.** $x^2 + y^2 = 289$
25. $x^2 + y^2 = t^2$ **27.** Yes; $AO = 17$ **29.** $7x +$
$6y = 24$; $5x - 18y = -20$; $19x - 6y = 28$
31. $x + y = 4$; $4x - 22y = -35$; $20x - 6y = 29$

Pages 550-551
Class Exercises **3.** $(-3, 2)$ **5.** $(0, 1)$ **Written**
Exercises **1.** $\left(-1, \frac{5}{2}\right)$

3. $\left(\frac{5}{3}, \frac{-5}{6}\right)$ **5.** $\left(\frac{6}{5}, -\frac{6}{5}\right)$ **7.** $(2, -1)$ **9.** $\left(\frac{3}{2}, \frac{11}{4}\right)$
11. $(-1, 1)$ **13.** No; lines coincide **15.** Yes
17. $(k, 2k - 7)$ **19.** $\left(\frac{14}{k}, 3\right)$
21. $4 - 3 = 1$;
$4^2 + 3^2 = 25$

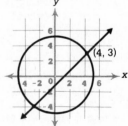

27. Yes; $(-2, 3)$ **29.** $\left(2, \frac{5}{3}\right)$ **31.** $\left(\frac{53}{26}, \frac{51}{26}\right)$

Pages 555-557

Class Exercises **1.** $A(-r, 0)$; $C(r, 2r)$; $D(-r, 2r)$
3. $N(t, t\sqrt{3})$ **5.** $Q(a + b, c)$ **7.** Zero **9.** Midpt.
$\overline{RO} = M_1(1, \frac{3}{2})$; midpt. $\overline{OC} = M_2(3, 0)$; midpt.
$\overline{CK} = M_3(\frac{11}{2}, \frac{3}{2})$; midpt. $\overline{KR} = M_4(\frac{7}{2}, 3)$ **11.** $y =$
$6x - 18$ **Written Exercises** **1.** $F(2k, 0)$;
$G(2k, 2k)$ **3.** $R(-a, 0)$; $T(0, a\sqrt{3})$ **5.** Typical
answer: $A(-a, a)$; $B(a, a)$; $C(a, -a)$; $D(-a, -a)$
7. Typical answer: $P(-a, 0)$; $Q(a, 0)$ **9.** $D(t - s, u)$
11. Let the vertices have coordinates $M(6r, 6s)$;
$N(6t, 0)$; and $O(0, 0)$. So the midpoints are
$A(3r + 3t, 3s)$; $B(3t, 0)$; and $C(3r, 3s)$.
From Part I, $D(2r + 2t, 2s)$ lies on $\overleftrightarrow{AO}$, $\overleftrightarrow{BM}$,
and $\overleftrightarrow{CN}$. By the distance formula, $DO =$
$2\sqrt{(r + t)^2 + s^2}$; $AO = 3\sqrt{(r + t)^2 + s^2}$; $DM =$
$2\sqrt{(t - 2r)^2 + (2s)^2}$; $BM = 3\sqrt{(t - 2r)^2 + (2s)^2}$;
$DN = 2\sqrt{(r - 2t)^2 + s^2}$; and $CN =$
$3\sqrt{(r - 2t)^2 + s^2}$. Therefore, $\dfrac{DO}{AO} = \dfrac{2}{3}$;
$\dfrac{DM}{BM} = \dfrac{2}{3}$; $\dfrac{DN}{CN} = \dfrac{2}{3}$. Thus,
$\dfrac{DO}{AO} = \dfrac{DM}{BM} = \dfrac{DN}{CN} = \dfrac{2}{3}$.
13. Place the vertices
at $A(0, 0)$; $B(b, 0)$;
$C(b + a, d)$; and
$D(a, d)$. By the
distance formula,
$DB = \sqrt{(b - a)^2 + d^2}$
and $AC =$
$\sqrt{(b + a)^2 + d^2}$. Since
$DB = AC$,
$(b - a)^2 + d^2 =$
$(b + a)^2 + d^2$, or $-a = a$. This occurs if and only
if $a = 0$. Thus $\overline{AD} \perp \overline{AB}$ and $ABCD$ is a
rectangle.
15. Place the vertices at $A(-a, 0)$, $B(b, 0)$, and
$C(0, c)$. Then $\overline{CO}$ is the alt. from C. The
equation for $\overleftrightarrow{CO}$ is $x = 0$. Since the slope of $\overleftrightarrow{BC}$
is $-\dfrac{c}{b}$, the slope of the alt. from A is $\dfrac{b}{c}$, and
the equation of this alt. is $y = \dfrac{b}{c}(x + a)$ or
$bx - cy = -ba$. Then the alts. from C and A
intersect at $P\left(0, \dfrac{ab}{c}\right)$. Since the slope of
the $\overleftrightarrow{AC}$ is $\dfrac{c}{a}$, the slope of the alt. from B is
$-\dfrac{a}{c}$, and the equation of the alt. is $y =$
$-\dfrac{a}{c}(x - b)$ or $ax + cy = ab$. Since the coords.

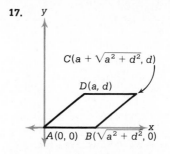

of P satisfy this equation, P is also on this alt.
Thus the 3 alts. are concurrent at P.

17.

Place two vertices at $A(0, 0)$ and $D(a, d)$. By
the Pythagorean Thm. and the def. of rhombus,
the other vertices are $B(\sqrt{a^2 + d^2}, 0)$ and
$C(a + \sqrt{a^2 + d^2}, d)$. The slope, m_1, of $\overline{AC}$ is
$\dfrac{d}{a + \sqrt{a^2 + d^2}}$. The slope, m_2, of $\overline{BD}$ is
$\dfrac{d}{a - \sqrt{a^2 + d^2}}$. Since $m_1 m_2 = -1$, the diagonals
are perpendicular.
19. Use the rhombus from Exercise 17. Then
the midpts. of $\overline{AB}$, $\overline{BC}$, $\overline{CD}$, and $\overline{DA}$ are M_1
$(\frac{1}{2}\sqrt{a^2 + d^2}, 0)$, $M_2(\frac{1}{2}a + \sqrt{a^2 + d^2}, \frac{1}{2}d)$,
$M_3(a + \frac{1}{2}\sqrt{a^2 + d^2}, d)$, and $M_4(\frac{1}{2}a, \frac{1}{2}d)$,
respectively. The slope of $\overleftrightarrow{M_1 M_2}$ is
$\dfrac{d}{a + \sqrt{a^2 + d^2}}$; the slope of $\overleftrightarrow{M_3 M_4}$ is also
$\dfrac{d}{a + \sqrt{a^2 + d^2}}$. So $\overleftrightarrow{M_1 M_2} \| \overleftrightarrow{M_3 M_4}$. The slope of
$\overleftrightarrow{M_2 M_3}$ is $\dfrac{d}{a - \sqrt{a^2 + d^2}}$; the slope of $\overleftrightarrow{M_4 M_1}$ is
also $\dfrac{d}{a - \sqrt{a^2 + d^2}}$. So $\overleftrightarrow{M_2 M_3} \| \overleftrightarrow{M_4 M_1}$. Thus
$M_1 M_2 M_3 M_4$ is a $\square$. But the prod. of the slopes
of $\overline{M_1 M_2}$ and $\overline{M_2 M_3}$ is -1, so $\overline{M_1 M_2} \perp \overline{M_2 M_3}$.
Therefore $M_1 M_2 M_3 M_4$ is a rectangle.

Page 559

Class Exercises **1.** $AB = 4\sqrt{17}$; $M(4, 2, 1)$
3. Yes **Written Exercises** **1.** $AB = 9$;
$M(\frac{9}{2}, 1, 5)$ **3.** $EF = \sqrt{94}$; $M(\frac{7}{2}, \frac{1}{2}, 4)$
5. $AB = 5$; $BD = 15$; $AD = 20$; yes **7.** Yes

Postulates and Theorems

Chapter 1 Introduction to Geometry

Postulate 1

Points Postulate Space contains at least four noncoplanar, noncollinear points. A plane contains at least three noncollinear points. A line contains at least two points. page 14

Postulate 2

Line Postulate Two points are contained in one and only one line. page 14

Postulate 3

Plane Postulate Three noncollinear points are contained in one and only one plane. page 14

Postulate 4

Flat Plane Postulate If two points are contained in a plane, then the line through them is contained in the same plane. page 15

Postulate 5

Plane Intersection Postulate If two planes intersect, they intersect in a line. page 15

Postulate 6

Ruler Postulate For every pair of points there is a unique positive real number called the *distance* between them. page 24

Postulate 7

Segment Construction Postulate On any ray, there is exactly one point at a given distance from the endpoint of the ray. page 25

Postulate 8

Segment Addition Postulate If point P is between points A and B, then $AP + PB = AB$. page 25

Postulate 9

Midpoint Postulate A segment has exactly one midpoint. page 26

Postulate 10

Protractor Postulate For every angle there is a unique real number r called its *degree measure* such that $0 < r < 180$. page 33

Postulate 11

Angle Construction Postulate Let $\mathcal{H}_1$ be a half-plane with edge $\overleftrightarrow{PA}$. There is exactly one ray, $\overrightarrow{PB}$ with B, in $\mathcal{H}_1$ such that $\angle APB$ has a given measure. page 33

Postulate 12

Angle Addition Postulate If B is in the interior of $\angle APC$, then $m \angle APB + m \angle BPC = m \angle APC$. page 33

Postulate 13

Angle Bisector Postulate An angle has exactly one bisector. page 34

Postulate 14

Supplement Postulate The angles in a linear pair are supplementary. page 41

Chapter 2 Proof in Geometry

Theorem 2.1

All right angles are congruent. page 68

Theorem 2.2

Congruence of segments is reflexive, symmetric, and transitive. page 68

Theorem 2.3

Congruence of angles is reflexive, symmetric, and transitive. page 68

Theorem 2.4

If two lines intersect, they intersect in one and only one point. page 72

Theorem 2.5

A line and a point not on the line are contained in one and only one plane. page 73

Theorem 2.6

Two intersecting lines lie in one and only one plane. page 73

Theorem 2.7

Supplements of congruent angles are congruent. page 79

Theorem 2.8
Supplements of the same angle are congruent.
page 79

Theorem 2.9
Complements of congruent angles are
congruent. page 79

Theorem 2.10
Complements of the same angle are congruent.
page 79

Theorem 2.11
Vertical angles are congruent. page 84

Theorem 2.12
If one angle of a linear pair is a right angle,
then the other angle is also a right angle.
page 86

Theorem 2.13
Two perpendicular lines form four right angles.
page 92

Theorem 2.14
If the angles of a linear pair are congruent,
then the lines containing their sides are
perpendicular. page 93

Chapter 3   Parallel Lines and Planes

Postulate 15
Parallel Lines Postulate Two coplanar lines cut
by a transversal are parallel if and only if
corresponding angles are congruent. page 112

Theorem 3.1
If a transversal is perpendicular to one of two
parallel lines, then it is perpendicular to the
other. page 113

Theorem 3.2
In a plane, if two lines are perpendicular to the
same line, then they are parallel. page 113

Theorem 3.3
If two parallel lines are cut by a transversal,
then alternate interior angles are congruent. (2
lines $\parallel \Rightarrow$ alt. int. $\angle$s $\cong$) page 116

Theorem 3.4
If two lines are cut by a transversal so that
alternate interior angles are congruent, then
the lines are parallel. (Alt. int. $\angle$s $\cong \Rightarrow$ 2 lines $\parallel$)
page 116

Theorem 3.5
If two parallel lines are cut by a transversal,
then interior angles on the same side of the
transversal are supplementary. (2 lines $\parallel \Rightarrow$ int.
$\angle$s on the same side supp.) page 117

Theorem 3.6
If two lines are cut by a transversal so that
interior angles on the same side of the
transversal are supplementary, then the lines
are parallel. (Int. $\angle$s on same side supp. $\Rightarrow$ 2
lines $\parallel$) page 117

Theorem 3.7
Through a point not on a given line, there is
exactly one line parallel to the given line.
page 126

Theorem 3.8
In a plane, if two lines are parallel to the same
line, then they are parallel to each other.
page 127

Theorem 3.9
In a plane, through a point on a given line,
there is one and only one line perpendicular to
the given line. page 127

Theorem 3.10
In a plane, a segment has exactly one
perpendicular bisector. page 128

Theorem 3.11
Through a point not on a given line, there is
one and only one line perpendicular to the
given line. page 128

Theorem 3.12
If two planes are perpendicular to the same
line, then the planes are parallel. page 134

Theorem 3.13
If two parallel planes are cut by a third plane,
then the lines of intersection are parallel.
page 135

Theorem 3.14
The sum of the measures of the angles of a
triangle is 180. page 142

Theorem 3.15
If two angles of one triangle are congruent to two angles of another triangle, then the remaining angles are congruent. page 143

Theorem 3.16
The acute angles of a right triangle are complementary. page 143

Theorem 3.17
Each angle of an equiangular triangle has measure 60. page 143

Theorem 3.18
The measure of an exterior angle of a triangle is equal to the sum of the measures of its two remote interior angles. page 143

Theorem 3.19
The measure of an exterior angle of a triangle is greater than the measure of either of its remote interior angles. page 143

Theorem 3.20
The sum of the measures of the angles of a convex polygon of n sides is $(n - 2)180$. page 153

Theorem 3.21
The sum of the measures of the exterior angles of a convex polygon, one angle at each vertex, is 360. page 154

Chapter 4   Congruent Triangles

Postulate 16
SSS Postulate If three sides of one triangle are congruent to the corresponding parts of another triangle, then the triangles are congruent. page 172

Postulate 17
SAS Postulate If two sides and the included angle of one triangle are congruent to the corresponding parts of another triangle, then the triangles are congruent. page 173

Postulate 18
ASA Postulate If two angles and the included side of one triangle are congruent to the corresponding parts of another triangle, then the triangles are congruent. page 173

Theorem 4.1
Congruence of triangles is reflexive, symmetric, and transitive. page 167

Theorem 4.2
AAS Theorem If two angles and the side opposite one of the angles in one triangle are congruent to the corresponding parts of another triangle, then the triangles are congruent. page 177

Theorem 4.3
LL Theorem If two legs of one right triangle are congruent to the corresponding parts of another right triangle, then the triangles are congruent. page 178

Theorem 4.4
HA Theorem If the hypotenuse and an acute angle of one right triangle are congruent to the corresponding parts of another right triangle, then the triangles are congruent. page 178

Theorem 4.5
LA Theorem If a leg and an acute angle of one right triangle are congruent to the corresponding parts of another right triangle, then the triangles are congruent. page 178

Theorem 4.6
Isosceles Triangle Theorem If two sides of a triangle are congruent, then the angles opposite those sides are congruent. page 197

Theorem 4.7
If two angles of a triangle are congruent, then the sides opposite those angles are congruent. page 198

Theorem 4.8
An equilateral triangle is also equiangular. page 198

Theorem 4.9
An equiangular triangle is also equilateral. page 198

Theorem 4.10
HL Theorem If the hypotenuse and a leg of one right triangle are congruent to the corresponding parts of another right triangle, then the triangles are congruent. page 198

Theorem 4.11
If the lengths of two sides of a triangle are unequal, then the measures of the angles opposite those sides are unequal in the same order. page 202

Theorem 4.12
If the measures of two angles of a triangle are unequal, then the lengths of the sides opposite those angles are unequal in the same order. page 202

Theorem 4.13
Triangle Inequality Theorem The sum of the lengths of any two sides of a triangle is greater than the length of the third side. page 203

Theorem 4.14
Points A, B, and C are collinear and B is between A and C if $AB + BC = AC$. page 204

Theorem 4.15
The perpendicular segment from a point to a line is the shortest segment from the point to the line. page 204

Theorem 4.16
The perpendicular segment from a point to a plane is the shortest segment from the point to the plane. page 204

Theorem 4.17
Hinge Theorem If two sides of one triangle are congruent to two sides of another triangle and the measures of the included angles are unequal, then the lengths of the third sides are unequal in the same order. page 208

Theorem 4.18
If two sides of one triangle are congruent to two sides of another triangle and the lengths of the third sides are unequal, then the measures of the angles included between the congruent sides are unequal in the same order. page 209

Chapter 5   Using Congruent Triangles

Theorem 5.1
A diagonal and the sides of a parallelogram form two congruent triangles. page 223

Theorem 5.2
Opposite sides of a parallelogram are congruent. page 223

Theorem 5.3
Opposite angles of a parallelogram are congruent. page 224

Theorem 5.4
The diagonals of a parallelogram bisect each other. page 224

Theorem 5.5
The distance between two given parallel lines is constant. page 225

Theorem 5.6
If two sides of a quadrilateral are parallel and congruent, then the quadrilateral is a parallelogram. page 229

Theorem 5.7
If both pairs of opposite sides of a quadrilateral are congruent, then the quadrilateral is a parallelogram. page 230

Theorem 5.8
If the diagonals of a quadrilateral bisect each other, then the quadrilateral is a parallelogram. page 230

Theorem 5.9
If a segment joins the midpoints of two sides of a triangle, then it is parallel to the third side, and its length is one-half the length of the third side. page 234

Theorem 5.10
If three or more parallel lines cut off congruent segments on one transversal, then they cut off congruent segments on every transversal. page 235

Theorem 5.11
A parallelogram is a rectangle if and only if its diagonals are congruent. page 240

Theorem 5.12
A parallelogram is a rhombus if and only if its diagonals are perpendicular. page 241

Theorem 5.13
A parallelogram is a rhombus if and only if each diagonal bisects a pair of opposite angles of the parallelogram. page 241

Theorem 5.14
Each pair of base angles of an isosceles trapezoid is congruent. page 246

Theorem 5.15
The diagonals of an isosceles trapezoid are congruent. page 247

Theorem 5.16
The median of a trapezoid is parallel to the bases, and its length is one-half the sum of the lengths of the bases. page 247

Theorem 5.17
The locus of points in a plane equidistant from two given points is the perpendicular bisector of the segment joining the two points. page 254

Theorem 5.18
The locus of points equidistant from two given points is the perpendicular bisecting plane of the segment joining the given points. page 255

Theorem 5.19
In a plane, the locus of points equidistant from the sides of an angle is the bisecting ray of the angle, excluding its endpoint. page 255

Theorem 5.20
If a line is perpendicular to each of two intersecting lines at their point of intersection, then it is perpendicular to the plane containing the two lines. page 255

Chapter 6   Similarity

Postulate 19
AA Postulate If two angles of one triangle are congruent to two angles of another, the triangles are similar. page 273

Theorem 6.1
The ratio of the perimeters of two similar polygons is equal to the ratio of the lengths of any pair of corresponding sides. page 269

Theorem 6.2
SAS Similarity Theorem If an angle of one triangle is congruent to an angle of a second triangle, and if the lengths of the sides including these angles are proportional, then the triangles are similar. page 274

Theorem 6.3
SSS Similarity Theorem If the lengths of the sides of one triangle are proportional to the lengths of the sides of a second triangle, the triangles are similar. page 275

Theorem 6.4
Similarity of polygons is reflexive, symmetric, and transitive. page 275

Theorem 6.5
If a line parallel to one side of a triangle intersects the other two sides, it divides them proportionally. page 281

Theorem 6.6
On any two transversals, parallel lines cut off segments whose lengths are proportional. page 282

Theorem 6.7
The bisector of an angle of a triangle divides the opposite side into two segments whose lengths are proportional to the lengths of the other two sides. page 289

Theorem 6.8
In similar triangles, the lengths of bisectors of corresponding angles are in the same ratio as the lengths of corresponding sides. page 289

Theorem 6.9
In similar triangles, the lengths of the altitudes from corresponding vertices are in the same ratio as the lengths of corresponding sides. page 290

Theorem 6.10
In similar triangles, the lengths of medians from corresponding vertices are in the same ratio as the lengths of corresponding sides. page 290

Theorem 6.11
If an altitude is drawn to the hypotenuse of a right triangle, the new triangles formed are similar to each other and to the given triangle. page 293

Theorem 6.12
The length of the altitude to the hypotenuse of a right triangle is the geometric mean of the lengths of the segments into which the altitude separates the hypotenuse. page 294

Theorem 6.13

If the altitude to the hypotenuse is drawn in a right triangle, the length of either leg is the geometric mean of the lengths of the hypotenuse and the segment on the hypotenuse which is adjacent to that leg. page 294

Chapter 7   Right Triangles

Postulate 20

Coordinate Plane Postulate There is a one-to-one correspondence between points in a plane and ordered pairs of real numbers such that:
1. If P and Q have coordinates (x_1, a) and (x_2, a), then $PQ = |x_2 - x_1|$, and
2. If R and S have coordinates (b, y_1) and (b, y_2), then $RS = |y_2 - y_1|$. page 327

Theorem 7.1

Pythagorean Theorem In a right triangle, the square of the length of the hypotenuse equals the sum of the squares of the lengths of the legs. page 315

Theorem 7.2

If the sum of the squares of the lengths of two sides of a triangle is equal to the square of the length of the third side, then the triangle is a right triangle. page 316

Theorem 7.3

In a 30-60-90 triangle, the length of the hypotenuse is twice the length of the shorter leg, and the length of the longer leg is $\sqrt{3}$ times the length of the shorter leg. page 319

Theorem 7.4

The length of the altitude of an equilateral triangle with sides of length s is $\frac{1}{2}s\sqrt{3}$. page 320

Theorem 7.5

In a 45-45-90 triangle, the length of the hypotenuse is $\sqrt{2}$ times the length of a leg. page 320

Theorem 7.6

Distance Formula If the coordinates of P and Q are (x_1, y_1) and (x_2, y_2) respectively, then the distance between them is given by the formula $PQ = \sqrt{(x_2 - x_1)^2 + (y_2 - y_1)^2}$. page 330

Theorem 7.7

Midpoint Formula If the coordinates of P and Q are (x_1, y_1) and (x_2, y_2), respectively, then the midpoint of $\overline{PQ}$ has coordinates $\left(\dfrac{x_1 + x_2}{2}, \dfrac{y_1 + y_2}{2}\right)$. page 331

Theorem 7.8

In a right triangle ABC with right $\angle C$, $(\sin A)^2 + (\cos A)^2 = 1$. page 337

Chapter 8   Circles

Postulate 21

Arc Addition Postulate If P is on $\overarc{AB}$, then $m\overarc{AP} + m\overarc{PB} = m\overarc{APB}$. page 375

Theorem 8.1

A line that lies in the plane of a circle and contains an interior point of the circle is a secant. page 355

Theorem 8.2

In a plane, a line is tangent to a circle if and only if it is perpendicular to a radius at a point on the circle. page 359

Theorem 8.3

Tangent segments drawn from an exterior point to points on the circle are congruent. page 360

Theorem 8.4

If a line through the center of a circle is perpendicular to a chord, it bisects the chord. page 363

Theorem 8.5

In the same circle or in congruent circles, two chords are congruent if and only if they are the same distance from the center(s) of the circle(s). page 364

Theorem 8.6

The perpendicular bisectors of the sides of a triangle are concurrent in a point equidistant from the vertices of the triangle. page 368

Theorem 8.7

A circle can be circumscribed about any triangle. page 368

Theorem 8.8
The angle bisectors of a triangle are concurrent in a point equidistant from the sides of the triangle. page 369

Theorem 8.9
A circle can be inscribed in any triangle. page 369

Theorem 8.10
In the same circle or in congruent circles, two minor arcs are congruent if and only if their corresponding chords are congruent. page 376

Theorem 8.11
The measure of an inscribed angle is one-half the measure of its intercepted arc. page 380

Theorem 8.12
If two inscribed angles intercept the same arc or congruent arcs, then the angles are congruent. page 380

Theorem 8.13
If a quadrilateral is inscribed in a circle, then its opposite angles are supplementary. page 381

Theorem 8.14
If an angle is inscribed in a semicircle, then it is a right angle. page 381

Theorem 8.15
The measure of an angle formed by two secants which intersect in the interior of a circle is one-half the sum of the measures of the arcs intercepted by the angle and its vertical angle. page 385

Theorem 8.16
The measure of an angle formed by two secants that intersect in the exterior of a circle is one-half the difference of the measures of the intercepted arcs. page 386

Theorem 8.17
The measure of an angle formed by a tangent and a secant that intersect at the point of tangency is one-half the measure of the intercepted arc. page 386

Theorem 8.18
The measure of an angle formed by a secant and a tangent that intersect in the exterior of a circle is one-half the difference of the measures of the intercepted arcs. page 387

Theorem 8.19
The measure of an angle formed by two intersecting tangents is one-half the difference of the measures of the intercepted arcs. page 387

Theorem 8.20
If two chords intersect in a circle, then the product of the lengths of the segments on one chord is equal to the product of the lengths of the segments on the other. page 390

Theorem 8.21
If two secants are drawn to a circle from an exterior point, the product of the lengths of one secant segment and its external secant segment is equal to the product of the lengths of the other secant segment and its external secant segment. page 391

Theorem 8.22
If a tangent and a secant are drawn to a circle from an exterior point, the square of the length of the tangent segment is equal to the product of the lengths of the secant segment and its external secant segment. page 391

Chapter 9   Area of Polygons and Circles

Postulate 22
Area Postulate To every polygonal region there corresponds a unique positive number, called the area of the region. page 400

Postulate 23
Area Postulate for Congruent Triangles If two triangles are congruent, then the triangles have equal areas. page 400

Postulate 24
Area Addition Postulate The area of the union of two or more nonoverlapping polygonal regions is the sum of the areas of these polygonal regions. page 401

Postulate 25
Area Postulate for Rectangles The area, A, of a rectangle is equal to the product of the length, b, of a base and the corresponding height, h. $A = bh$ page 401

Theorem 9.1
The area, A, of a square is equal to the square of the length, s, of a side. $A = s^2$ page 401

Theorem 9.2
The area, A, of a parallelogram is equal to the product of the length, b, of a base and the corresponding height, h. $A = bh$ page 404

Theorem 9.3
The area, A, of a triangle is equal to one-half the product of the length, b, of any side and the corresponding height, h. $A = \frac{1}{2}bh$
page 405

Theorem 9.4
The area, A, of an equilateral triangle with side length, s, is equal to $\frac{s^2}{4}\sqrt{3}$. $A = \frac{s^2}{4}\sqrt{3}$
page 405

Theorem 9.5
The area, A, of a trapezoid is equal to one-half the product of the height, h, and the sum of the lengths, b_1 and b_2, of the bases. $A = \frac{1}{2}h(b_1 + b_2)$ page 410

Theorem 9.6
The area, A, of a rhombus is equal to one-half the product of the lengths, d_1 and d_2, of its diagonals. $A = \frac{1}{2}d_1d_2$ page 411

Theorem 9.7
If two triangles are similar, then the ratio of their areas is equal to the square of the ratio of the lengths of any two corresponding sides.
page 416

Theorem 9.8
If two polygons are similar, the ratio of their areas is equal to the square of the ratio of the lengths of any two corresponding sides.
page 418

Theorem 9.9
A circle can be circumscribed about any regular polygon. page 422

Theorem 9.10
A circle can be inscribed in any regular polygon. page 423

Theorem 9.11
The area, A, of a regular polygon is equal to one-half the product of the apothem, a, and the perimeter, p. $A = \frac{1}{2}ap$ page 423

Theorem 9.12
The ratio of the circumference to the diameter is the same for all circles. page 428

Theorem 9.13
The circumference, C, of a circle is equal to the product of π and the diameter, d. $C = \pi d$ or $C = 2\pi r$ page 428

Theorem 9.14
The area, A, of a circle is equal to the product of π and the square of the radius, r, of the circle. $A = \pi r^2$ page 428

Theorem 9.15
In a circle of radius r, the ratio of the length, s, of an arc to the circumference, C, of the circle is the same as the ratio of the arc measure, m, to 360. $\frac{s}{C} = \frac{m}{360}$ or $s = \frac{m}{360}(2\pi r)$ page 432

Theorem 9.16
In a circle of radius r, the ratio of the area, A_s, of a sector to the area, A_c, of the circle is the same as the ratio of the arc measure, m, to 360.
$\frac{A_s}{A_c} = \frac{m}{360}$ or $A_s = \frac{m}{360}(\pi r^2)$ page 432

Chapter 10   Solids

Postulate 26
Volume Postulate To every solid polyhedron there corresponds a unique positive real number, called the *volume* of the solid polyhedron. page 452

Postulate 27
The volume, V, of a rectangular solid is equal to the product of its length, l, width, w, and height, h. $V = lwh$ page 453

Postulate 28
Cavalieri's Principle Given a plane and two solids. If every plane that is parallel to the given plane and intersects one of the solids also intersects the second solid, and if the cross sections formed have the same area, then the solids have the same volume. page 453

Theorem 10.1
The bases of a prism have corresponding sides and corresponding angles congruent. page 445

Theorem 10.2
The bases of a prism have equal area. page 445

Theorem 10.3
The lateral area, L.A., of a right prism is the product of the length of a lateral edge, h, and the perimeter, p, of the base. L.A. $= hp$
page 448

Theorem 10.4
All cross sections of a prism have equal area.
page 453

Theorem 10.5
The volume, V, of a prism is equal to the product of the height, h, and the area of a base, B. $V = Bh$ page 454

Theorem 10.6
The lateral area, L.A., of a right cylinder is equal to the product of the circumference, C, of a base and the height, h. L.A. $= Ch$ or L.A. $= 2\pi rh$ page 458

Theorem 10.7
The volume, V, of a cylinder is equal to the product of the height, h, and the area, B, of a base. $V = Bh$ or $V = \pi r^2 h$ page 458

Theorem 10.8
The lateral faces of a regular pyramid are congruent isosceles triangles. page 464

Theorem 10.9
The lateral area, L.A., of a regular pyramid is equal to one-half the product of the perimeter, p, of the base and the slant height, s. L.A. $= \frac{1}{2}sp$ page 465

Theorem 10.10
The volume, V, of a pyramid is equal to one-third the product of the area, B, of the base and the height, h. $V = \frac{1}{3}Bh$ page 465

Theorem 10.11
The lateral area, L.A., of a right cone is equal to one-half the product of its slant height, s, and the circumference, C, of its base. L.A. $= \frac{1}{2}sC$ or L.A. $= \pi rs$ page 468

Theorem 10.12
The volume, V, of a cone is equal to one-third the product of its height, h, and the area of its base, B. $V = \frac{1}{3}Bh$ page 468

Theorem 10.13
The volume, V, of a sphere of radius, r, is $\frac{4}{3}\pi r^3$. $V = \frac{4}{3}\pi r^3$ page 473

Theorem 10.14
The area, A, of a sphere of radius, r, is $4\pi r^2$. $A = 4\pi r^2$ page 473

Chapter 11   Using Transformations in Geometry

Theorem 11.1
A line reflection is an isometry. page 485

Theorem 11.2
A point reflection is an isometry. page 486

Theorem 11.3
An isometry preserves collinearity and betweenness of points. page 490

Theorem 11.4
If an isometry maps A onto A' and B onto B', then the image of $\overleftrightarrow{AB}$ is $\overleftrightarrow{A'B'}$, the image of $\overrightarrow{AB}$ is $\overrightarrow{A'B'}$, and the image of $\overline{AB}$ is $\overline{A'B'}$. page 491

Theorem 11.5
An isometry preserves angle measure. page 491

Theorem 11.6
Under an isometry, a triangle and its image are congruent. page 491

Theorem 11.7
A translation is an isometry. page 499

Theorem 11.8
Under a translation, a line and its image are parallel. page 499

Theorem 11.9
If a translation maps A onto A' and B onto B', then $\overline{AA'}\|\overline{BB'}$ and $\overline{AA'} \cong \overline{BB'}$. page 499

Theorem 11.10
A rotation is an isometry. page 500

Theorem 11.11

If a rotation with center P maps A onto A' and B onto B' (and P is not on $\overline{AA'}$ or $\overline{BB'}$), then $m\angle APA' = m\angle BPB'$. page 501

Theorem 11.12

Under a half-turn, a line and its image are parallel. page 501

Theorem 11.13

If a dilation with center C and scale factor k maps A onto A' and B onto B', then $A'B' = k(AB)$. page 511

Theorem 11.14

A dilation preserves collinearity and betweenness of points. page 511

Theorem 11.15

If a dilation maps A onto A' and B onto B', then the image of $\overleftrightarrow{AB}$ is $\overleftrightarrow{A'B'}$, the image of $\overrightarrow{AB}$ is $\overrightarrow{A'B'}$, and the image of $\overline{AB}$ is $\overline{A'B'}$. page 514

Theorem 11.16

A dilation preserves angle measure. page 514

Theorem 11.17

Under a dilation, a triangle and its image are similar. page 514

Theorem 11.18

Under a dilation, a line and its image are parallel. page 514

Theorem 11.19

In a plane, if $\triangle ABC \cong \triangle A'B'C'$, then there is a unique isometry that maps $\triangle ABC$ onto $\triangle A'B'C'$. page 517

Theorem 11.20

Every isometry can be expressed as a composite of at most three line reflections. page 518

Theorem 11.21

In a plane, if $\triangle ABC \sim \triangle A'B'C'$, then there is a unique similarity transformation that maps $\triangle ABC$ onto $\triangle A'B'C'$. page 520

Chapter 12   Using Coordinates in Geometry

Theorem 12.1

If two nonvertical lines are parallel, then they have equal slopes. page 532

Theorem 12.2

If two nonvertical lines have equal slopes, then they are parallel. page 532

Theorem 12.3

Two nonvertical lines are perpendicular if and only if the slope m_1 of one line is the negative reciprocal of the slope m_2 of the other line.

$$m_1 = -\frac{1}{m_2}, \text{ or } m_1 m_2 = -1 \quad \text{page 533}$$

Theorem 12.4

The graph of the equation $y - y_1 = m(x - x_1)$ is the nonvertical line ℓ that has slope m and contains $P(x_1, y_1)$. page 537

Theorem 12.5

The graph of the equation $y = mx + b$ is the nonvertical line with slope m and y-intercept b. page 538

Theorem 12.6

The graph of an equation in x and y is a line if and only if the equation is a linear equation. page 542

Theorem 12.7

The equation of a circle with center (h, k) and radius r is $(x - h)^2 + (y - k)^2 = r^2$. page 544

Glossary

Acute angle An angle whose measure is less than 90. Page 40

Acute triangle A triangle with three acute angles. Page 139

Adjacent angles Two coplanar angles with a common side and no common interior points. Page 41

Alternate interior angles In the diagram, transversal t cuts lines ℓ and m. $\angle 3$ and $\angle 5$, $\angle 4$ and $\angle 6$ are pairs of alternate interior angles. Page 109

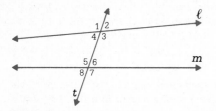

Altitude of a cone The segment from the vertex perpendicular to the plane of the base. Page 467

Altitude of a parallelogram A segment perpendicular to the base with endpoints on the base and the opposite side (or on the lines containing them). Page 401

Altitude of a prism A segment from a point in one base perpendicular to the plane of the other base. The length of the altitude is the *height* of the prism. Page 445

Altitude of a pyramid The segment from the vertex perpendicular to the plane of the base. Page 464

Altitude of a trapezoid A perpendicular segment from any point in one base to a point on the line containing the other base. Page 410

Altitude of a triangle The perpendicular segment from any vertex of the triangle to the line containing the opposite side. Page 193

Angle The union of two noncollinear rays which have the same endpoint. The rays are called the *sides* of the angle and their common endpoint is the *vertex*. Page 31

Angle bisector of a triangle The segment from any vertex of the triangle to the opposite side on the ray bisecting the angle. Page 193

Angle inscribed in a circle An angle whose sides contain the endpoints of an arc and whose vertex is a point on the arc other than the endpoints. Page 379

Apothem of a regular polygon The distance from the center to each side. Page 423

Area of a circle The limit of the areas of the inscribed regular polygons. Page 427

Area of a polygonal region A unique positive number which corresponds to the polygonal region. Page 400

Auxiliary line A line introduced to aid in the proof of a theorem. Page 126

Axis of a cone The segment from the vertex to the center of the base of the cone. Page 467

Axis of a cylinder The segment joining the centers of its bases. Page 457

Base angle of an isosceles triangle See *isosceles triangle*. Page 139

Base of a cone See *circular cone*. Page 467

Base of a cylinder See *circular cylinder*. Page 457

Base of an isosceles triangle See *isosceles triangle*. Page 139

Base of a parallelogram Any side of the parallelogram. Page 401

Base of a prism A face in one of the parallel planes. Page 444

Base of a pyramid See *pyramid*. Page 464

Base of a trapezoid One of the parallel sides of the trapezoid. Page 246

Bisector of an angle Ray $\overrightarrow{PB}$ is the bisector of $\angle APC$ if and only if B is in the interior of $\angle APC$ and $m\angle APB = m\angle BPC$. Page 34

Bisector of a segment A set of points whose intersection with the segment is the midpoint of the segment. Page 26

Center of a circle See *circle.* Page 354

Center of a dilation See *dilation.* Page 510

Center of a regular polygon The center of its circumscribed circle. Page 423

Center of a rotation See *rotation.* Page 500

Central angle of a circle An angle in the plane of the circle whose vertex is the center of the circle. Page 374

Central angle of a regular polygon An angle formed by two radii drawn to the endpoints of one side. Page 423

Centroid of a triangle Point of concurrency of the medians of the triangle. Page 369

Chord A segment whose endpoints lie on a circle. Page 355

Circle The set of coplanar points at a given distance from a given point in the plane. The given point is called the *center.* Page 354

Circular cone A circular cone contains a vertex, V, not in a plane E, a circular region in plane E, and all segments joining a point of the circle to V. The circular region in plane E is the *base* of the cone. Page 467

Circular cylinder The union of two congruent circles and their interiors, lying in parallel planes, and all segments that have one endpoint on each circle and that are parallel to the line joining the centers of the circles. The circular regions are the *bases* of the cylinder. Page 457

Circumference of a circle The limit of the perimeters of the inscribed regular polygons. Page 427

Circumcenter of a triangle The point of concurrency of the perpendicular bisectors of the sides of the triangle. Page 368

Circumscribed polygon A polygon whose sides are tangent to a circle. The circle is *inscribed* in the polygon. Page 367

Collinear points Points that are contained in one line. Page 9

Common external tangent A common tangent that does not intersect the segment joining the centers of the circles. Page 360

Common internal tangent A common tangent that intersects the segment joining the centers of the circles. Page 360

Common tangent A line that is tangent to each of two coplanar circles. Page 360

Complementary angles Two angles whose measures have a sum of 90. Page 40

Composite of two transformations Let F and G be transformations. The composite of F and G is the transformation which maps each point P onto a point P' as follows: First, P is mapped onto P_1 under F. Then P_1 is mapped onto P' under G. Page 498

Concentric circles Coplanar circles with the same center. Page 375

Conclusion The "then" clause of a conditional statement. Page 77

Concurrent lines Two or more lines that intersect in a single point. The point is the *point of concurrency.* Page 368

Conditional statement A statement of the form "If p, then q." Page 77

Cone See *circular cone.* Page 467

Congruent angles Angles that have the same measure. Page 34

Congruent arcs Arcs that have the same measure and lie on the same or on congruent circles. Page 375

Congruent circles Circles with congruent radii. Page 363

Congruent figures Two plane figures are congruent if and only if there is an isometry that maps one figure onto the other. Page 518

Congruent segments Segments that have the same length. Page 26

Congruent triangles Two triangles in which there is a correspondence between the vertices such that each side and each angle is congruent to its corresponding side or angle. Page 166

Consecutive angles of a polygon Two angles such that the same side of the polygon is contained in a side of each angle. Page 147

Consecutive sides of a polygon Two sides with a common endpoint. Page 147

Contrapositive A statement formed from the original statement by negating the hypothesis and the conclusion and then interchanging them. Page 100

Converse A statement formed by interchanging the hypothesis and the conclusion of the original statement. Page 96

Convex polygon A polygon such that each line that contains a side of the polygon contains no points in the interior of the polygon. Page 148

Coplanar points (lines) Points (lines) that are contained in one plane. Page 9

Corollary A theorem that follows directly from another theorem. Page 79

Corresponding angles In the diagram, transversal t cuts lines ℓ and m. $\angle 1$ and $\angle 5$, $\angle 2$ and $\angle 6$, $\angle 3$ and $\angle 7$, $\angle 4$ and $\angle 8$ are pairs of corresponding angles. Page 109

Cosine ratio In right $\triangle ABC$ with acute $\angle A$:
$$\cos A = \frac{\text{length of side adjacent } \angle A}{\text{length of hypotenuse}}.$$
Page 336

Counterexample A statement or diagram that shows that a given statement is not always true. Page 26

Cross section of a solid The intersection of the solid and a plane parallel to a base of the solid. Page 453

Cube A prism in which all faces are squares. Page 445

Cylinder See *circular cylinder.* Page 457

Deductive reasoning The use of logical principles to draw conclusions. Page 60

Degree measure of a major arc $360 -$ the measure of the related minor arc. Page 375

Degree measure of a minor arc The measure of its central angle. Page 375

Degree measure of an angle The unique real number r that corresponds to the angle such that $0 < r < 180$. Page 33

Degree measure of a semicircle The degree measure of a semicircle is 180. Page 375

Diagonal of a polygon A segment joining two nonconsecutive vertices of the polygon. Page 148

Diameter of a circle A segment that contains the center and has its endpoints on the circle. Also the length of this segment. Page 354

Diameter of a sphere A segment that contains the center and has its endpoints on the sphere. Page 356

Dihedral angle The union of two noncoplanar half-planes with a common edge, together with the common edge. Page 53

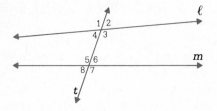

Dilation Let C be a point and k a positive real number. A dilation is a transformation that maps each point of the plane onto an image point as follows: C is its own image. For any point P other than C, the image of P is the point P' on $\overrightarrow{CP}$ for which $CP' = k(CP)$. C is the *center* and k, the *scale factor* of the dilation. Page 510

Distance between two parallel lines The length of a segment drawn from any point on one line perpendicular to the other line. Page 225

Distance between two points A unique positive real number that corresponds to the pair of points. Page 24

Distance from a point to a line (plane) not containing the point The length of the perpendicular segment from the point to the line (plane). Page 204

Edge of a polyhedron See *polyhedron*. Page 444

Enlargement A dilation in which the scale factor is greater than one. Page 511

Equiangular polygon A polygon in which all the angles are congruent. Page 148

Equiangular triangle A triangle with three congruent angles. Page 139

Equilateral polygon A polygon in which all the sides are congruent. Page 149

Equilateral triangle A triangle with three congruent sides. Page 139

Equivalence relation A relation which is reflexive, symmetric, and transitive. Page 171

Exterior angle of a triangle An angle which forms a linear pair with one of the angles of the triangle. Page 143

Exterior angles In the diagram, transversal t cuts lines ℓ and m. $\angle 1$, $\angle 2$, $\angle 7$, and $\angle 8$ are exterior angles. Page 109

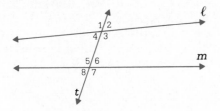

Exterior of a circle The set of points in the plane whose distance from the center is greater than the radius. Page 355

Exterior of an angle The set of points in the plane which do not belong to the interior of the angle or to the angle itself. Page 32

Externally tangent circles Two tangent circles such that the segment joining the centers of the circles intersects the tangent line. Page 361

External secant segment See *secant segment*. Page 390

Face of a polyhedron See *polyhedron*. Page 444

Geometric mean The positive number x such that $\dfrac{a}{x} = \dfrac{x}{b}$ where a and b are two positive real numbers. Page 293

Great circle of a sphere The intersection of a sphere and a plane containing the center of the sphere. Page 356

Half-turn See *reflection through point O*. Page 486

Height of a cone The length of its altitude. Page 467

Height of a parallelogram for a given base The length of an altitude. Page 401

Height of a prism The length of its altitude. Page 445

Height of a pyramid The length of its altitude. Page 464

Hypotenuse The side opposite the right angle in a right triangle. Page 139

Hypothesis The "if" clause of a conditional statement. Page 77

Identity transformation The transformation that maps each point of the plane onto itself. Page 501

Image If A is mapped onto A', A' is called the image of A. A is the *preimage* of A'. Page 484

Incenter of a triangle The point of concurrency of the angle bisectors of the triangle. Page 369

Included angle An included angle for two sides of a triangle is an angle whose rays contain the two sides of the triangle. Page 167

Included side An included side for two angles of a triangle is a side whose endpoints are the vertices of the angles. Page 167

Inductive reasoning The process of forming a conclusion based upon examination of several specific cases. Page 48

Inscribed angle An angle whose sides contain the endpoints of an arc and whose vertex is a point on the arc other than the endpoints. Page 379

Inscribed polygon A polygon whose vertices lie on a circle. The circle is *circumscribed* about the polygon. Page 367

Intercepted arc An arc whose endpoints lie on different sides of an angle and whose other points lie in the interior of the angle. Page 379

Interior angles In the diagram below, transversal *t* cuts lines ℓ and *m*. ∠3, ∠4, ∠5, and ∠6 are interior angles. Page 109

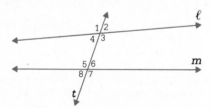

Interior angles on the same side of the transversal In the diagram above, ∠4 and ∠5, ∠3 and ∠6 are pairs of interior angles on the same side of the transversal. Page 117

Interior of a circle The set of points in a plane whose distance from the center is less than the radius. Page 355

Interior of an angle The interior of ∠APB is the intersection of two half-planes; the side of $\overleftrightarrow{PA}$ containing B and the side of $\overleftrightarrow{PB}$ containing A. Page 32

Internally tangent circles Two tangent circles such that the segment joining the centers of the circles does not intersect the tangent line. Page 361

Intersection of two sets The set of elements that the two sets have in common. Page 10

Inverse A statement formed from the original statement by negating both the hypothesis and the conclusion. Page 100

Isometry A transformation that preserves distance. Page 485

Isosceles trapezoid A trapezoid whose legs are congruent. Page 246

Isosceles triangle A triangle with at least two sides congruent. In an isosceles triangle, the congruent sides are the *legs;* the third side is the *base*. The angle opposite the base is the *vertex angle*. The angles opposite the congruent sides are the *base angles*. Page 139

Kite A quadrilateral such that exactly one diagonal is the perpendicular bisector of the other. Page 411

Lateral area of a prism The sum of the areas of its lateral faces. Page 448

Lateral edge of a prism The intersection of two lateral faces of the prism. Page 444

Lateral face of a prism A face of the prism other than a base. Page 444

Leg of an isosceles triangle See *isosceles triangle*. Page 139

Leg of a right triangle One of the sides that is not the hypotenuse of the right triangle. Page 139

Leg of a trapezoid One of the nonparallel sides of the trapezoid. Page 246

Length of an arc An arc can be divided into *n* arcs of equal measure. If chords are drawn in these *n* arcs, the length of the arc is the limit of the sum of the lengths of the *n* chords as *n* gets very large. Page 432

Length (linear measure) of a segment The distance between its endpoints. Page 24

Line of symmetry See *line symmetry*. Page 506

Line parallel to a plane A line and a plane are parallel if and only if they do not intersect. Page 108

Line perpendicular to a plane A line and a plane that intersect are perpendicular if and only if every line in the given plane which passes through the point of intersection is perpendicular to the given line. Page 134

Line symmetry A plane figure has line symmetry if and only if there is a line ℓ such that the figure coincides with its reflection image over ℓ. Line ℓ is a *line of symmetry* or a *symmetry line* for the figure. Page 506

Linear equation An equation that can be written in the form $Ax + By = C$, with A and B not both zero and A, B, and C real numbers. Page 542

Linear pair of angles A pair of adjacent angles whose noncommon sides are opposite rays. Page 41

Locus The set of all points, and only those points, that satisfy a given condition. Page 250

Magnitude of a rotation If a rotation with center P maps A onto A', then the measure of $\angle APA'$ is the magnitude of the rotation. Page 501

Major arc of a circle The set of points on the circle that lie on a central angle or in the exterior of the central angle. Page 374

Mapping See *transformation*. Page 484

Median of a trapezoid The segment joining the midpoints of the legs of the trapezoid. Page 247

Median of a triangle The segment from any vertex of the triangle to the midpoint of the opposite side. Page 193

Midpoint of a segment A point S is the midpoint of segment $\overline{RT}$ if and only if R, S, and T are collinear and $RS = ST$. Page 26

Minor arc of a circle The set of points on the circle that lie on a central angle or in the interior of the central angle. Page 374

Noncollinear points Points that are not contained in one line. Page 9

Noncoplanar points (lines) Points (lines) that are not contained in the same plane. Page 10

Oblique cone A cone in which the axis is not perpendicular to the base. Page 467

Oblique cylinder A cylinder in which the axis is not perpendicular to the planes of the bases. Page 457

Oblique prism A prism in which the lateral edges are not perpendicular to the planes of the bases. Page 445

Obtuse angle An angle whose measure is greater than 90. Page 40

Obtuse triangle A triangle with an obtuse angle. Page 139

Opposite rays Rays $\overrightarrow{AB}$ and $\overrightarrow{AC}$ are opposite rays if points A, B, and C are collinear and A is between B and C. Page 19

Opposite sides of a quadrilateral Two sides that do not have a common vertex. Page 218

Orthocenter of a triangle Point of concurrency of the lines containing the altitudes of the triangle. Page 369

Parallel lines Lines which are coplanar and do not intersect. Page 108

Parallel planes Planes that do not intersect. Page 108

Parallelopiped A prism in which all faces are parallelograms. Page 445

Parallelogram A quadrilateral in which both pairs of opposite sides are parallel. Page 218

Perimeter of a polygon The sum of the lengths of its sides. Page 148

Perpendicular bisecting plane of a segment The plane that is perpendicular to the segment at its midpoint. Page 251

Perpendicular bisector of a segment A line which is perpendicular to the segment and contains its midpoint. Page 42

Perpendicular lines Lines that intersect to form a right angle. Page 42

Platonic solids Five polyhedrons which Plato described fully in his writings: tetrahedron, hexahedron, octahedron, dodecahedron, and icosahedron. Page 470

Point reflection See *reflection through point O.* Page 486

Point symmetry A plane figure has point symmetry if and only if there is a point *P* such that the figure and its image coincide under a reflection through *P.* Page 507

Point of tangency See *tangent to a circle.* Page 355

Polygon The union of three or more coplanar segments such that each segment intersects exactly two other segments, one at each endpoint, and no two intersecting segments are collinear. Page 147

Polygonal region A plane figure formed by the union of a finite number of coplanar, nonoverlapping triangular regions. Page 400

Polyhedron A union of polygons, not all coplanar, with their interiors, which encloses a region of space. The enclosed space is the *interior* of the polyhedron. A *solid polyhedron* is the union of a polyhedron and its interior. Each polygon is a *face* of the polyhedron. The intersection of two faces is an *edge* of the polyhedron. The intersection of three or more edges is a *vertex* of the polyhedron. Page 444

Postulate A statement that is assumed to be true. Page 14

Preimage See *image.* Page 484

Prism A polyhedron with two congruent polygonal faces contained in parallel planes. These faces are called the *bases* of the prism. The other faces are called *lateral faces.* Page 444

Proportion An equation which states that two or more ratios are equal. Page 267

Pyramid A polyhedron with all but one vertex, *V,* contained in a plane *E.* The polygonal region determined by the vertices in plane *E* is the *base* of the pyramid. The lateral faces of a pyramid are triangles. Page 464

Quadrilateral A polygon with four sides. Page 148

Radius of a circle A segment determined by the center and a point on the circle. Also the length of this segment. Page 354

Radius of a regular polygon A segment from the center to a vertex. Page 423

Radius of a sphere A segment determined by the center and a point on the sphere. Page 356

Ray A ray, $\overrightarrow{RT}$, is the set of points $\overline{RT}$ and all points *S* such that *T* lies between *R* and *S.* Page 18

Rectangle A parallelogram with four right angles. Page 219

Rectangular solid A solid right rectangular prism. Page 452

Reduction A translation in which the scale factor is less than one. Page 511

Reflection over line ℓ A transformation that maps each point *P* of the plane onto a point *P′* as follows: If *P* is not on *ℓ*, then *ℓ* is the perpendicular bisector of $\overline{PP'}$. If *P* is *ℓ*, then *P′* coincides with *P.* *ℓ* is the *line of reflection.* *P′* is the *reflection image* of *P.* Page 475

Reflection through point O A transformation that maps each point *P* of the plane onto a point *P′* as follows: If *P* does not coincide with *O,* then *O* is the midpoint of $\overline{PP'}$. If *P* coincides with *O,* then *P′ = P.* Page 486

Regular polygon A convex polygon which is both equiangular and equilateral. Page 148

Regular polyhedron A polyhedron in which each pair of its dihedral angles is congruent, and all the polygons in its faces are congruent regular polygons. Page 470

Regular prism A right prism whose bases are regular polygons. Page 445

Regular pyramid A pyramid which has a regular polygon for a base, and lateral edges that are congruent. Page 464

Remote interior angles of a triangle The two angles of a triangle which are not adjacent to a given exterior angle. Page 143

Rhombus A parallelogram with four congruent sides. Page 219

Right angle An angle whose measure is 90. Page 40

Right cone A cone in which the axis is perpendicular to the base. Page 467

Right cylinder A cylinder in which the axis is perpendicular to the bases. Page 457

Right prism A prism in which the lateral edges are perpendicular to the bases. Page 445

Right triangle A triangle with a right angle. The side opposite the right angle is the *hypotenuse*. The other two sides are the *legs*. Page 139

Rotation A composite of two reflections over two intersecting lines. The point of intersection of the two lines is the *center* of the rotation. Page 500

Rotational symmetry A plane figure has rotational symmetry if and only if there is a rotation such that the figure and its image coincide under the rotation. Page 507

Scale factor See *dilation*. Page 510

Scalene triangle A triangle with no two sides congruent. Page 139

Secant A line that intersects a circle in two points. Page 355

Secant segment In the diagram, $\overleftrightarrow{AC}$ is a secant of circle P. $\overline{AC}$ is a secant segment and $\overline{AB}$ is an *external secant segment*. Page 390

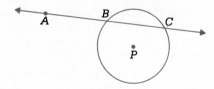

Sector of a circle A region bounded by two radii and either the major arc or the minor arc that is intercepted. Page 432

Segment A segment, $\overline{RT}$, is the set of points R and T and all the points between R and T. Page 18

Segment of a circle A region bounded by a chord and either the major arc or the minor arc that is intercepted. Page 433

Semicircle The union of the endpoints of a diameter and the points of the circle in a given half-plane formed by the line containing the diameter. Page 374

Sides of an angle See *angle*. Page 31

Similar convex polygons Convex polygons for which there is a correspondence between their vertices such that the corresponding angles are congruent, and the ratios of the lengths of their corresponding sides are equal. Page 266

Similarity Two plane figures are similar if and only if there is a similarity transformation that maps one figure onto the other. Page 520

Similarity transformation A composite of a dilation and an isometry. Page 519

Sine ratio In right $\triangle ABC$ with acute $\angle A$:

$$\sin A = \frac{\text{length of side opposite } \angle A}{\text{length of hypotenuse}}.$$

Page 336

Skew lines Two lines that are not coplanar. Page 108

Slant height of a regular pyramid The length of the altitude of any lateral face from the vertex of the pyramid. Page 464

Slant height of a right cone The length of a segment from the vertex to a point of the circle. Page 467

Slope of a line The slope, m, of a nonvertical line that contains two points $P(x_1, y_1)$ and $Q(x_2, y_2)$ is $m = \dfrac{y_2 - y_1}{x_2 - x_1}$. Page 530

Small circle of a sphere The intersection of a sphere and a plane containing an interior point of the sphere, but not containing the center. Page 356

Solid polyhedron The union of a polyhedron and its interior. Page 444

Space The set of all points. Page 8

Sphere The set of all points in space that are a given distance from a given point. The given point is the *center* of the sphere. Page 356

Square A rectangle with four congruent sides. Page 219

Statement A sentence that is either true or false but not both. Page 100

Supplementary angles Two angles whose measures have a sum of 180. Page 41

Symmetry line See *line symmetry*. Page 506

Tangent circles Two coplanar circles that are tangent to the same line at the same point. Page 361

Tangent ratio In right $\triangle ABC$ with acute $\angle A$:

$$\tan A = \frac{\text{length of side opposite } \angle A}{\text{length of side adjacent to } \angle A}.$$

Page 336

Tangent ray A ray which is a subset of a tangent line and which contains the point of tangency. Page 355

Tangent segment A segment which is a subset of a tangent line and which contains the point of tangency. Page 355

Tangent to a circle A line in the plane of the circle that intersects the circle in exactly one point. The point of the intersection is called the *point of tangency*. Page 355

Tessellation An arrangement of polygonal shapes that completely covers a plane surface without overlapping and without leaving gaps. Page 156

Theorem A statement that is proved. Page 67

Total area of a prism The sum of its lateral area and the areas of its two bases. Page 448

Transformation of a plane A one-to-one correspondence between the points of the plane and themselves. Also called a *mapping*. Page 484

Translation A composite of two reflections over two parallel lines. Page 498

Transversal A line which intersects two coplanar lines in two distinct points. Page 109

Trapezoid A quadrilateral with exactly one pair of opposite sides parallel. Page 218

Triangle The union of three segments determined by three noncollinear points. Page 138

Triangular region The union of a triangle and its interior. Page 400

Unequal in the same order For real numbers a, b, c, and d: a and b are unequal in the same order as c and d if (1) $a > b$ and $c > d$, or (2) $a < b$ and $c < d$. Page 202

Vertex angle of an isosceles triangle See *isosceles triangle*. Page 139

Vertex of an angle The common endpoint of the rays which are its sides. Page 31

Vertex of a polyhedron See *polyhedron*. Page 444

Vertical angles Two angles whose sides form two pairs of opposite rays. Page 42

Volume of a solid polyhedron A unique positive real number which corresponds to the solid polyhedron. Page 452

x-intercept The x-coordinate of the point of intersection of a line and the x-axis. Page 539

y-intercept The y-coordinate of the point of intersection of a line and the y-axis. Page 538

Acknowledgments

All photographs not credited are the property of Scott, Foresman & Company.

For permission to reproduce photographs on the pages indicated, acknowledgment is made to the following:

Cover © Norman Prince
Page xii Tom Pantages **Page 2** Artstreet
Page 3 Photo of honeycomb, Art Pahlke **Page 5** Photo of rainbow, Candee Associates; photo of starfish, Michael Collier **Page 9** M. C. Escher, *Cubic Space Division,* © BEELDRECHT, Amsterdam/V.A.G.A., New York, Collection Haags Gemeentemuseum—The Hague **Page 16** Photo of cove molding, Jay Wolke **Page 18** Copyright The University of Texas McDonald Observatory **Page 25** David R. Frazier **Page 31** Julian Baum **Page 39** E. Michael James, by permission of Republic Airlines **Page 40** Ray F. Hillstrom/Hillstrom Stock Photo **Page 48** Photo of pendulum clock, Jay Wolke **Page 55** James Buddenbaum **Page 58** Stephen J. Krasemann/Peter Arnold, Inc. **Page 60** Jay Wolke **Page 66** Jay Wolke **Page 76** Photo of furniture designer © Freda Leinwand **Page 77** Photo of student taking test, Jay Wolke; photo of crowd at ball game, James Buddenbaum **Page 78** NASA **Page 100** Steve Lissau **Page 114** James Buddenbaum **Page 121** M. C. Escher, *Ascending and Descending,* © BEELDRECHT, Amsterdam/V.A.G.A., New York, Collection Haags Gemeentemuseum—The Hague **Page 128** Jerry Wachter/Focus On Sports **Page 137** Michael D. Sullivan **Page 138** © 1982 Walt Disney Productions **Page 147** E. R. Degginger **Page 157** Photo on left, M. C. Escher, *Study of Regular Division of the Plane with Bird,* 1955. © BEELDRECHT, Amsterdam/V.A.G.A., New York, Collection Haags Gemeentemuseum—The Hague; photo on right, M. C. Escher, *Study of Regular Division of the Plane with Reptiles,* 1939. © BEELDRECHT, Amsterdam/V.A.G.A., New York, Collection Haags Gemeentemuseum—The Hague **Page 187** photo of starfish, Art Pahlke; photo of flower, Wendy Watriss/Woodfin Camp **Page 191** Artstreet **Page 197** James Buddenbaum **Page 207** Jay Wolke **Page 216** Theodore L. Manekin **Page 218** Dennis Kucharzak **Page 227** Dennis Kucharzak **Page 229** Imagery **Page 232** Artstreet **Page 234** Ray F. Hillstrom/Hillstrom Stock Photo **Page 240** James Buddenbaum **Page 246** A. F. Rohrer/Shostal Assoc. **Page 250** Dennis Kucharzak **Page 264** NASA **Page 272** Artstreet **Page 299** Photo of bronze statue, Hirmer Fotoarchiv Munchen; photo of nautilus shell, W. S. Nawrocki/Hillstrom Stock Photo **Page 300** Artstreet **Page 312** Rene Pauli/Shostal Assoc. **Page 319** Ray F. Hillstrom/Hillstrom Stock Photo **Page 320** Jerry Wachter/Focus On Sports **Page 336** Artstreet **Page 340** Artstreet **Page 347** Gerald F. Jarosz **Page 352** Frederic Lewis, Inc. **Page 354** David R. Frazier **Page 359** Chuck Pefley **Page 398** G. Halary/Shostal Assoc. **Page 409** Steve Lissau **Page 431** Tom Pantages **Page 442** Karen Luksich **Page 457** Mark Bolster/Int'l Stock Photo **Page 459** James Buddenbaum **Page 468** © Jim Pickerell **Page 470** E. R. Degginger **Page 474** NASA **Page 477** © Jim Pickerell **Page 482** M. C. Escher, *Magic Mirror,* © BEELDRECHT, Amsterdam/V.A.G.A., New York, Collection Haags Gemeentemuseum—The Hague **Page 506** Photo of moth, Dennis Kucharzak; photo of beetle, Jorge Sole **Page 508** Photo of diatoms, Manfred Kage/Peter Arnold, Inc.; photo of flower, Artstreet; photo of snowflake, © Roger J. Cheng/Atmospheric Sciences Research Center, State University of New York at Albany **Page 518** M. C. Escher, *Symmetry Drawing No. 99,* © BEELDRECHT, Amsterdam/V.A.G.A., New York, Collection Haags Gemeentemuseum—The Hague **Page 519** M. C. Escher, *Smaller and Smaller,* © BEELDRECHT, Amsterdam/V.A.G.A., New York, Collection Haags Gemeentemuseum—The Hague **Page 543** NOAA

For permission to reproduce drawings on the page indicated, acknowledgement is made to the following:
Page 165 From THE STANDARD BOOK OF QUILT MAKING AND COLLECTING by Marguerite Ickis. Copyright 1949, 1977 by Marguerite Ickis. Reprinted by permission of Dover Publications, Inc.

Index

Right triangle(s), 139, 198, 313-316
  hypotenuse of, 139, 314-315
  isosceles (45-45-90), 320
  legs of, 139, 314-315
  Pythagorean Theorem, 314-316,
    323-324, 330-331, 336-337
  similar, 293-295
  30-60-90, 319
  trigonometric ratios, 336-337,
    340-341
Rotation, 500-501
Rotational symmetry, 507
Ruler Postulate, 24

SAS Postulate, 173
SAS Similarity Theorem, 274
Scale drawing, 268
Scale factor (dilation), 510
Scalene triangle, 138
Secant (of circle), 355, 385-387
Secant segment, 390
Sector (of circle), 432
Segment(s), 18
  bisector of, 26
  and circles, 390-391
  of circle, 433
  congruent, 26
  endpoints of, 18
  length of, 24-26
  midpoint of, 26
  postulates pertaining to, 25-26
  proportional division of, 281-282
Segment Addition Postulate, 25
Segment Construction Postulate, 25
Semicircle, 374-376
Side(s)
  of angle, 31
  corresponding, 166-167
  of polygon, 147-148
Similarity, 265-269
  congruence and, 273
  diagonal test for, 279
  of polygons, 266-269
  problems involving, 300-301
  transformations and, 519-520
  of triangles, 273-276, 289-290,
    293-295
Similar polygons. See also *Similarity.*
  area of, 416-418
Similar triangles. See also *Similarity.*
  area of, 416-417
Sine ratio, 336

Skew lines, 108
Slant height
  of cone, 467
  of pyramid, 464
Slope-intercept form, 538
Slope of line, 530-533, 537-539
Small circle of sphere, 356
Solids, 443, 444. See also
  Polyhedron; Prism; Pyramid.
  cross section of, 453
Space, 8
  coordinates in, 558
Sphere, 356, 472-474
  area of, 473-474
  center of, 356
  diameter of, 356
  great circle of, 356
  radius of, 356
  small circle of, 356
  volume of, 472-473
Square, 219, 240-242, 401
SSS Postulate, 172-173
SSS Similarity Theorem, 275
Standard form, 542
Statement(s), 100. See also
  Conditional statements.
  contrapositive of, 100-101
  equivalent, 101
  converse of, 100-101
  negation of, 100
Substitution principle, 61
Supplementary angles, 41
Supplement Postulate, 41
Symmetric property, 61
Symmetry, 506-507
  line, 506
  point, 507
  rotational, 507

Tangent
  to circle, 355, 359-360, 385-387
  common, 360
Tangent circles, 361
Tangent ratio, 336
Tessellations, 156-157, 245
Tests
  chapter, 57, 105, 161, 215, 263,
    307, 351, 397, 439, 481, 527,
    565
  cumulative, 162-163, 308-311,
    440-441, 566-569
Tetrahedron, 470-471

Theorem(s)
corollary, 79
diagrams for, 71-72
meaning of, 67
proving, 66-68, 71-73, 84-86, 92-93
Total area, 448-449, 458
Transformation(s), 483, 484-486
composite of, 498-500
congruence and, 517-518
dilation, 510-511
distance-preserving, 485
identity, 501, 511
isometry, 485-486, 498-502
reflection, 483, 484-486
rotation, 500
similarity and, 519-520
translation, 498-499
Transitive property, 61
Translation(s), 498-499
Transversal, 109, 112-113, 116-118
Trapezoid, 218, 246-247
altitude of, 410
area of, 410
base angles of, 246
bases of, 246
isosceles, 246-247
legs of, 246
median of, 247
Triangle(s), 138-139, 142-143. See
also *Right triangle.*
acute, 139
altitude of, 193
angle bisector of, 193
angle measures, sum of, 142
angles of, 138-139, 142-143
area of, 405-406, 409, 416-417
base of, 139
centroid of, 369
circumcenter of, 368
circumscribed, 367-369
classification of, 139
congruence of, 165-167, 172-174,
177-178, 183-184, 400
coordinate plane and, 553-555
corresponding parts of, 166-167
equiangular, 139, 198
equilateral, 139, 198
exterior of, 138
45-45-90, 320
incenter of, 369
included angle, 167
included side, 167

inequalities in, 202-204, 208-209
inscribed, 367-369
interior of, 138
isosceles, 139, 197-198
median of, 193
obtuse, 139
orthocenter of, 369
overlapping, 187-188
right, 139, 198, 313-316, 319-320
scalene, 139
sides of, 138-139
similar, 273-276, 289-290, 293-295
30-60-90, 319
vertices of, 138
Triangle Inequality Theorem, 203
Triangular region, 400. See also
Triangle.
Trichotomy property, 61
Trigonometric ratios, 336-337, 340-341
problems involving, 344-345
table of, 343
Trigonometry. See *Trigonometric
ratios.*

Undefined terms, 8
Using BASIC, 47, 91, 258-259, 334,
426, 462-463, 560-561

Vertex
of angle, 31
of cone, 467
of polygon, 147
of polyhedron, 444
of triangle, 138
Vertical angles, 42
Volume
of cone, 468
of cylinder, 458
of polyhedron, 452-453, 464-465
of prism, 452-453
of pyramid, 465
of sphere, 472-473
Volume Postulate, 452

x-**axis,** 327, 558
x-**coordinate,** 327-328
x-**intercept,** 539

y-**axis,** 327, 558
y-**coordinate,** 327-328
y-**intercept,** 538